The Great Father

FRANCIS PAUL PRUCHA

The Great Father

The United States Government

and the American Indians

I

UNIVERSITY OF NEBRASKA PRESS

LINCOLN AND LONDON

Publication of this work
was aided by a grant from De Rance, Inc.

Acknowledgments for the use of
copyrighted material appear on pp. xxxi–xxxii.

The paper in this book
meets the guidelines for permanence
and durability of the Committee
on Production Guidelines for Book
Longevity of the Council
on Library Resources.

Library of Congress
Cataloging in Publication Data

Prucha, Francis Paul.
The great father.

Includes index.
⅟. Indians of North America –
Government relations.
I. Title.
E93.P9654   1984
323.1'197073   83-16837
ISBN 0-8032-3668-9 (alk. paper)

*For the Jesuits of Marquette University,
with whom I have lived and worked
for many years*

When your GREAT FATHER and his chiefs see those things, they will
know that you have opened your ears to your GREAT FATHER'S voice,
and have come to hear his good Councils.

Lewis and Clark, in presenting American flags
and medals to Oto chiefs, 1804

Friends and Brothers,—The business part of our Council is closed.
But we have seen who are your great men. We stand here to put medals
around their necks. . . . All these medals have on one side of them
your GREAT FATHER'S face, and on the other side is his pipe, his
peace hatchet, and his hand.

Friends and Brothers,—You are never to forget that this is a great gift. It
comes from your GREAT FATHER himself, who sends it to you by our
hands. It is a new heart. Your GREAT FATHER has told us to come up here,
and put it in the breast of his great Chippeway children. No bad blood
belongs to this heart. It is an American heart, and is full of good blood;
and if you will open your ears and listen well, and never forget your
GREAT FATHER'S message, it will make you all happy.

Thomas L. McKenney at treaty negotiations
with the Chippewa Indians, 1826

They [the Indians] look to our government for protection; rely upon
its kindness and its power; appeal to it for relief to
their wants; and address the president as their GREAT FATHER.

John Marshall in
Cherokee Nation v. *Georgia,* 1831

This is a great day for you and for us. A day of peace and friendship
between you and the whites for all time to come. You are about to be
paid for your lands, and the GREAT FATHER has sent me today to treaty
with you concerning the payment. . . . And the GREAT FATHER wishes you
to have homes, pastures for your horses and fishing places. He wishes you
to learn to farm and your children to go to a good school; and he now
wants me to make a bargain with you, in which you will sell your lands
and in return be provided with all these things.

Isaac I. Stevens at a council with Nisqually,
Puyallup, and Squaxon Indians, 1854

My friends: Your GREAT FATHER whose heart is right, and who loves his red as well as his white children, has heard there is trouble between the whites and Indians on the plains. He has heard that there is war and that blood has been shed. He is opposed to war and loves peace and his heart is sad. He has sent all these big Chiefs to see you and to ascertain what is wrong. . . . Now, if your GREAT FATHER did not love you, he would not send all these big Chiefs so many hundred of miles to hunt you up and converse with you. We are sent here to enquire of you and find out what is the trouble between the white men and you.

Nathaniel G. Taylor, president of the Indian Peace
Commission, speaking to Sioux Indians, 1867

Nothing is more indispensable than the protecting and guiding care of the Government during the dangerous period of transition from savage to civilized life. . . . [The Indian] is overcome by a feeling of helplessness, and he naturally looks to the "GREAT FATHER" to take him by the hand and guide him on. That guiding hand must necessarily be one of authority and power to command confidence and respect. It can be only that of the government which the Indian is accustomed to regard as a sort of omnipotence on earth. Everything depends upon the wisdom and justice of that guidance.

Secretary of the Interior Carl Schurz in an
article in the *North American Review*, 1881

[The Indians] are the wards of the Nation. From time immemorial, the Indians have been taught to call the President of this mighty republic the "GREAT FATHER," and all communications from them to the Indian Office are addressed in that way. In their speeches, they say that they regard the President as a father, that they are his children, and they look to him for protection, for justice, for succor, for advice.

Commissioner of Indian Affairs Thomas J. Morgan
in an address entitled "A Plea for the Papoose"

Contents

Andrew Jackson and Removal. Motivation for Removal.
Controversy and Debate. The Cherokee Cases.

VOLUME II

Maps

VOLUME I

VOLUME II

Illustrations

Tables

Preface

The relations of the federal government of the United States with the American Indians through two centuries form a major component of American political history. From the beginnings of the nation, when some Indian tribes were political and military entities of power and independence with whom the young nation had to come to terms, to the present, when newly energized tribal organizations once again emphasize a government-to-government relation with the United States, Indians as tribes or as individuals have been persistently in the consciousness of officials of all three branches of the federal government.

I have long recognized the need for a comprehensive history of the relations between the United States government and the Indians. Excellent one-volume surveys of the subject exist, and there are now a great many scholarly studies of selected periods or particular aspects of American Indian policy. But what I have attempted here is a survey of the full scope of American Indian policy from the time of the Revolutionary War to 1980. I have sought to provide a reasonably complete discussion of the course of Indian policy development and implementation, with its many vicissitudes, and to indicate in the footnotes the essential documents and secondary works in which this history is set forth.

Because federal policies have rested on past experience, no full understanding of any part of the story is possible without seeing what went before or without examining the working out of the programs. I have learned from this comprehensive study that there was much more fundamental unity and continuity in the government's policy than I had previously thought from looking only at selected partial aspects or at limited chronological periods.

The officials of the federal government in the executive branch and in Congress faced a serious problem as greatly diverse cultures came into contact and often conflict within the expanding territorial limits of the United States. The Indian cultures were amazingly rich and diverse; but the Indian groups quickly fell far behind the white society in numbers and technical skills, and they were in general no match for the economically and militarily powerful United States. When the Indian tribes, early in the nineteenth century, lost their powerful European allies in the New World—with whose assistance they might have hoped to hold off the onslaught of white American advance—it was clear to both Indians and whites that the United States dealt with the Indians from a position of dominance.

Cries for extermination of the Indians occasionally sounded by aggressive frontiersmen and exasperated frontier commanders were rejected by United States officials responsible for Indian affairs. These officials instead sought to treat the Indians honorably, even though they acted within a set of circumstances that rested on the premise that white society would prevail. The best term for this persistent attitude is *paternalism*, a determination to do what was best for the Indians according to white norms, which translated into protection, subsistence of the destitute, punishment of the unruly, and eventually taking the Indians by the hand and leading them along the path to white civilization and Christianity. The relationship was sometimes described, as it was by Chief Justice John Marshall in 1832, as resembling that of a ward and its guardian. The modern emphasis on the trust responsibility of the federal government toward the Indians has elements of the same attitude.

In the nineteenth century, it was common for Indians to refer to the president (head and symbol of the United States government) as the Great Father, and the term was adopted by government officials as well. It was an appropriate usage for the paternalistic attitude of the federal government toward the Indians as dependent children. The Great Father rhetoric largely disappeared after 1880, but paternalism continued and sometimes increased. Federal concern for the education, health, and economic development of its wards colored the history of Indian policy in the twentieth century. And when, in the decades of the 1960s and 1970s, the renewal of Indian self-determination came to the fore, it was protest against continuing governmental paternalism that gave form to the movement.

Paternalism was considered by its white practitioners as a humane Christian approach to the serious problems that faced the nation in its relations with the Indians, and it was accepted by many Indians as welcome and necessary support. But paternalism also had its oppressive aspects, and criticism of it has frequently arisen, sometimes in the form of a desire to get the government out of the Indian business and let the Indians fend for themselves within the larger white society and sometimes in the form of criticism of the weakening of the Indians' ability to direct their own destiny. Throughout the two centuries covered by this study, however, the controlling force in Indian-white relations has been the policy determined by the white government, not the wishes of the Indians.

This history is divided into two volumes at roughly 1880. The year is a neat chronological dividing point, for each volume thus covers a century, but it is more than that, too. Although nothing of startling historical importance happened in that precise year, the date can be used to note the end of an era marked by diplomatic dealings with the Indian tribes and marred by almost incessant military encounters with them in one region or another. The century after 1880, in contradistinction, was dominated by a new movement to destroy old tribal relations and traditional customs and to accomplish the ultimate acculturation and assimilation of individual Indians into white society.

As in my previous historical studies of Indian-white relations in the United States, large parts of which are incorporated in this book, I concentrate on the history of federal Indian policy and do not treat in detail the history of the Indian communities. I do this in part as a matter of expediency, because it is possible to survey the course of government policy in a single work, whereas it is not possible to treat the "Indian story" in such a unified way, given the great diversity of Indian groups and of individual responses within those groups. But my approach is justified also, I think, because the policies and programs of the United States have had a determining influence on the history of the Indian tribes. In the period of Indian-white contact that I cover, no history of a tribe can be understood without a detailed consideration of treaties, land cessions, the reservation system, and Indian educational programs, for example, which formed the substance of government policy and action.

I have boldly carried the story to 1980, for historical studies of Indian affairs have for too long emphasized events of the nineteenth century. Indian communities, like all human societies, have changed and developed through time, and their relations with the United States government have also changed. The policies and programs of the twentieth century are as important for understanding the status of Indians today in American society as are those of the nineteenth. There are difficulties, of course, in moving so close to the present in the writing of history, before the outcome of laws and decisions can be evaluated. Readers will appreciate that, in the case of many recent events, I have been unable to give the proportion of attention to them that later historians may find appropriate. But I have attempted to describe the multifarious developments that occurred and to indicate the arguments and purposes that lay behind them.

FRANCIS PAUL PRUCHA, S.J.
Marquette University

Acknowledgments

In a study of this size, reliance on the work of other scholars and the assistance of archivists and librarians is manifest. I cannot begin to thank adequately the staffs of the National Archives, Library of Congress, Milwaukee Public Library, Harvard University Library, State Historical Society of Wisconsin, Newberry Library, Huntington Library, Department of the Interior Library, and Marquette University Library, as well as many others, who have helped in one way or another. Historians and other scholars who have contributed to my knowledge and understanding are altogether too many to name, for I have spoken or corresponded with a great many persons interested in Indian-white relations in the United States, and I have read their books and articles. I owe special mention, however, to Robert F. Berkhofer, Ray Allen Billington, William T. Hagan, Reginald Horsman, Robert M. Kvasnicka, Frederick Merk, Robert Pennington, Martin Ridge, Robert M. Utley, Herman J. Viola, Wilcomb E. Washburn, and Mary E. Young. To my students, too, I owe much gratitude.

My research in Indian affairs has been materially aided by grants and fellowships from the Social Science Research Council, National Endowment for the Humanities, John Simon Guggenheim Foundation, Charles Warren Center for the Study of American History, and Huntington Library. De Rance, Incorporated, has generously provided research funds and has added a sizable subvention for the publication of these volumes. Marquette University, the Marquette Jesuit Community, and the Wisconsin Province of the Society of Jesus have supported my studies in many ways.

In writing this comprehensive history of the federal government's relations with the American Indians, I have drawn on several of my own previously published studies. For permission to use sections verbatim from the following works, I thank the editors and publishers:

American Indian Policy in the Formative Years: The Indian Trade and Intercourse Acts, 1790–1834. Harvard University Press. Copyright © 1962 by the President and Fellows of Harvard College.

The Sword of the Republic: The United States Army on the Frontier, 1783–1846. Macmillan Company. Copyright © by Francis Paul Prucha.

"Andrew Jackson's Indian Policy: A Reassessment." *Journal of American History* 56 (December 1969): 527–39.

Indian Peace Medals in American History. Copyright © 1971 by the State Historical Society of Wisconsin.

"The Image of the Indian in Pre-Civil War America," in *Indiana Historical Society Lectures, 1970–1971.* Copyright © 1971 Indiana Historical Society.

"American Indian Policy in the 1840s: Visions of Reform," in *The Frontier Challenge: Responses to the Trans-Mississippi West,* ed. John G. Clark. Copyright © 1971 by the University Press of Kansas.

American Indian Policy in Crisis: Christian Reformers and the Indian, 1865–1900. Copyright 1976 by the University of Oklahoma Press.

The Churches and the Indian Schools, 1888–1912. Copyright © 1979 by the University of Nebraska Press.

Introduction to *Cherokee Removal: The "William Penn" Essays and Other Writings,* by Jeremiah Evarts. Copyright © 1981 by the University of Tennessee Press.

Indian Policy in the United States: Historical Essays. Copyright © 1981 by the University of Nebraska Press.

The maps were prepared by the Cartographic Laboratory of the University of Nebraska–Lincoln. Picture and map credits are listed separately on pp. 607–8 and 1259–60.

The Great Father

ABBREVIATIONS

ASP:IA	*American State Papers: Indian Affairs*, 2 vols. (Washington: Gales and Seaton, 1832–1834).
CIA Report	Annual Report of the Commissioner of Indian Affairs. For the period 1824–1920, the edition in the congressional serial set is used and the serial number is given.
GPO	United States Government Printing Office.
JCC	*Journals of the Continental Congress*, 34 vols. (Washington: U.S. Government Printing Office, 1904–1937).
Kappler	Charles J. Kappler, comp., *Indian Affairs: Laws and Treaties*, 5 vols. (Washington: U.S. Government Printing Office, 1904–1941). Unless otherwise indicated, references are to vol. 2.
OIA	Records of the Office [Bureau] of Indian Affairs, National Archives, Record Group 75.
OIA CCF	Records of the Office [Bureau] of Indian Affairs, Central Classified Files, National Archives, Record Group 75.
OIA Circulars	Records of the Office [Bureau] of Indian Affairs, Procedural Issuances: Orders and Circulars, National Archives, Record Group 75 (M1121).
OIA LR	Records of the Office [Bureau] of Indian Affairs, Letters Received, National Archives, Record Group 75 (M234).
OIA LS	Records of the Office [Bureau] of Indian Affairs, Letters Sent, National Archives, Record Group 75 (M21).
OSI	Records of the Office of the Secretary of the Interior, National Archives, Record Group 48.
OSI CCF	Records of the Office of the Secretary of the Interior, Central Classified Files, National Archives, Record Group 48.
SW IA LS	Records of the Office of the Secretary of War, Letters Sent, Indian Affairs, National Archives, Record Group 75 (M15).
WNRC	Washington National Records Center, Suitland, Md.

Note: For documents in the congressional serial set the number of the Congress and session are given in this abbreviated form: 92–1.

The Colonial
Experience

Images of the Indians. Christianization.

Invasion of the Indian Lands.

Trade Relations. British Imperial Policy.

The United States government in its relations with the American Indians built upon English colonial and imperial experience. The policy it developed was in many respects, of course, a response to specific conditions on the frontier, but little if anything was begun entirely de novo. Two centuries of English contact with the natives in the New World had provided a rich set of conceptions about the Indians and numerous examples of policies and programs concerning the interaction of the two cultures. There were colonial precedents for all the interfaces between white government and Indian groups—missionary contacts, military encounters, trade relations, and land transfers—upon which the new nation could draw. And after individual colonies seemed unable to regulate the settlers and maintain honorable and tranquil relations with the Indians, imperial programs of control furnished models of centralized management of Indian affairs that were clear in the minds of the Founding Fathers. To understand the foundation on which the United States erected its complex and evolving policy, one must look, however sketchily, at English and other European beginnings in America.[1]

1. There is an immense literature dealing with Indian affairs in the European colonial period. Douglas Edward Leach, *The Northern Colonial Frontier, 1607–1763* (New York: Holt, Rinehart and Winston, 1966), and W. Stitt Robinson, *The Southern Colonial Frontier, 1607–1763* (Albuquerque: University of New Mexico Press, 1979), offer general accounts that place Indian relations in a broad context. Recent general works of value are

IMAGES OF THE INDIANS

When Christopher Columbus struck the Western Hemisphere by chance in his attempt to sail west around the world to the riches of the Orient, he found not only land but peoples. Unable to comprehend that he was opening up a "new" world and confident that he had touched some outlying reaches of the Indies, he called the inhabitants *Indians*, a name that has lasted for five centuries despite its descriptive inaccuracy and the occasional attempts to substitute a more suitable name. These peoples were numerous and magnificently diverse, and it was immediately evident that they were different from the Europeans who came in contact with them. The Indians had to be accommodated into the intellectual patterns of the Western European mind, and practical conventions for dealing with them had to be developed.

The Europeans dealt with the Indians as they perceived them, and this perception came ultimately from detailed observation. Explorers, churchmen, traders, governors, scientists, and casual travelers all were fascinated by the strange land and its inhabitants and produced a voluminous literature about the Indians. No aspect of Indian life and customs was unexamined or unreported. The early Spanish reports were eagerly devoured by curious Europeans, who translated them into their own languages. And as the Portuguese, French, English, and Dutch followed the Spanish to America, they created their own reservoir of facts, surmises, and fanciful tales about the Indians.[2] The accumulated images of the Indians, however, were

Gary B. Nash, *Red, White, and Black: The Peoples of Early America* (Englewood Cliffs, New Jersey: Prentice-Hall, 1974), and Wilbur R. Jacobs, *Dispossessing the American Indian: Indians and Whites on the Colonial Frontier* (New York: Charles Scribner's Sons, 1972). Two works that present sharply conflicting views of the Puritans and the Indians are Alden T. Vaughan, *New England Frontier: Puritans and Indians, 1620–1675*, rev. ed. (New York: W. W. Norton and Company, 1979), and Francis Jennings, *The Invasion of America: Indians, Colonialism, and the Cant of Conquest* (Chapel Hill: University of North Carolina Press, 1975). An excellent study on the middle colonies is Allen W. Trelease, *Indian Affairs in Colonial New York: The Seventeenth Century* (Ithaca: Cornell University Press, 1960). Views of southern Indians are well treated in Richard Beale Davis, *Intellectual Life in the Colonial South, 1585–1763*, 3 vols. (Knoxville: University of Tennessee Press, 1978), 1: 103–256. A perceptive analysis of writings on colonial Indian matters is James Axtell, "The Ethnohistory of Early America: A Review Essay," *William and Mary Quarterly*, 3d series 35 (January 1978): 110–44. See also Axtell, *The European and the Indian: Essays in the Ethnohistory of Colonial North America* (New York: Oxford University Press, 1981).

2. A number of historians have recently examined the writings of Englishmen in the early period of colonization to extract views about Indians and their relations to Europeans. The fullest compendium of such views is H. C. Porter, *The Inconstant Savage: England and the North American Indian, 1500–1600* (London: Duckworth, 1979), but it offers few clear themes. Bernard W. Sheehan, *Savagism and Civility: Indians and English-*

not free of preconceptions. The Europeans already had established patterns into which to cast the inhabitants of the New World, who, since they lived in or close to the state of nature, were commonly called "savages."[3] Two basic images developed, contradictory in content.

The first was that of the "noble savage," natural man living without technology and elaborate societal structures. Naked without shame, unconcerned about private ownership and the accumulation of material wealth but sharing all things unselfishly, and free from the problems of government, the Indian represented an idyllic state from which the European had strayed or fallen. Dwelling in an earthly paradise, the Indians were a living example of a golden age, long past in European history but now suddenly thrust again upon the world's consciousness. John Donne in 1597 wrote, "The unripe side of the earth produces men like Adam before he ate the apple." And Marc Lescarbot, a Frenchman who visited the New World in 1606 and whose report was quickly published in an English translation, noted that the Indians lived in common, "the most perfect and most worthy life of man," a mark of the "ancient golden age." This good Indian welcomed the European invaders and treated them courteously and generously. He was handsome in appearance, dignified in manner, and brave in combat, and in all he exhibited a primitivism that had great appeal to many Europeans.[4]

The second pattern was that of the "ignoble savage," treacherous, cruel, perverse, and in many ways approaching the brute beasts with whom he shared the wilderness. In this view, incessant warfare and cruelty to captives marked the Indians. Ritual cannibalism and human sacrifice were the ultimate abominations; but countless descriptions of Indian life noted the squalor, the filth, the indolence, the lack of discipline, the thievery, and the hard lot accorded Indian women. Not a few Englishmen saw the

---

men in Colonial Virginia (Cambridge: Cambridge University Press, 1980), emphasizes the disparity that Englishmen saw between the savagism of the Indians and their own civility. Karen Ordahl Kupperman, *Settling with the Indians: The Meeting of English and Indian Cultures in America, 1580–1640* (Totowa, New Jersey: Rowman and Littlefield, 1980), in contrast, argues that the English writers recognized civility in the Indians and judged them basically as a "common sort" of person similar to the common sort of Englishmen. An excellent general account of white conceptions of the Indians is Robert F. Berkhofer, Jr., *The White Man's Indian: Images of the American Indian from Columbus to the Present* (New York: Alfred A. Knopf, 1978).

3. The term *savage* must be understood in its early meaning of a person who lived in the wilderness in a state of nature, without necessary connotations of cruelty and ruthlessness. There is an extended discussion of the terms *Indian* and *savage* in Berkhofer, *White Man's Indian,* pp. 3–31. See also Jennings, *Invasion of America,* pp. 73–81.

4. Donne and Lescarbot are quoted in Sheehan, *Savagism and Civility,* pp. 22, 31. Paradisiacal imagery, primitivism, and the noble savage concept are discussed in Sheehan, pp. 9–36, and in Berkhofer, *White Man's Indian,* pp. 28, 72–80.

Indians with their superstitions and inhuman practices as literally children of the Devil.[5]

The threads of these two conceptions intertwined in strange ways, and
one or the other was drawn upon as suited the occasion. What persisted,
however, were the notions of otherness, dependency, and inferiority. "Savagism" (whether noble or ignoble) was contrasted with "civility"; natural
life in the wilds was opposed to disciplined life in civil society. There was
little doubt in the minds of the Europeans (pace those who used the noble
savage concept to condemn evils in their own society) that savagism was
an inferior mode of existence and must give way to civility (civilization).
The Indians were "younger brethren," dependents whom persons in superior positions claimed the right and obligation to shape into a new and civilized mold, by persuasion if possible and ultimately by force.[6]

The concept of savagism and inferiority did not imply racism, that is, a
belief that the Indian was an inherently different kind of being incapable of
rising out of an inferior condition. There was little question in the minds
of Englishmen that the Indians were human beings like themselves, a belief firmly planted in the scriptural account of Adam as the single progeni-
tor of all men. Nor was color an obstacle, for the brownness or tawny complexion of the Indians was considered to be the result of conditioning by
the elements or by the use of cosmetics on persons born basically white.
Not until the very end of the seventeenth century was there any reference
to Indians as red, and then the term may have had symbolic meaning or
arisen from the use of war paint.[7] The dichotomy between noble and ignoble savagism was never completely resolved, for the a priori images were
fixed, and from time to time these simplistic positions resurfaced in theoretical discussions of the Indians.

As the English experience deepened, the theoretical concepts of noble
and ignoble savagery (though long continued in imaginative literature)
were replaced by more realistic and complex appraisals based on practical
encounters. Remnants of Indian tribes remained in the developing colonies, often in a state of abject dependency, but the Indians who received the
attention of the English colonial authorities in the century preceding the

5. Sheehan, *Savagism and Civility*, pp. 37–88.

6. Sheehan, *Savagism and Civility*, makes a strong case for the contrast between the
two states, but he crystallizes the concepts unduly. Kupperman, *Settling with the Indians*, especially pp. 170–71, discusses the tutelary role of the English in regard to the
natives. She argues that the exploitation of the Indians came not because of ideas of racial
superiority on the part of the English but because of the ultimate powerlessness of the
natives.

7. See Wesley Frank Craven, *White, Red, and Black: The Seventeenth-Century Vir-
ginian* (Charlottesville: University Press of Virginia, 1971), pp. 39–41; Vaughan, *New
England Frontier*, rev. ed., p. xv.

independence of the United States were separate groups existing outside the areas of concentrated English settlement. More or less independent "nations" (like the Cherokees and other southern Indians and the Six Nations of the Iroquois in the north) entered into the diplomatic relations of the age along with a multiplicity of other political entities—French and Spanish as well as English colonies. These Indian groups were recognized and dealt with as distinct political entities, and forms of political structure familiar to Europeans were frequently attributed to them whether or not they accurately reflected the actual political organization of the tribes.[8] Yet the white goal continued to be the ultimate transformation of the Indians with whom they came into contact, a "civilizing" process that reached its apogee in the United States at the end of the nineteenth century.

CHRISTIANIZATION

The civility toward which the English hoped to bring the savages of the New World had as its companion Christianity. Although the two could be separated in theory, in practice they were nearly always combined. Thus an Englishman promoting colonization in 1583 could speak of doing "a most excellent worke, in respect of reducing the savage people to Christianity and civilitie." Or, as William Crashaw phrased it in 1610: "We give the Savages what they most need. 1. Civilitie for their bodies. 2. Christianitie for their soules." With sincere convictions, although without much actual success in the end, the English colonizers placed conversion of the Indians high among their objectives.[9]

Indeed, God's providence in permitting the discovery of the New World by the Christian nations of Europe was considered a mandate for Christianization. A writer reasoned in 1577 "that Christians have discovered these countries and people, which so long have byen unknowne, and they not us: which plainly may argue, that it is Gods good will and pleasure, that they should be instructed in his divine service and religion, whiche from the beginning, have been nouzeled and nourished in Atheisme, gross ignorance, and barbarous behavior." Despite repeated fears and assertions that the Indians were the children of Satan, Europeans generally believed

8. Edward H. Spicer, *A Short History of the Indians in the United States* (New York: Van Nostrand Reinhold Company, 1969), pp. 11–44, has a good discussion of the "many nations" interacting.

9. Christopher Carleill, "A Briefe and Summary Discourse upon the Intended Voyage to the Hithermost Parts of America," and "Crashaw's Sermon," quoted in Sheehan, *Savagism and Civility*, pp. 117, 124. See Sheehan's chapter on conversion, pp. 116–43, and Davis, *Colonial South*, 1: 176–96.

that conversion was possible and repeatedly asserted missionary motives for colonization. The first charter of the Virginia Company of 1606 included the declaration that propagation of the gospel was a principal purpose of the enterprise, and instructions to Governor Thomas Gates directed conversion of the natives "as the most pious and noble end of this plantation." Attempts were made to provide schools in which the Indian children could learn both religion and civil manners. Plans and collection of funds for a college at Henrico in Virginia were an early indication of the attempts in the southern colonies, and the idea never died. The results, to be sure, were minimal, for the Indians remained attached to their old ways, and missionary enthusiasm waned in the face of so little success. Frontier settlers had little interest in converting the natives, and what initiative there was came from the coastal areas or England.[10]

The Puritans of New England, of course, made conversion of the Indians a major justification of their undertaking. The Massachusetts charter charged the officers to "Wynn and incite the Natives . . . [to] the onlie true God and Saviour of Mankinde," and the oath of the governor directed him to "doe your best endeavor to draw on the natives of this country . . . to the true God." The seal of the Governor and Company of Massachusetts Bay, 1629, shows an Indian crying out, "Come over and help us."[11]

The goal of conversion remained throughout the period of settlement. Impressive work was done by the missionary Thomas Mayhew on Martha's Vineyard, and John Eliot, the "apostle to the Indians," won fame for his missionary zeal and effectiveness among the Indians as he established "praying towns" of natives. Parliament promoted the good work by chartering in 1649 the Society for Propagation of the Gospell in New-England. Education was at the heart of the endeavor, and the establishment of an Indian college at Harvard was an indication of the Puritans' determination. But even with the determination, zeal, and notable success of a few missionaries, the total number of converted Indians remained small, in part, no doubt, because of the total transformation required by the Puritans of their converts.[12]

10. Dionyse Settle, *A True Reporte of the Laste Voyage into West and Northwest Regions*, quoted in Sheehan, *Savagism and Civility*, p. 119; Davis, *Colonial South*, 1: 188–90.

11. Vaughan, *New England Frontier*, pp. 235–308; quotations p. 236. The seal is reproduced in Jennings, *Invasion of America*, p. 229.

12. A harsh view of Puritan missionary efforts, contrasting with that of Vaughan, is found in Jennings, *Invasion of America*, pp. 228–53. Jennings is especially critical of Eliot, whose fame as an Indian missionary he labels fraudulent. A similarly critical view is expressed in Neal E. Salisbury, "Red Puritans: The 'Praying Indians' of Massachusetts Bay and John Eliot," *William and Mary Quarterly*, 3d series 31 (January 1974): 27–54. Sympathetic portraits of Eliot are provided in Ola Elizabeth Winslow, *John Eliot: "Apostle*

Of particular note among Christians who preached to the Indians were the Quakers, members of the Society of Friends. Their founder, George Fox, instructed his American followers in 1667 to "go and discourse with some of the *Heathen Kings,* desiring them to gather their Council and People together, that you may declare *God's Everlasting Truth,* and his *Everlasting Way of Life and Salvation* to them, knowing that *Christ* is the promise of *God* to them, *a Covenant of Light to the Gentiles.*" The Friends followed that admonition and did missionary and educational work among the Indians with a gentleness and lack of arrogance that maintained mutual good feelings even though it did not result in any converts to Quakerism. The Quakers followed a policy of nonviolence toward the Indians and showed a willingness to accept Indian culture unknown among other groups of colonists; the common dichotomy between "savagery" and "civilization" had no place in their worldview. The Quaker colony established by William Penn had peaceful relations with the Indians, the result in part of Penn's insistence that lands be fairly purchased from the Indians; and the reputation of Penn and his followers for fair dealing was strong in the nineteenth century and has lasted to the present day.[13]

The great missionary upsurge in the United States after 1800 had a long history of colonial efforts as precedent, but in the English colonies, as later, mundane affairs overshadowed missionary work and at times seemed to obliterate it altogether.

INVASION OF THE INDIAN LANDS

The great distinguishing feature of English relations with the Indian groups was replacement of the Indians on the land by white settlers, not conversion and assimilation of the Indians into European colonial society. The

---

to the Indians" (Boston: Houghton Mifflin Company, 1968), and Samuel Eliot Morison, "John Eliot, Apostle to the Indians," in *Builders of the Bay Colony* (Boston: Houghton Mifflin Company, 1930), pp. 289–319. A strong emphasis on Puritan relations with the Indians as sacral rather than secular history is given in the documents and commentary in Charles M. Segal and David C. Stineback, *Puritans, Indians, and Manifest Destiny* (New York: G. P. Putnam's Sons, 1977). See also William Kellaway, *The New England Company, 1649–1776: Missionary Society to the American Indians* (New York: Barnes and Noble, 1961).

13. Frederick B. Tolles, "Nonviolent Contact: The Quakers and the Indians," *Proceedings of the American Philosophical Society* 107 (April 15, 1963): 93–101; Rayner Wickersham Kelsey, *Friends and the Indians, 1655–1917* (Philadelphia: Associated Executive Committee of Friends on Indian Affairs, 1917); Thomas E. Drake, "William Penn's Experiment in Race Relations," *Pennsylvania Magazine of History and Biography* 68 (October 1944): 372–87.

Spanish colonies to the south were marked by subjugation of a massive concentrated native population and its use as a primary labor force in exploiting the mineral and agricultural resources of the conquered lands. The Spaniards, in addition, carried on large-scale missionary efforts to Christianize the Indians, and the church was as significant as the state in the development of Spanish America. The preponderantly male Spanish colonists, moreover, took Indian women as wives and concubines, incorporating the Indians biologically as well as socially into Spanish society. None of these situations obtained in the English colonies to any large extent. The difference can be explained in part by the diverse attitudes toward other peoples of the southern and the northern Europeans, but it was the fundamental nature and place of English colonization that determined the case. The Indians did not present the same usefulness to the English that they did to the Spanish. There were no heavy Indian populations to be turned into a labor force and at the beginning no real need, for the English came to settle and cultivate the land. Nor was intermarriage or other liaison between the whites and Indians called for on a large scale among the family-oriented English colonists.[14]

An underlying condition of English settlement was the depopulation that had previously occurred among the Indian tribes with whom the first Englishmen had come in contact. European diseases, of which smallpox was only the most important among many, struck the Indians with devastating force, for the inhabitants of the New World had developed no immunity to Old World diseases. Large areas were stripped of once heavy populations, and the cleared fields of the former inhabitants were taken over by white settlers, who often saw the hand of Providence in their good fortune.[15]

The replacement of the Indians on the land became the basis for enduring conflict with the Indians who remained, and Indian wars marked the English experience as they did that of the United States. In the very beginning, the natives received the English colonists hospitably, greeted them

14. Nash, *Red, White, and Black*, pp. 65–67.

15. Indian demography has become a subject of great interest, and new estimates of aboriginal populations have greatly increased previous figures. A now classic article is Henry F. Dobyns, "Estimating Aboriginal American Population: An Appraisal of Techniques with a New Hemispheric Estimate," *Current Anthropology* 7 (October 1966): 395–416; see also Dobyns, *Native American Historical Demography: A Critical Bibliography* (Bloomington: Indiana University Press, 1976). There is a discussion of the effect of European diseases on the Indians in Alfred W. Crosby, Jr., *The Columbian Exchange: Biological and Cultural Consequences of 1492* (Westport, Connecticut: Greenwood Publishing Company, 1972), pp. 35–63. See also Wilbur R. Jacobs, "The Tip of an Iceberg: Pre-Columbian Indian Demography and Some Implications for Revisionism," *William and Mary Quarterly*, 3d series 31 (January 1974): 123–32.

with signs of friendship, and supplied them with food. But the image of savagism in the minds of the Europeans included a strong element of treachery on the part of the savages, and English behavior toward the Indians soon brought real enmity to the surface. It became evident to the Indians that the colonists were moving in to stay, and as the English expanded, encroaching upon Indian lands and in many cases treating the inhabitants despicably, the Indians resisted with force; sometimes young warriors acted without tribal approval, sometimes considered attacks were planned and executed by skilled tribal leaders. Indian rivalries, too, contributed to the conflicts, for by aiding one or another group that eagerly sought help against its enemies, the English became involved in intertribal wars. The Europeans for their part looked for Indian allies in their own conflicts. Sooner or later most tribes became attached in some fashion to French, Spanish, or British imperial systems. The pattern of hostility and open war thus began early and was a dominant part of Indian-white relations until almost the end of the nineteenth century.[16]

The first case was the massacre of 1622 in Virginia, in which the Indians under Opechancanough rose up against the white settlers who had invaded their lands and quickly killed a quarter to one-third of the population. English reaction was immediate and vengeful; the massacre was used as an excuse for a massive retaliation against the Indians, for it was looked upon as proof that Indians could not be trusted, even when professing friendship. Soon after, in New England, the Pequot War of 1637 began formal conflicts between the Indians and the English. The Pequots, moving into the Connecticut River Valley, met Puritans migrating into the same region and posed a threat to the peaceful expansion of the Massachusetts Bay Colony. Pequot harassment of the settlements brought war as the English attacked the hostile Indians in order to protect the nascent colony in Connecticut. Such conflicts set a pattern. A new surprise attack by Indians in Virginia in 1644, which killed five hundred whites, brought new reprisals, and Bacon's Rebellion of 1676 had strong anti-Indian origins. In 1675–1676 King Philip's War in New England furnished still another case of warfare instigated by the Indians in a desperate attempt to stop the advancing tide of English settlement.[17]

16. An excellent comprehensive study that covers colonial Indian wars is Douglas Edward Leach, *Arms for Empire: A Military History of the British Colonies in North America, 1607–1763* (New York: Macmillan Company, 1973); see especially pp. 42–79.

17. Alden T. Vaughan, "'Expulsion of the Savages': English Policy and the Virginia Massacre of 1622," *William and Mary Quarterly*, 3d series 35 (January 1978): 57–84; Vaughan, "Pequots and Puritans: The Causes of the War of 1637," ibid. 21 (April 1964): 256–69; Douglas Edward Leach, *Flintlock and Tomahawk: New England in King Philip's War* (New York: Macmillan Company, 1958). Most accounts of the English colonial experience deal with these conflicts.

These wars were brutal encounters—"savage" warfare on both sides—
and confirmed the English in attitudes of fear and hatred toward the Indians. The terms of peace imposed on the defeated Indians were harsh and
drawn up to ensure the future security of expanding white settlements. As
in the aftermath of the Virginia massacre of 1622, the Indians were killed
or forced out of the areas of white settlement. In some cases reserved lands
with set boundaries were marked out for them, but white pressures against
these reservations were incessant. Hopes for intermingling and coexis-
tence of the whites and the Indians eventually collapsed.

Forced conquest, of course, was not the only means by which lands
were transferred to white ownership. There was much theoretical discussion about the rights of savage, non-Christian peoples to the land they
occupied, of whether the Indians and similar people could claim lands
against Christian nations; and the idea that the lands in the New World
were a *vacuum domicilium,* a wasteland, open for the taking, had wide
acceptance. The God-fearing Puritans of Massachusetts Bay Colony found
religious justification for dispossessing the Indians, and John Winthrop,
the colony's first governor, declared: "The whole earth is the lords Garden
& he hath given it to the sonnes of men, wᵗʰ a general Condicion, Gen:
1.28. Increase & multiply, replenish the earth & subdue it. . . . And for the
Natives of New England they enclose noe land neither have any settled
habitation nor any tame cattle to improve the land by, & soe have noe
other but a naturall right to those countries Soe as if we leave them sufficient for their use wee may lawfully take the rest, there being more than
enough for them & us."[18] This argument echoed through the decades in the
words of later religion-minded men.

The supremacy of the cultivator over the hunter was a classic weapon in
the arsenal of the dispossessors. The argument was given legal expression
in the writings of the eighteenth-century Swiss jurist Emmerich de Vattel,
whose *Law of Nations* became a standard handbook. He wrote:

> There is another celebrated question, to which the discovery of
> the new world has principally given rise. It is asked if a nation may
> lawfully take possession of a part of a vast country, in which there are
> found none but erratic nations, incapable by the smallness of their
> numbers, to people the whole? We have already observed in estab-
> lishing the obligation to cultivate the earth, that these nations can-

18. *Conclusions for the Plantation in New England,* quoted in Albert K. Weinberg,
Manifest Destiny: A Study of Nationalist Expansionism in American History (Bal-
timore: Johns Hopkins Press, 1935), pp. 74–75; Wilcomb E. Washburn, "The Moral and
Legal Justifications for Dispossessing the Indians," in James Morton Smith, ed., *Seven-
teenth-Century America: Essays in Colonial History* (Chapel Hill: University of North
Carolina Press, 1959), pp. 15–32.

not exclusively appropriate to themselves more land than they have occasion for, and which they are unable to settle and cultivate. Their removing their habitations through these immense regions, cannot be taken for a true and legal possession; and the people of Europe, too closely pent up, finding land of which these nations are in no particular want, and of which they make no actual and constant use, may lawfully possess it, and establish colonies there. We have already said, that the earth belongs to the human race in general, and was designed to furnish it with subsistence; if each nation had resolved from the beginning, to appropriate to itself a vast country, that the people might live only by hunting, fishing, and wild fruits, our globe would not be sufficient to maintain a tenth part of its present inhabitants. People have not then deviated from the views of nature in confining the Indians within narrow limits.[19]

Aside from conquest in a "just war" and the aggressive encroachment of individual settlers, however, the English colonies generally did not simply dispossess the Indians as though they had no rights of any kind to the land. The vast claims in the New World made by European monarchs on the slightest pretence of "discovery" were claims against other European monarchs, not against the aboriginal inhabitants of those lands, and the handsome grants made to trading companies or individual proprietors in the form of colonial charters (with their extravagant language of lands extending from sea to sea) were of the same nature. The English settlers took steps to "quiet the Indian title" to the land before they took possession— "extinguishing the Indian title" was the terminology commonly used in later times by the United States.[20] But this did not solve all problems, for the Indian and the white systems of land tenure were quite different. The Indians had a notion of communal ownership of land, the English one of individual ownership in fee simple; neither fully understood the concept of the other.

Many years of actual contact between the groups were necessary before settled relations were agreed upon. But as European exploration and colonization increased, a theory in regard to the territory in America gained general acceptance, a theory developed by the European nations without consultation with the natives but one that did not totally disregard the In-

19. Emmerich de Vattel, *The Law of Nations; or, Principles of the Law of Nature, Applied to the Conduct and Affairs of Nations and Sovereigns* (Northhampton, Massachusetts: Simeon Butler, 1820), pp. 158–59 (bk. 1, chap. 18, para. 209).

20. There is a long discussion of colonial practices in regard to Indian lands in Cyrus Thomas, "Introduction," in Charles C. Royce, comp., *Indian Land Cessions in the United States*, Eighteenth Annual Report of the Bureau of American Ethnology, 1896–1897, part 2 (Washington: GPO, 1899), pp. 527–639.

dians' rights. According to this theory, the European discoverer acquired the right of preemption, the right to acquire title to the soil from the natives in the area—by purchase if the Indians were willing to sell or by conquest—and to succeed the natives in occupying the soil if they should voluntarily leave the country or become extinct. Discovery gave this right against later discoverers; it could hardly make claim against the original possessors of the soil, the native Indians. In practice, nevertheless, and eventually in theory, absolute dominion or sovereignty over the land rested in the European nations or their successors, leaving to the aborigines the possessory and usufructuary rights to the land they occupied and used.[21]

Although there were many cases in which individual colonists acquired land directly from Indians by purchase or some other sort of deed, abuses arose in these private arrangements. Colonial laws struck at the difficulty by declaring null and void all bargains made with the Indians that did not have governmental approval.[22] Not only did such laws seek to remove causes of resentment among the Indians by preventing unjust and fraudulent purchases, but they aimed as well at preserving the rights of the Crown or the proprietor to the land, which would be seriously impaired by extinguishment of Indian titles in favor of private persons. The preamble of the South Carolina act of December 18, 1739, called attention to this double motivation behind the restrictive legislation of the colonial governments, noting that "the practice of purchasing lands from the Indians may prove of very dangerous consequence to the peace and safety of this Province, such purchases being generally obtained from Indians by unfair representation, fraud and circumvention, or by making them gifts or presents of little value, by which practices, great resentments and animosities have been created amongst the Indians towards the inhabitants of this Province," and that "such practices tend to manifest prejudice of his Majesty's just right and title to the soil of this Province, vested in his Majesty by the surrender of the late Lords Proprietors."[23]

A common vehicle for dealing with the Indians for land, as also for more generalized relations of trade and of peace and war, was the treaty negotiation. Formal and stately ceremonials marked the interchanges, in which

21. Washburn, "Moral and Legal Justifications for Dispossessing the Indians," pp. 16–18, points out the "speculative" nature of the claims advanced by the European discoverers.

22. *The Colonial Laws of Massachusetts* (Boston, 1889), p. 161; *The Colonial Laws of New York from the Year 1664 to the Revolution*, 5 vols. (Albany: J. B. Lyon, 1894–1896), 1: 149; James T. Mitchell and Henry Flanders, eds. *The Statutes at Large of Pennsylvania from 1682 to 1801*, 16 vols. (Harrisburg, 1896–1911), 4: 154–56; Thomas Cooper, ed., *The Statutes at Large of South Carolina*, 10 vols. (Columbia: A. S. Johnston, 1836–1841), 3: 526.

23. *Statutes at Large of South Carolina*, 3: 525–26.

the English colonists adapted their proceedings to the deliberate and highly metaphorical patterns of the Indians. The eighteenth-century treaties with the Iroquois, for example, were dramatic documents indicating a shrewdness and eloquence on the part of the Indians that were often a match for the self-interest of the whites. It is in the treaties that one sees best the acceptance by Europeans of the nationhood of the Indian groups that became a fixed principle in the national policy of the United States, although the colonial treaties for the most part were in the form of reports of the speeches and negotiations as well as articles of agreement (all sealed with the presentation of strings and belts of wampum or other gifts), rather than in the cold legal contract form in which United States treaties were cast.[24]

The treaties did not solve the problem of the steady pressure of white settlers on the Indian hunting grounds, and it is difficult to explain the slowness with which the imperial government came to realize the danger of these white encroachments. Continuing to rely on presents in order to keep the Indians attached to the English cause, officials only gradually awakened to the realization that the way to keep the Indians happy would be to remove the causes of their resentment and discontent.

Conferences between the Indians and the Albany Congress in 1754 emphasized the point, for the Indians made known their resentment in unmistakable terms. "We told you a little while ago," said one speaker for the Mohawks, "that we had an uneasiness on our minds, and we shall now tell you what it is; it is concerning our land." Again and again in the course of the conferences, Indians complained of the steady encroachment of whites onto their lands through purchases that the Indians refused to acknowledge or without any semblance of title at all.[25] No matter how great the

24. There is an intelligent discussion of colonial treaty making in Davis, *Colonial South*, 1: 239–54; the process of treaties and gift giving in the north is treated in Wilbur R. Jacobs, *Diplomacy and Indian Gifts: Anglo-French Rivalry along the Ohio and Northwest Frontier, 1747–1763* (Stanford: Stanford University Press, 1950); Dorothy V. Jones, *License for Empire: Colonialism by Treaty in Early America* (Chicago: University of Chicago Press, 1982), discusses British treaty making after 1763. A useful list with synopses of printed Indian treaties is given in Henry F. DePuy, *A Bibliography of the English Colonial Treaties with the American Indians, Including a Synopsis of Each Treaty* (New York: Lenox Club, 1917), but it is necessary to read the full treaties to appreciate their nature. A handsomely printed compilation is Julian P. Boyd, ed., *Indian Treaties Printed by Benjamin Franklin, 1736–1762* (Philadelphia: Historical Society of Pennsylvania, 1938). An ongoing compilation is *Early American Indian Documents: Treaties and Laws, 1607–1789* (Washington: University Publications of America, 1979–). The dramatic quality of the treaties is analyzed in Lawrence C. Wroth, "The Indian Treaty as Literature," *Yale Review* 17 (July 1928): 749–66.

25. E. B. O'Callaghan, ed., *Documents Relative to the Colonial History of the State of New-York*, 15 vols. (Albany: Weed, Parsons and Company, 1853–1887), 6: 853–92.

presents made to the tribes, gifts could not cover over the fundamental reasons for Indian hostility to the English.

TRADE RELATIONS

Colonial bargaining with the Indians for land was but one aspect of the
transactions between the two races. Trade in general was the great point of
contact, and the exchange of goods became a complex mixture of economic, political, and military elements. Trade was of inestimable importance to the colonies economically, but political considerations came to
overshadow all else. Peace and at times the very existence of the colonies
depended on Indian attachment to the English. Presents to the Indians
were long a favored method of ensuring the allegiance of the tribes, and
constant efforts to prevent abuses in dealing with the Indians aimed to secure peace on the frontiers. But the fundamental policy in Indian affairs
was to make the Indians dependent on the English in their trade. The colonists were instructed to encourage the Indians to trade with them "SO
THAT they may apply themselves to the English trade and NATION rather
than to any other OF EUROPE."[26] This was especially true in the case of the
Iroquois, whom the English determined to attach to themselves at all costs
in their conflict with the French. Because trade became the great means of
cementing political alliance, the object was to get the trade; it was less important whether the furs and other goods were needed or not.[27] But the
rivalry to capture the Indian trade was not limited to that between the
European nations in the New World. It existed, too, among the English
colonies.

Important as trade was to both the English and the Indians, it was also
the source of almost endless trouble, and it became necessary for the colonial governments to protect the interests of the commonwealth against
uncontrolled private gain. Fraud and illegal practices on the part of traders
stirred up Indian indignation and anger and thus led to frequent retaliations against the white community. In an attempt to prevent abuses, multifarious legislation regulating the conditions of the trade was enacted.
Different systems were tried, modified, abandoned, and tried again. Some-

26. Leonard W. Labaree, ed., *Royal Instructions to British Colonial Governors,*
1670–1776, 2 vols. (New York: D. Appleton-Century Company, 1935), 2: 464.

27. See the introduction in Peter Wraxall, *An Abridgment of the Indian Affairs Con-*
tained in Four Folio Volumes: Transacted in the Colony of New York, from the Year
1678 to the Year 1751, ed. Charles H. McIlwain (Cambridge: Harvard University Press,
1915). My discussion on trade is taken largely from Francis Paul Prucha, *American In-*
dian Policy in the Formative Years: The Indian Trade and Intercourse Acts, 1790–1834
(Cambridge: Harvard University Press, 1962), pp. 6–10.

times a strict public monopoly of the trade was set up; more often, the trade was in the hands of private traders, who were hedged about by strict and detailed regulations. Because the Indian trade had such close bearing on the public welfare, the colonial governments insisted on strict measures of control.

The universal means of regulation was a licensing system. This was the only way to keep trade open to all qualified persons and at the same time provide protection against traders of bad character. The need for such protection was manifest, for, as a South Carolina law of 1707 declared, "the greater number of those persons that trade among the Indians in amity with this Government, do generally lead loose, vicious lives, to the scandal of the Christian religion, and do likewise oppress the people among whom they live, by their unjust and illegal actions, which if not prevented may in time tend to the destruction of this Province."[28] Often bond was required of traders, and violators of the regulations were punished by revocation of license, forfeiture of bond and stores, or some specified fine. Frequently trade was restricted to designated localities, the better to enforce the licensing system. Commissioners and agents were appointed to manage trade, issue licenses, enforce laws, and adjudicate disputes arising from trade.[29]

Regulation of trade was critical in the case of two items—firearms and liquor—because of their explosive potentialities. Just as the colonists were forbidden to buy land from the Indians, so were they restricted in the sale of arms and rum. For obvious reasons it was necessary to prevent the supplying of hostile Indians with weapons, and laws were enacted for that purpose, especially in the early days of the colonies, when survival against the Indians was of primary concern.[30] Of far greater moment, however, were the restrictions placed on the sale of liquor to the natives. The Indian propensity toward strong drink and the disastrous results that inevitably followed were universal phenomena. Traders throughout the long history of

28. *Statutes at Large of South Carolina*, 2: 309–16.

29. An example of an orderly and comprehensive law was the South Carolina "Act for the better regulation of the Indian Trade, and for appointing a Commissioner for that purpose" of August 20, 1731. It came after years of controversy among various elements of the colony for control of the trade and bitter experience with Indian wars resulting from ill-managed affairs. Ibid., 3: 327–34. Verner W. Crane, *The Southern Frontier, 1670–1732* (Durham: Duke University Press, 1928), pp. 202–3, asserts that under this law the regulation of the Indian trade was "probably as well planned and as efficiently enforced as any such system could have been under colonial conditions, and in view of the vast extent of the Carolina Indian country." The law became an Indian trading code for the whole southern frontier, for Georgia modeled its regulations on it.

30. Francis X. Moloney, *The Fur Trade in New England, 1620–1676* (Cambridge: Harvard University Press, 1931), pp. 102–4; *Archives of Maryland*, 62 vols. (Baltimore: Maryland Historical Society, 1883–1945), 1: 346.

the fur trade relied upon rum and whiskey in their dealings with the Indians. The unscrupulous merchant did not hesitate to debauch the Indian with liquor in order to cheat him out of his furs. And the Indians' revenge more often than not was taken out indiscriminately upon the settlers close at hand. Governor George Thomas of Pennsylvania sensed the danger that was common to all the colonies. "I cannot but be apprehensive," he told the assembly in 1744, "that the Indian trade as it is now carried on will involve us in some fatal quarrel with the Indians. Our Traders in defiance of the Law carry Spirituous Liquors amongst them, and take Advantage of their inordinate Appetite for it to cheat them out of their skins and their wampum, which is their Money, and often to debauch their wives into the Bargain. Is it to be wondered at then, if when they Recover from the Drunken fit, they should take severe revenges?"[31]

In an attempt to meet the difficulty, the colonies enacted prohibitions against the sale of rum and other liquors to the Indians. Often the prohibition was absolute. Stiff fines were provided for violators, forfeiture of stores was common, and in some cases authorization was given to destroy the liquor. Such absolute prohibitions met with opposition even from the respectable traders, who could not then compete with the irregular traders or the Dutch and the French. Prohibitions were often relaxed and sometimes removed altogether.[32]

Unfortunately, the whole business of liquor restriction was largely futile, for the Indians' thirst would be quenched by foul means if fair means were denied. The moral fiber of the general run of traders was too frayed to permit a stand against liquor when the profits were so enticing, and even the colonial authorities at times found it necessary or expedient to give the Indians rum. The experience of the colonies showed the seemingly insatiable thirst of the Indians and the willingness of depraved traders to quench it.

Despite all the concern, regulation of the Indian trade by the individual colonies was a failure. The frontiers were too extensive and the inhabitants too widely scattered to permit adequate control of intercourse with the Indians. The Indians could not be induced or forced to bring their furs to central markets where the trade could be supervised and regulations enforced, so trade was left practically free and unrestricted. Anyone could engage in it by obtaining a license. The fur trade was thus in the hands of a great

31. Quoted in George Arthur Cribbs, "The Frontier Policy of Pennsylvania," *Western Pennsylvania Historical Magazine* 2 (January 1919): 25.

32. *Colonial Laws of Massachusetts*, p. 161; *Statutes at Large of South Carolina*, 2: 190; *Statutes at Large of Pennsylvania*, 2: 168–70; *Colonial Laws of New York*, 1: 657, 888. See Moloney, *Fur Trade in New England*, pp. 104–8, for discussion of liquor in the New England fur trade.

number of individuals, many of them lawless, unprincipled, and vicious. Even if one leaves out of the picture the offensive traders and focuses on the respectable merchants and colonial officials, there is little to praise, for Indian regulations could become hopelessly entangled in factional politics. There was no uniformity among the colonies, no two sets of like regulations. Abuses prohibited by one colony were tolerated by the next, and the conditions could hardly be amended while each colony was left to govern its own trade and to be guided in part by rivalry with its neighbors. The failure was apparent to all. The corruption, fraud, and mischievous dealings of the traders continually aroused the resentment of the Indians.

BRITISH IMPERIAL POLICY

The important precedents in Indian affairs for the patriot leaders who established the government of the United States were the recent actions and plans of the British government looking toward imperial control. For there was no question that colonial management had failed. Trade was not adequately controlled; the English settlers steadily moved into Indian lands; the Indians were resentful and showed their ill humor by incessant attacks upon the settlements. The hardest fact of all had to be faced: the Indians by and large adhered to the French in the imperial war that broke out between England and France in 1754.[33]

In 1755 the first step was taken to remove Indian affairs from the incompetent hands of the colonists and center political control in the hands of the imperial government. On April 15 William Johnson, longtime friend of the Iroquois, was appointed superintendent of Indian affairs for the northern department, and in the following year Edmond Atkin was named to a similar post in the south; he was replaced in 1762 by the more famous John Stuart. The superintendents had full charge of political relations between the British and the Indians. Their responsibilities were numerous: protecting the Indians as well as they could from traders and speculators, negotiating the boundary lines that were called for after 1763, distributing presents given to the Indians in the attempt to gain and maintain their goodwill, and enlisting Indians in wartime to fight on the British side. The superintendents, too, exercised what control they could over the fur trade, although management of the trade remained to a great extent in colonial hands.[34] The problems of the Indian trade caught the eye of the Board of

33. My discussion of imperial policy is taken from Prucha, *American Indian Policy in the Formative Years*, pp. 11–25.
34. A modern scholarly biography of Johnson is Milton W. Hamilton, *Sir William Johnson: Colonial American, 1715–1763* (Port Washington, New York: Kennikat Press,

Trade in London, but the intricate nature of the trade and the sensitiveness of the colonies to their longtime prerogatives caused the board to move slowly. Although indications of the movement toward imperialization of the trade can be seen in the declarations of the board, nothing substantial had been done by 1763.

The purchase of Indian lands also engaged the attention of the Board of Trade. Restrictions placed by individual colonies upon the purchase of Indian lands by private persons had not worked well, for single colonies could not grasp the overall pressure along the frontier, and the provincial governments themselves were causing alarm among the tribes by their own purchase of lands. Imperial control was imperative if peace and harmony with the Indians was to be maintained.

As early as 1753, in its instructions to the governor of New York, the board initiated a new policy in regard to the purchase of Indian lands. The governor was instructed to permit no more purchases of land by private individuals, "but when the Indians are disposed to sell any of their lands the purchase ought to be made in his Majesty's name and at the publick charge." A similar measure for improving the regulation of Indian affairs was proposed at the Albany Congress. Then on December 2, 1761, a general order was issued to the governors in the royal colonies that forbade them to issue grants to any Indian lands. All requests to purchase land from the Indians would have to be forwarded to the Board of Trade and would depend upon directions received from the board. The governors, furthermore, were to order all persons who "either wilfully or inadvertently" had settled on Indian lands to leave at once and were to prosecute all persons who had secured titles to such lands by fraud.[35]

1976); it is to be supplemented with a second volume that is to carry the life beyond 1763. Of older biographies, the best is Arthur Pound, *Johnson of the Mohawks: A Biography of Sir William Johnson, Irish Immigrant, Mohawk War Chief, American Soldier, Empire Builder* (New York: Macmillan Company, 1930). See also *The Papers of Sir William Johnson,* 14 vols. (Albany: University of the State of New York, 1921–1965). On Atkin, see Wilbur R. Jacobs, ed., *Indians of the Southern Colonial Frontier: The Edmond Atkin Report and Plan of 1755* (Columbia: University of South Carolina Press, 1954), and John C. Parish, "Edmond Atkin, British Superintendent of Indian Affairs," in *The Persistence of the Westward Movement and Other Essays* (Berkeley: University of California Press, 1943), pp. 147–60. John R. Alden, *John Stuart and the Southern Colonial Frontier: A Study of Indian Relations, War, Trade, and Land Problems in the Southern Wilderness, 1754–1775* (Ann Arbor: University of Michigan Press, 1944), treats fully Stuart's career; chapter 9 gives a good discussion of the office of superintendent.

35. Oliver M. Dickerson, *American Colonial Government, 1696–1765: A Study of the British Board of Trade in Its Relation to the American Colonies, Political, Industrial, Administrative* (Cleveland: Arthur H. Clark Company, 1912), p. 340; Labaree, *Royal Instructions,* 2: 467–68; O'Callaghan, *New York Colonial Documents,* 7: 478–79.

Little by little the idea grew of establishing an official and defined boundary line to separate Indian lands from lands of the whites. Pennsylvania, in fact, provided a precedent in the Treaty of Easton, October 24, 1758, by which the governor returned to the Indians all of the trans-Allegheny lands that had been purchased from the Six Nations in 1754 at Albany. A line was drawn between the whites and the Indians, and neither was to violate the territory of the other. The British ministry ratified this colonial agreement, accepting it under the stress of war, it is true, but binding itself by a solemn commitment that could not be ignored at the conclusion of the hostilities.[36]

Conciliation of the Indians was of prime importance to the British government at the end of the war with the French. British officials knew that justice in the treatment of the Indians was required and that justice demanded strong measures to restrain, if not prevent, encroachment on Indian lands. A document drawn up in May 1763 explicitly proposed an Indian boundary line along the western edge of the colonies, although the motive behind it seems to have been to forestall the formation of western colonies (which would not fit in well with a mercantilist scheme of empire) rather than to placate Indians. A similar document, drawn up by the secretary of the Board of Trade, while considering the wisdom of limiting the extent of the colonies, saw also the need to designate the land between the ridge of the Appalachians and the Mississippi "as lands belonging to the Indians." Both documents were incorporated into a report of the Board of Trade of June 8, 1763.[37] There were in fact two groups in the ministry: expansionists, who were eager for the spread of the colonists to the west, and anti-expansionists, who wished to restrict settlements to the seaboard. The boundary line was agreed to by both, the latter looking upon it as a permanent western wall for the colonies, the former as a temporary expedient needed at once to satisfy the Indians and to be the basis from which an ordered and regulated movement westward could be made.[38]

36. Lawrence H. Gipson, *The British Empire before the American Revolution*, vol. 9: *The Triumphant Empire: New Responsibilities within the Enlarged Empire, 1763–1766* (New York: Alfred A. Knopf, 1956), p. 51. A facsimile reproduction of Franklin's printing of "Minutes of Conferences, held at Easton, in October, 1758," is in Boyd, *Indian Treaties Printed by Franklin*, pp. 213–43.

37. The documents are cited in Prucha, *American Indian Policy in the Formative Years*, pp. 16–17.

38. See chapters 6–8 in Clarence W. Alvord, *The Mississippi Valley in British Politics: A Study of the Trade, Land Speculation, and Experiments in Imperialism Culminating in the American Revolution*, 2 vols. (Cleveland: Arthur H. Clark Company, 1917), 1: 157–228. A more recent study, which revises some of Alvord's conclusions, is Jack M. Sosin, *Whitehall and the Wilderness: The Middle West in British Colonial Policy, 1760–1775* (Lincoln: University of Nebraska Press, 1961).

The theoretical deliberations were interrupted by news from America, which, though it did not change the basic direction in which British policy was moving, demanded emergency action. Word arrived in August of Pontiac's Rebellion, with its threat of disaster to the whole back country. Sir William Johnson wrote to the Lords of Trade on July 1 reporting the blockade of Detroit, the defeat of a detachment on the way there from Niagara, the destruction of the fort at Sandusky with its garrison (and the apprehension that a similar fate had befallen the other outposts), the cutting off of communications with Fort Pitt, the destruction of several settlements, the murder of many traders, and in general "an universal pannic throughout the Frontiers."[39]

This was no time for debating where the line should be drawn, for running a carefully surveyed boundary, or for solving the disputed point about the wisdom of westward expansion for the colonies. Some action was needed at once to pacify the Indians. They must be convinced that the encroachment of the whites was at an end and that they could return with confidence to their peaceful ways, assured that they need no longer fear a steady and ruthless expulsion from their hunting grounds. The Indians must be convinced that the British government meant to honor the commitments made to them in both the north and the south. A boundary line needed to be drawn quickly, and the ridge of the Appalachians was accepted as the dividing line. On October 7, George III incorporated it into his famous Proclamation of 1763. The document proclaimed three things: it established the boundaries and the government for the new colonies of Florida and Nova Scotia acquired by the Peace of Paris; it offered specific encouragement to settlement in the new areas; and it established the boundary line as a new policy in Indian affairs.[40]

By this proclamation, the governors and commanders in chief of the new colonies were forbidden to issue any warrants for survey or patents for lands beyond the boundaries set for their colonies. The officials of the older colonies were forbidden "for the present, and until our further Pleasure be known," to permit surveys or to grant lands beyond the watershed of the Appalachians. Second, the proclamation formally reserved the Indian country for the Indian nations—"all the Lands and Territories lying to the Westward of the Sources of the Rivers which fall into the Sea from the West and North West." The king's subjects were prohibited from making purchases or settlements in the restricted territory, and any person who had already moved into the Indian country was ordered to leave at once.

The Appalachian boundary line proclaimed in 1763, occasioned by the

39. O'Callaghan, *New York Colonial Documents*, 7: 526.
40. The Proclamation of 1763 is printed in Adam Shortt and Arthur G. Doughty, eds., *Documents Relating to the Constitutional History of Canada, 1759–1791*, rev. ed. (Ottawa: J. de L. Taché, 1918), pp. 163–68.

war whoop of the Indians, was provisional. The Lords of Trade realized that the ordinary process of instructions to the governors was too slow for a time of crisis. They knew, too, that it was impossible during an Indian war (especially one as serious as the uprising of Pontiac) to proceed with the detailed surveying necessary for laying out the line itself. But the point-by-point negotiation with the Indians over the location of the line was only postponed, not abandoned. In 1764, in its outline of a plan for the management of Indian affairs, the Board of Trade emphasized the necessity of a carefully drawn line, to be worked out by the agents with the Indians.[41]

Almost immediately the laborious work began. In 1765 the line was marked out in South Carolina and continued into North Carolina in 1767. During 1768–1769 the line was drawn west of Virginia's settlements— with some reluctance on the part of Virginia, which did not want to appear to give up its claims to the western regions. In the north the responsibility lay with Sir William Johnson. At a conference with the Six Nations in the spring of 1765 he obtained the approval of the Indians, and in 1768, by the Treaty of Fort Stanwix, he settled the northern boundary line. By 1768 then, the boundary line, determined by solemn agreements with the Indians, extended from Canada to Florida. The concept of such a line by then had become ineradicable; but the line itself moved constantly westward as new treaties and new purchases drove the Indians back before the advancing whites.[42]

The Proclamation of 1763 was not a carefully worked out plan for management of the West and regulation of affairs with the Indians, and it did not remove the confusion in colonial Indian trade regulations. The Board of Trade recognized the necessity "of speedily falling upon some method of regulating Indian commerce & polity, upon some more general and better established system than has hitherto taken place." At the same time that it proposed the boundary line to the king it undertook to gather information on which to build an adequate set of regulations for the trade by writing to Sir William Johnson and to John Stuart for their opinions and proposals.[43] When the reports of the superintendents were in, the board set about to formulate a comprehensive imperial program for the fur trade.

41. O'Callaghan, *New York Colonial Documents,* 7: 641. The British government augmented the proclamation with special instructions to the colonial governors to enforce its restrictions. See instructions to the governors of East Florida, West Florida, and Quebec, 1763, and to the governors of Virginia and Pennsylvania, 1765, in Labaree, *Royal Instructions,* 2: 473–74, 479–80.

42. Max Farrand, "The Indian Boundary Line," *American Historical Review* 10 (July 1905): 782–91; John C. Parish, "John Stuart and the Cartography of the Indian Boundary Line," in *Persistence of the Westward Movement,* pp. 131–46; O'Callaghan, *New York Colonial Documents,* 7: 665; 8: 111–37.

43. Lords of Trade to Sir William Johnson, August 5, 1763, O'Callaghan, *New York Colonial Documents,* 7: 535–36.

On July 10, 1764, the board proposed a plan that had as its object "the regulation of Indian Affairs both commercial and political throughout all North America, upon one general system, under the direction of Officers appointed by the Crown, so as to sett aside all local interfering of particular Provinces, which has been one great cause of the distracted state of Indian affairs in general." The plan included an imperial department of Indian affairs independent both of the military commander in America (whose control had irked the Indian superintendents) and of the colonial governments. The board honestly faced the problems that existed in America and provided a competent set of rules for carrying on an orderly and peaceful trade.[44]

The fur trade was declared to be free and open to all British subjects, and to better regulate it two districts were designated, with lists of tribes to be considered in each district. For the southern district, all trade was to be carried on at the Indian towns; in the north, fixed posts for trade were to be designated. The trade would be taken completely out of the hands of the colonies, all colonial laws regulating Indian affairs repealed, and control placed with the agent or superintendent of each district, who was to be assisted by deputies, commissaries, interpreters, smiths, and missionaries. So that the superintendents could have a free hand, the plan expressly forbade interference in the conduct of Indian affairs by the commander in chief of His Majesty's forces in America and by the governors and military commanders of the separate colonies, although the cooperation of these officials was enjoined. It empowered agents or their deputies to visit the tribes yearly and to act as justices of the peace.

Persons wishing to trade would be required to obtain licenses from the governor or commander of their respective colonies and to give bonds for the observance of the regulations. The licenses would run for one year only, and each trader was required to specify in his license the town or post at which he intended to trade. Fines and imprisonment would hold for those trading without a license. Trade would be governed by tariffs of prices "established from time to time by the commissaries . . . in concert with the Traders and Indians." No trader could supply Indians with liquor or rifled guns or give them credit for goods beyond the sum of fifty shillings.

Affairs continued to drift, for unfortunately the Plan of 1764 was never formally adopted, and in 1768 it was officially abandoned. The sum of twenty thousand pounds a year, which the plan was estimated to cost, was too heavy for the British government to bear, and the Stamp Act troubles had shown the impossibility of raising the money in the colonies. Colonial

44. Lords of Trade to Sir William Johnson, July 10, 1764, ibid., pp. 634–36. The "Plan for the Future Management of Indian Affairs" is printed ibid., pp. 637–41. The Plan of 1764 was sent to Johnson and Stuart for their criticisms and "further lights" and to numerous other colonial officials as well.

opposition, too, contributed to the decision to put aside the imperial program and return affairs to the colonies.[45] But the superintendents used the plan as a guide in the conduct of Indian affairs, and it foreshadowed later legislation of the United States.

The return of regulation of the fur trade to the colonies was a strange reversal. The Board of Trade was aware that the colonies had failed, and that the misconduct of the ill-regulated traders had "contributed not a little to involve us in the enormous expences of an Indian war." Undaunted, with eyes consciously or unconsciously blinded to reality, the board trusted that the ill effects of past neglect and inattention would induce colonial officials in the future to more caution and better management.

The results were what might have been expected. The ministry perhaps thought the Indian boundary line alone would forever remove the causes of friction between the Indians and the English, but the American settlers could not be restrained. Control of the fur trade was no more exact. The failure of the colonies to enact the necessary legislation caused great restlessness among the Indians. Superintendent Stuart described the conditions in his department as chaotic, for the old lawless traders were still at work, and settlements were constantly appearing across the boundary line. The failure of the colonies to agree upon any sort of general regulations resulted in intolerable conditions in the West. Some interposition of Parliament for the regulation of the fur trade on an imperial basis was necessary, and one last attempt was made. By the Quebec Act of 1774 the western areas were placed under the Quebec government. In this way the Board of Trade hoped to provide the necessary regulation.

The mind of the British ministry was revealed in the instructions sent to Governor Guy Carleton of Quebec at the beginning of January 1775. They enunciated again the freedom of the fur trade for all His Majesty's subjects and directed that regulations be drawn up, "giving every possible facility to that Trade, which the nature of it will admit, and as may consist with fair and just dealing towards the Savages." The need for fixed times and places for the trade, for tariffs of prices for goods and furs, and for prohibiting the sale of rum and other liquors was again indicated. Governor Carleton received a copy of the Plan of 1764, which was to serve as his guide when drawing up the rules for trade.[46] It was a return to the former plan for imperializing the West, but it came too late. The Revolutionary War and the establishment of the independent United States threw these problems into the hands of the new nation.

It was certainly not clear at the time that the United States would

45. Peter Marshall, "Colonial Protest and Imperial Retrenchment: Indian Policy, 1764–8," *Journal of American Studies* 5 (April 1971): 1–17.

46. Instructions to Carleton, January 3, 1775, Shortt and Doughty, *Canadian Constitutional Documents*, pp. 419–33.

quickly grow to a position of dominance and threaten not only the lands but the tribal existence of Indians living east of the Mississippi. The vast majority of the Indians, who lived west of the Appalachians, were neither subjected politically nor dominated culturally by the United States; they continued to maintain their independence and to seek a secure place in the international circumstances of the time by fighting or by negotiation. Their ability to obtain material and moral support from the British in the north and the Spanish in the south made them a force that the United States government could not ignore but had to respect and conciliate. When the nation entered on its independent existence, Indian relations were a very important item on its agenda.

PART ONE

Formative
Years

The United States, on declaring its independence from the British Empire, inherited a responsibility that had not been well fulfilled by either the Crown or the individual colonies—a responsibility to maintain just and peaceful relations with the Indian tribes while at the same time allowing (if not indeed encouraging) the expansion of white society west from the Atlantic coast. Building on past experience and experimenting with new policies and procedures as problems arose, the nation little by little developed a set of principles to follow in its dealings with the Indians. The form of this federal program had been determined by 1834, when Congress codified previous legislation.

The program was carried out in an age when land was the most important element in the economic life of the nation. The population was largely rural, subsisting on the land. Accumulation of land was a means to wealth, power, and prestige, and land speculation was a big business. On a continent that seemed illimitable, "free land" was beckoning toward the west, and few could withstand the pull. "Land was the nation's most sought-after commodity in the first half-century of the republic," one historian of the public domain has written, "and the effort of men to acquire it was one of the dominant forces of the period."[1] It seemed only reasonable to the land-hungry

1. Malcolm J. Rohrbough, *The Land Office Business: The Settlement and Administration of American Public Lands, 1789–1837* (New York: Oxford University Press,

whites that the Indians, who made little use of their vast territories, should somehow give way to them.

American statesmen were part of this milieu, but they were determined that the advance of the frontier should be orderly and peaceful. Order was to be achieved, in the first place, by restrictions and regulations governing the intercourse between whites and Indians. These measures were intended as a tight web to hold back unruly frontiersmen, thus preserving the honor of the nation by enforcement of the agreements made between the United States and the Indians in formal treaties. The major restrictive elements were the following:

1. Protection of Indian rights to land by setting definite boundaries for the Indian country, prohibiting whites from entering the area except under certain controls, and removing illegal intruders.

2. Control of the disposition of Indian lands by denying the right of private individuals or local governments to acquire land from the Indians by purchase or any other means.

3. Regulation of Indian trade by determining the conditions under which individuals might engage in the trade, prohibition of certain classes of traders, and competition with private traders in the form of government trading houses.

4. Control of the liquor traffic by regulating the flow of intoxicating liquor into the Indian country and later prohibiting it altogether.

5. Provision for the punishment of crimes committed by members of one race against the other and compensation for damages suffered by one group at the hands of the other, in order to remove the occasions for private retaliation that led to frontier hostilities.[2]

Behind this legislative program stood the military force of the United States. The army was small and often not well disciplined (for heavy reliance was placed on militia), but power was there in fact or potentially to enforce the laws against obstreperous whites and to subjugate hostile Indians when attempts at peaceful relations failed.

The government policy had positive features as well as negative ones, however. It was the goal of the United States to civilize, Christianize, and

---

1968), p. xii. See also chapter 7, "The People and the Land," in Curtis P. Nettels, *The Emergence of a National Economy, 1775–1815* (New York: Holt, Rinehart and Winston, 1962), pp. 130–55, and Paul W. Gates, *The Farmer's Age: Agriculture, 1815–1860* (New York: Holt, Rinehart and Winston, 1960). There is stimulating discussion of the importance of land in Michael Paul Rogin, *Fathers and Children: Andrew Jackson and the Subjugation of the American Indian* (New York: Alfred A. Knopf, 1975), pp. 76–110.

2. These points are taken from Francis Paul Prucha, *American Indian Policy in the Formative Years: The Indian Trade and Intercourse Acts, 1790–1834* (Cambridge: Harvard University Press, 1962), p. 2.

educate the Indians so that they could ultimately be absorbed into the mainstream of American society. To this end, the government and Christian missionary societies cooperated to bring the "blessings of Christian civilization" to the Indians. Their programs and activities rested upon an intellectual or theoretical base that held that the Indian was inherently equal to the white man, but the belief in the potentiality of the Indians for civilization should not obscure the concomitant view that the existing condition of Indian society was far inferior to that of the whites. Innate equality of all men did not mean actual equality of diverse cultures. The Indians, it was clear to the whites, did not yet enjoy the advantages of civilization, and descriptions of their unflattering state abound, no doubt often exaggerated because seen through the ethnocentric eyes of the whites or played up to make the demand for educational civilizing programs more urgent. The result in white society was the growth of benevolence (an inclination to perform charitable acts toward the "untutored savages") and philanthropy (an effort to increase the well-being of the less fortunate Indians), which coalesced into an abiding paternalism (providing for the Indians' needs in a fatherly way without giving them responsibility).

It is true that the Indian tribes during and after the Revolutionary War were treated by the United States as independent sovereign nations. Treaties of peace were signed with them, and land cessions were acquired only through formal diplomatic mechanisms. Yet to emphasize such events is to mistake the true status of the United States in relation to the Indian tribes. The Indians, who had once been able to play off one European power against another for their own security and advantage, now faced a *single* power, the United States, a political state that soon greatly overshadowed them in population and resources. The United States knew it was superior to the Indians, not only in religious beliefs, literary accomplishments, and other cultural patterns, but also in population, in technological and agricultural achievements, and ultimately, therefore, in power. Even Thomas Jefferson had no illusion on this score and assumed that the Indians also had none. He urged humanity in dealing with the tribes, but he was willing to fall back upon fear if necessary. He wrote to a territorial governor in 1803: "We presume that our strength and their weakness is now so visible, that they must see we have only to shut our hand to crush them."[3]

As the century advanced, the disparity between the white and Indian societies became more pronounced. John C. Calhoun, as secretary of war, was outspoken. Although he promoted the education of the Indians and

3. Jefferson to William Henry Harrison, February 27, 1803, *The Writings of Thomas Jefferson*, ed. Andrew A. Lipscomb, 20 vols. (Washington: Thomas Jefferson Memorial Association, 1903–1904), 10: 370–71.

acknowledged "partial advances" in the attempts to civilize them, he saw the need for more radical measures. "They must be brought gradually under our authority and laws," he reported to Congress in 1820, "or they will insensibly waste away in vice and misery. It is impossible, with their customs, that they should exist as independent communities, in the midst of civilized society. They are not, in fact, an independent people, (I speak of those surrounded by our population,) nor ought they to be so considered. They should be taken under our guardianship; and our opinion, and not theirs, ought to prevail, in measures intended for their civilization and happiness. A system less vigorous may protract, but cannot arrest their fate." He asserted that "nominal independence" of the Indians was opposed to their happiness and civilization, for they had none of the advantages of real independence but suffered all the disadvantages of a state of complete subjugation.[4]

William Clark, too, from his vantage point as superintendent of Indian affairs in the west, pointed to changes that had occurred in relations between the United States and the Indians as a result of the military victories by American troops. Once a "formidable and terrible enemy," the Indians were no longer to be feared, he wrote; their "power had been broken, their warlike spirit subdued, and themselves sunk into objects of pity and commiseration." Clark outlined a paternal system of education for the Indians and urged their removal outside the states and territories to accomplish it.[5]

The view of the Indians that these men had—and many others shared it—did not call for extermination of the Indians but for humanity and benevolence. The policy makers, from George Washington and Henry Knox on, were imbued with a vision of the United States as the great republican model for the world, and they were continually conscious of the duties of justice toward a less favored people. Secretary of War Knox did not want the world to class the United States with Spain, which had destroyed the Indians of Mexico and Peru. Almost forty years later, John Quincy Adams's secretary of war, James Barbour, declared: "Next to the means of self-defence, and the blessings of free government, stands, in point of importance, the character of a nation. Its distinguishing characteristics should be, justice and moderation. To spare the weak is its brightest ornament."[6]

Added to this basically secular concern was the immense weight of Christian concern. The goal of the rising Protestant missionary endeavors was to evangelize the whole world, to bring Christ's message to all man-

4. Report of January 15, 1820, ASP:IA, 2: 200–201; Report of February 8, 1822, *House Report* no. 59, 17–1, serial 66, pp. 6–7.
    5. Report of March 1, 1826, *House Report* no. 124, 19–1, serial 138.
    6. Report of Knox, December 29, 1794, ASP:IA, 1: 543–44; Report of Barbour, February 3, 1826, *House Document* no. 102, 19–1, serial 135, p. 5.

kind. And the instrument for that great work was to be a United States committed to Christian principles. Deeply imbued with a sense of mission, of carrying out God's commands of justice and compassion, active Christians reinforced the national policy of paternalism to the Indians. It was not enough to lament past failings in regard to the Indians. A committee of the American Board of Commissioners for Foreign Missions in 1824 condemned failures to improve the civil, moral, and religious condition of the Indians, injustices in acquiring Indian lands and furs, and devastating wars against the natives. It viewed these acts as "national sins, aggravated by our knowledge and their ignorance, our strength and skill in war and their weakness; by our treacherous abuse of their unsuspicious simplicity, and especially by the light and privileges of Christianity, which we enjoy, and of which they are destitute." The only way to avert the just vengeance of God for these wrongs—and "to elevate our national character, and render it exemplary in the view of the world"—was to speed the work of civilizing and elevating the Indians.[7]

Thus the formative years brought into sharp focus the anomalies in relations between the United States and the Indian tribes that would persist through the decades. The federal government promoted the expansion of settlers westward, thus exerting great pressure on Indian lands, while it tried to ease the resulting conflict by regulating the whites and acculturating the Indians. The United States signed treaties with the Indian tribes, recognized an independent nationhood, and in many ways acted as though the Indian chiefs were in fact the rulers of sovereign political entities. Yet it hedged the tribes around with restrictions on their freedom of action, dictated treaty terms to chiefs unable or afraid to reject them, and set about to change the fundamental cultural patterns of the Indians in a self-righteous paternal manner.

7. Memorial of the American Board of Commissioners for Foreign Missions, March 3, 1824, ASP:IA, 2: 446.

CHAPTER I

Peace after
the Revolution

The Policy of the Continental Congress.
Early Treaties and Ordinances. The Constitution
and Indian Policy. Treaty-Making Principles
and Practices. Indian Rights to the Land.

The colonies, engaged in a war with the mother country, were much concerned about the Indian nations at their backs. Unless the Indians could be neutralized or persuaded to join the patriots, the struggle for independence would be seriously jeopardized. And when the Revolutionary War had been won, Indian problems remained an important business in the establishment of the new nation.

THE POLICY OF THE CONTINENTAL CONGRESS

A coordinated Indian policy began to take shape during the Revolutionary War, even before independence was declared.[1] The individual colonies were well aware of Indian matters, and some of them sent commissioners to the tribes. But the Indian problem could not be handled adequately by disparate provincial practices, and on July 12, 1775, less than three months after Lexington and Concord, the Continental Congress inaugurated a federal Indian policy with a report from a committee on Indian affairs. Declaring that "securing and preserving the friendship of the Indian Nations, ap-

1. Much of the material in this chapter is taken from Francis Paul Prucha, *American Indian Policy in the Formative Years: The Indian Trade and Intercourse Acts, 1790–1834* (Cambridge: Harvard University Press, 1962), pp. 27–43. See also Walter H. Mohr, *Federal Indian Relations, 1774–1788* (Philadelphia: University of Pennsylvania Press, 1933).

pears to be a subject of the utmost moment to these colonies" and noting
that there was reason to fear that the British would incite the Indians
against the rebelling colonies, the committee recommended that steps be
taken to maintain the friendship of the Indians. Congress thereupon established three departments: a northern department including the Six Nations and the Indians to the north of them; a southern department including the Cherokees and all others to the south of them; and a middle
department containing the tribes living in between. It appointed commissioners for each department, who were to treat with the Indians "in the
name, and on behalf of the united colonies"; they were to work to preserve
peace and friendship with the Indians and, in the quaint understatement of
the report, "to prevent their taking any part in the present commotions."
Agents appointed by the commissioners would spy out the conduct of the
British superintendents and their men and seize any British agents who
were stirring up the Indians against the patriots.[2]

Congress on July 13 appointed the commissioners for the northern and
middle departments, but it left the nomination of those for the southern
department to the council of safety of South Carolina. That Benjamin
Franklin, Patrick Henry, and James Wilson were chosen for the middle department is an indication of the importance attached to the matter.[3]

Indian matters were entwined with the still greater problem of the western lands, for administration of the lands and management of the Indians
who were on the lands went hand in hand. Washington observed in 1783,
"The Settlmt. of the Western Country and making a Peace with the Indians are so analogous that there can be no definition of the one without
involving considerations of the other."[4] But the questions of managing the
Indians and controlling trade with them did have a separate identity and
were considered separately by the Continental Congress. The decisions
made by that Congress and the principles incorporated into the Articles of
Confederation gave a decisive turn to American Indian policy.

As with all the major questions involved in forming the new government, so with Indian policy the basic decision concerned the authority to

2. JCC, 2: 174–77. The great extent of Indian concerns can be seen in *Index, Journals
of the Continental Congress*, comp. Kenneth E. Harris and Steven D. Tulley (Washington: National Archives and Records Service, 1976), and *Index: The Papers of the Continental Congress*, comp. John P. Butler, 5 vols. (Washington: National Archives and Records Service, 1978).

3. JCC, 2: 183, 192, 194.

4. Washington to James Duane, September 7, 1783, *The Writings of George Washington from the Original Manuscript Sources, 1745–1799*, ed. John C. Fitzpatrick, 39 vols.
(Washington: GPO, 1931–1934), 27: 139–40. See Merrill Jensen, *The Articles of Confederation: An Interpretation of the Social-Constitutional History of the American Revolution* (Madison: University of Wisconsin Press, 1940), for details of the western land
problem and how it was tied in with the Indian question.

be given to the federal government. The imperial experiment in unified management of the Indians had made its mark on the minds of the delegates to Congress, and a majority believéd that Indian affairs belonged to the central government. Benjamin Franklin, the leading personality in the Congress, had offered a plan of union at Albany in 1754 that provided that the president-general, with the advice of the grand council, should control Indian affairs. Now he included the idea in a draft for a confederation that he proposed to Congress on July 21, 1775. He offered two articles. First, no colony could engage in offensive war against the Indians without the consent of Congress, which would be the judge of the justice and necessity of the war. Second, a perpetual alliance, both offensive and defensive, should be made with the Six Nations. For them, as well as for all other tribes, boundaries should be drawn, their land protected against encroachments, and no purchases of land made except by contract drawn between the great council of the Indians and the Congress. Agents residing among the tribes would prevent injustices in the trade and provide for the "personal Wants and Distresses" of the Indians by occasional presents. The purchase of land from the Indians was to be "by Congress for the General Advantage and Benefit of the United Colonies."[5]

The committee appointed to draft the Articles of Confederation put the task into the hands of the able writer John Dickinson, a Pennsylvanian like Franklin and an advocate of congressional control of the western lands. His draft, submitted on July 12, 1776, elaborated Franklin's plan; in the general enumeration of powers granted the central government, Dickinson included "Regulating the Trade, and managing all Affairs with the Indians."[6]

Congressional control of Indian affairs, however, was not accepted by all, and the debate on July 26 indicated a decided divergence of views. The opposition came chiefly from South Carolina, which wanted to handle Indian affairs as a colony. Georgia, on the other hand, was quite willing for Congress to assume the burden because the state could not afford the presents for the Indians that its position as a buffer against hostile tribes demanded. In the end, the overall necessities of controlling the Indians prevailed, for, as James Wilson pointed out, the Indians refused to recognize any superior authority, and only the United States in Congress assembled

5. The Albany proposal of June 28, 1754, "Short Hints toward a Scheme for a General Union of the British Colonies on the Continent," is in *The Papers of Benjamin Franklin*, ed. Leonard W. Labaree, 21 vols. to date (New Haven: Yale University Press, 1959–), 5: 361–64; it is based on an earlier sketch of a union drawn up by Franklin, June 8, 1754, ibid., pp. 335–38. The 1775 draft is in JCC, 2: 197–98. Jensen, *Articles of Confederation*, p. 152, points out that Franklin's draft reflected his views as a Pennsylvanian and a land speculator, siding with the landless states in insisting on control of the western lands by Congress.

6. Dickinson's draft is in JCC, 5: 546–54.

could have any hope of dealing with them adequately. Above all else, rivalries between colonies in treating with the Indians had to be avoided.[7]

On August 20 Congress accepted an amended draft. The Franklin-Dickinson articles about alliances with the Indians, about maintaining their boundaries, and about purchase of their lands—as well as Dickinson's strong statements about federal control of boundaries of colonies and of the western lands—were omitted. Only the following simple statement appeared: "The United States Assembled shall have the sole and exclusive right and power of . . . regulating the trade, and managing all affairs with the Indians, not members of any of the States."[8]

Even this did not satisfy the advocates of state control, who were jealous of individual state authority within their own territories, and corrective amendments were offered. Congress rejected two alternative amendments before agreeing to the provision that appeared in the ratified document. In its long enumeration of the powers of Congress, the Articles of Confederation declared: "The United States in Congress assembled shall also have the sole and exclusive right and power of . . . regulating the trade and managing all affairs with the Indians, not members of any of the States, provided that the legislative right of any State within its own limits be not infringed or violated."[9]

Thus the management of Indian affairs and the regulation of Indian trade fell to the federal government. The principle was enunciated, but it was not crystal clear, for the proviso cast a heavy blur over the article and the power that it actually gave to Congress and prohibited to the states. James Madison in Number 42 of *The Federalist* poked fun at the article, ridiculing it as "obscure and contradictory," as "absolutely incomprehensible," and as inconsiderately endeavoring to accomplish impossibilities. It must be admitted that Madison was moved to make the Articles of Confederation look black so that the new Constitution would look so much the brighter. But practical experience gave him and other critics of the Articles a sound foundation for their opposition. At critical moments in Indian affairs, some of the states refused to abdicate in favor of Congress.

The debates over the Articles of Confederation and the subsequent practice under this frame of government, nevertheless, clarified one element of Indian relations: the concept of the Indian country was strengthened. Not only was the Indian country the territory lying beyond the boundary lines, forbidden to settlers and to unlicensed traders, but it was also the area over which federal authority extended. Federal laws governing the Indians and

7. JCC, 6: 1077–79; Jensen, *Articles of Confederation*, p. 155; Mohr, *Federal Indian Relations*, pp. 182–84.
8. JCC, 5: 674–89.
9. Ibid., 9: 844–45.

the Indian trade took effect in the Indian country only; outside they did not hold.

The Articles of Confederation were approved by Congress in 1777, but they did not take effect until 1781, for Maryland refused to ratify until the landed states had ceded their western claims to the United States. Meanwhile, the course of the war was in the hands of the Continental Congress and its committees.[10]

The British had the more advantageous position in the war and in large measure retained the allegiance of the Indians. John Stuart and his deputies in the south and the successors of Sir William Johnson in the north made use of their authority and influence with the Indians to prevent them from following the colonists in opposition to the king. The British not only had better agents than the patriots could muster; they had powerful arguments, too, which they did not fail to exploit.[11] It was plain that the causes of complaint among the Indians—the abuses of traders and the encroachment of white settlers—all came from the colonists. The British imperial officials, on the other hand, had a good record of trying to deal justly with the Indians, of protecting their rights to their lands and their peltries, and of furnishing the goods needed for trade. The British agents did not hesitate to call these facts to the attention of the Indians. One deputy reminded the Cherokees, "But for the care of the Great King they could not have had a foot of land left them by the White." John Stuart, haranguing the Choctaws and Chickasaws at Mobile in May 1777, urged them to follow the Cherokees in taking up the hatchet against the Americans. He pointed out the difficulties that the royal superintendents had experienced in protecting Indian rights against the colonists, and he concluded that "as it is the declared intention of the Rebels to possess themselves of your Lands, it also becomes your duty and interest to unite yourselves with other nations for your mutual defense and protection and to attach yourselves firmly to the King's cause, to whose goodness and protection you have been and are so much indebted."[12]

The ineffectiveness of the revolutionary government in supplying the Indians with essential trade goods was a serious disadvantage in seeking Indian support. It was all well and good to urge the Indians to desert the British by remaining neutral or by actively joining the colonial forces, but these positions (certainly the latter) meant loss of trade ties with the Brit-

10. The Indians' part in the war is treated extensively in Barbara Graymont, *The Iroquois in the American Revolution* (Syracuse: Syracuse University Press, 1972), and James H. O'Donnell III, *Southern Indians in the American Revolution* (Knoxville: University of Tennessee Press, 1973).

11. Mohr, *Federal Indian Relations*, pp. 42–43.

12. The quotations are in Helen L. Shaw, *British Administration of the Southern Indians, 1756–1783* (Lancaster, Pennsylvania: Lancaster Press, 1931), pp. 96–97, 109–10.

ish, who alone could adequately supply the Indians' needs. The Americans could not honestly promise to replace the British as suppliers of goods, and this the Indians undoubtedly knew.

At first, the best the patriots could hope for was to keep the Indians neutral in the conflict. As delegates of the Continental Congress told the Iroquois in July 1775, "This is a family quarrel between us and Old England. You Indians are not concerned in it. We don't wish you to take up the hatchet against the king's troops. We desire you to remain at home, and not join on either side, but keep the hatchet buried deep."[13] That sentiment gradually changed, however, and the colonists, like the British, began to seek positive assistance from the Indians. In this they had little success. Some New England tribal remnants, it is true, aided Washington in the siege of Boston. But the only important groups to espouse the cause of the patriots were the Tuscaroras and Oneidas of the Six Nations, largely, it seems, because of the influence among them of the New England missionary Samuel Kirkland.

Although there was no consolidated uprising of Indians along the western frontier—which could have been a serious if not fatal blow to colonial aspirations—there were sporadic outbreaks, enough to keep settlers on edge and give consternation to the Congress that was directing the war. This phase of the Revolutionary War, perhaps, can best be considered a continuation of the tension between the two races that had already become a way of life in the West. But there is little doubt that the borderland warfare was aggravated by British encouragement of the Indians.[14]

There were only a few instances of formal entry into the war by Indians. The Cherokees in 1776, against the advice of John Stuart, mounted an attack on the back country of the Carolinas. It was a disastrous venture. In an unusual show of intercolonial cooperation, militia from Virginia, North Carolina, and South Carolina united to crush the Indians. The Cherokees signed treaties in which they ceded large sections of land. This was the end of organized Indian harassment in the south.[15]

In the north, the protagonists were members of the Iroquois confederacy who elected to side actively with the British. Ably directed by Guy John-

13. JCC, 2: 182.
14. The matter of who was to blame for the use of Indians is considered in Jack M. Sosin, "The Use of Indians in the War of the American Revolution: A Re-assessment of Responsibility," *Canadian Historical Review* 46 (June 1965): 101–21. He concludes: "To [General Thomas] Gage belongs the major blame for exaggerating the involvement on the patriot side and encouraging the wise-scale employment of the savages. Fortunately for the American Frontier, Carleton and John Stuart did not initially follow his orders and the settlers were thus given two years to prepare. At that point both sides, seeking to increase their manpower, actively tried to obtain warriors for offensive operations, but the British were more successful than the Americans in enlisting them."
15. O'Donnell, *Southern Indians*, pp. 34–53.

son, who had succeeded his uncle as superintendent in the north, and greatly influenced by the remarkable Mohawk chief Joseph Brant, the Mohawks and Senecas and their friends took an active part in the attempt in 1778 to cut off New England from the rest of the colonies. As General St. Leger drove east from Niagara along the Mohawk Valley to meet General Burgoyne coming from the north toward Albany, his army was heavily augmented by Indian allies. They played a significant role in the battle of Oriskany, as colonial troops sought to relieve the beleaguered garrison at Fort Stanwix.[16]

Burgoyne's defeat at Saratoga signaled the failure of the British plans, but the Iroquois power remained a distinct threat aimed at the heart of the colonies. It was to destroy this danger and to show the Indians that the colonial government could and would strike strongly against the tribes who had decided to fight with the British that Washington sent a well-planned expedition into Iroquois country in 1779 under General John Sullivan. Following a deliberate scorched earth policy, Sullivan's army moved north into the heart of the Iroquois confederacy. Swinging wide through western New York, the troops destroyed villages and crops, without, however, managing to destroy the Indians, who faded away ahead of the approaching army. The policy of destruction left blackened ruins and a bitterness that was not easily erased.[17] Retaliatory raids by the Indians heightened the hatred.

The British from their post at Detroit instigated Indian war parties against the settlements south of the Ohio. To cut off this danger, George Rogers Clark, sent out by Virginia, attacked the Illinois towns and then recaptured Vincennes from the British commander Henry Hamilton, greatly bolstering the morale of western patriots. It was less than a total victory, for the Indians continued to be dependent on trade with the whites; and it was the British, not the Americans, who could provide the needed trading system. Moreover, Clark did not receive the reinforcements he required to proceed against Detroit, and for the last two years of the war he was on the defensive against continual Indian attacks.[18]

Although the Indian campaigns in the war had little effect on the out-

16. These campaigns are treated in general histories of the Revolutionary War. See, for example, Christopher Ward, *The War of the Revolution*, 2 vols. (New York: Macmillan Company, 1952), 2: 477–91.

17. A brief account of the expedition is Donald R. McAdams, "The Sullivan Expedition: Success or Failure," *New-York Historical Society Quarterly* 54 (January 1970): 53–81. See also George S. Conover, comp., *Journals of the Military Expedition of Major General John Sullivan against the Six Nations of Indians in 1779* (Auburn, New York: Knapp, Peck and Thomson, 1887).

18. The war in the west is discussed in Don Higginbotham, *The War of American Independence: Military Attitudes, Policies, and Practice, 1763–1789* (New York: Macmillan Company, 1971), pp. 319–31, and Ward, *War of the Revolution*, 2: 850–65.

come, they did leave a lasting heritage. On the one side, Indian participation in the Revolutionary War had far-reaching effects upon the Indian communities themselves. The war, with the pull in opposite directions by the British and the colonists, fragmented the Iroquois confederacy and in general demoralized the eastern and southern tribes. Those who had agreed to aid Great Britain had succumbed to promises of support of land claims and generous provisions for trade. They discovered to their astonishment that at the end of the war these were disregarded. The British did not insist that Indian rights be protected in the Treaty of Paris that ended the war in 1783, and the Indians were left on their own to deal with the victorious colonists. Important, too, was the heritage of hostility between whites and Indians to which the war contributed so strongly. It is true that such fundamental causes of conflict as white desire for land existed independently of the war, but the atrocities on the frontiers, on the part of both Indians and whites, intensified antagonism and reinforced a pattern that might, in other circumstances, have been modified if not eliminated. It seemed only natural and proper to the founders of the nation that Indian affairs be placed under the War Department.

After the war had run its course and peace loomed on the horizon, the problem of the Indians and the western lands again came to the fore. The ascendency and unique authority of Congress in regard to Indian affairs had to be asserted again and again. The committee appointed to report on the land cessions of the states and on the petitions of various land companies declared on May 1, 1782, that a clearer definition of congressional jurisdiction over Indian affairs was imperative. The recommendations of the committee indicate that the authority given Congress in the Articles of Confederation was not well understood by the states and their citizens. Among a series of resolutions dealing with the creation of new states to the west, the committee felt obliged to include two that reasserted the principle that the sole right of "superintending, protecting, treating with, and making purchases of" the Indian nations living beyond the boundaries of the states belonged to Congress.[19]

When the Revolutionary War ended, the Treaty of Paris signed with Great Britain in 1783 recognized the independence of the United States and designated the Mississippi River and the Great Lakes as the western and northern boundaries of the new nation. But because the treaty made no provision for the Indian tribes, they were considered technically still at war. It behooved the new nation to come to terms with the tribes at once, for the great desideratum was peace. Prolonged hostilities on the frontier could well have collapsed the young nation in the first precarious years of its existence.

19. JCC, 22: 230–31.

The Congress under the Articles of Confederation, aware of the unrest and threatened dangers in the north, south, and west, acted quickly and responsibly to ensure peace. A committee report to Congress on April 21, 1783, made a series of recommendations: suspension of all offensive movements against the Indians as preparation for a final peace; appointment of four commissioners (eastern, northern, western, and southern) to inform the Indians of the decision; and purchase of presents to have on hand when the Indians assembled for a treaty of peace. Congress was also concerned about the steady encroachment onto Indian lands. A proclamation of September 22, 1783, forbade settling on lands inhabited or claimed by the Indians outside of state jurisdiction and purchasing or otherwise receiving such lands without the express authority and direction of Congress. It declared, moreover, that any such purchases or cessions were null and void.[20]

A new report submitted by a committee on Indian affairs on October 15, 1783, proposed a policy for dealing with the Indians of the northern and middle departments only, for the committee disclaimed competency in regard to the southern Indians because of insufficient data. The first problem to be faced was that of drawing the proper boundary lines to designate lands reserved to the Indians. The lines should be drawn "convenient to the respective tribes, and commensurate to the public wants"; that is, restricting the Indians enough so that the lands would be available to fulfill pledges made to soldiers during the war for land bounties. This land should be obtained from the Indians without any considerable expenditure, which the state of public finances would in no case allow. After all, the committee argued, the Indians had been on the losing side in the war. They could with justice be treated as conquered nations and their lands taken from them by right of conquest. And even if the right of conquest were waived, the destruction wrought by Indians and the outrages and atrocities they had committed required atonement and a reasonable compensation for the expenses incurred by the United States. The Indians could accomplish this act of justice only by agreeing to the boundaries proposed. The committee, however, was composed of realists, who recommended some compensation for Indian claims rather than risk another Indian war and the tremendous expense it would bring.[21]

The committee proposed further that a general conference be held with the tribes in order to receive them back into the favor and friendship of the United States. The conference should determine the boundary lines that would divide the white settlements from the villages and hunting grounds

20. Ibid., 24: 264; 25: 602.
21. Ibid., 25: 680–94. The committee that drew up this report relied heavily on the opinions and advice of George Washington, expressed in a letter to the committee head, James Duane, September 7, 1783, *Writings of George Washington*, 27: 133–40. Much of the wording of the report is identical with that in Washington's letter.

of the Indians and thus remove as far as possible the occasion for "future animosities, disquiet and contention." The government commissioners should demand hostages for the return of all prisoners but indicate at the same time the nation's preference for clemency instead of rigor in dealing with the defeated Indians. They should tell the Indians that the government was disposed to be kind to them, to supply their wants through trade, and to draw a veil over the past.

The committee drew up in detail the line to be proposed to the Indians. For the Oneida and Tuscarora tribes, who had adhered to the colonial cause during the war, it recommended special assurances of friendship and recognition of their property rights. And the importance of the Indian trade was not forgotten; to prevent violence, fraud, and injustice toward the Indians, the trade must be regulated and the traders required to give security that they would follow the regulations. To this end, the committee recommended that a group be appointed to draw up an ordinance for regulating the Indian trade.

The committee appointed to consider Indian affairs in the south returned an almost identical report on May 28, 1784.[22]

EARLY TREATIES AND ORDINANCES

Outlining a policy in the halls of Congress was easy enough; the test came in carrying out the actual negotiations with the Indians. In the north and west this was accomplished shortly by the treaties of Fort Stanwix, October 22, 1784, Fort McIntosh, January 21, 1785, and Fort Finney (at the mouth of the Great Miami), January 31, 1786. The first, drawn up with the Six Nations, limited the Indians to an area in western New York and distributed goods to them pursuant to "the humane and liberal views of the United States." The second was a treaty with Delawares, Wyandots, Chippewas, and Ottawas by which these western Indians were allotted an area of land and by which they ceded to the United States other lands formerly claimed by them. The last was a similar agreement with the Shawnees. In these negotiations the idea of a boundary line was taken for granted; the basic problems were exact determination of the line, the conflict of state and federal authority in dealing with the tribes, and the grounds for demanding cessions from the Indians.[23]

The sole and exclusive right of Congress to treat with the Indian tribes was challenged by New York commissioners, who had already come to an agreement with the Six Nations and who caused trouble at the Fort Stan-

22. JCC, 27: 453–64.
23. The treaties are printed in Kappler, pp. 5–8, 16–18.

wix negotiations, but the federal commissioners completed the treaty. No provisions were made for trade, however.[24]

The United States in these first treaties after the Revolutionary War thought it was dealing with conquered tribes or nations. Although Congress spoke of liberality toward the vanquished and realized that some moderation of claims might be necessary to avoid a renewal of fighting, its commissioners dictated the boundary lines and offered no compensation for the ceded lands. To this highhanded arrangement the Indians, abetted by the British, continued to object. They had never asked for peace, they insisted, but thought that the Americans desired it, and they had had no idea that they were to be treated as conquered peoples.[25]

Furthermore, although the lands west of the boundary lines were guaranteed to the Indians and the United States promised to restrict the encroachment of whites, white aggressions continued. George Washington, after a tour of the West in 1784, reported the extent of the menace:

> Such is the rage for speculating in, and forestalling of Lands on the No. West side of Ohio, that scarce a valuable spot within any tolerable distance of it, is left without a claimant. Men in these times, talk with as much facility of fifty, a hundred, and even 500,000 Acres as a Gentleman formerly would do of 1000 acres. In defiance of the proclamation of Congress, they roam over the Country on the Indian side of the Ohio, mark out lands, Survey, and even settle them. This gives great discontent to the Indians, and will unless measures are taken in time to prevent it, inevitably produce a war with the western Tribes.[26]

The government seemed powerless to hold back the onslaughts of the advancing whites, and by 1786 the northwest Indians, out of disgust with the whole policy of the United States, were ready to repudiate all the engagements made with them since the close of the war.

In the south, the difficulties were, if anything, even greater because of the tenacity with which the Indians held to their lands, the mounting pressure of white settlers on the lands, the history of hostility of the tribes

24. For a discussion of troubles with the New York commissioners, see Henry S. Manley, *The Treaty of Fort Stanwix, 1784* (Rome, New York: Rome Sentinel Company, 1932). Barbara Graymont, "New York State Indian Policy after the Revolution," *New York History* 57 (October 1976): 438–74, shows how New York continued to treat with the Indians within its borders, contrary to federal policy, and in the end largely stripped the Indians of their lands.

25. Mohr, *Federal Indian Relations*, pp. 93–138; Reginald Horsman, "American Indian Policy in the Old Northwest, 1783–1812," *William and Mary Quarterly* 18 (January 1961): 35–39.

26. Washington to Jacob Read, November 3, 1784, *Writings of George Washington*, 27: 486.

against the whites, and the serious interference by state officials in the federal government's handling of Indian affairs. A special committee again reported recommendations for dealing with these southern tribes similar to those proposed a year earlier. Emphasis was placed on the precise determination of a boundary line marking the Indian country, and the Indians were authorized to drive off unlawful intruders, who would forfeit the protection of the United States.[27] After troubles with North Carolina and Georgia, which objected to the composition of the board of commissioners, a series of treaties was negotiated with the Cherokees, Choctaws, and Chickasaws at Hopewell, South Carolina, at the end of 1785 and the beginning of 1786. These treaties fixed boundaries for the Indian country, withdrew United States protection from settlers on the Indian lands who did not leave within six months, made arrangements for the punishment of criminals, and declared in solemn tones that "the hatchet shall be forever buried." They stipulated further that "the United States in Congress assembled shall have the sole and exclusive right of regulating the trade with the Indians, and managing all their affairs in such manner as they think proper," and declared that "until the pleasure of Congress be known," any citizen of the United States could trade with the tribes.[28]

The new nation faced innumerable difficulties, and it was imperative that the Indians remain at peace. This happy end could be attained only by a policy of justice toward the Indians and protection of their rights and property against unscrupulous traders, avaricious settlers, and ubiquitous speculators. With this in mind, Congress on August 7, 1786, enacted an Ordinance for the Regulation of Indian Affairs. With an eye, no doubt, to North Carolina and Georgia, the exclusive right of Congress under the Articles of Confederation to deal with the Indians was once more reasserted. The ordinance established southern and northern Indian departments, divided by the Ohio River, and authorized a superintendent of Indian affairs for each. These men were to hold office for two years unless sooner removed, reside in or near their districts, and "attend to the execution of such regulations, as Congress shall, from time to time, establish respecting Indian Affairs." The plan placed the superintendents under the secretary of war and directed them to correspond regularly with him and to obey his instructions. The superintendents and their deputies had power to grant trading licenses. They could not engage in the trade themselves, however, and had to take an oath to fulfill their obligations and to post a

27. JCC, 28: 118–20.

28. Kappler, pp. 8–16. Details on the appointment of commissioners are in JCC, 27, and in Merritt B. Pound, *Benjamin Hawkins: Indian Agent* (Athens: University of Georgia Press, 1951). See also Mohr, *Federal Indian Relations*, pp. 139–72, and Kenneth Coleman, "Federal Indian Relations in the South, 1781–1789," *Chronicles of Oklahoma* 35 (Winter 1957–1958): 435–58.

bond for the faithful discharge of their duties. All traders needed a license, good for one year at a fee of fifty dollars, and had to give bond of three thousand dollars for strict observance of the laws and regulations. Only citizens of the United States could reside among the Indians or trade with them.[29]

The Ordinance of 1786 was backed up in February 1787 by a set of instructions sent to the superintendents. "The United States are fixed in their determination," the instructions read in part, "that justice and public faith shall be the basis of all their transactions with the Indians. They will reject every temporary advantage obtained at the expence of these important national principles." The directive told the superintendents to seek out the causes of Indian unrest and correct them as much as possible; to cultivate trade with the Indians as an object of special importance but to allow no traders to engage in the trade without the proper licenses; and to investigate the character and conduct of the traders. To aid in the enforcement of the ordinance, the commanding officers of frontier posts were ordered to render such assistance as was necessary and as the state of their commands would allow. These were general instructions; the fine points of treating with the Indians and managing the trade were left to the "prudence, fidelity and judgment" of the agents.[30]

The regulations and grand utterances of the general government were largely ignored, and affairs got out of hand. The frontier was too extensive, the enforcing agencies inadequate, and the concern with other matters more pressing. Georgia on November 3, 1786, less than three months after the ordinance had restated the sole and exclusive right of Congress to deal with the Indian tribes, signed the Treaty of Shoulderbone, in which a small body of Creeks pretending to speak for the nation signed and gave up the Indian claims to all lands in Georgia east of the Oconee River. The encroachments continued apace, and the trade regulations of the ordinance were not followed; there is no record of any licenses being issued in the south under its provisions.

Again, in the Northwest Ordinance of July 13, 1787, the federal government voiced its position: "The utmost good faith shall always be observed towards the Indians, their lands and property shall never be taken from them without their consent; and in their property, rights and liberty, they shall never be invaded or disturbed, unless in just and lawful wars authorised by Congress; but laws founded in justice and humanity shall from time to time be made, for preventing wrongs being done to them, and for preserving peace and friendship with them."[31]

The continual reassertion by Congress of its ideas of justice toward the Indians began to have a hollow sound. Part of the problem undoubtedly came from the haziness (at least professed in the minds of some) about the

29. JCC, 31: 490–93.   30. Ibid., 32: 66–69.   31. Ibid., pp. 340–41.

exact authority of Congress, and the intermeddling of the states in Indian affairs aggravated the difficulties of the general government.

Mincing no words, a congressional committee on southern Indian affairs in August 1787 went to the heart of the matter. It insisted on the authority of Congress over independent Indian tribes and condemned the acts of states (specifically Georgia and North Carolina) in dealing with Indian tribes. It demanded that Congress give serious attention to the repeated complaints of the Indians about encroachments upon their lands, "as well because they [the encroachments] may be unjustifiable as on account of their tendency to produce all the evils of a general Indian war on the frontiers." It urged an investigation of the causes of hostilities and a policy of strict justice to both sides. "An avaricious disposition in some of our people to acquire large tracts of land and often by unfair means," the committee noted, "appears to be the principal source of difficulties with the Indians," and it made note of the settlements that were appearing on the lands of the Cherokees and Creeks contrary to treaties made with those tribes.[32]

Admittedly it was difficult to determine accurately the titles to land, but more embarrassing was the misunderstanding about the extent of federal power in governing Indian matters. It was on this point that the committee made its strongest comments. It insisted upon the just claims of the Indians to their lands and asserted that the power needed to manage affairs with the Indians could not be divided between the states and the federal government.[33]

Still the encroachments continued. General Henry Knox, secretary of war under the Confederation, reported to Congress in July 1788 the unprovoked and direct outrages against Cherokee Indians by inhabitants on the frontier of North Carolina in open violation of the Treaty of Hopewell. The outrages were of such extent, Knox declared, "as to amount to an actual although informal war of the said white inhabitants against the said Cherokees." The action he blamed on the "avaricious desire of obtaining the fertile lands possessed by said indians of which and particularly of their ancient town of Chota they are exceedingly tenacious," and he urged Congress to take action to uphold the treaty provisions and thus the reputation and dignity of the Union. He recommended that Congress issue a proclamation warning the settlers to depart, and if they did not, to move in troops against them. "Your Secretary begs leave to observe," he concluded his report, "that he is utterly at a loss to devise any other mode of correct-

---

32. Ibid., 33: 455–62.
33. Ibid., pp. 458–59. The precise point at issue was the meaning of the proviso in the Articles of Confederation about not restricting the legislative right of any state within its own borders.

ing effectually the evils specified than the one herein proposed. That he conceives it of the highest importance to the peace of the frontiers that all the indian tribes should rely with security on the treaties they have made or shall make with the United States."[34]

Congress did not disappoint Knox. On September 1 it issued the recommended proclamation—that universal but generally useless prescription for such ills as the secretary of war described. The proclamation cited the provisions of the Treaty of Hopewell and the boundary lines drawn therein, and it ordered the intrusions and the outrages to cease, enjoining all who had settled on the Cherokee lands to leave at once. It directed the secretary of war to have troops in readiness to disperse the intruders.[35]

That Knox and Congress were not sure of their ground is shown by the deference they both paid to the state of North Carolina. Knox assumed that North Carolina would place no obstruction in the way of federal action, but he recommended nevertheless that the state be requested to concur. Congress sent copies of the proclamation to the executives of North Carolina and Virginia, asking their cooperation.

Congress did not retreat from the position that Indians were a uniquely federal concern. The hazy proviso in the ninth Article of Confederation and the highhanded action of New York and North Carolina caused difficulties, it is true, but the high councils of state, by constant reiteration of the principles, managed to make it stick. The centrifugal force of state sovereignty and state pride was never strong enough to destroy the centralization of Indian control.

The new federal government had to tread with great care, and it could not always act according to the theories it propounded. The practical problems of dealing with the Indians at the end of the war had to be met by practicable measures, not high-flown theory. The one basic requirement of the new government that never faded from the consciousness of its leaders was peace on the frontier. The government needed peace in which to get firmly established, and it had to tailor its practice to this great end.

Knox came to realize that agreements with the Indians based upon the right of conquest did not work and that adherence to such a policy would continually endanger the peace of the frontier. The British and colonial practice of purchasing the right of the soil from the Indians was the only method to which the Indians would peaceably agree, and Knox urged a return to that policy. To establish claims by the principle of conquest would mean continuous warfare. He recommended, therefore, that the land ceded by the northwest Indians be compensated for and that future cessions be acquired by purchase. By the treaties signed at Fort Harmar on January 9, 1789, with the Six Nations and some of the northwest Indians, the lands

34. JCC, 34: 342–44. 35. Ibid., pp. 476–79.

granted to the United States at Fort Stanwix and Fort McIntosh were paid for. Small as the payments were, they marked the abandonment of the policy that the lands from the Indians had been acquired by conquest.[36]

THE CONSTITUTION AND INDIAN POLICY

After the concern of the Continental Congress with Indian affairs and the discussion aroused when the Articles of Confederation were drawn up, it is surprising to find so little about Indian matters in the Constitutional Convention of 1787. It was almost as if the presence of Indians on the frontiers had slipped the minds of the Founding Fathers and provisions were made for carrying on relations with them only as an afterthought. The lack of debate on the question indicates, perhaps, the universal agreement that Indian affairs should be left in the hands of the federal government. It was not the purpose of the men who wrote the Constitution, of course, to provide explicit details for congressional or executive action. Grants of powers and responsibilities were made to the federal government, enabling Congress to work out the detailed laws that were necessary to achieve the end proposed, but the Constitution is meager indeed on the subject of Indians, and what does appear was not the product of long debate.

The statesmen who gathered in Philadelphia in the summer of 1787 had come together to correct weaknesses in the federal compact. It was natural, then, that disregard of federal authority in Indian matters by the states should find a place in the discussions. In James Madison's mind, at least, the problem was clear, and when the Committee of the Whole discussed the Paterson plan on June 19, he asked, "Will it prevent encroachments on the federal authority?" The Articles of Confederation had failed in this regard, and one of the examples adduced by Madison was that "by the federal articles, transactions with the Indians appertain to Congs. Yet in several instances, the States have entered into treaties & wars with them." When the Committee of Detail presented its draft of a constitution to the convention on August 6, however, no provision was made for dealing with the Indians. To remedy this omission, Madison proposed on August 28, among other additions to the powers of the federal legislature, that Congress have power "to regulate affairs with the Indians, as well within as without the limits of the United States." His proposal was referred to the Committee of Detail.[37]

36. Mohr, *Federal Indian Relations*, p. 132; Kappler, pp. 18–25.

37. Max Farrand, ed., *The Records of the Federal Convention of 1787*, 4 vols. (New Haven: Yale University Press, 1911–1937), 1: 316; 2: 321. Madison had Georgia specifically in mind. In his "Preface to Debates in the Convention of 1787" he wrote: "In certain cases the authy of the Confederacy was disregarded, as in violations not only of the

This broad grant of power, "to regulate affairs with the Indians," was considerably cut down by the committee, which merely added to the clause granting Congress the power "to regulate commerce with foreign nations, and among the several States" the words "and with the Indians, within the Limits of any State, not subject to the laws thereof." In the report of the Committee of Eleven, submitted on September 4, the Indian clause was reduced again, this time to the simple phrase "and with the Indian tribes." The convention agreed to this wording the same day without any opposition.[38]

These five words would seem to be scant foundation upon which to build the structure of federal legislation regulating trade and intercourse with the Indian tribes. Yet through them, plus treaty-making and other powers, Congress exercised what amounted to plenary power over the Indian tribes. John Marshall noted in *Worcester* v. *Georgia*: "[The Constitution] confers on Congress the powers of war and peace; of making treaties, and of regulating commerce with foreign nations, and among the several States, and with the Indian tribes. These powers comprehend all that is required for the regulation of our intercourse with the Indians. They are not limited by any restrictions on their free action. The shackles imposed on this power, in the confederation, are discarded." There have been questions about the precise derivation of congressional power over the Indians, of course. Some jurists emphasize the commerce clause; others find the bulk of congressional power in the treaty clause; some add authority from the general welfare, national defense, and national domain clauses of the Constitution. In 1886 the Supreme Court spoke of federal power that grew out of the peculiar nature of the relations between the two races, independent of grants of authority in the Constitution. But whatever the ultimate source of congressional power, the federal legislature established by the Constitution has never felt hampered for want of authority.[39]

Treaty of peace; but of Treaties with France & Holland, which were complained of to Congs. In other cases the Fedl authy was violated by Treaties & wars with Indians, as by Geo." Ibid., 3: 548.

38. Ibid., 2: 367, 493, 495, 499. There is little evidence that Indian matters entered into the debates over ratification of the Constitution. Georgia, however, seems to have quickly ratified because of a desire to gain stronger protection against hostile Indians. James Jackson, Georgia's representative in Congress, declared on August 11, 1789, as he was demanding federal aid against the Creeks, that the Georgians "must procure protection here or elsewhere. In full confidence that a good, complete, and efficient Government would succor and relieve them, they were led to an early and unanimous adoption of the Constitution." Quoted in Randolph C. Downes, "Creek-American Relations, 1782–1790," *Georgia Historical Quarterly* 21 (June 1937): 172–73.

39. *Worcester* v. *Georgia*, 6 Peters 559. An analysis of the scope of federal power over Indian affairs is in *Felix S. Cohen's Handbook of Federal Indian Law*, 1982 edition (Charlottesville, Virginia: Michie, Bobbs-Merrill, 1982), pp. 207–28.

TREATY-MAKING PRINCIPLES AND PRACTICES

The Constitution, with its division of powers among the three branches of government, necessitated a working out in practice of the grants of authority only briefly enumerated in the document itself. This was particularly true in regard to treaty making, which was stated in these terms: "[The President] shall have power, by and with the advice and consent of the Senate, to make treaties, provided two thirds of the senators present concur." Two questions arose: Were agreements with the Indian tribes to follow regular treaty procedures? How precisely did the Senate advise and consent in regard to treaties? Both questions were answered in 1789 and 1790 as President Washington dealt with the Senate concerning the treaties at Fort Harmar of January 1789 and the treaty with the Creeks at New York of August 1790.[40]

The Fort Harmar treaties, although negotiated before the government under the Constitution was set up, were submitted to the Senate on May 25, 1789, by Henry Knox, who went to the Senate in person as a representative of the president to explain the circumstances under which the treaties had been concluded. When the Senate postponed action on the treaties, President Washington sent a communication to that body on September 17, 1789, in which he expressed his opinion about the nature of Indian treaties and their ratification. He argued that it was the custom among nations to have the treaties negotiated by commissioners ratified by the government that had appointed them. "This practice has been adopted by the United States, respecting their treaties with European Nations," he noted, "and I am inclined to think it would be adviseable to observe it in the conduct of our treaties with the Indians: for tho' such treaties, being on their part, made by their Chiefs or Rulers, need not be ratified by them, yet being formed on our part by the agency of subordinate Officers, it seems to be both prudent and reasonable, that their acts should not be binding on the Nation until approved and ratified by the Government."[41]

A committee appointed to consider the president's message reported the following day that it did not consider formal ratification of Indian

40. Ralston Hayden, *The Senate and Treaties, 1789–1817: The Development of the Treaty-Making Functions of the United States Senate during Their Formative Period* (New York: Macmillan Company, 1920), pp. 11–39. The pertinent documents are carefully edited in *Documentary History of the First Federal Congress of the United States of America, March 4, 1789–March 3, 1791*, ed. Linda Grant De Pauw, vol. 2: *Senate Executive Journal and Related Documents* (Baltimore: Johns Hopkins University Press, 1974).

41. *Senate Executive Journal and Related Documents*, pp. 40–41.

treaties by the Senate necessary, for the signing of the treaties by both parties without further ratification by the governments had been the common practice. But the Senate rejected this opinion and proceeded on September 22 to "advise and consent that the President of the United States ratify" the Treaty of Fort Harmar with the northwest tribes.[42] Thus was the precedent established, in accordance with Washington's view, that Indian treaties—like those with foreign nations—be formally approved by the Senate before they took effect.

While the case of the Fort Harmar treaties was still pending, the Senate and the president began to work out the functioning of the treaty-making power. On August 6 a committee of the Senate was appointed "to wait on the President of the United States, and confer with him on the mode of communication proper to be pursued between him and the Senate, in the formation of Treaties, and making appointments to Offices." On August 8 and again on August 10, the committee conferred with the president. Although Washington believed that nominations to office could be made by written communications, he felt differently about treaties. "In all matters respecting Treaties," as the report of the conference expressed his sentiment, "oral communications seemed indispensably necessary; because in these a variety of matters are contained, all of which not only require consideration, but some of them may undergo much discussion; to do which by written communications would be tedious without being satisfactory." Although Washington did not want a hard and fast rule that would not permit accommodation to varying circumstances, in the matter of treaties he looked upon the Senate as a council with whom he would discuss in person any pending negotiations.[43] The procedure was put to the test in the case of a treaty with the Creek Indians.

On August 22 and August 24, 1789, President Washington and Secretary of War Knox met with the Senate in the Senate chamber and laid before the members a set of facts concerning relations with the southern tribes.

> To conciliate the powerful tribes of Indians in the southern District, amounting probably to fourteen thousand fighting Men, and to attach them firmly to the United States, may be regarded as highly worthy of the serious attention of government.
>
> The measure includes, not only peace and security to the whole southern frontier, but is calculated to form a barrier against the Colonies of an European power, which in the mutations of Policy, may one day become the enemy of the United States. The fate of the

42. Ibid., pp. 42–43.
43. Ibid., pp. 24, 29–30; notes on conference of August 8, 1789, *Writings of George Washington*, 30: 373–74; Washington to Madison, August 9, 1789, ibid., pp. 374–75.

southern States therefore, or the neighbouring Colonies, may principally depend on the present measures of the Union towards the
southern Indians.

The serious encroachment into Cherokee lands in violation of the Treaty
of Hopewell, Washington believed, could not be immediately resolved because North Carolina, whence the incursions came, had not yet ratified
the Constitution and joined the Union, and the Chickasaws and Choctaws
were far enough to the west to prevent immediate conflicts with white settlers. But the Creek problem needed immediate attention because of hostilities between the Creeks and the Georgians.[44]

The Creek situation illustrates well the complicated Indian affairs that
faced President Washington. The Creeks were the strongest and best organized of the southern Indians, although they maintained the nature of a
federation of somewhat independent towns organized as the Upper Towns
and the Lower Towns. They formed a buffer between the new states and
the Spanish, who had regained jurisdiction over Florida in 1783. The Creeks,
like other Indian tribes, were increasingly dependent upon trade goods procured from white centers, and they had established patterns of trade to the
south, largely though the firm of Panton, Leslie, and Company, with headquarters at Pensacola. Their relations with the state of Georgia were critical. Georgia, ignoring the established principle that only the federal government could negotiate with the Indian nations for cessions of land, had
concluded a series of treaties with a minority of Creek chiefs in which the
Indians had ceded land for white use. These treaties of Augusta (1783),
Galphinton (1785), and Shoulderbone (1786) were contested by a majority
of the Creeks, who denied their validity.[45] The spokesman for the Creeks
was the astute leader Alexander McGillivray, the son of a Scottish Loyalist
trader and a French-Indian mother. Although he got his support largely
from the Upper Towns, he represented himself successfully as chief of all
the Creeks. He refused to accept the Georgia treaties and bolstered his
position by strong ties with Panton and with Spanish officials, from whom
he customarily received a pension.[46]

Washington outlined for the Senate his proposed solution to this im-

---

44. *Senate Executive Journal and Related Documents*, pp. 31–37.

45. The treaties are printed ibid., pp. 165–69, 180–83. American relations with the
Creek Indians are covered in Downes, "Creek-American Relations, 1782–1790," pp.
142–84, and Randolph C. Downes, "Creek-American Relations, 1790–1795," *Journal of
Southern History* 8 (August 1942): 350–73. See also Clyde R. Ferguson, "Andrew Pickens
and U.S. Policy toward the Creek Indians, 1789–1793," *Kansas Quarterly* 3 (Fall 1971):
21–28.

46. On McGillivray, see John Walton Caughey, *McGillivray of the Creeks* (Norman:
University of Oklahoma Press, 1938); Arthur Preston Whitaker, "Alexander McGillivray,
1783–1789," *North Carolina Historical Review* 5 (April 1928): 181–203; Whitaker,

passe—to negotiate with the Creeks for conveyance of the lands actually occupied by the Georgians through a federal treaty, in case commissioners sent to investigate the claims of the two parties should decide against Georgia—and he posed seven questions about the pending negotiations, to which he asked for and received answers from the Senate.[47]

The conferences between the president and the Senate were marked by constraint and tension, and the procedure proved unsatisfactory to both parties. The Senate wanted to examine the documents of the case at leisure, and Washington was irked by such delay. When he left the chamber, the president declared that "he would be damned if he ever went there again." And in fact he never did, although he continued to keep the Senate informed about the progress of negotiations with the Creeks.[48]

It was the goal of the United States to come to an agreement with McGillivray and the Creeks in order to settle the peace on the southwest frontier, to vindicate federal authority against Georgia in dealing with the Indian nations, and to draw the Creeks away from the Spanish into American channels of trade. In the fall of 1789 the government sent commissioners to meet with the Creeks at Rock Landing, Georgia, but when it became apparent that the commissioners were going to stand behind Georgia's claims, the Indians withdrew and the conference broke up with nothing accomplished.[49] In 1790 another attempt was made. Through the good offices of Senator Benjamin Hawkins of North Carolina (who later gained fame as agent to the Creeks), Washington sent Colonel Marinus Willett to persuade McGillivray to come to the seat of government in New York. The chief agreed, and with great fanfare he and his party of chiefs and warriors arrived in New York to negotiate with Washington and Knox. Although he was carefully watched and to some extent importuned by Span-

---

"Alexander McGillivray, 1789–1793," ibid. (July 1928): 289–309; and J. Leitch Wright, Jr., "Creek-American Treaty of 1790: Alexander McGillivray and the Diplomacy of the Old Southwest," *Georgia Historical Quarterly* 51 (December 1967): 379–400. A sprightly, popular article is Gary L. Roberts, "The Chief of State and the Chief" (Washington and McGillivray), *American Heritage* 26 (October 1975): 28–33, 86–89.

47. *Senate Executive Journal and Related Documents*, pp. 33–36.

48. The story of Washington's encounter with the Senate is reported in *Memoirs of John Quincy Adams*, ed. Charles Francis Adams, 12 vols. (Philadelphia: J. B. Lippincott and Company, 1874–1877), 6: 427, and told in detail in William Maclay, *The Journal of William Maclay: United States Senator from Pennsylvania, 1789–1791* (New York: Albert and Charles Boni, 1927), pp. 125–29. Material on the Creek treaty matter appears in *Senate Executive Journal and Related Documents*, pp. 55, 86–87, 88–89, 90–91.

49. Instructions to the commissioners, August 29, 1789, and the long report of the commissioners, November 17, 1789 (which includes transcriptions of pertinent documents) are in *Senate Executive Journal and Related Documents*, pp. 202–41. See also Lucia Burk Kinnaird, "The Rock Landing Conference of 1789," *North Carolina Historical Review* 9 (October 1932): 349–65.

ish and British representatives, who followed the proceedings with considerable self-interest, McGillivray signed a treaty of peace and land cession on August 7, 1790.[50]

In the treaty the Creeks acknowledged themselves "to be under the protection of the United States of America and of no other sovereign whosoever" and agreed not to hold treaties with individual states or persons. For a small annuity, the Indians agreed to cede lands actually occupied by Georgia settlers, but they refused to accede to the rest of Georgia's claims based on her treaties with the Creeks. The United States solemnly guaranteed the Creek lands lying beyond the boundary line established by the Treaty of New York. It promised also to furnish "useful domestic animals and implements of husbandry," in order that the Creek nation might be led "to a greater degree of civilization and to become herdsmen and cultivators instead of remaining in a state of hunters." There is no doubt that the treaty was made possible by a number of secret articles. One of these authorized duty-free trade through United States ports if Creek trade channels through Spanish territories were cut off (which effectively guaranteed to McGillivray control over Creek trade through American ports, which he then held over trade through Spanish). Another made McGillivray an agent of the United States in the Creek nation with the rank of brigadier general and an annuity of twelve hundred dollars. Others presented medals, commissions, and one hundred dollars a year to lesser Creek chiefs and promised to educate and clothe Creek youths.[51]

When it came time to negotiate with the Cherokees, Washington again sought Senate advice before the negotiations were carried out. But this time all was done by written communication; neither Washington nor Knox met personally with the Senate. The questions proposed for advice and consent were very general and did not deal with alternatives that might arise in the negotiations. The Senate, too, replied briefly. But it was noted in ratification that the completed treaty conformed to the instructions given to the commissioners by the president and that those instructions were founded upon the prior advice and consent of the Senate.[52]

50. Wright, "Creek-American Treaty of 1790." This article analyzes the influence of the Nootka Sound controversy between England and Spain and the Yazoo land grants on McGillivray's decision to go to New York to treat with the United States, and it traces the activities of the Spanish and British in New York.

51. The Senate ratified the treaty on August 12, 1790, *Senate Executive Journal and Related Documents*, pp. 96–97. The original treaty and the secret articles are reprinted ibid., pp. 241–50. The treaty is in Kappler, pp. 25–28; the secret provisions are printed in Hunter Miller, ed., *Treaties and Other International Acts of the United States of America*, 8 vols. (Washington: GPO, 1931–1948), 2: 344.

52. Hayden, *The Senate and Treaties*, pp. 33–34; *Senate Executive Journal and Related Documents*, pp. 94–96; ASP:IA, 1: 123–29.

Later treaties during Washington's administration for the most part dispensed with prior consultation, and when the president's cabinet, in considering the Treaty of Greenville in 1795, was asked whether the executive should consult ahead of time with the Senate, the members unanimously said no.[53] It became the established procedure in treaties with the Indians, as in other treaties, for the executive to negotiate and sign the treaties and only then to submit them to the Senate for action.

The United States government thus treated with Indian tribes with the same legal procedures used for foreign nations, a practice that acknowledged some kind of autonomous nationhood of the Indian tribes. When Chief Justice John Marshall in 1831 and 1832 examined the history of American relations with the Cherokees and other tribes, he strongly emphasized that point. "They [the Cherokees] have been uniformly treated as a state from the settlement of our country," Marshall said in *Cherokee Nation* v. *Georgia*. "The numerous treaties made with them by the United States recognize them as a people capable of maintaining the relations of peace and war, of being responsible in their political character for any violation of their engagements, or for any aggression committed on the citizens of the United States by an individual of their community."[54] In *Worcester* v. *Georgia* Marshall was even more explicit.

> The Constitution, by declaring treaties already made, as well as those to be made, to be the supreme law of the land, has adopted and sanctioned the previous treaties with the Indian nations, and consequently admits their rank among those powers who are capable of making treaties. The words "treaty" and "nation" are words of our own language, selected in our diplomatic and legislative proceedings, by ourselves, having each a definite and well understood meaning. We have applied them to Indians, as we have applied them to the other nations of the earth. They are applied to all in the same sense.[55]

However the theory was expressed—and there were those like Andrew Jackson who early argued that it was a mistake to sign treaties with Indians—the practice became deeply ingrained. Many of the basic relations between the United States and the tribes were determined by treaties, and the obligations incurred endured after the treaty-making process itself ended.

53. Hayden, *The Senate and Treaties*, pp. 34–37.
54. *Cherokee Nation* v. *Georgia*, 5 Peters 16.
55. *Worcester* v. *Georgia*, 6 Peters 559. For a discussion of the scope and legal force of treaties, see *Cohen's Handbook of Federal Indian Law*, 1982 ed., pp. 62–70. For a discussion of the importance of treaty making, see Dorothy V. Jones, *License for Empire: Colonialism by Treaty in Early America* (Chicago: University of Chicago Press, 1982), pp. 157–86.

Although Indian treaties and those with foreign nations had a legal similarity, it would be a mistake to push the sameness too far. In fact, the Indian groups were not like foreign nations, and the negotiations with them often differed markedly from those with England or France. The Indian tribes, either willingly or because forced to do so, acknowledged in the very treaties themselves a degree of dependence upon the United States and a consequent diminution of sovereignty. In the treaties at Hopewell in 1785–1786, the Cherokees, Chickasaws, and Choctaws acknowledged themselves "to be under the protection of the United States of America, and of no other sovereign whosoever." Similar clauses appeared in the treaties of Fort McIntosh and Fort Harmar with the northwest Indians, in the Treaty of Fort Stanwix with the Six Nations, and in the Creek treaty of New York. And the Hopewell treaties proclaimed: "For the benefit and comfort of the Indians, and for the prevention of injuries or oppressions on the part of the citizens or Indians, the United States in Congress assembled shall have the sole and exclusive right of regulating the trade with the Indians, and managing all their affairs in such manner as they think proper." Other clauses specified provisions for trade and for the extradition of whites who committed crimes within the Indian nations.[56]

Although the treaties did not touch the autonomy of the tribes in internal affairs, they made it clear that in relations with whites, the Indian nations accepted significant restrictions. The tribes were not free to deal directly with European nations, with individual states, or with private individuals, a point enunciated by Marshall in his Cherokee decision in 1831 in unequivocal fashion. "They and their country are considered by foreign nations, as well as by ourselves," he said, "as being so completely under the sovereignty and dominion of the United States, that any attempt to acquire their lands, or to form a political connexion with them, would be considered by all as an invasion of our territory, and an act of hostility." It was such considerations that led the chief justice to denominate the Indian tribes, not independent foreign nations, but "domestic dependent nations."[57]

INDIAN RIGHTS TO THE LAND

One indication of the lack of full sovereignty among the Indian tribes was the insistence by the United States on the principle of preemption of In-

56. Kappler, pp. 9–16. Similar statements appeared in subsequent treaties. See, for example, the treaty with the Cherokees, 1791, ibid., pp. 29–32.

57. *Cherokee Nation* v. *Georgia*, 5 Peters 17–18. The Creeks in 1790 agreed that they would "not hold any treaty with an individual State, or with individuals of any State"; the Cherokees in 1791 agreed that they would "not hold any treaty with any foreign power, individual state, or with individuals of any state." Kappler, pp. 25, 29.

dian lands, inherited from the European nations who had developed it in the course of their New World settlement. Thomas Jefferson relied upon this accepted view when the British minister asked him in 1792 what he understood to be the American right in the Indian soil. The secretary of state replied: "1st. A right of pre-emption of their lands; that is to say, the sole and exclusive right of purchasing from them whenever they should be willing to sell. 2d. A right of regulating the commerce between them and the whites. . . . We consider it as established by the usage of different nations into a kind of *Jus gentium* for America, that a white nation settling down and declaring that such and such are their limits, makes an invasion of those limits by any other white nation an act of war, but gives no right of soil against the native possessors." The following year he was even more emphatic in replying to queries posed by Washington to his cabinet. "I considered our right of pre-emption of the Indian lands," Jefferson remarked, "not as amounting to any dominion, or jurisdiction, or paramountship whatever, but merely in the nature of a reminder after the extinguishment of a present right, which gave us no present right whatever, but of preventing other nations from taking possession, and so defeating our expectancy; that the Indians had the full, undivided and independent sovereignty as long as they choose to keep it, and that this might be forever."[58]

Henry Knox entertained the same views, although he based them less on theoretical reasoning about the law of nations than did Jefferson. For the secretary of war, the common principles of human decency and the honor and dignity of the nation were reason enough to protect the rights of the Indians. "It is presumable," he wrote to Washington on June 15, 1789, "that a nation solicitous of establishing its character on the broad basis of justice, would not only hesitate at, but reject every proposition to benefit itself, by the injury of any neighboring community, however contemptible and weak it might be, either with respect to its manners or power. . . . The

58. *The Writings of Thomas Jefferson*, ed. Andrew A. Lipscomb, 20 vols. (Washington: Thomas Jefferson Memorial Association, 1903), 1: 340–41; 17: 328–29. See also the strong statement in support of Indian rights in Jefferson to Henry Knox, August 10, 1791, ibid., 8: 226–27; and Jefferson to Knox, August 26, 1790, *The Papers of Thomas Jefferson*, ed. Julian P. Boyd, 19 vols. to date (Princeton: Princeton University Press, 1950–), 17: 430–31. Jefferson's proposed amendment to the Constitution to ratify the Louisiana Purchase contained a statement of respect for Indian rights: "The right of occupancy in the soil, and of self-government, are confirmed to the Indian inhabitants, as they now exist. Pre-emption only of the portions rightfully occupied by them, & a succession to the occupancy of such as they may abandon, with the full rights of possession as well as of property & sovereignty in whatever is not or shall cease to be so rightfully occupied by them shall belong to the U.S." Quoted in Annie H. Abel, "The History of Events Resulting in Indian Consolidation West of the Mississippi," *Annual Report of the American Historical Association for the Year 1906* (Washington, 1908), 1: 241. Abel argues that in 1803 Jefferson looked upon the Indian possession as only temporary.

Indians being the prior occupants, possess the right of the soil. It cannot be taken from them unless by their free consent, or by the right of conquest in case of a just war." Knox adverted to the opinion that the Indians had indeed lost their rights by reason of defeat with the British in the Revolution, but he pointed out that Congress in 1788 and 1789 had waived the right of conquest and had conceded to the Indians rights to the lands they possessed. "That the Indians possess the natural rights of man, and that they ought not wantonly to be divested thereof, cannot be well denied," Knox declared, and he recommended that these rights be ascertained and declared by law. "Were it enacted that the Indians possess the right to all their territory which they have not fairly conveyed," he wrote, "and that they should not be divested thereof, but in consequence of open treaties, made under the authority of the United States, the foundation of peace and justice would be laid."[59]

The principle of preemption was vital in Washington's policy. General Rufus Putnam concluded a treaty of peace with the Wabash and Illinois Indians in 1793 that included the following article: "The United States solemnly guaranty to the Wabash, and the Illinois nations, or tribes of Indians, all the lands to which they have just claim; and no part shall ever be taken from them, but by a fair purchase, and to their satisfaction. That the lands originally belonged to the Indians; it is theirs, and theirs only. That they have a right to sell, and a right to refuse to sell. And that the United States will protect them in their said just right." In sending the treaty to the Senate for consideration, the president requested a change in this statement of absolute Indian ownership "to guard . . . the exclusive pre-emption of the United States to the land of the said Indians." The Senate, reluctant to amend the document without further negotiations with the Indians involved, in the end rejected the treaty, but not because of any disagreement with the principle of preemption.[60]

Such views of Indian rights to the land were the basis of the dealings of the United States with the Indians. However great the pressures for dispossession of the Indians, the legal principles were clear. Judicial decisions regarding Indian rights to the land stressed either the possessory right of the Indians or the limitations of that right—the "sacred" right of occupancy or the "mere" right of occupancy—but all agreed that the aboriginal title involved an exclusive right of occupancy but not the ultimate ownership.[61]

59. Knox to Washington, June 15, 1789, and January 4, 1790, ASP:IA, 1: 13, 61. See also Knox to Washington, July 7, 1789, ibid., pp. 52–54.

60. ASP:IA, 1: 338; Hayden, *The Senate and Treaties*, pp. 34–37.

61. Felix S. Cohen, *Handbook of Federal Indian Law* (Washington: GPO, 1942), p. 293.

CHAPTER 2

War and Defense

Subjugating the Indians Northwest of the Ohio River.

Unrest and Retaliation in the South.

Probing the New West. The War of 1812.

American Dominion—North, West, and South.

The goal of Washington and Knox was peace, a peace to be obtained and preserved by just and humane treatment of the Indians. Yet there was war on the frontiers, undeclared war between the frontiersmen and the Indians in raids and counterraids. The federal government soon came to realize that military might was an indispensable ingredient of the policy it pursued. When treaties, laws, proclamations, and trade provisions by themselves failed to ensure tranquility on the frontier, military force was needed to enforce the stipulations of the treaties and the legislation and to back up the decisions of the agents and the War Department. Moreover, from time to time it was employed to crush resisting hostile tribes and force them to submit to land cessions and other demands of white society.[1]

The United States, of course, absolutely rejected a war of extermination against the Indians. Henry Knox, in a long memoir relative to the Indians northwest of the Ohio that was sent to President Washington on June 15, 1789, weighed carefully the two alternatives: overwhelming the Indians by military force or treating them with justice in seeking cessions of land. He concluded that to crush the Indians would require men and money "far exceeding the ability of the United States to advance, consistently with a

---

1. This chapter relies heavily on Francis Paul Prucha, *The Sword of the Republic: The United States Army on the Frontier, 1783–1846* (New York: Macmillan Company, 1969)—especially chapters 2–8, pp. 17–137—and some sections are taken directly from the book. The book has more extensive documentation than is presented here.

due regard to other indispensable objects." To treat the Indians by a "conciliatory system" would not only cost far less but, more important, would absolve the nation from "blood and injustice which would stain the character of the nation . . . beyond all pecuniary calculation."[2]

Yet conditions on the frontiers again and again got out of hand, and the United States not only called up militia but, contrary to its republican pronouncements against a standing army, built a regular army to serve on the frontier. The purpose of this army was to enforce peaceful measures for regulating relations between whites and Indians and, when these failed, to provide a defense against hostile Indians and occasionally a striking force to subdue them.[3]

SUBJUGATING THE INDIANS NORTHWEST OF THE OHIO RIVER

A crisis approached in the Old Northwest as waves of white settlers appeared along the Ohio, floating down the river by the thousands in flatboats and barges. Major John Doughty at Fort Harmar wrote to Knox that between April 6 and May 16, 1788, "181 boats, 406 souls, 1,588 horses, 314 horned cattle, 223 sheep and 92 wagons" had passed his post. "It will give you some idea," he added, "of the amazing increase flowing into the western world from the old Atlantic states."[4]

The Indians refused to accept this invasion. They did not acknowledge the treaties of Fort McIntosh and Fort Finney, which had not been approved by the confederacy of the northwest Indians, and they refused to accept the idea that they had been defeated along with the British in the Revolutionary War. Supported by the British in Canada, they maintained that the Ohio River was the boundary that the Americans should not cross. But they were willing to treat again with the United States, provided that all land cessions were "by the united voice of the confederacy" and that partial treaties be considered null and void. Protesting a sincere desire for friendship and peace, the confederated Indians begged the United States "to prevent your surveyors and other people from coming upon our side [of] the Ohio river."[5]

2. ASP:IA, 1: 12–14.
3. An excellent study of the creation of the regular army is Richard H. Kohn, *Eagle and Sword: The Federalists and the Creation of the Military Establishment in America, 1783–1802* (New York: Free Press, 1975).
4. Quoted in North Callahan, *Henry Knox: General Washington's General* (New York: Rinehart and Company, 1958), p. 317.
5. "Speech of the United Nations, at their Confederate Council, held near the mouth of the Detroit river, the 28th November and 18th December, 1786," ASP:IA, 1: 8–9. The speech is also printed in *Documentary History of the First Federal Congress of the United States, March 4, 1789–March 3, 1791,* ed. Linda Grant De Pauw, vol. 2: *Senate*

The issue was joined. The Americans were intent on settling north of the Ohio, and the Indians were equally resolved that the Ohio was to be a permanent and irrevocable boundary between the white settlers and themselves. The Treaty of Fort Harmar, in which the United States benefited from rifts among the Indians, renewed the land cessions and paid for them, and Arthur St. Clair, governor of the Northwest Territory, ended the council on a pious note as he told the Indians: "I fervently pray to the Great God that the peace we have Established may be perpetual."[6] His words were soon echoing in mockery through the forests.

Although the War Department was not to be pushed precipitously into military action, pressure for war became too strong for Knox to resist as reports of Indian incursions and atrocities poured in from the west, and the military engagements with the northwest tribes began.[7] General Josiah Harmar, having been directed by the secretary of war to "extirpate, utterly, if possible," the banditti who were wreaking havoc on the frontier, on September 20, 1790, launched a punitive attack against the Miami towns. His expedition, formed mostly of militia from Kentucky and Pennsylvania, was routed by the Indians. Rufus Putnam at the Ohio Company settlement declared: "Our prospects are much changed. in stead of peace and friendship with our Indian neighbours a hored Savage war Stairs us in the face. the Indians in stead of being humbled by the Destruction of the Shawone Towns & brought to beg for peace, appear ditermined on a general War, in which our Settlements are already involved." The Indians, Putnam reported, "were much elated with there success & threatened there should not remain a Smoak on the ohio by the time the Leaves put out."[8]

Executive Journal and Related Documents (Baltimore: Johns Hopkins University Press, 1974), pp. 146–48. Knox's discussion of the document in the Senate on May 25, 1789, is given ibid., pp. 3–6.

6. Quoted in Randolph C. Downes, *Frontier Ohio, 1788–1803* (Columbus: Ohio State Archaeological and Historical Society, 1935), p. 16.

7. Reports on Indian disturbances are in ASP:IA, 1: 84–96. There are many histories dealing with the Indian wars in the Northwest. See James Ripley Jacobs, *The Beginning of the U.S. Army, 1783–1812* (Princeton: Princeton University Press, 1947), pp. 40–188; Randolph C. Downes, *Council Fires on the Upper Ohio: A Narrative of Indian Affairs in the Upper Ohio Valley until 1795* (Pittsburgh: University of Pittsburgh Press, 1940), pp. 310–38; Downes, *Frontier Ohio*; Kohn, *Eagle and Sword*, pp. 91–127; William H. Guthman, *March to Massacre: A History of the First Seven Years of the United States Army, 1784–1791* (New York: McGraw-Hill Book Company, 1975). See also the discussion of Indian policy in terms of the northwest campaign in Reginald Horsman, *Expansion and American Indian Policy, 1783–1812* (East Lansing: Michigan State University Press, 1967), pp. 84–103.

8. Quotations are in Knox to Harmar, June 7, 1790, ASP:IA, 1: 97–98, and *The Memoirs of Rufus Putnam and Certain Official Papers and Correspondence*, ed. Rowena Buell (Boston: Houghton, Mifflin and Company, 1903), pp. 113, 247. Special works on Harmar's campaign include Randolph G. Adams, "The Harmar Expedition of 1790,"

The next to try to chastise the Indians was Governor St. Clair, who was given command with a commission as major general. He was a man of parts, with a substantial if not distinguished military career in the Revolutionary War, and Congress gave him additional troops. His chances of success in a punitive expedition against the Indians were greater than those of the hapless Harmar, but delays in getting supplies and in establishing a chain of posts north of Fort Washington led to a late fall campaign, and the troops, still largely militia, fared no better than Harmar's. An attack by the Indians on November 4, 1791, destroyed St. Clair's army. The general was exonerated of blame for the failure of the campaign, which was laid in large part on the undisciplined troops. John Cleves Symmes, one of the three judges of the Northwest Territory, wrote to a friend in Philadelphia after the debacle: "Too great a proportion of the privates appeared to be totally debilitated and rendered incapable of this service, either from their youth (mere boys) or by their excessive intemperance and abandoned habits. These men who are to be purchased from the prisons, wheelbarrows and brothels of the nation at two dollars per month, will never answer our purpose for fighting of Indians."[9]

St. Clair's defeat was a national disaster, and it proved that a makeshift force was not enough to face the competent chiefs and warriors of the Indians. Knox called for an adequate military force of disciplined troops, and Congress responded on March 5, 1792, with an "Act for making farther and more effectual Provision for the Protection of the Frontiers of the United States" that authorized more regular infantry and militia cavalry. President Washington appointed another Revolutionary War general, Anthony Wayne, to lead a new campaign against the Indians.[10]

Ohio State Archaeological and Historical Quarterly 50 (January–March 1941): 60–62; Howard H. Peckham, "Josiah Harmar and His Indian Expedition," ibid. 55 (July–September 1946): 227–41; John P. Huber, "General Josiah Harmar's Command: Military Policy in the Old Northwest, 1784–1791" (Ph.D. dissertation, University of Michigan, 1968).

9. Symmes to Elias Boudinot, January 12, 1792, *Quarterly Publication of the Historical and Philosophical Society of Ohio* 5 (July–September 1910): 95–96. A study of St. Clair's campaign and reaction to it is William Patrick Walsh, "The Defeat of Major General Arthur St. Clair, November 4, 1791: A Study of the Nation's Response, 1791–1793" (Ph.D. dissertation, Loyola University of Chicago, 1977). Official documents of the campaign are in ASP:IA, 1: 136–202.

10. ASP:IA, 1: 197–202; 1 *United States Statutes* 241–43; *Annals of Congress*, 2d Congress, 1st session, pp. 337–55. General Wayne has received extensive treatment by historians; see Harry Emerson Wildes, *Anthony Wayne: Trouble Shooter of the American Revolution* (New York: Harcourt, Brace and Company, 1941); Thomas Boyd, *Mad Anthony Wayne* (New York: Charles Scribner's Sons, 1929); Dwight L. Smith, "Wayne's Peace with the Indians of the Old Northwest, 1795," *Ohio State Archaeological and Historical Quarterly* 59 (July 1950): 239–55. Extensive correspondence between Wayne and the secretaries of war is in Richard C. Knopf, ed., *Anthony Wayne, A Name in Arms: The*

As Wayne set about to organize and discipline his troops for war, a new peace offensive was begun. The chances for success were not auspicious, for the victory over St. Clair had greatly heightened the Indians' spirit and reunited the tribes in their determination to defend their lands and their civilization against the whites. "The Indians began to believe them Selves invinsible, and they truly had great cause of triumph," as General Putnam observed.[11] In these views the Indians got full support from the British until they had developed an exaggerated opinion of the aid they could count on in their struggle with the Americans. The Indians adopted an adamant stand that rejected all compromise. The United States, for its part, was now willing to withdraw its insistence on the Fort Harmar Treaty line, and its commissioners were sent deep into the Indian country to treat with the Indians. In July 1793 the commissioners arrived at Detroit, but their meeting with the Indians did not ensure peace. The arrogant chiefs on August 16 insisted that the Americans withdraw from all the lands north of the Ohio. The ultimatum was unacceptable to the commissioners, and they returned empty-handed.[12] Wayne in the meantime had reorganized the troops into the Legion of the United States, assembled raw material for an army, and with extreme measures to ensure military discipline, worked diligently to whip the soldiers into shape for Indian fighting.

To Wayne's irritation, Knox kept hoping that peaceful measures would obviate the need for a new campaign to chastise the Indians. He tried to explain to Wayne at the beginning of 1793 that all avenues for peace must be explored before the signal for war could be sounded. "We shall always possess the power of rejecting all unreasonable propositions," he wrote. "But the sentiments of the great mass of the Citizens of the United States are adverse in the extreme to an Indian War and although these sentiments would not be considered as sufficient cause for the Government to conclude an infamous peace, yet they are of such a nature as to render it adviseable to embrace every expedient which may honorably terminate the conflict." Knox cited the president's hope that fair and humane motives exhibited by the United States would themselves pacify the tribes and his fear that with war "the extirpation and destruction of the Indian tribes" was inevitable. Nor could the young nation afford to ignore world opinion. "The favorable opinion and pity of the world is easily excited in favor of the oppressed," Knox noted. "The indians are considered in a great degree of this description—If our modes of population and War destroy the tribes

---

Wayne-Knox-Pickering-McHenry Correspondence (Pittsburgh: University of Pittsburgh Press, 1960); official documents are in ASP:IA, 1: 487–95, 524–29.

11. *Memoirs of Rufus Putnam*, p. 116.

12. An account of the peace negotiations, with extensive citation of sources, is given in Kohn, *Eagle and Sword*, pp. 148–54.

the disinterested part of mankind and posterity will be apt to class the effects of our Conduct and that of the Spaniards in Mexico and Peru together—." Nevertheless, if every measure for peace was found unavailing without a "sacrifice of national character," Knox "presumed" the citizens would unite to prosecute the war with vigor.[13]

What Knox called the "procrastinated and fruitless, but absolutely necessary negociations with the hostile Indians" consumed the summer of 1793.[14] But when it became clear in September that the peace overtures were a failure, Wayne prepared for an active campaign. He moved north of Fort Washington and spent the winter building a post he called Fort Greenville. From there in the spring and summer of 1794 he prepared his advance against the tribes, and on August 20 at the Battle of Fallen Timbers the Indians fled headlong in defeat. The British at nearby Fort Miami, not willing to risk open conflict with United States troops, closed their gates in the face of the retreating Indians and with this action ended the Indians' final hope of succor from those who had encouraged their defiance of the Americans.[15]

Wayne at once set about to consolidate his victory. He built Fort Wayne at the headwaters of the Wabash and by November was back at his headquarters at Greenville. He negotiated with the Indians, who were stunned by their defeat and the failure of the British to support them; he was determined to conclude a treaty even if he had to treat at a place chosen by the Indians. In the summer the chiefs began to assemble at Greenville. Their hope of maintaining the Ohio boundary was now gone, and on August 3, 1795, they agreed to Wayne's terms, giving up once and for all the two-thirds of Ohio and the sliver of Indiana marked by the Treaty of Greenville line.[16]

Peace with the Indians in the northwest was supported by diplomatic negotiations with the British, whose occupation of military posts on American soil after the Revolutionary War encouraged the Indians and exasperated the United States. Jay's Treaty, signed in 1794, although highly un-

13. Knox to Wayne, January 5, 1793, Knopf, *Anthony Wayne*, pp. 165–66.

14. Knox to Wayne, November 25, 1793, ibid., p. 285.

15. There is a detailed description of the battle, with references to primary sources, in Jacobs, *Beginning of the U.S. Army*, pp. 173–76. The part played by the British in encouraging the Indians to resist Wayne is shown in Reginald Horsman, "The British Indian Department and the Resistance to General Anthony Wayne, 1793–1795," *Mississippi Valley Historical Review* 49 (September 1962): 269–90. Relations between the British and the Indians, both north and south, is thoroughly treated, to a large extent from British sources, in J. Leitch Wright, Jr., *Britain and the American Frontier, 1783–1815* (Athens: University of Georgia Press, 1975).

16. Kappler, pp. 39–45. For a careful analysis of the terms of the treaty and their origin, see Dwight L. Smith, "Wayne and the Treaty of Green Ville," *Ohio State Archaeological and Historical Quarterly* 63 (January 1954): 1–7.

popular among some segments of the population because it failed to settle maritime grievances against Great Britain, was an effective instrument for peace in the West, for the British agreed to evacuate the troublesome posts and turn them over to the United States on June 1, 1796. The provision in the treaty that permitted Indian traders from Canada to operate unrestricted within American territory was a continuing threat to American sovereignty because of the inimical influence of the traders upon the Indians, yet the transfer of Fort Mackinac, Detroit, and the other posts was a significant recognition of American authority that was not lost upon the Indians.[17]

UNREST AND RETALIATION IN THE SOUTH

In the region south of the Ohio River, American sovereignty was maintained as precariously as in the Old Northwest. Much of the present state of Tennessee, most of Alabama and Mississippi, and large parts of Georgia were held by the Cherokees, Creeks, Chickasaws, and Choctaws. Spain, in possession of the Floridas and Louisiana and claiming jurisdiction as far north as the Tennessee River, sought to control the trade of the southern tribes and, by entering into alliances with them, to use the Indians as a barrier against the advancing American settlers. Baron de Carondelet, who became governor of Louisiana at the end of 1791, if he did not indeed encourage an American-Indian war would at least have welcomed such a conflict.[18]

Despite serious provocation and the clamor for military support from whites in the region, the federal government refused to declare war in the south. It had committed its meager regular army to resolving the question of effective American sovereignty in the Northwest Territory, and it had no resources to commit in another direction. Nor could the United States afford to antagonize or irritate Spain while delicate negotiations were under way over the southern boundary of the United States and navigation of the Mississippi. The Indian problem was merged with the boundary dispute, and one could not be negotiated or solved without the other.

17. On Jay's Treaty, see Samuel Flagg Bemis, *Jay's Treaty: A Study in Commerce and Diplomacy*, rev. ed. (New Haven: Yale University Press, 1962).

18. A survey of conditions in the Old Southwest is Thomas P. Abernethy, *The South in the New Nation, 1789–1819* (Baton Rouge: Louisiana State University Press, 1961). Specifically on Indian problems, see Jane M. Berry, "The Indian Policy of Spain in the Southwest, 1783–1795." *Mississippi Valley Historical Review* 3 (March 1917): 462–77; Randolph C. Downes, "Indian Affairs in the Southwest Territory, 1790–1796," *Tennessee Historical Magazine*, 2d series 3 (January 1937): 240–68; Arthur P. Whitaker, "Spain and the Cherokee Indians, 1783–1798," *North Carolina Historical Review* 4 (July 1927): 252–69; Horsman, *Expansion and American Indian Policy*, pp. 66–83.

With the northwestern tribes emboldened by their victories over Harmar and St. Clair, Knox hastened to conciliate the southern nations, lest they be drawn into the war against the United States. At least to keep them neutral was his aim, at best to induce them to join the American forces against the tribes of the northwest. To this end early in 1792 he sent Leonard Shaw, a young Princeton graduate, as a special emissary to the Cherokees, bearing medals for the chiefs and presents for the nation and a speech of friendship from President Washington. He entrusted to Shaw similar gifts and messages for delivery to the Choctaws and Chickasaws. The annuities due the Cherokees were quietly increased by 50 percent.[19]

Indian attacks and white retaliation continued. A group of Cherokees who had broken away from the parent nation, the Chickamaugas, were forced to seek new hunting lands along the Cumberland River and incessantly pressed upon the growing white settlement there. They were joined by Creeks, whose predilections of hostility against the Americans were aggravated by the activities of the Spanish and by English adventurers in their midst.[20]

In the face of impending war, William Blount, governor of the Territory South of the River Ohio (or Southwest Territory), called up the militia until in the fall of 1792 he had fourteen companies of infantry and a troop of cavalry in service. He fully expected an offensive move by the federal government against the hostile tribes. Instead he got a warning and then a stinging rebuke from the secretary of war. In August, before the worst of the storm, Knox had told him that war in the territory would be considered "by the general government as a very great, and by the mass of the citizens of the middle and eastern States as an insupportable evil," and Blount was urged to remove every just pretence of grievances on the part of the Indians. This was not very encouraging, and although Blount then described in detail the disturbances with which he was faced, Knox's reply was extremely critical. In the first place, the president did not feel authorized to direct offensive operations against the Indians. Declaring war was a power reserved to Congress, which hesitated to act because "the extension of the Northern Indian War to the Southern Tribes would be a measure into which the Country would enter with extreme reluctance." Second, Knox

---

19. ASP:IA, 1: 203–6, 247–48, 265–66; Kappler, pp. 32–33. The presentation of American medals to these Indians (among whom the Choctaws and Chickasaws, at least, were considered by Spain to be within its sphere of interest) greatly incensed Spanish officials, and Secretary of State Jefferson had some explaining to do to the Spanish agents in Philadelphia. Some of the certificates, signed by Governor William Blount, presented to the Choctaws with medals are now in the Archivo General de Indias in Madrid. The story is told in Francis Paul Prucha, *Indian Peace Medals in American History* (Madison: State Historical Society of Wisconsin, 1971), pp. 6–8.

20. See James P. Pate, "The Chickamaugas: A Forgotten Segment of Indian Resistance on the Southern Frontier" (Ph.D. dissertation, Mississippi State University, 1969).

strongly suggested that it was the whites, not the Indians, who were responsible for the frontier encounters. The United States, he told Blount, "never will enter into a War to justify any sort of encroachment of the Whites." He then criticized Blount for calling out more militia and keeping them in service for a longer time than was necessary.[21]

Blount continued to hope for offensive war against the Indians, but the failure of peace negotiations with the northern Indians in the summer of 1793 and the extreme measures taken by the whites destroyed the chances that the federal government would come in aggressively on the side of the frontiersmen. The governor and the Tennesseeans then moved ahead on their own with an invasion into the Cherokee and Creek country more extensive than any since the Revolutionary War. Mounted militia under General John Sevier penetrated the Indian country, defeated the Indian warriors, and laid waste their towns. The failure to get adequate federal support maddened the frontiersmen, and when news of victory at Fallen Timbers was received, an offensive force was sent to destroy the Chickamauga towns. Before Blount could stop these illegal movements, the deed was done by Major James Ore and the territorial militia.[22]

The chastisement of the Chickamaugas and the triumph of Anthony Wayne—which left the military forces of the United States free to deal with the southern Indians if need be—brought peace to the Cherokee frontier, for the body of the Cherokees had already been appeased by the increase in their annuities. The Creeks still remained a problem, but Blount's efforts to stir up the Cherokees and Chickasaws against them were quashed by the federal government. "It is plain that the United States are determined, if possible, to avoid a direct or indirect war with the Creeks," Knox's successor, Timothy Pickering, told Blount. "Congress alone are competent to decide upon an offensive war, and congress have not thought fit to authorize it."[23]

While the Southwest Territory and its governor were contending with the Cherokees and Creeks, another border contest was being fought in Georgia, where continuing conflict between state and national jurisdiction over Indian affairs further complicated matters. The Treaty of New York with the Creeks in 1790 had been ineffective, for Georgia had not been consulted about the treaty and refused to back down on her claims to In-

21. Correspondence between Blount and Knox, August 1792 to January 1793, printed in Clarence E. Carter, ed., *The Territorial Papers of the United States*, 26 vols. (Washington: GPO, 1934–1962), 4: 163–64, 175, 208–16, 220–34.

22. The failure of the peaceful federal Indian policy, which led to military action by the settlers in Tennessee, is discussed in Craig Symonds, "The Failure of America's Indian Policy on the Southwestern Frontier, 1785–1793." *Tennessee Historical Quarterly* 35 (Spring 1976): 29–45. For Ore's campaign, see Downes, "Indian Affairs in the Southwest Territory," pp. 260–61.

23. Pickering to Blount, March 23, 1795, Carter, *Territorial Papers*, 4: 386–93.

dian lands. Independent action by Georgia to overwhelm the Creeks was severely condemned by the federal government, and Georgia was reined in.[24] The United States agreed, however, to negotiate again with the Creeks in June 1796 at Colerain on the St. Mary's River, but to no avail. The Creeks refused to cede their lands, and this treaty did no more than ratify the Treaty of New York and reassert peace between the nation and the United States.[25]

When Henry Knox retired at the end of 1794, he left a forthright statement about defense of the western frontiers, both north and south.[26] He reasserted his policy of peace through justice, which meant calming Indian fears for their lands by control of the avaricious whites. Until the Indians could be quieted on this point and rely upon the United States government to protect their country, he argued, "no well grounded hope of tranquillity can be entertained." He sought to constrain the war in the northwest and prevent its spread to the south, where the Indians were stronger and where an open war could lead to serious diplomatic repercussions. In ending his public career he sounded the same high note of moral righteousness that had always marked his hope for peaceful relations with the Indians. "As we are more powerful, and more enlightened than they are," he wrote, "there is a responsibility of national character, that we should treat them with kindness, and even liberality." He noted the "melancholy reflection" that the United States in its dealings with the aborigines had been more destructive than the conquerors of Mexico and Peru, and he feared that future historians might mark the causes of this destruction in "sable colors."

In practical terms, Knox proposed a line of military posts garrisoned by regular army troops along the frontier within the Indian country. He wanted fifteen hundred men at posts on the southwestern frontier stretching from the St. Mary's River on the border of Georgia to the Ohio. North of the Ohio, in addition to the posts on American soil soon to be surrendered by the British, he advocated one at the Miami village on the Wabash and connecting posts south on the Wabash toward the Ohio and northeast on the Maumee toward Lake Erie, plus a post at Presque Isle. Knox outlined here a cordon of military posts strung along the border of contact between the Indians and the whites that became a staple of American defense policy. Regular army garrisons, at the crucial meeting points of the two cultures, were to restrain the whites and overawe the Indians and protect the two

24. See correspondence between Governor Edward Telfair of Georgia and Knox, April–September 1793; ASP:IA, 1: 264–65, 368–70. See also John K. Mahon, "Military Relations between Georgia and the United States, 1789–1794," *Georgia Historical Quarterly* 43 (June 1959): 138–55.

25. Kappler, pp. 46–49.

26. Knox to Washington, December 29, 1794, ASP:IA, 1: 543–44. The following quotations are from this document.

races from each other. "If to these vigorous measures," Knox concluded, "should be combined the arrangement for trade, recommended to Congress, and the establishment of agents to reside in the principal Indian towns, . . . it would seem that the Government would then have made the fairest experiments of a system of justice and humanity, which, it is presumed, could not possibly fail of being blessed with its proper effects—an honorable tranquillity of the frontiers."

Knox's wise plans called for adequate regular troops to man the posts, troops whose very presence on the frontier would uphold American authority without war. With the cessation of hostilities in the northwest, however, Congress turned to consider whether the military establishment that had been called into being to pacify the Indians should be continued. Secretary of War Pickering and his successor James McHenry submitted observations and recommendations to guide the lawmakers. Congress did not listen. The committee on the military establishment, viewing the end of hostilities against the Indians, decided that "the force to be provided for the defensive protection of the frontiers, need not be so great as what had been contemplated for carrying on the war against the different tribes of hostile Indians, and which is the basis of the present military establishment," and Congress on May 30, 1796, reduced the size of the army.[27]

In the Treaty of San Lorenzo (Pinckney Treaty), signed with Spain on October 27, 1795, the United States won recognition of the thirty-first parallel as its southern boundary and navigation rights on the Mississippi. Then the Louisiana Purchase in 1803 changed the whole complexion of Mississippi valley defense and Indian relations, for the withdrawal of the Spanish from New Orleans and the acquisition of the right bank of the Mississippi from its source to its mouth removed the obstacles to western commerce that had long irritated frontiersmen. Spain, however, was still present in the Floridas, which cut off the south from the Gulf of Mexico, and the southern Indians maintained their hold on vast stretches of territory. The Creeks, supported by British traders and the Spanish, remained a special problem, but there was relative quiet until the approach of the War of 1812.[28]

PROBING THE NEW WEST

The Louisiana Purchase nearly doubled the territorial size of the United States and provided a new empire of unmeasured extent and almost totally

27. Pickering to Committee on the Military Establishment, February 3, 1796, and McHenry to the committee, March 14, 1796, *American State Papers: Military Affairs*, 1: 112–14; committee report, ibid., p. 112; 1 *United States Statutes* 483–86.

28. On the treaty with Spain, see Samuel Flagg Bemis, *Pinckney's Treaty: A Study of America's Advantage from Europe's Distress, 1783–1800* (Baltimore: Johns Hopkins

unknown character. Occupying and establishing American sovereignty over the land and its people brought new problems and new opportunities in government relations with the Indians.

In the southern part of the Louisiana Purchase, with its concentrations of white population in New Orleans and outlying regions, the United States moved quickly to replace the Spanish and French and to institute civil government of its own. There were few Indians in the area. But north of the thirty-third parallel, a region first erected into the District of Louisiana (attached for administration to Indiana Territory) and then into the Territory of Louisiana, the land was largely wilderness and, aside from St. Louis and a few other small settlements along the Mississippi and its tributaries, the Indians were the lords of the land.

To serve as first governor of the new territory, President Jefferson appointed General James Wilkinson, who combined in his one person both civil and military authority over the region. The War Department, which directed his duties on military and Indian matters, charged Wilkinson in vague terms to "conciliate the friendship & esteem, of the Indian generally of that extensive Country, & to produce peace & harmony, as well among the several nations and tribes, as between them & the white inhabitants," but at the same time demanded of him strict adherence to "the most riged economy" and forbade him to establish any permanent military posts.[29]

Although Wilkinson's fame has been tarnished by his association with Aaron Burr and his machinations with Spanish officials in the western regions, he had a fundamental grasp of the problems facing the United States with its new empire, in regard to the British and the Spanish and the influence of these powers through their traders upon the Indians. His experience in campaigns in the Old Northwest had given his mind a distinctly anti-British set, and what he learned at his post in St. Louis did little to change it. Of immediate concern was the danger from British traders. Wilkinson knew that he could not suddenly cut off the British merchandise that furnished the regular supplies of the Indians, but he urged the

---

Press, 1926), pp. 280–355, and Arthur P. Whitaker, *The Mississippi Question, 1795–1803: A Study in Trade, Politics, and Diplomacy* (New York: D. Appleton-Century, 1934), pp. 51–78.

29. Secretary of war to Wilkinson, April 19, 1805, Carter, *Territorial Papers*, 12: 116–17. There are three biographies of Wilkinson, all critical of the man, as their titles show: Thomas Robson Hay and M. R. Werner, *The Admirable Trumpeter: A Biography of General James Wilkinson* (Garden City, New York: Doubleday, Doran, and Company, 1941); James Ripley Jacobs, *Tarnished Warrior: Major-General James Wilkinson* (New York: Macmillan Company, 1938); Royal Ornan Shreve, *The Finished Scoundrel* (Indianapolis: Bobbs-Merrill, 1933). A more favorable view of Wilkinson is presented in Francis S. Philbrick, *The Rise of the West, 1754–1830* (New York: Harper and Row, 1965).

secretary of state and the secretary of war to warn the British that the trade would be stopped and to make the warning public. To enforce the interdiction Wilkinson recommended the immediate establishment of a military post at the mouth of the Wisconsin River and another at the Mandan villages or at the falls of the Missouri, with customs officers to seize contraband goods. "These arrangements being once accomplished," he predicted, "in a very few years the trade of the Mississippi and Missouri, would take its ancient and natural course to New Orleans."[30]

Officials in Washington did not move as strongly as Wilkinson wanted to occupy the new regions, and the government did no more than build Fort Belle Fontaine near the confluence of the Missouri with the Mississippi. The general did not let up. He issued a proclamation prohibiting foreign citizens from trading along the Missouri River, and then he poured out his concern about Spanish dangers to the secretary of war, proposing an apt analogy from his experience on the Ohio frontier a decade earlier:

> The relative position of the Spaniards in New Mexico, of the United States on the Mississippi, & the intermediate hordes of Savages, may be compared to the former relations of the British Posts on the Lakes, our settlements on the Ohio, & the intervening tribes of savages, who so long Jeopardized our frontier & defied our Force; and the Policy is so obvious, we ought not to doubt, that the Spaniards (however blind) will exert themselves to Erect a strong Barrier of hostile Savages, to oppose us in time of War, & to harrass our frontier in time of Peace.—The Anology of circumstances fails indeed, in several important essentials unfavourable to us,—The Theatre before us is much more extensive—we are here feeble & far removed from substantial succour—The Savages are as ten to one—They are known to the Spaniards & unknown to us—and their Habits of Life, put it out of our Power to destress or destroy them.[31]

No doubt Wilkinson perceived political dangers that never would materialize, but he saw with a clear eye the importance of the Indians in the scheme of western empire.

While Wilkinson was worrying about the effect of British and Spanish influence on the western Indians, President Jefferson, fired by a dream of empire of his own, set about to gain accurate information about the land and its inhabitants. How could one *possess* the new land if he did not *know* it?

The most daring and dramatic of the expeditions was that of Meriwether

30. Wilkinson to the secretary of war and Wilkinson to the secretary of state, July 28, 1805, Carter, *Territorial Papers*, 12: 169, 173–74.

31. Proclamation and related documents, ibid., 13: 200–203; Wilkinson to the secretary of war, September 22 and December 30, 1805, ibid., pp. 230, 357–58.

Lewis and William Clark and their corps of discovery to the Pacific and back in 1804–1806. Along with the gathering of scientific data, trade with the Indians and peaceful relations with them were uppermost in Jefferson's mind as he sent the explorers out. Lewis emphasized to Clark "the importance to the U. States of an early friendly and intimate acquaintance with the tribes that inhabit that country, that they should be early impressed with a just idea of the rising importance of the U. States and of her friendly dispositions towards them, as also her desire to become usefull to them by furnishing them through her citizens with such articles by way of barter as may be desired by them or usefull to them."[32]

As they ascended the Missouri, Lewis and Clark carefully informed the Indians that the French and Spanish had withdrawn from the waters of the Missouri and the Mississippi and that the "great Chief of the Seventeen great nations of America" was now the one to whom they must turn: "He is the only friend to whom you can now look for protection, or from whom you can ask favours, or receive good council, and he will take care that you shall have no just cause to regret this change; he will serve you, & not deceive you." Lewis described the power and great number of the Americans, and he promised to arrange for trade. With considerable ceremony the chiefs were given silver medals with Jefferson's image on one side and symbols of peace and friendship on the other, along with American flags, chiefs' coats, and other presents, with the admonition from the president: "He has further commanded us to tell you that when you accept his flag and medal, you accept therewith his hand of friendship, which will never be withdrawn from your nation as long as you continue to follow the council which he may command his chiefs to give you, and shut your ears to the councils of Bad birds." The chiefs were told to turn in their French, Spanish, and British flags and medals, for it was no longer proper for them to keep these emblems of attachment to any great father except the American one.[33]

When Lewis returned, he discussed the problems of protecting the region and its fur trade. He pointed to the dangers of giving British traders a free hand on the upper Missouri, thus allowing the Indians to fall under the traders' influence and permitting them "to be formed into a rod of iron,

32. Lewis to Clark, June 19, 1803, Donald Jackson, ed., *Letters of the Lewis and Clark Expedition with Related Documents, 1783–1854,* 2d ed., 2 vols. (Urbana: University of Illinois Press, 1978), 1: 59. The literature on Lewis and Clark is voluminous. The most complete edition of their journals is Reuben Gold Thwaites, ed., *Original Journals of the Lewis and Clark Expedition, 1804–1806,* 8 vols. (New York: Dodd, Mead and Company, 1904–1905), but it needs to be supplemented with editions of more recently discovered documents. See the enlightening study by Paul Russell Cutright, *A History of the Lewis and Clark Journals* (Norman: University of Oklahoma Press, 1976).

33. Lewis and Clark to the Oto Indians, August 4, 1804, Jackson, *Letters of the Lewis and Clark Expedition,* 1: 203–8.

with which, for Great Britain, to scourge our frontier at pleasure." He proposed restricting British traders, opening the trade under fair competition to American merchants, and prohibiting Americans themselves from unrestricted hunting and trapping in the Indian country. It was his hope, he wrote, to combine "philanthropic views toward those wretched people of America," with means "to secure to the citizens of the United States, all those advantages, which ought of right exclusively to accrue to them, from the possession of Upper Louisiana." This would take a delicate balance, Lewis knew, and in his rough outline of points to be considered he included this shrewd observation: "The first principle of governing the Indians is to govern the whites—the impossibility of doing this without establishments, and some guards at those posts."[34]

While Lewis and Clark were still working their way across the Great Divide, General Wilkinson himself sent out two exploratory expeditions with similar goals. On July 30, 1805, he ordered a young lieutenant of the First Infantry, Zebulon Montgomery Pike, up the Mississippi River to seek its source. Pike was told to gather geographical and scientific knowledge, to locate proper points for military posts, and "to spare no pains to conciliate the Indians and to attach them to the United States." The written orders said nothing about counteracting the influence of British traders in the northwest, but it is clear from the attention given to the matter that Pike had strong directions from Wilkinson to this effect. Pike got as far as Leech Lake (somewhat short of the source of the Mississippi), where he found a British trader operating on American soil. He asserted American rights in no uncertain terms in a letter to the trader, and in council with the Chippewas he directed them to turn in their British medals and flags. But a single expedition to the upper Mississippi was not enough to undo the British traders' influence over the Indians. Pike's remonstrances meant little after he had disappeared downriver, and the power of the British traders over the Indians at the outbreak of the War of 1812 is proof that Pike's expedition alone was not enough.[35]

Pike in 1806 made a second trip, this time to probe the activities of the Spanish and their influence over the Indians in the southwest. He was instructed to make contact with the Comanches, to make peace between them and other tribes, and to induce some of their chiefs to visit Washing-

34. Thwaites, *Journals of the Lewis and Clark Expedition*, 7: 378, 387–88.

35. For journals and other documents of Pike's two expeditions, see Donald Jackson, ed., *The Journals of Zebulon Montgomery Pike with Letters and Related Documents*, 2 vols. (Norman: University of Oklahoma Press, 1966); also W. Eugene Hollon, *The Lost Pathfinder: Zebulon Montgomery Pike* (Norman: University of Oklahoma Press, 1949). Wilkinson's directive to Pike, July 30, 1805, is in Jackson, *Pike*, 1: 3–4; Pike's letter to trader Hugh McGillis, February 6, 1806, and his speech to the Chippewas, February 16, 1806, appear ibid., pp. 257–58, 263–64.

ton, where their friendship could be cultivated and they could be impressed with the power and authority of the United States.[36] Pike found clear evidence of Spanish influence over the Indians; and when he ventured too far west, he was arrested by Spanish troops, taken into Mexico, and not released for several weeks.

Acquaintance with the Indians in the vast Trans-Mississippi West was just beginning, but the importance of the tribes and their trade in the diplomatic relations of the continent was clearly seen. The War of 1812 soon emphasized the point.

THE WAR OF 1812

As the century advanced, there were new signs of Indian unrest on the frontiers, and the fragile peace achieved by a combination of negotiation and military force began to crumble. William Clark, who on his return from the expedition of discovery began a long career as Indian agent and superintendent at St. Louis, noted in late 1807 that the Indians on the upper Missouri "Shew Some hostile Simtoms," which he attributed to British action, and he feared that British traders had already made inroads on the upper Missouri.[37]

The War Department could not be entirely quiet in the face of continued remonstrances from responsible men of good judgment on the frontier, and it began to push trading houses and military garrisons into the Mississippi Valley. Factories and posts were established in 1808 among the Osages (Fort Osage) and near the mouth of the Des Moines River on the upper Mississippi (Fort Madison). "The principal object of the Government in these establishments," the superintendent of Indian trade wrote, was "to secure the Friendship of the Indians in our country in a way the most beneficial to them and the most effectual & economical to the United States."[38] The new posts did not prevent the drift toward open war, yet Congress refused to strengthen the military defense of that remote frontier, doing no more than to authorize six companies of rangers for the protection of settlers from Indian incursions. Meanwhile, farther east, advancing white settlement pushed against the Treaty of Greenville line and revived the temporarily quieted antagonisms of the Indians.

The celebrated Shawnee chief Tecumseh and his brother, the Prophet, soon appeared on the scene. Tecumseh by all accounts was a great man, noted for his humanity and uprightness of character. The Prophet preached resistance to the whites and a return to primitive ways, and Tecumseh be-

36. Wilkinson to Pike, June 24, 1806, Jackson, *Pike,* 1: 285–87.

37. Clark to the secretary of war, June 1, September 12, and December 3, 1807, Carter, *Territorial Papers,* 14: 126–27, 146–47, 153–54.

38. John Mason to John Johnson, May 20, 1808, ibid., pp. 185–87.

came a political leader, determined to stop the westward advance of the whites. Arguing that no sale of Indian land could be valid unless approved by all the tribes, he set about to form a confederacy that would unite the Indians in blocking white aggrandizement. For aid in this great project Tecumseh depended upon the British and from them drew arms and ammunition.[39] With the increased tension between Great Britain and the United States that grew out of the *Chesapeake* affair in 1807, the British in Canada were quite willing to renew the active allegiance of the Indians. The vision of Tecumseh thus reopened problems that the Americans thought had been resolved at Fallen Timbers and Greenville. American sovereignty north of the Ohio had not yet been secured in the face of rising Indian apprehensions, and from 1807 to the War of 1812 Indian relations in Indiana and Illinois territories steadily worsened.

Tecumseh and his brother won many supporters among the northwest Indians, and in 1808 the Prophet and his followers moved to the upper Wabash at the mouth of Tippecanoe Creek. This concentration of warriors on the Wabash alarmed William Henry Harrison, governor of Indiana Territory, who was convinced that serious trouble was brewing. Yet in the face of growing Indian intransigence, Harrison concluded a treaty at Fort Wayne on September 30, 1809, with the Miamis, Weas, and Delawares by which he purchased a large tract of land in Indiana. The treaty greatly agitated Tecumseh even though no Shawnee lands were involved, and in 1810 he visited Harrison at Vincennes, where he threatened the governor with hostile gestures and announced that he would never submit to the Fort Wayne treaty. A truce was arranged, but no ultimate compromise seemed possible. The following summer Tecumseh appeared again with a large retinue. He told Harrison he was on his way south to bring the southern nations into his confederacy.[40]

Harrison made use of the opportune absence of the Shawnee leader to advance against the Prophet's town. With regular troops, militia, and volunteers, he moved north from Vincennes in September 1811. In early November he sought a parley with the Indians, which failed to materialize. On November 7 the Indians attacked Harrison's army and were repulsed

39. On Tecumseh, see Glenn Tucker, *Tecumseh: Vision of Glory* (Indianapolis: Bobbs-Merrill, 1956). A brief popular account is Alvin M. Josephy, Jr., "'These Lands Are Ours . . . ,'" *American Heritage* 12 (August 1961): 14–25, 83–89. A scholarly study that emphasizes the importance of the Prophet is R. David Edmunds, *The Shawnee Prophet* (Lincoln, University of Nebraska Press, 1983).

40. The troubles between Harrison and Tecumseh and the Prophet are discussed in Dorothy Burne Goebel, *William Henry Harrison: A Political Biography* (Indianapolis: Historical Bureau of the Indiana Library and Historical Department, 1926), pp. 109–27, and Tucker, *Tecumseh*, pp. 134–231. See also *Messages and Letters of William Henry Harrison*, ed. Logan Esarey, 2 vols. (Indianapolis: Indiana Historical Commission, 1922); ASP:IA, 1: 776–80, 797–811.

only after severe fighting in which Harrison's losses were heavy. This Battle of Tippecanoe was described by Harrison as "a complete and decisive victory," but in the end it settled nothing. The Prophet's town was burned and his followers were scattered, but enmity against the whites only increased. Another step had been taken toward all-out war to see who would control the Old Northwest.[41]

The causes of the War of 1812 have been argued by historians at great length, but frontier disquiet cannot be discounted. Indian components of the war were a continuation of the prewar conflict, and they set the stage for the military history of the American frontier in the decades after 1815. The Indians, by and large, maintained or renewed their allegiance to the British, and the armies that the Americans met on the northwestern frontier were composed of more Indian troops than white. Tecumseh's dream of an Indian confederation, maintaining a united front against American territorial advance, seemed possible when the British were once again openly fighting the Americans.[42]

In the territory stretching west of Lake Michigan, the British and their Indian allies immediately reasserted control. Fort Mackinac fell on July 17, 1812, and Fort Dearborn (established in 1803 on the site of future Chicago) was evacuated on August 15 and most of its inhabitants massacred by the Indians as they marched out. More important was the disastrous surrender of Detroit on August 16 by General William Hull, who feared the massacre of the women and children by the Indian allies of the British if the city were taken by force.

The surrender of Hull's army left consternation and confusion on the frontier, and the Indians were emboldened by the American disaster. In Ohio, where settlement was heavy and concentrated, little was to be feared, but in thinly settled Indiana and Illinois fears of Indian raids were

41. Reports of Harrison to the secretary of war, November 8 and 18, 1811, *Messages and Letters of Harrison*, 1: 614–15, 618–30. Accounts of the drift toward war are in Jacobs, *Beginning of the U.S. Army*, pp. 356–63, and Louise Phelps Kellogg, *The British Regime in Wisconsin and the Northwest* (Madison: State Historical Society of Wisconsin, 1935). See also Christopher B. Coleman, "The Ohio Valley in the Preliminaries of the War of 1812," *Mississippi Valley Historical Review* 7 (June 1920): 39–50.

42. For British Indian policy before the war and the part played by the Indians in the war, see Reginald Horsman, "British Indian Policy in the Northwest, 1807–1812," *Mississippi Valley Historical Review* 45 (June 1958): 51–66; Horsman, "The Role of the Indian in the War," in Philip P. Mason, ed., *After Tippecanoe: Some Aspects of the War of 1812* (East Lansing: Michigan State University Press, 1963), pp. 60–77; and George F. G. Stanley, "The Indians in the War of 1812," *Canadian Historical Review* 31 (June 1950): 145–65. On the general course of the war, see Henry L. Coles, *The War of 1812* (Chicago: University of Chicago Press, 1965); Alec R. Gilpin, *The War of 1812 in the Old Northwest* (East Lansing: Michigan State University Press, 1958); Reginald Horsman, *The War of 1812* (New York: Alfred A. Knopf, 1969); and John K. Mahon, *The War of 1812* (Gainesville: University of Florida Press, 1972).

well-founded. The governors of the two territories ordered mounted militia to patrol the frontier, and a camp was established in southern Illinois for militia and the United States rangers. But clearly a new northwestern army would have to be organized to repair the damage done by Hull's defeat. The work fell to William Henry Harrison, who moved successfully against the British in upper Canada as soon as Admiral Oliver H. Perry had won control of the supply lines in the Great Lakes. At the Battle of the Thames on October 5, 1813, Harrison defeated Colonel Henry Proctor and his Indian allies. The Indians, ably led by Tecumseh, offered stiff resistance, but Tecumseh was soon killed and the Indians followed the British in flight. The Americans had made a great step toward redeeming the northwest, but attempts to regain Fort Mackinac and control of the upper Mississippi were rebuffed. The upper Mississippi remained in British hands, and the assertion of United States authority there had to await the post-war era.

Meanwhile a parallel story unfolded in the south. The hostile Creeks with their Spanish allies were the counterpart to Tecumseh's confederacy, and the Battle of Horseshoe Bend destroyed the Indians' hopes as did the Battle of the Thames and the death of Tecumseh. Whereas the Chickasaws and Choctaws took little part in the war and some of the Cherokees joined the United States forces, the Creeks developed a hostile faction that posed a serious threat. Certain of the young Creeks were influenced by Tecumseh, who visited the nation in 1811 and again in 1812 to solicit southern Indian support for his confederacy. Although older chiefs warned against Tecumseh, the great Shawnee came with a bagful of magic tricks and on his second visit brought encouraging news of American defeats. With promises that Spanish and British aid would support the Indians he won over the young warriors, or Red Sticks, among them William Weatherford (Red Eagle), a nephew of Alexander McGillivray. When a party of Red Sticks returning from a trip to Pensacola (where the Spanish governor had supplied them with ammunition) were attacked by white frontiersmen, the Indians retaliated by massacring the men, women, and children at Fort Mims, a stockade forty miles north of Mobile. The United States was electrified, and campaigns to crush the hostile Red Sticks were immediately mounted.[43]

The most important of these was led by Andrew Jackson, commander of the Tennessee militia. He quickly assembled volunteers, augmented them with regular infantry, and prepared to strike the Creeks in their stronghold in eastern Alabama. On March 27, 1814, aided by a contingent of Cherokees, Jackson crushed the hostile Creeks at Horseshoe Bend, a fortified position on the Tallapoosa River in the heart of the Creek country. Jackson

43. A recent detailed and well-documented account of Indian matters in the south during the War of 1812 is Robert V. Remini, *Andrew Jackson and the Course of American Empire, 1767–1821* (New York: Harper and Row, 1977), pp. 187–245.

did not intend to lose his advantage. He moved down the river and built Fort Jackson where the Coosa and Tallapoosa rivers join to form the Alabama. From this headquarters his troops scoured the country for hostile Indians. Not many were found, for most of the Red Sticks fled into Spanish Florida and some, including William Weatherford, turned themselves in at Fort Jackson. Jackson now forsook his militia status and accepted a commission as brigadier general in the regular army. He was almost immediately promoted to major general and given command of the Seventh Military District, which included Tennessee, Louisiana, and Mississippi Territory. In this position he concluded a treaty with the Creeks at Fort Jackson on August 9. It was the friendly Creeks who attended the council, for the hostiles had been killed or had fled, and the chiefs protested the terms of the treaty. Jackson insisted, nevertheless, on large land cessions west of the Coosa and along the Florida border, as buffers between the Creeks and Chickasaws and Choctaws on the west and the Spanish on the south.[44]

On August 27 Jackson was at Mobile, where he strengthened defenses constructed a year earlier and enabled the garrison to drive back an attack of the British. In early November, after receiving a new increment of mounted volunteers, he seized Pensacola, driving out the British who had been using it as a port and military depot. These southern escapades confirmed the action at Horseshoe Bend, for the Creeks might now well despair of active assistance from the British or the Spanish in the south. Jackson was ready to protect New Orleans if any British general should be so foolhardy as to make a direct attack by sea.

The treaty of peace signed at Ghent on December 27, 1814, provided for a return to the status quo before the war and left unmentioned the basic maritime problems that had done so much to bring on the war, and it is easy to assert that the war accomplished nothing. This was certainly not the case on the frontier in the northwest and the southwest. The crushing defeats of the Indians at the Thames and at Horseshoe Bend and the failure of the British (or the Spanish) to substantiate Indian claims against the Americans put a new complexion on the Indian problems in the West.

AMERICAN DOMINION—NORTH, WEST, AND SOUTH

The Indians, against whom so much of the American force in the War of 1812 had pressed, were not a party to the Treaty of Ghent. The ninth arti-

44. Kappler, pp. 107–10. A detailed history of the Creek War is Frank Lawrence Owsley, Jr., *Struggle for the Gulf Borderlands: The Creek War and the Battle of New Orleans, 1812–1815* (Gainesville: University Presses of Florida, 1981).

cle of the treaty, however, provided that the United States would undertake to put an end to all hostilities with Indian tribes with whom it might still be at war at the time of ratification of the treaty and to restore to those tribes "all the possessions, rights, and privileges" that they had enjoyed previous to the war.[45] Accordingly, President Madison on March 11, 1815, appointed three commissioners to treat with the Indians who had fought against the United States, to notify all the tribes on the Mississippi and its tributaries who were at war with the United States that peace had been concluded with Great Britain, and to invite them to a council to sign a treaty of peace and amity. Peace was to be the only purpose of the treaties; other matters could be attended to at a later time. The commissioners were to inform the Indians that the government intended to establish strong military posts high up the Mississippi and between the Mississippi and Lake Michigan and to open trading houses at these posts or at other suitable places for their accommodation. Twenty thousand dollars' worth of presents was placed at the disposal of the commissioners—"blankets, strouds, cloths, calicoes, handkerchiefs, cotton stuffs, ribands, gartering, frock coats, flags, silver ornaments, paints, wampum, looking-glasses, knives, fire-steels, rifles, fusils, flints, powder, tobacco, pipes, needles, &c.," according to the enumeration of the secretary of war, who specified that the goods should equal in quality those that the Indians were accustomed to get from the British.[46]

On May 11 the commissioners met at St. Louis and prepared talks to be sent out to the Indian chiefs. News of continuing hostility among the tribes made it difficult to find messengers to carry the tidings into the Indian nations, but eventually thirty-seven talks were dispatched by means of army officers, Indian agents, Frenchmen, or Indians themselves (who promised to deliver the messages to more remote tribes with whom they were in contact). The Indians gathered at Portage des Sioux, a convenient spot on the west bank of the Mississippi above the mouth of the Missouri and a few miles below the mouth of the Illinois. There, between July 18 and October 28, 1815, thirteen treaties were signed with the western Indians. These were peace pacts, providing that "every injury or act of hostility by one or either of the contracting parties against the other shall be mutually forgiven and forgot," promising "perpetual peace and friendship"

45. There is a detailed account of the negotiations at Ghent, including Indian matters, in Bradford Perkins, *Castlereagh and Adams: England and the United States, 1812–1823* (Berkeley: University of California Press, 1964), pp. 81–127. See also A. L. Burt, *The United States, Great Britain, and British North America: From the Revolution to the Establishment of Peace after the War of 1812* (New Haven: Yale University Press, 1940), pp. 345–72.

46. Monroe to commissioners, March 11, 1815, ASP:IA, 2: 6; Monroe to John Mason, March 27, 1815, ibid., p. 7.

between the Americans and the Indians, agreeing to the exchange of prisoners, and confirming previous treaties. In the next three years, other
western tribes, absent from Portage des Sioux, signed similar treaties.[47]

Meanwhile, other negotiations were carried on with the Indians of Ohio,
Indiana, and Michigan. These Indians had technically been at peace with
the United States when the Treaty of Ghent had been ratified, and the provisions of that treaty did not apply; but "hostile excitement" among the
Indians induced the secretary of war to appoint a commission to conciliate
them and explain to them the provisions of the treaty. "The object of these
explanations will be to counteract any suppositions that the treaty of
peace has placed Great Britain in a new and more advantageous relation to
the Northwest Indians," the acting secretary of war wrote to the commissioners on June 9, 1815; "to supersede the idea that the Indians have acquired by the treaty a more independent political character than they possessed before; and to beget a just confidence in the power as well as the
resolution of our Government to maintain its rights against every opposition." The War Department considered the introduction of military posts
and factories into the Indian country of increasing importance, and it directed the commissioners to inform the Indians that "in order to aid and
protect them, and also to guard against encroachment upon the property
and people of the United States" the president intended to establish a
chain of posts from Chicago to St. Louis. A treaty was signed with the Indians on September 8 at Spring Wells near Detroit, in which peace was re-
affirmed and the Indians who had continued hostilities after 1811 were
pardoned.[48]

These treaties of friendship would be no more than paper documents
unless the United States carried out its resolve to establish military posts
on the Great Lakes and in the upper Mississippi Valley. Such action was
imperative if the United States did not want to forfeit for a second time its
control over the Indian tribes of the northwest. Americans in the West
pleaded for military establishments that would check the Indians, weaken
or destroy their adherence to the British, and protect and extend the American fur trade in the region. The point was well made by Governor Lewis
Cass of Michigan Territory, who traced most of the difficulties he had with
Indians to the problem of British traders among the northwestern tribes.
He asserted that the British were about to renew their activities with increased energy, for large supplies of trade goods had arrived at Malden,

47. Kappler, pp. 126–33, 138–40, 156–59. For an excellent account of the treaty negotiations, see Robert L. Fisher, "The Treaties of Portage des Sioux," *Mississippi Valley
Historical Review* 19 (March 1933): 495–508. Copies of the treaties and related documents about the negotiations are in ASP:IA, 2: 1–12.
48. Kappler, pp. 117–19. Documents dealing with these negotiations are in ASP:IA,
2: 12–25.

across from Detroit, and there had been an influx of agents and subordinate officers. As an effective check on their operations, Cass proposed blocking off with military posts the channels of communication by which the British traders and their goods infiltrated into the United States.[49]

The War Department quickly moved to establish new military posts and reestablish old ones at strategic spots. In 1816 the post at Chicago (Fort Dearborn) was reoccupied and Fort Howard at Green Bay was constructed. At the same time troops pushed up the Mississippi to build Fort Crawford at the mouth of the Wisconsin River. Indian agencies were established in the shadows of these posts.[50]

That was but a beginning. When John C. Calhoun accepted the post of secretary of war in October 1817, he brought to the office a pronounced spirit of nationalism and a dream of vindicating American authority over its largely nominal empire west of the Mississippi. With the disasters of the recent war etched deeply in his memory, he presented his arguments. The Indians in the West, composed of warlike and powerful tribes, were unacquainted with American power and at the same time were "open to the influence of a foreign Power"; with the expansion of American settlements, they were becoming close neighbors. A new thrust of American force into the region was thus necessary to overawe the tribes and to cut off once and for all the intercourse between the Indians and the British trading posts. "This intercourse," Calhoun said, "is the great source of danger to our peace; and until that is stopped our frontiers cannot be safe." The Treaty of Ghent had ended the British right to trade with the Indians, and Congress in 1816 had prohibited foreigners from trading with the Indians within the territory of the United States, but Calhoun admitted that "the act and instructions to Indian agents can have but little efficacy to remedy the evil." He would have preferred to persuade the British through diplomatic means to end the trade and the generous distribution of presents to the Indians, but until the British acted, new military posts would "put in our hand the power to correct the evil."[51]

Calhoun wanted military posts at Sault Ste. Marie, on the Mississippi at the mouth of the Minnesota (St. Peter's), and on the Missouri at the Mandan villages or even the mouth of the Yellowstone. He believed that re-

49. Cass to A. J. Dallas, July 20, 1815, Carter, *Territorial Papers,* 10: 573–75.

50. For general histories of the military expansion into the northwest after the War of 1812, see Henry P. Beers, *The Western Military Frontier, 1815–1846* (Philadelphia, 1935); Edgar B. Wesley, *Guarding the Frontier: A Study of Frontier Defense from 1815 to 1825* (Minneapolis: University of Minnesota Press, 1935); and Francis Paul Prucha, *Broadax and Bayonet: The Role of the United States Army in the Development of the Northwest, 1815–1860* (Madison: State Historical Society of Wisconsin, 1953).

51. Calhoun to Alexander Smyth, December 29, 1819, *American State Papers: Military Affairs,* 2: 33–34.

straining and overawing the Indians and destroying their contacts with the British traders and posts were primarily military matters. "Trade and presents, accompanied by talks calculated for the purpose," he noted, "are among the most powerful means to control the action of savages; and so long as they are wielded by a foreign hand our frontiers must ever be exposed to the calamity of Indian warfare." Of two great objects in view, he said, "the permanent security of our frontier is considered by far of the greatest importance." But the second object was also much in his mind: the enlargement and protection of the American fur trade. The military posts, by enforcing the prohibition on foreign traders, would permit unrestricted access to the trade by American traders. When the posts were all established and occupied, asserted Calhoun with a certain tone of exultation, "the most valuable fur trade in the world will be thrown into our hands."[52]

In 1818 Calhoun issued orders for the implementation of his plan. General Thomas A. Smith was to move up the Missouri to build a permanent post at the mouth of the Yellowstone, but the expedition faltered—hampered by congressional opposition to the cost—and the troops got no farther than Council Bluffs, above present-day Omaha, where they constructed Fort Atkinson. Calhoun's call for a strong post on the upper Mississippi was better answered. Troops moving from Detroit to Green Bay, then along the Fox-Wisconsin waterway and up the Mississippi, established in 1819 the impressive fort at the mouth of the Minnesota that eventually was named Fort Snelling.[53]

The failure to fulfill Calhoun's plan for advancing high up the Missouri emboldened the Indians of the region and lessened the chances of attaching them to the American government. The Indians were alert to what they considered American failures, and their arrogance seemed to grow whenever American force or resolution weakened. Attacks on St. Louis fur traders along the Missouri and its tributaries in 1823 by Arikaras and Blackfeet caused a special outcry. Benjamin O'Fallon, the United States Indian agent at Fort Atkinson, wrote in intemperate language to his superior in July, 1823: "I was in hopes that the British traders had some bounds to their rapacity—I was in hopes that during the late Indian war, in which they were so instrumental in the indiscriminate massacre of our people,

52. Calhoun to Henry Atkinson, March 27, 1819, *Correspondence of John C. Calhoun*, ed. J. Franklin Jameson, Annual Report of the American Historical Association for the Year 1899, vol. 2 (Washington, 1900), p. 159.

53. For this military advance, see Prucha, *Sword of the Republic*, pp. 140–51, and works cited there. See also Roger L. Nichols, "The Army and the Indians, 1800–1830: A Reappraisal, the Missouri Valley Example," *Pacific Historical Review* 41 (May 1972): 151–68, which challenges my view of the army's success.

they had become completely satiated with our blood, but it appears not to have been the case.—Like the greedy wolf, not yet gorged with the flesh, they guard over the bones—they ravage our fields, and are unwilling that we should glean them—although barred by the treaty of Ghent, from participating in our Indian trade, they presume [to do so]. . . becoming alarmed at the individual enterprise of our people, they are exciting the Indians against us."[54]

At the same time, General Edmund P. Gaines, commanding the Western Division, wrote to the secretary of war: "If we quietly give up this trade, we shall at once throw it, and with it the friendship and physical power of near 30,000 efficient warriors, into the arms of England, who has taught us in letters of blood (which we have had the magnanimity to forgive, but which it would be treason to forget) that this trade forms the rein and curb by which the turbulent and towering spirit of these lords of the forest can alone be governed." Gaines argued that to let the Arikaras and Blackfeet go unpunished would be to surrender the trade and the influence it exerted over the Indians to England.[55]

Colonel Henry Leavenworth and a company of 220 men from the Sixth Infantry, augmented by fur traders and Sioux, moved up the Missouri to the Arikara villages, where Leavenworth came to terms with the Indians. On his return to Fort Atkinson, he announced the successful outcome of the expedition: "The blood of our countrymen have been honorably avenged, the Ricarees humbled, and in such a manner as will teach them and other Indian tribes to respect the American name and character."[56]

Leavenworth's dealings with the Indians were not considered severe enough by the traders, who were more insistent than either the agents or the army officers in cries for strong government action. The trading interests had a powerful advocate in Senator Thomas Hart Benton, who broadcast their petitions in a national arena. In March 1824 Benton introduced a bill authorizing commissioners to negotiate treaties of friendship with the

54. Quoted in Donald McKay Frost, *Notes on General Ashley, the Overland Trail, and South Pass* (Worcester: American Antiquarian Society, 1945), pp. 83–84. Other information on the problems of the upper Missouri fur trade after the War of 1812 is in Dale L. Morgan, *The West of William H. Ashley: The International Struggle for the Fur Trade of the Missouri, the Rocky Mountains, and the Columbia, with Explorations beyond the Continental Divide, Recorded in the Diaries and Letters of William H. Ashley and His Contemporaries, 1822–1838* (Denver: Old West Publishing Company, 1964).

55. Gaines to John C. Calhoun, July 28, 1823, *American State Papers: Military Affairs*, 2: 579.

56. Leavenworth's final report and other documents are in Doane Robinson, ed., "Official Correspondence Pertaining to the Leavenworth Expedition of 1823 into South Dakota for the Conquest of the Ree Indians," *South Dakota Historical Collections* 1 (1902): 179–256.

Missouri River tribes and directing that a military post be built on the upper Missouri. It is interesting to note that Benton entitled his measure a bill "to enable the President to carry into effect the treaty made at Ghent, the 24th of December, 1814, excluding foreigners from trade and intercourse with Indian tribes within the United States, and to preserve the fur trade within the limits of the said United States." Not all of the Senate, however, was as convinced of the need as was Benton. His provision for building a fort was stricken out, and the title of the bill was changed. The most that he could get was authorization for a military escort to accompany the treaty commissioners.[57]

The expedition, led by Henry Atkinson and Benjamin O'Fallon, signed treaties of friendship in the summer of 1825 with the tribes they met along the way, but they discovered no British influence in the area they covered.[58] The dangers so loudly proclaimed by the American fur traders had evaporated as the British traders had shifted westward toward the rich beaver of the Rockies.

In the south, the federal government presumed that all Indian difficulties had ended with the Treaty of Fort Jackson with the Creeks. Besides the huge land cession, the Indians had promised to abandon all communication or intercourse with any British or Spanish posts and to permit the establishment of American forts and roads in the territory they still retained. It was a harsh peace, imposed, as the preamble to the treaty stated, because of the "unprovoked, inhuman, and sanguinary war" waged by the Creeks against the United States. But many Indians, unwilling to accept defeat, joined the Seminoles in Florida, where they continued to be a lively threat to white settlers moving onto the vacated lands. Here they were encouraged by British adventurers in their belief that the lands taken away from them at Fort Jackson would be returned now that the War of 1812 had ended. The American government, however, did not consider that the Treaty of Ghent in any way negated the treaty made with the Creeks at Fort Jackson.[59]

To maintain peace on this perilous frontier was the task of General

57. *Senate Journal*, 18–1, serial 88, pp. 239, 281, 432; *Annals of Congress*, 18th Congress, 1st session, pp. 432–45, 450–61.

58. For the Atkinson–O'Fallon expedition, see Roger L. Nichols, *General Henry Atkinson: A Western Military Career* (Norman: University of Oklahoma Press, 1965), pp. 90–108; Nichols, ed., "Report of the Yellowstone Expedition of 1825," *Nebraska History* 44 (June 1963): 65–82; ASP:IA, 2: 595–609. The journal of the expedition is in Russell Reid and Clell G. Gannon, eds., "Journal of the Atkinson–O'Fallon Expedition," *North Dakota Historical Quarterly* 4 (October 1929): 5–56; the treaties signed are in Kappler, pp. 225–46.

59. Kappler, pp. 107–9. For a scholarly account of the southern frontier from 1815 to 1821, see James W. Silver, *Edmund Pendleton Gaines, Frontier General* (Baton Rouge: Louisiana State University Press, 1949), pp. 54–88.

Gaines, who attempted to overawe the warlike Indians with a show of force. He built Fort Scott at the confluence of the Flint and Chattahoochee rivers, almost on the Florida border, and from there and from Fort Montgomery in Alabama (to which he moved in January 1817) Gaines carried on a running war with recalcitrant Indians along the border. He was soon joined by General Andrew Jackson, who, convinced that the Spanish were encouraging the Indians, boldly invaded Florida. There he seized two British traders, tried them by court-martial, and summarily executed them.[60]

Unmindful of the storm of controversy that would soon arise because of his execution of the two British subjects on Spanish soil, Jackson moved next against Pensacola. On May 25 he invested the Spanish post and three days later accepted its surrender. His proclamation of May 29 announced the appointment of one of his army officers as civil and military governor of Pensacola and the application of the revenue laws of the United States. His justification was explicit: "The Seminole Indians inhabiting the territories of Spain have for more than two years past, visited our Frontier settlements with all the horrors of savage massacre—helpless women have been butchered and the cradle stained with the blood of innocence. . . . The immutable laws of self defense, therefore compelled the American Government to take possession of such parts of the Floridas in which the Spanish authority could not be maintained."[61]

Jackson moved north to Fort Montgomery, where on June 2, 1818, he sent long letters to President Monroe and to Secretary of War Calhoun reporting what he had done and insisting upon the necessity of holding the posts in Florida he had taken. He told Calhoun: "The Seminole War may now be considered at a close. Tranquility [is] again restored to the Southern Frontier of the United States, and as long as a cordon of military posts is maintained along the gulf of Mexico America has nothing to apprehend from either foreign or Indian hostilities."[62]

Jackson returned to Nashville in triumph, leaving the diplomats to pick up the pieces. The Spanish minister, Don Luis de Onís, demanded the prompt restitution of St. Marks, Pensacola, and all other places wrested from Spain by Jackson's forces, as well as an indemnity for all losses and the punishment of the general. The posts were returned, but the general was not punished, and resolutions in Congress condemning his action were voted down.[63]

General Gaines meanwhile kept watch on the southern frontier, where

60. Jackson's role is treated in Remini, *Andrew Jackson*, pp. 341–424, and in other biographies of Jackson.

61. *Correspondence of Andrew Jackson*, ed. John Spencer Bassett, 6 vols. (Washington: Carnegie Institution of Washington, 1926–1933), 2: 374–75.

62. Jackson to Monroe and Jackson to Calhoun, June 2, 1818, ibid., pp. 377, 380.

63. See the references cited in Prucha, *Sword of the Republic*, p. 133 n; the political

the problems were not as completely solved as Jackson had asserted. The Indians had not been decisively beaten in combat, and until Florida finally passed into American possession in 1821, there was a continual threat of Spanish intrigue with the Indians. St. Augustine was a point of special concern, and Gaines was all for moving against it. His hands were tied against aggressive action, however, lest the delicate negotiations with Spain for the purchase of Florida become still more entangled.

---

repercussions of Jackson's highhanded operations in Florida are discussed in Remini, *Andrew Jackson*, pp. 366–77.

CHAPTER 3

Trade and
Intercourse Laws

Legislation to Control the Frontier Whites.

Regulating the Trade in Furs. The Crusade against

Ardent Spirits. Crimes in the Indian Country.

Removal of Intruders on Indian Lands.

Military action against the Indians to push them back before the advancing whites was not a suitable basis for governing the relations between the United States and the Indians. Washington and Knox, both men of high integrity and experienced in Indian affairs, rejected an all-out war of subjugation against the tribes. The alternative was conciliation of the Indians by negotiation, a show of liberality, express guarantees of protection from encroachment beyond certain set boundaries, and a fostered and developed trade. But it was not enough to deal only with the Indians, for white settlers and speculators ignored the treaties and guarantees. Plainly, something more was needed than the treaties, which had been so largely disregarded.[1]

LEGISLATION TO CONTROL THE FRONTIER WHITES

In response to the insistent pleas of the executive, Congress supplied a series of laws for regulating trade and intercourse with the Indians. These laws, originally designed to implement the treaties and enforce them

1. This chapter is a condensation of material in Francis Paul Prucha, *American Indian Policy in the Formative Years: The Indian Trade and Intercourse Acts, 1790–1834* (Cambridge: Harvard University Press, 1962), pp. 43–50, 66–84, 93–212, and some parts are taken directly from that work.

against obstreperous whites, gradually came to embody the basic features of federal Indian policy. The first law was approved on July 22, 1790. Continuing the pattern set in the Ordinance of 1786 and earlier colonial legislation, it first of all provided for the licensing of traders and established penalties for trading without a license. Then it struck directly at the current frontier difficulties. To prevent the steady eating away of the Indian country by individuals who privately acquired lands from the Indians, it declared such purchases invalid unless made by a public treaty with the United States. To put a stop to the outrages committed against Indians by whites who invaded the Indian country, the act provided punishment for murder and other crimes committed by whites against the Indians in the Indian country.[2]

The bill as it was introduced called for the appointment of a military officer as superintendent, but strong opposition to this in the House of Representatives because it "blended the civil and military characters" forced its elimination. In the Senate an article to authorize the purchase of trade goods by the government for sale to the Indians through the superintendents and agents was likewise removed.[3] The law in its final form was to be in force "for the term of two years, and from thence to the end of the next session of Congress, and no longer." Congress was feeling its way and was not ready to commit the nation to a permanent measure.

Despite the legislation, frontier disturbances continued in both north and south, and military force had to be used to restrain the Indians and defend the whites. Washington, however, did not abandon his hope for a rule of law and justice. In his message to Congress in October 25, 1791, he laid down basic principles to govern the relations of the United States with the Indians. The president hoped to avoid all need of coercion, and to this end he sought "to advance the happiness of the Indians, and to attach them firmly to the United States." He offered a six-point program:

1. an "impartial dispensation of justice" toward the Indians;

2. a carefully defined and regulated method of purchasing lands from the Indians, in order to avoid imposition on them and controversy about the reality and extent of the purchases;

3. promotion of commerce with the Indians, "under regulations tending to secure an equitable deportment toward them";

4. "rational experiments" for imparting to the Indians the "blessings of civilization";

5. authority for the president to give presents to the Indians;

6. an "efficacious provision" for punishing those who infringed Indian rights, violated treaties, and thus endangered the peace of the new nation.

2. 1 *United States Statutes* 137–38.
3. *Annals of Congress*, 1st Congress, 2d session, p. 1575.

"A system corresponding with mild principles of religion and philanthropy toward an unenlightened race of men, whose happiness materially depends on the conduct of the United States," Washington concluded, "would be as honorable to the national character as conformable to the dictates of sound policy."[4] The president's message was referred to a special committee in the House, which in turn reported a bill, but the legislation died without debate or action.

Although the act of 1790 still continued in force, its life was about to expire, and Washington in his annual message of 1792 called this fact to the attention of Congress. His report was not optimistic, for troops were being raised and measures taken to put down the continuing hostilities, but he still hoped that legislation could be provided that would eliminate the causes of the conflict, and he again urged the matter upon Congress. It was necessary first of all, he told the lawmakers, to enforce the laws on the frontier and to check the outrages committed by the whites, which led to reprisals on the part of the Indians. The government should employ qualified agents, promote civilization among the friendly tribes, and develop some plan for carrying on trade with them "upon a scale equal to their wants."[5]

A new law, approved March 1, 1793, was a considerably stronger and more inclusive piece of legislation than its predecessor of 1790, for the seven sections of the earlier law were now expanded to fifteen. New sections authorized the president to give goods and money to the tribes "to promote civilization . . . and to secure the continuance of their friendship," and a long section was aimed at horse stealing, but the bulk of the new material was intended to stop criminal attacks of whites against the Indians and the irregular acquisition of their lands. This law, too, was temporary, with the same time limitations as the first one.[6]

A good part of Washington's program was written into these laws, which at least set up the machinery for the protection of Indian rights. Complaints of the Indians about encroachments could now be met by prosecutions for outrages committed by the whites. Peace, nevertheless, was not yet firmly won, and at the end of 1793 Washington urged still further congressional action. In addition to the immediate emergency, which certainly required attention, the president was looking ahead to measures

4. Fred L. Israel, ed., *The State of the Union Messages of the Presidents, 1790–1966,* 3 vols. (New York: Chelsea House, 1966), 1: 8–9. *House Journal,* 2d Congress, 1st session, pp. 445, 462.

5. Israel, *State of the Union Messages,* 1: 14. Citations to the *House Journal* for the first thirteen Congresses are from the reprint edition published by Gales and Seaton (Washington, 1826). A facsimile reprint of the original editions of the journals has been published by Michael Glazer, Inc. (Wilmington, Delaware, 1977).

6. 1 *United States Statutes at Large* 329–32.

that would "render tranquillity with the savages permanent, by creating ties of interest." He came back again to the second part of his two-pronged program. "Next to a rigorous execution of justice on the violators of peace," he said, "the establishment of commerce with the Indian nations, on behalf of the United States, is most likely to conciliate their attachment." Advocating a system of government trading houses that would replace the profit-seeking private traders, he hammered at the point again and again until he was finally heeded by Congress.[7]

The trade and intercourse laws were necessary to provide a framework for the trade and to establish a licensing system that would permit some control and regulation, but this was merely a restatement of old procedures. The vital sections of the laws were in answer to the crisis of the day on the frontier, and the provisions pertained to the tribes of Indians with whom the nation dealt as independent bodies. Neither President Washington nor the Congress was concerned with the remnants of tribes that had been absorbed by the states and had come under their direction and control. The laws sought to provide an answer to the charge that the treaties made with the tribes on the frontiers, which guaranteed their rights to the territory behind the boundary lines, were not respected by the United States. The laws were not primarily "Indian" laws, for they touched the Indians only indirectly. The legislation, rather, was directed against lawless whites and sought to restrain them from violating the sacred treaties. Even when severe crises were resolved by force, the restrictive elements of the intercourse laws were maintained, augmented, refined, and applied to later frontiers.

At first an attempt was made to combine the restrictive or protective features of Washington's program (that is, the regulation of traders, the prohibition of land purchases, the prevention and punishment of outrages against the Indians) with the positive features (the promotion of trade through government trading houses and the civilization of the Indians). But in the course of events the two elements of the president's plan for maintaining peaceful relations with the Indians became embodied in separate series of legislation. The laws "to regulate trade and intercourse with the Indian tribes, and to preserve peace on the frontier" became the main current that carried along the federal policy, which was in large measure one of controlling contact between the two races.

By the end of 1795 the hostile Indians north of the Ohio had been defeated by General Wayne, but the largely unrestrained invasion of the lands of the Creeks and Cherokees in Tennessee and Georgia caused a constant disruption of the peace, and Washington again asked Congress to act. He

7. Israel, *State of the Union Messages*, 1: 19–20. The trading factories are treated in detail in chap. 4 below.

repeated his plea for measures to protect the Indians from injuries inflicted by whites and to supply the necessities of the Indians on reasonable terms.[8] In response Congress passed the intercourse law of May 19, 1796. The new law specified in detail the boundary line between the whites and the Indians, the first designation of the Indian country in a statute law. The delineation was meant to indicate once again the government's intention to uphold the treaties, and though the line met with opposition in the House, efforts to remove it from the bill failed. Violent debate erupted over sections in the law aimed specifically at intruders on Cherokee lands, but again the supporters of the bill were able to maintain their ground. The measure was the only way, they argued, to satisfy the Indians and prevent invasion of their lands. As the bill finally emerged, unscathed by the attacks upon it, it was almost double the length of the law it replaced; but it, too, was only a temporary measure.[9]

Despite dissatisfaction with the law on the part of frontiersmen whose encroachments it curtailed, the law of 1796 did not wreak the havoc on the frontier that its opponents had feared, and it gave assurance to the Indians that the federal government was doing what it could to protect their rights. In 1799, two days before the law was due to expire, it was reenacted, passing both houses without amendment and with little debate.[10]

When Thomas Jefferson sent his first annual message to Congress in December 1801, he could remark that "a spirit of peace and friendship generally prevails" among the Indian tribes. The new president saw no need to depart from the Indian policies of his predecessors, and when the temporary laws for trading houses and for governing trade and intercourse expired, he asked Congress to renew them. The only modification he suggested was some restriction of the liquor traffic among the Indians, which he said the Indians themselves wanted. Accordingly, on March 30, 1802, a new trade and intercourse law was passed. It was for the most part merely a restatement of the laws of 1796 and 1799, but now the period of trial was over. The law of 1802 was no longer a temporary measure; it was to remain in force, with occasional additions, as the basic law governing Indian relations until it was replaced by a new codification of Indian policy in 1834.[11]

8. Israel, *State of the Union Messages*, 1: 30.

9. 1 *United States Statutes at Large* 469–74; *House Journal*, 4th Congress, 1st session, pp. 426, 433, 508, 510; *Senate Journal*, 4th Congress, 1st session, pp. 256–57; *Annals of Congress*, 4th Congress, 1st session, pp. 286–88, 893–905. Citations to the *Senate Journal* for the first thirteen Congresses are to the reprint edition published by Gales and Seaton (Washington, 1820–1821).

10. 1 *United States Statutes* 743–49.

11. Israel, *State of the Union Messages*, 1: 58; James D. Richardson, comp., *A Compilation of the Messages and Papers of the Presidents, 1789–1897*, 10 vols. (Washington: GPO, 1896–1899), 1: 334–35; 2 *United States Statutes* 139–46.

REGULATING THE TRADE IN FURS

The fur trade remained an important source of legitimate contact between the Indians and the whites, but after the removal of British and Spanish influence in the early years of the nineteenth century the political importance of the trade disappeared, for it was no longer necessary to win over the Indians from rival allegiances by drawing them into the American circuit of trade. Economically, too, the trade declined in importance, and by 1834 John Jacob Astor, the great fur mogul, had withdrawn from the business after complaining for years about its economic liabilities. Governmental interest in the trade then tended to become colored more and more by humanitarian interest, by the desire to protect the Indians from the injustices of wily traders and thus assure contentment and peace on the frontier. But under all the changing conditions trade regulation was an essential element in federal Indian policy, as the title "trade and intercourse" laws suggests.[12]

Congress did not have to look far for a method of regulation. It simply adopted the principles of the licensing system used for decades past, although it softened somewhat the requirements set forth in the Ordinance of 1786. The intercourse laws required licenses of all traders, bonds for the faithful observance of regulations governing the trade, and forfeiture of goods taken illegally into the Indian country. From time to time the legislation was strengthened by additional restrictions or increased fines, and the law of 1796 and subsequent laws authorized the use of military force to apprehend offenders.[13] These laws supplemented and strengthened the treaties signed with the tribes, which often dealt with trade and the federal government's right to regulate it.

The provisions of both the laws and the treaties seem unexceptionable. The licensing system was meant to furnish a check on the traders and make them abide by the rules of the trade. The bonds were high enough to eliminate the unstable, and the threat of confiscation of goods—with one-half to the informer—should have dampened any hopes for profitable trading outside the law. The facts, however, belied the surface impression. Year after year reports poured in about illegal trading and the inability of anyone to prevent it. Both north and south of the Ohio the territorial governors, serving ex officio as superintendents of Indian affairs, found it impossible

12. Useful information on the fur trade is found in Paul Chrisler Phillips, *The Fur Trade*, 2 vols. (Norman: University of Oklahoma Press, 1961). On John Jacob Astor and the American Fur Company, see Kenneth Wiggins Porter, *John Jacob Astor: Business Man*, 2 vols. (Cambridge: Harvard University Press, 1931), and David Lavender, *The Fist in the Wilderness* (Garden City, New York: Doubleday and Company, 1964).

13. 1 *United States Statutes* 137–38, 329–30, 473; 3 *United States Statutes* 682.

to cope with the illicit trade. With the addition of the Louisiana Purchase, the problems of regulating the trade spread over a vaster area and one where the legal lines were even less clearly drawn.

The problem of enforcing the intercourse laws can be understood and appreciated only in light of the character of the men with whom the enforcing agents had to contend. The traders were divided roughly into two classes. There were the licensed traders, often attached to some organized and responsible firm like the American Fur Company. They frequently were substantial men in the frontier communities, but their business tactics and the character of many of their employees were not above reproach, and they could interfere seriously with the process of the law by their political pressure and their astute discovery of legal technicalities. But there were also hordes of independent little traders, large numbers of whom were unlicensed—a breed of men irresponsible, lawless, in some cases depraved—who lived off clandestine intercouse with the Indians. The very nature of the fur trade called forth men to whom the restraints of civilized living meant little. They went off into the wilderness with their packs of goods and sought out the peltries of the Indians. Often they took Indian wives and adopted Indian ways, yet their loyalties were not transferred to the tribe, for they mercilessly exploited the Indians, debauched them with whiskey, and then robbed them of their furs. The fines and forfeitures of the laws meant little to them, for they had no property to lose. If they were temporarily driven off in one area, they quickly appeared again in another. There was trouble enough from both groups when it came to enforcing the intercourse laws—one lobbied to get favorable laws and interpretations and was intransigent in local courts against government officials who were too solicitous in the enforcement of the law, and the other totally disregarded legalities.

It seemed well-nigh impossible to stop the illegal trading by judicial process. The intercourse laws provided machinery, designating the action to be taken and the courts to be used, but the machinery was shaky and not very effective. Distances were too great, the time lag too long, and the difficulties of arranging for witnesses too serious for the laws to provide an effective deterrent or remedy for the illicit traffic. If some diligent and conscientious officer or agent did make the effort to bring a violator to trial, chances were that the judges would dismiss the case on a technicality or the jury side with the defendant. Too often the only reward for an officer who attempted to enforce the law was to be called into court himself to answer to charges of illegal trespass or arrest.[14]

14. Examples of the problems of enforcing officers are given in Prucha, *American Indian Policy in the Formative Years*, pp. 74–76.

The mischievous, unscrupulous, unlicensed trader caused untold troubles along the whole frontier, yet he was unorganized, and his total volume of trade was perhaps of little moment. It was his ubiquity and his furtive ways that made him such a nuisance, and it was his reliance on the illegal introduction of liquor to gain his ends that caused such consternation. More serious in many respects than his infractions, however, were the inroads on the trade made by foreign traders, chiefly the British along the Great Lakes and the upper reaches of the Mississippi and the Missouri.

British traders had deeply infiltrated the northwest area after the French were driven out in 1763. Operating under the direction of powerful companies, they exerted great influence over the Indians, who accepted their presents and depended upon them for goods. These traders were unmolested after the Revolutionary War, chiefly because the Americans were not prepared to replace them, and Jay's Treaty of 1794 specifically guaranteed their right to be there. Their posts at Michilimackinac and Prairie du Chien were important gathering points for Indians. There had always been irritation on account of these foreigners, and little by little they were pushed out of the trade south of the Great Lakes; but it was the War of 1812 that fully opened American eyes to the danger, for it was through the influence of traders that the Indians fought with the British against the United States in the war.

It is understandable that agitation should have arisen to eliminate the British traders altogether. By a law of April 29, 1816, licenses to trade with the Indians within the territorial limits of the United States were refused to noncitizens, although the president could permit such licenses if he thought the public interest demanded it. All goods taken into the Indian country by foreigners were subject to seizure and forfeiture if not yet traded to the Indians, and all peltries purchased from the Indians by foreigners were liable to seizure while still in the Indian country. The president was authorized to use military force to seize the goods or furs and to arrest violators of the act. Even foreigners who wished merely to pass through the Indian lands were required first to obtain a passport.[15]

The discretionary power of the president was invoked to allow some foreigners to continue in the trade. A sudden and absolute cutting off of noncitizens from the trade was impolitic, if not impossible, because there were not enough Americans to fill the vacuum that would have been created. The Indians had to be supplied with the goods on which they had become dependent, and for the time being it was necessary to rely on foreign traders. The president granted authority to Governor Lewis Cass of

15. 3 *United States Statutes* 332–33. There was little debate on the measure in Congress and apparently no opposition. *House Journal*, 14th Congress, 1st session, pp. 402, 647, 654; *Senate Journal*, 14th Congress, 1st session, p. 603.

Michigan Territory and to the Indian agents at Michilimackinac, Green Bay, and Chicago to issue licenses to foreigners, but only to reputable characters who were above suspicion.[16]

This presidential discretion in issuing licenses to foreigners was criticized in Congress, and on November 26, 1817, the president withdrew the power he had granted earlier to Cass and the agents. The law of 1816 was now to be carried fully into effect, and no licenses in the future were to be granted to anyone who was not an American citizen.[17] The exigencies of the trade, however, would not allow this drastic move. The traders themselves, no doubt, should be American citizens, but where could enough citizens be found to serve as boatmen and interpreters? It was necessary to rely on foreigners for these essential jobs—chiefly men of French extraction but of British citizenship, who congregated at such centers as Mackinac, Green Bay, and Prairie du Chien—and the president, after "farther information and reflection," permitted the use of such men under careful restrictions.[18] Yet, by the effects of the restrictive legislation and the steady growth of the power and influence of the American Fur Company, the British were generally forced out of the trade within the territory of the United States.

For some years after the War of 1812, the government sought to eliminate abuses in the fur trade by supplying the Indians through the government trading houses, or factories, but when Congress struck down the factory system in 1822, it was necessary to return to direct legislation. In fact, on the very day that the factories were abolished, Congress approved an amendment to the intercourse law of 1802 that raised the bonds required of licensed traders, demanded an annual report of licenses granted, and strengthened the restrictions on the whiskey trade. The law also protected Indians in suits over property with white citizens by placing the burden of proof upon the whites, and it authorized the appointment of a superintendent of Indian affairs at St. Louis.[19]

There was continued agitation to strengthen the hand of the government over the traders. One demand was for discretionary power on the part of the agents in issuing licenses, so that they could exclude unsavory characters, but such exclusion of citizens from the trade seemed to go against

16. William H. Crawford to Cass, May 10, 1816, *Wisconsin Historical Collections*, 19: 406–7; George Graham to Cass, October 29, 1816, Clarence E. Carter, ed., *The Territorial Papers of the United States*, 26 vols. (Washington, GPO, 1934–1962), 10: 667–68; Graham to Cass, May 4, 1817, SW IA LS, vol. D, p. 35 (M15, reel 4).

17. George Graham to Cass, November 26, 1817, SW IA LS, vol. D, p. 101 (M15, reel 4).

18. Calhoun to Cass, March 25, 1818, ibid., pp. 320–21; Cass to agents, April 23, 1818, *Wisconsin Historical Collections*, 20: 42–46.

19. 3 *United States Statutes* 682–83.

the American spirit of free enterprise. And any discretionary power over licenses greatly frightened the American Fur Company, which suspected there would be a severe limiting of the number of licenses granted; it fought through its political friends to quash such a "new-fangled obnoxious Indian system."[20] When Lewis Cass and William Clark, relying on their long experience as Indian superintendents, in 1829 repeated the recommendation of discretionary authority, the fur company did everything it could to block the proposal.

Another suggested panacea was to permit trading in the Indian country at designated sites only, where, with fewer places to keep an eye on, the agents could be more efficient in enforcing the law. In 1824 the proposal became law, and Secretary of War John C. Calhoun set up strict norms for the agents to follow: no more than one site for each tribe, no changes in designated sites without War Department approval, and forfeiture of bonds if trading was done at places not indicated on one's license.[21] There was an immediate outcry against the law from the American Fur Company, which found the designated sites neither convenient nor suitable, and some adjustments were made to accommodate the traders, but the law and the principle remained. Attempts to change the 1824 law failed, and the trade and intercourse law of 1834 continued to specify that no trade was to be carried on except at designated sites.

THE CRUSADE AGAINST ARDENT SPIRITS

The greatest source of difficulty in the Indian trade was whiskey. The "ardent spirits" smuggled into the Indian country made madmen of the Indians, yet the flow could not easily be stanched. It was an elemental problem, rooted in strong human drives—the Indians' fondness for drink and the heartless avarice of the whites. To protect the Indian from his own weakness the government needed to clamp down on the whiskey dealer.

The problem of the liquor traffic was as old as white settlement in America. Yet the first federal laws governing intercouse with the Indians made no mention of intoxicating liquors, just as there had been no discussion of the matter in the Continental Congress and no specific enactments in regard to it. This may seem like a strange omission in view of the past troubles that had grown out of laxness in the matter, but it is likely that the legislators hoped that the licensing provisions of the laws would pro-

20. Ramsay Crooks to John Jacob Astor, May 30, 1820, American Fur Company Letter Books, 1: 305–6, photostatic copies at the State Historical Society of Wisconsin.

21. 4 *United States Statutes* 35–36; Calhoun to superintendents and agents, June 5, 1824, OIA LS, vol. 1, pp. 96–97 (M 21, reel 1).

vide the necessary restraints. They looked to the superintendents of Indian affairs and to the Indian agents to place the necessary brake upon the liquor trade. Nor was it clear at first that state or territorial ordinances could not take care of the problem. Officials on the frontier were in fact well aware of the whiskey menace, even though territorial governors and legislators took little action. That their steps were halting was due more to the dim twilight of authority between federal and local governments and to hesitation to act against the economic interests of the infant communities than to any malice toward the Indians or indifference to their plight.

The Territory North West of the River Ohio was still in its first stage of territorial government when the governor and judges proclaimed a comprehensive law governing Indian trade, not only forbidding under penalty of fine the distribution of intoxicating liquor to the Indians, but excluding foreigners from the trade and setting the high penalty of five hundred dollars for trading without a license. The law set a pattern for ineffectiveness. There was an uneasiness about the restrictions, and five years after enactment the law was quietly repealed with the notation that it was "partly supplied by an act of the United States." The governor of the territory found that his authority as superintendent of Indian affairs in large measure evaporated because it did not affect white settlements to which the Indians freely resorted for liquor.[22]

The inability or unwillingness of the territorial governments to cope with the whiskey problem brought numerous complaints to the federal officials as the nefarious traffic flourished. Even the Indians themselves, becoming aware of the evil effects of the liquor on their morals, health, and very existence, pleaded with President Jefferson for protection. When Jefferson in turn recommended to Congress that it restrict the trade, Congress inserted a special provision in the intercouse law of 1802 that authorized the president "to prevent or restrain the vending or distributing of spirituous liquors among all or any of the said Indian tribes." To implement the law, the secretary of war sent a circular of instructions to Indian officials, forbidding traders to vend ardent spirits. He addressed special letters as well to territorial governors, telling them not to allow traders to supply the Indians with spirituous liquors on any pretext whatever and to take licenses away from traders who disturbed the peace and harmony existing between the Indians and the whites.[23]

22. Theodore C. Pease, ed., *The Laws of the Northwest Territory, 1788–1800* (Springfield: Illinois State Historical Library, 1925), pp. 26–28, 256; letter of Winthrop Sargent, July 22, 1793, Carter, *Territorial Papers*, 3: 412; proclamation of Sargent, September 10, 1794, ibid., p. 423.

23. Jefferson to Congress, January 27, 1802, Richardson, *Messages and Papers*, 1: 334–35; 2 *United States Statutes* 146; Henry Dearborn to superintendents and agents,

The distinction between the Indian country and ceded territory was a major obstacle in the enforcement of the restrictions on whiskey, for it was accepted opinion that the federal regulations applied only to the lands still owned and occupied by Indians. Thus the territories and states had to take action themselves to extend prohibition against the liquor traffic to the ceded lands, but the legislatures were halfhearted in their measures. In 1808 President Jefferson pleaded with the governors to propose to the lawmakers the wisdom and humanity of restraining citizens from vending spirituous liquors to the Indians, and some action was taken in response to the request by most of the western territories.[24]

All the laws and regulations for regulating the trade were considered important in large measure because they would help to check the whiskey menace. The system of government trading houses, too, was strongly supported by humanitarians because it might squeeze out the petty traders, who were the primary distributors of liquor. When Congress struck down the factories, it made a new attempt to prevent the introduction of liquor into the Indian country. The 1822 amendment to the intercourse law of 1802 that accompanied the act abolishing the trading houses authorized the president to direct Indian agents, superintendents of Indian affairs, and military officers to search the goods of all traders in case of suspicion or information that ardent spirits were being carried into the Indian lands. If liquor was found, all the goods were to be forfeited, the trader's license was to be canceled, and his bond was to be put in suit.[25] But the new amendment availed little. There were still ambiguities and loopholes in the law, and the American Fur Company was able to overreach the government agents and army officers in executing it when they received permission from Governor Cass to import liquor in order to compete with British traders along the northern border.[26]

Then in February 1827 came a new tightening of the prohibition against liquor. "Upon this point," the head of the Indian Office wrote to Cass, "any discretion which may have been heretofore given not provided for by law, you will consider as withdrawn. The laws will govern." Cass objected to

---

September 14, 1802, SW IA LS, vol. A, p. 276 (M15, reel 1); Dearborn to William Henry Harrison, September 3, 1802, Carter, *Territorial Papers*, 7: 74; Dearborn to William C. C. Claiborne, September 11, 1802, Dunbar Rowland, ed., *The Mississippi Territorial Archives*, vol. 1 (Nashville: Brandon Printing Company, 1905), p. 552.

24. Jefferson to executives, December 31, 1808, *The Writings of Thomas Jefferson*, ed. Andrew A. Lipscomb, 20 vols. (Washington: Thomas Jefferson Memorial Association, 1903), 12: 223–24. For state and territorial response, see Prucha, *American Indian Policy in the Formative Years*, pp. 106–8.

25. 3 *United States Statutes* 682–83.

26. Prucha, *American Indian Policy in the Formative Years*, pp. 110–14.

the order because he had permitted whiskey only to prevent the utter ruin of American trade. Furthermore, Cass pointed out, his use of the discretionary power was not contrary to the laws, but was expressly allowed by the acts of 1802 and 1822. But he assumed that the president's intention now was to allow no more exceptions, so he discontinued such licenses.[27] The American Fur Company did not accept this rebuff. It soon made a new application for the privilege it had previously enjoyed, and on June 15, 1831, Secretary of War John H. Eaton restored to Cass the discretionary power that had been withdrawn in 1827. This was a temporary respite, for a new law of 1832 destroyed altogether the possibility of a discretionary grant.[28]

There were other ways to take liquor into the Indian country under the protection of authority. Permission was granted to carry in whiskey for use of the boatmen employed in trading, as the prohibition under the laws of 1802 and 1822 was only against introducing the article for use in trade with the Indians. This was a loophole through which large amounts of liquor poured into the Indian country, and any ruse to get by inspecting officers seemed to succeed. A second method was to demand liquor for the white settlements, such as Green Bay or Prairie du Chien, which were not, strictly speaking, Indian country.[29]

However diligent the agents and army officers were, the whiskey merchants were always one step ahead. The licensed traders used whatever schemes they could concoct to gain permission to take in liquor, and they slipped easily into illegal practices. The unlicensed traders operated altogether beyond the law. No section of the frontier was free of disturbance. From Florida, Alabama, Mississippi, Michigan, Arkansas, and Missouri reports flowed into the War Department from officers and agents lamenting the state of affairs, which all the current laws were quite inadequate to remedy. The legislation to date had concentrated on regulating the trade; because such measures were ineffective, the next step would be absolute prohibition of spirituous liquor in the Indian country.

This step was taken in 1832, when Congress bluntly declared: "No ardent spirits shall be hereafter introduced, under any pretence, into the Indian country." It was an all-inclusive prohibition that allowed for no exceptions and that applied to traders and nontraders alike.[30] For a short period

27. Thomas L. McKenney to Cass, February 20, 1827, OIA LS, vol. 3, p. 390 (M21, reel 3); Cass to McKenney, March 25, 1827, OIA LR, Michigan Superintendency (M234, reel 419); McKenney to Cass, April 19, 1827, OIA LS, vol. 4, p. 24 (M21, reel 4).

28. Eaton to Cass, June 15, 1831, Carter, *Territorial Papers*, 12: 294 and n.

29. Prucha, *American Indian Policy in the Formative Years*, pp. 115–20.

30. 4 *United States Statutes* 564. The law said that no liquor could be *introduced* into Indian country, and the agent of the American Fur Company on the upper Missouri

the strong prohibition seemed to have a good effect. The War Department sent strongly worded instructions to the Indian agents to carry out the provisions of the new law, and army officers were given new energy in searching out the forbidden goods, even though they still faced the possibility of legal action against them by the American Fur Company for their diligence.

Attempts were made to get permission to introduce limited amounts of whiskey as exceptions to the law, but the War Department was now adamant. Lewis Cass, who as governor of Michigan Territory had looked with favor upon such requests under the earlier laws, as secretary of war firmly refused permission even to his friends of the American Fur Company, although he continued to be bothered about details in the execution of the new law.

CRIMES IN THE INDIAN COUNTRY

When the white and red races met on the American frontier, there occurred innumerable violations of the personal and property rights of one group by members of the other. Murders and robberies were all too frequent between peoples who were nominally at peace, and some provision had to be made to preserve law and order or constant warfare would result. If private retaliation was not to be the rule, then crimes had to be defined and legal machinery established to mete out justice. These provisions for criminal court procedure formed an essential part of the Indian intercourse laws.

No matter how the sovereignty of the Indian nations might be defined, the establishment of an Indian country outside the jurisdiction of the states created special problems. Here was another indication of the anomaly of the Indian situation, for there were no formal precedents to go by. As in other elements of federal Indian policy, the legislation dealing with crimes in the Indian country grew bit by bit, until in the law of 1834 the main pieces were finally assembled into a whole.

The first measures taken to regularize criminal procedure in cases arising between Indians and white citizens were special articles included in the early treaties for the apprehension and punishment of criminals. Indians, or whites taking refuge among Indians, who had committed murder or other serious crimes against any citizen of the United States were to be delivered up to American authorities by the tribe and punished according to the laws of the United States. If, on the other hand, a white citizen committed the crime against an Indian, he was to be punished just as though

---

sought to evade it by distilling whiskey *within* the Indian country. The story is told in Prucha, *American Indian Policy in the Formative Years*, pp. 136–37.

the crime had been against another white citizen, and this punishment according to some of the treaties was to be exacted in the presence of the Indians. A special section added the injunction that private retaliation was not to be practiced on either side.[31]

The earlier intercourse laws, in an attempt to guarantee respect for the treaties on the part of whites, were concerned particularly with whites who committed crimes against Indians in the Indian country. The act of 1790 equated a crime against an Indian with the same deed committed against an inhabitant of one of the states or territories. The white offender was to be subject to the same punishment and the same procedure was to be followed as though the offense had been committed outside the Indian country against a white. Procedures for apprehending, imprisoning, and bailing in such crimes were to follow the Judiciary Act of 1789.[32]

These basic provisions of 1790 were expanded in succeeding acts because, as Washington pointed out in his annual message of 1792, "more adequate provision for giving energy to the laws throughout our interior frontier, and for restraining the commission of outrages upon the Indians" was necessary. The bill that was introduced in response to the message contained much that the president wished for, but strong opposition developed to the section of the bill that provided for punishment of crimes committed in the Indian country—the very heart of the measure if it were to bring an end to the outrages caused by the whites. The argument was advanced that the treaties or the laws of the states already provided for these cases and that it would be an absurdity to enact them again. The law, furthermore, would operate unfairly by striking whites without reaching out equally to Indians. But wiser counsels carried the day. "If the Government cannot make laws to restrain persons from going out of the limits of any of the States, and commit murders and depredations," one congressman asserted, "it would be in vain to expect any peace with the Indian tribes."[33]

In the intercourse law of 1793, "murder, robbery, larceny, trespass or other crimes" were named, and a new section specified the proper courts to be used. Yet this was not strong enough. Washington bluntly told Congress in December 1795: "The provisions heretofore made with a view to the protection of the Indians from the violences of the lawless part of our frontier inhabitants, are insufficient. It is demonstrated that these violences can now be perpetrated with impunity, and it can need no argument

31. See, for example, treaties with the Cherokees (1785), Choctaws (1786), Chickasaws (1786), Shawnees (1786), Wyandots (1789), and Creeks (1790), Kappler, pp. 8ff.
32. 1 *United States Statutes* 138.
33. Israel, *State of the Union Messages*, 1: 14; *Annals of Congress*, 2d Congress, 2d session, pp. 750–51.

to prove that unless the murdering of Indians can be restrained by bringing the murderers to condign punishment, all the exertions of the Government to prevent destructive retaliations by the Indians will prove fruitless and all our present agreeable prospects illusory."[34]

Acting on Washington's recommendation, Congress wrote into the intercourse law of 1796 detailed provisions for restraining outrages on both sides, including the death penalty for anyone convicted of going into Indian country and there murdering an Indian. Property taken or destroyed was to be paid for by the culprit or by the United States Treasury, and if Indians crossed over the line into white lands and committed crimes, satisfaction was to be demanded from the tribe. All of this was predicated on the condition that no private satisfaction be exacted. The provisions of the 1796 law were reenacted with little change in the temporary law of 1799 and in the permanent law of 1802. But it was not until 1817 that Congress ordained punishment for Indians who committed crimes against whites within the Indian country.[35]

The United States government was determined to provide an adequate judicial system for the Indian country and intended that Indians and whites be treated with equal justice. In practice, however, there were serious discrepancies, for the universal resort to legal procedures to gain satisfaction and justice envisaged by the laws simply did not obtain. Serious disturbances were solved by crushing defeats of the Indians and by their removal to lands farther away rather than by strict enforcement of the laws.

The laws, however, were by no means completely ineffective. Against Indian criminals they were invoked again and again. If an Indian committed a crime against a white—and murder was the offense foremost in mind—the criminal was demanded from the tribe for punishment by the United States. If the accused Indian was not delivered up, a military expedition was sent to apprehend him, or hostages were seized and held until the criminal appeared. The culprit was guarded by the federal troops and turned over by them to a civil court in a nearby territory or state for trial. In many cases this procedure worked satisfactorily. However reluctant the Indian tribes might have been to turn over their members to the United States for punishment, they had a remarkably good record in doing so. Whether this was due to their sense of justice or to the threat or use of military force cannot be determined, and it is impossible to tell what percentage of Indian murderers were actually brought to trial. Certainly many murders went unpunished. In 1824, Thomas L. McKenney, head of the Indian Office, wrote to both Lewis Cass and William Clark about the "alarm-

34. 1 *United States Statutes* 329–31; Israel, *State of the Union Messages*, 1: 30.
35. 1 *United States Statutes* 470–73, 744–48; 2 *United States Statutes* 39–40, 141–45; 3 *United States Statutes* 383.

ing extent to which murders are committed in the North and West," and he urged them to take special action to prevent recurrence.[36]

Even when court action was initiated, the simple frontier communities frequently became tied up in the legal proceedings. To find suitable counsel, to call adequate witnesses, to empanel a proper jury—all this was a complicated and time-consuming process. The local courts had insufficient means to confine prisoners while awaiting trial, it was not always easy to determine which court had proper jurisdiction, and collection of evidence was a difficult and thankless task. The whole process was expensive and, in the minds of army officers upon whom much of the responsibility fell, wrongly conceived. Some officers wanted to throw out the legal procedures of white civilization and punish Indian offenders on the spot. This sort of action the Indians would understand, and it would be effective in checking their depredations. But the government refused to modify the policy of treating Indians on a par with whites as far as legal forms were concerned. All along the frontier, army officers sought out criminals in the Indian country, confined them in the post guardhouses, and then sent them under military guard to civil authorities for trial.[37]

For crimes committed by whites against Indians the laws made specific provision, gradually becoming more explicit. If the offenses were committed within a territory or a state, the criminal code of that civil jurisdiction sufficed. Within the Indian country, offenses of whites against Indians were punishable in federal courts when the offenses were specified in the federal statutes, and the intercourse laws declared that crimes in any of the states or territories against a white citizen should also be considered crimes if committed in the Indian country against an Indian. But the crimes were so numerous and widespread that their control by judicial means proved impossible. The frequency of offenses committed against Indians by frontier whites, among which outright murder was commonplace, was shocking. It was often a question of who was more aggressive, more hostile, more savage—the Indian or the white man. The murders and other aggressions of whites against Indians provided one of the great sources of friction between the two races. Lack of enforcement made a mockery of the statutes. The typical frontier community could not be brought to convict a man who injured or murdered an Indian, and confusion as to the status of the federal courts in the territories delayed effective action.

Letters and directives and official proclamations, even when backed by

36. McKenney to Cass and Clark, November 1, 1824, OIA LS, vol. 1, p. 214 (M21, reel 1).

37. See Francis Paul Prucha, *Broadax and Bayonet: The Role of the United States Army in the Development of the Northwest, 1815–1860* (Madison: State Historical Society of Wisconsin, 1953), pp. 84–88.

all the goodwill in the world, were no match for the singular Indian-hating mentality of the frontiersmen, upon whom depended conviction in the local courts. In Indiana Territory, for example, the criminal law broke down, and Governor Harrison lamented the sad state of justice toward the Indians. In his message to the legislature in 1806 he unhesitatingly admitted that, although the laws provided the same punishment for offenses committed against Indians as against white men, "experience . . . shows that there is a wide difference in the execution of those laws. The Indian always suffers, and the white man never."[38]

The federal government made repeated efforts to bring white offenders to justice, and no doubt some Indians were influenced by the good intentions of the United States, even though white citizens were never kept in check. One measure taken to appease the Indians was to issue a proclamation in the name of the president, offering a handsome reward for the apprehension of the criminal. The ineffectiveness of such proclamations in actually bringing the criminals to justice in the frontier communities can be presumed, and the government more frequently resorted to compensating the families of murdered Indians by payment of a fixed sum of money or goods. The War Department directed the Indian agents to offer such pecuniary satisfaction in cases where the murderers could not be apprehended, in order to satisfy the families and show the willingness of the government to do justice. A sum of one to two hundred dollars for each Indian murdered by whites was suggested by the secretary of war in 1803, and this amount was regularly given.[39]

Theft was another cause of conflict, and the chief concern was horses. Aside from outright murders and massacres by the Indians, nothing was so likely to embroil the two races on the frontier as horse stealing, for horses were of elemental necessity for the frontiersman. The white's need and the Indian's cupidity and stealth made for an explosive combination that threatened to blow up one frontier after another. The petitions that reached the War Department regularly coupled horse stealing with murder as the scourge of living near the Indians.[40]

It was necessary to get at the evil indirectly, first of all by eliminating the market for the stolen stock. If the Indians could not dispose of the horses by ready sale, there would be no further incentive for large-scale

38. *Messages and Letters of William Henry Harrison*, ed. Logan Esarey, 2 vols. (Indianapolis: Indiana Historical Commission, 1922), 1: 199–200.

39. See proclamations dated February 27 and March 1, 1804, SW IA LS, vol. A, pp. 443, 447 (M15, reel 1). For use of compensation, see letters of Dearborn to various agents, ibid., pp. 352–53, 373, 417; Calhoun to Thomas Forsyth, March 15, 1819, ibid., vol. D, p. 269 (M15, reel 4); Calhoun to John McKee, July 21, 1819, Carter, *Territorial Papers*, 18: 657.

40. Carter, *Territorial Papers*, 4: 72, 129; 16: 188–89.

thefts. Such was the logic behind the provisions that were written into the intercourse laws, beginning with the law of 1793 and repeated in subsequent laws. To purchase a horse from any Indian or from any white person within the Indian country required a special license, and a report of all horses purchased was to be made to the agent who issued the license. For every horse purchased or brought out of the Indian country without a license, a fine was imposed. Furthermore, to plug another loophole, any person who purchased a horse that he knew had been brought out of the Indian country without a license was to forfeit the value of the horse.[41] But there were no convictions under these licensing and forfeiture provisions of the intercourse laws, and the laws soon became a dead letter.

The intercourse law of 1796, though it continued the restrictions on the purchase of horses in the Indian country, tried a new approach to the problem, one aimed less at justice than at preventing injustice from causing frontier disturbances. This was a guarantee of government compensation for theft of horses or other injuries if satisfaction could not be obtained from the guilty party, either by application to the tribe in the case of thefts by Indians or by recourse to the courts in the case of injuries perpetrated by whites. The War Department was eventually flooded with claims for stolen horses and occasionally for other property, and it did not know just what to do about the claims because often they were submitted on the least provocation without clear evidence that Indians were the real culprits and without going through the procedure prescribed by the laws. Yet faulty as the operation of the law was, it regularized this point of contact between the two races. By providing machinery for recovery of losses by peaceful means, it eliminated any justification for private retaliation and was largely successful in removing this friction, except on the rawest frontiers before they were amenable to juridical procedures. In numerous cases injured whites received compensation for their losses out of the annuities due the Indians, and in some cases—although apparently far fewer—the Indians were paid for injuries sustained from the whites. Frequently large numbers of claims on both sides were summarily provided for in treaties made with specific tribes.[42]

Because it was generally admitted that offenses among Indians within the tribe or nation were tribal matters that were to be handled by the tribe and were of no concern to the United States government, crimes committed by Indians against other Indians did not fall within the scope of the intercourse laws. The sovereignty of an Indian tribe, no matter how it might be circumscribed in other respects, was certainly considered to ex-

41. 1 *United States Statutes* 330.

42. Cases regarding horse stealing are discussed in Prucha, *American Indian Policy in the Formative Years*, pp. 205–11.

tend to the punishment of its own members. Up to the mid-nineteenth century, indeed, there were no laws or treaty provisions that limited the powers of self-government of the tribes with respect to internal affairs. Indian tribal sovereignty existed long before the coming of the whites and did not depend upon federal legislation. Yet the United States formally indicated its respect for this tribal authority by embodying in the law of 1817 that established federal jurisdiction over Indian offenses the declaration that the law did not extend "to any offense committed by one Indian against another, within any Indian boundary."[43] Intertribal wars, however, were of continuing interest to the United States, for they could endanger the lives and property of white citizens on the frontier. Indian agents were directed to use whatever advice, persuasion, or presents might be needed to prevent hostilities between tribes, but they were not to involve the United States on either side.[44]

REMOVAL OF INTRUDERS ON INDIAN LANDS

The conflict between the whites and Indians that marked American Indian relations was basically a conflict over land. Although the American government recognized Indian rights to the land and attempted by law, treaty, and special proclamation to ensure justice to the aborigines, the views of the frontiersmen were of a different nature altogether. Theorizing about rights of preemption played little part in the thinking of the settler or of the eastern speculator in western lands. Their doctrine was simpler and earthier, and they had their own ideas about *jus gentium*: they saw the rich lands of the Indians and they wanted them. Their philosophy was summed up by John Sevier, one of the most aggressive of the frontier leaders. "By the law of nations, it is agreed that no people shall be entitled to more land than they can cultivate," he said. "Of course no people will sit and starve for want of land to work, when a neighbouring nation has much more than they can make use of."[45]

In the conflict with the frontiersmen, the government did not back down in its principles; it in fact tightened its restrictions and strengthened the machinery of enforcement. But as the spearhead of settlement fluctu-

---

43. 3 *United States Statutes* 383.

44. John Smith to William Clark, September 8, 1810, SW IA LS, vol. C, pp. 49–50 (M15, reel 3); Calhoun to James Miller, June 29, 1820, ibid., vol. D, pp. 458–59 (M15, reel 4).

45. Sevier to James Ore, May 12, 1798, Robert H. White, ed., *Messages of the Governors of Tennessee*, 5 vols. (Nashville: Tennessee Historical Commission, 1952–1959), 1: 58,

ated back and forth across the West, driving ever deeper into territories once solely Indian, the pious principles of the legislators ran into the un- principled practices of the settlers. The men actually on the land generally had the better of it, for they again and again deflected the enforcing army of government and in the end forced the Indians off the land. This is the story that has attracted so many writers and led to a widely held opinion that the Indians were ruthlessly dispossessed with nothing done to protect their rights. Quite the contrary, for the Indians were not completely de- serted. Explicit treaties were made guaranteeing their rights, and stringent laws were enacted to ensure respect for the treaties. Various measures were undertaken to enforce the laws, which were not completely ineffec- tive. It is true that in the end the Indians were pushed back by the onrush of whites, but what order and peace there was on the frontier came in large part from the enforcement of the intercourse laws against unlawful en- croachment on Indian lands.

The prohibition of private purchase of lands from the Indians, which had been part of the colonial and imperial policy, continued as a fixed pol- icy of the United States. The First Congress incorporated this principle into the intercourse law of 1790. The restriction entered as section 4 read: "no sale of lands made by any Indians, or any nation or tribe of Indians within the United States, shall be valid to any person or persons, or to any state, whether having the right of pre-emption to such lands or not, unless the same shall be made and duly executed at some public treaty, held un- der the authority of the United States." The same prohibition was included in the act of 1793, with an added clause setting a fine and imprisonment for any person treating directly or indirectly with the Indians for title to land. The law recognized, however, the right of agents of the states, with the approval of the United States commissioners, to be present at treaty making and to propose and adjust with the Indians the compensation for lands within the states whose Indian title would be extinguished by the treaty. This section was reenacted in the laws of 1796, 1799, and 1802.[46] The principle was clearly stated, and the practice had been uniform for decades. Federal commissioners were appointed to treat with the Indians for their lands, and Congress appropriated funds for compensating the Indians.

Treaties entered into with the Indians for cessions of land had the uni- versal corollary that the unceded lands would be guaranteed against inva-

46. 1 *United States Statutes* 138, 330–31, 472, 746; 2 *United States Statutes* 143. Despite arguments in the 1970s that these provisions applied also to acquisition of lands from remnants of Indian tribes by such states as Massachusetts, the context in which the laws were passed indicates that the legislators did not have such cases in mind. See dis- cussion below, "Land Claims and Conflicts," in chapter 46.

sion by whites. Thus all the treaties entered into by the Continental Congress guaranteed the remaining lands of the Indians, and the later ones expressly forbade whites to settle on Indian land under sanction of forfeiting the protection of the United States and becoming subject to punishment by the Indians. The same provisions were written into the first treaties made under the Constitution. Congress, therefore, in drawing up the intercourse law of 1790, considered it unnecessary to make specific prohibition of encroachment on the Indian country.

The open violations of the treaties, however, necessitated additional legislative measures against the illegal settlers, and the intercourse law of 1793 provided a maximum fine of one thousand dollars and imprisonment for twelve months for anyone who settled on Indian lands or surveyed or marked boundaries on such lands with a view to settlement. The president, furthermore, was authorized to remove all unlawful settlers by such measures as he might judge necessary. From that time on, the successive laws included sections aimed specifically at the aggressive frontiersmen. The act of 1796, which was copied in substance by the subsequent acts, forbade whites to cross over the Indian boundary line to hunt or to drive their livestock there to graze. Even to enter the Indian country south of the Ohio required a special passport issued by the governor of one of the states or by a commander of a frontier military post. Unauthorized settlers would lose any claim they might have to the lands they settled on or surveyed and suffer fine and imprisonment as well, and the president could use force to remove them.[47]

The federal government was determined to defend the integrity of the Indian country, but the United States itself was sometimes forced to seek concessions from the Indians. This occurred particularly in two cases: the acquisition of land within the Indian country for military posts, agencies, and trading houses, and acquisition for roads connecting important settlements or major segments of American territory. Getting land for the military posts and other government establishments caused little trouble because the troops of the United States were generally looked upon with respect by the Indians. Military forces within the Indian lands were more a protection than a threat and did not form a wedge for whites to intrude into the forbidden lands. The agencies and factories also worked for the benefit of the Indians.

The running of roads through the Indian country was a more controversial question, for the Indians frequently objected to such invasion of their lands. The War Department instructed its agents to proceed with great caution in persuading the Indians to grant permission for the roads and to offer

47. 1 *United States Statutes* 330, 470.

suitable inducements and compensation. With requests for the roads also went requests for sites of land on which "houses of entertainment" might be set up for the refreshment of the travelers, and one inducement used to win the agreement of the Indians was that the Indians themselves might profit from running such establishments. Though permission was sometimes delayed, the United States generally won its point, and treaties with the Indians contained specific articles authorizing the roads. Some of the intercourse laws mentioned roads when outlining the lands reserved to the Indians.[48]

Such small and authorized encroachments on Indian lands were insignificant in comparison with the illegal onrush of settlers, whose pressure was usually so great that the United States could not enforce the intercourse laws with any complete success. The Indians, who made valiant attempts to stave off the onslaught when it became apparent that the federal government was powerless to protect their rights, were little by little crushed, liquidated, or driven west. But the laws of Congress, the proclamations of the president, and the orders issued by the War Department did provide a brake on the westward rolling juggernaut.[49]

In the end, the force of the intruders was too great to be held back. Temporarily it could be halted, but the intruders were a mobile lot. They had moved in easily the first time, and if they were removed by military force, they could just as easily return. When the troops departed from the area, back streamed the settlers. Although the government repeatedly directed the Indian agents and the military commanders to carry out the law, little was accomplished. Then came the War of 1812 and the Creek War of 1813–1814, which turned attention to more serious troubles. The outcome of it all was what had already come to be expected—an expectation that no doubt took much of the edge off the zeal of officers responsible for removing the intruders. The more frequently the government acquiesced in the illegal settlements, the more difficult it became to take effective action. The settlers knew that they would be treated considerately. They had little fear that civil action would succeed against them, and there was an increasing number of examples of government action to cover such settlements through formal treaties that extinguished the Indian title.

A serious weakness in the protection of the Indian country was the shortage of troops to enforce the removal of intruders. The peacetime establishment of the regular army was altogether inadequate to the task. An

48. Secretary of war to William C. C. Claiborne, July 9, 1803, Carter, *Territorial Papers*, 5: 221–22; secretary of war to Benjamin Hawkins, February 11, 1804, ibid., pp. 306–7; Albert Gallatin to John Badollet, August 14, 1806, ibid., 7: 378–80; Kappler, pp. 30, 55, 56.
49. Prucha, *American Indian Policy in the Formative Years*, pp. 147–65.

attempt was made to use Indian troops, but because they were the bene-
ficiaries of the action, the government balked at paying them for their
military service. In Georgia, the incessant intrusion onto Cherokee lands
led finally to the enrollment of volunteer troops at regular army pay to
drive out the violators. Joseph McMinn, as Cherokee agent, ordered the
mustering in of the volunteers and dispatched them to drive out the settlers. Armed with large butcher knives to cut down the corn of the intruders and with many mounted on horses they themselves had supplied, the
volunteers drove into the trouble spots, destroying the crops and burning
fences and houses. The intruders showed considerable hostility, and in the
engagement one of the settlers was killed by the troops, for which the
officers and two of the privates were haled into court.[50]

Even where regular troops were available, the officers often hesitated
to act, for they risked court action. "Every subaltern in the command
knows," reported one civilian traveler, "that if he interferes between an Indian and a white man, he will be sued instantly in the courts of the State.
When I was at Prairie du Chien, there were several of the officers who had
been cited to appear in court for having, pursuant to order, removed 'squatters' from the Indian lands over the Mississippi. The Indians then despise
the agent, because he is clothed with no military authority; and the pioneer despises the military, because their hands are tied by the local civil
power, whatever it be."[51]

Certain elemental conditions formed the basis of these difficulties.
Given the nature of American western settlement, there was an inherent
antagonism between the frontiersmen and any governmental force that
tried to inhibit their activities. The deep-seated desire for land found the
restrictions of the government an obstruction. Americans were expansion-
minded; it seemed part of their very nature. Too often the government was
helpless, even had it had the will, to hold in check the men who squatted
on land not yet officially open to them, whether it was public land or Indian country.[52]

On top of this foundation there was often built a superstructure of personal animosity. Martinets of army officers who expected the free-living

50. Ibid., pp. 165–66. Examples of problems in enforcing the laws are given ibid., pp.
166–85.

51. Charles F. Hoffman, *A Winter in the West*, 2 vols. (New York: Harper and Brothers, 1835), 2: 86–87.

52. On March 3, 1807, a law was approved that forbade settling on public lands on
which the Indian title had been extinguished but which were not yet surveyed and
opened to settlement. 2 *United States Statutes* 445–46. The federal government had no
more success in restraining such squatters than it had in preventing settlement on Indian
lands. See Paul W. Gates, *History of Public Land Law Development* (Washington: Public
Land Law Review Commission, 1968), pp. 219–21.

citizens on the frontier to jump with military precision at the sound of their voice—commandants little loved by soldier and civilian alike—did not supply the diplomacy necessary for the smooth running of the frontier communities. Indian agents, zealous beyond measure, perhaps, for the interests of their charges and overbearing in their self-importance, who could not get along with either the military or the traders and settlers, added their own measure of intolerance. Frontier entrepreneurs or budding lawyers, who dreamed of their community as the future pride of the West (with whose ascent they too would be propelled upward), developed fanatical hatred of the army officers who attempted to clamp down on their manifold operations.

The history of intrusions on Indian lands, of course, raises the difficult question of the sincerity of the government in its policy of protecting Indian rights to the land. Certainly the legal basis was firm enough, and the doctrines of preemption and of Indian sovereignty were endorsed by the Supreme Court in a series of famous decisions. In *Fletcher* v. *Peck*, in 1810, the court asserted that the "nature of the Indian title, which is certainly to be respected by all courts, until it be legitimately extinguished, is not such as to be absolutely repugnant to seizin in fee on the part of the State."[53] In 1823, in *Johnson and Graham's Lessee* v. *McIntosh*, the court expanded this doctrine when it considered the case of two claimants to the same piece of land, one of whom had received the title directly from the Indians, the other by a patent from the government. Chief Justice Marshall, in giving the decision of the court, furnished a long disquisition about the nature of the Indian title to land and expatiated on the traditional doctrine of preemption. With numerous citations of colonial precedents to back up his contention, he maintained that the United States, or the several states, had the exclusive power to extinguish the Indian right of occupancy. Although the "absolute ultimate title" rested with the European discoverers, the Indians kept the right of occupancy. This right, Marshall declared, "is no more incompatible with a seizin in fee, than a lease for years, and might as effectually bar an ejectment." He continued, "It has never been contended that the Indian title amounted to nothing. Their right of possession has never been questioned."[54]

The laws and proclamations were explicit, and there were many instances of vigorous action to drive off illegal settlers. Yet in the long run, the settlers nearly always won out. Why did the government not take more effective measures to prevent encroachment? The answer lies partly in the insufficiency of the forces available to carry out the legislative measures and executive decisions. Indian agents simply lacked the necessary means.

53. *Fletcher* v. *Peck*, 6 Cranch 87.
54. *Johnson and Graham's Lessee* v. *McIntosh*, 8 Wheaton 543.

The civil authorities could not be relied upon to prosecute or convict violators; and the army on the frontier was too small to police the whole area
successfully.

But behind these failures was a larger issue. The federal government
was sincerely interested in preventing settlement on Indian lands only up
to a point, and it readily acquiesced in illegal settlement that had gone so
far as to be irremediable. The policy of the United States was based on an
assumption that white settlement should advance and the Indians withdraw. The federal government was interested primarily in seeing that this
process was as free of disorder and injustice as possible. It meant to restrain and govern the advance of the whites, not to prevent it forever. It
supported Indian claims as far as it could out of justice and humanity to
the Indians and above all as far as it was necessary to keep a semblance of
peace and to maintain Indian goodwill so that land could continue to be
ceded by the tribes. In the early decades of the nineteenth century the federal government was convinced that once the Indians had been permanently settled on lands west of the Mississippi, the problems of encroachment and of removing intruders would be unhappy memories of the past.
And in the end it looked for the civilization of the Indians and their assimilation into white society.

The energy of the government in removing intruders was, in fact, proportionate, either directly or inversely, to a number of other circumstances: to
the length of time during which the Indian claims were expected to be
maintained; to the seriousness of Indian objections to the intruders, as removal was often the only way to prevent an Indian war; to the necessity of
convincing the Indians of the government's good faith in order to keep
them in a proper frame of mind for some impending treaty at which more
concessions of land were to be sought; to the pressures of white settlement, for full-scale drives into an area usually led to new treaties of cession
rather than to removal of the whites; to the boldness and aggressiveness of
the agents and military commanders in enforcing the laws; to the military
forces available in the area where encroachment was threatened; to the
strength of frontier opposition to military action against the intruders; and
to the color of title that the settlers on Indian lands could display, as well
as the character of the settlers themselves.

CHAPTER 4

Government Trading
Houses (Factories)

Beginnings of the Factory System.

Jeffersonian Expansion.

Attack and Support.

The End of the Factories.

If military subjugation in the manner of Anthony Wayne was one way to assure peace on the frontier—and peace remained the great desire of President Washington—establishing friendship on the basis of trade was a preferable alternative. In his recommendations for a just and humane Indian policy at the end of the Revolutionary War, Washington wrote: "I think, if the Indian Trade was carried on, on Government Acct., and with no greater advance than what would be necessary to defray the expence and risk, and bring in a small profit, that it would supply the Indians upon much better terms than they usually are; engross their Trade, and fix them strongly in our Interest." The subsequent course of events did not change his mind about the benefits of a trading policy that would be fair to the Indians and free of abuses. He insisted that the trade must be free of fraud and extortion, supply goods plentifully and without delay, and provide a market for Indian commodities at a stated and fair price. Private traders were motivated by hope of profit and took advantage of the Indians to gain their end, Washington argued; therefore the government, which was interested only in reimbursement of costs, should undertake the trade itself. He looked to Congress for appropriate authorization, and when no action was forthcoming, he repeated his recommendation.[1]

1. George Washington to James Duane, September 7, 1783, *Writings of George Washington*, ed. John C. Fitzpatrick, 39 vols. (Washington: GPO, 1931–1944), 27: 137–38; annual messages of October 25, 1791, December 3, 1793, and November 19, 1794, Fred L.

BEGINNINGS OF THE FACTORY SYSTEM

The system of government trading houses that Washington envisaged was soon begun. A committee of the House of Representatives reported favorably on the president's proposal on December 1, 1794, noting that "it would conduce to the honor and prosperity of the United States to cultivate peace with the Indian tribes" and that "the establishment of trading houses, under the direction of the President of the United States, would have a tendency to produce this laudable and benevolent effect." On February 28, 1795, Congress took the plan under consideration. Congress was sympathetic, for as Josiah Parker of Virginia noted, some legislation of the sort was necessary "to conciliate the affections of a distressed and unhappy people, and as it might prevent the expenses of a war with them." The Indians, it was argued, "had common sense enough not to quit allies who supplied them with articles which they wanted, till we also made some effectual establishments of that kind." The measure, too, was seen as a part of a total system for dealing with the Indians: military force to protect the frontier from Indian incursions, laws to prevent white frontiersmen from "predatory invasion into the Indian country," and trading houses to supply the Indians' wants and to detach "their habits of trade and their affections from a foreign nation." Without the third element in the system, the first two would be ineffective. "It was clear as a sunbeam," one representative remarked, "that the establishment of a trade must be the foundation of amity."[2]

Congress was cautious, but it was willing to let the president try the matter as an experiment. It appropriated $50,000 to purchase goods for the Indians in 1795 and directed that the goods be sold under the direction of the president.[3]

With such small funds, only a small and experimental beginning could

Israel, ed., *The State of the Union Messages of the Presidents, 1790–1966*, 3 vols. (New York: Chelsea House, 1966), 1: 9, 19–20, 26. The government trading houses that resulted from Washington's insistence have been thoroughly studied by historians. Two extensive studies are Ora Brooks Peake, *A History of the United States Indian Factory System, 1795–1822* (Denver: Sage Books, 1954), which has many data but is not well presented; and Aloysius Plaisance, "The United States Government Factory System, 1796–1822" (Ph.D. dissertation, Saint Louis University, 1954), a careful, detailed study. See also Herman J. Viola, *Thomas L. McKenney: Architect of America's Early Indian Policy, 1816–1830* (Chicago: Swallow Press, 1974), pp. 6–70. Articles on individual factories are cited below.

    2. ASP:IA, 1: 524; *Annals of Congress*, 3d Congress, 2d session, pp. 1262–63, 1276.
    3. 1 *United States Statutes* 443. The laws generally speak of "trading houses" and "agents" in charge of them, but the terms "factory" and "factor" were also in common use. I use the terms interchangeably.

be made. Passing over the Six Nations, which were closely surrounded by white settlements, and the tribes north of the Ohio River, still negotiating for peace after Wayne's victory, the War Department decided to apply the money among the southern Indians only.[4] For the Creeks a factory was set up at Colerain, on the St. Marys River in Georgia, a point of easy access for goods and sufficiently close, it was mistakenly judged, to the Creeks.[5] To supply the Cherokees, and to a lesser extent the Chickasaws, another trading house was begun at Tellico Blockhouse in eastern Tennessee, where there was already a military post to which the Indians were accustomed to resort. There was some difficulty in obtaining supplies because of the need to provide General Wayne with goods for his treaty negotiations and for annuity payments to the Chickasaws, but goods were sent off in the fall as soon as they could be procured. Two-thirds of the funds were used for the Creek factory because it could be more easily supplied.

The success of this initial outlay prompted Congress in the next session to formalize the program of trading houses. The arguments in favor were much the same as they had been earlier—that private traders of the young nation were unable to compete with the strong British traders and that development of commerce with the Indians, whatever it might cost, was less expensive than war. Suggestions that it was no business of the government to engage in trade and motions for delay were overcome, and the measure became law on April 18, 1796.[6]

The law of 1796 gave the president authority to establish such trading houses on the southern and western frontiers or in the Indian country as he judged best for carrying on a "liberal trade" with the Indians. Money was provided for agents and clerks, to be appointed by the president, who were prohibited from engaging in any trade on their own account. To the fund of the previous year Congress now added $150,000, and the law di-

4. An account of the establishment of the first two houses is given in a report of Secretary of War Timothy Pickering, December 12, 1795, ASP:IA, 1: 583–84.

5. Colerain proved quite unsatisfactory, and in 1797 the factory was moved to Fort Wilkinson on the Oconee River. In 1806 it was moved to the site of Fort Hawkins and in 1817 to Fort Mitchell in Alabama. An excellent article on the Creek factory (in its various locations) is Ray H. Mattison, "The Creek Trading House: From Colerain to Fort Hawkins," *Georgia Historical Quarterly* 30 (September 1946): 169–84. Another account of Colerain, based on the William Eaton Papers in the Huntington Library, San Marino, California, is Louis B. Wright and Julia Macleod, "William Eaton, Timothy Pickering, and Indian Policy," *Huntington Library Quarterly* 9 (August 1946): 387–400. The relation of the United States Indian agent and the first two southern factories is explored in George D. Harmon, "Benjamin Hawkins and the Federal Factory System," *North Carolina Historical Review* 9 (April 1932): 138–52.

6. Debate on the bill is recorded in *Annals of Congress*, 4th Congress, 1st session, pp. 229–32, 240–43, 282–85.

rected that prices were to be set at such a level that this capital stock not be diminished. Lest the trade in any way hinder the ultimate goal of civilizing the Indians in the white man's pattern, the law forbade agents to accept in trade guns, clothing, cooking utensils, or "any instrument of husbandry" obtained by the Indians in their intercourse with whites. The act was to run for two years and to the end of the next session of Congress thereafter.[7]

For some unexplained reason, the new legislation did not result in an expansion of the system, perhaps because President John Adams, a New Englander, did not push it aggressively.[8] Colerain (moved to Fort Wilkinson in 1797 in order better to supply the Creeks) and Tellico continued to be the only trading houses in operation, and when the legislation lapsed on March 3, 1799, no one seemed to notice. The end of the legislation did not liquidate the capital fund or remove the factors from their positions, and the system continued, law or no law.

JEFFERSONIAN EXPANSION

Thomas Jefferson stirred up the whole matter anew when he became president, for unlike his predecessor he had a deep and abiding interest in Indian affairs. His secretary of war, Henry Dearborn, reporting on the operation of the factories up to the end of 1801, found that not only had the capital not diminished, but it had increased 3 or 4 percent. He judged that the system had had a "very salutary effect on the minds of the Indians," and that such commerce had "a powerful tendency toward strengthening and confirming the friendship of the Indians to the people and Government of the United States, and toward detaching them more and more from the influence of neighboring Governments." He urged extension of

7. 1 *United States Statutes* 452–53.

8. Adams appeared to have little interest in Indian problems while he was president, although he later prided himself on observing peace. "I was engaged in the most earnest, sedulous, and, I must own, expensive exertions to preserve peace with the Indians, and prepare them for agriculture and civilization, through the whole of my administration," he wrote. "I had the inexpressible satisfaction of complete success. Not a hatchet was lifted in my time; and the single battle of Tippecanoe has since cost the United States a hundred times more money than it cost me to maintain universal and perpetual peace. . . . My labors were indefatigable to compose all difficulties and settle all controversies with all nations, civilized and savage." Adams to James Lloyd, March 31, 1815, *The Works of John Adams*, ed. Charles Francis Adams, 10 vols. (Boston: Little, Brown and Company, 1850–1856), 10: 153. For a discussion of Adams's views and activities, see Frederick M. Binder, *The Color Problem in Early National America as Viewed by John Adams, Jefferson and Jackson* (The Hague: Mouton, 1968), pp. 32–47.

the system. Noting the lapse of authorization for the factories, Jefferson asked Congress to revive the system and to extend it.[9]

On April 30, 1802, Congress obliged by renewing the act of 1796 and extending it until March 4, 1803.[10] A new flurry of activity resulted. Trading houses were established in 1802 at Fort St. Stephens among the Choctaws on the Tombigbee River in Alabama, at Chickasaw Bluffs among the Chickasaws in western Tennessee, at Fort Wayne in Indiana, and at Detroit.[11]

There was no letup. Jefferson sent a special message to Congress at the beginning of 1803 in which he urged continuation of the trading houses, for they were an integral part of what he considered an essential Indian policy. The pressure on Indian lands had been so great that many Indians were resisting further diminution of their land. "It hazards their friendship and excites dangerous jealousies and perturbations in their minds," Jefferson said, "to make any overture for the purchase of the smallest portions of their land." Two measures, he believed, were called for. One was to encourage the Indians to abandon hunting and to adopt the agriculture and husbandry of the whites, proving to them that less land would maintain them better under such operations than their traditional mode of living. The second was to multiply trading houses among them and thus put within their reach means of domestic comfort. Jefferson hoped thus to arrange a mutually advantageous exchange—the Indians would give up unnecessary lands and receive the means to carry on the white man's agricultural existence. He pointed out to Congress that the system was succeeding with its liberal trade policies. Private traders, both foreign and domestic, were undersold and driven from the field, and the nation was ridding itself of a class of men who constantly endeavored to excite the

9. Report of Henry Dearborn, December 8, 1801, ASP:IA, 1: 654–55; Jefferson to Congress, January 28, 1802, ibid., p. 653.

10. 2 *United States Statutes* 173.

11. The Choctaw factory at Fort St. Stephens was moved to Fort Confederation, farther up the Tombigbee, in 1817; the factory at Chickasaw Bluffs was moved to Spadra Bluffs on the Arkansas River in 1818. A detailed history of the operation of the Choctaw factory is given in Aloysius Plaisance, "The Choctaw Trading House, 1803–1822," *Alabama Historical Quarterly* 16 (Fall–Winter 1954): 393–423. For the history of the Chickasaw Bluffs factory, see Plaisance, "The Chickasaw Bluffs Factory and Its Removal to the Arkansas River, 1818–1822," *Tennessee Historical Quarterly* 11 (March 1952): 41–57. Information on one of the factors at Spadra Bluffs is given in George L. Montagno, "Matthew Lyon's Last Frontier," *Arkansas Historical Quarterly* 16 (Spring 1957): 46–53. Invoices, inventories, and memorials from the factory at Fort Wayne, 1802–1811, are printed in Bert J. Griswold, ed., *Fort Wayne, Gateway of the West, 1802–1813* (Indianapolis: Historical Bureau of the Indiana Library and Historical Department, 1927), pp. 401–663. They furnish an exhaustive listing of the trade goods sent to the factory and of the furs received.

Indian mind with suspicions, fears, and irritations toward the Americans.[12]

In a private letter to William Henry Harrison, governor of Indiana Territory, the president spoke eloquently and candidly about his views. "Our system," he told Harrison, "is to live in perpetual peace with the Indians, to cultivate an affectionate attachment for them, by everything just and liberal which we can do for them within the bounds of reason, and by giving them effectual protection against wrongs from our own people." But fundamentally, he hoped "to draw them to agriculture, to spinning and weaving." Then, as they came to need less land they would willingly sell to the whites. "To promote this disposition to exchange lands, which they have to spare and we want, for necessaries, which we have to spare and they want," he said, "we shall push our trading houses, and be glad to see the good and influential individuals among them run in debt, because we observe that when these debts get beyond what the individuals can pay, they become willing to lop them off by a cession of lands." With the trading houses underselling private traders, the country would "get clear of this pest without giving offence or umbrage to the Indians."[13]

Congress kept the system afloat by renewing the 1796 act again in 1803, and in 1805 it appropriated $100,000 for additional trading houses. New factories appeared in 1805 at Chicago, at Belle Fontaine on the Missouri River just north of St. Louis, at Natchitoches on the Red River in Louisiana, and at Arkansas Post on the Arkansas River. A year later another was opened at Sandusky, Ohio.[14]

With such far-flung and increasing activity, it was necessary to do more than revive from time to time the original law of 1796, and in 1806 Congress supplied more comprehensive legislation for the system. In addition to repeating the main provisions of the earlier legislation, it set the sum for trading goods, including previous appropriations, at $260,000 and authorized a superintendent of Indian trade to take charge of the whole business

12. Message of January 18, 1803, James D. Richardson, comp., *A Compilation of the Messages and Papers of the Presidents*, 10 vols. (Washington: GPO, 1896–1899), 1: 340–41.

13. Jefferson to Harrison, February 27, 1803, *The Writings of Thomas Jefferson*, ed. Andrew A. Lipscomb, 20 vols. (Washington: Thomas Jefferson Memorial Association, 1903–1904), 10: 369–71. In a similar letter to Secretary of War Dearborn, August 12, 1802, Jefferson spoke of the trading houses as "the cheapest & most effectual instrument we can use for preserving the friendship of the Indians." Clarence E. Carter, ed., *The Territorial Papers of the United States*, 26 vols. (Washington: GPO, 1934–1962), 7: 67–69.

14. 2 *United States Statutes* 207, 338. There is an account of the Chicago factory in Milo Milton Quaife, *Chicago and the Old Northwest, 1673–1835* (Chicago: University of Chicago Press, 1913), pp. 296–309. For the history of the factory at Arkansas Post, see Aloysius Plaisance, "The Arkansas Factory, 1805–1810," *Arkansas Historical Quarterly* 11 (Autumn 1952): 184–200, and Wayne Morris, "Traders and Factories on the Arkansas Frontier, 1805–1822," ibid., 28 (Spring 1969): 32–40.

under the direction of the president. But Congress still could not see the trading houses as any more than a temporary expedient and provided that the act was to run for three years only.[15]

The creation of the Office of Indian Trade was a milestone in developing the federal machinery for dealing with Indian problems. Before 1806 there had been no official in the government whose full duties concerned the Indians; the secretary of war, under the president, looked after what business there was. The goods for the factories were purchased by a succession of purchasing agents operating in Philadelphia. Now, with the superintendent of Indian trade, there was someone who could attend to the important trading functions and who gradually became the focus for nonmilitary Indian matters.

The first superintendent was John Shee of Philadelphia, appointed on July 8, 1806. He was a shadowy figure who made no appreciable mark on the office, and he was replaced in October 1807 by John Mason, president of the Bank of Columbia in the District of Columbia. Mason was an able officer, and the factory system expanded in his early years, with additional houses established in 1808 at Fort Osage on the Missouri River, at Mackinac Island, and at Fort Madison on the west bank of the Mississippi at the mouth of the Des Moines River. These new posts reflected the advance of the American frontier; as the Indians were pushed westward by white settlement, old factories were closed, and new ones, more convenient for the changing circumstances of the trade, were substituted. In 1809, while extending the life of the system for another three years, Congress appropriated an additional $40,000 for the trade and authorized an additional clerk in the office of the superintendent.[16]

Much of the formalizing of the activities and duties of the factors was the work of Mason, who sent full instructions to these agents. He dictated the percentage of markup on the goods sold, where to ship their furs and peltries, restrictions on their trading activities, and the kind of accounts they were to keep. The factors were to sell to Indians only, except in "very particular and pressing cases" and then with an additional charge of 10 percent. Credit was allowed "with caution, to principal chiefs of good character." The sale of liquor was strictly prohibited.[17]

It was an active and relatively thriving business. At the beginning of 1812, Mason, reporting on the preceding four years, showed $290,000 employed out of the $300,000 of capital stock authorized and a profit for the period of $14,171.30. The southern factories were doing poorly, however,

15. 2 *United States Statutes* 402–4.
16. 2 *United States Statutes* 544–45.
17. Circular of Mason to agents, December 12, 1807, ASP:IA, 2: 520–21; Mason to Matthew Irwin, September 9, 1808, *Wisconsin Historical Collections*, 19: 326–30.

for they depended largely on deerskins, for which the home market was deficient, whereas the northern factories, dealing chiefly in hatters' furs, for which the home demand was greater than the supply, generally showed sizable profits. The northern posts also received other goods from the Indians—buffalo tallow and candles at Fort Osage, maple sugar at Mackinac, and lead at Fort Madison.[18] Mason and his successor carried on their activities from headquarters in Georgetown, whither the office had been moved from Philadelphia in 1807. Using the former Bank of Columbia building, a three-story brick building still standing on M Street in Georgetown, the Office of Indian Trade with its small staff and long hours conducted its manifold business.[19]

Apparently satisfied with the operation of the factories in these years, Congress continued the system in 1811 with a new basic law. Repeating most of the 1806 act and its supplements, the new law specifically authorized the factors and in a very general way described their duties. The capital stock of $300,000 was continued, and the president was authorized to open additional houses. An indication of the growing responsibility of the superintendent of Indian trade was the directive that in future he was to purchase and distribute, in addition to the goods for the trading houses, all the goods needed for annuities and presents to the Indians and for treaty purposes.[20]

Mason seems to have handled these duties effectively, but he and his successor operated within a bureaucratic snarl that must have been disconcerting at best. No clear administrative responsibility was given to the superintendent, although he seems to have operated vaguely within the War Department, which had general charge of Indian affairs. The secretary of war approved the dates for auctioning off the furs collected, and accounts relating to annuities and presents were reviewed by the War Department. The Indian trade accounts, on the other hand, had to be sent to the Treasury. Because the War Department and the Treasury Department were eventually serviced by different auditors and comptrollers, the separation of the paper work was troublesome. The appointment of factors and the opening and closing of factories, of course, had to be done under the eye of the president.[21]

18. Report of Mason, January 13, 1812, with attached documents, ASP:IA, 1: 782−94. A previous, less detailed report of April 12, 1810, showed a diminution of the capital amounting to roughly $44,500. Ibid., pp. 768−75.

19. An excellent description of the routine is given in Viola, *McKenney*, pp. 10−20. Extensive details on the operations of the Office of Indian Trade also appear in Peake, *Indian Factory System*, and Plaisance, "United States Government Factory System."

20. 2 *United States Statutes* 652−55.

21. Viola, *McKenney*, pp. 8−9, 306−7. Although the act of 1806 did not specify subordination of the superintendent of Indian trade to the secretary of war (his work was to be done under the direction of the president, with accounts sent to the Treasury Depart-

MAP I: United States Factory System, 1795–1822

(modern state lines shown)

The connection of the factory system with the War Department was important on the frontier, for the association of the factories and the military posts was very close. The success of the government trading operations was due in part to the protection and assistance given to the factories by

---

ment), it is interesting to note that Thomas L. McKenney's appointment as superintendent was signed by the secretary of war as well as by the president and bore the seal of the War Department. Commission, in Huntington Library, HM 1926.

TABLE 1: Government Trading Houses (Factories), 1795–1822

1. COLERAIN (Georgia)
   Established 1795; moved to Fort
   Wilkinson 1797

2. TELLICO (Tennessee)
   Established 1795; moved to
   Hiwassee 1807

3. FORT WILKINSON (Georgia)
   Established 1797; moved to
   Ocmulgee Old Fields 1806;
   designated Fort Hawkins 1808

4. FORT ST. STEPHENS (Alabama)
   Established 1802; moved to Fort
   Confederation 1817

5. CHICKASAW BLUFFS (Tennessee)
   Established 1802; moved to
   Spadra Bluffs 1818

6. FORT WAYNE (Indiana)
   Established 1802; closed 1812

7. DETROIT (Michigan)
   Established 1802; closed 1805

8. CHICAGO (Illinois)
   Established 1805; destroyed 1812;
   reopened 1815; closed 1821

9. BELLE FONTAINE (Missouri)
   Established 1805; closed 1808

10. NATCHITOCHES (Louisiana)
    Established 1805; moved to
    Sulphur Fork 1818

11. ARKANSAS POST (Arkansas)
    Established 1805; closed 1810

12. SANDUSKY (Ohio)
    Established 1806; destroyed 1812

13. OCMULGEE OLD FIELDS (Georgia)
    Established 1806; designated
    Fort Hawkins 1808

14. HIWASSEE (Tennessee)
    Established 1807; closed 1811

15. FORT OSAGE [Fort Clark] (Missouri)
    Established 1808; reopened at Arrow

Rock 1813; reestablished 1815;
closed 1822

16. FORT MACKINAC (Michigan)
    Established 1808; captured by
    British 1812

17. FORT MADISON (Iowa)
    Established 1808; closed 1812

18. FORT HAWKINS (Georgia)
    Designated 1808; moved to Fort
    Mitchell 1817

19. GREEN BAY (Wisconsin)
    Established 1815; closed 1821

20. PRAIRIE DU CHIEN (Wisconsin)
    Established 1815; closed 1822

21. FORT CONFEDERATION (Alabama)
    Established 1817; closed 1822

22. FORT MITCHELL (Alabama)
    Subagency of Fort Hawkins 1816;
    principal factory 1817; closed 1819

23. FORT JOHNSON [Le Moin] (Illinois)
    Branch of Prairie du Chien 1817;
    moved to Fort Edwards 1819

24. SPADRA BLUFFS (Arkansas)
    Established 1818; closed 1822

25. SULPHUR FORK (Arkansas)
    Established 1818; closed 1822

26. FORT EDWARDS (Illinois)
    Established 1819; moved to Fort
    Armstrong 1821

27. MARAIS DES CYGNES (Missouri)
    Branch of Fort Osage 1820; inde-
    pendent factory 1821; closed 1822

28. FORT ARMSTRONG (Illinois)
    Established 1821; closed 1822

29. ST. PETERS (Minnesota)
    Authorized 1821 as consolidation
    of Green Bay and Chicago; never
    opened

Note: Dates are approximate, for dates of authorization and actual opening, and dates
for termination and actual closing, were not always the same.

the regular army garrisons. All but four of the trading houses were in the shadow of an existing military post or were themselves the occasion for the building of a fort. The forts protected the factories, the presence of the soldiers enhanced the factors' prestige in the eyes of the Indians, and the troops were sometimes the only labor force on hand to build the factories, transport their goods, and aid in the beating and packing of furs.[22]

ATTACK AND SUPPORT

The promising state of the factories was devastated by the War of 1812. The British and the Indians seized the trading houses at Mackinac, Chicago, Sandusky, and Fort Wayne, and the army officer at Fort Madison ordered the destruction of the store there to prevent the goods from falling into the hands of the enemy. The estimated loss was $43,369.61.[23]

This serious economic blow was quickly overcome, however. When Mason reported on the operation of the system from 1811 through 1815, he was able to indicate a net gain of nearly $12,500, even accounting for the destruction during the war. In 1815 the post at Chicago was reopened, and two new ones—at Green Bay and at Prairie du Chien—were established. Congress in the same year continued its game of renewing the enabling legislation, this time until March 4, 1817.[24]

More dangerous than the physical losses of the war were the changed conditions of the American fur trade after the Treaty of Ghent. The spirit of enterprise blossomed forth with the rise of American nationalism that came at the end of the war. When foreign traders were prohibited from the fur trade in 1816, the American Fur Company of John Jacob Astor began to push steadily for control of the fur trade in the area of the Great Lakes and the upper Mississippi. The years between the War of 1812 and the abolition of the factories in 1822 were years of dramatic conflict between the increasingly powerful private fur trading interests—powerful both economically and politically—and the embattled but defiant supporters of the government trading houses. The attacks and counterattacks filled official reports and the public press and provide a detailed picture of the American fur trade in the years after the war.

Some of the criticism of the factories came from western officials, who,

22. Francis Paul Prucha, *The Sword of the Republic: The United States Army on the Frontier, 1783–1846* (New York: Macmillan Company, 1969), pp. 99–101, 207.

23. Mason to William H. Crawford, February 9, 1816, ASP:IA, 2: 67–68, also Table Fm, p. 59. These and numerous other reports on the factory system are attached to the report sent to the Senate by Secretary of War Crawford, March 13, 1816, ibid., pp. 26–88.

24. Report of Mason, February 9, 1816, ASP:IA, 2: 67–68; 3 *United States Statutes* 239.

although friendly with private fur traders, might have been expected to know enough about conditions on the frontier to offer objective and valuable advice. One such person was Ninian Edwards, governor of Illinois Territory since 1809, who flatly told the secretary of war: "For my part, I have never been able to discover, and I defy any man to specify, a solitary public advantage that has resulted from it [the factory system] in this country." The system, he said, was "neither calculated to conciliate and accommodate the Indians, nor for successful competition with British traders." It was not extensive enough to provide for all the Indian tribes, and defects in its functioning—such as restrictions on credit and the requirement that the Indians bring in their furs to the factories—made it "good policy to abandon it."[25]

Another critic was the governor of Michigan Territory, Lewis Cass. As early as 1814 Cass had noted that the trading factories and "our economy in presents" had led the Indians to scorn the United States. "The Government," he told the secretary of war, "should never Come in contact with them, but in cases where its Dignity, its strength or its liberality will inspire them with respect or fear." After the War of 1812 he argued that there was sufficient private American capital to carry on the fur trade effectively and that there was no need then for the government to engage in the business; that, in fact, such mercantile enterprise made the government "obnoxious and contemptible" to the Indians. Since the Indians, if sober, were shrewd bargainers, the private traders could not take undue advantage of them. All that was necessary on the part of the government was to exclude liquor from the Indian country. "Believing as I do," Cass asserted, "that the system itself is radically incorrect I cannot but recommend its abolition."[26]

The Reverend Jedidiah Morse, reporting to the secretary of war in 1821 on conditions in the Indian country, returned a similar verdict. He found that the general consensus was against the system, and he advocated its abolition.[27]

The government officials responsible for the program were not so ready

25. Edwards to William H. Crawford, November 1815, ASP:IA, 2: 62–67.

26. Cass to John Armstrong, September 3, 1814, Carter, *Territorial Papers*, 10: 476; Cass to John C. Calhoun, September 14, 1818, *Wisconsin Historical Collections*, 20: 82–86. Cass had no sooner written to the secretary of war than he had second thoughts about his absolute rejection of the factory system, admitting that his opinion was "more speculative than practical." Consequences of abolition, he admitted, might be equally injurious. Cass to Calhoun, October 1, 1818, Records of the Office of Indian Affairs, Field Office Records, Michigan Superintendency, Letters Sent by the Superintendent, National Archives, Record Group 75 (M1, reel 4).

27. Jedidiah Morse, *A Report to the Secretary of War of the United States: On Indian Affairs* (New Haven: S. Converse, 1822), pp. 60–61. For an extensive survey of the criticism, see Peake, *Indian Factory System*, pp. 184–203.

to give up. Secretary of War William Crawford in 1816 advocated not only its continuation but its extension, with capital stock increased to $500,000. He wanted to use some of the extra money to establish a supply depot at St. Louis under an assistant superintendent, who would furnish goods not only to the government trading houses, but to respectable private traders under strict regulations. The financial problems of the factories did not overly concern Crawford, however, for profits were not the inducement for continuing them. "That inducement, if it exists at all," he observed, "must be found in the influence which it gives the Government over the Indian tribes within our limits, by administering to their wants, increasing their comforts, and promoting their happiness. The most obvious effect of that influence is the preservation of peace with them, and among themselves." He hoped by trade to develop in the Indians a concern for private property, and he showed unmistakably the growing humanitarian concerns of the advocates of the factories. His views, he concluded, were "substantially founded upon the conviction that it is the true policy and earnest desire of the Government to draw its savage neighbors within the pale of civilization." If, on the contrary, the goal was to gain all their lands as quickly as possible, then the trade ought to be abandoned to private interests. "The result," Crawford asserted, "would be continued warfare, attended by the extermination or expulsion of the aboriginal inhabitants of the country to more distant and less hospitable regions." But not for a moment would he accept such a policy, an idea "opposed to every act of the Government, from the declaration of independence to the present day." He wanted a "humane and benevolent policy" that would ultimately incorporate the Indians into "the great American family of freemen."[28]

Crawford had the strong support of John Mason, whose views he was no doubt echoing. But Mason resigned on April 1, 1816, pleading the necessity of attending to his private business because of his large family.[29]

Mason was replaced by Thomas Loraine McKenney, one of the key figures in the development of American Indian policy, a sentimental and romantic man who could not always keep his accounts straight, who lived beyond his means, and who was continually trying to advance his importance in the political circles of the day, but withal a sincere humanitarian committed to the welfare and betterment of the Indians. McKenney, born in Maryland in 1785, was a merchant in Georgetown when the War of 1812 broke out. After military duty in the war, he sought a federal office suited to his talents. At last he obtained the superintendency of Indian trade. Taking office on Good Friday, April 12, 1816, the pious McKenney prayed: "Al-

28. Report of Crawford to the Senate, March 13, 1816, ASP:IA, 2: 26–28.
29. Mason to Crawford, March 6, 1816, ASP:IA, 2: 70; Records of the Office of Indian Trade, Letters Sent, vol. C, p. 495, National Archives, Record Group 75 (M16, reel 3).

mighty God! This day I have sworn faithfully and honestly, to discharge the duties of Superintendent of Indian Trade—but as man in his best estate is weak and helpless, always liable to err; and continually subject to the casualties which often involve his good name, and his dearest interests,—I do most humbly beseech Thee to grant me in all my labors the assistance of thy Holy Spirit, through Jesus Christ our Lord. Amen."[30] McKenney needed spiritual succor, for he bore the brunt of the growing attacks made by the American Fur Company, some of which were aimed at him personally, not merely at the factory system.

McKenney used his office to further two intense and abiding views. One was an abhorrence of private traders, whom he saw as the source of immeasurable evil in the Indian country. "In the course of my Superintendence of the trade established with the several Indian Tribes," he wrote to the chairman of the House Committee on Indian Affairs in 1818, "it has become part of my duty to take cognizance of such checks as are known to operate against it. Among these, and foremost in this train, is the conduct of the private traders, than which it is impossible to conceive of any thing more obnoxious, if viewed in relation to the morals of the Indians; or more destructive of that pacific result which the U.S. factories are or may be calculated to produce."[31]

An example of McKenney's concern were the reports he received from Arkansas, where the traders were "almost literally drown[ing] that country with whiskey" and stirring up the Indians against the government posts. McKenney told the secretary of war:

> Indeed I am of opinion that this influence destroyed, a power would exist in the Factory . . . in withholding from them their looked for supplies, or granting them, as their bad or good conduct should dictate. But the Traders not only make them independent of the Gov[t] supplies, (which however is done at the cost of exactions and the most unexampled debauchery) but stimulate them to become hostile, with a view to their entire monopoly of their trade, which the prostration of the Factory would enable them to realize upon terms even more enriching than those which their inebriating policy already ensures to them.

McKenney's views were strongly supported by Major Thomas Biddle and by Colonel Henry Atkinson from their experiences on the military expedition up the Missouri River. Biddle saw the "impossibility of civilizing the

---

30. Prayer by McKenney, April 12, 1816, written on the back of his commission from President Madison, dated April 2, 1816, Huntington Library, HM 1926.

31. McKenney to Henry Southard, January 6, 1818, *Wisconsin Historical Collections*, 20: 12–16.

Early Indian Policy

1. Jefferson Indian Peace Medal

Thomas Jefferson was a key figure in the formulation of early Indian policy. His view of the unity of mankind and thus the innate equality of Indians and whites became the basis of humanitarian concern for the Indians and of the drive to educate them in the white man's civilization. This large medal bearing the president's likeness was the beginning of a series of round silver medals presented to Indian chiefs as a symbol of their allegiance to the United States.

2. Hopethle-Mico, a Creek Chief

The famous American artist John Trumbull made this pencil sketch of Hopethle-Mico when a Creek delegation came to New York in 1790 to negotiate a treaty with the United States. The artist wrote: "I had been desirous of obtaining portraits of some of these principal men, who possessed a dignity of manner, form, countenance and expression, worthy of Roman senators."

When a delegation of Osages and other Indians from the West came east in 1804 to confer with officials of the United States, some of them were drawn in crayon by the French artist Charles B. Saint Mémin. Payouska, an Osage chief, wears a large medal, an arm band, and a military uniform—all gifts highly prized by the Indians.

Although Secretary of War Henry Knox hoped to maintain peace with the Indians by dealing fairly with them, warfare broke out in the area north of the Ohio River when whites invaded the Indian lands. Fort Washington was established in 1789 at the site of present-day Cincinnati to serve as a base for military expeditions against the hostile Indians. After the Indians defeated the troops led by Josiah Harmar and Arthur St. Clair, General Anthony Wayne crushed Indian resistance at the Battle of Fallen Timbers in 1794.

3. Payouska, an Osage Chief

4. Henry Knox

5. Anthony Wayne

6. Fort Washington

7. William Clark

8. Meriwether Lewis

9. Zebulon M. Pike

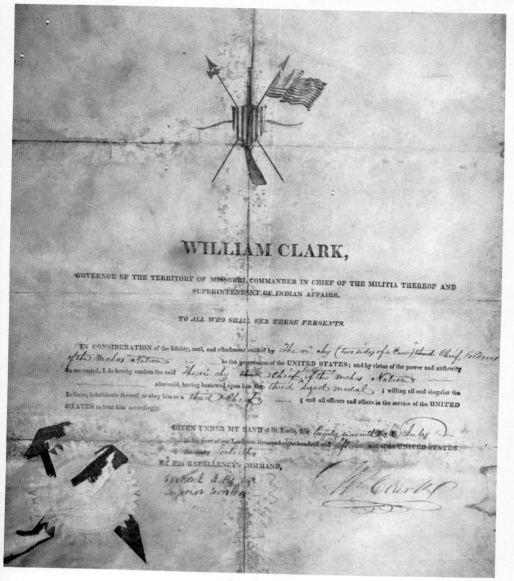

WILLIAM CLARK,

GOVERNOR OF THE TERRITORY OF MISSOURI, COMMANDER IN CHIEF OF THE MILITIA THEREOF AND SUPERINTENDENT OF INDIAN AFFAIRS.

TO ALL WHO SHALL SEE THESE PRESENTS.

IN CONSIDERATION of the fidelity, zeal, and attachment testified by *The ni chy (two sides of a Cow) third Chief Soldiers of the Mahas Nation* to the government of the UNITED STATES; and by virtue of the power and authority in me vested, I do hereby confirm the said *The ni chy third chief of the Mahas Nation* aforesaid, having bestowed upon him the *third sized medal*; willing all and singular the Indians, inhabitants thereof, to obey him as a *third Chief*; and all officers and others in the service of the UNITED STATES to treat him accordingly.

GIVEN UNDER MY HAND at St. Louis, this *twenty seaventh* day of *July* in the year of our Lord one thousand eight hundred and *fif* and of the UNITED STATES the thirty *fortieth*

BY HIS EXCELLENCY'S COMMAND,

10. Indian Certificate

Exploratory expeditions sought to convince the Indians in the West of the good-will of the United States government. The Lewis and Clark expedition of 1804–1806 was the most dramatic, and after its return Clark became a key official in dealing with the Indians. Pike's two expeditions—one to the upper Mississippi and another across the central plains—were means of extending the influence of the United States against the British and Spanish.

The portraits of these three men were painted in his Philadelphia studio by Charles Willson Peale.

As governor of Missouri Territory, William Clark presented medals and certificates to Indian chiefs who came to Portage des Sioux in the summer of 1815 to make peace after the War of 1812. This certificate with a small medal was given to a minor Omaha chief.

11. Pawnee Council

12. Fort Snelling

Samuel Seymour, official artist with Stephen H. Long's exploring expedition, painted a picture of the council with the Pawnee Indians held in October 1819. The painting served as the basis for this engraving from Edwin James's *Account of an Expedition from Pittsburgh to the Rocky Mountains.*

Fort Snelling, established in 1819, was a key post in the West. This painting by Captain Seth Eastman, who commanded Fort Snelling in the 1840s, was one of a series of pictures of military forts done by Eastman when he was called upon in the 1870s to decorate the room of the House Committee on Military Affairs in the United States Capitol.

McKenney (painted by Charles Loring Elliott) and Calhoun (painted by John Wesley Jarvis) were significant leaders in the formulation of American Indian policy. The former served as superintendent of Indian trade (1816–1822) and as first head of the Indian Office within the War Department (1824–1830) and the latter was secretary of war (1817–1825). The two men worked closely together to develop a policy that would lead the Indians toward the ways of white society.

13. Thomas Loraine McKenney

14. John C. Calhoun

15. Wisconsin Territorial Seal

16. Astor Indian Medal

17. Lewis Cass

The seal designed by William Wagner for the Territory of Wisconsin in 1838 showed by its Latin motto, *Civilitas successit barbarum*, the pervasive belief of the age in stages of society progressing from savagery to barbarism to civilization.

John Jacob Astor's American Fur Company, in its competition with the trading houses of the United States, produced silver medals for the Indians in imitation of the official medals distributed by the federal government.

Cass, as governor of Michigan Territory (1813–1831) and as secretary of war (1831–1836) was a dominant force in American Indian affairs. This daguerreotype of about 1850–1855 shows the firm character of the man that impressed the Indians and won their respect.

Indians, when exposed to the temptations and delusions of interested traders," and both he and Atkinson recommended that all private trading be prohibited and that the government take over the entire business.[32]

The second major interest of McKenney, in which he built upon the work of his predecessor but went far beyond it, was the use of the factories as positive agencies for promoting the education and civilization of the Indians. He expected the factors to be more than tradesmen; they were to be key men in spreading the gospel of agriculture and domestic arts, to supply necessary tools and information, and to be models of what could be done in taming the wilderness.[33] But in addition to his instructions to the men at the trading houses, McKenney hoped to inaugurate a federal policy of education and civilization, and in this he broadly expanded his position as superintendent of Indian trade.

When President Madison asked Congress to resume "the work of civilization" with the Indians and the House Committee on Indian Affairs requested information of McKenney, the superintendent not only urged expansion of the factory system ($200,000 for eight new factories and a supply depot at St. Louis), but he proposed a network of schools to be run by the missionary societies and supervised by the superintendent of Indian trade.[34]

McKenney and his friends worked hard to push the school system, but their maneuvering was conducted in an atmosphere of near desperation, for the defenders of the factories were being forced to the wall by their attackers. McKenney may, in fact, have hoped that turning the system into a great civilizing and Christianizing agency would increase the prospects of its staying alive and, if this were the case, that his salary would also be increased as the system expanded.[35]

Undoubtedly there were problems in the factory system after the War of 1812. Although the trading houses made a reasonable recovery from the devastation of the war, the panic of 1819, which struck a severe blow at the whole economy, brought losses to the factories and a call upon Congress to cut federal spending. Returns from the sale of furs declined, and charges of mismanagement were easy to make. McKenney made excuses for the factories: the short term authorizations for the system gave it no permanence

32. McKenney to John C. Calhoun, July 16, 1819, Carter, *Territorial Papers*, 19: 86; Thomas Biddle to Henry Atkinson, October 29, 1819, ASP:IA, 2: 201–3; Atkinson to Calhoun, November 26, 1819, ibid., p. 204.

33. See, for example, McKenney to George C. Sibley, October 21, 1816, in Office of Indian Trade, Letters Sent, vol. D, pp. 152–53 (M16, reel 4).

34. Viola, *McKenney*, pp. 33–35; see McKenney to Isaac Thomas, December 14 and 23, 1816, January 3, 1817, Office of Indian Trade, Letters Sent, vol. D, pp. 200–209, 209–15, 217–25 (M16, reel 4).

35. For the outcome of the education drive, see below, pp. 148–54.

and did not allow for major improvements; the restrictions on giving credit and presents to the Indians weakened its competitive stance against private traders; the prohibition against liquor turned many Indians toward more freehanded traders; and the machinations of the private traders harassed the factors in the field.[36]

McKenney continued to insist that an expanded factory system, with tightened control of private traders if they could not be excluded entirely from the trade, was the proper policy of the government. His emphasis was on the humanitarian effects of the government system, which were simply impossible under private traders motivated only by gain. He declared in 1818 that an end to the government factory system would cause the whole system of Indian reform to "tumble into ruins, and blast, at once, the happiness of thousands of Indians who now enjoy its benefits." He concluded:

> The existing Government system has its foundation in *benevolence*, and *reform*. Those are the two pillars, on which it rests. The Factors employed by the United States do not go to supply the more helpless parts of our Family with articles necessary for their support and security against the elements, and upon terms that embrace no more than a preservation of the capital employed, only, but also with implements of husbandry; with suitable instructions how to use them; and with invitations to seek their support from the Earth, and exchange, for her certain compensation, the uncertain products of the chase. The instructions [to] the Factors also, direct them to cultivate among the Indians a regard for, and attachment to our Government and Country.[37]

THE END OF THE FACTORIES

In the long run, McKenney's vision of benevolence and reform was overcome by John Jacob Astor and his political friends, who were alarmed by McKenney's efforts to maintain and expand the government system at the expense of private traders. Ramsay Crooks and Robert Stuart, Astor's lieutenants in the American Fur Company, wrote to Astor at the beginning of 1818 lamenting the competition of the factories, which had "become so

36. See the discussion of McKenney's defense of the factory system in Viola, *McKenney*, pp. 47–70.

37. McKenney to Calhoun, August 19, 1818, *Wisconsin Historical Collections*, 20: 69. Other statements of value are McKenney to Henry Southard, March 19, 1818, ibid., pp. 37–41; McKenney to Southard, November 30, December 30, 1820, March 17, 1821, Office of Indian Trade, Letters Sent, vol. F, pp. 99–104, 104–7, 151–53 (M16, reel 6); McKenney to Henry Johnson, December 27, 1821, ASP:IA, 2: 260–65.

numerous, and are of late provided with such extensive means, as threatens in a very few years more, to annihilate private competition, and throw the whole trade into the hands of Government." Astor was quick to pass on the complaint to Calhoun. "We have been great sufferers," he wrote, "so much so, that it would indeed be ruinous to continue the Trade under such circumstances."[38] And he sent Crooks to Washington to explain the "difficulties" in person. Crooks became a steady lobbyist against the factories, and a general harassment of the system started to come from Congress, beginning with a resolution asking the secretary of war to report "a system for providing for the abolition of the existing Indian trading establishment."[39]

That the concept of government trading houses had at best an uncertain hold on the mind of Congress is evident from the congressional refusal to extend the system more than a short period at a time. In March 1817 the factories were authorized until May 1, 1818; then their life was extended until March 1, 1819; in 1819 they were granted a reprieve for one more year, then for another one, and finally in 1821 for still another single year.[40] At each renewal the contest grew more bitter between the supporters of the factories and their opponents; after 1820 there was an all-out attempt on the part of the American Fur Company to have Congress do away with the system altogether. Crooks expressed his determination in a candid letter to Astor, who was then in Europe.

> I shall follow your advice in again visiting Washington, and will use every fair means to obtain a decision on the Public Trading House system. Last session a respectable majority voted against their continuance, but Congress had to rise on the 3d March without having time to act finally on the subject, in consequence of the Government Officers having resorted to every means in their power to delay its consideration. It will be brought forward early this session, and I have reason to think will be warmly supported, for enough is now known of the subject to excite enquiry, and if a thorough investigation is had, the abolition of these useless establishments is in my opinion sure. Great efforts will be made by Mr McKenney, & his

38. Crooks and Stuart to Astor, January 24, 1818, *Wisconsin Historical Collections*, 20: 26; Astor to Calhoun, March 4, 1818, *Papers of John C. Calhoun*, ed. Robert L. Meriwether, W. Edwin Hemphill, and Clyde N. Wilson, 14 vols. to date (Columbia: University of South Carolina Press, 1959–), 2: 191–92. There is an account of the American Fur Company's opposition to the factory system in Kenneth Wiggins Porter, *John Jacob Astor, Business Man*, 2 vols. (Cambridge: Harvard University Press, 1931), 2: 709–14.

39. *House Journal*, 15–1, serial 4, p. 420. Calhoun's reply of December 5, 1818, is in ASP:IA, 2: 181–85; it follows closely McKenney to Calhoun, August 14, 1818, *Wisconsin Historical Collections*, 20: 66–79.

40. 3 *United States Statutes* 363, 428, 514, 544, 641.

friends to save the Factories. His official reports to the Indian Committee will villify the Traders, and whine over the unfortunate & helpless conditions of the poor Indians, who will be left to the mercy of these unprincipled private traders; but all this will avail him little, for his canting is too well known, and his only resource will be falsehood, to which he has more than once resorted. Exposition will become necessary, and may involve us in a paper war, but the consequences must be encountered; for I cannot, and will not tamely submit to his scurilous abuse.[41]

The American Fur Company and the St. Louis fur traders enlisted the aid of Senator Thomas Hart Benton, who entered the Senate in 1821 and who became a great supporter of western interests. With vigorous rhetoric and biting sarcasm, he railed against the factories in 1822. He asserted that great abuses had been committed in the purchase of goods by the superintendent, who had bought some goods ill suited to the Indian trade and others of bad quality and had purchased goods at high prices in eastern markets when they would have cost less in western ones. He accused the superintendent of mismanagement in the disposition of goods to the Indians and in the sale of the furs and peltries taken in trade. Benton was at his best in ridiculing allegedly useless goods purchased for the factories. In the list of items sent out in 1820, he hit upon eight gross of jew's harps. He had fun regaling the Senate with examples of music that would sooth savage breasts. The jew's harps, he said, were

> precisely adapted to the purposes of the superintendent, in reclaiming the savage from the hunter state. The first state after that, in the road to refined life, is the pastoral, and without music the tawney-colored Corydons and the red-skinned Amaryllises, "*recubans sub tegmine fagi*," upon the banks of the Missouri and the Mississippi, could make no progress in the delightful business of love and sentiment. Even if the factories should be abolished, these harps might not be lost. They might be "hung upon the willows," and Æolus, as he passes by, might discourse upon them melancholy music, "soft and sad," adapted to the vicissitudes of human affairs, the death of the factories, and the loss of that innocent age they were intended to introduce.[42]

This was unfair, of course, for jew's harps were a standard article in the Indian trade, and Benton's friends of the American Fur Company sent large

---

41. Crooks to Astor, November 30, 1821, American Fur Company Letter Books, 2: 177–78, photostatic copies at the State Historical Society of Wisconsin.

42. *Annals of Congress*, 17th Congress, 1st session, pp. 319–20.

numbers of them to the frontier. But Benton offered more than amusing ridicule. He produced reports from Indian agents John Biddle and Benjamin O'Fallon, from John R. Bell, an army officer who had accompanied the expedition of Stephen H. Long in 1820, and from Ramsay Crooks himself, all denouncing the iniquities of the factory system. O'Fallon, in addition, condemned the misdeeds of McKenney and his agents, who were alleged to be growing rich in the service.[43]

Benton did his work well. He succeeded in amending a bill introduced for the abolition of the factories by providing that the business of liquidating the factories be taken out of the hands of McKenney and the factors and assigned to special agents. So amended, the bill to terminate the factory system became law on May 6, 1822.[44] Ramsay Crooks congratulated Senator Benton on the victory: "The result is the best possible proof of the value to the country of talents, intelligence, & perseverance; and you deserve the unqualified thanks of the community for destroying the pious monster, since to your unwearied exertions, and sound practical knowledge of the whole subject, the country is indebted for its deliverance from so gross and [un]holy an imposition."[45] The two had sufficient reason for rejoicing. The trade now became the unimpeded domain of the private traders and the powerful fur company.

Although the law specified that the factories be closed on June 3, 1822, in fact the process dragged out for a number of years. Benton's insistence that the closing be done by others than McKenney and his agents indicated his hope that evidence of fraud and mismanagement would be uncovered. McKenney tried in vain to get permission for the present employees to close out the business. Instead, George Graham, who at one time had served as acting secretary of war, was put in charge of the liquidation. He was familiar with the operations of the factory system, but the other special agents knew little about the business. Considerable losses were incurred as Graham and his men sought to sell or otherwise dispose of the property. An investigation by the House of Representatives exonerated McKenney in 1823 of any misdeeds in his handling of the factory business, but it was not until 1833 that all his accounts were straightened out.[46]

In the heyday of the factories during Jefferson's administration, the

43. The reports of these critics are printed in ASP:IA, 2: 326–32. A long rebuttal by McKenney with supporting documents appears ibid., pp. 354–64. The same material is printed in *Senate Document* no. 60, 17–1, serial 59.

44. 3 *United States Statutes* 679–80.

45. Crooks to Benton, April 1, 1822, American Fur Company Letter Books, 2: 241.

46. The story of the liquidation of the factories and of the charges brought against McKenney for mismanagement is told in Viola, *McKenney*, pp. 71–84. For documents on the closing of the factories, see *House Report* no. 104, 17–2, serial 87; *House Report* no. 129, 18–1, serial 106; and *House Document* no. 61, 18–2, serial 116.

United States had written into treaties with the Sacs and Foxes and with the Osages a promise to establish and permanently maintain trading houses near them. With the abolition of the factories, these obligations were quietly abrogated by new treaties, in which the tribes agreed to release the government from its promise in return for payment in goods—$1,000 worth for the Sacs and Foxes and $2,329.40 for the Osages—taken from the closing factories.[47]

It cannot be said that the conduct of the Indian trade by the federal government was a failure, for the system was never really given a full chance. Unable to concede that circumstances might demand a government monopoly of the trade in order to end abuses and to supply the Indians fairly with the goods they needed, the government admitted a dual system, allowing private traders to engage in the trade (under a less than rigorous licensing system) while at the same time engaging in the trade itself on a nonprofit basis. Once the private traders came into their own after the War of 1812, they squeezed out the factory system, which had never had more than halfhearted support from Congress, despite the strong rational arguments made in its behalf by McKenney, Calhoun, and other ardent supporters. The ineffectiveness of the factories, which their critics charged, was belied by the opposition itself, for the violence of the attacks is indication enough that the factories were offering serious competition. It may be that the proponents put too much burden on the system. Instead of working to correct recognized economic weaknesses, they intended to use the trading houses as a measure for benevolence and reform, humanitarian notions that could not stand up against the hardheaded, if not ruthless, economic policies of John Jacob Astor.[48] But the hope of some fair means by which the Indians could be supplied recurred again and again, and the dream of civilizing them came to depend on other means than the factory system, on which Thomas L. McKenney had pinned such high hopes.

47. Kappler, pp. 76, 95, 201–2.
48. The two final chapters in Peake, *Indian Factory System*, summarize the various reasons proposed for the system's failure.

CHAPTER 5

Civilization and Education

Civilization. Agriculture and Domestic Industry. Christianization. The Role of Thomas L. McKenney. The Civilization Fund and Indian Schools. Jedidiah Morse's Report.

Much of the legislative program that established Indian policy aimed to avoid conflicts between white citizens and the Indians. It was thus largely negative and restrictive, as it sought to regulate trade and intercourse between the two races. Even the government trading houses, although they contained certain positive features in supplying the Indians with useful goods at fair prices and with good example, had as their primary objective the elimination of abuses in the fur trade.

Parallel to these restraining activities was a positive constructive attempt to change the Indians and their cultural patterns. Operating under the principles of the Enlightenment and of Christian philanthropy, government officials proposed to bring civilization to the Indians. It is here that the benevolent and paternalistic aspects of Indian policy appear most clearly. Although the first attempts were feeble and sporadic, they foreshadowed increasingly powerful efforts through the nineteenth century to Americanize the Indians.

CIVILIZATION

The proposals made to better the condition of the Indians all gave evidence of a deepseated and common conviction of what *civilization* meant, even though most of the officials concerned never bothered to think philosophically about the concept. They relied on the accepted wisdom of the day, which reflected ideas that were part of their Western European heritage.[1] *To civilize* meant to bring to a state of civility out of a state of rudeness and barbarism, to enlighten and refine. It meant as a minimum to lead persons who lived a natural life in the wilderness, relying upon hunting and gathering, to a state of society dependent upon agriculture and domestic arts (spinning and weaving); to this was added instruction in reading, writing, arithmetic, and the truths of the Christian religion.

The place of American Indians in the scheme of civilization depended on the way Americans viewed the Indians. Opinions varied from the extreme disdain of the aggressive frontiersman, who equated the Indians with wild beasts of the forest fit to be hunted down at will, to the romantic ideas of novelists like James Fenimore Cooper and poets like Henry Wadsworth Longfellow, who exalted the superhuman qualities of the "noble savage." But in between, among the responsible and respected public figures in the first decades of United States development, there was a reasonable consensus that was the underpinning of official policy toward the Indians.[2]

Among the first generation of American statesmen, Thomas Jefferson was surely the most important theorizer about the aborigines. He was a man of tremendous speculative interests, a scientist (according to the definition of his age) as well as a political philosopher, and one who so influenced his generation that we correctly speak of his age in American history as "Jeffersonian." Jefferson, setting a pattern that was not to be successfully challenged, considered the Indian to be by nature equal to the white man. Although he strongly suspected that the black was an inferior creature, he never for a moment relegated the Indian to such status. Thus he wrote un-

1. An excellent analysis of the history and meaning of the term *civilization* is in Charles A. Beard and Mary R. Beard, *The American Spirit: A Study of the Idea of Civilization in the United States* (New York: Macmillan Company, 1942), especially chapters 3–5, pp. 62–276. .

2. Several works deal with images of the Indian and theoretical speculatons about race. The most comprehensive is Robert F. Berkhofer, Jr., *The White Man's Indian: Images of the American Indian from Columbus to the Present* (New York: Alfred A. Knopf, 1978). See also Roy Harvey Pearce, *The Savages of America: A Study of the Indian and the Idea of Civilization* (Baltimore: Johns Hopkins Press, 1953), and a critique of the book by David Bidney, "The Idea of the Savage in North American Ethnohistory," *Journal of the History of Ideas* 15 (April 1954): 322–27. There are valuable insights in Winthrop D. Jordan, *White over Black: American Attitudes toward the Negro, 1550–1812* (Chapel Hill: University of North Carolina Press, 1968), although the book touches on Indians only incidentally. I also rely in this section on Francis Paul Prucha, "The Image of the Indian in Pre-Civil War America," *Indiana Historical Society Lectures, 1970–1971* (Indianapolis: Indiana Historical Society, 1971), pp. 2–19, from which some parts are taken directly.

equivocally in 1785: "I believe the Indian then to be in body and mind equal to the whiteman."[3]

His arguments rested on two principles. In the first place, he believed in an essential, fixed human nature, unchangeable by time or place, and he applied his principle of unity of mankind to the Indians. In the second place, as an ardent American, Jefferson could not accept a position that would have made the American natives a basically ignoble breed. In fact, his most detailed and most eloquent defense of the qualities of the Indians came in his *Notes on the State of Virginia*, in which he refuted the criticism of things American that appeared in the celebrated work of the French naturalist Georges Louis Leclerc de Buffon, who described the Indian as deficient in stature, strength, energy, mental ability, and family attachments. These aspersions Jefferson answered fully, and he entered a point-by-point refutation of the slanders. He insisted that the Indian's "vivacity and activity" of mind was equal to that of the white in similar situations. And he quoted from the famous speech of Chief Logan, declaring that the whole orations of Demosthenes and Cicero could not produce a single passage superior to the chief's oratory. Physically, too, the Indians were a match for the whites. They were brave, active, and affectionate.[4]

Unable to ignore weaknesses in Indian life and customs as they existed before his eyes, Jefferson (like most of his contemporaries) explained the difference by environment. If the circumstances of their lives were appropriately changed, the Indians would be transformed. In that happy event, Jefferson asserted, "we shall probably find that they are formed in mind as well as in body, on the same module with the 'Homo sapiens Europeaus.'"[5]

So convinced was he of the racial equality or uniformity that he urged physical as well as cultural amalgamation of the Indians with the whites. "In truth," he wrote to the Indian agent Benjamin Hawkins, "the ultimate point of rest & happiness for them is to let our settlements and theirs meet and blend together, to intermix, and become one people." In his disappointment that during the War of 1812 the British had again stirred up Indian animosity toward the Americans, Jefferson lamented: "They would

---

3. Jefferson to François-Jean Chastellux, June 7, 1785, *The Papers of Thomas Jefferson*, ed. Julian Boyd, 19 vols. to date (Princeton: Princeton University Press, 1950–), 8: 186. The views of Jefferson and the Jeffersonians about the Indians are examined in Bernard W. Sheehan, *Seeds of Extinction: Jeffersonian Philanthropy and the American Indian* (Chapel Hill: University of North Carolina Press, 1973), part 1; Daniel J. Boorstin, *The Lost World of Thomas Jefferson* (New York: Henry Holt Company, 1948), pp. 81–88; Frederick M. Binder, *The Color Problem in Early National America as Viewed by John Adams, Jefferson, and Jackson* (The Hague: Mouton, 1968), pp. 82–119.

4. For Jefferson's refutation of Buffon, see his *Notes on the State of Virginia* (Richmond: J. W. Randolph, 1853), pp. 62–69, 215–18.

5. Ibid., p. 67.

have mixed their blood with ours, and been amalgamated and identified with us within no distant period of time. . . . but the interested and unprincipled policy of England has defeated all our labors for the salvation of these unfortunate people."[6]

Since the Indian by nature possessed the capacity for civilization, Jefferson admitted the responsibility of the whites to aid the natives in attaining that great goal. He knew, of course, that the Indians could not be transformed at a single stroke; but the movement toward civilization he held to be inexorable, and unless the Indians moved with the tide, they would surely be destroyed. That they would indeed move and eagerly accept white aid was judged to be a corollary of their rational nature. If there was a sense of urgency in Jefferson's hope for Indian melioration, it came from his conviction that haste was necessary because of the extraordinary pressures of white civilization.

Jefferson had a linear view of civilization; he saw an inevitable movement from the savagery of the Indians toward the European culture of his own coastal region. This he expressed in a striking comparison of geographical states with temporal ones. He wrote:

> Let a philosophic observer commence a journey from the savages of the Rocky Mountains, eastwardly towards our seacoast. These [the savages] he would observe in the earliest stage of association living under no law but that of nature, subsisting and covering themselves with the flesh and skins of wild beasts. He would next find those on our frontiers in the pastoral state, raising domestic animals to supply the defect of hunting. Then succeed our own semi-barbarous citizens, the pioneers of the advance of civilization, and so in his progress he would meet the gradual shades of improving man until he would reach his, as yet, most improved state in our seaport towns. This, in fact, is equivalent to a survey, in time, of the progress of man from the infancy of creation to the present day.[7]

Jefferson here expressed succinctly the "stages of society" theory that dominated the minds of the nineteenth century, the idea that the set stages of savagery, barbarism, and civilization followed one another inevitably, as the history of all human societies had shown. If the whites had gone through that process over the centuries, there was no reason to doubt that the Indians would follow the same route.[8]

6. Jefferson to Hawkins, February 18, 1803, *The Works of Thomas Jefferson*, ed. Paul Leicester Ford, 12 vols. (New York: G. P. Putnam's Sons, 1904–1905), 9: 447; and Jefferson to Baron von Humboldt, December 6, 1813, ibid., 11: 353.

7. Jefferson to William Ludlow, September 6, 1824, *The Writings of Thomas Jefferson*, ed. Andrew A. Lipscomb, 20 vols. (Washington: Thomas Jefferson Memorial Association, 1903–1904), 16: 74–75.

8. The long history of the theory of stages of society based on different modes of sub-

Jefferson and his contemporaries did not think that the Indians would take as long to reach civilization as had their own European ancestors. The process could be speeded up by radical changes in the conditions of Indian society, and the Jeffersonians and their heirs set about to make those changes. Jefferson strongly urged the Indians to accept the white man's ways. And for this he had a single formula. The hunter state must be exchanged for an agricultural state; the haphazard life dependent upon the chase must give way to a secure and comfortable existence marked by industry and thrift; private property must replace communal ownership. By example and by education these changes could be wrought. The central point was conversion to farming, which was proper enough in light of Jefferson's agrarian propensities.

In Jefferson's mind there was no contradiction or equivocation in working for the Indians' advancement and at the same time gradually reducing the land they held. It was not an opposition of policies, one working for the education and civilization of the Indians, the other seeking to relieve them of their land for the benefit of the whites. These were two sides of the one coin. At the same time that the whites called for more land, the Indians, by conversion to an agricultural existence, would need less land, and they would exchange their excess land for the trade goods produced by the whites. Nor was Jefferson unmindful of benevolence toward the Indians. "In leading them thus to agriculture, to manufactures, and civilization," he told Congress on January 18, 1803; "in bringing together their and our sentiments, and in preparing them ultimately to participate in the benefits of our Government, I trust and believe we are acting for their greatest good."[9]

Although Jefferson was the chief theorist, his view was common. In the early days of the Continental Congress the doctrine received formal approval in a resolution of 1776, which declared that "a friendly commerce between the people of the United Colonies and the Indians, and the propagation of the gospel, and the cultivation of the civil arts among the latter,

---

sistence is traced in Ronald L. Meek, *Social Science and the Ignoble Savage* (Cambridge: Cambridge University Press, 1976). A classic account of the theory came near the end of the nineteenth century in Lewis Henry Morgan, *Ancient Society; or, Researches in the Lines of Human Progress from Savagery through Barbarism to Civilization* (New York: Henry Holt and Company, 1877). An interesting example of the pervasiveness of the theory can be seen in the Territory of Wisconsin, which in 1838 adopted an official seal picturing an Indian surrounded by a farmer, a steamboat, a pile of lead ingots, a lighthouse, a schoolhouse, and a representation of the territorial capitol, with the Latin motto *Civilitas Successit Barbarum*. See John O. Holzheuter, "Wisconsin's Flag," *Wisconsin Magazine of History* 63 (Winter 1979–1980): 91–121.

9. Jefferson to Benjamin Hawkins, February 18, 1803, *Works*, ed. Ford, 9: 447; James D. Richardson, comp., *A Compilation of the Messages and Papers of the Presidents, 1789–1897*, 10 vols. (Washington: GPO, 1896–1899), 1: 352.

may produce many and inestimable advantages to both," and Congress directed the commissioners for Indian affairs to investigate places among the Indians for the residence of ministers and teachers. Secretary of War Knox, in his first report on Indian affairs under the Constitution, admitted that the civilization of the Indians would be "an operation of complicated difficulty," which would require deep knowledge of human nature and patient perseverance in wise policies, but he did not doubt its possibility. Missionaries, he thought, should be appointed to reside among the Indians and supplied with the necessary implements and stock for farming. In instructions to General Rufus Putnam, whom he sent in 1792 to treat with the Indians near Lake Erie, Knox directed Putnam to make clear to the Indians the desire of the United States to impart to them "the blessings of civilization, as the only mean[s] of perpetuating them on the earth" and to inform them that the government was willing to bear the expense of teaching them to read and write and to practice the agricultural arts of the whites.[10]

President Washington was moved by similar considerations when he outlined an Indian policy for the United States. He had asked Congress in 1791 to undertake experiments for bringing civilization to the Indians and in the following year repeated his plea. Thereupon Congress in the intercourse law of 1793 provided that "in order to promote civilization among the friendly Indian tribes, and to secure the continuance of their friendship," the president might furnish them with domestic animals and the tools of husbandry, as well as other goods and money. Temporary agents sent to the tribes would have the same purposes, and twenty thousand dollars a year was allowed for the gifts and for payment of the agents. Washington in 1795 noted with pleasure that the results of the law seemed promising, and the law of 1796 retained the civilization provision, although the appropriation was cut to fifteen thousand. This measure was repeated in the laws of 1799 and 1802.[11]

Even Lewis Cass, whose eighteen years as governor of Michigan Territory (1813–1831) had given him close contacts with the Indians and led him often to judge harshly the present conditions of the Indians, basically agreed with Jefferson. While leaving untouched as much as possible the peculiar aboriginal institutions and customs, he wanted to encourage the Indians to adopt individual ownership of property, assist them in opening farms and procuring domestic animals and agricultural implements, and employ honest and zealous men to instruct them as far and as fast as their

10. JCC, 4: 111; Knox to Washington, July 7, 1789, ASP:IA, 1: 53–54; Knox to Putnam, May 22, 1792, ibid., p. 235.

11. Washington's messages of October 25, 1791, November 6, 1792, and December 8, 1795, Fred L. Israel, ed., *The State of the Union Messages of the Presidents, 1790–1966*, 3 vols. (New York: Chelsea House, 1966), 1: 9, 14, 30.

capabilities permitted. Education was essential. Cass openly despaired of doing very much to change the habits or opinions of adult Indians. "Our hopes," he asserted, "must rest upon the rising generation. And, certainly, many of our missionary schools exhibit striking examples of the docility and capacity of their Indian pupils, and offer cheering prospects for the philanthropist." His aid to the missionary teacher Isaac McCoy indicated a willingness to promote in practice what he preached in principle. William Clark, Cass's counterpart on the Mississippi and Missouri rivers, has been characterized as a "Jeffersonian man on the frontier," who believed that Indian assimilation could be attained by altering the Indians' environment.[12]

Emphasis on the Enlightenment thought of the Jeffersonians in the formation of American policy, however, overlooks an even more important and enduring influence: the dominance of evangelical (that is, biblical) Christianity in American society. The views about the nature of the Indians and the possibility of their transformation held by the rationalists and the churchmen were much the same if not identical. But the basis was different. One built on the philosophy of the Enlightenment, on the laws of nature discovered in God's creation by rational man. The other was a product of a surge of evangelical religion that came with the Second Great Awakening at the turn of the century, a new missionary spirit, a revivalism that was to be a dominant mark of Protestant Christian America for a full century and more. The unity of mankind, firmly anchored in the story of man's creation in Genesis, became and remained a fundamental tenet in the nation's Indian policy.

Thomas L. McKenney, as superintendent of Indian trade and then head of the Office of Indian Affairs, whose influence on federal Indian affairs was unmatched between the War of 1812 and the removal of the Indians to west of the Mississippi after 1830, was a good example of the strong Christian influence among the policy makers. McKenney, of Quaker background, can hardly be considered a man of the Enlightenment. He was a *Christian* humanitarian, for whom the civilization and Christianization of the Indians was of great moment. He was unequivocal in his stand on the equality of the races and the reasons for his opinion. In a letter of 1818 asking for a copy of a manuscript by Lewis Cass on Indian relations, McKenney said: "I will be gratified, I am sure, with a perusal of Gov. Gass's view of our Indian relations. I hope he has considered them as Human Beings,—because, if he has not, I shall believe the good book is profane to him, which says, 'of *one blood*,' God made all the nations to dwell upon

12. Report of the secretary of war, November 31, 1831, *House Executive Document* no. 2, 22–1, serial 216, pp. 27–34; Cass, "Indians of North America," *North American Review* 22 (January 1826): 115, 118–19; Jerome O. Steffen, *William Clark: Jeffersonian Man on the Frontier* (Norman: University of Oklahoma Press, 1977).

the face of the earth.'"[13] As a tireless instigator of missionary efforts for the Indians, McKenney cooperated with the missionary societies that sprang up or were revitalized at the beginning of the century.

AGRICULTURE AND DOMESTIC INDUSTRY

The work of civilization got well under way first among the Cherokees, for the secretaries of war told the agents to that nation that it would be a principal object of their work to introduce among the women the art of spinning and weaving and among the men "a taste for raising of stock and Agriculture." They enjoined the agents to operate a school to teach the women and promised them spinning wheels and other apparatus necessary for producing linen and cotton cloth and the agricultural implements and livestock essential for the farms. A specified sum of money was authorized for these projects.[14]

The civilization of the Indians by instructing them in agricultural and household arts, of course, received vigorous support from Thomas Jefferson. In his first annual message to Congress, Jefferson enthusiastically reported success in the program under the intercourse laws; that the Indians had already come to realize the superiority of these means of obtaining clothing and subsistence over the precarious resources of hunting and fishing; and that instead of decreasing in numbers they were beginning to show an increase. The president expressed his views freely in his talks to the Indians. He told the Miamis, Potawatomis, and Weas, for example, on January 7, 1802: "We shall with great pleasure see your people become disposed to cultivate the earth, to raise herds of useful animals and to spin and weave, for their food and clothing. These resources are certain, they will never disappoint you, while those of hunting may fail, and expose your women and children to the miseries of hunger and cold. We will with pleasure furnish you with implements for the most necessary arts, and with persons who may instruct how to make and use them."[15]

13. McKenney to Christopher Vandeventer, June 21, 1818, Christopher Vandeventer Collection, Clements Library, University of Michigan (note supplied by Herman J. Viola). McKenney's humanitarianism is fully discussed in Herman J. Viola, *Thomas L. McKenney: Architect of America's Early Indian Policy, 1816–1830* (Chicago: Swallow Press, 1974).

14. James McHenry to Thomas Lewis, March 30, 1799, and Henry Dearborn to Return J. Meigs, May 15, 1801, SW IA LS, vol. A, pp. 29–35, 43–49 (M15, reel 1). The importance of these civilizing measures can be seen from the prominent position they are given in the long instructions to the agents.

15. Message of December 8, 1801, Israel, *State of the Union Messages*, 1: 58; SW IA LS, vol. A, p. 143 (M15, reel 1).

Jefferson's views were ardently promoted by Secretary of War Henry Dearborn, who kept up a constant battery of instructions to the agents on the use of implements made available under the intercourse laws. He wrote in the name of the president to the territorial governors of the Northwest Territory, Mississippi Territory, and Indiana Territory to encourage them to promote energetically the government's plan for civilizing the Indians, and he authorized the employment of blacksmiths and carpenters, necessary to keep the plows and other implements in working order.[16] Dearborn expressed his optimism to the Creek agent in 1803:

> The progress made in the introduction of the arts of civilization among the Creeks must be highly pleasing to every benevolent mind, and in my opinion is conclusive evidence of the practicability of such improvements upon the state of society among the several Indian Nations as may ultimately destroy all distinctions between what are called Savages and civilized people. The contemplation of such a period however distant it may be is highly pleasing, and richly compensates for all our trouble and expense; and to those Gentlemen who have and shall be the individual agents in effecting such an honorable and benevolent system it must not only afford the most pleasant self approbation, but command the warmest plaudits of every good man.[17]

When word reached the War Department that one of the Indian agents was obstructing the work of civilization being carried on within his agency by a missionary establishment, he was warned that if he did not cease his opposition to the views of the government in this matter, he would be removed from his position.[18]

Jefferson, as he neared the end of his administration, saw in the state of Indian affairs a vindication of the policy of civilization. Those tribes who were "most advanced in the pursuits of industry" were the ones who were most friendly to the United States. The southern tribes, especially, were far ahead of the others in agriculture and the household arts and in proportion to this advancement identified their views with those of the United States.[19] It is impossible to know the full operation of the annual fifteen thou-

16. Dearborn to William Lyman, July 14, 1801, and to Charles Jouett, September 6, 1802, SW IA LS, vol. A, pp. 92–93 (M15, reel 1); Dearborn to William C. C. Claiborne, William H. Harrison, and Arthur St. Clair, February 23, 1802, ibid., p. 166. See also Dearborn to Silas Dinsmoor, May 8, 1802, in which the intentions of the government in its Indian policy are again clearly stated. Ibid., pp. 207–8.

17. Dearborn to Benjamin Hawkins, May 24, 1803, ibid., pp. 349–50.

18. John Smith to William Wells, July 9, 1807, ibid., vol. B, p. 324 (M15, reel 2). For a full account of the case, see Joseph R. Parsons, Jr., "Civilizing the Indians of the Old Northwest, 1800–1810," *Indiana Magazine of History* 56 (September 1960): 208–13.

19. Message of October 27, 1807, Israel, *State of the Union Messages*, 1: 91–92.

sand dollars authorized by the intercourse laws, for the Treasury Department kept no special account under that heading, and when the Senate in 1822 asked for information on the annual disposition of the fund, little was forthcoming from either the War Department or the Treasury. Secretary of War Calhoun, however, reported that he thought the principal expenditure had been made through the Cherokee, Creek, Chickasaw, and Choctaw agents for spinning wheels, looms, agricultural implements, and domestic animals.[20]

The annual fund provided by the intercourse laws for promotion of civilization among the Indians was not the only source from which the government could draw in providing plows and looms, blacksmiths and carpenters; for many of the treaties signed with the tribes also provided for such aid. The Treaty of New York with the Creeks and the Treaty of Holston with the Cherokees were early examples. The Delawares in 1804 were promised a yearly sum "to be exclusively appropriated to the purpose of ameliorating their condition and promoting their civilization," plus the employment of a person to teach them how to build fences, cultivate the earth, and practice the domestic arts. In addition, the United States agreed to deliver draft horses, cattle, hogs, and agricultural implements. Similar arrangements were made with other tribes, and sometimes the tribes were allowed to choose between annuities in the form of goods or money and special aids for developing agriculture. Furthermore, treaties often stipulated blacksmiths or other artificers and teachers in agricultural or domestic arts.[21]

Abortive attempts were made in 1821 and 1822 to make the licensed traders responsible for promoting the agricultural advance of the tribes they served. A bill introduced in January 1821, aiming primarily at the abolition of the factories and the tighter control of independent Indian traders, also included special features to promote the civilization of the Indians. The bill directed traders to live in fixed abodes on the land leased from the Indians, to set up blacksmith shops there for the Indians, to cultivate grain and fruit and raise domestic animals, to sell seed and stock to the Indians, and to induce them to become cultivators and livestock breeders. For his license, each trader would pay an annual fee that was to be used to buy seed and stock for the Indians and to build mills for them. Congress, however, did not act on the bill, and when the measure was reintroduced in January 1822, it again made no progress through the House.[22]

20. Calhoun to James Monroe, February 21, 1822, and report of William Lee, February 19, 1822, ASP:IA, 2: 326.

21. Kappler, pp. 28, 31, 36, 42, 70–71, 75, 93, 95, 186, 200.

22. *Annals of Congress*, 16th Congress, 2d session, pp. 958–59; *House Journal*, 17–1, serial 62, pp. 157, 543; original bill (H.R. 41), 17th Congress, 1st session.

CHRISTIANIZATION

The United States government accepted as allies in its work of civilization the Christian churches of the land, whose missionary energies were directed in part toward the Indians. These were in the main Protestant efforts; the early Catholic missionary work within the boundaries of the United States was sparse, and not until the end of the nineteenth century did Catholic missionaries come into prominence. But even Protestant missionaries at the beginning of the new nation were not much in evidence. Only a dozen missionaries survived at the end of the Revolutionary War to Christianize the Indians. But the Second Great Awakening that began at the end of the century stimulated new endeavors, and soon there was a group of eager missionary societies whose purpose it was to evangelize the heathen, including the Indians in their own nation. The most important of these groups was the American Board of Commissioners for Foreign Missions, founded in Boston in 1810 by Presbyterians and Congregationalists. Their goal, in good Protestant fashion, was to bring the gospel to the unenlightened.[23]

The churches engaged in a long and inconclusive debate over the precedence to be given to civilizing and to Christianizing. Did an Indian need to be civilized first, so that Christianity could "take"? "The Gospel, plain and simple as it is, and fitted by its nature for what it was designed to effect," one missionary wrote, "requires an intellect above that of a savage to comprehend. Nor is it at all to the dishonor of our holy faith that such men must be taught a previous lesson, and first of all be instructed in the emollient arts of life." Others held as firmly that the gospel itself was the greatest civilizing power. "Instead of waiting till Civilization fit our Indian neighbors for the gospel," one advocate said, "let us try whether the gospel will not be the most successful means of civilizing them."[24] But it was largely a theoretical squabble, for the two processes, civilizing and Christianizing, were inextricably mixed. When missionaries went among the Indians, they went to educate and to convert, and it would be difficult to tell where one activity ended and the other began. Nor did it matter to the government, which came to depend upon the church societies for civilizing work among the Indians without intending to promote any particular religion.

23. The best study of Protestant missionary efforts among the Indians before the Civil War is Robert F. Berkhofer, Jr., *Salvation and the Savage: An Analysis of Protestant Missions and American Indian Response, 1787–1862* (Lexington: University of Kentucky Press, 1965; reprinted with a new preface, New York: Atheneum, 1972).

24. Thaddeus M. Harris, *A Discourse, Preached November 6, 1823* (Boston, 1823), p. 8, and John M. Mason, *Hope for the Heathen: A Sermon Preached . . . before the New*

It was quietly understood, by government officials as well as by church leaders, that the American civilization offered to the Indians was *Christian* civilization, that Christianity was a component of civilization and could not and should not be separated from it. By the end of the nineteenth century, concepts of religion and civilization became entwined in the Americanism of the Protestants, but the seeds of such a union were well sprouted at the beginning of the nation's life. The missionary's goal, seen in this light, differed little from the goal of Washington, Jefferson, and other public statesmen. Take, for example, this statement of the United Foreign Missionary Society in 1823:

> Let then, missionary Institutions, established to convey to them the benefits of civilization and the blessings of Christianity, be efficiently supported; and, with cheering hope, you may look forward to the period when the savage shall be converted into the citizen; when the hunter shall be transformed into the mechanic; when the farm, the work shop, the School-House, and the Church shall adorn every Indian village; when the fruits of Industry, good order, and sound morals, shall bless every Indian dwelling; and when throughout the vast range of country from the Mississippi to the Pacific, the red man and the white man shall everywhere be found, mingling in the same benevolent and friendly feelings, fellow citizens of the same civil and religious community, and fellow-heirs to a glorious inheritance in the kingdom of Immanuel.[25]

To achieve such ideals, the mission stations among the Indians were primarily educational institutions, instructing the Indian children not only in piety, but in traditional learning and in industrious work habits.[26] As such, they were actively encouraged and supported by the United States government. Thus when the Presbyterian missionary Gideon Blackburn approached Jefferson and Dearborn in 1803 about aid for a school among the Cherokees, he was warmly received and permitted to open his school. Although he was told that he could expect no compensation from the government for his services, the secretary of war nevertheless instructed the Cherokee agent to erect a schoolhouse and to give necessary aid to start

---

York Missionary Society . . . , *November 7, 1797* (New York, 1797), p. 43, both quoted in Berkhofer, *Salvation and the Savage*, pp. 4–5. See the discussion in Berkhofer, pp. 4–15.

25. Records of the UFMS Board of Managers, May 5, 1823, quoted in Berkhofer, *Salvation and the Savage*, pp. 10–11.

26. Berkhofer, *Salvation and the Savage*, devotes a separate chapter to each of these areas of instruction and furnishes a detailed picture of the schools and other mission work of the church societies.

the project, "which should not require more than two or three hundred dollars for the first six months of its application."[27]

The first mission of the American Board of Commissioners for Foreign Missions was founded at Brainerd, Tennessee, in 1816 and received similar assistance from the government. Cyrus Kingsbury, founder of the school, applied to the War Department for support on the grounds that extending to the Indians the blessings that whites enjoyed was "not only a dictate of humanity, and a duty enjoined by the Gospel, but an act of justice." Secretary of War William H. Crawford greeted the request favorably; he told Kingsbury:

> the agent will be directed to erect a comfortable school-house, and another for the teacher and such as may board with him. . . . He will also be directed to furnish two ploughs, six hoes, and as many axes, for the purpose of introducing the art of cultivation among the pupils. Whenever he is informed that female children are received and taught in the school, and that a female teacher has been engaged, capable of teaching them to spin, weave, and sew, a loom and half a dozen spinning-wheels, and as many pair of cards, will be furnished. He will be directed, from time to time, to cause other school-houses to be erected, as they shall become necessary, and as the expectation of ultimate success shall justify the expenditure.

If the mission succeeded, Crawford assured the missionary, Congress would notice the good work and that "the means of forwarding your beneficent views will be more directly and liberally bestowed by that enlightened body."[28]

Kingsbury had explicit goals, which could easily be seconded by the War Department and the Indian agents. "I considered it to be the grand object of the present undertaking," he wrote to the American Board on November 26, 1816, "to impart to them that knowledge which is calculated to make them useful citizens, and pious Christians. In order to do this, it appeared necessary to instruct them in the various branches of common English

27. Dearborn to Meigs, July 1, 1803, SW IA LS, vol. A, pp. 354–55 (M15, reel 1); Dearborn to Blackburn, July 1, 1803, ibid., pp. 355–56; Dearborn to Blackburn, January 12, 1804, ibid., pp. 422–23. Blackburn continued his school until 1810, when ill health and financial difficulties forced him to withdraw.

28. Kingsbury to Crawford, May 2, 1816, and Crawford to Kingsbury, May 14, 1816, ASP:IA, 2: 477–78. Information on the Brainerd school is given in Viola, *McKenney*, pp. 32–33, and in Robert Sparks Walker, *Torchlights to the Cherokees: The Brainerd Mission* (New York: Macmillan Company, 1931). The Indian missionary work of Kingsbury is treated in Arthur H. DeRosier, Jr., "Cyrus Kingsbury: Missionary to the Choctaws," *Journal of Presbyterian History* 50 (Winter 1972): 267–87.

education, to form them to habits of industry, and to give them a competent knowledge of the economy of civilized life."[29]

THE ROLE OF THOMAS L. MCKENNEY

The close union of minds between government and the churches was exhibited in the attempt to make the factory system into a primary civilizing agency. Such was the dream, if not the obsession, of Thomas L. McKenney while he was superintendent of Indian trade from 1816 to 1822.[30] McKenney used his office to further his paramount interest, the civilization and Christianization of the Indians, and he sounded at times more like a missionary than a public official. "It is enough to know that Indians are Men," he wrote to a missionary of the American Board early in his tenure, "that like ourselves they are susceptible of pleasure, and of pain—that they have souls, the term of whose duration is co-extensive with our own—that like us they must live forever; and that we have the power not only to enhance their happiness in this world, but in the next also; and by our councils, and guidance, save souls that otherwise must perish!" He declared that the government was founded on pillars of mercy, that it was run by men who "would joyfully administer to them [the Indians] the cup of consolation, nor withhold it because of the color which an Indian Sun has burned upon their brothers."[31] As superintendent of Indian trade McKenney worked in close concert with missionaries to the Indians, prodding, encouraging, and supporting their efforts and interceding for them with the secretary of war.

McKenney's first goal was to turn the Indians toward agriculture, which would promote an interest in private property, stimulate hard work, and provide the stability and settled existence that the missionaries needed to build Christian communities. Despite a considerable lack of enthusiasm on the part of the Indians, he sent agricultural equipment and seeds to the factories and wanted the factors to encourage the Indians to trade for such goods by setting up model gardens and farms. "This is the way you will most effectually promote the *great object of the Govt.* towards these unenlightened people," he wrote. "Invite their attention to agriculture and the arts, and help them, for they are helpless. Our object is not to keep these Indians hunters eternally. We want to make citizens out of them, and

29. Quoted in Walker, *Torchlights*, p. 22.

30. There is ample discussion of McKenney's interest in civilizing the Indians through the factory system in Viola, *McKenney*, chap. 3, "The Factories and Indian Reform," pp. 21–46.

31. McKenney to Elias Cornelius, July 26, 1817, Records of the Office of Indian Trade, Letters Sent, vol. D, pp. 374–75, National Archives, Record Group 75 (M16, reel 4).

they must be first anchored to the soil, else they will be flaying about whilst there is any room for them in the wilderness or an animal to be trapped."[32]

McKenney also helped the missionaries directly. He sent letters and packages for them under his franking privilege, urged factors to support missionaries visiting their regions, and persuaded Secretary of War Calhoun to endorse missionary activities.[33]

Cyrus Kingsbury's work at Brainerd so impressed McKenney that he soon was actively promoting a network of similar schools in the Indian country. As he urged an expansion of the factory system to "serve the great object of humanity" by fostering cultural improvement among the Indians, he added to the proposal a system of schools to be run by the missionary societies under his supervision. He worked closely with the Kentucky Baptist Society for Propagating the Gospel among the Heathen and the American Board of Commissioners for Foreign Missions, who hoped to get government support for the Indian educational work they planned.[34]

McKenney was much encouraged by President James Monroe, who in his first annual message to Congress in December 1817 noted the rapid extinguishment of Indian titles in both north and south, and said:

> In this progress, which the rights of nature demand and nothing can prevent, marking a growth rapid and gigantic, it is our duty to make new efforts for the preservation, improvement, and civilization of the native inhabitants. The hunter state can exist only in the vast uncultivated desert. It yields to the more dense and compact form and greater force of civilized population; and of right it ought to yield, for the earth was given to mankind to support the greatest number of which it is capable, and no tribe or people have a right to withhold from the wants of others more than is necessary for their own support and comfort. It is gratifying to know that the reservations of land made by the treaties with the tribes on Lake Erie were made with a view to individual ownership among them and to the cultivation of the soil by all, and that an annual stipend has been pledged to supply their other wants. It will merit the consideration of Congress whether other provision not stipulated by treaty ought to be made for these tribes and for the advancement of the liberal and humane policy of the United States toward all the tribes within our limits, and more particularly for their improvement in the arts of civilized life.[35]

32. McKenney to Matthew Lyon, May 18, 1821, ibid., vol. F, p. 197 (M16, reel 6).
33. See the case of the Osage mission of the United Foreign Missionary Society, discussed in Viola, *McKenney*, pp. 27–32.
34. Ibid., pp. 33–37.
35. Israel, *State of the Union Messages*, 1: 152–53.

Working with Henry Southard, chairman of the House Committee on Indian Affairs, and other sympathetic congressmen, McKenney fought hard for a national school system for the Indians, to be supported by profits from an expanded factory system. "I certainly think," he told Southard, "Congress has it completely in its power to erect out of the materials of Indian reform a monument more durable and towering than those of ordinary dimensions, a monument as indestructible as justice, interesting as humanity—and lasting in time."[36] He and his missionary friends lobbied earnestly for the measure, and the House committee reported a bill on January 22, 1818, to extend the factory system with the addition of eight new factories and to provide schools for the Indians. The committee's arguments were typical of those advanced by the humanitarians: "In the present state of our country, one of two things seems to be necessary: either that those sons of the forest should be moralized or exterminated. Humanity would rejoice at the former, but shrink with horror from the latter. Put into the hands of their children the primer and the hoe, and they will naturally, in time, take hold of the plough; and, as their minds become enlightened and expand, the Bible will be their book, and they will grow up in habits of morality and industry, leave the chase to those whose minds are less cultivated, and become useful members of society." The committee noted the success of missionary societies in Africa and Asia and pointed out that the obstacles to be overcome among the Indians were considerably less.[37]

The bill submitted by the committee proposed to use profits from the factory system to support education of the Indians by directly endowing schools and by helping missionary societies to support their schools. The second provision was removed by amendment and a limit was set on the first of $10,000 annually, but the bill still did not pass. Perhaps it departed too much from the basic principle of the factory system, which specified that no profits were to be made out of the government trade with the Indians in order to undersell and gradually force out the petty traders.[38]

This was but a temporary delay, for McKenney did not waver in his resolve, and he stimulated a flood of petitions to Congress from religious groups in behalf of a measure (now left unspecified) for "the *security, preservation,* and *improvement* of the Indians." President Monroe reasserted the need to civilize the Indians, and the House committee reporting on the president's message in January 1819 praised the successful work being done by missionary societies among the Indians, asserting that "a more en-

36. McKenney to Southard, January 15, 1818, Office of Indian Trade, Letters Sent, vol. E, pp. 99–100 (M16, reel 5).

37. Report of January 22, 1818, ASP:IA, 2: 150–51.

38. *House Journal*, 15–1, serial 4, p. 169; original bill (H.R. 50), 15th Congress, 1st session.

ergetic and extensive system is necessary, to improve the various Indian tribes, in agriculture, education, and civilization." At the same time, it reported a bill authorizing the president to select such tribes as he thought best prepared for the change and to use whatever means seemed proper to civilize them.[39] When Senator Jeremiah Morrow of Ohio, chairman of the Senate Committee on Indian Affairs, asked McKenney how much money should be appropriated yearly for the civilization of the Indians, McKenney was quick to reply: "One hundred thousand dollars, annually. It is little enough since we got the Indians' land for an average of 2¾ cents the acre." The prudent senator cut the sum to ten thousand dollars and introduced a bill to that effect, which replaced the House bill.[40] What was won, however, was not an elaborate school system tied to the factories, but an annual appropriation for a civilization fund independent of the factories, which continued after the factories themselves were destroyed.

THE CIVILIZATION FUND AND INDIAN SCHOOLS

The "act making provision for the civilization of the Indian tribes adjoining the frontier settlements" became law on March 3, 1819. It appropriated ten thousand dollars annually for use at the president's discretion to further the civilization of the tribes wherever practicable by employing "capable persons of good moral character, to instruct them in the mode of agriculture suited to their situation; and for teaching their children in reading, writing, and arithmetic." The president and the secretary of war decided not to use the fund directly, but rather to spend it through the "benevolent societies" that had already established schools for the education of Indian children or would do so in future (under the encouragement of the fund). Secretary of War Calhoun issued a special circular that invited interested individuals or groups to apply for a share of the fund and called for information about their resources, the kind of education they proposed to impart, and the number of students to be instructed.[41]

The civilization fund was not without its critics. Congress repeatedly asked for reports on the functioning of the program and passed resolutions inquiring into the expediency of repealing the law. On May 4, 1822, Repre-

39. Message of Monroe, November 16, 1818, Israel, *State of the Union Messages,* 1: 163–64; report of Henry Southard, January 15, 1819, ASP:IA, 2: 185–86.

40. Congressional action can be followed in *House Document* no. 91, 15–2, serial 22; *Senate Journal,* 15–2, serial 13, pp. 288, 289, 323; and *House Journal,* 15–2, serial 16, pp. 188, 331, 333, 339. Morrow's interchange with McKenney is reported in Viola, *McKenney,* pp. 41–43.

41. 3 *United States Statutes* 516–17; report of Calhoun, January 15, 1820, ASP:IA, 2: 200–201; circular of September 3, 1819, ibid., p. 201.

sentative Thomas Metcalfe of Kentucky sought to eliminate the measure altogether by amendments to the supplementary intercourse act of 1822. He inveighed against the civilization fund on the grounds of inutility and cited numerous historical examples to show that all such attempts to civilize the Indians had ended in failure. Despite such attacks the annual appropriation continued, and the House Committee on Indian Affairs in 1824 reported enthusiastically on the program. The committee noted the twenty-one schools then in existence, all but three of which had been established after the act of 1819, and the more than eight hundred pupils "whose progress in the acquisition of an English education exceeds the most sanguine expectations that had been formed." It believed that the large contributions made toward the schools by the missionary societies had been stimulated by the annual appropriation of the government.[42]

When McKenney was appointed to head the Office of Indian Affairs in 1824, he continued to fight aggressively for the program. One of his early acts was to send a blistering circular to the Indian superintendents and agents reminding them of the solicitude of the government for the improvement of the Indians by means of the school system and the ten thousand dollars' annual appropriation for its support. It was the duty of the superintendents, McKenney declared, to "*sanction*, and *second*, this plan of renovating the morals and enlightening and improving these unfortunate people." Those who opposed the plan were opposing the government itself, paralyzing its program, and bringing the program into contempt in the eyes of the Indians, whom it was designed to benefit. McKenney continued to be enthusiastic about the program and its salutary effects. In November 1824 he reported 32 schools in operation, with 916 children, and he accepted the optimistic reports of the school directors as proof that nothing insuperable stood in the way of complete reformation of the Indians' lives. A year later he had lost none of his enthusiasm, and in 1826 he recommended that the annual allotment be increased, so great were the benefits being derived from the schools. Annual reports showed a steady increase in the number of schools, the enrollment of Indian pupils, and the religious groups taking part. These groups, encouraged by the government aid, devoted more and more from their private funds to the enterprise.[43]

Indian schools were materially aided also by special treaty provisions.

42. *Annals of Congress*, 17th Congress, 1st session, pp. 1792–1801; *House Report* no. 92, 18–1, serial 106.

43. Circular of August 7, 1824, OIA LS, vol. 1, p. 170 (M21, reel 1); McKenney to James Barbour, December 13, 1825, ibid., vol. 2, pp. 298–306 (M21, reel 2); McKenney to Calhoun, November 24, 1824, ASP:IA, 2: 522–24; McKenney to Barbour, November 20, 1826, ibid., pp. 671–72. A complete account of disbursements of the civilization fund, showing amounts, to whom payments were made, and purposes of grants, 1820–1844, is given in *House Document* no. 247, 28–1, serial 443.

Treaties with the Chippewas and the Potawatomis in 1826, for example, authorized an annual grant for schools, to be continued as long as Congress thought proper. Similarly, treaties with Winnebagos, Menominees, Kickapoos, Creeks, Cherokees, and others stipulated money for education. As the policy continued, sizable funds were provided. In the year 1834, thirty-five thousand dollars was due for schools under treaty provisions.[44]

Of special note among the attempts to provide white education for Indian youths was the Choctaw Academy, established in 1825 under the sponsorship of Richard M. Johnson, representative and senator from Kentucky and later vice president of the United States. Under the Choctaw Treaty of Doak's Stand in 1820, funds for education were provided from the sale of ceded lands, and in 1825 a new treaty added a six-thousand-dollar annuity for twenty years to support Choctaw schools. The chiefs desired to use part of the funds for a school outside the Choctaw Nation, where the influence of white civilization would be stronger. When the federal government approved the request, Johnson quickly seized upon the occasion to have the school established on his property near Great Crossings, in Scott County, Kentucky. The Baptist General Convention undertook the venture, and the Reverend Thomas Henderson was engaged to superintend the school. What developed was a boarding school for Indian boys that taught the standard elements of an English education and supplied training in mechanic arts. The students were primarily Choctaws, sent from the Indian Territory, but the school was open to other Indians and to local white boys as well. Johnson was a good promoter, no doubt in part because he profited from the venture, and Henderson an able director, and the school flourished for fifteen years. It reached its top enrollment of 188 in 1835.[45]

The goal of the Choctaw Academy was well expressed in 1831 by Elbert Herring, head of the Office of Indian Affairs:

> Many Indian youths . . . have already returned to their respective tribes, carrying with them the rudiments of learning, the elements of

44. Kappler, pp. 36, 193, 220, 274, 282, 287, 304, 307; George Dewey Harmon, *Sixty Years of Indian Affairs: Political, Economic, and Diplomatic, 1789–1850* (Chapel Hill: University of North Carolina Press, 1941), p. 380.

45. Kappler, pp. 193, 212. The history of the Choctaw Academy can be traced in the documents printed in *House Document* no. 109, 26–2, serial 384; expenses are tabulated in *House Document* no. 231, 27–2, serial 404. An excellent series of letters from Johnson to Henderson is in Thomas Henderson Papers (photostats), State Historical Society, Madison, Wisconsin. See also Mrs. Shelley D. Rouse, "Colonel Dick Johnson's Choctaw Academy: A Forgotten Educational Experiment," *Ohio Archaeological and Historical Publications* 25 (1916): 88–117; Carolyn Thomas Foreman, "The Choctaw Academy," *Chronicles of Oklahoma* 6 (December 1928): 543–80; Foreman, "The Choctaw Academy," ibid. 9 (December, 1931): 382–411; 10 (March 1932): 77–114.

morals, and the precepts of religion; all apparently calculated to subdue the habits, and soften the feelings of their kindred, and to prepare
the way for the gradual introduction of civilization and Christianity.
That such will be the result of the intellectual and moral cultivation
of a portion of the young of their respective tribes, on the life and
character of the Indians in their confederacies, cannot be predicted
with certainty. It is, however, an experiment creditable to our national council, and meriting its further patronage. It is an experiment
consecrated by our best feelings, delightful to the view of the patriot,
and dear to the heart of philanthropy; but time alone can disclose its
efficacy.[46]

The efficacy of the Indian schools was in fact not always evident. In the
formative years the system was inadequate, and even enthusiastic promoters like Thomas McKenney came to realize that. Because of the small
number of schools provided, only a few children in each tribe could be educated, and they were not enough to influence the character of the whole
tribe. Even those who enrolled in school often did not profit because at the
completion of their studies they had no means and little incentive to pursue a new life. So the student's only alternative was, as McKenney noted,
"to turn Indian again; and too often by his improved intelligence he becomes the oppressor of his less cultivated brothers." McKenney wanted to
furnish the educated Indians with land, a house, and agricultural implements, but no funds for the purpose were available.[47]

As the 1820s advanced, the initial expansion of Indian education occasioned by the civilization fund began to slacken. By 1830, there were fifty-
two schools with 1,512 students, but that was not a large proportion of the
total number of Indian children, even of the tribes where schools had been
established.[48] It had been McKenney's hope that once the system had
proved itself, Congress would increase the annual fund, but Congress refused to do so. When McKenney left office in 1830, he saw how far short of
his optimistic goals the reality was, and he came to support voluntary removal of the tribes as necessary for their preservation and improvement.
The deepseated conviction that the destiny of the Indians was acculturation and assimilation into white society had not changed; if it could not be
accomplished east of the Mississippi, then it would have to be pursued in
the West.

46. CIA Report, 1831, serial 216, p. 172.
47. Viola, *McKenney*, p. 194.
48. CIA Report, 1830, serial 206, pp. 166–68.

JEDIDIAH MORSE'S REPORT

The congruence of missionary and government endeavors on behalf of the Indians is well illustrated in the inspection of Indian tribes made in 1820 by the Reverend Jedidiah Morse, noted Congregational clergyman, editor, and geographer. Then in his sixtieth year, Morse had accepted commissions from two missionary societies to visit the Indians in order to acquire knowledge about them that would aid in devising plans for advancing their civilization and welfare. He proposed as well to serve as an agent of the federal government in his tour. President Monroe approved the plan, and Secretary of War Calhoun sent Morse an official commission, with an allowance of five hundred dollars and the promise of more if his expenses should exceed that amount. Calhoun expressed a desire for a prompt report so that the government could "avail itself of it in the future application of the fund for the civilization of the Indians."[49]

Morse received detailed instructions about what he was to look for: "the actual condition of the various tribes . . . in a religious, moral, and political point of view." Calhoun wanted information on the number of the Indians, the extent of their territory, their mode of life, and the character and disposition of their chiefs. He further directed Morse:

> You will also particularly report on the number of schools, their position, the number and character of the teachers, the number of scholars of each sex, the plan of education, with the degree of success which appears to attend the respective schools, and the disposition which appears to exist in the tribes, and with their chief men, to promote among them education and civilization. You will also report your opinion as to the improvements which may be made, and the new establishments, to promote the object of the government in civilizing the Indians, which can be advantageously formed.

Calhoun asked as well for a report on the character of the Indian trade and on any other points that might be useful to the government.[50]

Morse reported to Congress and the president on various parts of his charge from time to time and then in 1822 published a full report with extensive appendixes. It was an illuminating view by an intelligent and sympathetic observer, and no doubt it was well received by the federal officials.[51]

49. Calhoun to Morse, February 7, 1820, Jedidiah Morse, *A Report to the Secretary of War of the United States on Indian Affairs* (New Haven: S. Converse, 1822), p. 11. Calhoun included a copy of this letter in a report to the House of Representatives on the civilization of the Indians, January 19, 1822, ASP:IA, 2: 273–74.
50. Calhoun to Morse, February 7, 1820, Morse, *Report*, p. 12.
51. Calhoun in his report of February 8, 1822, on civilization of the Indians referred

Morse had a high view of the Indians, "an intelligent and noble part of our race, and capable of high moral and intellectual improvement," and he firmly declared: "They are a race who on every correct principle ought to be saved from extinction, if it be possible to save them." He did not hesitate to offer plans to the government for this great end. He proposed an Indian college, liberally endowed by the government and run by a missionary society, in which Indian youth could be trained as teachers and leaders of their own peoples. His main plan, however, was for the establishment of "education families" composed of missionaries, teachers, and mechanics, who would serve among the Indians to instruct them and lead them into the paths of civilization by example as well as by precept. The government agents, too, would be members of these families and if possible might be nominated by the missionary groups. Morse saw in the regulations sent by Calhoun to the agents on February 29, 1820, the inchoate form of what he was proposing, for Calhoun had directed: "It is considered to be the duty of all persons who may be employed or attached to any institution, not only to set a good example of sobriety, industry, and honesty, but, as far as practicable, to impress on the minds of the Indians the friendly and benevolent views of the Government towards them, and the advantage to them in yielding to the policy of Government, and co-operating with it in such measures as it may deem necessary for their civilization and happiness."[52]

Morse knew that there were persons who argued that the Indians were not capable of civilization, but he gave them little countenance. "It is too late to say that Indians cannot be civilized," he asserted. "The facts referred to [in his appendix], beyond all question, prove the contrary. The evidence of actual experiment in every case, is paramount to all objections founded on mere *theory* or . . . in naked and unsupported *assertions*."[53]

Nor would there be any lack of funds, if only the government would devote to the purpose a reasonable proportion of the money it gained from selling the Indian lands ceded by treaty to the United States. Morse admitted that "the work of educating and changing the manners and habits of nearly half a million Indians, as they are now situated, is acknowledged to be great, and arduous, and appalling." But he had great faith in God—and in the United States. His outlook in 1822 was not untypical of the new missionaries and of men like McKenney and Calhoun, who directed the Indian affairs of the nation. But their optimism and benevolence were cooled by the failure of Congress to respond fully and by the mundane economic desires of so many of their countrymen.

---

to Morse's *Report* for more detailed information. *House Document* no. 59, 17–1, serial 66.

52. Morse, *Report*, pp. 23, 65–96, 292. Calhoun's directive is also in ASP:IA, 2: 273.

53. Morse, *Report*, p. 81.

In order to aid the government in pursuing the good work, Morse dreamed up an elaborate American Society for Promoting the Civilization and General Improvement of the Indian Tribes within the United States, to be composed of members from each state and territory and from all religious denominations, under the patronage of the chief officers of the government. It was to be a scientific organization that would gather accurate information, identify past failures and their causes, and propose remedies, and it would look to Congress for the funds to carry on its work. The society would be "an eye to the Government, and act the part of pioneers and surveyors to them in pursuing an important object in an unexplored wilderness."[54]

Morse moved boldly ahead with his scheme. In February 1822 he sent a prospectus to important individuals, with a copy of the constitution of the society and an invitation to join and to subscribe funds. The list of goals to be pursued was formidable—gathering information about the character of the Indians and their country, conducting agricultural experiments to ascertain the best crops and domestic animals for Indian advancement, determining the most suitable locations for "education families"—in short, doing all "which such a Society can do, to accomplish its grand object THE CIVILIZATION OF THE INDIANS." The prospectus and the constitution set forth an amazing array of ex officio officers and members, including the past presidents of the United States, the vice president, members of Congress, cabinet officers, justices of the Supreme Court, governors of states and territories, Indian superintendents and agents, commanding officers of military posts, professors of colleges and seminaries, and on and on. Morse himself was shown as corresponding secretary and signed an attached circular that urged cooperation in the "arduous work."[55]

Morse made a strong argument for voluntary associations. "In extensive, complicated, and arduous works of benevolence, requiring large means, and powerful influence to carry them forward with success," he wrote, "individuals, associations, and whole communities, have each their appropriate duties. Individuals begin these works; they devise and suggest. Associations combine their wisdom, and ripen suggestions into plan and system; and thus the way is prepared for the nation to examine and approve; and then to lend the means and patronage necessary for their accomplishment."[56]

The argument had little effect. There was one meeting of the society in Washington in 1824. But none of the distinguished gentlemen listed in Morse's prospectus had been approached beforehand; and the important

54. Ibid., pp. 75–76.
55. *A New Society for the Benefit of Indians: Organized at the City of Washington, February, 1822* (n.p., n.d.). The constitution is also printed in Morse, *Report*, pp. 284–90.
56. *First Annual Report of the American Society for Promoting the Civilization and General Improvement of the Indian Tribes in the United States* (New Haven: S. Converse, 1824), p. 13.

men needed to make the organization a success begged to be excused. John Adams declined—although he hoped everything possible could be done for the happiness of the Indians—because he believed the responsibility and powers to effect those ends lay with the officials of government, not with a voluntary organization. Thomas Jefferson refused to participate for much the same reasons, denying the need of a "collateral power" to achieve functions already being handled by government officials under law and fearing that "this *wheel within a wheel* is more likely to produce collision than aid." He also feared the magnitude of the organization with all its ex officio members and the fact that clergymen would make up nineteen-twentieths of the whole. "Can this formidable array be reviewed without dismay?" he asked. All the Supreme Court justices also refused. Secretary of War Calhoun accepted, as did James Madison. But the society collected no funds with which to carry on its activities. Yet it had done some good, Morse believed, in awakening the community to look at the condition of the Indians and preparing it to act for their relief.[57]

Morse, of course, had strong allies among his fellow churchmen. At the same time that he was promoting his society to aid the Indians, he joined with others of the American Board of Commissioners for Foreign Missions to memorialize Congress "to extend the blessings of civilization and Christianity, in all their variety, to the Indian tribes within the limits of the United States." Asserting that "the object of the Government and of the board is one, and, indeed, is common to the whole community," the memorial expressed forcefully Christian humanitarian views. It noted past neglect of the Indians, which would bring down God's vengeance upon the nation if reform was not undertaken. It offered "indubitable evidence of the practicability of educating Indians" for full civilization. And it repeated Morse's plan for a college to educate Indian teachers.[58]

Morse died in 1826, and no more was heard of his society. It was but one in a long line of voluntary associations organized and supported by Christian philanthropy specifically for the improvement and welfare of the Indians. The American Board of Commissioners for Foreign Missions, a well-organized and well-supported missionary organization, in many ways fulfilled the purposes that Morse had in mind for his abortive society.

Whether the initiative came from government officials like Thomas L. McKenney and John C. Calhoun or from zealous citizens like Jedidiah Morse and the missionaries of the American Board, the goal of civilizing and Christianizing the Indians remained an important element in government policy well into the twentieth century and helped to give that policy its strongly paternalistic bent.

57. Ibid., pp. 20–24 and passim.
58. The memorial, presented in the House on March 3, 1824, is in *House Document* no. 102, 18–1, serial 97, and in ASP:IA, 2: 446–48.

CHAPTER 6

The Indian
Department

Superintendents and Agents. Headquarters

Organization. Assistance from Military

Commanders. Presents and Annuities.

Peace Medals and Delegations.

Implementation of United States Indian policy depended upon special personnel within the War Department appointed to deal with the Indians. The aggregate of these persons was given the general designation "Indian department," a term covering the officials and clerks in the office of the secretary of war who were assigned to Indian matters and the superintendents, agents, subagents, interpreters, clerks, and mechanics who carried on the work in the field. The term did not necessarily indicate a fixed organization, and it seems to have been used in the first place as a category for accounting for funds. The word *department* was initially applied also to geographical units, such as the northern and southern districts or departments designated in the Ordinance of 1786, but the geographical divisions of Indian administration soon came to be known as superintendencies, agencies, and subagencies, corresponding to the title of the persons in charge. As the laws governing intercourse with the Indians expanded in scope and were expressed with greater precision, so the official standing and duties of the men in the Indian department also became more clearly defined, until in 1834 a definitive organization was established by law.[1]

---

1. This chapter is based in large part on Francis Paul Prucha, *American Indian Policy in the Formative Years: The Indian Trade and Intercourse Acts, 1790–1834* (Cambridge: Harvard University Press, 1962), pp. 51–65, 250–74, and sections are taken directly from that work. General accounts of the development of the Indian department can be found in Laurence F. Schmeckebier, *The Office of Indian Affairs: Its History, Activities and*

SUPERINTENDENTS AND AGENTS

Antecedents of the Indian department are found in the colonial agents sent among the Indians, the British superintendents, the special commissioners sent out by the Continental Congress, and the Indian superintendents authorized by the Ordinance of 1786. Most directly concerned were the superintendents, for their office was quietly carried over when the Constitution replaced the Articles of Confederation. On September 11, 1789, Congress provided two thousand dollars for the governor of the Northwest Territory, both as his annual salary and "for discharging the duties of superintendent of Indian affairs in the northern department," thus beginning the practice of making territorial governors ex officio superintendents of Indian affairs. In 1790 the law establishing the Territory South of the River Ohio declared that "the powers, duties and emoluments of a superintendent of Indian affairs for the southern department, shall be united with those of the governor." This office of southern superintendent lapsed in 1796 when Tennessee became a state, but in the same year Benjamin Hawkins was appointed "principal temporary agent for Indian affairs south of the Ohio River"; Hawkins exercised wide supervision over the southern Indians, although he was especially responsible for the Creeks. When Mississippi Territory was set up in 1798, the office of southern superintendent was joined to the office of governor of the new territory. The law of May 7, 1800, which established Indiana Territory by dividing the original Northwest Territory, declared that "the duties and emoluments of superintendent of Indian affairs shall be united with those of governor"; subsequent laws setting up new territories included a similar clause.[2]

The first trade and intercourse law (1790) authorized the superintendents to issue licenses for trade and to enforce the licensing provisions, and it referred to "such other persons as the President of the United States shall appoint" to issue and recall licenses. But no specific provision was made for appointing agents or establishing agencies. To care for particular Indian problems, however, special agents were appointed in 1792. These men—three sent to the southern Indians and one to the Six Nations—had no connection with the intercourse law. They were charged instead with special diplomatic missions. The primary object of the agent sent to the

---

Organization (Baltimore: Johns Hopkins Press, 1927), pp. 1–42, and Felix S. Cohen, *Handbook of Federal Indian Law* (Washington: GPO, 1942), pp. 9–12. An extensive historical account of legislation dealing with Indian agencies is in *House Report* no. 474, 23–1, serial 263. *House Document* no. 60, 23–1, serial 255, gives data on persons employed in the Indian department.

  2. 1 *United States Statutes* 50, 54, 68, 123, 550; 2 *United States Statutes* 59, 309, 331, 515.

Cherokees was to keep the southern Indians from joining the warring tribes north of the Ohio and attach the Indians more firmly to the interests of the United States. The agent sent to the Creeks sought to quiet disturbances among them, to see that the Treaty of New York was complied with, and finally to obtain three hundred Creek warriors to join the federal troops against the northern Indians. The duties of the agents sent to the Chickasaws and the New York Indians were of a similar nature.[3]

A new turn in the development of Indian agencies came with the second intercourse law (1793). A section dealing with measures to civilize the Indians authorized the president "to appoint such persons, from time to time, as temporary agents, to reside among the Indians, as he shall think proper." The commissions and instructions sent to these agents emphasized their responsibility to civilize the Indians by means of agriculture and domestic arts and referred to them officially as "temporary agents." The duties assigned them ran the wide range of Indian relations set forth in the intercourse laws, and eventually the word *temporary* was dropped from their title.[4] Under this authorization appeared the permanent Indian agents, assigned to particular tribes or areas, who became indispensable in the management of Indian affairs.

The work of the agents paralleled the development of the intercourse laws. At first their duties were set down in very general terms: to maintain the confidence of the Indians, to keep them attached to the United States, and to impress upon them the government's desire for peace and justice. As the intercourse laws made more specific the means by which peace was to be preserved and justice maintained, the agents' duties were also specified, in order to see that the laws were carried out.

The government also appointed subagents, but there seems to have been no special authorization for them as distinct from the agents. They were appointed at first as assistants to the agents; eventually they were assigned to separate locations with duties similar to those of the agents. All these men came under the general superintendence of the territorial gover-

3. Instructions to Leonard Shaw, February 17, 1792, ASP:IA, 1: 247–48; Henry Knox to James Seagrove, February 20, 1792, ibid., pp. 249–50; Knox to William Blount, April 22, 1792, ibid., p. 253; instructions to Israel Chapin, April 28, 1792, ibid., pp. 231–32.

4. 1 *United States Statutes* 331. Benjamin Hawkins in 1796 was appointed "Principal Temporary Agent for Indian Affairs South of the Ohio River." Thomas Lewis in 1799 was appointed "Temporary Indian Agent in the Cherokee Nation," William Lyman in 1801 was appointed "Temporary Agent for Indian Affairs in the Northwestern and Indiana Territories," and Silas Dinsmoor in 1802 was appointed "Temporary Agent for the Choctaw Nation." But the commissions issued to Charles Jouett and Richard Graham in 1815 called them simply "Agent of Indian Affairs." Appointments of these men are in SW IA LS, vol. A, pp. 29–35, 44–49 (M15, reel 1); and Clarence E. Carter, ed., *The Territorial Papers of the United States*, 26 vols. (Washington: GPO, 1934–1962), 5: 146–50; 7: 26–29; 17: 190–91, 196–200.

nors and reported through them to the War Department. They were directed to keep records of the happenings at their agencies and to note the condition of the Indians, the natural history of the area, and the progress of the Indians in civilization.[5]

In 1818 there were fifteen agents and ten subagents among the Indians, and on April 16 of that year Congress regularized the appointment of these men; they were to be nominated by the president and appointed by and with the consent of the Senate, but the law did not actually establish the offices that the appointees were to fill. Nor did the law of April 20, 1818, which set the pay of agents and subagents, formally establish the agencies. These laws and the succeeding appropriation bills that provided "for pay of the several Indian agents as allowed by law" merely took the agencies for granted.[6]

The 1822 amendment to the intercourse law of 1802 repeatedly mentioned agents, their authority in restricting the whiskey traffic, their duties in issuing licenses, and the reports required of them by the War Department. The act, furthermore, authorized the appointment of a superintendent of Indian affairs at St. Louis with power over the Indians who frequented that place (a necessary arrangement after the admission of Missouri as a state), and a special agent for the tribes in Florida.[7]

However indefinite and insecure their legislative foundation was before 1834, the agents were accepted as a regular part of the Indian service; the War Department came to rely on them more and more heavily in the enforcement of Indian policy, a reliance explicitly indicated in the instructions and regulations given to them. Of these instructions, the most important were the detailed ones drawn up for the early agents, which—with some necessary changes in geographical names and territorial officers—continued to be sent to Indian agents until 1815. After a preamble which enjoined upon the agent zealous endeavors to introduce the civilized arts of agriculture and spinning and weaving (an injunction worked into the body of the instructions in the 1815 version), the document directed the agent point by point in his enforcement of the laws and in the records and

5. Dearborn to Governors William C. C. Claiborne, William H. Harrison, and Arthur St. Clair, February 23, 1802, SW IA LS, vol. A, pp. 166–68 (M15, reel 1); Dearborn to Agents William Lyman, Samuel Mitchell, John McKee, and William Wells, February 27, 1802, ibid., pp. 172–73.

6. 3 *United States Statutes* 428, 461.

7. 3 *United States Statutes* 682–83. In the interval between the end of Missouri Territory with its governor as ex officio superintendent of Indian affairs and the commission to William Clark, who became superintendent under the act of 1822, the Indian agents were charged to correspond directly with the War Department. This was a general practice, but in some cases agents within states were made subordinate to a nearby territorial governor.

reports required.[8] The War Department augmented these initial instructions with specific directives, either to promulgate some change in policy or to answer questions of policy and procedure posed by the agents themselves. From time to time, too, the secretary of war issued additional general instructions to the superintendents of Indian affairs for their own guidance and for transmittal to the agents under their charge.

An agent's duties were in large part reportorial. He was to keep an eye out for violations of the intercourse laws and to report them to the superintendents, to the military commanders of the frontier posts, or to the War Department. Action and further directions to the agent in most cases came from his superior officers. But the critical work of dealing with the Indians and the frontier whites devolved upon the agent, and the success of the work depended upon the character of the man, the respect he won from the tribes among whom he lived, and the authority of his position in the eyes of the whites. Fortunately, the United States had a number of capable and distinguished men of a character and integrity that gave stature to the office of Indian agent and that enabled the agents by their personal influence alone to ease the conflicts between whites and Indians without reliance on either civil court procedures or military force.[9]

HEADQUARTERS ORGANIZATION

The work of directing the superintendents and agents rested upon the secretary of war and the clerks of the War Department whom he chose to as-

8. The instructions of James McHenry to Thomas Lewis, March 30, 1799, SW IA LS, vol. A, pp. 29–35 (M15, reel 1), is the oldest extant copy. It is possible that McHenry merely transcribed instructions that had been issued earlier to other agents. Other instructions are cited in n. 4 above.

9. The work of the agents is discussed in Edgar B. Wesley, *Guarding the Frontier: A Study of Frontier Defense from 1815 to 1825* (Minneapolis: University of Minnesota Press, 1935), pp. 16–30; Ruth A. Gallaher, "The Indian Agent in the United States before 1850," *Iowa Journal of History and Politics* 14 (January 1916): 3–55. For the work and character of two important agents for the early period, see Merritt B. Pound, *Benjamin Hawkins: Indian Agent* (Athens: University of Georgia Press, 1951); Frank L. Owsley, Jr., "Benjamin Hawkins, the First Modern Indian Agent," *Alabama Historical Quarterly* 30 (Summer 1968): 7–13; Lawrence Taliaferro, "Auto-biography of Major Lawrence Taliaferro: Written in 1864," *Minnesota Historical Collections* 6 (1887–1894): 189–225. For the two most important superintedents, see John L. Loos, "William Clark, Indian Agent," *Kansas Quarterly* 3 (Fall 1971): 29–38; Jerome O. Steffen, *William Clark: Jeffersonian Man on the Frontier* (Norman: University of Oklahoma Press, 1977); Francis Paul Prucha, *Lewis Cass and American Indian Policy* (Detroit: Wayne State University Press, 1967); Ronald Gregory Miriani, "Lewis Cass and Indian Administration in the Old Northwest, 1815–1836" (Ph.D. dissertation, University of Michigan, 1975).

sign to the task, for in the first decades of the new nation there was no formally established office charged specifically with Indian affairs. Dealings with the Indians were considered a special category of the War Department's activities, however, and separate letterbooks were maintained for correspondence concerned with Indian matters.

When the office of superintendent of Indian trade was established in 1806, it became an unofficial focus for Indian affairs, supplying information and advice to the secretary of war and corresponding with citizens who were interested in the Indians. But the abolition of the factories in 1822 removed even this semblance of an Indian center in the War Department.[10]

Then on March 11, 1824, Secretary of War Calhoun, by his own order and without special authorization from Congress, created in the War Department what he called the Bureau of Indian Affairs. Calhoun appointed his friend Thomas L. McKenney to head the office and assigned him two clerks as assistants. The duties of the new position were set forth in the letter of appointment: to take charge of the appropriations for annuities and current expenses, to examine and approve all vouchers for expenditures, to administer the fund for the civilization of the Indians, to decide on claims arising between Indians and whites under the intercourse laws, and to handle the ordinary Indian correspondence of the War Department.[11]

Despite Calhoun's designation, the new section was not commonly called the Bureau of Indian Affairs. McKenney for the first few months headed his letters Indian Office and then uniformly used Office of Indian Affairs. Indian matters from the superintendents and agents passed through his hands, as well as business with persons outside the government. The correspondence was voluminous, and McKenney was generally also called upon to prepare the reports on Indian affairs requested by Congress of the secretary of war. He and his clerks formed a sort of Indian secretariat within the War Department, but it did not take him long to become dissatisfied with this setup. The work of handling disbursements, immense correspondence with the agents, preparation and execution of treaties, care for Indian schools, and regulation of Indian trade all rested with McKenney, but the authority and responsibility still resided in the secretary of war. "It was the weight of these concerns, added to their importance, which led to the creation, *by the Executive*, of this office. But, with its constitution, no power was conveyed," McKenney complained. "The business, though it be arranged, has yet, at every step, to be carried up to the head of the Department, without regard to its importance, otherwise the most unimportant

10. The manifold work of the Office of Indian Trade under Thomas L. McKenney is well treated in Herman J. Viola, *Thomas L. McKenney: Architect of America's Early Indian Policy, 1816–1830* (Chicago: Swallow Press, 1974).

11. *House Document* no. 146, 19–1, serial 138, p. 6.

correspondence upon matters of mere detail, is not authorized, *except by the general confidence of the head of the Department in the Officer in charge of the Indian business."* What McKenney wanted was for Congress to create an office of Indian affairs, with a responsible head, to whom would be referred all matters arising out of Indian relations.[12]

McKenney drew up a bill embodying his suggestions that was introduced in the House of Representatives on March 31, 1826. It called for the appointment of a general superintendent of Indian affairs who would have the responsibility for keeping the records on Indian affairs, conducting all correspondence arising out of Indian relations, handling and adjusting financial accounts before transmitting them to the Treasury, and, in general, for doing all things in relation to Indian affairs that had hitherto rested with the secretary of war directly. The bill was committed to the Committee of the Whole, but there was no further action in that Congress, and subsequent attempts to get the bill passed also failed.[13]

McKenney's proposal for congressional action was picked up by Lewis Cass and William Clark and included in their plan for reorganizing Indian affairs, which they prepared at the behest of the secretary of war in 1829. In the Twenty-second Congress the measure was introduced again, this time by the Senate Committee on Indian Affairs, and it passed both houses without difficulty. The bill, which became law on July 9, 1832, authorized the president to appoint a commissioner of Indian affairs, under the secretary of war, who was to have "the direction and management of all Indian affairs, and of all matters arising out of Indian relations." The secretary of war was to assign clerks to the new office, without, however, increasing the total number of clerks in the War Department, and an annual salary of three thousand dollars was specified for the commissioner. Ironically, the new position was established only after McKenney had been removed from office.[14]

ASSISTANCE FROM MILITARY COMMANDERS

The army on the frontier was sent there for military defense and to uphold American authority in remote regions of the nation, but the military men who commanded the frontier forts had an important role as the power be-

12. McKenney to James Barbour, November 15, 1825, ibid., pp. 6–9.

13. *House Journal*, 19–1, serial 130, p. 394; original bill (H.R. 195), 19th Congress, 1st session, March 31, 1826; *House Journal*, 20–1, serial 168, pp. 72–73, 105; original bill (H.R. 29), 20th Congress, 1st session, January 2, 1828.

14. 4 *United States Statutes* 564. The first commissioner of Indian affairs was Elbert Herring; authoritative biographical sketches of Herring and the succeeding commissioners appear in Robert M. Kvasnicka and Herman J. Viola, eds., *The Commissioners of Indian Affairs, 1824–1977* (Lincoln: University of Nebraska Press, 1979).

hind the decisions and policies of the Indian agents and as the last resort of the territorial governors in dealing with hostile Indians or recalcitrant whites. It was no accident that Indian agencies and government trading houses were usually in the shadow of a military post.

The instructions sent to the Indian agents directed them to apply to the military commanders for aid in carrying out their duties, and the army officers received explicit directives time after time from the War Department to assist the agents in the enforcement of the laws and treaties. The legal justification for this assistance was written into the intercourse laws beginning with the law of 1796, which provided that the president of the United States could employ such military force as he judged necessary to remove illegal settlers on lands belonging to the Indians or secured to them by treaty and to apprehend any person found in the Indian country in violation of the laws. Furthermore, the law directed the military force of the United States, when called upon by civil magistrates, to assist in arresting offenders against the law and committing them to safe custody for trial according to law.[15]

The army officers' hands, however, were pretty well tied, for any hint of militarism was deeply feared. Recommendations made by Knox and others for use of courts-martial to try frontier offenders were never accepted by Congress, and the intercourse laws carefully provided that, in apprehending persons who were in the Indian country illegally, military troops should convey them immediately by the nearest convenient and safe route to the civil authority of the United States in an adjoining state or territory for trial. The law of 1796 directed that persons apprehended by the military could be detained no more than ten days between arrest and removal to the civil authorities. In 1799 the period of detention was reduced to five days, and as a further precaution against tyrannical action (which American frontiersmen always suspected on the part of the military) the law directed that the officers and soldiers having custody of a prisoner should treat him "with all the humanity which the circumstances will possibly permit; and every officer and soldier who shall be guilty of maltreating any such person, while in custody, shall suffer such punishment as a court-martial shall direct." Military officers, if requested to do so by the persons in custody, were required to conduct those persons to the nearest judge of the supreme court of any state, who, if the offense were bailable, might take proper bail if offered. By a special supplement to the intercourse laws in 1800, this provision was extended to justices of inferior or county courts, unless the defendant had been charged with murder or some other capital offense.[16]

Close cooperation was required of the agents and the military command-

15. 1 *United States Statutes* 470, 473–74.
16. 1 *United States Statutes* 748; 2 *United States Statutes* 40.

ers, not only by the intercourse laws themselves, but also by the repeated directives coming from the secretary of war, the general in chief, and the head of the Office of Indian Affairs. Unfortunately, the official directives could not smooth out all the rough edges in human relations between the army officers and the civilian Indian agents. Both groups were under the direction and surveillance of the secretary of war, but frequent conflicts of authority arose, to the detriment of efficient enforcement of the intercourse laws. Legally, and according to accepted practice, routine peacetime Indian relations were to be in the hands of the civilian superintendents and agents. Troops were to be called upon by them only when physical force or the threat of its use was necessary. Alexander Hamilton, then major general in the "provisional army" authorized to meet a threat of war from France, expressed the policy in a letter to a frontier commander in 1799:

> You are aware that the Governors of the North Western Territory and of the Mississippi Territory are severally *ex officio* Superintendants of Indian Affairs. The management of those affairs under the direction of the Secretary of War appertains to them. The military in this respect are only to be auxiliary to their plans and measures. In saying this, it must not be understood that they are to direct military dispositions and operations; But they are to be the organs of all negociations and communications between the Indians and the Government; they are to determine when and where supplies are to be furnished to those people and what other accommodations they are to have. The military in regard to all such matters are only to aid as far as their Cooperation may be required by the superintendants; avoiding interferences without previous concert with them, or otherwise than in conformity with their views. This will exempt the military from a responsibility which had better rest elsewhere: And it will promote a regular and uniform system of Conduct towards the Indians, which Cannot exist if every Commandant of a Post is to intermeddle separately and independently in the management of the concerns which relate to them.[17]

Yet many army officers were unwilling to take orders directly from civilian officers of the government, even from the superintendents and agents who were, like them, under the War Department. Specific orders coming explicitly from the secretary of war or down through the chain of command to the post commandant were considered necessary before military officers would heed the requests of agents for help. Such orders were a normal procedure, however, and the agents were supported by the War Department in their call for military assistance, although the post comman-

17. Hamilton to J. F. Hamtramck, May 23, 1799, Carter, *Territorial Papers*, 3: 24–25.

ders could be slow to respond and quick to find excuses for taking no action.[18]

Difficulties sometimes arose because of interference in Indian affairs on the part of army officers, who did not always wait to get a cue from the agents and whose garrisons were at times a point of infection in the Indian country, to which the Indians flocked for free food and even liquor. One Indian agent recommended to Governor Lewis Cass in 1815 that the relative powers of the agents and the commanding officers be more clearly pointed out. "For want of this definition of powers," he asserted, "the officers of the two departments are very apt to fall out, and the publick interest receive much injury." Lawrence Taliaferro, the able Indian agent at St. Peter's, for example, had been directed when he assumed his post to consult with the post commander at Fort Snelling and keep him informed of all his proceedings as agent. "It is of the first importance," Secretary of War Calhoun had written him, "that, in such remote posts, there should be a perfect understanding between the officers, civil and military, stationed there, to give energy and effect to their operations." Nevertheless, in his long tenure in the office of agent, Taliaferro was often at odds with the commander of Fort Snelling.[19]

The disputes and controversies between agents and officers were more than balanced by the energy and zeal with which most of the frontier commanders undertook to carry out the federal government's Indian policy. In removing intruders, confiscating liquor, restraining Indian hostilities, and conducting treaties and conferences, the army officers were able and devoted supporters of the government and of the intercourse laws.

PRESENTS AND ANNUITIES

Whatever the legal formality of treaties between sovereign nations, the relations between the United States government and the Indian tribes called forth procedures and practices that indicated special relationships that hardly existed even analogously between the United States and the nations of Europe. One was the widespread use of presents to Indian leaders. It had been European practice during the colonial era and continued to be British

18. The travail of the military commanders in dealing with Indian affairs is described in Francis Paul Prucha, *Broadax and Bayonet: The Role of the United States Army in the Development of the Northwest, 1815–1860* (Madison: State Historical Society of Wisconsin, 1953), pp. 53–103, and in Prucha, *The Sword of the Republic: The United States Army on the Frontier, 1783–1846* (New York: Macmillan Company, 1969), pp. 193–209.

19. Benjamin F. Stickney to Cass, September 27, 1815, Carter, *Territorial Papers*, 10: 597; Calhoun to Taliaferro, December 27, 1819, SW IA LS, vol. D, p. 350 (M15, reel 4).

practice among the Indians in Canada and along the border to provide gifts to Indian tribes and their chiefs. As the Indians came to depend more and more upon European goods, such gifts formed an indispensable diplomatic tool in gaining the good will and allegiance of Indian tribes. Great amounts of money were expended to "brighten the chain of friendship," and as the outlay of free goods continued, many Indians became almost completely dependent upon them.[20]

The young United States could not eliminate the practice. If it wanted to win the adherence of crucial Indian nations, it would have to continue gift giving—and it did. The Continental Congress beginning in 1776 provided for the purchase of goods to be distributed to the Indians as presents in order to cultivate their goodwill and friendship. And early treaties negotiated under the Articles of Confederation provided "in pursuance of the humane and liberal views of Congress" for the distribution of goods to the tribes for their use and comfort.[21]

President Washington was alert to the need for presents, and in the six-point program for advancing the happiness of the Indians and attaching them to the United States proposed in 1791, he asked that the president "be enabled to employ the means to which the Indians have been long accustomed for uniting their immediate interests with the preservation of peace." The presents were to be employed also as a means of bringing the Indians around to the civilization of the whites. Secretary of War Knox, in his first long report on Indian affairs, recommended gifts of sheep and other domestic animals for chiefs and their wives in an attempt to instill in the Indians a "love for exclusive property." And the intercourse laws provided that "in order to promote civilization among the friendly Indian tribes, and to secure the continuance of their friendship," the president could furnish them with domestic animals and the implements of husbandry.[22]

Competition with the British offered a strong incentive for distributing presents to Indians. Lewis Cass, as governor of Michigan Territory, gave the matter great emphasis, and in a memorandum of 1816 concerning In-

20. An excellent study of the use of presents in colonial times is Wilbur R. Jacobs, *Diplomacy and Indian Gifts: Anglo-French Rivalry along the Ohio and Northwest Frontier, 1748–1763* (Stanford: Stanford University Press, 1950). Jacobs provides great detail not only on the use and significance of the presents but on the kinds of goods provided. The use of presents among the southern tribes is indicated in Wilbur R. Jacobs, ed., *Indians of the Southern Colonial Frontier: The Edmond Atkin Report and Plan of 1755* (Columbia: University of South Carolina Press, 1954).

21. JCC, 4: 378, 410; 7: 127; 8: 542, 550; 24: 225; 25: 688–89; Kappler, pp. 6, 8.

22. Fred L. Israel, ed., *The State of the Union Messages of the Presidents, 1790–1966*, 3 vols. (New York: Chelsea House, 1966), 1: 9; Knox to Washington, July 7, 1789, ASP:IA, 1: 53–54; 1 *United States Statutes* 331, 472, 746–47; 2 *United States Statutes* 143; 4 *United States Statutes* 738.

dian affairs he provided a detailed rationale for giving presents. In the first place, he saw a moral obligation to provide for the Indians who had given up "the fairest portion of their Country" to the whites and who now found it difficult to subsist by means of hunting. Without the "annual gratuities" they had come to expect from the government, Cass found it "difficult to conceive how they could support and clothe themselves." Cass, charged with maintaining peace on his remote frontier, looked upon the distribution of presents as essential for that end. "Whatever has a tendency to conciliate the minds of the Indians and to render less unpleasant those obnoxious circumstances in our intercourse with them, which cannot be removed," he wrote, "will have a powerful effect in continuing our existing relations with them. The importance of presents in this point of view is too striking to require any particular illustration." This was especially true in competition with the British, and Cass pointed to the experience of the War of 1812, in which the British had used presents to great advantage. Moreover, presents were required to secure the attachment of influential chiefs and to prevent Indians from committing depredations on the property of white citizens. Finally, the distribution of presents by agents of the United States was necessary "to give dignity, influence and importance to the Agent, and attention to his representations." Governor Cass added a detailed proposal for procedures in distributing presents to get the most good out of them and suggested $20,000 a year in presents for the Indians of his region.[23]

Cass's proposal was not fully implemented, and as annuities under treaties and trade goods from the factory system provided alternatives, the use of presents as a wholesale means of supplying the needs of the Indians declined. But the influence of presents upon chiefs, to get them to agree to American proposals, continued unabated. The appropriate distribution of gifts where they would do the most good, in a thinly veiled form of bribery, became an accepted part of treaty making.

A special form of gift giving was rations, distributed gratuitously from time to time to the Indians. These were generally provided at treaty negotiations for the large groups of participating Indians, and the reorganization of the Indian department in 1834 authorized the president to grant such rations as could be spared from army provisions to Indians visiting military posts or Indian agencies on the frontier.[24]

As more and more land was ceded by the Indians in treaties with the

23. Francis Paul Prucha and Donald F. Carmony, eds., "A Memorandum of Lewis Cass: Concerning a System for the Regulation of Indian Affairs," *Wisconsin Magazine of History* 52 (Autumn 1968): 40–41, 45–50.

24. 2 *United States Statutes* 85. The provision, with the addition of the words "or agencies," was repeated in the law of 1834. 4 *United States Statutes* 738.

United States, the payments for these lands in the form of annuities proportionately increased. The annuities, together with rations and other gratuities that continued through the decades, became an essential means of support for many tribes. The distribution of the annuities—either in cash or in goods—became one of the primary activities of the Indian department and one of its biggest headaches.

The annuities, as the name suggests, were annual payments either for a specified period of years or in perpetuity. At first the payments were small, mere token payments, such as the $1,500 a year to the Creeks in the Treaty of New York in 1790 and the $1,000 a year to the Cherokees in the Treaty of Holston in 1791, although both those treaties also provided for "certain valuable goods" to be delivered immediately to the nation.[25] But year by year, as the treaties of cession multiplied, considerable sums were appropriated annually to meet the treaty obligations. When Cass and Clark in 1829 recommended consolidation of annuity appropriations into a single bill, the list of funds due under various treaties totaled $214,590.[26]

In some cases the treaties specified a money payment to the tribe; in many other cases the annuity was to be in the form of goods or services. Thus in the treaty of 1794 with the Six Nations, in addition to $10,000 worth of goods delivered at once, the United States agreed to expend "yearly forever" a sum of $4,500 "in purchasing clothing, domestic animals, implements of husbandry, and other utensils suited to their circumstances, and in compensating useful artificers, who shall reside with or near them, and be employed for their benefit." Stipulations that annuity payments be used for education were also common in the treaties.

To procure the goods needed for annuity payments was no small task. The work was entrusted by a law of 1792 to an agent of the Treasury Department who supervised the purchases of supplies for the military, naval, and Indian services. In 1795 Congress created the office of purveyor of public supplies for the procurement of government goods.[27] In 1811, after the office of superintendent of Indian trade had been established, the superintendent was charged with the purchase and distribution of annuity goods as well as of goods needed for the trading houses. The great variety of items

25. Kappler, pp. 26, 30.

26. *Senate Document* no. 72, 20–2, serial 181, pp. 52–57.

27. 1 *United States Statutes* 280, 419. A letterbook of the commissioner of the revenue, 1794–1796, is in Records of the Revenue Office Relating to the Treasury of the War Department, National Archives, Record Group 75. The work of the purveyor is discussed in the biography of the man who held the job from 1803 to 1812: Jacob E. Cooke, *Tench Coxe and the Early Republic* (Chapel Hill: University of North Carolina Press, 1978), pp. 413–21. For details on annuity goods, see Journal of Superintendent of Military Stores, Annuity Goods, 1794–1811, Records of the Indian Tribal Claims Branch, WNRC, Suitland, Maryland.

required and the frequent difficulties in locating appropriate stocks created an immense amount of work and worry for his office. After the dissolution of the factory system and the institution of the Office of Indian Affairs in the War Department, the head of that office carried on the work. The fact that Thomas L. McKenney, the last superintendent of Indian trade, became the first head of the Indian Office made possible some continuity in the enterprise.[28]

No matter who was responsible for distributing goods or money to the Indians, accounting for both was a major task. When the annuities and presents were added to funds appropriated for the salaries of agents and their supporting personnel, for transportation, for buildings, and for contingent expenses, the sums involved were large, and it seemed impossible (granted the problems of communication and the incompetence of some of the men who handled accounts) to keep the records straight. McKenney had great trouble clearing his accounts for annuities and presents, as well as for trade goods, when the factories were closed. When he became head of the Indian Office, he had even more money to account for; in some years he was responsible for the disbursement of up to a million dollars.[29]

Regulations and laws dealing with accounting for funds were extensive and became increasingly detailed. When Lewis Cass printed a two-page broadside in Detroit, dated September 15, 1814, called "Regulations for the Indian Department," he prescribed in detail the procedures for distributing presents and keeping accounts on them, details that took up most of the broadside. The law of 1822 tightening the regulation of trade had a special section on accounting for Indian department funds, and judging from the correspondence it called forth, that part of the law most interested the secretary of war.[30]

Accounting procedures remained a special problem and seemed to give officials of the Indian department more trouble than did the actual dealings with the Indians. Henry R. Schoolcraft, the longtime Indian agent at Sault Ste. Marie, expressed a general view when he wrote graphically in 1828, "The derangements in the fiscal affairs of the Indian department are in the extreme. One would think that appropriations had been handled with a pitchfork. . . . And these derangements are only with regard to the

28. An account of McKenney's work in procuring Indian supplies is in Viola, *McKenney*, pp. 12–16.

29. Ibid., pp. 80–84, 105, 175–76. Indian office disbursements in 1824 amounted to $424,978.50 and in 1825 to $671,470.59; McKenney estimated that they would be $1,082,474.68 in 1826. McKenney to James Barbour, April 21, 1826, OIA LS, vol. 3, pp. 44–45 (M21, reel 3). In attached statements, McKenney gives a breakdown for each year.

30. Calhoun to Clark, May 28, 1822, SW IA LS, vol. E, pp. 258–61 (M15, reel 5); Calhoun to William P. DuVal, June 11, 1822, Carter, *Territorial Papers*, 22: 452–55; Calhoun to the territorial governors, March 18, 1823, ibid., 19: 502.

north. How the south and west stand, it is impossible to say. But there is a screw loose in the public machinery somewhere." Such criticisms McKenney was willing to accept; he knew well enough, he said, "how slip-shod almost every thing is," but he insisted that only Congress could remedy the situation.[31] In 1834 the president was authorized "to prescribe such rules and regulations as he may think fit . . . for the settlement of the accounts of the Indian department." The distribution of annuities usually took place at the Indian agencies, to which the Indians were summoned for the occasion. There the agent, with the support of the military post commander, gave the money or goods to the chiefs, who in turn distributed them to the Indians. In some cases the annuities went directly to individuals, but in 1834 Congress stipulated that annuities were to be paid to the chiefs or to such other persons as the tribe designated. At the request of the tribe, according to the same legislation, money annuities could be commuted to goods.[32]

Cash annuities, although easier to provide than goods, came under frequent attack, for the money quickly passed from the Indians' hands into the pockets of traders. McKenney called the payment of money a "radical defect." It was a practice, he said, that "furnishes a lure to the avaricious— and gives the means of indulgence to these untutored people, in all their propensities to drunkenness & idleness; & is known, to have produced from the beginning, *no other fruits.*"[33] Annuities continued to be of great concern to the government officials responsible for Indian affairs.

PEACE MEDALS AND DELEGATIONS

One practice in dealing with the Indian chiefs that the United States took over from the British and other European nations was the presentation of silver medals to chiefs and warriors as tokens of friendship and as signs of allegiance and loyalty on the part of those who accepted them. These peace medals came to play a prominent part in American Indian policy.[34] Medals were given to Indian chiefs on such important occasions as the

31. Henry R. Schoolcraft, *Personal Memoirs of a Residence of Thirty Years with the Indian Tribes on the American Frontier* (Philadelphia: Lippincott, Grambo and Company, 1851), p. 319; McKenney to P. S. Duponceau, October 1, 1828, OIA LS, vol. 5, pp. 140–42 (M21, reel 5).

32. 4 *United States Statutes* 737–38.

33. McKenney to William P. DuVal, December 26, 1825, OIA LS, vol. 2, p. 330 (M21, reel 2); McKenney to Eli Baldwin, October 8, 1829, ibid., vol. 6, p. 105 (M21, reel 6).

34. A complete history of the peace medals, their production, and their use is Francis Paul Prucha, *Indian Peace Medals in American History* (Madison: State Historical Society of Wisconsin, 1971). Sections of that book are used here.

signing of a treaty, a visit of Indians to the national capital, or a tour of Indian country by some federal official. They were distributed, too, by Indian agents on the frontier at their own discretion but according to established norms. The proposed regulations for the Indian department drawn up in 1829 by Cass and Clark set forth a simple outline of rules to govern the use of medals:

> In the distribution of medals and flags, the following rules will be observed:
> 1. They will be given to influential persons only.
> 2. The largest medals will be given to the principal village chiefs, those of the second size will be given to the principal war chiefs, and those of the third size to the less distinguished chiefs and warriors.
> 3. They will be presented with proper formalities, and with an appropriate speech, so as to produce a proper impression upon the Indians.
> 4. It is not intended that chiefs should be appointed by any officer of the department, but that they should confer these badges of authority upon such as are selected or recognized by the tribe, and as are worthy of them, in the manner heretofore practised.
> 5. Whenever a foreign medal is worn, it will be replaced by an American medal, if the Agent should consider the person entitled to a medal.[35]

Although these regulations were never formally adopted, they represented the generally accepted practice on the frontier.

The practice became so firmly established, indeed, that it was impossible to conduct satisfactory relations with the Indians without medals. Thomas L. McKenney made this clear to the secretary of war at the end of 1829. "So important is its continuance esteemed to be," he wrote, "that without medals, any plan of operations among the Indians, be it what it may, is essentially enfeebled. This comes of the high value which the Indians set upon these tokens of Friendship. They are, besides this indication of the Government Friendship, badges of power to them, and trophies of renown. They will not consent to part from this ancient *right*, as they esteem it; and according to the value they set upon medals is the importance to the Government in having them to bestow."[36]

When the United States was in competition with the British for the friendship of the tribes, the medals were of supreme importance, for the chiefs signified their switch from adherence to the British to loyalty to

35. *Senate Document* no. 72, 20–2, serial 181, pp. 77–78.
36. McKenney to John H. Eaton, December 21, 1829, OIA LS, vol. 6, p. 199 (M21, reel 6).

the United States by formally turning in their British medals and accepting in their place those bearing the likeness of the American president. The medals, perhaps even more than the flags that also were presented to chiefs, carried the full weight of national allegiance. They were personal marks, worn with pride upon the breasts of the chiefs, and unlike flags were nearly indestructible. Within the tribes, too, possession of a medal gave rank and distinction; and despite protestations of government officials to the contrary, by awarding medals the United States commissioners sometimes designated or "made" the chiefs with whom they dealt.

President Washington presented large oval silver medals to Alexander McGillivray and his Creek associates by the secret clauses of the Treaty of New York in 1790 and sent similar medals to the Cherokees, Choctaws, and Chickasaws in subsequent years and to the Seneca chief Red Jacket in 1792. General Wayne distributed Washington medals at Greenville. When Lewis and Clark ascended the Missouri in 1804, they took along a large supply of medals, mostly Jefferson medals (in three sizes) with the bust of the president on the obverse and clasped hands with the words PEACE AND FRIENDSHIP on the reverse. The explorers confiscated Spanish and British medals and replaced them with American ones. As the years passed, these medals flooded the frontier, especially after the War of 1812, when they played a significant part in the campaign to gain the loyalty of the Indians in the Great Lakes region and on the upper Mississippi and Missouri.[37] The urgency appears in a letter of William Clark to the secretary of war in 1831:

> I beg leave to S[t]ate to you the necessity of my being Supplied with *Medals* for Indian Chiefs, within the Superintendency of St. Louis. At the Treaties which have been latterly negotiated, with various Tribes of the Indians of the Missouri and Mississippi rivers, application was made in council by their chiefs "for *Medals* with the face of the President (their great father) to place near their heart, which would give them power and Strength to follow his Councils, and enforce the provisions of their Treaties"—as I had no medals, and the commissioners being in favour of their application, a promise was made to those Chiefs, that I would ask the President (their great father) to grant their request, and that we had no doubt of his bestowing Medals, on Such Chiefs as were worthy of receiving that mark of distinction.[38]

Clark reported that British medals had been delivered up to the commissioners who had treated with the tribes on the upper Missouri in 1825

---

37. Prucha, *Indian Peace Medals*, pp. 3–53.

38. Clark to John H. Eaton, January 22, 1831, OIA LR, St. Louis Superintendency (M234, reel 749).

and that the chiefs were still waiting for the United States medals prom- ised them. "I must beg leave to observe," he said, "that all western Tribes of Indians consider *Medals* of the bust of the President, one of the greatest marks of distinction which they can receive from the government and which is worn suspended from their neck as authority in important coun- cil with the white people, their negotiations with other tribes, and in mak- ing themselves known to Strangers. Medals & Flags are the greatest *boast* of a chief among those distant Tribes, who considers himself supported by the Gov᛬ bestowing on him those marks of distinction, in ad[d]ition to the influence he has with his own tribe and is so considered by other tribes.

The distribution of medals to the chiefs of the northwestern and west- ern tribes, Clark believed, had had a salutary effect in gaining security for American traders and in easing tensions among the tribes themselves. "To effect in part these objects," he concluded, "a proper distribution of *Medals,* Flags & Chief Coats will give an influence which no other means within my knowledge can be applied with as little expense."[39]

Federal officials took great pains to procure medals of respectable artis- tic merit, for as McKenney noted in connection with the John Quincy Adams medals, "they are intended, not for the Indians, only, but for pos- terity." Notable artists and diesinkers were hired to design and produce the medals, and the United States Mint in Philadelphia handled the striking of them.[40]

Another device for attaching Indians to the United States government was to invite delegations of important tribal leaders to the seat of govern- ment to confer with the president, the secretary of war, and the commis- sioner of Indian affairs. These Indian delegates sometimes came to negoti- ate treaties and sometimes to present grievances, but the occasions were used also to impress them with the size and power of the United States and its people. The Indians visited the sights of the capital, met dignitaries at the White House, inspected navy yards and fortifications, and often stopped to see Philadelphia and New York before they returned home. The trials of entertaining the Indians in Washington were many, but the practice con- tinued—often at the insistence of the Indians.[41]

39. Ibid.

40. McKenney to Samuel Moore, October 13, 1825, OIA LS, vol. 2, p. 188 (M21, reel 2). For details on production of the medals, see Prucha, *Indian Peace Medals,* pp. 73–138.

41. There is considerable literature on delegations. The best account is Herman J. Vi- ola, *Diplomats in Buckskins: A History of Indian Delegations in Washington City* (Washington: Smithsonian Institution Press, 1981). See also Katharine C. Turner, *Red Men Calling on the Great White Father* (Norman: University of Oklahoma Press, 1951), and John C. Ewers, "'Chiefs from the Missouri and Mississippi,' and Peale's Silhouettes of 1806," *Smithsonian Journal of History* 1 (Spring 1966): 1–26.

The Indian Office, which entertained the delegations and performed the steadily increasing duties that federal relations with the Indians entailed, was a modest bureau in the early years of the nineteenth century. Its organization and much of its work began informally, but as the years passed its role became ever more critical, and like other bureaucracies it grew and grew. The Indian Office assumed the paternalistic mantle that theoretically belonged to the Great Father, the president.

PART TWO

Indian Removal

American Indian policy is sometimes thought of as a movement between two extremes. On one hand was the idea of assimilating the Indians into white American society through the acculturative processes of private property, an agricultural (as opposed to a hunter) economy, formal education in English letters, and Christianization. On the other was the idea of segregation or separateness; the Indians could maintain their limited political autonomy, their special languages, and their customs and religions but only outside the limits of white society, either in protected enclaves or, preferably, beyond the western frontier of white settlement. In the nineteenth century at least, there was no concept of a truly pluralistic society.

The removal of the eastern Indians that dominated the second quarter of the century, if the dichotomy above is accepted, falls of course on the side of separateness. It was an admission that the speedy acculturation and absorption of the Indians into white society (and even the biological intermingling of the races) that was the goal of the Jeffersonians had not been attained and was perhaps unattainable. Yet this was not a simple matter of either assimilation or segregation. Removal was the policy adopted to solve the problem of alien groups claiming independence within established states and territories of the United States, the problem of groups of human beings with communal cultures still only partially dependent upon agriculture owning large areas of land that were coveted for the dynamic white agricultural systems of both the north and the south, and the problem of friction that occurred along the lines of contact between the two societies and the deleterious effect that contact almost universally had upon Indian individuals and Indian society.

These problems were real problems for both the United States government and its people and for the Indian tribes. They could not be easily waved aside simply by appeals to public morality and justice. They resulted in a great complexity of practical situations that confounded sincere Christian statesmen as well as zealous missionaries and for which even aggressive and ruthless white expansionists found no easy answers. Indian leaders, too, saw the complexity, and they arrived at a variety of adaptive responses as they sought to maintain some degree of self-determination in the face of the obvious power and advantages of the United States. Nor was removal complete segregation, a cutting off of the Indian groups from white contact and connections by banishment beyond the Mississippi. In some respects the policy and the process brought increased rather than lessened interference in domestic Indian affairs on the part of the Great Father. And when the emigrant Indians were settled in their western homes, the drive for educating, civilizing, and Christianizing them took on new vigor. Acculturation and to a large extent assimilation was still the ultimate goal, slowed down and delayed as it seemed to have been in the East.

Indian removal has been popularly associated with the Five Civilized Tribes of the southeastern United States and dramatized in the Cherokees' Trail of Tears, but it was a phenomenon that affected Indians north of the Ohio River as well. The total picture must encompass both groups, and it must include in addition the developments in the Indian department and its administration that were occasioned by the massive relocation of the tribes.

The debates over removal policy touched fundamental questions. In 1828 Secretary of War Peter B. Porter had complained that there was no clear definition of the nature of the relations between the United States and the Indians. On one side he saw advocates of "primitive and imprescriptible rights in their broadest extent" contending that the tribes were independent nations with sole and exclusive right to the property and government of the territories they occupied. On the other side he recognized extremists who considered the Indians "mere tenants at will, subject, like the buffalo of the prairies, to be hunted from their country whenever it may suit our interests or convenience to take possession of it."[1]

The controversy over removal in the 1830s might have been expected to widen the split between the opposing forces, for each side presented an extreme position. Yet when the dust stirred up by the debates began to settle, the definition that Porter had asked for began to appear. It is true that the

1. Report of Peter B. Porter, November 24, 1828, *American State Papers: Military Affairs*, 4: 3.

supporters of the removal bill won their point in Congress and that the Indians were ejected from the eastern states. Hostile attitudes toward the Indians were often victorious in practice on much of the frontier, too, but official United States Indian policy had a firmer and more balanced foundation than the selfish interests of frontiersmen. That policy came to rest on treaties (including the removal treaties), which uniformly guaranteed Indian rights, as well as on the intercourse laws and War Department regulations, which implemented the treaties and restricted the contacts between whites and Indians in order to protect both parties, and on the decisions of the Supreme Court, such as those of 1831 and 1832 dealing with the Cherokees, which vindicated Indian rights. The tremendous weight of the arguments put forth in the 1830s by those who opposed forced and ruthless removal stirred the conscience of much of the nation and to a large extent reinforced the concern for Indian welfare and improvement that had been part of official attitudes from the beginning.

Ultimate evaluation of Indian removal is difficult. Removal brought neither the utter collapse of Indian society and culture direly predicted by the critics of Jackson's program nor the utopia in the West that advocates envisaged. Like so many human affairs, it had elements of good and evil, of humanitarian and philanthropic concern for the Indians and fraud and corruption practiced by unscrupulous men. How it might finally have turned out cannot be determined, for the development of the emigrant Indians in the West was cut short by new forces of expansion in the 1840s and 1850s and then by the cataclysm of the Civil War.

CHAPTER 7

The Policy of
Indian Removal

Formulation of the Policy. Andrew Jackson and

Removal. Motivation for Removal. Controversy

and Debate. The Cherokee Cases.

Although it has been common to ascribe the removal of the Indians in the
1830s to Andrew Jackson, his aggressive removal policy was in fact the
culmination of a movement that had been gradually gaining momentum
in government circles for nearly three decades. Whites had steadily encroached upon Indian lands, and new treaties of cession had been negotiated from time to time to validate the incursions. But this was a piecemeal
process, and there were dreams that the problems could be eliminated
once and for all by inducing the eastern Indians to exchange their lands for
territory west of the Mississippi, leaving the area between the Appalachians
and the Father of Waters free of encumbrance for white exploitation.[1]

FORMULATION OF THE POLICY

The idea of exchange of lands originated with Thomas Jefferson in 1803,
when the addition of the vast Louisiana Purchase created conditions that
would make removal feasible. Before the end of Jefferson's administration

1. The development of the removal policy has received extended treatment from historians. I follow here my earlier discussion in Francis Paul Prucha, *American Indian Policy in the Formative Years: The Indian Trade and Intercourse Acts, 1790–1834* (Cambridge: Harvard University Press, 1962), pp. 224–49. See also the old but still useful
treatise by Annie H. Abel, "The History of Events Resulting in Indian Consolidation

gentle pressure was being placed on the Cherokees, to introduce to them the notion of exchanging their present country for lands in the West. The secretary of war directed the Indian agent to sound out the chiefs and let the subject be discussed in the nation so that prevailing opinion could be ascertained. Those who chose to live by hunting were to be especially encouraged to emigrate, but care was to be taken that the removal was the result of their own inclinations and not of force.[2]

Some Cherokees did go west, at first to hunt and then to settle, but the problems of the War of 1812 crowded out any serious thought of orderly emigration of the tribes. Not until Monroe's administration was the proposal discussed again in earnest. In January 1817 the Senate Committee on the Public Lands reported on the expediency of exchanging lands with the Indians and proposed that an appropriation be made to enable the president to enter into treaties with the Indians for that purpose. The aim of the measure was to obviate the "irregular form of the frontier, deeply indented by tracts of Indian territory," to consolidate the settlement of the whites, and to remove the Indians from intimate intercourse with the whites, a contact "by which the civilized man cannot be improved, and by which there is ground to believe the savage is depraved."[3]

President Monroe and Secretary of War John C. Calhoun worked earnestly for a change in the enduring situation of the Indians. The anomaly of large groups of savage or semicivilized tribes surrounded by civilized whites struck them with special force. The solution was either removal to the open western regions or a change from the hunter state. In a letter to Andrew Jackson in October 1817, Monroe asserted that "the hunter or savage state requires a greater extent of territory to sustain it, than is compatible with the progress and just claims of civilized life, and must yield to it." He returned to the same views in his annual message to Congress in December, adding that it was right that the hunter should yield to the farmer. The prickly question of land tenure would disappear if only the Indians could be removed beyond the Mississippi, and the War Department authorized its commissioners to make liberal offers to the eastern tribes in an attempt to induce them to accept willingly an exchange of lands. Monroe

---

West of the Mississippi," *Annual Report of the American Historical Association for the Year 1906*, 1: 233–450; also the more recent, heavily documented study, Ronald N. Satz, *American Indian Policy in the Jacksonian Era* (Lincoln: University of Nebraska Press, 1975), pp. 1–63. An example of popular treatments that are almost universally very sympathetic to the Indian cause is Dale Van Every, *Disinherited: The Lost Birthright of the American Indian* (New York: William Morrow, 1966).

  2. Secretary of war to Return J. Meigs, March 25 and May 5, 1808, SW IA LS, vol. B, pp. 364, 377 (M15, reel 2).

  3. *Senate Journal*, 14th Congress, 2d session, p. 95; report of Senate Committee on Public Lands, January 9, 1817, ASP:IA, 2: 123–24.

and Calhoun, as well as Jackson, were convinced that the good of the Indians demanded an end to their independent status within the white settlements and urged some action on Congress.[4]

The removal question was then given a new and dangerous twist by special circumstances surrounding the Cherokees in Georgia (and to a lesser extent the Creeks, Chickasaws, and Choctaws in Alabama and Mississippi). The Cherokees were settled within the boundaries of Georgia on lands which they had always held. These Indians were not nomads; they had an abiding attachment to their lands and were determined to hold them at all costs, no matter what the United States might offer them as an inducement to move. One of the ironies of the situation was that the very progress in civilization of the Cherokees made them less willing to depart. The United States, through government officials directly and through the encouragement given to missionary societies, had urged the Indians to adopt white ways by tilling the soil and developing the domestic arts of spinning and weaving. Formal education in English language schools, also, had led to a cadre of leaders—mostly mixed-bloods—who could deal effectively with white society. The remarkable invention of a Cherokee syllabary by Sequoyah made it possible for great numbers of Cherokees to learn to read in their native tongue. Assisted by the missionaries of the American Board, the Cherokees at the end of the decade of the 1820s began to publish their own newspaper, the *Cherokee Phoenix*, which printed material in English and in the Cherokee language and which became an important vehicle for disseminating views of the Cherokees, both within their own nation and to the white world. Some of the Indian leaders, too, had adopted the whites' system of black slavery and had established extensive plantations, rivaling their white counterparts. Contemporaries differed in their opinions about the actual extent of progress in white cultural patterns. Was it evident only in the small group of mixed-bloods, who sought to manipulate the destinies of the Indian nations for their own interests, or was the general mass of the population also affected? Whatever the case, the "civilized tribes" of the southeastern United States did not correspond to the Indian tribes pictured as hunters who needed to transform themselves into agriculturalists that was a common part of the rhetoric justifying removal.[5]

4. Monroe to Jackson, October 5, 1817, *Correspondence of Andrew Jackson*, ed. John Spencer Bassett, 6 vols. (Washington: Carnegie Institution, 1926–1933), 2: 331–32; message of December 2, 1817, Fred L. Israel, ed., *The State of the Union Messages of the Presidents, 1790–1966*, 3 vols. (New York: Chelsea House, 1966), 1: 152–53; C. Vandeventer to Lewis Cass, June 29, SW IA LS, vol. D, pp. 176–79 (M15, reel 4); Calhoun to Joseph McMinn, July 29, 1818, ibid., pp. 191–94. See also Monroe's message of November 16, 1818, Israel, *State of the Union Messages*, 1: 163–64; Calhoun's report of January 15, 1820, ASP:IA, 2: 200–201.

5. Most accounts of the Cherokees and other southern tribes note their cultural

Georgia and the United States had signed a compact on April 24, 1802, by which Georgia ceded to the United States its western land claims. In return, the United States agreed to extinguish the Indian title to lands within the state and turn them over to Georgia as soon as this could be done peaceably and on reasonable terms. As the land greed of the Georgians increased through the years, the federal government was accused of failing in its part of the bargain, for the government had not extinguished the Indian title to the Georgia lands. Complaints reached Washington both from the Cherokees—who looked with apprehension on the threats of Georgia and on the federal government's renewed appropriations for a treaty to extinguish the Indian claims—and from the Georgians. The governor of Georgia censured the federal government for its tardiness and weakness, asserting that the Indians were mere tenants at will who had only a temporary right to use the lands for hunting; he insisted that Georgia was determined to gain the Cherokee lands.[6]

To these criticisms President Monroe replied in a special message to Congress on March 30, 1824, defending the course of the government, asserting that the Indian title was in no way affected by the compact with Georgia, and denying any obligation on the part of the United States to force the Indians to move against their will. He reiterated his strong opinion that removal would be in the best interests of the Indians, but he refused to be pushed by Georgia beyond the strict import of the compact. The president's message did nothing to soothe the irritation of the Geor-

---

transformation, but the description is frequently based on enthusiastic accounts of the missionaries and other whites. See, for example, Grace Steele Woodward, *The Cherokees* (Norman: University of Oklahoma Press, 1963), pp. 139–56. For insight into white acculturated Indians, see Ralph Henry Gabriel, *Elias Boudinot, Cherokee, and His America* (Norman: University of Oklahoma Press, 1941). Much information about the state of Cherokee acculturation is given in William G. McLoughlin and Walter H. Conser, Jr., "The Cherokees in Transition: A Statistical Analysis of the Federal Cherokee Census of 1835," *Journal of American History* 64 (December 1977): 678–703. Studies of Indian slave-holders are Theda Perdue, *Slavery and the Evolution of Cherokee Society, 1540–1866* (Knoxville: University of Tennessee Press, 1979); Perdue, "Cherokee Planters: The Development of Plantation Slavery before Removal," in *The Cherokee Indian Nation: A Troubled History*, ed. Duane H. King (Knoxville: University of Tennessee Press, 1979), pp. 110–28; R. Halliburton, Jr., *Red over Black: Black Slavery among the Cherokee Indians* (Westport, Connecticut: Greenwood Press, 1977); Daniel F. Littlefield, Jr., *Africans and Creeks: From the Colonial Period to the Civil War* (Westport, Connecticut: Greenwood Press, 1979).

6. Charles C. Royce, "The Cherokee Nation of Indians: A Narrative of Their Official Relations with the Colonial and Federal Governments," *Annual Report of the Bureau of Ethnology, 1883–1884* (Washington: GPO, 1887), pp. 233–38. The compact of 1802 is printed in Clarence E. Carter, ed., *The Territorial Papers of the United States*, 26 vols. (Washington: GPO, 1934–1962), 5: 142–46.

gians, whose governor in another communication to the president commented with much severity upon the bad faith that for twenty years had characterized the conduct of the executive officers of the United States.[7]

As Monroe neared the end of his term, he increased his insistence that steps be taken to preserve the rapidly degenerating tribes, now increasingly threatened by Georgia. He told Congress on December 7, 1824, of the Indians' deplorable conditions and the danger of their extinction. To civilize them was essential to their survival, but this was a slow process and could not be fully attained in the territory where the Indians then resided. Monroe had no thought of forceful ejection; even if it aimed at the security and happiness of the Indians, he said, it would be "revolting to humanity, and utterly unjustifiable." There was only one solution: the Indians must be invited and induced to take up their home in the West. The plan would be expensive, Monroe admitted, but he saw no other solution.[8]

Before Congress had time to act, Monroe sent it a special message on removal based upon a report of Calhoun dated January 24, 1825. The president urged a liberal policy that would satisfy both the Cherokees and the Georgians. He asked for "a well-digested plan" for governing and civilizing the Indians, which would not only "shield them from impending ruin, but promote their welfare and happiness." He was convinced that such a plan was practicable and that it could be made so attractive to the Indians that all, even those most opposed to emigration, would be induced to accede to it in the near future. The essence of his proposal was the institution of a government for the Indians in the West, one that would preserve order, prevent the intrusion of the whites, and stimulate civilization. "It is not doubted," Monroe told Congress, "that this arrangement will present considerations of sufficient force to surmount all their prejudices in favor of the soil of their nativity, however strong they may be." To convince the Indians of the sincere interest of the government in their welfare, he asked Congress to pledge the solemn faith of the United States to fulfill the arrangements he had suggested, and he recommended sending commissioners to the various tribes to explain to them the objects of the government.[9]

Congress acted at once to implement the president's message. On the day following the message, Senator Thomas Hart Benton wrote to Calhoun that the Committee on Indian Affairs in the Senate had unanimously adopted the system recommended by Monroe, and Calhoun sent Benton a

7. Monroe's message and numerous documents relating to the compact of 1802 are printed in *Senate Document* no. 63, 18–1, serial 91. See also Royce, "Cherokee Nation of Indians," pp. 238–40.

8. Israel, *State of the Union Messages*, 1: 228.

9. Report of Calhoun, January 24, 1825, ASP:IA, 2: 542–44; message of Monroe, January 27, 1825, James D. Richardson, comp., *A Compilation of the Messages and Papers of the Presidents, 1789–1897*, 10 vols. (Washington: GPO, 1896–1899), 2: 280–83.

draft of a bill. The measure, introduced by Benton on February 1, followed precisely the recommendations Monroe had made, authorizing the president to acquire land from the western Indians and to treat with the eastern tribes for removal. It directed the president, furthermore, "to pledge the faith of the nation" that the emigrating tribes would be guaranteed permanent peace, protection from intrusion, and aid in improving their condition and in forming a suitable government, and to appoint commissioners to visit the tribes to induce them to move. A sum of $125,000 was to be appropriated to carry out the provisions of the bill. It was a promising beginning, but although the bill passed the Senate, it failed in the House.[10]

The matter was by no means dead, however. In December 1825 a House resolution charged the Committee on Indian Affairs to inquire into the expediency and practicability of establishing a territorial government for the Indians west of the Mississippi, and on February 21, 1826, a new bill was introduced.[11] This bill represented the current view of the administration, for John Cocke, chairman of the House committee, had sent a copy of the earlier bill to Secretary of War James Barbour, asking for his opinion. "The Committee are desirous," Cocke said, "to cooperate with the views of the President in relation to the Indians within the limits of the U. States." Barbour in reply argued for removal of the Indians as the only means to preserve them. He suggested the following outline for a bill:

1. The country west of the Mississippi to be set aside for the exclusive use of the Indians.

2. Removal of the Indians as individuals, instead of as tribes.

3. Establishment of a territorial government for the Indians, to be maintained by the United States.

4. When circumstances permitted, extinction of tribes and distribution of property among individuals.

5. The condition of those Indians who remained in the East to be left unchanged.[12]

Barbour's letter was read and discussed in a cabinet meeting on February 7. Although President Adams noted that Barbour's paper was "full of benevolence and humanity," he wrote: "I fear there is no practicable plan by which they can be organized into one civilized, or half-civilized, Government. Mr. Rush, Mr. Southard, and Mr. Wirt all expressed their doubts

10. Benton to Calhoun, January 28, 1825, OIA LR, Miscellaneous (M234, reel 429); Calhoun to Benton, January 31, 1825, OIA LS, vol. 1, pp. 334–35 (M21, reel 1). The course of the bill (S. 45) can be followed in the Senate and House *Journals*, in serials 107 and 112.

11. *House Journal*, 19–1, serial 130, pp. 97, 276 (H.R. 113).

12. Cocke to Barbour, January 11, 1826, OIA LR, Miscellaneous (M234, reel 429); Barbour to Cocke, February 3, 1826, ASP:IA, 2: 646–49.

of the practicability of Governor Barbour's plan; but they had nothing more effective to propose, and I approved it from the same motive."[13]

The bill failed to pass, however, and at the beginning of the following session of Congress, the House called upon the secretary of war for detailed information on the condition of the Indians, their willingness to migrate, and the probable expense of removal. McKenney answered the request for Barbour in a serious and reasonable document in which he honestly admitted lack of information on much of what the House wanted to know and recognized the difficulties involved in carrying out removal. Yet he insisted strongly that the program was possible and that the Indians could be brought to accept it if they were approached in the right way.[14]

On July 26, 1827, the Cherokee Nation adopted a written constitution patterned after that of the United States in which the Indians asserted that they were one of the sovereign and independent nations of the earth with complete jurisdiction over their own territory. This move on their part caused great alarm. The secretary of war wrote to the Cherokee agent, warning that the constitution could not be understood as changing the relations that then existed between the Indians and the government of the United States. In the House of Representatives the Committee on the Judiciary and then the Committee on Indian Affairs were directed to inquire into the matter, and a special report was requested from the president. Georgia, of course, was indignant and angered by the "presumptuous document."[15]

Because Congress provided no legislation to relieve the situation, Georgia finally began to move against the Cherokees, contending that it could not abide an *imperium in imperio* within the state. Georgia's line of action was to extend the authority of the state and its laws over the Cherokee lands. This would in effect withdraw the Cherokee territory from the status of Indian country, bring control of the lands into Georgia's hands, and by overt as well as subtle pressure force the Indians out. The resolutions of a committee of the Georgia legislature that were approved on December 27, 1827, gave an indication of the direction of the wind. After condemning the bad faith of the federal government for not having extinguished the

13. *Memoirs of John Quincy Adams, Comprising Portions of His Diary from 1795 to 1848*, ed. Charles Francis Adams, 12 vols. (Philadelphia: J. B. Lippincott and Company, 1874–1877), 7: 113. William Clark in his long comments on Barbour's letter showed general agreement. Clark to Barbour, March 1, 1826, ASP:IA, 2: 653–54.

14. McKenney to Barbour, December 27, 1826, OIA LS, vol. 3, pp. 273–85 (M21, reel 3).

15. The Cherokee Constitution is printed in *House Document* no. 91, 23–2, serial 273, pp. 10–19. For congressional action, see *House Journal*, 20–1, serial 168. The president's report with accompanying documents is in *House Executive Document* no. 211, 20–1, serial 173.

Cherokee title, the committee put forth Georgia's position, that the lands within the limits of the state belonged to it absolutely and that because the Indians were merely tenants at will, the state could end that tenancy at any time. The committee insisted that Georgia had the right to extend its authority and laws over the whole territory and to exact obedience to them from all. Another resolution was a thinly veiled threat of the use of force, if necessary, to accomplish Georgia's aims.[16]

The situation grew steadily more serious. How could the claims of the state of Georgia be reconciled with justice to the Indians? John Quincy Adams in his final message to Congress reviewed the problem:

> As independent powers, we negotiated with them [the Indians] by treaties; as proprietors, we purchased of them all the lands which we could prevail upon them to sell; as brethren of the human race, rude and ignorant, we endeavored to bring them to the knowledge of religion and of letters. The ultimate design was to incorporate in our own institutions that portion of them which could be converted to the state of civilization. In the practice of European States, before our Revolution, they had been considered *as children* to be governed; as tenants at discretion, to be dispossessed as occasion might require; as hunters to be indemnified by trifling concessions for removal from the grounds from which their game was extirpated. In changing the system it would seem as if a full contemplation of the consequences of the change had not been taken. We have been far more successful in the acquisition of their lands than in imparting to them the principles or inspiring them with the spirit of civilization. But in appropriating to ourselves their hunting grounds we have brought upon ourselves the obligation of providing them with subsistence; and when we have had the rare good fortune of teaching them the arts of civilization and the doctrines of Christianity we have unexpectedly found them forming in the midst of ourselves communities claiming to be independent of ours and rivals of sovereignty within the territories of the members of our Union. This state of things requires that a remedy should be provided—a remedy which, while it shall do justice to those unfortunate children of nature, may secure to the members of our confederation their rights of sovereignty and of soil.[17]

The House Committee on Indian Affairs, which considered the proposals of President Adams and Secretary of War Peter B. Porter, agreed that

16. *Acts of the General Assembly of the State of Georgia, 1827* (Milledgeville, 1827), pp. 249–50.

17. Message of December 2, 1828, Israel, *State of the Union Messages,* 1: 287. For a study of Adams's changing views about the Indians, see Lynn Hudson Parsons, "'A Per-

removal was necessary because of the crisis growing out of the controversy with the states. The elementary question to be answered was, How are the Indians to be preserved? The committee found only one way: to remove the Indians from the states and establish them on lands beyond the limits of any state or territory. "The policy of urging them to leave their country for another would be deplored," the committee asserted, "if it were not believed to be the only effectual measure to secure the prosperity and happiness of themselves and their posterity." The committee reported a bill to appropriate fifty thousand dollars to enable the president to aid the Indians in their migration westward, but the measure was not passed.[18]

ANDREW JACKSON AND REMOVAL

Then Andrew Jackson—a man of forthright views who did not hesitate to speak his mind and a man who had ample Indian experience to give weight to his utterances—became president of the United States. Jackson had early decided that it was farcical to treat with the Indian tribes as though they were sovereign and independent nations, and he could point to considerable evidence to show that treaties had never been a success.[19]

Jackson himself had been a United States commissioner in drawing up treaties with the southern Indians. As his experience with the Indians

---

petual Harrow upon My Feelings': John Quincy Adams and the American Indian," *New England Quarterly* 46 (September 1973): 339–79.

18. *House Report* no. 87, 20–2, serial 190, pp. 1–3.

19. Jackson's relations with the Indians and his role in their removal from east of the Mississippi have been variously commented upon. Many historians have viewed his opinions and his actions harshly, heaping on him most of the opprobrium for the removal policy. For an extreme example, see Edward Pessen, *Jacksonian America: Society, Personality, and Politics*, rev. ed. (Homewood, Illinois: Dorsey Press, 1978), p. 296, which describes Jackson's position as "a blending of hypocrisy, cant, and rapaciousness, seemingly shot through with contradictions. Inconsistencies however are present only if the language of the presidential state papers is taken seriously. . . . When the lofty rhetoric is discounted and viewed for what is was—sheer rationale for policy based on much more mundane considerations—then an almost frightening consistency becomes apparent." A more seious and balanced appraisal of Jackson's policy, is Satz, *American Indian Policy in the Jacksonian Era.* The events get a special twist in the psychohistory by Michael Paul Rogin, *Fathers and Children: Andrew Jackson and the Subjugation of the American Indian* (New York: Alfred A. Knopf, 1975). Rogin suggests that Jackson was a victim of separation anxiety because of his parents' early death and that he proved his manhood by destroying Indians. Although the book has much good material, its argument is not convincing. A favorable view that attempts to understand the complex situation facing Jackson is Francis Paul Prucha, "Andrew Jackson's Indian Policy: A Reassessment," *Journal of American History* 56 (December 1969): 527–39.

grew, he began to question openly the wisdom of the traditional procedure. In March 1817, while military commander in the South, he had complained to President Monroe about the absurdity of making treaties with the Indians, whom he considered subjects of the United States with no sovereignty of their own. Congress, Jackson maintained, had as much right to legislate for the Indians as for the people of the territories, and he strongly urged—for the good of the Indians, he insisted, as well as for the good of the nation—that Congress make use of this right to prescribe the Indian bounds and to occupy and possess parts of their lands when the safety, interest, or defense of the country should render it necessary. Due compensation was to be given, of course, just as in any exercise of the right of eminent domain. The Indians, he said, "have only a possessory right to the soil, for the purpose of hunting and not the right of domain, hence I conclude that Congress has full power, by law, to regulate all the concerns of the Indians."[20]

Monroe had found Jackson's view "new but very deserving of attention," and, encouraged no doubt by the favorable reception of his views in high circles, Jackson had stuck to his position. In 1820 he wrote to Secretary of War Calhoun on the subject of Indian affairs. The message was the same. It was absurd to treat with the Indians rather than legislate for them. It was "high time to do away with the farce of treating with the Indian tribes." Again his views were approved, but Calhoun was unable to get Congress to modify the treaty system.[21] During the seven and one-half years that Calhoun held the position of secretary of war, with the conduct of Indian affairs under his department, forty treaties were signed with the Indian nations. The picture had not changed. The solemnities were still observed; the documents spoke formally of grants and guarantees as though the great powers of the world were negotiating.

Jackson brought his early views with him when he entered the White House. He was convinced that the Indians could no longer exist as independent enclaves within the state. They must either move west or become subject to the laws of the states.

Assured of presidential sympathy, Georgia took new action against the Cherokees. At the end of 1828 the Georgia legislature added Cherokee lands to certain northwestern counties of Georgia. A year later, it extended the laws of the state over these lands, effective June 1, 1830. Thereafter the Cherokee laws and customs were to be null and void.[22] The Cherokees

20. *Correspondence of Andrew Jackson*, 2: 279–81.

21. Monroe to Jackson, October 5, 1817, ibid., pp. 331–32; Jackson to Calhoun, September 2, 1820, and January 18, 1821, ibid., 3: 32, 36–38; Calhoun to Jackson, November 16, 1821, ibid., p. 132.

22. William C. Dawson, comp., *A Compilation of the Laws of the State of Georgia* (Milledgeville: Grantland and Orme, 1831), pp. 198–99.

immediately protested and made representations to the president and to Congress.

Jackson, whatever his shortcomings in dealing with the Indians, was not one to hide his realistic intentions behind pleasant phrases, for, as he had written to an Indian commissioner a few years earlier, "with all Indians, the best plan will be to come out with candor."[23] Through the instrumentality of Secretary of War John H. Eaton, Jackson answered the Cherokees. Bluntly he told them that they had no hope of succor from the federal government. The letter of Eaton to the delegation of the Cherokees on April 18, 1829, was an unequivocal statement of the Jackson policy.[24]

Eaton informed the Indians that by the Declaration of Independence and the treaty of 1783 all the sovereignty which pertained to Great Britain had been conferred upon the states of the Union. "If, as is the case," he told the Indians, "you have been permitted to abide on your lands from that period to the present, enjoying the right of the soil, and privilege to hunt, it is not thence to be inferred, that this was any thing more than a permission, growing out of compacts with your nation; nor is it a circumstance whence, now to deny to those states, the exercise of their original sovereignty." The treaties with the Indians, which for the supporters of Indian rights were a great arsenal of arguments, were turned to his own uses by the secretary of war. The "emphatic language" of the Treaty of Hopewell, he told the Cherokees, could not be mistaken. The United States *gave peace* to the Indians and took them again into favor and under her protection. The treaty *allotted* and *defined* the hunting grounds. It secured to the Indians the privilege of pursuing game and protection from encroachment. "No right, however, save a mere possessory one, is by the provisions of the treaty of Hopewell conceded to your nation. The soil, and the use of it, were suffered to remain with you, while the Sovereignty abided precisely where it did before, in those states within whose limits you were situated." Later treaties, after renewed hostilities, were similar to the Treaty of Hopewell, guaranteeing occupancy and possession of the Indian country. "But the United States, always mindful of the authority of the States, even when treating for what was so much desired, peace with her red brothers, forbore to offer a guarantee adverse to the Sovereignty of Georgia. They could not do so; they had not the power." The compact of 1802, Eaton added, had nothing to say about sovereignty. Both parties to the compact knew well where it lay: with the state. There was nothing to be offered to the Cherokees but the urgent recommendation that they move west of the Mississippi.

23. Jackson to John D. Terrill, July 29, 1826, *Correspondence of Andrew Jackson*, 3: 308–9.

24. Eaton to Cherokee delegation, April 18, 1829, OIA LS, vol. 5, pp. 408–12 (M21, reel 5). This document was seen at the time—by both friends and foes of Jackson—as epitomizing Jackson's position.

The same doctrine was set forth by Jackson's attorney general, the Georgian John M. Berrien, who insisted that the United States had granted peace to the Cherokees in 1785 as a "mere grace of the conqueror."[25] The argument might have sounded plausible in 1830, but in 1783 and the years following, Congress did not look much like a conqueror imposing terms on the conquered Indians. With nervous anxiety, the United States then sought to keep the Indians at peace at all costs rather than risk any more hostilities, which a new nation in its weakness could ill afford.

Jackson moved ahead boldly. In his first message to Congress, on December 8, 1829, he addressed himself to the problems of the "condition and ulterior destiny of the Indian tribes within the limits of some of our States." He called attention to the fact that some of the southern Indians had "lately attempted to erect an independent government within the limits of Georgia and Alabama," that the states had countered this infringement on their sovereignty by extending their laws over the Indians, and that the Indians in turn had appealed to the federal government. Did the federal government have a right to sustain the Indian pretensions, he asked. His answer was forthright. The Constitution forbade the erection of a new state within the territory of an existing state without that state's permission. Still less, then, could it allow a "foreign and independent government" to establish itself there. On these grounds, he told Congress, he had informed the Indians that their attempt to establish an independent government would not be countenanced by the executive of the United States, and he had advised them either to emigrate beyond the Mississippi or to submit to the laws of the states. He came back to the old argument: if the Indians remained in contact with the whites they would be degraded and destroyed. "Humanity and national honor demand that every effort should be made to avert so great a calamity." The solution was to set apart an ample district west of the Mississippi, to be guaranteed to the Indian tribes as long as they occupied it. There they could be taught the arts of civilization.[26]

Jackson denied any intention to use force. "This emigration should be voluntary, for it would be as cruel as unjust to compel the aborigines to abandon the graves of their fathers and seek a home in a distant land." The protestation had a hollow ring, for the Indians were to be informed that if they remained they would be subject to the state laws and would lose much of their beloved land. With a touch of sarcasm, the president pronounced it visionary for the Indians to hope to retain hunting lands on

25. "Opinion of the Attorney General as to the Right Acquired to the Soil under Existing Treaties with the Cherokees," March 10, 1830, *House Executive Document* no. 89, 21–1, serial 197, pp. 45–46.

26. Israel, *State of the Union Messages*, 1: 308–10.

which they had neither dwelt nor made improvements, "merely because they had seen them from the mountain or passed them in the chase."[27]

Following the suggestion of the president, the House and the Senate each introduced an Indian removal bill. The bills were similar in nature, and the House version was dropped in favor of the Senate bill. The measure, like the president's message, made no mention of coercion to remove the Indians, and on the surface it seemed harmless and humane enough, with its provisions for a permanent guarantee of possession of the new lands, compensation for the improvement left behind, and aid and assistance to the emigrants. But those who knew the policy and practice of Jackson and the Georgians and the adamant stand of the Indians against removal understood that force would be inevitable.

MOTIVATION FOR REMOVAL

The strongest pressure for removal of the Indians from Georgia and the other southeastern states came from the land hunger of the whites. When the cotton plantation system began its dynamic drive west across the gulf plains after the War of 1812, a movement stimulated by the invention of the cotton gin and the seemingly endless demand for cotton to feed the new mills in England and the Northeast, the lands held by the Indians seemed an enormous obstacle. All of the Five Civilized Tribes—Cherokee, Creek, Choctaw, Chickasaw, and Seminole—had sloughed off rims of territory by treaties of cession in the period 1815–1830, a paring down that opened much good land to white exploitation. But all the tribes insisted on retaining their heartlands, sizable blocks of territory that seemed to Georgia and the new states of Mississippi and Alabama (admitted to the Union in 1817 and 1819, respectively) to be alien enclaves in their midst. It was possible for some years to postpone the conflict, as free land was taken up and as Georgia continued to expect action from the federal government in regard to Cherokee lands under the compact of 1802. But in the 1820s the push for new lands intensified, and the vehemence of the demands of the southern states increased. An added element was the discovery of gold within the Cherokee Nation in 1829. As would be the case with strikes in the Far West later in the century, the word of gold fired the Georgians with new enthusiasm for Cherokee lands, and many rushed into the region in violation of the Indians' territorial rights.

There was no effective check upon the covetousness for land. Land was the most important commodity in early nineteenth-century America, and

27. Ibid., p. 310.

the sale of the public domain was a major source of funding for the national government before the Civil War. White society, both northern and southern, had a fundamental belief that the land was there to be exploited and that the Indians were not making full use of its possibilities. Governor George C. Gilmer of Georgia declared in 1830 that "treaties were expedients by which ignorant, intractable, and savage people were induced without bloodshed to yield up what civilized peoples had a right to possess by virtue of that command of the Creator delivered to man upon his formation—be fruitful, multiply, and replenish the earth, and subdue it." To the House Committee on Indian Affairs, which reported the removal bill in 1830, the practice of extinguishing Indian titles by money payments was "but the substitute which humanity and expediency have imposed, in place of the sword, in arriving at the actual enjoyment of property claimed by the right of discovery, and sanctioned by the natural superiority allowed to the claims of civilized communities over those of savage tribes." Semiliterate frontiersmen justified their encroachment on Chickasaw lands by challenging the government to remove them from "fine fertile countrys lying uncultivated."[28]

There were strong arguments made for the rights of the Indians to their lands, but they ultimately foundered on the deepseated conviction that the white man had a superior right to the land. The Jacksonian and Georgian contention that the Indians had only a possessory right to the soil—a "mere right of occupancy"—was not a spur-of-the-moment argument to cover white cupidity for Indian lands. There had long been an overriding reluctance to admit any title in fee for Indians. Despite the Jeffersonian principle that the salvation of the Indians lay in private ownership of land, treaties negotiated with them generally had fallen short of providing fee simple ownership either to individual Indians or to tribes.[29]

The Jacksonian drive to relocate the Indians west of the Mississippi, however, failed to appreciate their attachment to their ancestral homes. The ancestors of the whites who now sought Indian lands had themselves emigrated from their homelands, and thousands of white citizens each year were pulling up their roots and moving west. If whites, seeking a better condition, could adjust to the pains of removal, why not the Indians. Jackson told a Choctaw leader in 1830:

> The attachment you feel for the soil which encompasses the bones of
> your ancestors is well known. Our forefathers had the same feeling

28. Gilmer statement quoted in Albert K. Weinberg, *Manifest Destiny: A Study of Nationalistic Expansionism in American History* (Baltimore: Johns Hopkins Press, 1935), p. 83; *House Report* no. 227, 21–1, serial 200, pp. 6–7; petition of intruders on Chickasaw lands, September 5, 1810, in Carter, *Territorial Papers*, 6: 107.

29. Robert W. McCluggage, "The Senate and Indian Land Titles, 1800–1825," *Western Historical Quarterly* 1 (October 1970): 415–25.

when a long time ago, to obtain happiness, they left their lands beyond the great waters, and sought a new and quiet home in those distant and unexplored regions. If they had not done so, where would have been their children? And where the prosperity they now enjoy? The old world would scarcely have afforded support for a people who, by the change their fathers made, have become prosperous and happy. In future time, so will it be with your children.[30]

By liberal terms and inducements, the promoters of removal hoped to persuade the Indian tribes that it would be to their benefit to move away from the stresses and pressures that came from existence within the state and that the advantages would overcome the attachment to their ancestral lands. Such a voluntary move was made by considerable numbers of Indians, but the great majority preferred to stay where they were, and they insisted on their right to do so.

Desire for Indian lands was not the only motivation for removal. The concern about states' rights and the fear of a bitter federal-state jurisdictional contest that might even lead to military conflict was not simply a rationalization for base economic motives but a very real issue in the pre-Civil War period. The demands made for federal protection of the Indians in their own culture on their ancestral lands within the states in the East ran up against the hard fact that the United States government could not risk an all-out confrontation with Georgia. The federal government did not have a standing army of sufficient strength to protect the enclaves of Indian territory from the encroachments of the whites. Jackson could not withstand Georgia's demands for the end of the *imperium in imperio* represented by the Cherokee Nation and its new constitution, not because of some inherent immorality on his part but because the political situation of America would not permit it.

The jurisdictional dispute cannot be simply dismissed. Were the tribes independent nations? The question received its legal answer from the Supreme Court when John Marshall defined the Indian tribes as "domestic dependent nations." But aside from the judicial decision, were the Indians, in fact, independent, and could they have maintained their independence without the support—political and military—of the federal government? The answer, clearly, was no, as writers at the time pointed out. The federal government could have stood firm in defense of the Indian nation against Georgia, but this would have brought it into head-on collision with a state that insisted its sovereignty was being impinged upon by the Cherokees. This was not a conflict that anyone in the federal government wanted.

30. Jackson to Greenwood LeFlore, August 23, 1830, quoted in Arthur H. DeRosier, Jr., *The Removal of the Choctaw Indians* (Knoxville: University of Tennessee Press, 1970), p. 119.

President Monroe had been slow to give in to the demands of the Georgians. He had refused to be panicked into hasty action before he had considered all the possibilities. But eventually he became convinced that stubborn resistance to the southern states would solve nothing, and from that point on he and his successors, Adams and Jackson, sought to solve the problem by removing the cause. They wanted the Indians to be placed in some area where the problem of federal versus state jurisdiction would not arise, where the Indians could be granted land in fee simple by the federal government and not have to worry about what some state thought were its rights and prerogatives.

There was also, it must be admitted, genuine humanitarian concern for the Indians, in which their voluntary removal out of contact with whites appeared to be a viable, indeed perhaps the only, answer. Despite the optimism of supporters of the programs for civilizing the Indians, an uncomfortable conclusion had become increasingly clear: the contact of Indians with white civilization had deleterious effects upon the Indians. The efforts at improvement were vitiated or overbalanced by the steady pressure of white vices, to which the Indians succumbed. Instead of prospering under white tutelage, Indians in many areas were degenerating and disappearing. That men as knowledgeable in Indian ways as Thomas L. McKenney, William Clark, and the Baptist missionary Isaac McCoy were longtime and ardent promoters of Indian removal should give us pause in seeing only insatiable land hunger or Jacksonian villainy behind the policy.[31] The promoters of the program argued that only if the Indians were removed beyond contact with whites could the slow process of education, civilization, and Christianization take place. Insofar as removal was necessary to safeguard the Indian, to that extent the intercourse laws had failed.

A shift of attitude can be seen in Thomas L. McKenney. His enthusiastic reports on the progress of the Indian schools and Indian civilization in general were replaced by more dismal reporting. Although he had for some time been favorable to the voluntary removal of groups of Indians, he asserted that his tour through the Indian country in 1827 had opened his eyes to the degradation of the eastern tribes. When asked to report in 1830 on the previous eight years of the program for civilizing the Indians, he no longer considered salvation possible in the present location of the tribes. The condition of the Florida Indians he described as "in all respects truly deplorable. It is not known that they have advanced a single step in any

31. Recent scholarly studies of these three men make clear their humanitarian concern for the Indians. See Herman J. Viola, *Thomas L. McKenney: Architect of America's Early Indian Policy, 1816–1830* (Chicago: Swallow Press, 1974); Jerome O. Steffen, *William Clark: Jeffersonian Man on the Frontier* (Norman: University of Oklahoma Press, 1977); George A. Schultz, *An Indian Canaan: Isaac McCoy and the Vision of an Indian State* (Norman: University of Oklahoma Press, 1972).

sort of improvement; and as to the means of education, when offered to them, they were refused." The Indians in the Northwest, he reported, "pretend to nothing more than to maintain all the characteristic traits of their race. They catch fish, and plant patches of corn; dance, paint, hunt, get drunk, when they can get liquor, fight, and often starve." Their condition, however, was far better than that of the Creeks and better than most of the Choctaws. McKenney agreed that those Choctaws who had benefited by instruction were better off than they had been before. "But these were, to my eye," he said, "like green spots in the desert. The rest was cheerless and hopeless enough. Before this personal observation, I was sanguine in the hope of seeing those people relieved, and saved, where they are. But a sight of their condition, and the prospect of the collisions which have since taken place, and which have grown out of the anomalous relations which they bear to the States, produced a sudden change in my opinion and my hopes."[32]

The paternalism of this position, of course, is inescapable. In a typically benevolent frame of mind McKenney wrote in 1829: "Seeing as I do the condition of these people, and that they are bordering on destruction, I would, were I empowered, take them *firmly* but *kindly* by the hand, and tell them they must go; and I would do this, on the same principle that I would take my own children by the hand, firmly, but kindly and lead them from a district of Country in which the plague was raging." President Jackson expressed a similar view in private correspondence in 1829. He said: "You may rest assured that I shall adhere to the just and humane policy towards the Indians which I have commenced. In this spirit I have recommended them to quit their possessions on this side of the Mississippi, and go to a country to the west where there is every probability that they will always be free from the mercenary influence of White men, and undisturbed by the local authority of the states: Under such circumstances the General Government can exercise a parental control over their interests and possibly perpetuate their race."[33]

The idea of parental or paternal care was pervasive. Once removal was accomplished, Jackson told Congress in 1832, "there would be no question of jurisdiction to prevent the Government from exercising such a general control over their affairs as may be essential to their interest and safety."[34]

An example of humanitarian support of removal (although interwoven

---

32. Report of McKenney, March 22, 1830, *Senate Document* no. 110, 21–1, serial 193, pp. 2–3. For a critical, but unconvincing, appraisal of McKenney, see Richard Drinnon, *Facing West: The Metaphysics of Indian-Hating and Empire-Building* (Minneapolis: University of Minnesota Press, 1980), pp. 165–90.

33. McKenney to Eli Baldwin, October 28, 1829, OIA LS, vol. 6, p. 140 (M21, reel 6); Jackson to James Gadsden, October 12, 1829, *Correspondence of Andrew Jackson*, 4: 81.

34. Richardson, *Messages and Papers of the Presidents*, 2: 565–66.

with political interests) was the organization set up in New York City to promote Jackson's removal policy. When prominent church groups spoke out against that policy, McKenney gathered a group of clergymen and lay-men (mostly Dutch Reformed) to counteract the cry that the government was embarked upon an un-Christian enterprise. On July 22, 1829, the Board for the Emigration, Preservation, and Improvement of the Aborig-ines of America was established. McKenney, in addressing the board on August 12, argued removal in humanitarian and religious terms; his con-cern was to preserve the Indians from complete degradation and to enable them to improve and civilize themselves outside of contact with whites. The board, however, was short-lived. It sent a memorial to Congress and issued a pamphlet containing addresses and other documents; but when McKenney was removed from office by Jackson in August 1830, the organi-zation collapsed.[35]

CONTROVERSY AND DEBATE

The Cherokee Indians strongly protested Georgia's action and carried their arguments to the federal government. The politically astute leaders, gener-ally mixed-bloods who were wise in the ways of whites, kept delegations in Washington to watch developments and to present the Cherokee posi-tion to federal officials. On February 17, 1829, the Cherokee delegation ad-dressed a letter to the secretary of war, pointing to the tribes' national and territorial rights and to Georgia's violations of these rights in extending jurisdiction over the Indian lands. Ten days later the Cherokees presented a memorial to Congress in which they made the same points, appealing to the federal government to protect them in their legal rights and to uphold the treaty obligations that the United States had entered into with the tribe.[36]

The Indian action was ineffective in reversing the position of the Jack-son administration. The removal bill introduced in February 1830 was re-

35. Francis Paul Prucha, "Thomas L. McKenney and the New York Indian Board," *Mississippi Valley Historical Review* 48 (March 1962): 635–55. McKenney's address and other pertinent documents are printed in *Documents and Proceedings Relating to the Formation and Progress of a Board in the City of New York, for the Emigration, Preserva-tion, and Improvement, of the Aborigines of America* (New York, 1829). Some of the material is also printed in Thomas L. McKenney, *Memoirs, Official and Personal* (New York: Paine and Burgess, 1846).

36. The letter of February 17 could not be located, but its contents can be determined by the specific reply it occasioned, Eaton's letter of April 18, 1829. The Cherokee memo-rial of February 27, 1829, is printed in *House Document* no. 145, 20–2, serial 187. See also Cherokee memorials of November 5, 1829, and December 18, 1829, in *House Report* no. 311, 21–1, serial 201, pp. 2–9; and Creek memorial of February 3, 1830, against the actions of Alabama, in *House Report* no. 169, 21–1, serial 199.

ported favorably by the Committee of Indian Affairs in both the House and the Senate. The Senate committee urged removal of the Indians to the west, "where they can be secured against the intrusion of any other people; where, under the protection of the United States, and with their *aid*, they can pursue their plan of civilization, and, ere long, be in the peaceable enjoyment of a civil government of their own choice, and where Christian and philanthropist can have ample scope for their labors of love and benevolence." The House committee, in a long exposition of the administration's views, spoke in the same benevolent terms.[37]

This position was countered by a campaign in support of the Cherokees' rights that sought, even before the congressional committees had made their formal reports, to arouse the public conscience against the removal scheme and to convince Congress to support the Indian nations against Georgia and the other states. The campaign, although on the surface a great outpouring of Christian sentiment and a spontaneous upsurge of public opinion, was in fact largely the inspiration and the work of one man, the secretary of the American Board of Commissioners for Foreign Missions, Jeremiah Evarts.

Evarts, born in Vermont in 1781 and a graduate of Yale University, was a lawyer, but he devoted most of his short life to the cause of religion and especially Christian missions. He became associated with the American Board shortly after its founding in 1810 and in 1821 became its secretary. Evarts had close acquaintance with the Cherokees and other southern tribes because of the American Board's missions among them. He had traveled through the Indian country, counted numerous Indian leaders among his personal friends, and had studied their history and legal claims. If any man ever held an absolutely sure position, it was Jeremiah Evarts in regard to the rights of the Cherokee Indians to stay where they were in Georgia and the obligation of the United States to protect those rights without delay or equivocation. But Evarts was more than an expert on the legal rights of the Cherokees. He was a man with a vision of a world fully evangelized, of universal conversion to Christ, and he saw the new American nation as the vehicle of this great work. The movement of Christian benevolence, reaching its height as the Indian question came to the fore, became for Protestant Americans of Evarts's persuasion a great national mission. Evarts insisted upon Christian influence on civil society and upon the obligation of committed Christians to call to task civil rulers if they departed from the path of justice and morality. It was no self-righteous, carping attitude that motivated such criticism but a profound patriotic view that God had called this nation to a special mission—to be a special beacon of good-

37. *Senate Document* no. 61, 21–1, serial 193; *House Report* no. 227, 21–1, serial 200.

ness in a corrupt world—and that God in his vengeance would rain disaster and destruction on America if it, as a nation, sinned against that covenant.[38]

Evarts was convinced that the federal government's refusal to protect the Cherokees against the clamors of Georgia would be a moral wrong, a sin of great magnitude. The only way to prevent it would be through an outcry by the Christians of the nation, protesting against the threatened action with such a loud and persistent voice that the national leaders would turn aside from their sinful plans. Evarts set about to stir up the conscience of the nation and to direct its indignation and sense of outrage into effective channels in the national councils.

The first and most significant work of Evarts in support of the Cherokees was a series of twenty-four articles that appeared in the *National Intelligencer* between August 5 and December 19, 1829, under the pseudonym William Penn. The articles began with a statement of the moral crisis facing the nation in the removal question, the national sin that would bring God's sure punishment if the obligations to the Indians were cast aside, and then moved to a detailed analysis of the Cherokee treaties and their recognition of the Cherokees as a nation. The Penn essays were the fullest and best statement of the Cherokee case and the obligations of the United States to support it. They were reprinted in numerous newspapers and periodicals and widely circulated in pamphlet form. Churchmen and congressmen alike drew their arguments from Evarts's writings, and they looked to him to instruct them as they moved against the Jackson policy and Georgia's actions.[39]

Evarts initiated a widespread campaign of submitting memorials to Congress in favor of the Cherokees and against the removal bill. His strategy was to enlist individuals or groups to organize in major cities public meetings that would endorse a memorial written by Evarts. The first such memorial came from New York City at the end of December 1829. It presented information on the rights of the Indians and their treaties, drawn

38. I follow here the introduction by Francis Paul Prucha to Jeremiah Evarts, *Cherokee Removal: The "William Penn" Essays and Other Writings* (Knoxville: University of Tennessee Press, 1981). Biographical material on Evarts is found in E. C. Tracy, *Memoir of the Life of Jeremiah Evarts, Esq.* (Boston: Crocker and Brewster, 1845); J. Orin Oliphant, ed., *Through the South and West with Jeremiah Evarts in 1826* (Lewisburg, Pennsylvania: Bucknell University Press, 1956); "Biography: Sketch of the Life and Character of Jeremiah Evarts, Esq.," *Missionary Herald* 27 (October 1831): 305–13; (November 1831): 337–46; *Dictionary of American Biography*, s.v. Evarts, Jeremiah, by H. W. Howard Knott. There is an excellent discussion of Evarts' world view in Oliphant, *Jeremiah Evarts*, pp. 8–19.

39. Jeremiah Evarts, *Essays on the Present Crisis in the Condition of the American Indians: First Published in the National Intelligencer, under the Signature of William Penn* (Boston: Perkins and Marvin, 1829).

largely from the Penn essays, and ended with an earnest plea that Congress intervene on the behalf of the Indians in order to "save the nation, by prompt and decisive measures, from the calamity that hangs over it." The memorial did not get a friendly reception in Congress, where Georgia senators and congressmen lashed out against it for impeaching the character and conduct of the southern states. Representative Richard H. Wilde was especially vehement, ridiculing the attempt of the memorialists to meddle in other people's business, and he voiced his disgust over "these everlasting political homilies—this mawkish mixture of sentiment and selfishness—this rage for instructing all the world in their appropriate duties."[40]

Evarts and his friends were chastened, and they moderated their condemnatory language in future memorials, but they were undaunted and stepped up their petition campaign. Another long memorial prepared in Boston was submitted on February 8; then short petitions in the same vein were distributed to friends around the country, to be signed by concerned Christians and forwarded to Congress. Evarts made use of the network of parishes already in touch with the American Board offices and enlisted the aid of special zealots like George B. Cheevers, later to be a well-known abolitionist, who as a student at Andover Seminary pushed with great vigor the campaign to save the Cherokees and thus the sacred honor of the nation.[41]

The final argument of Evarts and other opponents of Indian removal shifted away from the question of legal rights to the inexpediency of emigration. While the supporters of the policy spoke of exchanging eastern lands for lands of equal or better quality in the West, the critics described in the most dismal terms those districts set aside to receive the emigrants. Thus Evarts in the final number of the Penn essays spoke of the misery that removal would bring to thousands of innocent persons, and a memorial he prepared in early 1831 described how the despondent Indians would sink into anarchy and how the temptations of the open land to the west would counteract the forces that had led them to adopt agriculture in the East. Vagrant white men and savage Indians would press upon them, and

40. "Memorial unanimously adopted by a meeting of citizens of the City of New York, convened by a public notice," December 28, 1829, in Records of the U.S. Senate, Memorials and Petitions, Committee on Indian Affairs, 21A–G8, National Archives, Record Group 46; *Register of Debates in Congress*, 6: 7–8.

41. The Boston memorial is in *House Report* no. 245, 21–1, serial 200. Cheever's work can be followed in the Cheever Family Papers, American Antiquarian Society, Worcester, Massachusetts; see also Robert M. York, *George B. Cheever: Religious and Social Reformer, 1807–1890*, University of Maine Studies, 2d ser. no. 69 (Orono, Maine: University Press, 1955). The petitions are in Records of the U.S. Senate, Memorials and Petitions, Committee on Indian Affairs (RG 46), and Records of the U.S. House of Representatives, Memorials and Petitions, Committee on Indian Affairs (RG 233). A good many are published in the serial set of congressional documents.

the very nature of the land assigned them was unknown. That little was in fact known about the lands in the West did not stop fanciful descriptions to suit the purpose of Jackson's opponents.[42]

While Evarts was masterminding the petition campaign, he was simultaneously engaged in another publicity endeavor on behalf of his particular views on the Indian question. This was caused by the appearance in the *North American Review* for January 1830 of a long article by Lewis Cass, governor of Michigan Territory. In the article, which was nominally a review of the pamphlet published by the New York Board for the Emigration, Preservation, and Improvement of the Aborigines of America, Cass came out strongly in favor of Jackson's program of removal, even though he had in the past been critical of the policy. Evarts called the article "the most important thing that has transpired of late, on this subject," and he declared that the piece was "distinguished for servility and sycophancy." He told a friend, "This man wishes to trim his sails, in such a manner as to catch the breeze of government favor and patronage." Evarts succeeded in evoking articles and pamphlets that refuted Cass's position, and Congress and the public were thus made more fully aware of the Boston missionaries' position.[43]

Through all this agitation, Evarts kept in close touch with what was going on in Congress. His chief point of contact in Washington was Theodore Frelinghuysen, Whig senator from New Jersey, a man of similar Christian outlook whose active promotion of such Christian programs as the Sunday School Union and temperance brought him the title of the "Christian statesman." Frelinghuysen corresponded frequently with Evarts about the Indian question and about another of Evarts's campaigns, prohibition of the Sunday mails. Evarts corresponded also with other sympathetic members of Congress, some of whom regularly solicited his advice.[44] As the debate on removal intensified in Congress, Evarts went to

42. A good many historians have accepted the arguments of Jackson's opponents without careful examination, and some have gone so far as to assert that the United States government turned to removal when Major Stephen H. Long submitted his report in 1820 on the desert conditions west of the Mississippi. See the refutation of this position in Francis Paul Prucha, "Indian Removal and the Great American Desert," *Indiana Magazine of History* 59 (December 1963): 299–322.

43. Lewis Cass, "Removal of the Indians," *North American Review* 30 (January 1830): 62–121; Evarts to Eleazar Lord, January 8, 1830, Evarts Family Papers, Yale University Library. An example of the anti-Cass pamphlets was George B. Cheever, *Removal of the Indians: An Article from the American Monthly Magazine; An Examination of an Article in the North American Review; and an Exhibition of the Advancement of the Southern Tribes, in Civilization and Christianity* (Boston: Peirce and Williams, 1830).

44. Frelinghuysen to Evarts, January 11 and February 22 and 24, 1830, Evarts Family Papers; Frelinghuysen to Evarts, February 1, 1830, Letters to Jeremiah Evarts, Library of Congress. See also correspondence with Isaac C. Bates, Edward Everett, and Ambrose

Washington to follow the course of events from close at hand and to offer advice and assistance to the Indians and their defenders. The debates, most of which he listened to from the gallery, increased his concern and confirmed the harsh judgments he had already made—both about the callousness of the Jackson party and about the apathy of the well-meaning Christians of the nation. He applauded the speeches of Senator Frelinghuysen, who spoke for six hours against the administration measure, and of Senator Peleg Sprague of Maine, as well as the similar speeches in the House of Henry R. Storrs of New York, William E. Ellsworth of Connecticut, and Edward Everett and Isaac C. Bates of Massachusetts; and he condemned the arguments of those who spoke in favor of removal.[45]

Jeremiah Evarts and his friends tried to make the removal question simply a moral issue. Would the United States government honor its treaty obligations to the Cherokees, recognize their nationhood, and protect them against the illegal pretensions of Georgia? Or would Jackson and the Georgians drive ahead in their evil ways and make the nation liable to God's punishment? "Nothing can save us," George Cheever wrote, "unless the public mind be universally aroused from its lethargy, and an appeal made, so loud, simultaneous, and decisive, as shall astonish the world at the power of moral feeling in the heart of the country, and cause the most inveterate and bold supporters of national iniquity to tremble."[46]

Yet beneath the surface of this bombast was a strong party feeling; each side accused the other of operating not on moral principles but on political ones. Evarts was particularly pointed in charging the supporters of removal with acting in "the spirit of party." It is clear, nevertheless, that Evarts got all his support from Whigs and other anti-Jackson men and that the fight against removal was used as one means to embarrass the Jackson administration. The administration's supporters, indeed, insisted that the op-

---

Spencer in Evarts Family Papers. Evarts's concern to prohibit the distribution of mail on Sunday was almost as deep as his concern for the Indians—and for the same reason: he feared that the nation, by desecrating the Sabbath, would incure divine wrath. His campaign of petitions against the Sunday mails was comparable to that against Cherokee removal and no more successful.

45. The anti-removal speeches are printed in Jeremiah Evarts, ed., *Speeches on the Passage of the Bill for the Removal of the Indians, Delivered in the Congress of the United States, April and May, 1830* (Boston: Perkins and Marvin, 1830); they are reported in *Register of Debates in Congress*, 6: 305ff and 580ff. Evarts wrote an account of the debate that appeared in seven issues of the *New-York Observer* in the summer and fall of 1830 under the title "History of the Indian Bill." Evarts's stay in Washington is fully reported, in large part through quotations from letters and reports of Evarts, in Tracy, *Jeremiah Evarts*, pp. 353–82. See also Satz, *American Indian Policy in the Jacksonian Era*, pp. 20–31.

46. Cheever, *Removal of the Indians*, p. 10.

position to the removal bill was a matter of party politics and that the sudden feeling for the Indians was a ruse to defeat the president on an important measure. Wilson Lumpkin of Georgia declared that every one of the supporters of the Cherokees was an opponent of Jackson on political grounds, and Jackson himself claimed that the opposition to the bill was part of the "secrete workings of Duff Green, Calhoun and Co."[47]

The Senate passed the removal bill 28 to 19 on April 24 and the House by the narrower margin of 102 to 97 on May 26, and Jackson signed it on May 28, 1830. On its face it was a "liberal" measure that Jackson hoped would win over the Indians. It authorized the president to mark off lands west of the Mississippi "not included in any state or organized territory, and to which the Indian title has been extinguished," and to exchange such districts for lands held by the eastern Indians. The president was "solemnly to assure the tribe or nation with which the exchange is made, that the United States will forever secure and guaranty to them, and their heirs or successors, the country so exchanged with them." The act provided payment for improvements made on present lands, for aid and assistance in emigrating and for the first year after removal, and for protection of the Indians in their new home and the "same superintendence and care" over the tribes that was authorized in their present places of residence. The act specifically noted that it did not authorize or direct the violation of any existing treaties. For carrying out these provisions, Congress appropriated five hundred thousand dollars.[48] The symbol that the act had become was perhaps more important than its specific provisions. Its passage meant congressional authorization of the removal policy that Jackson's administration had announced, and steps were quickly taken to begin treaty negotiations for removal.

The opponents of removal did not admit defeat, however. They noted the slim margin of victory in the House and that Jackson's Maysville Road bill veto on May 27 lost him some of his supporters. Evarts declared that "there is great reason to hope for an expression of public opinion, that will compel the government to be cautious, and will ultimately vindicate the rights of the Indians." Congress adjourned on May 31, three days after Jackson signed the Removal Act, and Evarts pinned his hopes on repeal of the law in the next session of Congress, or at least on the prevention of any further appropriations.[49]

47. Wilson Lumpkin, *The Removal of the Cherokee Indians from Georgia*, 2 vols. (Wormsloe, Georgia, 1907; New York: Dodd, Mead and Company, 1907), 1: 74; Jackson to John Coffee, April 24, 1831, *Correspondence of Andrew Jackson*, 4: 269. The political maneuvering is well described in Satz, *American Indian Policy in the Jacksonian Era*, chapters 1 and 2, pp. 9–63.

48. 4 *United States Statutes* 411–12.

49. Tracy, *Jeremiah Evarts*, pp. 374–81.

While in Washington, Evarts, who conferred frequently with the Cherokee delegates, wrote an address to be signed by the Cherokees on their departure from the capital, a statement that was ultimately issued instead by the Cherokee National Council and published in the *Cherokee Phoenix* of July 24, 1830. It was addressed to the people of the United States as a plea for support against removal, and it offered a succinct and compelling statement of the Cherokee position in opposition to the arguments of Georgia and President Jackson.[50]

Passage of the removal bill did not resolve the controversy. If anything, agitation against the administration measure grew stronger as Jackson began to get the movement under way. During 1830 Evarts redoubled his efforts. He edited and published a collection of the chief speeches in Congress against the Indian bill, and he continued his writing against removal.[51] When the second session of the Twenty-first Congress approached (it opened on December 6), Evarts began a new campaign of petitioning in favor of the Indians, the most significant result of which was a memorial in late January 1831 from the Prudential Committee of the American Board. It was Evarts's last effort, for he was seriously ill. After a futile attempt to regain his health in Cuba, he died on May 10, three months after his fiftieth birthday.[52]

For all practical purposes, the Christian crusade against the removal of the Indians died with Evarts. There were, to be sure, a large number of petitions sent to Congress in early 1831, a sizable proportion of them undoubtedly the result of his agitation. Many of these memorials simply repeated the arguments and pleas of the previous year. Others called for the outright repeal of the Removal Act and for refusal to ratify treaties made under it. Still others emphasized the enforcement of the Indian intercourse law of 1802, which prohibited encroachment on Indian lands. Although many were referred to the committees on Indian affairs, others were merely tabled. They had little or no effect on Congress or the administration. Jackson was further goaded by the Senate, which demanded an accounting of his enforcement of the intercourse law in Georgia. The president replied with a strong vindication of his course of action in withdrawing federal

50. "Address of the 'Committee and Council of the Cherokee nation in General Council convened' to the people of the United States," *Cherokee Phoenix and Indians' Advocate*, July 24, 1830; Tracy, *Jeremiah Evarts*, p. 432. The address is printed in Tracy, pp. 442–48. Tracy notes that the last two paragraphs were added by the Cherokee council.

51. Included among these writings were "Removal of the Indians," *North American Review* 31 (October 1830): 396–442, and two new "William Penn" articles, *National Intelligencer*, November 24 and 27, 1830.

52. "Memorial of the Prudential Committee of the American Board of Commissioners for Foreign Missions," January 26, 1831, *Senate Document* no. 50, 21–2, serial 204. Evarts's illness and death is treated in Tracy, *Jeremiah Evarts*, pp. 410–17.

troops from the Cherokee lands as soon as Georgia had extended her laws over the area.[53] Soon the petitions and the pamphlets and the press agitation died away almost entirely. Opposition to the removal policy by then had moved to the courts.

THE CHEROKEE CASES

Having failed in their appeals to the president and to Congress, the Cherokees took their case to the Supreme Court.[54] At the urging of Senators Daniel Webster and Frelinghuysen and Representative Ambrose Spencer of New York, the Indians engaged William Wirt as their legal adviser. Wirt, who as attorney general in the Monroe and Adams administrations had approved the removal policy, had changed his mind and was convinced that a court decision in favor of the Cherokees would embarrass Jackson. With the aid and advice of such important Whig lawyers as Webster and James Kent, with funds provided by the Cherokee Nation, and with an encouraging statement of sympathy for the Indians' cause from Chief Justice John Marshall, Wirt (aided by John Sergeant) prepared a case. The Cherokee Nation filed suit in the Supreme Court against the state of Georgia; it sought an injunction against Georgia's encroachment on the Indian territory in violation of the tribe's treaty rights. Wirt contended that the Cherokees were a sovereign nation, not subject to Georgia's territorial jurisdiction, and that the laws of Georgia were null and void because they were repugnant to treaties between the United States and the Cherokees, to the intercourse law of 1802, and to the Constitution by impairing contracts arising from the treaties and by assuming powers in Indian affairs that belonged exclusively to the federal government.[55]

53. Jackson's message to the Senate, February 22, 1831, and accompanying documents, *Senate Document* no. 65, 21–2, serial 204.

54. I follow here in large measure the article by Joseph C. Burke, "The Cherokee Cases: A Study in Law, Politics, and Morality," *Stanford Law Review* 21 (February 1969): 500–531. See also Satz, *American Indian Policy in the Jacksonian Era*, pp. 44–50, and William F. Swindler, "Politics as Law: The Cherokee Cases," *American Indian Law Review* 3, no. 1 (1975): 7–20. All these accounts stress the political implications of the Cherokee cases. The crisis for the Supreme Court that these cases occasioned is the theme of Charles Warren, *The Supreme Court in United States History*, rev. ed., 2 vols. (Boston: Little, Brown and Company, 1937), 1: 729–79.

55. Wirt's views were expressed in *Opinion on the Right of the State of Georgia to Extend Her Laws over the Cherokee Nation* (Baltimore: F. Lucas, Jr., 1830). The arguments of Sergeant and Wirt before the Supreme Court were printed in Richard Peters, *The Case of the Cherokee Nation against the State of Georgia* (Philadelphia: John Grigg, 1831). Wirt's interest in the case and his unusual request for a show of opinion from John Marshall before undertaking the case are reported in John P. Kennedy, *Memoirs of the*

Marshall's decision in *Cherokee Nation* v. *Georgia*, March 18, 1831, began with a statement of concern for the Cherokees. "If Courts were permitted to indulge their sympathies," he said, "a case better calculated to excite them can scarcely be imagined." But rather than look at the merits of the case, he moved instead to "a preliminary inquiry." Did the Supreme Court have jurisdiction? Was the Cherokee Nation a foreign state and thus, under the Constitution, able to sue as a plaintiff in the Supreme Court? Marshall admitted that the Cherokees formed "a distant political society, separated from others, capable of managing its own affairs and governing itself." He noted the treaties by which the United States recognized the tribe as capable of maintaining the relations of peace and war and of being responsible for violations of their political engagements. But were the Indians, in fact, a *foreign* state? Marshall's answer was no, that the relation of the Cherokees and the United States was something different, "perhaps unlike that of any other two people in existence." He noted that the commerce clause of the Constitution listed foreign nations, the several states, and Indian tribes and concluded that the three categories were distinct. He wrote:

> The Indian territory is admitted to compose a part of the United States. In all our maps, geographical treatises, histories, and laws, it is so considered. In all our intercourse with foreign nations, in our commercial regulations, in any attempt at intercourse between Indians and foreign nations, they are considered as within the jurisdictional limits of the United States, subject to many of those restraints which are imposed upon our own citizens. They acknowledge themselves in their treaties to be under the protection of the United States; they admit that the United States shall have the sole and exclusive right of regulating the trade with them, and managing all their affairs as they think proper. . . .
>
> Though the Indians are acknowledged to have an unquestionable, and, heretofore, unquestioned right to the lands they occupy, until that right shall be extinguished by a voluntary cession to our government; yet it may well be doubted whether those tribes which reside within the United States, can, with strict accuracy, be denominated foreign nations. They may, more correctly, perhaps, be denominated domestic dependent nations. They occupy a territory to which we assert a title independent of their will, which must take effect in point

---

Life of William Wirt: Attorney-General of the United States, rev. ed., 2 vols. in 1 (Philadelphia: J. B. Lippincott and Company, 1860), 2: 253–58. See also Marvin R. Cain, "William Wirt against Andrew Jackson: Reflection on an Era," *Mid-America* 47 (April 1965): 113–38.

of possession when their right of possession ceases. Meanwhile they are in a state of pupilage. Their relation to the United States resembles that of a ward to his guardian.

They look to our government for protection; rely upon its kindness and its power; appeal to it for relief to their wants; and address the president as their great father. They and their country are considered by foreign nations, as well as by ourselves, as being so completely under the sovereignty and dominion of the United States, that any attempt to acquire their lands, or to form a political connexion with them, would be considered by all as an invasion of our territory, and an act of hostility.[56]

Associate Justices John McLean, Henry Baldwin, and William Johnson concurred with the decision that the court lacked jurisdiction. Baldwin and Johnson did not agree, however, with Marshall's analysis of the status of the Indian tribes, for they denied that the Cherokees had any political or property rights in Georgia.[57] Thus the court for the present sidestepped a critical confrontation with Jackson and Georgia, and the Jacksonites looked upon the decision as a vindication of their position.

Two justices, Smith Thompson and Joseph Story, dissented, for they believed that the Cherokees were a foreign state, but they did not deliver formal opinions. To counteract the publicity given the decisions of Baldwin and Johnson, Marshall urged Thompson and Story to make public their views; Thompson wrote out his opinion, which Story also accepted.[58] The Thompson opinion renewed hope for the Indian cause, for it indicated the possibility that the court might favor the Cherokees if another case were brought before it. The documents of *Cherokee Nation* v. *Georgia* were publicly aired in a publication for private sale by the court reporter, Richard Peters. In addition to the opinions of the justices, the book included the briefs of the Cherokees' counsel, the treaties with the Cherokees, the opinion of James Kent on the Cherokee claims, ·and the trade and intercourse law of 1802.[59] Anti-Jackson agitation took on new life, and Jackson was painted as a "nullifier" who refused to enforce the intercourse law. At the meeting of the National Republicans in Baltimore in December 1831, called in order to name candidates for the 1832 election, much was made of Jackson's villainy regarding the Cherokee issue.

The legal cause of the Indians, meanwhile, entered a new stage. Georgia, under a law that took effect on March 1, 1831, forbade whites to reside in

56. 5 Peters 15–20.
57. The concurring opinions of Baldwin and Johnson are printed ibid., pp. 20–50.
58. Thompson's dissent, although not written until the court had rendered its decision, is printed ibid., pp. 50–80.
59. Peters, *Case of the Cherokee Nation.*

the Cherokee country without a license, for the state hoped to remove the missionaries who encouraged and advised the Indians in their adamant stand against removal. When the missionaries did not leave, they were arrested and imprisoned. Two of them, Samuel A. Worcester and Elizur Butler, refused to accept pardons or licenses. The American Board of Commissioners for Foreign Missions, with which these men were affiliated, hired William Wirt and John Sergeant again to bring the Cherokee cause against Georgia to the Supreme Court. Here was a case to test the Georgia-Cherokee controversy that was clearly within the jurisdiction of the court. It was also a case with important political implications, for both Sergeant and Wirt accepted nomination for public office before the Supreme Court took up the case, the former as vice presidential candidate for the National Republican Party and the latter as presidential candidate for the Anti-Masonic Party. They had much at stake in a decision that would reflect adversely upon Jackson as he sought a second term.

Marshall's decision in the case of *Worcester* v. *Georgia*, delivered on March 3, 1832, was a forthright vindication of the Cherokee position, for he declared unconstitutional the extension of state law over Cherokee lands. In his long opinion, the chief justice again examined the status of the Indian tribes and now came to a conclusion that emphasized the political independence of the Cherokees considerably more than had his decision of the previous year.

> The Indian nations had always been considered as distinct, independent political communities, retaining their original natural rights, as the undisputed possessors of the soil, from time immemorial with the single exception of that imposed by irresistible power, which excluded them from intercourse with any other European potentate than the first discoverer of the coast of the particular region claimed; and this was a restriction which those European potentates imposed on themselves, as well as on the Indians. The very term "nation," so generally applied to them, means "a people distinct from others." The Constitution, by declaring treaties already made, as well as those to be made, to be the supreme law of the land, has adopted and sanctioned the previous treaties with the Indian nations, and consequently admits their rank among those powers who are capable of making treaties. The words "treaty" and "nation" are words of our own language, selected in our diplomatic and legislative proceedings, by ourselves, having each a definite and well understood meaning. We have applied them to Indians, as we have applied them to the other nations of the earth. They are applied to all in the same sense.

Marshall argued that the nationhood of the Indians was not destroyed by treaties acknowledging the protection of the United States, for "the settled doctrine of the law of nations is, that a weaker power does not surrender its independence—its right to self-government, by associating with a stronger, and taking its protection." The Cherokee Nation, therefore, was "a distinct community, occupying its own territory, with boundaries accurately described, in which the laws of Georgia can have no force, and which the citizens of Georgia have no right to enter, but with the assent of the Cherokees themselves, or in conformity with treaties, and with the acts of Congress." All intercourse with the Indian nations was vested, not in the state, but in the federal government.[60]

The Supreme Court issued a special mandate ordering the Georgia court to reverse its conviction of Worcester and release him, but there were loopholes in federal laws that made the court's action ineffective. United States marshals could not be sent to free the prisoners until the state judge had refused formally to comply with the order. But Georgia completely ignored the court's proceedings, and no written refusal was forthcoming. Anyway, the Supreme Court adjourned before it could report Georgia's failure to conform. Nor was there any other procedure that Jackson could adopt, even if he had wanted to. He himself declared that "the decision of the supreme court has fell still born, and they find that they cannot coerce Georgia to yield to its mandate."[61]

William Wirt and other opponents of Jackson made use of the *Worcester* decision to charge the president with failure to enforce federal laws, even though they knew that he was powerless to act in the case, and anti-Jacksonites made much of the continual imprisonment of the missionaries. In typical campaign rhetoric, the *Boston Daily Advertiser* asked: "Will the Christian people of the United States give their sanction, by placing him again in office, to the conduct of a President who treats the ministers of the Christian religion with open outrage, loads them with chains, drags them from their peaceful homes to prison, commits them to defiance of law like common criminals to the penitentiary, and violently keeps them there, against the decision of the highest law authority affirming their innocence?"[62]

For his part, Jackson hoped that the impossibility of enforcing the Supreme Court's decision might help to convince the Indians that voluntary removal would be the only practicable solution. He urged Governor Wil-

60. 6 Peters 559–63.

61. Jackson to John Coffee, April 7, 1832, *Correspondence of Andrew Jackson*, 4: 430. Historians still like to quote an alleged Jackson aphorism—"Well, John Marshall has made his decision; now let him enforce it!"—even though it is extremely unlikely that he made such a statement and it is clear that he had no legal grounds for acting. The matter is laid to rest effectively in Warren, *Supreme Court*, 1: 755–68; see also Burke, "Cherokee Cases," pp. 524–28.

62. Quoted in Burke, "Cherokee Cases," p. 528.

son Lumpkin of Georgia not to act in any way that would exacerbate the conflict, and Lumpkin agreed to act in concert with the federal government. The president asked Georgia to pardon the missionaries, and the American Board persuaded them to accept the release.[63]

The rapprochement was due in large part to the nullification threat from Georgia's neighboring state South Carolina, which came in the critical months after *Worcester* v. *Georgia*. Jackson moved cautiously lest he drive Georgia into the nullification camp; but more important, Jackson's opponents saw the danger to the Union that arose from South Carolina's action, and they tempered their criticism of Jackson as he stood firm against nullification. In the end, unionist sentiment proved greater than sympathies for the Cherokees, and the Indians' devoted friends on the American Board urged them to sign a removal treaty. Even Senator Frelinghuysen in April 1832 came to the conclusion that the Indians should move if offered a liberal treaty.[64]

Undoubtedly the Cherokee controversy lost votes for the Democratic Party in the election of 1832, but it was not an issue of sufficient weight to defeat the popular president. When Jackson was handily reelected in November 1832, hope for preserving the Cherokees in their old homes practically vanished.

63. Ibid., p. 530.
64. Edwin A. Miles, "After John Marshall's Decision: *Worcester* v. *Georgia* and the Nullification Crisis," *Journal of Southern History* 39 (November 1973): 519–44.

CHAPTER 8

The Emigration of the Southern Tribes

Choctaws. Creeks. Chickasaws.

Investigating the Lands in the West.

Seminoles and the Florida War.

Cherokees and the Trail of Tears.

The test of the removal policy was not the passage of the Removal Act or the legal decisions in the Cherokee cases of the Supreme Court. It came in the implementation of the policy during the administrations of Jackson and Martin Van Buren. The decade of the 1830s was matched by no other in American history as a dramatic period in relations between the United States government and the Indians. Removal treaties with the Five Civilized Tribes were negotiated—under various levels of duress—between 1830 and 1835, and by 1840 the bulk of the southeastern Indians, some sixty thousand tribesmen, were settled in the Indian Territory, now the state of Oklahoma, to continue their national existence. This uprooting of Indian nations from their ancestral homes was a traumatic experience and has become for many the most powerful symbol of white inhumanity toward the Indians. It was, however, a complex and confusing event, and the government was ill prepared for the tremendous physical task of moving so many thousands of men, women, and children and establishing them in the undeveloped regions west of the Mississippi.[1]

---

1. A long-accepted descriptive work on the removal process of the southern tribes is Grant Foreman, *Indian Removal: The Emigration of the Five Civilized Tribes of Indians* (Norman: University of Oklahoma Press, 1932); it is not a well-balanced account, however, for it overemphasizes the hardships and miseries.

CHOCTAWS

The first of the southern Indians to emigrate were the Choctaws, who moved from their homes in Mississippi to the region assigned them in what is now southeastern Oklahoma. Their removal was a sort of test case that exhibited the governmental pressures, tribal factionalism, hardships on the march, and troubles in establishing the nation in the West that marked the whole removal process.[2]

The Choctaws had long experienced white pressures upon their nation. In 1801, 1803, 1805, and 1816 they had reluctantly signed treaties of cession with the United States by which large areas passed into the hands of the whites.[3] Although the Indians had retained most of central Mississippi, the creation of the state in 1817 brought increased demands for the Indian lands. After some unsuccessful attempts at negotiations, the United States (with Andrew Jackson as principal commissioner) signed the Treaty of Doak's Stand with the Choctaws on October 18, 1820. The preamble noted that it was "an important object with the President of the United States, to promote the civilization of the Choctaw Indians, by the establishment of schools amongst them; and to perpetuate them as a nation, by exchanging, for a small part of their land here, a country beyond the Mississippi River, where all, who live by hunting and will not work, may be collected and settled together." The Choctaws, in exchange for five million acres in west central Mississippi, received some thirteen million acres between the Arkansas and Canadian rivers and the Red River, partly in Arkansas Territory and partly to the west. The residents of Arkansas were hostile to the treaty, which would bring more Indians into the territory, and the Choctaws for their part were reluctant to leave Mississippi. In 1825, by a treaty signed in Washington, a new boundary line was drawn along the western border of Arkansas and additional annuities were provided for the Choctaws.[4]

Under the Removal Act of 1830, Jackson sought to eliminate the re-

2. The fullest work on Choctaw removal is Arthur H. DeRosier, Jr., *The Removal of the Choctaw Indians* (Knoxville: University of Tennessee Press, 1970), but it gives too much weight to differences between the removal policies of Calhoun and Jackson. A good brief account is Muriel H. Wright, "The Removal of the Choctaws to the Indian Territory, 1830–1833," *Chronicles of Oklahoma* 6 (June 1928): 103–28. Ronald N. Satz, *American Indian Policy in the Jacksonian Era* (Lincoln: University of Nebraska Press, 1975), pp. 64–96, treats Choctaw removal as a "test case." See also Foreman, *Indian Removal*, pp. 19–104.

3. Kappler, pp. 56–58, 69–70, 87–88, 137. These treaties are discussed in DeRosier, *Removal of the Choctaw Indians*, pp. 28–37.

4. Kappler, pp. 191–95, 211–14; DeRosier, *Removal of the Choctaw Indians*, pp. 53–99.

maining Choctaws from Mississippi by the cession of all the lands they still owned in the state, and some of the Choctaws were receptive to the idea. Greenwood LeFlore, a mixed-blood Choctaw courted by the government and encouraged by the Methodist missionary Alexander Talley, drafted a removal treaty very favorable to the Indians and sent it to the president for acceptance. Although Jackson took the unprecedented step of submitting the "treaty" to the Senate for its advice, nothing came of the move, for the Senate refused to consider the document. Jackson then sent Secretary of War John Eaton and his old friend John Coffee to treat with the Choctaws in Mississippi, where they met with a huge gathering of five to six thousand Indians at Dancing Rabbit Creek in September 1830. Having sent the missionaries away from the treaty grounds lest they influence the Indians, Eaton and Coffee warned the Indians that if they did not move they would have to submit to state laws and thus lose their tribal existence. By providing generous land allotments and other benefits to tribal leaders, the commissioners were able to sign a treaty with the Choctaws on September 27.[5] The Choctaws agreed to relinquish all their lands east of the Mississippi and in return received "in fee simple to them and their descendants, to inure to them while they shall exist as a nation and live on it" the territory that had already been marked out in the treaty of 1825. The national existence of the Indians in the West was strongly guaranteed by the United States in the fourth article:

> The Government and people of the United States are hereby obliged to secure to the said Choctaw Nation of Red People the jurisdiction and government of all the persons and property that may be within their limits west, so that no Territory or State shall ever have a right to pass laws for the government of the Choctaw Nation of Red People and their descendants; and that no part of the land granted them shall ever be embraced in any Territory or State; but the U.S. shall forever secure said Choctaw Nation from, and against, all laws except such as from time to time may be enacted in their own National Councils, not inconsistent with the Constitution, Treaties, and Laws of the United States; and except such as may, and which have been enacted by Congress, to the extent that Congress under the Constitution are required to exercise a legislation over Indian Affairs. But the Choctaws, should this treaty be ratified, express a wish that Congress may grant to the Choctaws the right of punishing by their own laws, any

5. Kappler, pp. 310–19; DeRosier, *Removal of the Choctaw Indians,* pp. 116–28. Older accounts of the treaty are Henry S. Halbert, "The Story of the Treaty of Dancing Rabbit," *Publications of the Mississippi Historical Society* 6 (1902): 373–402; George Strother Gaines, "Dancing Rabbit Creek Treaty," *Historical and Patriotic Series of Alabama State Department of Archives and History,* 10 (1928): 1–31.

white man who shall come into their nation, and infringe any of their national regulations.

The United States, moreover, agreed to protect the Choctaws from domestic strife and from foreign enemies "on the same principle that the citizens of the United States are protected." Annuities from older treaties would continue, and the treaty authorized an additional twenty thousand dollars for twenty years. In addition, the United States was to provide houses for chiefs, schools, mechanics, and miscellaneous goods, and to educate forty Choctaw youth for a period of twenty years.

The treaty showed the ambivalence of the removal policy: whereas it made every effort to clear Mississippi of tribal Indians and included all sorts of inducements to encourage emigration, it at the same time allotted lands to Indians within the ceded territory east of the Mississippi. There were three categories of such allotments. First, 80 to 320 acres went to heads of families, according to the amount of land they had under cultivation. They were expected to sell these lands in order to pay for their improvements and to have money to pay debts or to aid in beginning a new life in the West. If no private sale was made, the United States would buy the allotments for fifty cents an acre. A second type of reservation went to persons who had some claim upon the government. These "special reservations" ranged from 320 to 2,560 acres, and some were floating claims that could be located anywhere within the cession; many of these grants were made in supplementary articles to the treaty signed on September 28. Most of these allottees sold their lands to speculators. The third type of grant was intended for those who desired to stay in the state—640 acres to heads of families and lesser amounts to others—to be granted in fee simple after five years of residence. The agent, William Ward, did not register all such claims as the treaty directed, however, seriously upsetting the intended operation of the system. All in all, the disposition of these lands and the settlement of claims arising from their sale led to nearly interminable conflicts between the Indians, bona fide settlers, and land speculators that delayed removal and unsettled land titles for years following the treaty.[6]

The Choctaw treaty was the sort of treaty, recognizing Indian political and property rights, that the Jackson administration hoped would make removal easy to swallow. There was considerable grumbling about its provisions among some of the Choctaws and a flaring up of intratribal animosities, however, and the government moved to counteract opposition.

6. The best discussion of these problems is Mary E. Young, *Redskins, Ruffleshirts, and Rednecks: Indian Allotments in Alabama and Mississippi, 1830–1860* (Norman: University of Oklahoma Press, 1961), pp. 47–72. Documents concerning Choctaw reservations are in *Senate Document* no. 266, 23–1, serial 240.

It promised to give the position of removal agent east of the Mississippi to George S. Gaines, a longtime trader among the Choctaws who was highly respected by them. Gaines led an exploration party west to investigate the nature of the lands designated for the tribe, and the party bought back a favorable report. The attitude of the tribe toward the treaty was ultimately neither enthusiasm nor opposition, but resignation. Chief David Folsom wrote: "We are exceedingly tired. We have just heard of the ratification of the Choctaw Treaty. Our doom is sealed. There is no other course for us but to turn our faces to our new homes toward the setting sun."[7]

The treaty specified emigration in three groups, the first in the fall of 1831 and the others in 1832 and 1833. The federal government would remove the Indians "under the care of discreet and careful persons, who will be kind and brotherly to them" and furnish them with ample corn and beef or pork for twelve months in their new homes. Some of the Indians, estimated at about one thousand, moved on their own before the official emigrant groups were organized, but most awaited the government's assistance. The operation, directed by the army's commissary general of subsistence, George Gibson, was carefully planned, with supplies accumulated along the route of travel and civilian agents and army officers appointed to oversee the actual movement. But confusion soon appeared, as the agents and army officers bickered among themselves and as maldistribution of rations caused delays. Late departures exposed the emigrants to unusually severe winter storms, and the Indians experienced great misery en route, even though the army officers who met them in the West exerted extraordinary efforts to meet the needs of the desperate travelers. Alexis de Tocqueville, who observed the Choctaws crossing the Mississippi at Memphis in 1831, wrote:

> It was then in the depths of winter, and that year the cold was exceptionally severe; the snow was hard on the ground, and huge masses of ice drifted on the river. The Indians brought their families with them; there were among them the wounded, the sick, newborn babies, and old men on the point of death. They had neither tents nor wagons, but only some provisions and weapons. I saw them embark to cross the great river, and the sight will never fade from my memory. Neither sob nor complaint rose from that silent assembly. Their afflictions were of long standing, and they felt them to be irremediable.[8]

In an attempt to better organize the removal process, Secretary of War Cass in April 1832 relieved all civilian agents and put the entire removal

7. Quoted in DeRosier, _Removal of the Choctaw Indians,_ p. 128.
8. Alexis de Tocqueville, _Democracy in America,_ ed. J. P. Mayer and Max Lerner, trans. George Lawrence (New York: Harper and Row, 1966), pp. 298–99. See also the

operation in military hands under General Gibson, and on May 15 he issued a set of regulations to govern the later removals.[9] The removals of 1832 and 1833 went more smoothly, but jurisdictional disputes disrupted the emigration, and in 1832 the appearance of cholera in the Mississippi Valley caused still further alarm and hardship. Altogether about 12,500 Choctaws settled in the Indian Territory; some 600 more remained in Mississippi, on allotments provided by the treaty or simply as vagrants. Little by little, many of them drifted west to join their brethren, but Choctaws still remain in the state today. The total expenditure for the Choctaw removal, including the treaty negotiations, was more than $5 million, a larger sum than the Jackson administration had estimated for the removal of all the eastern tribes. From the sale of the Choctaw cession, however, the federal government received more than $8 million, and after long negotiations about that sum and about other Choctaw claims, the United States paid the Choctaws about $3 million.[10]

The Choctaw emigration was not the model removal project that Jackson had intended—administrative mixups, high costs, bad weather, and tribal factionalism saw to that—but neither was it so disastrous as to form a hindrance to other removals.

CREEKS

The situation of the Creeks in Alabama and Georgia was much like that of the Choctaws. The Creek Nation had had long dealings with the federal government and with the southern states and in 1790 under the leadership of Alexander McGillivray had come to terms with the United States and placed itself under federal protection. But the Creeks were deeply divided, and when the Red Sticks became openly hostile during the War of 1812, their resounding defeat by Andrew Jackson at the Battle of Horseshoe Bend led to the massive cession of territory in Georgia and Alabama at the

---

account quoted in George Wilson Pierson, *Tocqueville in America* (Garden City, New York: Doubleday and Company, 1959), pp. 379–81.

9. *Senate Document* no. 512, 23–1, serial 244, pp. 343–49. The five volumes of *Senate Document* no. 512, serials 244–248, contain correspondence and other documents assembled by the commissary general of subsistence in response to Senate resolutions and cover the period between November 30, 1831, and December 27, 1833. These volumes are a very rich resource for the removal operations in 1832 and 1833. A description of the contents is provided in George Gibson to Cass, October 31, 1834, in serial 244, p. 3.

10. DeRosier, *Removal of the Choctaw Indians*, p. 163. For an account of the Choctaw claims controversy, see W. David Baird, *Peter Pitchlynn: Chief of the Choctaws* (Norman: University of Oklahoma Press, 1972).

MAP 2: Land Cessions of the Five Civilized Tribes

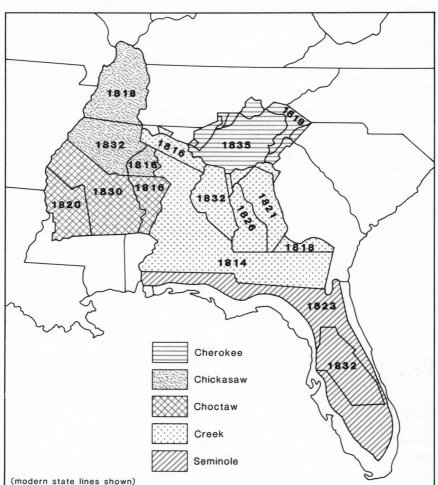

Treaty of Fort Jackson in 1814. In 1818 and 1821 other parcels of land were ceded in Georgia.[11]

In 1825 another large cession was made at the Treaty of Indian Springs, which included a provision for a grant of land in the Indian Territory in exchange for the ceded lands. This treaty had been negotiated by a small pro-removal faction led by William McIntosh against the clear stipulation of Creek law providing for the execution of any chief who subscribed to an unauthorized land cession, and McIntosh and some of his associates were

11. Kappler, pp. 107–10, 155–56, 195–98.

killed by order of the Creek council. When President John Quincy Adams learned of the fraudulent nature of the treaty, he determined to make a new treaty, which he did in Washington in 1826. This treaty validated the cession of land in Georgia, sought to adjust amicably the dissension between the Creek factions, and provided for removal to lands to be selected in the West. Prosperous mixed-blood members of the McIntosh faction migrated to the Indian Territory and laid out plantations in the Arkansas and Verdigris valleys.[12]

The Creeks who remained in Alabama were soon subjected to pressures from the state, which added the Creek territory to organized counties and extended the jurisdiction of local courts over the Indians, and from white intruders on their lands. Federal officials used such actions to support their arguments that the only salvation for the Creeks lay in removal from the state. Finally, on March 24, 1832, Chief Opotheyahola and other Creek leaders signed a treaty in Washington with Lewis Cass.[13]

The treaty was not specifically a removal treaty. Although the Creeks ceded to the United States all their lands east of the Mississippi, they were to receive allotments within the cession (a full section to each of ninety principal chiefs and a half-section to all other heads of families). The Indians were authorized to sell these allotments "to any other persons for a fair consideration," or to remain on the lands themselves and after five years receive a fee simple title. The United States was "desirous that the Creeks should remove to the country west of the Mississippi and join their countrymen there" and agreed to pay for the emigration and one year's subsistence in the West, but the treaty specifically stated that it was "not to be construed so as to compel any Creek Indian to emigrate but they shall be free to go or stay, as they please." The Creek territory west of the Mississippi was solemnly guaranteed to the Indians, and their right to govern themselves free from interference by any state or territory was recognized "so far as may be compatible with the general jurisdiction which Congress may think proper to exercise over them."

The treaty stipulated that intruders on the Creek lands in Alabama would be removed until the lands were surveyed and allotments selected (except for whites who had made improvements without expelling Creeks

---

12. Ibid., pp. 214–17, 264–68. A subsequent treaty of November 15, 1827, provided for the cession of Creek lands in Georgia that had not been included in the 1826 treaty. Ibid., pp. 284–86. For discussion of the treaty, see Annie H. Abel, "The History of Events Resulting in Indian Consolidation West of the Mississippi," *Annual Report of the American Historical Association for the Year 1906,* 1: 344–57; and Angie Debo, *The Road to Disappearance* (Norman: University of Oklahoma Press, 1941), pp. 88–95.

13. Kappler, pp. 341–43. Creek memorials prior to the treaty that complained of the acts of Alabama and demanded protection are printed in *Senate Document* no. 53, 21–1, serial 193, and *House Document* no. 102, 22–1, serial 218.

from theirs, who could remain to gather their crops). When all the reservations had been made, they would amount to a little more than two million acres out the approximately five million in the cession. The surplus land would be open to white entry.

The treaty, on its face, seemed like a reasonable document, for it supported Creeks who chose to emigrate and provided for those who preferred to stay; but its actual operation was disastrous for the Creeks. Despite its promises to evict intruders, the federal government in fact was unwilling or unable to do so, and the Creek lands were quickly overrun. Moreover, the Indians, unused to handling financial matters, were victimized by speculators, who moved in to gain title to the allotments and force the Indians off the land. The frauds were spectacular and widespread, making a mockery of the treaty intentions, and the government seemed impotent to stem the speculators' chicanery. The commissioner of Indian affairs, on receiving the report of a commission sent to investigate, declared in exasperation in 1838: "It is shocking to reflect on the disclosures elicited. They embrace men of every degree. Persons, heretofore deemed respectable, are implicated in the most disgraceful attempts to defraud those who are incapacitated from protecting their own interests; whose presence, as far from being any interruption to the plundering of themselves, was sometimes sought, as their instrumentality was used to effect their own ruin. This conduct, derogatory to civilized men, was not inaptly termed 'land stealing.'"[14]

Whites intimidated the Indians, who looked in vain for their promised protection. The whole Creek Nation was in a state of turmoil and bitterness resulting from the premature and illegal action of the whites, and a government attempt to get the Creeks to sign a new treaty that would provide for immediate removal came to nothing. Only a small number migrated in 1834, but the Indians, hoping that everything would be adjusted satisfactorily, continued their preparations for removal. Prospects looked good until the Indians discovered that the contract for their removal had been let to a company of men who had been active in defrauding them of their lands. The tension on both sides mounted, and destitute Indians sought refuge wherever they could find it, some moving into Cherokee country in Alabama and Georgia. The smoldering situation broke into open fire in the spring of 1836. Georgia militia attacked Creeks who had encamped on Georgia soil, and roving bands of Creeks began to attack and kill whites and destroy their property.[15]

14. T. Hartley Crawford to Joel R. Poinsett, May 11, 1838, *House Document* no. 452, 25–2, serial 331, p. 15. A detailed history of the Creek frauds is given in Young, *Redskins, Ruffleshirts, and Rednecks*, pp. 73–113. See also Foreman, *Indian Removal*, pp. 129–39.

15. I follow here the discussion of the Creek troubles in Francis Paul Prucha, *The*

As the alarming reports reached Washington, Secretary of War Cass issued orders to remove the Creeks as a military measure. He ordered General Thomas S. Jesup to inaugurate a military operation against the Indians, subdue them, and force their removal to the West. In the "Creek War" of 1836 several thousand troops were ordered into the Creek country. General Winfield Scott, leaving behind his Seminole difficulties in Florida, arrived at Savannah on May 22 and assumed general command of the war. He sent Jesup to Alabama to direct the operations of the Alabama militia toward the Creeks on the Chattahoochee River, and he himself planned to advance toward the same objective from the east. Between them, the two forces would find and defeat the Indians. Before Scott could perfect his preparations, however, Jesup acted on his own against the hostiles. Fearing that he could no longer restrain the militia, who were eager for action as reports of new Indian ravages came in, he moved directly into the heart of the Indian country. In a few days he had located the principal Creek camp and had captured the leader, Eneah Micco, and three or four hundred of the warriors. The whites' success quieted the Indians, and Jesup wrote to Scott that he had brought tranquility once more to the frontier.[16]

The subdued Creeks were now removed to the West. Dejected warriors, handcuffed, chained, and guarded by soldiers, left Fort Mitchell on July 2, followed by wagons and ponies carrying the children and old women and the sick. On July 14 almost 2,500 Indians, including 800 warriors, were embarked at Montgomery and conveyed down the Alabama River to Mobile, thence to New Orleans and up the rivers to the western lands of the Creeks. The remainder of the hostiles left Montgomery on August 2. The friendly Creeks soon followed their brothers west. In all, 14,608 Creeks were removed in 1836, including 2,495 enrolled as hostile. A number of Creek warriors who had enlisted for service in Florida against the Seminoles were released too late to emigrate in 1836 and followed the next year.[17]

CHICKASAWS

The Chickasaw Nation in northern Mississippi and northwestern Alabama suffered the same disabilities in relations with its white neighbors as

Sword of the Republic: The United States Army on the Frontier, 1783–1846 (New York: Macmillan Company, 1969), pp. 258–61.

16. The military strategy and campaign are treated in Charles W. Elliott, *Winfield Scott: The Soldier and the Man* (New York: Macmillan Company, 1937), pp. 310–21. Letters and reports dealing with the operations are in *House Document* no. 154, 24–2, serial 304, and *American State Papers: Military Affairs*, 7: 168–365.

17. Foreman, *Indian Removal*, pp. 152–90; "Statements of the Probable Number of

did the other southern tribes. Because they blocked white expansion into rich lands, the Chickasaws were ultimately forced to give in to the pressures put upon them by the states and the federal government, to cede all their lands east of the Mississippi, and to move west. Their removal, however, was more tranquil and the return they got for their lands more equitable than was the case with the other tribes.[18]

In 1816 and 1818, in treaties for which Andrew Jackson was one of the United States commissioners, the Chickasaws had ceded lands in Alabama, Tennessee, and Kentucky north of the Mississippi boundary in return for annuities and reservations of land for certain chiefs.[19] But they were firm in their refusal to part with the heart of their domain in northern Mississippi, and attempts of the government to win their agreement to removal in 1826 came to naught. The nation was politically and economically in the control of mixed-bloods, of whom the Colbert family was dominant. These leaders, although identifying themselves with tribal interests and thus gaining support of the full-bloods, managed to run the nation for their own benefit as well as that of the tribe, and they dealt skillfully with federal officials.

Immediately after the passage of the Removal Act, President Jackson himself met the Chickasaw leaders at Franklin, Tennessee, where the Indians signed a provisionary treaty on August 31, 1830, with Secretary of War John Eaton and John Coffee, the United States commissioners. By it the Indians ceded their lands east of the Mississippi in return for sizable individual allotments within the ceded territory, but the cession was contingent upon the location of a suitable territory in the West as the ultimate home of the Chickasaws. Because the Indians' investigating party failed to agree upon such a district, the treaty was null and void, and Jackson did not submit it to the Senate for ratification.[20]

The will of the Chickasaws not to move from Mississippi had been broken by encroachments of whites on their lands and by the action of the state in extending jurisdiction over the nation, erasing the tribal government and destroying the power of the chiefs. The Indians' appeal to Jackson against these evils met the same response given to the Cherokees, Choctaws, and Creeks: "To these laws, where you are, you must submit;— there is no preventive—no other alternative. Your great father cannot, nor can congress, prevent it. . . . [Your great father's] earnest desire is, that you

---

Creek Warriors Engaged in Hostilities against the United States during the Years 1836 and 1837," *American State Papers: Military Affairs*, 7: 951–52.

18. Chickasaw removal is treated in Arrell M. Gibson, *The Chickasaws* (Norman: University of Oklahoma Press, 1971), pp. 122–83, and Foreman, *Indian Removal*, pp. 193–226.

19. Kappler, pp. 135–37, 174–77.

20. This unratified treaty is printed ibid., pp. 1035–40.

may be perpetuated and preserved as a nation; and this he believes can only be done and secured in your consent to remove to a country beyond the Mississippi."[21]

With the failure of the Franklin treaty, the United States moved quickly to new negotiations carried on by John Coffee, and on October 20, 1832, at the Chickasaw council house at Pontotoc Creek, a new treaty was signed. "The Chickasaw Nation," the preamble read, "find themselves oppressed in their present situation; by being made subject to the laws of the States in which they reside. Being ignorant of the language and laws of the white man, they cannot understand or obey them. Rather than submit to this great evil, they prefer to seek a home in the west, where they may live and be governed by their own laws."[22]

The new treaty was similar to the Franklin treaty. Chickasaw lands were ceded to the government; they would be surveyed immediately and placed on sale, to be sold for what the market would bring. Meanwhile, each adult Indian received a temporary homestead (ranging from one section to four sections, depending on the size of the family). The money from the sale of these temporary reservations and of the surplus lands would be placed in a general fund of the Chickasaw Nation, and from it would come the costs of survey and of removal. In 1834 amendments were made to the Pontotoc treaty for the benefit of the Chickasaws; the size of the temporary homesteads was increased and provision was made for land for orphans. Moreover, the temporary lands were granted in fee simple, and the proceeds from their sale would now go to the individuals holding the land. The treaty provided for a tribal commission to supervise the sales and to judge the competence of individuals to assume direct control over the sale money.[23]

As the survey and sale of the lands in Mississippi proceeded, Chickasaw commissioners sought a satisfactory territory in the West. It had always been the intention of the United States that the Chickasaws would share the western lands assigned to the Choctaws, but the two tribes had been unable to come to an agreement. Finally, on January 17, 1837, at Doaksville in the Choctaw Nation, a treaty was signed; it provided for the purchase by the Chickasaws of the central and western sections of the Choctaw lands for $530,000, and it granted the Chickasaws certain privileges within the Choctaw Nation.[24] The Chickasaws then began their emigra-

---

21. *Niles' Register*, September 18, 1830, quoted in Gibson, *Chickasaws*, p. 154.

22. Kappler, pp. 356–62.

23. Ibid., pp. 418–25.

24. Ibid., pp. 486–88. The Chickasaw district was more specifically defined in treaties of November 5, 1854, and June 22, 1855, and the region west of the ninety-eighth meridian was leased to the United States as a home for other Indians. Ibid., pp. 652–53, 706–14.

tion; a roll of the tribe prepared for the removal showed 4,914 Chickasaws and 1,156 slaves.

The Chickasaws left Mississippi in relatively prosperous financial condition. A minimum price of $1.25 an acre had been set for the sale of their individual homesteads, and some of the land brought more, for an upturn in the business cycle made abundant capital available for investment in the Indian lands. The unallotted lands—over 4,000,000 acres out of the entire cession of 6,422,400 acres—were sold at public auction under a graduation principle and brought about $3.3 million to the Chickasaw general fund. The movement was placed in charge of A. M. M. Upshaw, from Tennessee, who enrolled tribesmen from four districts of the nation, and the movement proceeded in orderly fashion. But there were delays in the migration and the inevitable problems of cheating and exploitation in the contracting for supplies, and the Chickasaws did not escape misery and suffering in the emigrant camps, on the way, and in the establishment of their new homes. Ethan Allen Hitchcock, sent to Indian Territory to investigate charges of fraud, reported defective supplies at exorbitant prices and found bribery, perjury, and forgery in the transactions.[25]

INVESTIGATING THE LANDS IN THE WEST

As the removal process moved into full gear with the treaties made with the Choctaws, Creeks, and Chickasaws, the United States government took steps to ease the process by turning its attention to the lands to which the emigrating Indians were directed. In order to make sure that the Indians located on suitable lands and that no conflicts arose among the different tribes, Congress in July 1832 authorized the appointment of three commissioners to investigate the western lands, to select tracts for the incoming Indians, and to adjudicate conflicting claims. The commission, composed of Montfort Stokes, former governor of North Carolina, the Dutch Reformed minister John F. Schermerhorn, and a Connecticut businessman, Henry I. Ellsworth, received from Secretary of War Cass a detailed set of instructions, in which Cass urged them to satisfy the Indians

---

25. Young, *Redskins, Ruffleshirts, and Rednecks*, pp. 114–54; Gibson, *Chickasaws*, pp. 163–83. Hitchcock's investigations covered Creeks, Choctaws, and Cherokees as well as Chickasaws, and his report was a severe indictment of the contract system of supplying the emigrating Indians. See Hitchcock to Secretary of War J. C. Spencer, April 28, 1842, *House Report* no. 271, 27–3, serial 428, pp. 28–43; his observations are reported also in *Fifty Years in Camp and Field: Diary of Major-General Ethan Allen Hitchcock*, ed. W. A. Croffut (New York: G. P. Putnam's Sons, 1909), and *A Traveler in Indian Territory: The Journal of Ethan Allen Hitchcock, Late Major-General in the United States Army*, ed. Grant Foreman (Cedar Rapids, Iowa: Torch Press, 1930).

and thus preserve peace in the area. He told them particularly to welcome the Indian delegations sent to look at the land to see that they were pleased. "You will perceive," Cass said, "that the general object is to locate them all in as favorable positions as possible, in districts sufficiently fertile, salubrious & extensive, & with boundaries, either natural or artificial, so clearly defined, as to preclude the possibility of dispute. There is country enough for all, & more than all. And the President is anxious, that full justice should be done to each, & every measure adopted be as much to their satisfaction, as is compatible with the nature of such an arrangement."[26]

The Stokes Commission, in its report of 1834, judged the land favorably. It declared that the country acquired from the western Indians for the purpose of providing land for the Indians coming from the East was "very extensive," running from the Red River to 43° 30' north latitude, and from the western boundary of Missouri and Arkansas to the hundredth meridian. The climate did not "materially vary from the climate, in the corresponding degrees of latitude, in the Atlantic States, some distance in the interior from the seaboard," and the soil was of great diversity, such "as generally is found in the States bordering on the Mississippi." The commissioners reported considerable game but predicted that it would soon be destroyed as the eastern Indians moved in. They wrote:

> The question then arises, "is the country able to furnish them a support in any other way; and particularly is it calculated for the purposes of agriculture?" And this question the commissioners answer unhesitatingly in the affirmative. They are of opinion that there is a sufficiency of good first rate soil, now belonging to those tribes who already have lands assigned to them, and in sufficient quantity still undisposed of, to assign to such tribes as may hereafter choose to remove there, to support them, if they will settle down like our white citizens and become agriculturists.[27]

The Stokes Commission was perhaps bound to support the government's contention that lands west of the Mississippi were suitable for the emigrant Indians, but its report fitted into a pattern of favorable comments on the land from other men who knew the region firsthand. As early as 1826, when removal was recommended by Secretary of War Barbour, William Clark at St. Louis commented on the proposal as follows: "The country west of Missouri and Arkansas, and west of the Mississippi river, north

26. *House Executive Document* no. 2, 22–2, serial 233, pp. 32–37. The question of the quality of the land assigned to the emigrant Indians is discussed in Francis Paul Prucha, "Indian Removal and the Great American Desert," *Indiana Magazine of History* 59 (December 1963): 299–322.

27. Report of the commissioners, February 10, 1834, *House Report* no. 474, 23–1, serial 263, pp. 82–84.

of Missouri, is the one destined to receive them. From all accounts, this country will be well adapted to their residence; it is well watered with numerous small streams and some large rivers; abounds with grass, which will make it easy to raise stock; has many salt springs, from which a supply of the necessary article of salt can be obtained; contains much prairie land, which will make the opening of farms easy; and affords a temporary supply of game."[28]

In May 1828 Congress appropriated fifteen thousand dollars for an exploration of the country west of the Mississippi and authorized commissioners to accompany the Indians. The commissioners in their reports described the territory as far as they had examined it and set forth both advantages and disadvantages. In general, however, the reports were favorable. One of the commissioners—Isaac McCoy, a longtime advocate of colonizing the Indians in the West—declared that "the country under consideration is adequate to the purpose of a permanent and comfortable home for the Indians; and whatever may be the obstacles which at present oppose, they may nevertheless be located there without recourse to any measure not in accordance with the most rigid principles of justice and humanity." George B. Kennerly, who led the expedition composed of deputations of the Choctaws, Chickasaws, and Creeks, reported, "There is a sufficient quantity of well timbered and watered land on the Arkansas and its tributaries for the whole of the southern Indians, if a proper distribution be made."[29]

Other reports on inspection of the lands proposed for the eastern Indians were of like tenor. A treaty with the Delaware Indians for removal west of Missouri provided that the land be inspected and agreed upon before the treaty would take effect. The agent appointed to accompany the Indians in their tour was again Isaac McCoy. His report to the secretary of war in April 1831 described in some detail the lands extending about two hundred miles west of the Missouri and Arkansas lines. "I beg leave, sir, to state distinctly," he reported, "that I am confirmed in an opinion often expressed, that the country under consideration may safely be considered favorable for settlement: [in] the distance, on an average of two hundred miles from the State of Missouri and Territory of Arkansas, water, wood, soil, and stone, are such as to warrant this conclusion." McCoy noted that the Delawares were so anxious to move to the new tract that they did not wait for the United States aid promised in the treaty. This, he asserted, furnished *"the best comment on the suitableness of that country for the permanent residence of the Indians."*[30]

28. ASP:IA, 2: 653.

29. 4 *United States Statutes* 315; *House Report* no. 87, 20–2, serial 190, pp. 24–25.

30. Kappler, pp. 204–5; *Senate Document* no. 512, 23–1, serial 245, pp. 435–36. Another report of McCoy, February 1, 1832, is printed in *House Document* no. 172, 22–1,

Such positive reports, which in fact accurately described the lands that were designated to receive the emigrant Indians, substantially refuted the cries of alarm made by such men as Jeremiah Evarts and George B. Cheever. The negative reports brought back by some Indian groups who went west to look at the lands are understandable, for the Indians found undeveloped wilderness in contrast with the improved lands in their old homes. But the Indians after relocation did not find the agricultural potential of the region insufficient for their economic well-being and development. The injustice came, not from having to settle on poor lands, but from the ultimate lack of secure and permanent enjoyment of the lands they did receive.

SEMINOLES AND THE FLORIDA WAR

The Seminoles, an amalgam of Creeks who had gradually drifted into Florida and native tribes there with whom they mixed, numbered no more than five thousand, but they showed a resistance to removal that kept the United States army occupied for seven years and that was never completely overcome. The United States government had made a decision that the Seminoles were to be removed; then it tried with main force to carry out the decision, even though it soon became apparent that the land thus to be freed of the Indians was not of significant value to the whites and that if the Seminoles had been left alone the expense and grief of the conflict might have been avoided.[31]

---

serial 219; journals of McCoy's exploring expeditions are printed in *Kansas Historical Quarterly* 5 (August 1936): 227–77; 5 (November 1936): 339–77; 13 (August 1945): 400–462. McCoy's exploring work is discussed in George A. Schultz, *An Indian Canaan: Isaac McCoy and the Vision of an Indian State* (Norman: University of Oklahoma Press, 1972), pp. 101–22. See also J. Orin Oliphant, ed., "Report of the Wyandot Exploring Delegation, 1831," *Kansas Historical Quarterly* 15 (August 1947): 248–62.

31. I follow here the discussion in Prucha, *Sword of the Republic*, pp. 269–306. The Seminole removal and the war it caused have had extended historical treatment. A full scholarly account is John K. Mahon, *History of the Second Seminole War, 1835–1842* (Gainesville: University of Florida Press, 1967). An older history by a participant that contains a good many documents is John T. Sprague, *The Origin, Progress, and Conclusion of the Florida War* (New York: D. Appleton and Company, 1848). A recent careful study of relations of the United States and the Seminoles is Virginia Bergman Peters, *The Florida Wars* (Hamden, Connecticut: Archon Books, 1979). See also Mark F. Boyd, "The Seminole War: Its Background and Onset," *Florida Historical Quarterly* 30 (July 1951): 3–115. The printed government documents dealing with the war are voluminous, for as the war dragged on and the promised terminations did not materialize, Congress repeatedly called for explanations from the president and the secretary of war. The reports, often with extensive reprinting of correspondence, orders, and other documents, make it possible to reconstruct the war in great detail. See annual reports of the War Department; *American State Papers: Military Affairs*, volumes 5–7; serial set of congressional docu-

The removal of the Seminoles had complications that were not present in the removal of the other tribes. It was not simply a matter of exchanging the lands that the Indians claimed in Florida for lands beyond the Mississippi—although, indeed, this might have been matter enough for dispute. The Seminole problem was also a problem of black slaves. For many years slaves from the southern states had fled as fugitives to the Indian settlements in Florida, where they often became slaves of the Seminoles. The Indians may have augmented the number of slaves by the purchase of others in the white manner; but whatever their origin, the blacks enjoyed a less restrictive existence among the Seminoles than with white masters in Georgia or Alabama. They lived in a kind of semi-bondage, more like allies than slaves of the Indians. Many lived in their own villages as vassals of the chief whose protection they enjoyed, contributing shares of the produce from their own fields rather than labor on the lands of the owner.

The demands of the white masters of the fugitives became increasingly insistent. Claims were presented which the Seminoles, who kept no legal records of their slaves, could not easily refute in court. More and more frequently raiding parties from the north invaded the Seminole lands and attempted to carry off by force the blacks who were claimed as slaves. The Seminole War was perhaps as much a movement on the part of the slave owners to recover the property they claimed as it was a war to acquire Indian land for white use. And the blacks clearly sensed that fact. Although about a tenth of the Seminoles sided with the United States in the conflict over removal, acting as guides and interpreters against their blood brothers, the blacks all fought bitterly against the whites until assurance was given that enrollment for removal to the West did not mean placing oneself within the clutches of some white slave owner who stood by waiting to enforce his claims.[32]

The removal issue proper can be traced in three treaties between the Seminoles and the United States. The first of these was the Treaty of

---

ments; and Clarence E. Carter, ed., *The Territorial Papers of the United States*, 26 vols. (Washington: GPO, 1934–1962), vols. 25 and 26.

32. All the serious accounts of the war call attention to the importance of the blacks. The best consideration of the problem is in a series of articles by Kenneth W. Porter of which the following are the most general: "Florida Slaves and Free Negroes in the Seminole War, 1835–1842," *Journal of Negro History* 28 (October 1943): 390–421; "Osceola and the Negroes," *Florida Historical Quarterly* 33 (January–April 1955): 235–39; and "Negroes and the Seminole War, 1835–1842," *Journal of Southern History* 30 (November 1964): 427–50. The abolitionist Joshua R. Giddings claimed that the war was instigated by slave-holders; see his *The Exiles of Florida; or, The Crimes Committed by Our Government against the Maroons, Who Fled from South Carolina and Other Slave States, Seeking Protection under Spanish Laws* (Columbus, Ohio: Follett, Foster and Company, 1858), pp. 270–71.

Camp Moultrie, signed on September 18, 1823, in which the Florida Indians were induced to give up all their claims to Florida and in return were granted a reservation of land in central Florida, which by executive proclamation was slightly increased in 1824 and 1826 to include more tillable land. By the treaty the Indians agreed to prevent runaway slaves from entering their country and to aid in the return of slaves who had escaped. They were granted $6,000 worth of livestock and an annuity of $5,000 for twenty years.[33]

Much of the land thus reserved for the Indians was not well suited for cultivation, and the Indians did not abide by the reservation lines. The Seminoles were irritated by whites who were allowed to invade the reservation in search of slaves, and they retaliated by raids upon white settlements outside the reservation boundaries. Many of the Indians remained in their old homes when whites came into the area to settle, and there was increasing agitation for the removal of the Indians altogether from Florida. When the Removal Act of 1830 made provision for removal treaties, the Seminoles were also pressured into moving. A treaty was signed with the Indians on May 9, 1832, at Payne's Landing. The Indians were near destitution, and the promise of food and clothing in the treaty eased the negotiations. But the Seminoles would not agree to removal until they had had an opportunity to inspect the land and determine its suitability. The treaty, accordingly, provided that the government would send a party of the Indians to the West, where they could themselves judge the land that would be set aside for them. The members of the Seminole delegation arrived at Fort Gibson in November 1832, and they were shown the territory that was to be theirs in the Creek country. They were persuaded to sign an agreement stating that they approved the land. This Treaty of Fort Gibson, March 28, 1833, although it was not accepted by the Seminoles as a whole, was considered by the United States as fulfilling the provisions of the Payne's Landing treaty, and the government demanded that the Indians carry out the treaty and move out of Florida.[34]

The Seminoles did not think that the Fort Gibson agreement expressed the approval of their whole nation, and they did not want to be an integral part of the Creek Nation as the United States desired. The usual impasse had arrived. The government pointed to the treaty and insisted that it be

33. Kappler, pp. 203–7. For a detailed, reasonable account of the treaty and its background that is less condemnatory than most accounts, see John K. Mahon, "The Treaty of Moultrie Creek, 1823," *Florida Historical Quarterly* 40 (April 1962): 350–72.

34. Kappler, pp. 344–45, 394–95. John K. Mahon, "Two Seminole Treaties: Payne's Landing, 1832, and Ft. Gibson, 1833," *Florida Historical Quarterly* 41 (July 1962): 1–21, is a careful analysis of the treaties and the charges of fraud. Because the evidence is "fragmentary and often contradictory," Mahon arrives at no apodictic judgments. But he concedes that the Seminoles did not regard the treaties as just and that their refusal to abide by them led to war.

fulfilled. The Indians denied that they had made the agreements specified and refused to move. As the tension increased, the stage was set for war.

Indian Agent Wiley Thompson made plans for concentrating the Indians in preparation for emigration, and the Indians were told that if they did not come voluntarily, military force would be used. As the army closed in to force removal, the Indians struck. Thompson was murdered on December 28, 1835, outside Fort King, and on the same day Major Francis L. Dade and a company of troops were ambushed and killed. The uprising electrified the Florida frontier, and the War Department hastened to act, but the Indians could not easily be routed from their fastnesses in the Everglades. One commander after another tried his best to bring the embarrassing affair to a successful conclusion, yet the war dragged on and on, despite optimistic announcements from the commanding generals and the War Department that the war had finally been brought to an end. It was a sad and distressing affair, and it included episodes—such as the capture and imprisonment of the Seminole leader Osceola when he came in to parley under a white flag and the hiring of bloodhounds from Cuba to track down the elusive Indians—that roused strong public criticism of the war. Even a delegation of Cherokees who offered their good services in an attempt to bring the war to a conclusion was ineffective.[35]

In 1838 General Thomas S. Jesup, then directing the war, concluded that the removal of the Seminoles was not practicable and that to insist upon it would prolong a useless war without any hope of a satisfactory outcome. "In regard to the Seminoles," he told Secretary of War Joel R. Poinsett in February 1838, "we have committed the error of attempting to remove them when their lands were not required for agricultural purposes; when they were not in the way of the white inhabitants; and when the greater portion of their country was an unexplored wilderness, of the interior of which we were as ignorant of as of the interior of China. We exhibit, in our present contest, the first instance, perhaps, since the commencement of authentic history, of a nation employing an army to explore a country (for we can do little more than explore it), or attempting to remove a band of savages from one unexplored wilderness to another." But the secretary of war would not relent in carrying out the removal policy as em-

35. For the course of the war, see the accounts in Prucha, *Sword of the Republic*, pp. 273–300; Mahon, *Second Seminole War*; and Peters, *Florida Wars*, pp. 105–263. Osceola, the most famous of the Seminole leaders, has been given considerable attention; see the articles (including those on his capture) in *Florida Historical Quarterly* 33 (January–April 1955). A general account of the use of bloodhounds is James W. Covington, "Cuban Bloodhounds and the Seminoles," ibid. 33 (October 1954): 11–19. An extended discussion of the Cherokee mission is in Edwin C. McReynolds, *The Seminoles* (Norman: University of Oklahoma Press, 1957), pp. 197–206. See also "Report of Cherokee Deputation into Florida," *Chronicles of Oklahoma* 9 (December 1931): 423–38; and *House Document* no. 285, 25–2, serial 328.

bodied in the Treaty of Payne's Landing. "The treaty has been ratified," he told Jesup, "and is the law of the land; and the constitutional duty of the president requires that he should cause it to be executed. I cannot, therefore, authorize any arrangement with the Seminoles, by which they will be permitted to remain, or assign them any portion of the Territory of Florida as their future residence."[36]

So the war continued. Little by little some bands of Indians gave up and were moved from Florida, but others continued their desperate raids in the hope of driving off the white invaders. In the end, under Colonel William Jenkins Worth, the army harried most of the Indians into removal. In February 1842 Worth wrote to the commanding general of the army suggesting that a halt be called to the hostilities. "I believe there has been no instance," he began, "in which, in the removal of Indians, some, more or less, have not been left." And he declared the "utter impracticability" of securing by force the few Seminoles still left in Florida.[37] His observations were heeded, after some hesitation lest the honor of the country and the gallantry of the army be compromised, and the president on May 10 announced the decision in a special message to Congress. He noted the presence in Florida of only about 240 remaining Indians, of whom 80 were judged to be warriors, and asserted that "further pursuit of these miserable beings by a large military force seems to be as injudicious as it is unavailing." He continued that he therefore had authorized the commanding officer in Florida to declare that hostilities against the Indians had ceased. In accordance with these directives, Colonel Worth on August 14, 1842, declared the war at an end.[38] An estimated 2,833 Seminole Indians had been located in new lands in the Indian Territory.

So ended the bitterest episode in the annals of Indian removal. All but the irremovable remnant tallied by Worth had been killed or removed. In addition, more than 1,500 white soldiers had lost their lives and the costs of the war reached the staggering total of $20 million.

CHEROKEES AND THE TRAIL OF TEARS

Just as the Cherokee Nation was the chief focus of the controversy over the removal policy, so it furnished the most controversial episode in the

36. Jesup to Poinsett, February 11, 1838, quoted in Sprague, *Florida War*, pp. 200–201; Poinsett to Jesup, March 1, 1838, ibid., pp. 201–2. For a similar statement of the secretary of war, see Poinsett to Jesup, July 25, 1837, *House Document* no. 78, 25–2, serial 323, pp. 32–33.

37. Worth to Scott, February 14, 1842, quoted in Sprague, *Florida War*, pp. 441–44. Worth's correspondence on the Florida campaign is in *House Document* no. 262, 27–2, serial 405.

38. Message of President Tyler, May 10, 1842, James D. Richardson, comp., *A Com-*

actual emigration to the West.[39] The agitation of the 1830s, however, obscures the fact that many Cherokees had already emigrated and established themselves in the Indian Territory. Some had migrated west with the permission of the government during the administrations of Jefferson and Madison, and by 1816 the agent estimated that at least two thousand Cherokees were in Arkansas.[40] Their status there was precarious, for they were challenged by Osage Indians in the region and by incoming white settlers as well. To regularize the situation, the Cherokees, by treaties of July 8, 1817, and February 27, 1819, ceded large sections of their holdings in the East in return for a guaranteed tract in Arkansas between the Arkansas and White rivers. The treaties provided that all white citizens were to be removed from the western districts, but there were the usual difficulties as the whites looked with covetous eyes upon the rich Indian lands.[41] Then in 1828 the western Cherokees exchanged their lands in what is now Arkansas for seven million acres in the northeastern corner of the present state of Oklahoma, and they were granted as well the so-called Cherokee Outlet, extending west to the limits of United States jurisdiction at the hundredth meridian. This was in intent a removal treaty; its purpose was

> to secure to the Cherokee nation of Indians, as well those now living within the limits of the Territory of Arkansas, as those of their friends and brothers who reside in States East of the Mississippi, and who may wish to join their brothers of the West, *a permanent* home, and which shall, under the most solemn guarantee of the United States, be, and remain, theirs forever—a home that shall never, in all future time, be embarrassed by having extended around it the lines, or placed over it the jurisdiction of a Territory or State, or pressed upon by the extension, in any way, of any of the limits of any existing Territory or State.[42]

pilation of the Messages and Papers of the Presidents, 10 vols. (Washington: GPO, 1896–1899), 4: 154; Order no. 28, Headquarters Ninth Military Department, August 14, 1842, quoted in Sprague, *Florida War,* p. 486. The emigration of the Seminoles is recounted in Foreman, *Indian Removal,* pp. 364–86.

39. A recent retelling of the Cherokee story is Samuel Carter III, *Cherokee Sunset, a Nation Betrayed: A Narrative of Travail and Triumph, Persecution and Exile* (Garden City, New York: Doubleday and Company, 1976).

40. Return J. Meigs to William H. Crawford, February 17, 1816, enclosed in John Mason to Crawford, March 2, 1816, Carter, *Territorial Papers,* 15: 121–23.

41. Kappler, pp. 140–44, 177–79. For a discussion of Cherokee problems in Arkansas, see Francis Paul Prucha, *American Indian Policy in the Formative Years: The Indian Trade and Intercourse Acts, 1790–1834* (Cambridge: Harvard University Press, 1962), pp. 173–78.

42. Kappler, pp. 288–92.

The Indians west of Arkansas were known as the Old Settlers or Cherokees West, and they developed their own government and a prosperous agricultural economy along the rivers of the area. Here they were joined from time to time by small parties of eastern Cherokees who enrolled for emigration before a total removal treaty had been negotiated. By 1836 more than six thousand Cherokees had moved west.[43]

Despite the success of the Cherokees in the West, the great bulk of the nation adamantly refused to consider removal. Encouraged by the favorable decision of the Worcester case and influenced by political leaders who controlled the national councils, they repeatedly importuned the federal government—both the executive and Congress—to protect them where they were.[44]

Jackson's administration was embarrassed by the Cherokees' failure to accept the inducements to emigrate. Secretary of War Cass met again and again with the Cherokee delegations and explained the president's desire to aid them, but he insisted that if they chose to remain in the East, they must accept both the privileges and disabilities of other citizens. The unwillingness of the Cherokees to emigrate exasperated the secretary of war. "It was hoped that the favorable terms offered by the Government would have been accepted," he wrote to Wilson Lumpkin, then governor of Georgia. "But some strange infatuation seems to prevail among these Indians. That they cannot remain where they are and prosper is attested as well by their actual condition as by the whole history of our aboriginal tribes. Still they refuse to adopt the only course which promises a cure or even an alleviation for the evils of their present condition." Little by little Cass grew less patient in his dealings with the Cherokees, telling them curtly in 1834 that there was little use in reviving discussion with them, since the government's position had not changed. Jackson himself in March 1835 spoke bluntly to the Cherokees: "I have no motive, my friends, to deceive you. I am sincerely desirous to promote your welfare. Listen to me therefore while I tell you that you cannot remain where you now are. Circumstances that cannot be controlled and which are beyond the reach of human laws render it impossible that you can flourish in the midst of a civilized community. You have but one remedy within your reach. And that is to remove to the west and join your countrymen who are already

43. CIA Report, 1836, serial 301, p. 402. Emigration 1829–1835 totaled 2,698. *Senate Document* no. 403, 24–1, serial 283, pp. 1–2. There is a brief account of the Old Settlers in Morris L. Wardell, *A Political History of the Cherokee Nation, 1838–1907* (Norman: University of Oklahoma Press, 1938), pp. 4–7.

44. Memorial of January 5, 1832, *House Document* no. 45, 22–1, serial 217. Other memorials are the following: May 3, 1830, *House Report* no. 397, 21–1, serial 201; January 15, 1831, *House Document* no. 57, 21–1, serial 208; May 17, 1834, *Senate Document* no. 386, 23–1, serial 242.

established there. And the sooner you do this the sooner will commence your career of improvement and prosperity."[45]

Andrew Jackson and his supporters seemed convinced that there were two groups of Cherokees, the "real" Indians making up the majority of the Cherokee Nation, whose deplorable conditions made them willing and eager to migrate, and the mixed-blood chiefs, who selfishly opposed removal and threatened their subjects with reprisals if any agreed to removal. Thomas L. McKenney advanced the argument in 1829 as part of his program for the New York board that supported Jackson's removal policy. When the *Cherokee Phoenix* flatly denied his assertion and declared that "the great body of the tribe are *not anxious to remove*," McKenney took pains to gather together a number of documents from persons in the Indian country that substantiated his claims of the Indians' desire to emigrate and the use of threats to stop those who wanted to go and had them published in the New York *Evening Post*. As late as 1835, Commissioner of Indian Affairs Elbert Herring reported, "There can be little doubt that bad advisement, and the intolerant control of chiefs adverse to the measure, have conduced to the disinclination of a large portion of the nation to emigrate, and avail themselves of the obvious benefit of the contemplated change."[46]

Whatever the truth of this analysis, only a few Indians enrolled for emigration; the main body of the nation would not budge. The condition of the Cherokees in the East steadily worsened, as white encroachments continued to destroy their property and threaten their lives, and the federal government showed no signs of weakening its stand. A part of the Cherokees, thereupon, decided that the inevitable had to be faced and prepared to negotiate for removal. This group, known as the "treaty party," was led by Major Ridge, who had fought with Andrew Jackson against the Creeks at Horseshoe Bend; his educated and politically active son John Ridge; and his two nephews, the brothers Elias Boudinot and Stand Watie. Its appearance, beginning in 1832–1833, split the Cherokee Nation into factions of bitter opposition that persisted for decades. The "anti-treaty party," representing the bulk of the nation, was led by the elected principal chief, John Ross, a mixed-blood who was one-eighth Cherokee.[47]

45. Cass to John Martin, John Ridge, and William S. Coodey, January 10, 1832, OIA LS, vol. 8, p. 407 (M21, reel 8); Cass to Lumpkin, December 24, 1832, ibid., vol. 9, pp. 486–89 (M21, reel 9); Cass to John Ross and others, February 2, 1833, and March 13, 1834, ibid., vol. 10, pp. 18–21, and vol. 12, pp. 187–88 (M21, reels 10 and 12); Jackson to the Cherokees, March 16, 1835, ibid., vol. 15, p. 169 (M21, reel 15).

46. Francis Paul Prucha, "Thomas L. McKenney and the New York Indian Board," *Mississippi Valley Historical Review* 48 (March 1962): 649; CIA Report, 1835, serial 286, p. 262. See also CIA Report, 1832, serial 233, p. 161. The question is discussed in Mary E. Young, "Indian Removal and Land Allotment: The Civilized Tribes and Jacksonian Justice," *American Historical Review* 64 (October 1958): 33–35.

47. A history of the Ridge party that presents a reasonable and sympathetic account

This factionalism was used by the Reverend John F. Schermerhorn, appointed United States commissioner to treat with the Cherokees. When the Ross party rejected his overtures, he signed a removal treaty with the Ridge faction at New Echota on December 29, 1835. In an unusual preamble to the treaty, the government sought to justify its dealing with what was only a small portion of the whole tribe. The commissioners, the statement said, had called a meeting of the general council for December 21 at New Echota, at which they would be prepared to make a treaty with the Cherokees who assembled there. Those who did not come would be considered to have given their assent and sanction to whatever was transacted at the council. Ross and his supporters boycotted the meeting, so the Ridge party alone attended and signed the treaty. On this shaky foundation the United States procured its removal treaty with the Cherokees. A vehement protest came from the Cherokee national council, which passed a resolution condemning the work of the unauthorized New Echota meeting; and in a memorial to the Senate, Ross elaborated his position, protesting that "the instrument entered into at New Echota, purporting to be a treaty, is deceptive to the world, and a fraud upon the Cherokee people." There was a public outcry as well and a vigorous debate in the Senate; but on May 18, 1836, the Senate approved the treaty by a single vote.[48]

By the treaty, the Cherokees ceded all their lands east of the Mississippi and for $5 million released their claims upon the United States. The seven million acres of land granted the Cherokees in the treaty of 1828 plus the outlet to the west were confirmed, and additional lands were granted. Articles excluding the western lands from state or territorial jurisdiction and granting protection against unauthorized intruders and against domestic and foreign enemies, similar to those in the other removal treaties, were included. Provision was made also for the emigration, for one year's subsistence, and for allotments for Indians who desired to stay in the East. The treaty specified that the removal was to be accomplished within two years after ratification of the treaty.

The treaty party emigrated with little trouble; the state officials treated them considerately, and they were, in general, economically well-off. They

---

of their arguments and decisions is Thurman Wilkins, *Cherokee Tragedy: The Story of the Ridge Family and the Decimation of a People* (New York: Macmillan Company, 1970). A memorial of November 28, 1834, is a good statement of the Ridge party's argument that removal was inevitable for preservation of the nation; *House Document* no. 91, 23–2, serial 273, pp. 1–7. The best work on Ross is Gary E. Moulton, *John Ross, Cherokee Chief* (Athens: University of Georgia Press, 1978).

48. Kappler, pp. 439–49; "Memorial and Protest of the Cherokee Nation," March 8, 1836, and other documents in *House Document* no. 286, 24–1, serial 292; memorial of December 15, 1837, *House Document* no. 99, 25–2, serial 325. See also the discussion of Ross's activities in Moulton, *John Ross*, pp. 73–79.

established their farms and plantations among the western Cherokees. The remainder, having rejected the treaty as a valid instrument, refused to move, and Ross used every opportunity in his attempts to reverse the treaty's provisions. He encouraged his followers to stand firm, and few enrolled for emigration. Numerous petitions poured into Congress from religious and philanthropic supporters of the Cherokees, protesting the execution of the 1835 treaty.[49]

A strenuous denial of the validity of the treaty was submitted to Congress in early April 1838. It bore the signatures of 15,665 Cherokees and appealed to Congress once more for protection against the throngs of Georgians invading their lands as the deadline for removal approached. It closed with this plea: "We never can assent to that compact; nor can we believe that the United States are bound, in honor or in justice, to execute on us its degrading and ruinous provisions. It is true, we are a feeble people; and, as regards physical power, we are in the hands of the United States; but we have not forfeited our rights, and if we fail to transmit to our sons the freedom we have derived from our fathers, it must not only be by an act of suicide, it must not be with our own consent."[50]

Ross also carried on a pamphlet campaign to stir up public support for his cause and to condemn and weaken the opposing treaty party.[51] Such actions brought a vigorous response from Elias Boudinot as spokesman for the Ridge faction, in memorials to Congress and appeals to the nation. In a statement "To the Public," January 1838, and in long open letters to John Ross, Boudinot set forth the position held by the treaty party:

> Without replying to these charges [of Ross] in this place, we will state what *we* suppose to be the great cause of our present difficulties—our present dissensions. *A want of proper information among the people.* We charge Mr. Ross with having deluded them with expectations incompatible with, and injurious to, their interest. He has prevented the discussion of this interesting matter, by systematic measures, at a time when discussion was of the most vital importance. By that reason the people have been kept ignorant of their true condition. They have been taught to feel and expect what *could not* be realized, and what Mr. Ross himself must have known *would not*

49. For memorials against the New Echota Treaty, see *House Documents* nos. 374, 384, 385, and 404, 25–2, serial 330; *Senate Documents* nos. 388, 389, 390, 402, 416, and 417, 25–2, serial 318.

50. Memorial of February 22, 1838, *House Document* no. 316, 25–2, serial 329.

51. John Ross, *Letter from John Ross, Principal Chief of the Cherokee Nation of Indians, in Answer to Inquiries from a Friend Regarding the Cherokee Affairs with the United States* (Philadelphia, 1836); Ross, *Letter from John Ross, the Principal Chief of the Cherokee Nation: To a Gentleman of Philadelphia* (Philadelphia, 1837).

be realized. This great delusion has lasted to this day. Now, in view of such a state of things, we cannot conceive of the acts of a *minority* to be so reprehensible or unjust as are represented by Mr. Ross. If one hundred persons are ignorant of their true situation, and are so completely blinded as not to see the destruction that awaits them, we can see strong reasons to justify the action of a minority of fifty persons to do what the majority *would do* if they understood their condition —to save a nation from political thraldom and moral degradation.[52]

As the crisis continued, Ross sought finally to replace the New Echota Treaty with one of his own design, but his proposals were unacceptable, and the government would not depart from the provisions of the 1835 treaty.[53]

The general air of dissension within the Cherokee country and the fear that the New Echota treaty would not be carried out by the mass of the Cherokees had caused Secretary of War Cass to assign Brigadier General John E. Wool to the Cherokee country on June 20, 1836. Wool was ordered to ascertain the designs of the Cherokees and to take command of Tennessee volunteers raised by the governor of Tennessee. Cass directed him to reduce the Cherokees to submission if they should begin any hostilities and if necessary to call for more troops from the governors of Tennessee, Georgia, and North Carolina.[54]

Wool, whose sympathies lay with the Indians, did not find his task an appealing one. "The whole scene since I have been in this country has been nothing but a heart-rending one, and such a one as I would be glad to get rid of as soon as circumstances will permit," he wrote on September 10, 1836.[55] He anxiously hoped for a force of regular troops to be sent to him that fall, but he received only a curt note from the War Department that "there is no portion of the regular army that can be placed at your disposal." He was told to make use of the volunteers. When Wool attempted

52. Statement of Boudinot, *Senate Document* no. 121, 25–2, serial 315; see also the other material printed in this document. Boudinot also resorted to pamphlets: *Documents in Relation to the Validity of the Cherokee Treaty of 1835: Letters and Other Papers Relating to Cherokee Affairs, Being in Reply to Sundry Publications Authorized by John Ross* (Washington: Blair and Rives, 1838); *Letters and Other Papers Relating to Cherokee Affairs: Being in Reply to Sundry Publications Authorized by John Ross* (Athens, Georgia: Southern Banner, 1837).

53. Poinsett to John Ross and others, May 18, 1838, *House Document* no. 376, 25–2, serial 330; report of Senate Committee on Indian Affairs, June 5, 1838, *Senate Document* no. 466, 25–2, serial 318.

54. My account of military action against the Cherokees relies on Prucha, *Sword of the Republic*, pp. 262–68.

55. Quoted in James Mooney, *Myths of the Cherokee*, Nineteenth Annual Report of the Bureau of American Ethnology, 1897–1898, part 1 (Washington: GPO, 1900), p. 127.

to protect the Indians in the Cherokee country in Alabama, where their oppression was particularly notorious, he was charged by the governor and legislature of the state with having usurped the powers of the civil tribunals, disturbed the peace of the community, and trampled upon the rights of the citizens. The president referred the charges to a military court of inquiry, whch met in Knoxville in September 1837. The court completely vindicated Wool, but such maneuverings to protect the reputation of the general did nothing to ease the tense situation in the Cherokee country.[56]

When the deadline for removal, May 23, 1838, approached and the Indians were still on their old lands, the government ordered General Winfield Scott to the Cherokee country "with a view to the fulfillment of the treaty." Scott, on May 10, issued an address to the Cherokee chiefs. "The President of the United States," he told them bluntly, "has sent me, with a powerful army, to cause you, in obedience to the Treaty of 1835, to join that part of your people who are already established in prosperity on the other side of the Mississippi." He stressed his determination to carry out his orders and pointed to the troops already occupying the Indian country and the "thousands and thousands . . . approaching from every quarter." He urged them to move with haste, thus to spare him "the horror of witnessing the destruction of the Cherokees." The general directed his troops to treat the Indians with kindness and humanity as they were rounded up and gathered in concentration points for the movement west, but contemporary reports included lurid stories of harshness and inhumanity.[57]

The emigrating Indians were organized into detachments, but only about three hundred had departed when Scott called a halt to the exodus for the rest of the hot summer season. The Cherokee leaders then made an agreement with Scott whereby they themselves would take charge of the emigration when it began again in the fall, and the operation became a project of the Rosses. Officers were appointed by the Cherokee council, and a quasi-military order was maintained on the march. When the drought that had further delayed the departure was broken in October, the caravans began their march overland to Nashville and Memphis. The emigrants numbered about thirteen thousand, including black slaves; they carried along whatever of their belongings they had managed to save. The Indian leaders themselves were responsible for the good behavior of the nation, and no

56. The proceedings of the court of inquiry are in *House Document* no. 46, 25−1, serial 311.

57. Documents on Scott's operations are in *House Document* no. 453, 25−2, serial 331; Scott's part in the removal is treated in Elliott, *Winfield Scott*, pp. 345−55. Examples of reports of harsh treatment of the Cherokees appear in *Niles' National Register* 54 (August 18, 1838): 385, and in Mooney, *Myths of the Cherokee*, p. 130.

military escort was deemed necessary. The journey, with its late start, occurred during the hardest months of the year, and this Trail of Tears reaped a heavy harvest of misery and death.[58]

The difficulties in implementing the removal policy in regard to the Cherokees and the other southern tribes—the fraudulent nature of some of the treaties, the dishonesty and chicanery involved in the disposition of the Indians' lands, the bitter military conflict in Florida, and the hardships and misery of the movement—did not weaken the resolve of federal officers, from the president down, who favored the policy. Having committed themselves absolutely to eliminating the Indian nations east of the Mississippi, Jackson and his associates and their successors in office continued to expound the advantages of the program for both the Indians and the whites. Jackson himself, the great father, gave his final benediction to the removal

58. Descriptions of the emigration are given in Foreman, *Indian Removal*, pp. 279–312. Moulton, *John Ross*, pp. 95–106, discusses the removal under Ross and the subsequent controversy over removal expenses.

The number of Cherokees who perished on the Trail of Tears is a historiographical problem. Because of the injustice involved in the removal and the hardships endured, it is easy to accept uncritically greatly exaggerated figures. The crusading secretary of the Indian Rights Association declared in 1890: "The march through the wilderness caused the death of at least half the tribe." Herbert Welsh, *The Indian Question: Past and Present* (Philadelphia, 1890), p. 7. The historian Ralph Henry Gabriel wrote in 1929, "A third of the people perished in the autumn and winter of 1838 when the Cherokee followed what they called the 'trail of tears.'" Gabriel, *The Lure of the Frontier: A Story of Race Conflict* (New Haven: Yale University Press, 1929), p. 128. A commonly accepted figure, however, is four thousand, or one-fourth of the sixteen thousand total presumed to have emigrated. Thus Annie Abel's influential and usually well-documented monograph makes the undocumented assertion, "More than one-fourth are said to have perished on the way." Abel, "Indian Consolidation," p. 404. And Grant Foreman's widely accepted history says in a footnote, "All told, about 4,000 died during the course of capture and detention in temporary stockades, and the removal itself." *Indian Removal*, p. 312 n. The "more than one-quarter died" statistic is accepted by Mary Young, who depends on the testimony in 1839 of Dr. Elizur Butler, whom she regards as "a reliable witness, and perhaps the best qualified of his contemporaries to make a general estimate," but then she admits that "the proportion of deaths which can be positively confirmed runs between five and six per cent of the emigrants." Mary Young, "Indian Removal and the Attack on Tribal Autonomy: The Cherokee Case," in *Indians of the Lower South: Past and Present*, ed. John K. Mahon (Pensacola: Gulf Coast History and Humanities Conference, 1975), pp. 135–37. Figures given for the twelve emigrating parties in T. Hartley Crawford to Joel R. Poinsett, August 8, 1840, *House Report* no. 1098, 27–2, serial 411, pp. 9–10, show that fewer than 10 percent died on the journey. This is a demographic problem and has been treated as such in the study of Donald R. Englund, "A Demographic Study of the Cherokee Nation" (Ph.D. dissertation, University of Oklahoma, 1973). By comparing different censuses and rates of natural increase before and after removal, Englund concludes that about two thousand of the sixteen thousand died in the removal.

policy in his "Farewell Address" of March 4, 1837. "The States which had so long been retarded in their improvement by the Indian tribes residing in the midst of them are at length relieved from the evil," he said, "and this unhappy race—the original dwellers in our land—are now placed in a situation where we may well hope that they will share in the blessings of civilization and be saved from that degradation and destruction to which they were rapidly hastening while they remained in the States; and while the safety and comfort of our own citizens have been greatly promoted by their removal, the philanthropist will rejoice that the remnant of that ill-fated race has been at length placed beyond the reach of injury or oppression, and that the paternal care of the General Government will hereafter watch over them and protect them.[59]

President Van Buren, upon whom rested the responsibility for removing the Cherokees and for the conduct of the Seminole War, asserted in 1837 that "the most sanguine expectations" of the friends and promoters of removal had been realized, and he contrasted the "certain destruction" that awaited the tribes within the states and territories with the near utopia that could be developed in the West. He spoke the following year of the "misrepresentation" and "unjust imputations" made about removal and declared that the wisdom and necessity of the policy had never been doubted by "any calm, judicious, disinterested friend of the Indian race accustomed to reflection and enlightened by experience."[60]

Whatever the views, whether the extreme praise of the Jacksonites, who seemed blinded to the evils that accompanied the policy, or the severe condemnation of the anti-removal critics, who ignored the real problems facing the United States in adjusting the rights and interests of the two races, the southern Indian nations in fact had been removed, and only scattered remnants remained east of the Mississippi. The relations of the United States government with them thereafter were based upon that fundamental condition.

59. Richardson, *Messages and Papers of the Presidents*, 2: 541.
60. Message of December 5, 1837, Fred L. Israel, ed., *The State of the Union Messages of the Presidents, 1790–1966*, 3 vols. (New York: Chelsea House, 1966), 1: 490–91; message of December 3, 1838, ibid., p. 509.

CHAPTER 9

Removal of the
Northern Indians

Clearing the Old Northwest. Potawatomi

Dispersal. Sacs and Foxes and the

Black Hawk War. Other Tribes.

New York Indians. The Role of the Traders.

Public attention focused on the removal of the Five Civilized Tribes from the southeastern states. It was the Cherokees' conflict with Georgia that held the attention of the federal government and of the public in the development of the removal policy and in the Removal Act of 1830. But this removal policy was also intended to apply to the Indians north of the Ohio River, who remained on lands sought by the expanding agricultural society of the North. They, like their southern brothers—with the notable exceptions of groups that migrated to Canada and others that remained on reservations within their old territories—were removed to the Indian country west of the Mississippi River.[1]

CLEARING THE OLD NORTHWEST

Whereas the southern Indians were organized into five sizable Indian nations, with relatively well-defined land holdings that stretched back to time immemorial, the northern tribes were numerous, sometimes frac-

1. Grant Foreman, *The Last Trek of the Indians* (Chicago: University of Chicago Press, 1946), pp. 17–158, deals with the removal of the northern tribes, but the book is principally concerned with the actual emigrations. Ronald N. Satz, "Indian Policy in the Jacksonian Era: The Old Northwest as a Test Case," *Michigan History* 60 (Spring 1976): 71–93, is an indictment of the removal policy that suffers from trying to prove a case.

tionalized into scattered bands, and often with land claims overlapping or ill-defined as the result of frequent migrations. In the removal period a great variety of Indian communities in the Old Northwest (Kaskaskias, Peorias, Shawnees, Ottawas, Wyandots, Miamis, Potawatomis, Menominees, Delawares, Sacs and Foxes, Piankashaws, Weas, Kickapoos, Chippewas, Sioux, and New York Indians) negotiated treaties with the United States, and in the same period treaties were signed with Indians holding lands in Iowa, Missouri, and Minnesota in order to clear those regions, or parts of them, of Indian inhabitants. It was a continuous and complicated process.

Most of the Indians involved had a long history of shifting locales. The Delawares, for example, at the beginning of the historic period were located in what is now New Jersey and Delaware, and in the course of time they established themselves along the Susquehanna River in eastern Pennsylvania, in the Allegheny valley in western Pennsylvania, and in eastern Ohio, central Indiana, southern Missouri, and eastern Kansas. At the end of three centuries of movement there are now surviving groups of Delawares in Oklahoma, Kansas, Wisconsin, and Ontario.[2] The Shawnees had a similar history, perhaps even more diverse, for they appeared in the southeast and in Pennsylvania as well as in the Old Northwest; there are "Shawneetowns" scattered across the eastern United States. Migration had been a way of life for the Shawnees until they were moved west of Missouri in 1832.[3] Although these may be extreme cases, none of the Indians north of Ohio occupied precisely the same lands in 1830 that their ancestors had held when French traders first came in contact with them in the seventeenth century. The emigration of these tribes in the Jacksonian era was part of their migration history, which continued even after their first settlements west of the Mississippi.

Nor was the relation of the United States government with these groups in the 1830s, after the passage of the Removal Act, a new departure. Rather, it was a continuation of policies and actions that had been going on for more than three decades (although without doubt new impetus was given by the 1830 legislation). Removal, in the sense of an exchange of lands within the states and territories east of the Mississippi for lands in the West, was only one part of the story. Many of the treaties provided for ces-

---

Useful articles on the individual tribes appear in *Handbook of North American Indians*, vol. 15: *Northeast*, ed. Bruce G. Trigger (Washington: Smithsonian Institution, 1978).

2. See C. A. Weslager, *The Delaware Indians: A History* (New Brunswick: Rutgers University Press, 1972). The endpaper maps graphically depict the Delaware migrations.

3. Jerry E. Clark, *The Shawnee* (Lexington: University Press of Kentucky, 1977), p. 3. An elaborate map of Shawnee locations and movements is in Charles Callender, "Shawnee," in Trigger, *Northeast*, p. 623.

sion of Indian lands to the United States and the concentration of the displaced Indians on remaining lands, with the privilege of hunting on the ceded lands until they were surveyed and sold—a process that had been taking place for many years.[4] Indeed, by 1830 most of Ohio, Indiana, and Illinois had already been freed of Indian title in a succession of treaties between Indian groups and the United States government. What remained in these states were enclaves of natives, subsisting on agriculture and government annuities, surrounded by whites. Pressures for the release of these final Indian holdings became irresistible. The attitude of the whites is sharply reflected in the repeated memorials sent to Congress by the legislature of Indiana. One of January 1829 was an epitome of frontier sentiment:

> The continuance of these few savages within our limits, who claim so large a space of the best soil, not only circumscribes, in its practical effects, the usefulness of the privileges we enjoy as a free and independent State, but tends materially to impede a system of internal improvements essential to the prosperity of our citizens, and in a degree jeopardizes the peace and tranquillity of our frontier, which it is our right and duty to secure. It is evident, that, although the Indians within our boundaries have been supported by large annuities, although the game has greatly decreased, yet agricultural pursuits are almost entirely neglected; and thus the large extent of country they yet claim is not only unprofitable to them, but, by its contiguity to the [Wabash] canal, is calculated to retard the settlement, the revenue, and the prosperity of the State.[5]

In the northern territories, Michigan and Wisconsin, on the other hand, white settlement, even after the opening of the Erie Canal in 1825, was confined to the southern and central tiers of counties. The rest of the region retained much of its Indian population and in addition became a refuge for Indians displaced from other areas. Secretary of War Calhoun's 1825 proposal on Indian removal, in fact, included the suggestion that the Indians living in the northern parts of Indiana and Illinois and in Michigan,

4. James A. Clifton classifies the treaties with the Indians in the Old Northwest, 1830–1839, as follows: seventeen provided for reduction of land base without removal; three provided for permissive removal; eight provided for obligatory removal. His low total of twenty-eight results from omitting treaties that confirmed or supplemented earlier ones and from combining a number of treaties made with separate bands of Potawatomis, which were in fact a single action of ceding reservations made earlier. Clifton, "Escape, Evasion, and Eviction: Adaptive Responses of the Indians of the Old Northwest to the Jacksonian Removal Policy in the 1830s," an unpublished paper furnished me by Clifton.

5. Memorial of the General Assembly of the State of Indiana, January 22, 1829, *Senate Document* no. 22, 21–2, serial 203, p. 3. See similar memorials in *House Document* no. 68, 21–2, serial 208, and *House Document* no. 129, 23–2, serial 273.

Ohio, and New York be moved to the region west of Lake Michigan and north of Illinois.[6]

The situation in the Old Northwest also differed from that in the South because of the proximity of British Canada. Many of the tribes in the region had had close economic and political ties with the British. They had sided with the British in the War of 1812 and after the war continued to frequent the British posts (notably at Malden across from Detroit). This friendly association of the Indians with the British north of the border would perhaps have given the United States pause had it planned the ruthless dispossession of the Indians pictured by some writers. But more important than the possibility of succor in time of trouble was the open haven that Canada offered for Indians in the United States. It would be wrong to think of removal from the Old Northwest only as a migration to the future states of Iowa, Kansas, or Oklahoma, for large numbers of Potawatomis, Ottawas, and Chippewas, as well as smaller numbers of other tribes, moved into Canada.[7]

In treaties with the Indians of the Old Northwest, provision was frequently made for reserves of land within the cession for individuals or small bands. The practice began with the treaties of 1817, and thereafter it was difficult not to follow that precedent, for such reservations were a means for the Indians to escape (at least for the time being) the nearly inexorable pressure for emigration to lands west of the Mississippi. The guaranteed reserves, however, were an awkward intrusion into the removal policy. At first they were patented in fee to the individuals, but the Senate, in ratifying treaties, came to look askance at this procedure, and later treaties specified either that these lands were to be held "in the same manner as Indian reservations had been heretofore held," with preemption rights in the United States government, or that individual grants could not be disposed of without the approval of the president. But in practice there was no objection to the sale of these lands, and permission was easy to obtain. Once the practice of reserves had been established, it was almost impossible to obtain a treaty of cession from the northwest Indians without them. The reserves were not only a hedge against removal; they were

---

6. Calhoun report, January 24, 1825, ASP:IA, 2: 542–44.

7. On the Potawatomis, see James A. Clifton, *The Prairie People: Continuity and Change in Potawatomi Indian Culture, 1665–1965* (Lawrence: Regents Press of Kansas, 1977), pp. 301–9; Clifton, *A Place of Refuge for All Time: Migration of the American Potawatomi into Upper Canada, 1830 to 1850* (Ottawa: National Museums of Canada, 1975). For Ottawa movement to Canada, see Robert F. Bauman, "Kansas, Canada, or Starvation," *Michigan History* 36 (September 1952): 287–99. There is discussion of Indians moving to Canada in the reports of T. Hartley Crawford of Janaury 15, 1839, *House Document* no. 107, 25–3, serial 346, and April 7, 1840, *House Document* no. 178, 26–1, serial 366.

also a means of individual profit, for the Indians could dispose of them for a reasonable price and sometimes more. Traders and other land speculators hoped to get the lands from the Indians by sale or in payment of debts.[8]

To the federal government, desirous of clearing the states of Indians altogether, the reservations became an irritant and an obstacle, yet so insistent were the Indians that there was great temptation to allow the individual grants in order to obtain new cessions. In 1833 Secretary of War Cass instructed the commissioners dealing with the Potawatomis at Chicago:

Decline, in the first instances, to grant any reservations either to the Indians or others, and endeavor to prevail upon them all to remove. Should you find this impracticable, and that granting some reservations will be unavoidable, that course may be taken in the usual manner, and upon the usual conditions. But I am very anxious that individual reservations should be circumscribed within the narrowest possible limits. The whites and half-breeds press upon the Indians, and induce them to ask for these gratuities, to which they have no just pretensions; and for which neither the United States nor the Indians receive any real consideration. The practice, though it has long prevailed, is a bad one, and should be avoided as far as possible.

In the Chicago case, cash payments were provided "to satisfy sundry individuals, in behalf of whom reservations were asked, which the Commissioners refused to grant." In 1843 the Senate resolved that no more individual reservations should be allowed in treaties.[9]

The passage of the Removal Act, of course, stimulated increased action in regard to the northern tribes. President Jackson in February 1831 appointed James B. Gardiner of Ohio to treat with the Ohio Senecas, and upon Gardiner's success the president commissioned him as a special agent to confer with other Indians in Ohio and explain to them the necessity of moving beyond the Mississippi. In July and August 1831 Gardiner negotiated removal treaties with the Shawnees and the Ottawas in which they ceded all their lands in Ohio and accepted designated districts in the western Indian country beyond the state of Missouri. With the Wyandots Gardiner had less success. Although pressed upon by white settlements, these Indians first demanded an investigation of the land proposed for their

8. Paul W. Gates, "Indian Allotments Preceding the Dawes Act," in John G. Clark, ed., *The Frontier Challenge: Responses to the Trans-Mississippi West* (Lawrence: University Press of Kansas, 1971), pp. 147–58. For a discussion of the type of tenure the Indians had in the reserves, see Robert W. McCluggage, "The Senate and Indian Land Titles, 1800–1825," *Western Historical Quarterly* 1 (October 1970): 415–25.

9. Cass to commissioners, April 8, 1833, *Senate Document* no. 512, 23–1, serial 246, p. 652; Kappler, p. 402 (see Schedule A for individuals so rewarded, pp. 404–6); *Journal of the Executive Proceedings of the Senate*, 6: 170, 184.

residence in the West. When an unfavorable report was returned, the Wyandots refused to emigrate. The treaty that Gardiner signed with them on January 19, 1832, authorized the cession of sixteen thousand acres for which the Indians would be paid $1.25 an acre as the land was sold. The treaty provided that the band "may, as they think proper, remove to Canada, or to the river Huron in Michigan, where they own a reservation of land, or to any place they may obtain a right or privilege from other Indians to go."[10]

Congress in 1832 authorized treaties to extinguish the title of the Kickapoos, Shawnees, and Delawares at Cape Girardeau in Missouri and of the Piankashaws, Weas, Peorias, and Kaskaskias in Illinois, as well as for dealing with the Shawnees and Menominees. In October the Indians concerned assembled at Castor Hill, the home of Superintendent William Clark near St. Louis, where treaties were signed between October 24 and 29 by which the lands in Missouri and Illinois were given up and new lands west of the Missouri accepted.[11] The northern part of the Indian country in the West was gradually taking shape as the home of the northern Indians.

POTAWATOMI DISPERSAL

The Potawatomi Indians were an example of drawn out, piecemeal removal of Indians from the Old Northwest.[12] Altogether, between 1789 and 1837, members of this tribe signed thirty-nine treaties with the United States. By 1828 the Potawatomis had given up most of their lands except for parcels in Indiana, Michigan, Illinois, and Wisconsin. In that year Lewis Cass and Pierre Menard met with the Winnebagos and united bands of Potawatomis, Chippewas, and Ottawas at Green Bay for a preliminary agreement on cession of the lead-mining regions on the east side of the Mississippi; and the next year at Prairie du Chien the united bands ceded their claims to a tract along the Mississippi south of Prairie du Chien in Wisconsin and Illinois, as well as a large parcel of land south of the Fox

10. Foreman, *Last Trek of the Indians*, pp. 65–85; Carl G. Klopfenstein, "The Removal of the Wyandots from Ohio," *Ohio Historical Quarterly* 66 (April 1957): 119–36. Pertinent documents from *Senate Document* no. 512 are cited in Foreman; the treaties are in Kappler, pp. 325–40.

11. 4 *United States Statutes* 564, 594; Kappler, pp. 365–67, 370–72, 376–77, 382–83. There is discussion of the treaties in Foreman, *Last Trek of the Indians*, pp. 60–65.

12. I have depended upon the general accounts of Potawatomi removal that appear in Clifton, *Prairie People*, pp. 179–245, 279–346; R. David Edmunds, *The Potawatomis: Keepers of the Fire* (Norman: University of Oklahoma Press, 1978), pp. 240–72; and Foreman, *Last Trek of the Indians*, pp. 100–125.

River and west of Chicago, in return for annuities, special grants for chiefs, and payment of debts to traders.[13]

Another broad grouping of Potawatomis, those in Indiana and Michigan, who had been extensively missionized and in many ways acculturated to the white man's ways, negotiated with Cass and Menard in 1828 at Carey Mission on the St. Joseph River in southwestern Michigan. There the Indians ceded their holdings in the region; annuities and other benefits were provided, traders' debts were covered, and grants of land (one-half to two sections in size) were stipulated for certain individuals.[14]

After the Black Hawk War of 1832, Potawatomi bands met United States commissioners again on the Tippecanoe River in Indiana. These Indians were split into bitter factions, each looking out for its own interests, and the commissioners solved the problem by signing three separate treaties between October 20 and 27, 1832, with different groupings of Indians. The Potawatomis of "the Prairie and Kankakee" band relinquished title to lands in eastern Illinois along the Kankakee River. Those from Indiana villages gave up their claims in that state, and the third faction, chiefly from the St. Joseph River region, ceded all claims to lands in Illinois, Indiana, and Michigan. In order to expedite the negotiations, the United States agreed to small reservations of land within the ceded districts for individuals and for village bands. Some 120 such reserves were stipulated in the three treaties; they satisfied the desire of the Indians to remain (even on reduced land holdings), but they seriously interfered with the government's intention of removing the Indians from the states. The Indians made use of the importunity of the government to drive a harder bargain than in previous negotiations, and large sums of money and goods were involved. The influence of traders, too, was evident, for the treaties provided generously for the payment of debts, and the purchase of large quantities of goods for the Indians further enriched the merchants.[15]

By these various treaties the Potawatomis ceded most of their land base, and the tribesmen were concentrated in small reservations of bands scattered through Michigan, Indiana, and Illinois. They now owned in common only a single large tract in northeastern Illinois and southeastern Wisconsin. The conditions of the Potawatomis were deteriorating, and it

13. Kappler, pp. 292–94, 297–300. Beginning with a treaty at Chicago in 1821, the United States dealt with the Illinois-Wisconsin Potawatomi in conjunction with small groups of Chippewas and Ottawas associated with them. For all practical purposes these "united bands" were Potawatomis; the treaties applied only to them and to the limited numbers of others in close association with them. The treaties confused this fact by sometimes listing the Ottawas or the Chippewas first.

14. Kappler, pp. 294–97.

15. Ibid., pp. 353–56, 367–70, 372–75. These treaties are discussed in the books by Clifton and Edmunds.

MAP 3: Potawatomi Land Cessions—An Example of
the Piecemeal Removal of the Northern Tribes

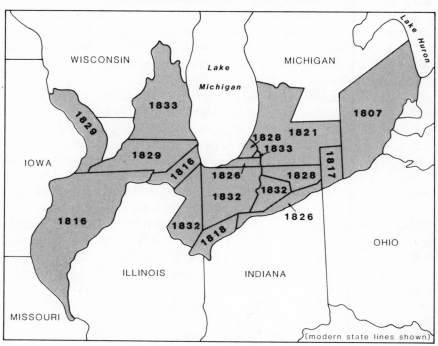

appeared inevitable that they would soon be pressured to remove altogether from the states and territories that had been their home. Some migrated voluntarily, joining Kickapoos who moved to Texas, settling in the Kickapoo reservation in Kansas, or establishing themselves on Manitoulin Island. For the rest, plans were soon under way for a treaty at Chicago in the fall of 1833.

The Chicago negotiation was a spectacular affair.[16] Large numbers of Indians appeared, and whites of all persuasions seeking personal fortunes were quickly on hand to gain whatever they could. The British traveler Charles Joseph Latrobe, passing through the village of Chicago, described the scene:

16. A general account of the treaty is Anselm J. Gerwing, "The Chicago Treaty of 1833," *Journal of the Illinois State Historical Society* 57 (Summer 1964): 117–42. An excellent portrayal of the many interests at work in the negotiations is in James A. Clifton, "Chicago, September 14, 1833: The Last Great Indian Treaty in the Old Northwest," *Chicago History* 9 (Summer 1980): 86–97. Documents pertaining to the treaty are printed in Milo M. Quaife, ed., "The Chicago Treaty of 1833," *Wisconsin Magazine of History* 1 (March 1918): 287–303.

You will find horse-dealers, and horse-stealers,—rogues of every description, white, black, brown, and red—half-breed, quarter-breeds,
and men of no breed at all;—dealers in pigs, poultry, and potatoes;—
men pursuing Indian claims, some for tracts of land, others, like our
friend Snipe, for pigs which the wolves had eaten;—creditors of the
tribes or of particular Indians, who know they have no chance of getting their money, if they do not get it from the Government agents;—
sharpers of every degree; pedlars, grog-sellers; Indian agents and Indian traders of every description, and Contractors to supply the Pot-
tawattomies with food. The little village was in an uproar from
morning to night, and from night to morning; for, during the hours of
darkness, when the housed portion of the population of Chicago
strove to obtain repose in the crowded plank edifices of the village,
the Indians howled, sang, wept, yelled, and whooped in their various
encampments. With all this, the whites seemed to me to be more
pagan than the red men.[17]

The forceful demands of the American commissioners, led by George B.
Porter, governor of Michigan Territory, were met by the skillful tactics of
the Indian negotiators, the mixed-bloods Billy Caldwell and Alexander
Robinson. The Wisconsin and Illinois Potawatomis signed first on September 26. Those from Michigan needed more persuading to part with their
small tracts and did so only with the proviso that they would not have to
migrate to the West; they affixed their signatures the next day. The treaty
stipulated the exchange of lands, some five million acres in the West, including a triangle between the original western boundary of the state of
Missouri and the Missouri River known as the Platte Purchase, for an
equal amount of land given up. Debts to traders were covered, payments
were made to specified Indians, and a twenty-year annuity was included.
The Indians agreed to emigrate as soon as possible, the cost to be borne by
the United States.[18]

The Senate was slow to ratify the treaty (which it finally did on February 21, 1835), for some of the traders' debts rightly looked suspicious. The
state of Missouri, moreover, desired the Platte Purchase for itself and at
the time of the Chicago treaty was already making plans to acquire it. The
Missouri senators succeeded in having the Senate amend the treaty to substitute land in Iowa for the Platte Purchase. It took some pains to get the
Potawatomis to agree to the amendment, and in the end a special commit-

17. Charles Joseph Latrobe, *The Rambler in North America, MDCCCXXXII–
MDCCCXXXIII*, 2 vols. (London: R. B. Seeley and W. Burnside, 1835), 2: 206–7.
18. Kappler, pp. 402–15. A biography of Billy Caldwell is James A. Clifton, "Merchant, Soldier, Broker, Chief: A Corrected Obituary of Captain Billy Caldwell," *Journal
of the Illinois State Historical Society* 71 (August 1978): 185–210.

tee of only seven men signed the revision in the name of the tribe. Even then the Indians insisted on occupying the Platte Purchase temporarily, and it was only after much irritation on both sides and the threat of military force that the emigrants moved into Iowa, where a subagency was established for them at Council Bluffs.[19]

While the united bands were struggling for some sort of stability west of the Mississippi, the United States began negotiations to eliminate the pockets of Potawatomis that remained in the states on the reserves stipulated in the 1832 treaties. Most of the lands allotted to individual Indians soon passed into white hands. Then, in a series of treaties in 1834 and 1836, the enclaves held by bands were ceded to the United States for considerations of goods, money, payment of debts, and annuities, and their inhabitants agreed to move off the land. A number of the treaties specified removal "to a country provided for them by the United States, west of the Mississippi river." Through the years many of the Indians affected by these treaties migrated into Kansas, settling on a reserve along the Osage River. In the removal of one band in 1838, that led by Chief Menominee, military force was used against the resisting Indians, and the hardships endured in the emigration were long remembered.[20] Other individuals and groups drifted northward in Michigan and Wisconsin and never left the eastern states at all, and about twenty-five hundred (nearly a third of the total Potawatomi population) moved into Canada.[21]

In 1846 a treaty was signed by both large groups of Potawatomis (those in Iowa and those on the Osage River reservation) in an attempt on the part of the United States to pull together into one unit the disparate strands of the Potawatomi people with whom it had been dealing—"to abolish all minor distinctions of bands by which they have heretofore been divided, and . . . to be known only as the Pottowautomie Nation, thereby reinstating the national character." The Indian signatories agreed to cede to the

19. The Platte Purchase issue is discussed in R. David Edmunds, "Potawatomis in the Platte Country: An Indian Removal Incomplete," *Missouri Historical Review* 68 (July 1974): 375–92. See also documents in *Senate Document* no. 206, 24–1, serial 281, and *Senate Document* no. 348, 24–1, serial 283.

20. Kappler, pp. 428–31, 457–61, 462–63, 470–72. There is a brief account of the removal of Menominee's band in Edmunds, *Potawatomis*, pp. 266–68. See also Irving McKee, ed., *The Trail of Death: Letters of Benjamin Marie Petit* (Indianapolis: Indiana Historical Society, 1941).

21. The Potawatomis were not simply shoved around by the paternal government of the United States, but they investigated and took advantage of options open to them in their adaptive response to white pressures. "A fair number of Potawatomis were shopping around in those days," Clifton notes, "inspecting, testing, and comparing the alternative possibilities of Iowa, Kansas, northern Wisconsin, or Canada before finally settling in somewhere. Their freedom of movement in this period was far greater than has generally been appreciated." *Prairie People*, p. 285.

United States their reservations in Iowa and eastern Kansas for $850,000. In return the United States sold them (for $87,000) a new reservation along the Kaw River, land recently ceded by the Kansa Indians.[22] The single national existence never materialized, however, for the united bands from Iowa (designated finally as the Prairie Potawatomi) did not coalesce with the more acculturated tribesmen who had moved to the Kaw from the Osage River (designated ultimately as the Mission or the Citizen Band).[23]

SACS AND FOXES AND THE BLACK HAWK WAR

The dispossession of the Sacs and Foxes, a confederation of once powerful tribes in the Great Lakes and upper Mississippi regions, was notable because it involved the Black Hawk War, a military conflict that in its small way was as embarrassing to the Jackson administration as the Florida War. The war was neither a planned aggression on either side nor a last-ditch stand of noble natives against Indian-hating frontiersmen. A disgruntled war chief, who sought ascendency over a rival chief of saner mind and who naively relied on the counsel of unreliable lieutenants, was opposed by reluctant and hesitant regular army commanders and undisciplined volunteers. A wiser decision here, a tighter rein there, would have obviated the dangers and provided a peaceful settlement.[24]

Black Hawk, the chief protagonist, was a Sac warrior with a long history of anti-American views and actions. In the War of 1812 he had joined actively with the British, and after the war he made regular trips to the British at Malden, which reinforced the hostilities toward the Americans of his followers, who became known as the British band. Black Hawk rejected the treaty made by William Henry Harrison with Sacs and Foxes at

22. Kappler, pp. 557–60.
23. Clifton, *Prairie People*, pp. 347–402. The history of the Citizen Band is given in Joseph Francis Murphy, "Potawatomi Indians of the West: Origins of the Citizen Band" (Ph.D. dissertation, University of Oklahoma, 1961).
24. I follow here the account in Francis Paul Prucha, *The Sword of the Republic: The United States Army on the Frontier, 1783–1846* (New York: Macmillan Company, 1969), pp. 211–31. The most complete history of the Black Hawk War is Frank E. Stevens, *The Black Hawk War, Including a Review of Black Hawk's Life* (Chicago: Frank E. Stevens, 1903); an excellent brief narrative and appraisal of the war is Reuben Gold Thwaites, "The Story of the Black Hawk War," *Wisconsin Historical Collections* 12 (1892): 217–65; a more recent retelling of the story is William T. Hagan, *The Sac and Fox Indians* (Norman: University of Oklahoma Press, 1958), pp. 92–204. For a recent popular account, see Cecil Eby, *"That Disgraceful Affair": The Black Hawk War* (New York: W. W. Norton Company, 1973). An exhaustive, carefully edited collection of documents is Ellen M. Whitney, ed., *The Black Hawk War, 1831–1832*, 2 vols. in 4 parts (Springfield: Illinois State Historical Library, 1970–1978).

St. Louis in 1804 by which the chiefs on hand ceded their extensive holdings east of the Mississippi, in western Illinois and southwestern Wisconsin. Although later treaties confirmed the cession and Black Hawk himself
signed at least one of them, he refused to depart from his village of Saukenuk and the lands in Illinois near the mouth of the Rock River.[25]

The treaty of 1804 had permitted the Indians to remain on the ceded
lands until they were surveyed and sold, and there was no crisis until Illinois settlers moved into the region in large numbers and at the end of the
1820s threatened the village of Saukenuk itself. Then removal of the Indians from Illinois became a political issue. Governor Ninian Edwards repeatedly called upon the federal government to move the Indians out altogether, and his political existence seemed to depend upon the success of
his endeavors.[26]

Many of the Sacs and Foxes considered removal west of the Mississippi
inevitable and, following the leadership of Keokuk, began to establish new
villages along the Iowa River. Keokuk continually preached acquiescence
in the demands of the United States, and he persuaded many to follow his
counsel. Not so Black Hawk. The older leader set himself squarely against
Keokuk. He refused to leave Saukenuk and rallied around himself the dis-
senters of like mind.[27]

A preliminary encounter occurred in 1831 as Black Hawk and his followers returned to Illinois after their winter hunt and began to plant corn.
General Edmund P. Gaines moved up the Mississippi to Rock Island with
new troops and called a council, attended by both Black Hawk and Keokuk. Keokuk pleaded with Black Hawk's followers to desert their leader
for more peaceful policies, and he succeeded in winning over some of the
band, but Black Hawk himself remained defiant. Only when militia called
out by Governor John Reynolds (who had succeeded Edwards in 1830) appeared to drive out the Indians did Black Hawk retreat quietly across the
Mississippi. In a new council called by Gaines, which Black Hawk reluctantly attended, the Sacs and Foxes signed Articles of Agreement and Ca-

25. Kappler, pp. 74–77, 120–22, 126–28, 250–55. The best source on Black Hawk is
Donald Jackson, ed., *Black Hawk (Ma-Ka-Tai-Me-She-Kia-Kiak): An Autobiography*
(Urbana: University of Illinois Press, 1955).

26. Correspondence on the matter can be found in *The Edwards Papers: Being a Portion of the Collection of the Letters, Papers, and Manuscripts of Ninian Edwards*, ed.
E. B. Washburne (Chicago: Fergus Printing Company, 1884). See also the letters of Edwards and Reynolds in Evarts B. Greene and Clarence W. Alvord, eds., *The Governors'
Letter-Books, 1818–1834* (Springfield: Illinois State Historical Library, 1909).

27. A masterful analysis of the background of the war is Anthony F. C. Wallace, *Prelude to Disaster: The Course of Indian-White Relations Which Led to the Black Hawk
War of 1832* (Springfield: Illinois State Historical Library, 1970). This appeared as the introduction to Whitney, *Black Hawk War*.

pitulation in which they agreed to stay west of the Mississippi and abandon all communication with the British. "I touched the goosequill to this treaty," Black Hawk admitted, "and was determined to live in peace."[28]

The quiet was short-lived. On July 31 a body of Sac and Fox warriors surprised an unarmed camp of Menominees near Fort Crawford and slew twenty-eight of the camp in vengeance for the massacre of Fox chiefs by Sioux and Menominees the year before. The outrage convinced many whites that they would be the next victims, and the government quickly demanded the murderers, ordering General Henry Atkinson with military reinforcements to Rock Island to restrain the Sioux and Menominees from an attack on the Sacs and Foxes. The intertribal conflict also reenergized Black Hawk. He championed those who refused to surrender the guilty braves and thus drew new elements into his depleted band and strengthened his position against his rival Keokuk, under whose domination he chafed. Advised by supporters that aid would be forthcoming from the British and from other Indian tribes, he and his band on April 6, 1832, recrossed the Mississippi into Illinois. There were about five hundred mounted warriors, together with the old men and the women and children of his band, who swelled the total number to an estimated two thousand.

Fearful of handling the explosive situation with his small regular force, Atkinson called upon Governor Reynolds for mounted militia. When Black Hawk refused to depart peacefully, the army began operations against the recalcitrant Indians, pursuing the Black Hawk band up the Rock River. The mounted Illinois militia moved faster than Atkinson's foot soldiers. Unfortunately, they were an undisciplined group, whose camp one regular officer described as a "multitude of citizen volunteers, who were as active as a swarming hive; catching horses, electioneering, drawing rations, asking questions, shooting at marks, electing officers, mustering in, issuing orders, disobeying orders, galloping about, 'cussing and discussing' the war, and the rumors thereof."[29] When they overtook the Indians near the Wisconsin border, Black Hawk, who realized now that he had been duped by his advisers and that no British or other aid was coming, sought to surrender. But the party he sent under a white flag was set upon by the excited volunteers. Believing that his peace overtures had been rejected, Black Hawk attacked and routed the militia camp. The war had now become a bloody affair, and there was no drawing back on either side.

28. Jackson, *Black Hawk: An Autobiography*, p. 129. Governor Reynolds tells the story of the Black Hawk War and his part in it in *My Own Times: Embracing Also, the History of My Life* (Belleville, Illinois, 1855), pp. 320–421. Documents are in *House Executive Document* no. 2, 22–1, serial 216, pp. 180–97.

29. Philip St. George Cooke, *Scenes and Adventures in the Army; or, Romance of Military Life* (Philadelphia: Lindsay and Blakiston, 1857), p. 158.

New volunteers were called up, and Atkinson began a slow pursuit of the Indians into Wisconsin. The delay was embarrassing to Jackson, who was seeking reelection. Going over the head of General Gaines, in whose department the conflict was raging, he ordered Major General Winfield Scott to assume general conduct of the war and ordered that all the troops that could be spared from the seacoast, the lakes, and the lower Mississippi be concentrated in the theater of war. Scott and his troops from the East never got into action, for they were caught by an epidemic of the dread Asiatic cholera as they traversed the Great Lakes and were quarantined in Chicago. Atkinson was left to push his campaign against the fleeing Indians, who soon realized that all was lost and sought only to find refuge across the Mississippi. Suffering desperately from want, they were finally overtaken just as they reached the Mississippi and were cut down at the mouth of the Bad Axe River. Some of the band made it across the Mississippi, but before they could reach safety with Keokuk, they were massacred by their old enemies the Sioux.[30]

Black Hawk, who had escaped the final carnage, was captured by a party of Winnebagos and turned in to the Indian agent at Prairie du Chien. He and his sons and two associates were sent in irons to Jefferson Barracks. In 1833 he and other prisoners were taken east, where they were briefly imprisoned at Fortress Monroe. They also saw President Jackson and enjoyed a triumphal tour of eastern cities in the process. On their release, Black Hawk was given into the custody of Keokuk and lived out his life in peaceful retirement.

The Black Hawk War need never have occurred, had there been honorable dealings with the Indians and a firm policy toward both the Indians and the whites. Squatters had been allowed to violate treaty obligations by invading the Sacs in their ancient lands before the area had been sold by the government. An earlier concentration of regular troops on the upper Mississippi might have kept the Indians better in check, and a less cautious commander than Atkinson might have successfully stopped the movement of Black Hawk's band up the Rock River before hostile acts had occurred. The shameful violation of the flag of truce by the volunteers precipitated open warfare just as Black Hawk had decided to surrender. Again at the Wisconsin River and at the Bad Axe River attempts of the Indians to surrender were misunderstood or rejected by the whites.

The war was a turning point in the history of the Sacs and Foxes. Once a

30. An excellent account of Scott's troop movement to Chicago with the difficulties encountered is in Charles W. Elliott, *Winfield Scott: The Soldier and the Man* (New York: Macmillan Company, 1937), pp. 259–73. The war from Atkinson's standpoint can be traced in Roger L. Nichols, *General Henry Atkinson: A Western Military Career* (Norman: University of Oklahoma Press, 1965), pp. 152–75.

powerful confederation that the United States was forced to respect, the Indians now succumbed to liquor and other white vices, declined precipitously in population, and were rent by internal factions. At the conclusion of the war in 1832 General Scott and Governor Reynolds, as United States commissioners, negotiated a treaty of cession with the Indians at Fort Armstrong. The preamble spoke fancifully of the Black Hawk War as "an unprovoked war upon unsuspecting and defenceless citizens of the United States, sparing neither age nor sex," carried on by "certain lawless and desperate leaders, a formidable band, constituting a large portion of the Sac and Fox nation." Accordingly, the United States demanded of the Indians a considerable cession of land: a wide strip along the Mississippi running almost the length of the future state of Iowa, "partly as indemnity for the expense incurred, and partly to secure the future safety and tranquillity of the invaded frontier." The Indians agreed to move from the cession, known as the Black Hawk Purchase, by July 1, 1833; and "to prevent any future misunderstanding," no one would be allowed to hunt, fish, or plant crops in the cession after that date. The government allowed a reserve of four hundred square miles along the Iowa River, including Keokuk's village, and provided an annuity of $20,000 for thirty years.[31]

This was the beginning of the complete liquidation of the estate of the Sacs and Foxes in Iowa. In 1836 they sold the reserve along the Iowa River, and in the following year, at a conference in Washington called to ease the conflicts between the Sacs and Foxes, the Sioux, and the Winnebagos, Keokuk sold another 1.25 million acres lying directly west of the Black Hawk Purchase. The United States commissioners repeatedly urged the Indians to move entirely from Iowa, where they suffered increasingly from the pressure of incoming white settlers. In 1841 unsuccessful negotiations attempted to persuade the Sacs and Foxes to accept a reserve in southwestern Minnesota. Then in October 1842, in negotiations with Governor John Chambers of Iowa Territory, the Indians gave in. They parted with their remaining lands in Iowa in return for the assignment of a "tract of land suitable and convenient for Indian purposes, to the Sacs and Foxes for a permanent and perpetual residence for them and their descendants" at some unspecified place on the Missouri River or its tributaries. They received also an annual payment of 5 percent of a sum of $800,000 and blacksmiths and gunsmiths. They refused to agree to payment in the form of funds set aside for agricultural and educational purposes, for the Sacs and Foxes consistently rejected the white man's schools and his religion. They were allowed three years to move from the western half of the cession, and they eventually gathered at the headwaters of the Osage River in Kansas.[32]

31. Kappler, pp. 349–51.

32. Ibid., pp. 474–78, 495–96, 546–49; Hagan, *Sac and Fox Indians*, pp. 205–24;

OTHER TRIBES

Each of the many tribes involved in removal from the Old Northwest had its own history, but many fitted a general pattern: a succession of treaties of cession following the War of 1812, increasing pressure on the remaining lands by white settlers supported by the state and federal governments, new cessions with reserved lands for chiefs and other individuals or bands that refused to migrate beyond the Mississippi, degradation and deterioration of the tribes because of drunkenness and indolence (often a result of the annuities on which many of the Indians depended for existence), and finally, as conditions worsened and pressures increased, acquiescence in treaties that demanded removal from the states to reservations laid out in the Indian country to the west.

Such was the case of the Miamis. In 1818 at the Treaty of St. Mary's, in Ohio, they relinquished the major part of their lands in central Indiana, accepting reservations of important tribal sites as well as reserves for individuals and a perpetual annuity of $15,000. Eight years later, under demands from citizens of Indiana who wanted Miami lands for canals and other transportation routes judged essential for the development of the state, the Miamis gave up claims to lands north and west of the 1818 cession (land also ceded by the Potawatomis) for increased annuities, some reserved land, payment of debts, and other considerations. But the treaty gave only temporary quiet to the Indians. The stimulus of the Removal Act, the canal-building fever that hit the state after the great success of the Erie Canal, and anti-Indian sentiment created by the Black Hawk War all contributed to new demands for Miami removal. Government attempts to get cessions in 1833 failed, but the Indians' resistance was weakened, and in October 1834 a new treaty was signed at the Forks of the Wabash. For considerable remuneration in cash, annuities, and payment of traders' debts, the Miamis ceded some of the reserves delineated in previous treaties. Jackson refused to approve the treaty because it did not provide for the removal of the Indians, but the Indians held firm, and the treaty was finally ratified on December 22, 1837. The inhabitants of Indiana strongly criticized the treaty for failing to rid the state of Indians, and it was clear that new negotiations would soon be undertaken. A tentative success for the United States came in November 1838. The Miamis ceded more land and the government promised to guarantee to the tribe "a country west of the

Donald J. Berthrong, "John Beach and the Removal of the Sauk and Fox from Iowa," *Iowa Journal of History* 54 (October 1956): 313–34. In 1851–1852 a group of Foxes, dissatisfied with the Kansas lands and tiring of confederation with the Sacs, returned to Iowa and located among the white settlers; their number was augmented from time to time, and they were finally recognized by the federal government.

Mississippi river, to remove to and settle on, *when the said tribe may be disposed to emigrate from their present country."* Although they did not then agree to leave Indiana, the Miamis did agree to explore the region in the West.[33]

Finally, in 1840, the chiefs (who had long adamantly resisted removal) agreed to accept emigration. A new treaty required the movement of about half the Miamis only because many of the tribe were exempted. But partial removal was accepted by the citizens of Indiana, for nearly all the tribal lands were made available for white exploitation. Although the treaty specified that removal was to take place within five years, that time was in the end extended; finally, in 1846–1847, the Miamis made the trek to a reservation in Kansas. The tribe by then was decimated; the agent at the reservation certified the arrival of only 323 persons.[34]

The fate of the Winnebago Indians, who were moved from place to place unconscionably, was particularly sad. Once having claimed a large area in what is now southwestern and south central Wisconsin, they, like the other tribes, were dispossessed to make room for white miners and farmers. The Winnebagos participated in the Treaty of Prairie du Chien of 1825, which set boundaries to their claims: roughly, the Rock River, the Black River, and the Wisconsin River. But the peace was interrupted in 1827 when Red Bird, taking vengeance for white assaults upon the Winnebagos, murdered members of a white family near Prairie du Chien. The government moved quickly with a show of military force to quell any widespread disturbance, and Red Bird and his accomplices surrendered to the United States commissioners.[35] Then, in quick succession, the Winnebagos signed treaties in 1829 and 1832 that extinguished their title to lands south of the Wisconsin River. By the 1832 treaty, the United States, realizing that the Wisconsin lands remaining to the Winnebagos would not support the tribe, granted to them the so-called Neutral Ground, a tract across the Mississippi lying between the lands of the Sacs and Foxes on the south and the Sioux on the north. Some Winnebagos moved to the new reservation, but they were insecure in the war zone between the hostile western tribes.[36]

The United States government wanted the Winnebagos to move en-

33. Kappler, pp. 278–81, 425–28, 519–24. The removal of the Miamis is thoroughly covered in Bert Anson, *The Miami Indians* (Norman: University of Oklahoma Press, 1970), pp. 177–233.

34. Kappler, pp. 531–34. An analysis of Miami population is given in Anson, *Miami Indians*, p. 226.

35. An elaborate description of Red Bird and his surrender is given in Thomas L. McKenney, "The Winnebago War of 1827," *Wisconsin Historical Collections* 5 (1868): 179–87.

36. Kappler, pp. 300–303, 345–48; Louise Phelps Kellogg, "The Removal of the Winnebago," *Transactions of the Wisconsin Academy of Sciences, Arts and Letters* 21 (1924): 23–29.

MAP 4: Indian Land Cessions in the North

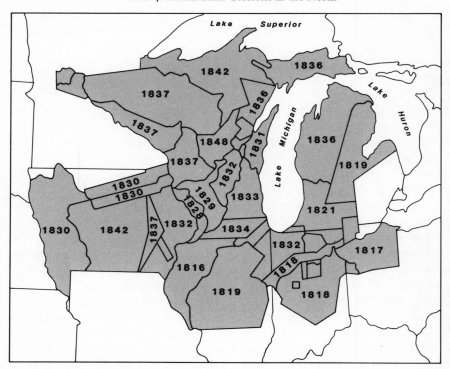

tirely beyond the Mississippi, which the tribe refused to do. In 1837, however, a delegation of Winnebagos was induced to travel to Washington.
There, in a clearly illegal treaty (for the delegation had no authority to sell),
they were pressured into signing away the rest of their Wisconsin land.
They were told, through the deception of the interpreter, that they would
have eight years to move, whereas in fact the treaty specified only eight
months. The treaty, pushed for execution by the United States, created a
permanent division in the tribe. One group decided it would be best to
abide by the treaty and in a series of subsequent treaties with the federal
government moved from one location to another—in 1846 from the Neutral Ground in Iowa to a reservation along the Mississippi at the Crow
Wing River in central Minnesota, in 1855 to a better spot farther south in
Minnesota at Blue Earth (half of which they ceded in 1859), and in 1862, as
a result of the agitation arising from the Sioux uprising of that year, from
Blue Earth to a barren spot along the Missouri River in Dakota, from which
they ultimately moved to Nebraska, where a reservation was provided for
them. The treaty-abiding faction, with whom these later negotiations were

conducted, amounted to about half the Winnebagos. The defiant remainder hid out in central Wisconsin, from which they were periodically rounded up and moved to join their fellow tribesmen, only to drift back to scattered enclaves in Wisconsin.[37]

The Chippewa (or Ojibway) Indians in Michigan, Wisconsin, and Minnesota did not take part in the general emigration of the northern tribes to the western Indian country. They also felt the pressures of white advance —farmers, lumbermen, and miners—and ceded most of their once large estate to the United States, but they managed to preserve reservations within their old territories, where they remain today.

The Chippewas of the Lake Superior region were inveterate foes of the Sioux, whom they at one time had driven out of lands east of the Mississippi. The incessant warfare of the two tribes was an unsettling condition on the frontier, and one of the purposes of the 1825 Treaty of Prairie du Chien was to adjudicate the rivalry and establish a line of demarcation between the hostile groups. That treaty, however, was but a prelude to further negotiations with the Chippewas, who faced aggressive whites coming into the region, as well as the Sioux. In 1837 at Fort Snelling, Henry Dodge, governor of Wisconsin Territory, signed a treaty with them in which they parted with a large tract of timberland in eastern Minnesota and north central Wisconsin in return for annuities, settlement of traders' claims, and cash to influential mixed-bloods. The Chippewas also retained the right to hunt, fish, and gather rice on the ceded lands until the president directed their removal. Meanwhile miners invaded the copper lands of the Indians along the southern shore of Lake Superior, and in 1842 by a treaty signed at La Pointe the Chippewas sold their hunting grounds as far east as Marquette, Michigan, for similar considerations. Not until 1850 did the president order the Indians to prepare for removal from the ceded lands, but even then the Indians refused to consider moving entirely from their homelands. The outcome was a new treaty in 1854 in which the Indians accepted a group of small permanent reservations scattered across northeastern Minnesota, northern Wisconsin, and the Upper Peninsula.[38]

37. Nancy Oestreich Lurie, "Winnebago," in Trigger, *Northeast*, pp. 697–700. See also the report of the Committee on Indian Affairs, March 17, 1836, *Senate Document* no. 252, 24–1, serial 281, which urges removal of the Winnebagos to south and west of the Missouri River; *House Document* no. 229, 25–3, serial 349, and *Senate Document* no. 297, 26–1, serial 359, which deal with Winnebago removal and the claims arising therefrom.

38. Negotiations with the western Chippewas are treated in Edmund Jefferson Danziger, Jr., *The Chippewas of Lake Superior* (Norman: University of Oklahoma Press, 1978), pp. 68–90; and Danziger, "They Would Not Be Moved: The Chippewa Treaty of 1854," *Minnesota History* 43 (Spring 1973): 175–85. The treaties are in Kappler, pp. 491–93, 542–45, 648–52.

The eastern bands of Chippewa met a similar fate in the state of Michigan. In 1819 they ceded a huge wedge of land extending from Lake Huron into central Michigan and in 1836 (with the Ottawas) gave up the northwest quarter of the Lower Peninsula. But no wholesale removal was involved, for reserves were provided, and the Indians retained the right to use the land until it was settled by whites.[39]

The Sioux Indians, too, succumbed to the forces demanding removal from the Old Northwest. They took part in the Treaty of Prairie du Chien in 1825, in which lines were drawn between them and the Sacs and Foxes to the south and their Chippewa enemies to the north, although the northern line was of little consequence in ending the hostilities between the two tribes. In 1830 they were again at Prairie du Chien, in negotiations aimed at ending conflicts between them and the Sacs and Foxes, and each tribe ceded a twenty-mile-wide strip of territory along the dividing line to create the Neutral Ground later given to the Winnebagos. The buffer strip was ineffective. Then at Washington in 1837 the Sioux were induced to cede their holdings east of the Mississippi (in what is now Wisconsin) in return for $300,000 to be invested at 5 percent, cash payments to relatives and friends of the tribe, $90,000 to pay debts due traders, and annuities in goods and provision for agricultural development. How much the Indians profited is questionable, for the annuities became a crutch for their subsistence and delayed the day when they could support themselves, and dependence upon the annuities created troubles if payment was late. For the government the treaty was one more advance in clearing the region east of the Mississippi of Indian titles. Not until the treaties of Traverse des Sioux and Mendota in 1851 were the Sioux forced to part with sizable tracts west of the river.[40]

The Menominee Indians resisted removal from their Wisconsin homes, but like others they were forced to relinquish vast territories of farmland and timberland to white pioneers, and they gave up valuable land as well to New York Indians migrating to Wisconsin. As participants in the Prairie du Chien Treaty of 1825, they had their claims defined, but the boundary between the Menominees and the Chippewas was not set. In 1827 at the Treaty of Butte des Morts, therefore, Lewis Cass and Thomas L. McKenney dealt anew with the tribe. The negotiations furnished a remarkable example of federal commissioners directing internal tribal matters, for Cass and McKenney in effect appointed a head chief with whom they could

39. Kappler, pp. 185–87, 540–56; Elizabeth Neumeyer, "Michigan Indians Battle against Removal," *Michigan History* 55 (Winter 1971): 275–88.
40. Kappler, pp. 305–10, 493–94; Roy W. Meyer, *History of the Santee Sioux: United States Indian Policy on Trial* (Lincoln: University of Nebraska Press, 1967), pp. 39–61. For a discussion of the 1851 treaties, see below, pp. 438–39.

deal. Cass told the assembled Indians that without a chief they appeared "like a flock of geese without a leader. Some fly one way & some another. Tomorrow at the opening of the Council, we will proceed to appoint a principal chief for the Menomonies." McKenney made the same point the following day in forceful rhetoric:

> Your great Father, who lives in the Great Village towards the rising sun, has heard confused sounds from the lands where his Menomonie children hunt. He thinks it is because there are too many mouths here & that all speak at once. He wants one mouth, that he may hear more distinctly, & one pair of ears to hear through, & a pair of eyes to see for him. He said to your father & me—*Go*, select from my Menomonie children the best man & make him Chief. Give him good things. Put a Medal around his neck, & a robe over his shoulders, & give him a flag. . . . Tell him his great Father takes him fast by the hand today—that this medal unites them.[41]

Oshkosh was named head chief and Caron second chief, and these men were the first to affix their marks to the treaty.[42] The treaty defined the boundaries between the Chippewas and the Menominees, but much of the discussion concerned the question of lands for Indians from New York who had migrated to Wisconsin. That question was deferred to the decision of the president. When the Senate in ratifying the treaty modified it to protect the interests of the New York Indians, the Menominees refused to accept the amended document. The issue was not settled until 1831, when the Menominees ceded specific lands along the Fox River to the New York Indians and specified tracts along the east shore of Lake Winnebago for the Stockbridge and Brotherton Indians. The Menominees also gave up their claims to the lands lying east of Green Bay, the Fox River, and Lake Winnebago. When the Indians objected to the 1831 treaty, a new agreement was drawn up in 1832 that somewhat modified the provisions. This was

41. Treaty journal, Documents Relating to the Negotiation of Ratified and Unratified Treaties with Various Indian Tribes, National Archives, Record Group 75 (T494, reel 2).

42. The designation of chiefs by the commissioners did not escape criticism. McKenney felt obliged to justify his action to the secretary of war: "I have already stated, that the persons employed to hold treaties with the Indian tribes in the Territory of Michigan, during the year 1827, did not undertake to 'constitute and appoint an Indian Chief,'" he wrote. "But in conformity to immemorial usage, as well of the British and French, as of our Government, the ceremony of recognizing those as chiefs who were reported by their bands as their acknowledged leaders, was observed by 'those persons' in putting medals around their necks. Further than this, and the giving of what was considered good advice, at the time, for their own and their people's government, nothing was done. All such signed the treaty, and after they received the medals." McKenney to James Barbour, March 24, 1828, OIA LS, vol. 4, pp. 362–63 (M21, reel 4).

but the beginning in the decline of the Menominee estate, for in 1836 the tribe ceded its land along the western shore of Green Bay and west of Lake Winnebago, as well as a strip of pinelands along the Wisconsin River.[43]

When Wisconsin became a state in 1848, new attacks were made on the Menominee holdings. In October, Indian Commissioner William Medill forced upon the now weakened tribe a removal treaty. The Indians gave up their remaining lands in Wisconsin and were assigned a tract on the Crow Wing River in central Minnesota. But ultimately they refused to move west. Exploring parties reported unfavorably on the Crow Wing land, and President Millard Fillmore extended the right of the Menominees to remain on their lands. With the support of white citizens, the Indians moved to new lands along the Wolf River in 1852. In 1854 the United States confirmed this reservation in place of the Minnesota tract. The adamant refusal of the Menominees to move across the Mississippi had succeeded, although the new Menominee Reservation amounted to but a fraction of the aboriginal holdings.[44]

NEW YORK INDIANS

The disposition of lands in Wisconsin was complicated by the emigration to that region of Indians from New York State at the very time the United States government was trying to extinguish the titles of the resident tribes. Federal officials like Secretary of War Calhoun, however, had spoken of the region west of Lake Michigan as a refuge for Indians from the East, and Lewis Cass wrote of the Iroquois in 1830: "It is very desirable to place them in that Country. Their habits and the strong pecuniary ties, which bind them to the United States would ensure their fidelity, and they would act as a check upon the Winnebagos, the worst affected of any Indians upon our borders."[45] Jedidiah Morse, too, in his report to Calhoun on his investigation of the West in 1820, praised the fertility of the Green Bay region. He told Calhoun: "Should it be thought expedient, and be found practicable, to collect the remnants of tribes now scattered, and languishing and wasting away among our white population, and to colonize them for the purpose of preserving them from utter extinction, and of educating them to the best advantage, and with the greatest economy, some portions

43. Kappler, pp. 281–83, 319–25, 377–82, 463–66; Patricia K. Ourada, *The Menominee Indians: A History* (Norman: University of Oklahoma Press, 1979), pp. 71–98.

44. Kappler, pp. 572–74, 626–27; Ourada, *Menominee Indians*, pp. 99–126.

45. Cass to Calhoun, November 11, 1820, quoted in Joseph Schafer, *The Winnebago-Horicon Basin: A Type Study in Western History* (Madison: State Historical Society of Wisconsin, 1937), p. 42. See also Albert G. Ellis, "Advent of the New York Indians into Wisconsin," *Wisconsin Historical Collections* 2 (1855): 415–49.

of these Territories will, I think, unquestionably be found better suited to these objects, than any other in our country, and as such I deliberately recommend them to the attention of the government."[46]

There was pressure, too, from the Ogden Land Company in New York, which held preemption rights to the Indian lands and which was eager to free the lands of Indian title. An additional and potent force was a mixed-blood named Eleazar Williams, a remarkable self-promoter (who among other things claimed to be the lost dauphin of France), who became the self-proclaimed leader of the emigration. Williams was able to interest only a group of Oneidas, however, for most of the Indians of the Six Nations refused to leave New York. To them he joined the Stockbridge Indians (Mohicans originally located in Massachusetts, and highly acculturated to white ways, who had migrated to New York in the 1780s and who now had a small admixture of Munsees). In addition, the Brotherton Indians, remnants of New England tribes that had settled in New York near the Stockbridges, joined the migration. In 1821 Williams led a mixed group of these Indians west to investigate possibilities, and arrangements were made with the local Indians (Menominees and Winnebagos) for grants of land along the Fox River. In 1822 the emigration began, and it continued through the decade.

The status of these intruding Indians was not well established, and their presence was resented by the local tribes. Because the negotiations at Butte des Morts in 1827 merely passed the problem to the president for resolution, it was not until the treaties of 1831–1832 with the Menominees (after a special commission had reported to the president on the issue) that the Oneidas, Stockbridges, and Brothertons were provided for. The Oneidas received a sizable tract west of the Fox River (which was severely reduced in 1836), and the Brothertons and Stockbridges were allotted lands along the eastern shore of Lake Winnebago.[47]

The Stockbridges, though a small group, furnish an excellent example of a sharp division of an Indian tribe into one faction seeking acculturation and citizenship (the Citizens Party) and another wishing to maintain traditional Indian community organization (the Indian Party) and the complications caused by the division in relations with the United States government. Each side attempted to win the government to its position with a steady stream of petitions and delegations sent to Washington. In a treaty

46. Jedidiah Morse, *A Report to the Secretary of War of the United States on Indian Affairs* (New Haven: S. Converse, 1822), appendix, p. 15. Schafer, *Winnebago-Horicon Basin*, pp. 35–57, gives a general account of the New York Indian immigration.

47. Kappler, pp. 319–25, 377–82; John H. Eaton to commissioners, June 9, 1830, in "McCall's Journal of a Visit to Wisconsin in 1830," *Wisconsin Historical Collections* 12 (1892): 172–77; report of the commissioners, September 20, 1830, in "Documents Illustrating McCall's Journal," ibid., pp. 207–14.

of 1839 half the Stockbridge reserve was sold and provisions were made for those who desired to maintain tribal cohesion to migrate west of the Mississippi, but few actually left Wisconsin. Then in 1843 Congress passed a law that granted citizenship to the Stockbridges and Brothertons and provided for the "subdivision and allotment in severalty" of the remaining lands. The Brothertons accepted the legislation and ended their federal status, but the Indian party of the Stockbridges strongly objected and refused citizenship. They were successful in 1846 in persuading Congress to repeal the 1843 law. This action, in turn, upset the members of the Citizens Party, who did not want to give up their citizenship, and the affairs of the tribe were in turmoil as each party sought to gain the federal money due the tribe. Finally in 1848 the tribe ceded all its lands in Wisconsin, and the Citizens Party patented tracts of land within the cession. The Indian Party was to move to Minnesota but in the end did not move across the Mississippi, and in 1856 they were provided land in the southwest corner of the Menominee Reservation. The configuration of Indian reservations in Wisconsin was thus set.[48]

THE ROLE OF THE TRADERS

It is easy to think of the treaties by which the Indian title to land was extinguished as compacts between two parties, the Indian tribe and the United States government—and such, legally, they were. But in fact there was sometimes an influential and occasionally dominating third party: traders. When the fur trade flourished, traders supplied the Indians with goods in return for furs, but as the hunting lands were circumscribed and the fur-bearing animals disappeared, the Indians paid the traders from their annuities, or the government bought large quantities of goods for the Indians directly from the traders. As cessions multiplied and annuities and other payments grew, the traders became more and more involved in the treaty process. Indians were indebted to the traders for goods received on credit; the debts could be recovered only by provisions in the treaties for cash annuities, by which the Indians could pay the debts, or by direct allotment of funds in the treaties to cover specified debts.[49]

48. Kappler, pp. 529–30, 574–82, 742–56; 5 *United States Statutes* 645–47; 9 *United States Statutes* 55–56. A detailed study of the Stockbridges is Marion Johnson Mochon, "Stockbridge-Munsee Cultural Adaptations: 'Assimilated Indians,'" *Proceedings of the American Philosophical Society* 112 (June 21, 1968): 182–219. The complicated relations with the United States can be followed in John Porter Bloom, ed., *The Territorial Papers of the United States*, vols. 27–28: *The Territory of Wisconsin* (Washington: National Archives and Records Service, 1969–1975), and in OIA LR, Green Bay Agency (M234, reels 315–36). See also Schafer, *Winnebago-Horicon Basin*, pp. 58–76.
    49. The best general account of the role of the trader is James L. Clayton, "The Im-

The allowance of traders' claims in the treaties began with the Osage treaty of 1825, in which the Indians, as a mark of friendship toward favorite traders, agreed to payment of certain debts by the United States. The practice became almost universal in the treaties signed in subsequent years with the Indians in the Old Northwest. And as the pressures for removal increased and removal treaties seemed necessary at any price, the rewards for the Indians and for the traders were considerable. The Potawatomi treaties of 1832, for example, together provided well over $100,000 for paying traders' claims, and the Winnebago treaty of 1837 authorized nearly twice that much.[50]

In addition, because the treaty negotiations were usually eased by generous handouts to the attending Indians, and because the treaties often specified large payments in goods as well as in cash, the traders profited by furnishing these supplies, often at inflated prices. The traders, moreover, had a deep interest in the lands allotted individual Indians in the treaties, for such lands often quickly fell into their hands. So much influence did traders have over the Indians that in many cases the government would have been unable to procure the treaties of cession it wanted without providing adequately for the traders' interests.

The exorbitance of many traders' claims called for government investigation and adjudication lest unscrupulous merchants grow inordinately rich at the expense of the Indians and the United States Treasury. The Senate from time to time refused to ratify treaties until the claims against the Indians were checked, and the War Department established regulations for the payment of claims. Special commissions were sometimes established to decide on claims and adjust the payments among diverse claimants, and they were given detailed instructions. Those investigating the claims under the Winnebago treaty of 1837 were told:

> You will require the respective creditors to deposit with you transcripts of their claims, exhibiting names, dates, articles, prices, and the original consideration in each claim. . . . If original books or en-

---

pact of Traders' Claims on the American Fur Trade," in David M. Ellis, ed., *The Frontier in American Development: Essays in Honor of Paul Wallace Gates* (Ithaca: Cornell University Press, 1969), pp. 299–322. Other studies, which deal with more restricted areas or tribes, are Paul Wallace Gates, "Introduction," in *The John Tipton Papers*, comp. Glen A. Blackburn and ed. Nellie Armstrong Robertson and Dorothy Riker, 3 vols. (Indianapolis: Indiana Historical Bureau, 1942), 1: 3–53; and Robert A. Trennert, "A Trader's Role in the Potawatomi Removal from Indiana: The Case of George W. Ewing," *Old Northwest* 4 (March 1978): 3–24. Trennert has expanded his account of the traders in *Indian Traders on the Middle Border: The House of Ewing, 1827–54* (Lincoln: University of Nebraska Press, 1981).

50. See table 15, "Fur Traders' Debt Claims Provided For by Treaty Funds, 1825–1842," in Clayton, "Traders' Claims," p. 303.

tries cannot be produced, their loss or destruction must be proved. The sale of spirituous liquors to Indians being prohibited by the laws of the United States, no item of charge on that account will, under any circumstances, be allowed. . . . If [the claim] be against an individual Indian, he should be called before you, and each item in the account be explained to him and his assent or dissent to it required.

The Indian Office recognized the forces pulling in two directions and instructed the commissioners further: "The moral duty of paying every just claim should be pressed upon the Indians; and, in receiving their statements, you will bear in mind the danger arising on the one hand from the disposition to evade an obligation; and on the other, from the exercise of improper influence by any of the claimants."[51] The commissioners found it impossible to carry out their duties with the exactitude wanted by the commissioner of Indian affairs, but they went about their business carefully and made judgments on the validity of the claims presented. In some cases claims were scaled down or disallowed altogether.

The attitude of the traders toward removal was often ambivalent. These men shared the sentiments of other white settlers that the Indians should be moved to the west to clear the land for white exploitation, and often they had a direct interest in the ceded lands. Yet it was not easy to part with the large profits they made in supplying the Indians where they were. Even though most traders realized that removal was inevitable, they worked to delay the emigration as much as possible. Each new treaty could be another bonanza. In 1838 the commissioner of Indian affairs asserted that disturbances arising in the removal of the Indians were caused "by the large indebtedness of the Indians to their traders, and to the undue influence of the latter over them." He said he was confident "that their influence is not only prejudicial to the Indians, but has been frequently exercised to defeat negotiations with them, and to prevent the accomplishment of objects sanctioned by treaties, and others devised and calculated to promote their welfare and permanent improvement."[52]

It was the government's unwavering objective to rid the East of Indians, and since it was necessary to get the traders' acquiescence if not active support, measures were taken to circumvent any obstructionism. Thus in the Potawatomi removal the government threatened to pay no more claims until the Indians had emigrated. Then on March 3, 1843, the Senate

51. C. A. Harris to commissioners, July 26, 1838, *House Document* no. 229, 25–3, serial 349, pp. 5–6; the undated report of the commissioners appears ibid., pp. 14–21. For other accounts of investigation of claims, see Trennert, "Traders's Role," and Clayton, "Traders' Claims."

52. C. A. Harris to J. R. Poinsett, February 12, 1838, *Senate Document* no. 198, 25–2, serial 316, p. 2.

resolved that in future negotiations of treaties with the Indians "no reservations of land should be made in favor of any person, nor the payment of any debt provided for."[53] But many old debts were still outstanding, and claims dragged on and on, much to the irritation of the overburdened Indian Office. In later treaties the claims of the traders against the Indians had to be recognized if the desired cessions were to be obtained. Even though the government did not pay the traders directly, large sums were provided to enable the Indians "to settle their affairs and comply with their present just engagements."[54]

53. *Journal of the Executive Proceedings of the Senate*, 6: 170, 184.
54. Sioux treaties of 1851, Kappler, pp. 589, 591; and Lucile M. Kane, "The Sioux Treaties and the Traders," *Minnesota History* 32 (June 1951): 65–80.

CHAPTER 10

The Emigrant Indians
in the West

Transplanted Indian Nations.

Military Defense of the Frontier.

Benevolence and Reform.

Advocates of removal justified the policy on the grounds that emigration to the West would benefit the Indians. Out of the reach of established states and territories, the Indian tribes could continue their national existence unmolested by encroaching whites and jurisdictional controversies. West of the Mississippi the federal government could provide for the protection and improvement of the Indians.

Because of the dramatic nature of the removal, especially of the southern tribes, it is easy to ignore the sequel of the removal itself and to assume that once the Indians had been shipped out of the way of the whites, the government breathed a sigh of relief and washed its hands of the whole affair. That was far from the case, for in the decade following removal the United States diligently—though not always effectively—worked to fulfill the vision Jackson had enunciated in his first annual message to Congress: "There [in the West] they may be secured in the enjoyment of governments of their own choice, subject to no other control from the United States than such as may be necessary to preserve peace on the frontier and between the several tribes. There the benevolent may endeavor to teach them, to raise up an interesting commonwealth, destined to perpetuate the race and to attest the humanity and justice of this Government."[1]

1. Fred L. Israel, ed., *The State of the Union Messages of the Presidents, 1790–1966,* 3 vols. (New York: Chelsea House, 1966), 1: 310.

Secretary of War Lewis Cass, in his first annual report on November 21, 1831, declared: "A crisis in our Indian affairs has evidently arrived, which calls for the establishment of a system of policy adapted to the existing state of things, and calculated to fix upon a permanent basis the future destiny of the Indians." Cass hoped by careful planning for the future to repair the errors and unpleasantness of the past. He was convinced that removal was the only means by which the Indians could be preserved and improved. But, granted the migration to the West, what steps should be taken to protect and encourage the Indians there? He suggested a seven-point program, a list of principles to govern relations with the Indians in their new circumstances.

1. A solemn declaration that the country assigned to the Indians would be theirs forever and a determination that white settlement should never encroach upon it.

2. A determination, accompanied by proper surveillance and proper police, to exclude all liquor from the Indians' new territory.

3. The employment of adequate military force in the vicinity of the Indians in order to prevent hostility between the tribes.

4. Encouragement to the Indians to adopt severalty of property.

5. Assistance to all who needed it for opening farms and procuring domestic animals and agricultural implements.

6. Restraint as much as possible from involvement with the peculiar institutions and customs of the Indians.

7. Employment of persons to instruct the Indians, moving as far and as fast as they were capable.

This, it was apparent, was not a detailed blueprint for Indian laws or regulations, but it offered a general policy background that the lawmakers would find useful.[2]

TRANSPLANTED INDIAN NATIONS

The Indian nations were not destroyed by removal, for the utter degradation and collapse predicted by the opponents of Jackson's removal program did not occur. Although most of the northern tribes that emigrated to the West were small in population and economically and politically weak, the Indian nations from the southeast moved to the Indian Territory in strength and with treaty guarantees that protected their land holdings and their political autonomy. The turmoil of removal brought great hardships to those who were forced to depart their traditional homes against their will, and

2. Report of the secretary of war, November 21, 1831, *House Executive Document no. 2*, 22–1, serial 216, pp. 27–34.

tribal divisions occasioned or aggravated by removal disrupted the tranquility of the communities. Yet the southern nations showed tremendous resilience in reestablishing an orderly and productive existence beyond the Mississippi. Organized governments continued, agricultural development (including large plantations run in part by slave labor) quickened, school systems were established, and missionary endeavors were renewed and encouraged.

The report of Ethan Allen Hitchcock, who was sent west by the War Department in 1841 to investigate charges of fraud and corruption in the business of removal, furnished a picture of established communities, which he compared favorably with those of white frontier Americans. "There was nothing to distinguish appearances from those of many of our border people," he wrote of a visit to a Cherokee home, "except the complexion (Cherokee) and superior neatness." Hitchcock described the homes, plantations, government, schools, Christian churches, and general society of the Indian groups, and he reported prosperity rather than depression or desperation among those with whom he came in contact. He noted, however, that the political and economic leadership was largely in the hands of mixed-bloods.[3]

Similar positive notes came from the government agents in contact with the tribes. The superintendent of the Western Territory wrote glowing reports of the progress and condition of the Choctaws, Chickasaws, Creeks, Seminoles, and Cherokees living under his jurisdiction. "Civilization is spreading through the Indian country," he noted as early as 1840, "and where but a few years past the forest was untouched, in many places good farms are to be seen; the whole face of the country evidently indicating a thrifty and prosperous people, possessing within themselves the means of raising fine stocks of horses, cattle, and hogs, and a country producing all the substantials of life with but a moderate portion of labor." The superintendent of Indian affairs at St. Louis in 1846 reported rapid improvement among many of the tribes in agriculture and the general comforts of life. He listed the Shawnees, Wyandots, Delawares, Kickapoos, Munsees, Stockbridges, Ottawas, and Potawatomis as the tribes among whom improvements were most visible, and he attributed this success to the influence of the missionaries and their schools.[4]

3. *A Traveler in Indian Territory: The Journal of Ethan Allen Hitchcock, Late Major-General in the United States Army,* ed. Grant Foreman (Cedar Rapids, Iowa: Torch Press, 1930); quotation is from p. 23. Excellent summary descriptions are given in a series of letters by Hitchcock to the secretary of war in 1841 and 1842, printed in appendix, pp. 233–62.

4. Report of William Armstrong, October 1, 1840, CIA Report, 1840, serial 375, p. 310; report of Thomas H. Harvey, September 5, 1846, CIA Report, 1846, serial 493, p. 282.

The Cherokees were the most important of the Indian nations in the West, and they best exemplified the rapid establishment of a viable society in the new lands. Yet they were sharply divided politically. The Old Settlers, Cherokees who had voluntarily emigrated to Arkansas and then into the Indian Territory before the agitation for removal in the 1830s, were economically well established in their western homes and had a loosely organized but effective government that dealt with the federal government as a distinct entity. In 1834 they numbered fifty-eight hundred. A second division was the treaty party of the Ridges, Elias Boudinot, and Stand Watie. Having promoted the Treaty of New Echota of 1835, they emigrated peacefully under its provisions and settled in the West with the Old Settlers. Because they had cooperated with the United States in the removal policy, they were generally favored by United States officials who became entangled in Cherokee intratribal conflicts. Finally, there was the Ross party, the group that had opposed removal and emigrated only when forced to do so in 1838. This was the most populous faction, with perhaps fourteen thousand adherents. John Ross considered himself the principal chief of *all* the Cherokees, thus irritating the treaty party and the Old Settlers, who feared his domination. The arrival of this anti-treaty group in the West brought dissension and conflict.[5]

The conflict was severely exacerbated by the vengeance taken by the Ross party against treaty party leaders for having ceded the eastern lands. On June 22, 1839, Major Ridge, John Ridge, and Elias Boudinot were brutally murdered; Stand Watie, also marked for death, escaped. Although it was clear that this was a planned political assassination, John Ross denied any complicity or approval of the deed; but he could not completely shake the accusations made against his party. The federal government remained critical of him and continually called for punishment of the murderers. Under the rubric of maintaining domestic peace within the Cherokee Nation, Matthew Arbuckle, commander at Fort Gibson in the Cherokee

5. Useful accounts of the Cherokees in the Indian Territory after removal are Morris L. Wardell, *A Political History of the Cherokee Nation, 1838–1907* (Norman: University of Oklahoma Press, 1938), pp. 3–117, and Grant Foreman, *The Five Civilized Tribes* (Norman: University of Oklahoma Press, 1934), pp. 281–426. The events from John Ross's viewpoint are told in Gary E. Moulton, *John Ross, Cherokee Chief* (Athens: University of Georgia Press, 1978), pp. 107–65; from that of Stand Watie of the treaty party in Kenny A. Franks, *Stand Watie and the Agony of the Cherokee Nation* (Memphis: Memphis State University Press, 1979), pp. 54–113. A brief treatment is Gerard Reed, "Postremoval Factionalism in the Cherokee Nation," in Duane H. King, ed., *The Cherokee Indian Nation: A Troubled History* (Knoxville: University of Tennessee Press, 1979), pp. 148–63. Documents dealing with the divisions among the Cherokees appear in *Senate Document* no. 347, 26–1, serial 359; *Senate Document* no. 140, 28–2, serial 457; *House Document* no. 185, 29–1, serial 485.

country, took an active part in Cherokee political affairs and openly represented the interests of the Old Settlers.[6]

Although members of the Cherokee factions agreed to an Act of Union in 1839 and 1840, the groups were still at odds among themselves and with United States military commanders, and the following years were filled with turmoil at times approaching civil war. All three parties sent delegations to Washington to plead their causes and to seek a settlement by the federal government, but the form that a solution might take was not easily agreed upon. Should the Cherokees be divided into two tribes (the Ross party in one and his opponents, the treaty party and the Old Settlers, in the other), or was a unified Cherokee Nation still possible? On April 13, 1846, President James K. Polk sent a special message to Congress on the matter. He noted the unprovoked murders and other disturbances in the Cherokee Nation that had gone unpunished, and he spoke approvingly of the army's attempts to suppress those outrages under the provision of the treaty of 1835, by which the United States had agreed "to protect the Cherokee Nation from domestic strife and foreign enemies." But in the end he concluded: "I am satisfied that there is no probability that the different bands or parties into which it [the Cherokee Nation] is divided can ever again live together in peace and harmony, and that the well-being of the whole requires that they should be separated and live under separate governments as distinct tribes." The House Committee on Indian Affairs reported a bill including all that Polk had asked for. It noted the obligations owed by the United States to the minority anti-Ross party, which had cooperated in the removal policy, and it justified the intervention of the United States against the Ross majority because of the wardship status of the Indians. It unanimously recommended division into two tribes. "The people must be separated," the report read; "the continuance of the present social compact, unchecked and unrestrained as it exists at present, will inevitably end in the fatal destruction of the minority parties."[7]

Such action led John Ross, who above all wanted a unified nation, to persuade Polk to approve a treaty that would keep the Cherokees intact. The president thereupon appointed commissioners to negotiate with

6. A balanced account of Arbuckle's action is given in Brad Agnew, *Fort Gibson: Terminal on the Trail of Tears* (Norman: University of Oklahoma Press, 1980), pp. 185–211; this book is a valuable study of Fort Gibson and Indian removal. An account unduly hostile toward Arbuckle is Foreman, *Five Civilized Tribes*.

7. James K. Polk to Congress, April 13, 1846, *House Document* no. 185, 29–1, serial 485, pp. 1–2; this document also contains a long report of the commissioner of Indian affairs on the Cherokee conflict, memorials from the three factions, and several other pertinent documents submitted to Congress by the president in support of his message. Further documents are in *Senate Document* no. 301, 29–1, serial 474. The report of the House Committee on Indian Affairs, June 2, 1846, is in *House Report* no. 683, 29–1, serial 490.

MAP 5: Location of Indians in the Indian Territory, after Removal

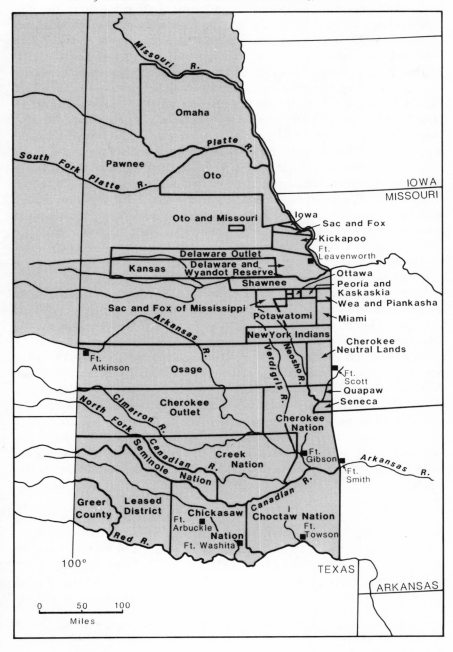

the three Cherokee delegations in Washington in order to heal all dissension. With able advisers and a firm intent to settle past differences, the three factions worked out an agreement. This treaty of 1846, debated and amended by the Senate and finally ratified by a majority of one vote, was approved in its modified form by the Indian delegates on August 14.[8]

The treaty provided for a unified Cherokee Nation and that "the lands now occupied by the Cherokee Nation shall be secured to the whole Cherokee people for their common use and benefit." A general amnesty and an end to party distinctions was proclaimed, and the treaty declared that "all difficulties and differences heretofore existing between the several parties of the Cherokee Nation are hereby settled and adjusted, and shall, as far as possible, be forgotten and forever buried in oblivion." The United States government agreed to adjust claims and pay indemnities to the treaty party.[9] The treaty was a compromise measure, for Ross now agreed to the legitimacy of the 1835 treaty, and the Old Settlers admitted that the Ross party had rights to the lands in the West. With the treaty, quiet returned to the Cherokee Nation, and a decade and more of prosperity and development ensued.

John Ross had frequently protested against actions of United States officials in what he considered strictly Cherokee matters, but he and other factional leaders were willing to use federal assistance in furthering their own goals. The military commanders and superintendents and agents in the Cherokee country were faced with difficult decisions in attempts to prevent civil war in the Cherokee Nation and to promote a workable accommodation among the parties. Officials of the Indian Office and the War Department, with whom rested the ticklish questions of adjudication of claims to annuities and other treaty funds, were torn between sympathy for John Ross's opponents and the fact that Ross commanded the allegiance of a majority of Cherokees. That the three delegations worked out the compromise of 1846 in Washington and embodied it in a formal treaty with the United States is an indication of the tremendous influence of the federal government in questions that were, in principle, internal concerns of the Cherokees.

The Choctaw Nation, the first to sign a removal treaty, reestablished itself in the southeastern section of the Indian Territory, west of Arkansas and along the Red River. This land had been assigned to the Choctaws by the Treaty of Doak's Stand in 1820, and an agency had been established for the western Choctaws, but not until after the Treaty of Dancing Rabbit Creek in 1830 did the Choctaws move en masse to the West. A govern-

8. Polk to the Senate, August 7, 1846, James D. Richardson, comp., *A Compilation of the Messages and Papers of the Presidents, 1789–1897*, 10 vols. (Washington: GPO, 1896–1899), 4: 458–59.

9. Kappler, pp. 561–65.

ment based on the three districts of the Choctaw Nation was set up, and agricultural development was promoted. Using funds specified in their treaties, the Choctaws built anew a flourishing school system, and Protestant missionaries zealously provided schools and churches.[10] The Choctaw leader Peter Pitchlynn drew a pleasant picture of the advances of his nation in 1849:

> Our constitution is purely republican, the gospel ministry is well sustained, and our schools are of a high order. Our people are increasing in numbers. Peace dwells within our limits, and plenteousness within our borders.
>
> Schools, civilization upon Christian principles, agriculture, temperance and morality are the only politics we have among us; and adhering to these few primary and fundamental principles of human happiness, we have flourished and prospered: hence we want none other. We wish simply to be let alone, and permitted to pursue the even tenor of our way.[11]

The Choctaws were joined by Chickasaws from northern Mississippi, who settled on the western section of the Choctaw lands (which they purchased from the Choctaws), with certain privileges in the Choctaw Nation. This condition dissatisfied the Chickasaws, for they wished to live under a strictly independent government, and in 1848 they adopted a formal constitution, in part as a means to prevent the diversion of their large tribal funds to the Choctaws. By 1854 contention between the two tribes had reached such a point that commissioners were appointed to seek agreement on separate jurisdictions and a set boundary line. A treaty signed that year at Doaksville in the Choctaw Nation defined the boundary; in 1855 a treaty concluded in Washington more carefully established relations between the two tribes.[12]

Chickasaw development in the West proceeded slowly, for with the death of Levi Colbert in 1834 there was no effective unified leadership, and the scattering of the settlements further fragmented the tribe. More serious was the general debilitation brought on, ironically, by the good terms received by the Chickasaws in their removal treaty. Hitchcock, who visited them in 1842, reported: "All accounts seem to agree that the Chickasaws are perhaps in a worse condition than either of the other emigrant

10. Angie Debo, *The Rise and Fall of the Choctaw Republic* (Norman: University of Oklahoma Press, 1934), pp. 58–79; Foreman, *Five Civilized Tribes*, pp. 17–94. Useful statistics on population and maps are provided in Jesse O. McKee and Jon A. Schlenker, *The Choctaws: Cultural Evolution of a Native American Tribe* (Jackson: University Press of Mississippi, 1980).

11. Remonstrance of Peter Pitchlynn, January 20, 1849, *House Miscellaneous Document* no. 35, 30–2, serial 544, p. 3.

12. Kappler, pp. 652–63, 706–14.

tribes resulting in part from their dependence upon what seemed in fact a more favorable treaty than that made by any other tribe." The Chickasaws seemed to lapse into a kind of apathy, depending on treaty annuities for their subsistence.[13]

Because of their exposed position, the Chickasaws suffered more than other tribes from raids by the warlike Kiowas, Comanches, and Kickapoos. "We are placed entirely on the frontier and surrounded by various bands of hostile Indians," Chickasaw leaders wrote to the president, "and we wish to know of our Great Father if he will not have some of his men placed at some suitable situation in our District to protect our lives and property, both of which are at the mercy of these roving bands."[14] In response to such pleas, the secretary of war in 1841 directed the construction of a new military post in the Chickasaw District to check the raiding tribes. Fort Washita was built near the mouth of the Washita River in 1842, and in 1851 another post, Fort Arbuckle, was established northwest of Fort Washita. Yet the Chickasaws were slow to move into their own district; a census of the tribe in 1844 showed a population of 4,111, three-fourths of whom still lived among the Choctaws. In 1853, however, a new count showed 4,709, with only one-tenth living outside the Chickasaw District.[15] By the mid-1850s the tribe appeared regenerated, with new leadership and social and economic development.

The Creek Indians moved to lands in the Indian Territory between the Cherokees and the Choctaws, although at first they clustered near Fort Gibson because they feared the wild tribes of the prairies. Like other tribes, they were divided, the Lower Creeks settling along the Arkansas River and the Upper Creeks along the Canadian. In 1840 the two groups united in a general council, but only later were the animosities between them quieted. Their factionalism, together with heavy population losses occasioned by the removal, delayed Creek development in the West.[16]

A further complication was the emigration of the Seminoles who had been forced out of Florida by the Seminole War. They were assigned a district within the Creek lands, between the Canadian River and its North Fork. But they objected to a union with the Creeks, and many stayed encamped near Fort Gibson. A principal bone of contention was the status of black slaves among the Seminoles, for these slaves enjoyed a good deal

13. Hitchcock, *Traveler in Indian Territory*, p. 176; Arrell M. Gibson, *The Chickasaws* (Norman: University of Oklahoma Press, 1971), pp. 184–226; Foreman, *Five Civilized Tribes*, pp. 97–144.

14. Quoted in Gibson, *Chickasaws*, p. 189.

15. Ibid., pp. 191–93.

16. Angie Debo, *The Road to Disappearance* (Norman: University of Oklahoma Press, 1941), pp. 108–41; Foreman, *Five Civilized Tribes*, pp. 147–219.

more freedom than the slaves of the Creeks, and they seemed to the Creeks to pose a threat to their own slave society. In a treaty signed at the Creek Agency on January 4, 1845, the difficulties were at least partially resolved, although the slavery problem continued and the Seminoles were irked by their incomplete independence from the Creeks. Finally, in 1856, following the pattern of separating the Choctaws and Chickasaws, a treaty was concluded in Washington by which the Seminoles received a new tract of land west of the Creek settlements. Once they had moved to these lands they were no longer subject to Creek laws.[17]

In spite of internal dissensions, the growth of these nations in the Indian Territory presaged an era of peace and prosperity that was taken as a sign of the wisdom of removal and the potentialities of the Indians to adapt to white ways. Such hopes were cut short by the Civil War, which reopened old animosities within the tribes and brought new economic and social disruptions.

MILITARY DEFENSE OF THE FRONTIER

Development of the Indian communities in the West depended upon a peaceful existence, free of attacks by outside enemies whether white or Indian. Critics of the removal policy had voiced a fear that the emigrant Indians would be insecure in their new homes, facing wild Indians of the plains who would resist the intrusion of tens of thousands of eastern Indians, most of them unprepared to fend off attacks. The emigrant Indians, moreover, would need protection against the encroachments of whites, protection that the Jackson administration had asserted was impossible in the East because of state jurisdictional problems but which the government could and would provide in the Trans-Mississippi West, where its authority was unchallenged. The federal government was mindful, also, of white citizens on the western frontier who, rightly or wrongly, feared the new heavy concentration of Indians on their borders. As removal proceeded, therefore, the United States developed elaborate plans for western defense to meet these needs.[18]

17. Kappler, pp. 550–52, 756–63. The problem of the slaves is thoroughly treated in Daniel F. Littlefield, Jr., *Africans and Seminoles: From Removal to Emancipation* (Westport, Connecticut: Greenwood Press, 1977), pp. 36–179; much of the same material is used in Littlefield, *Africans and Creeks: From the Colonial Period to the Civil War* (Westport, Connecticut: Greenwood Press, 1979), pp. 110–232.

18. I use here material from Francis Paul Prucha, *The Sword of the Republic: The United States Army on the Frontier, 1783–1846* (New York: Macmillan Company, 1969), pp. 339–60.

The removal of the eastern Indians, which poured thousands of tribes-men into the region west of Missouri and Arkansas, upset the haphazard system of establishing one fort at a time for frontier protection as local conditions required. What was needed now was a comprehensive, coordinated plan for the whole western frontier that would both maintain peace and fulfill the obligations the federal government had assumed to protect the transplanted Indians. The first full-scale plan came from Secretary of War Cass shortly before he left that office to become minister to France. On February 19, 1836, Cass presented a detailed proposal to House and Senate committees on military affairs. He estimated that when the re-moval of the eastern Indians was complete, about 93,500 emigrants would have been added to the indigenous tribes of the plains for a total of 244,870 between the Mississippi and the Rocky Mountains. These numbers were bound to increase the difficulties among the tribes and between the Indians and the whites. A sufficient military force along the frontier was needed to overawe the Indians, to intercept any bands that might attempt raids on white settlements, and to provide the means of concentrating troops wherever they might be needed.[19]

To accomplish these ends, Cass proposed the building of a military road along the frontier, running from the Red River near Fort Towson in the south to the Mississippi near Fort Snelling in the north. Along this line he wanted to construct stockaded posts. Forts east of the line would be aban-doned as quickly as possible and their troops transferred to the western line. The plan met immediate approval, and on July 2, 1836, Congress passed "an act to provide for the better protection of the western frontier" that embodied his proposals and appropriated the hundred thousand dol-lars he had requested to carry them out. The president was authorized to survey and open a military road from the Mississippi to the Red River and to have military posts constructed along the road wherever they would be judged most proper for the protection of the frontier. Two weeks later Cass sent instructions to the commission of army officers selected to lay out the road and determine the posts.[20] But then the whole project bogged down, for new councils in the War Department rejected the plan as an an-swer to western defense problems.

Benjamin F. Butler, who replaced Cass as secretary of war, expressed only reserved approval of the line of posts, noting that "though it will be sufficient, if well garrisoned, to protect our own frontier, [it] will not be all

19. Report of Cass, February 19, 1836, and accompanying papers, *American State Papers: Military Affairs*, 6: 149–55; the documents also appear in *House Report* no. 401, 24–1, serial 294.

20. 5 *United States Statutes* 67; Cass to commissioners, July 16, 1836, *House Document* no. 278, 25–2, serial 328, pp. 9–12.

that caution and good faith will require." Butler had in mind the solemn pledges given to the emigrating Indians that they would be protected in their new homes, and he wrote an eloquent appeal for the fulfillment of those promises. To preserve peace among the different tribes of emigrant Indians and to protect them from their savage neighbors would require posts inside the Indian country as well as on the exterior line. But Butler's greatest concern was to protect the Indians from the encroachments of whites. The pledges given by the government to prevent whites from intruding on Indian lands had been given in the utmost sincerity, he said, and they could not be fulfilled without a strong military force—"a force adequate to repress the encroachments of the civilized and more powerful race."[21]

Butler served only an interim term and was not in office long enough to carry on a successful fight for his highly honorable proposals. He was succeeded by Joel R. Poinsett, whose primary concern was to protect whites from hostile Indians and who shortly drew up a plan for western defense based on principles that he considered diametrically opposed to the underpinnings of Cass's proposal. Basing his plan on a report of Acting Quartermaster General Trueman Cross, Poinsett rejected Cass's idea of a road running north and south along the frontier and insisted that proper defense demanded lines of communication running *perpendicular* to the line of settlement, from the populated interior of the country to the exposed frontier. With a view both to protecting the border settlements from incursions of savage tribes and to fulfilling obligations toward the emigrant Indians, Cross had asked for 7,000 men to protect the border settlements, including large disposable forces at Fort Leavenworth, Fort Gibson, and Fort Towson, and a reserve of 1,500 men at Jefferson Barracks. Poinsett supported this request; he called for 5,000 troops to man the exterior and interior lines of posts, plus reserves at Jefferson Barracks and at Baton Rouge, which he thought would "both insure the safety of the western frontier, and enable the government to fulfill all its treaty stipulations, and preserve its faith with the Indians." He added a proposal, however, for an auxiliary force of volunteer troops, to be instructed a certain number of days each year by regular army officers at regular army posts, in order to have on hand a trained reserve force.[22]

21. Report of Butler, December 3, 1836, *American State Papers: Military Affairs*, 6: 815.

22. Poinsett's plan of December 30, 1837, and accompanying documents, *American State Papers: Military Affairs*, 7: 777–86, and *House Document* no. 59, 25–2, serial 322. Another plan was submitted by General Edmund P. Gaines, which is in *House Document* no. 311, 25–2, serial 329; it is discussed at length in James W. Silver, *Edmund Pendleton Gaines, Frontier General* (Baton Rouge: Louisiana State University Press, 1949), pp. 216–57.

All the proposals suggested a series of military posts as a military cordon in the West, and a line of forts was maintained that corresponded roughly with the master plans, even though specific locations often were determined by local circumstances. By 1844 the pre-Mexican War defense arrangements were set. In that year Fort Wilkins was established on Keweenaw Peninsula in Lake Superior to meet defense needs arising from the influx of miners into that copper region. To the secretary of war for whom the post was named, the new fort formed "one point in a new cordon, which the general extension of our settlements and the enlargement of our territories by Indian treaties" made necessary.[23] With Fort Wilkins the top link in the chain, the exterior line of posts in that year comprised Fort Snelling, Fort Leavenworth, Fort Scott, Fort Gibson, Fort Towson, and Fort Washita. The interior posts were Fort Mackinac and Fort Brady on the Great Lakes, Fort Winnebago at the portage between the Fox and Wisconsin rivers, Fort Crawford at Prairie du Chien, Forts Atkinson and Des Moines in Iowa, and Jefferson Barracks. In the south Fort Smith and Fort Jesup also served the Indian frontier.

The officers and men of these posts gave a sense of security to the whites in the West, and they furnished an available military force that was called upon to restrict white encroachments on Indian lands and lessen (although they could not control) the machinations of whiskey vendors. In this they carried out the stipulations of Indian treaties, fulfilling many promises made by the United States to the tribes. Although there were clashes between the plains Indians and the emigrants, there were no serious intertribal wars, and the maps of the Census Bureau that show frontier lines testify to the success of the line of forts in restraining white advance, for there is a sharp line between white settlement and regions reserved for the emigrated and indigenous tribes.

Although the emigrated Indians were much on the minds of government officials as they established the defense line in the West, the army did not neglect the plains Indians, with whom new contacts were continually being made. With the organization of a dragoon regiment in 1832 —the first regular mounted troops on the frontier—the army began a series of summer expeditions into the prairies and plains west of the emigrated tribes in order to overawe and keep at peace the western tribes. From Fort Gibson, Fort Leavenworth, and Fort Des Moines, the dragoons between 1834 and 1845 crisscrossed the Indian country and invaded the lands of the Comanches, Kiowas, Pawnees, Sioux, Cheyennes, and other western Indians, bringing a show of power into their lands and on occasion meeting with the tribes in council. In all this, the army served as an agent

23. Report of William Wilkins, November 30, 1844, *Senate Document* no. 1, 28–2, serial 449, p. 114.

of the federal government in regulating the advance of the white frontier and easing the intercultural conflicts that inevitably resulted.[24]

Army commanders on the frontier played a significant role in the management of Indian affairs, both between the Indians and the federal government and within the tribes themselves. Imbued with the same paternalistic spirit that marked the civilian officials of the government, the army officers felt called upon to impress and control Indians as they would unruly children. But they were also a significant buffer between the frequently helpless Indians and unscrupulous frontier whites or warlike Indians to the west, and they could be a source of support and influence that was cultivated by tribal factions for their own purposes.

BENEVOLENCE AND REFORM

When Indian removal was over—or nearly so—the federal government returned to a concentrated effort at civilization and Christianization.[25] By 1840 the bulk of the eastern Indians had emigrated, and as they settled into their new lives, new humanitarian efforts were made to move them rapidly into the white man's ways. With relative tranquility on the frontier and the traumas of the removal process over, the wounds began to heal as the tribes adjusted to their new conditions. Under such circumstances, it is understandable that concerns for Indian advancement should have assumed something of their old prominence.

The 1840s were a decade of intense reforming spirit in America, a decade that saw the "first great upsurge of social reform in United States history," a high point in reform movements that began about 1815 and continued to the Civil War.[26] Betterment for all mankind seemed within easy

24. Prucha, *Sword of the Republic*, pp. 365–94.

25. Much of the material in this section is taken from Francis Paul Prucha, "American Indian Policy in the 1840s: Visions of Reform," in John G. Clark, ed., *The Frontier Challenge: Responses to the Trans-Mississippi West* (Lawrence: University Press of Kansas, 1971), pp. 81–110.

26. The quotation is from Arthur M. Schlesinger, *The American as Reformer* (Cambridge: Harvard University Press, 1950), p. 3. The reform movements in antebellum America have received much attention. For surveys, see Alice Felt Tyler, *Freedom's Ferment: Phases of American Social History to 1860* (Minneapolis: University of Minnesota Press, 1944); Ronald G. Walters, *American Reformers, 1815–1860* (New York: Hill and Wang, 1978); and Clifford S. Griffin, *Their Brothers' Keepers: Moral Stewardship in the United States, 1800–1865* (New Brunswick: Rutgers University Press, 1960). A useful collection of contemporary essays is Walter Hugins, ed., *The Reform Impulse, 1825–1850* (Columbia: University of South Carolina Press, 1972); modern essays are reprinted with an excellent introduction in David Brion Davis, ed., *Ante-Bellum Reform* (New York: Harper and Row, 1967). The intellectual setting in which movements for

reach, and concern for society's unfortunates (the delinquent, the insane, the indigent poor, the deaf, and the blind) appeared everywhere. Crusades for peace, women's rights, temperance, education, and the abolition of slavery marched with reforming zeal and a strange naiveté through the land. Words like *benevolence, philanthropy,* and *perfectability* slipped easily from men's tongues. The plans for civilizing and Christianizing those Indians who had been moved from the main arena of American life partook of this evangelizing spirit. It was part of the continuing revivalist atmosphere that so marked America in the nineteenth century and made Americans into a reforming people.

Indian welfare in the 1840s was not the object of a formal "reform movement," with voluntary organizations and national attention—as were temperance, women's rights, or abolition, and as Indian reform became in the last decades of the century. But the men who directed Indian affairs reflected their times. They spoke the same evangelical Protestant perfectionist rhetoric that distinguished the other reformers. They shared in the vital optimism of the age and hoped for no less for the Indians than the professional reformers did for other unfortunate groups within the nation. The policies of the 1840s must be understood in this context.

Removal itself continued to be seen as part of the total drive to civilize the Indians. The men in charge of Indian affairs in the 1840s were convinced of the wisdom of the removal policy and eager to make it work for the Indians. "It will be the end of all," T. Hartley Crawford, the commissioner of Indian affairs appointed by President Van Buren, wrote after his first year in office, "unless the experiment of the Government in the Indian territory shall be blessed with success." He admitted that the outcome was uncertain, but he was not disheartened, and he urged perseverance.[27]

As Crawford warmed to his job, he became bolder in his praise of removal as essential for Indian betterment. He considered other alternatives that might have been pursued—assimilation of Indians into the mass of white society and life as farmers on their lands in the East—and rejected them as infeasible. Removal to the West, he judged, was "the only expedient—the wisest, the best, the most practicable and practical of all." His view of the advantages to the Indians was idyllic, his goals utopian. The Indians, he prophesied, would find "a home and a country free from the apprehension of disturbance and annoyance, from the means of indulging a most degrading appetite [for liquor], and far removed from the temptations of bad and sordid men; a region hemmed in by the laws of the United

---

bettering the conditions of the Indians must be placed is treated in Perry Miller, *The Life of the Mind in America from the Revolution to the Civil War* (New York: Harcourt, Brace and World, 1965); see especially the section on benevolence, pp. 78–84.

27. CIA Report, 1839, serial 363, p. 346.

States and guarded by virtuous agents, where abstinence from vice, and the practice of good morals, should find fit abodes in comfortable dwellings and cleared farms, and be nourished and fostered by all the associations of the hearthstone. In no other than this settled condition can schools flourish, which are the keys that open the gate to heaven and God." Imbued with this attitude, he could not but urge the speedy removal of those Indians who had not yet migrated.[28]

The great means to bring about the transformation in the Indians that the reformers wanted—as it had been since early in the century—was education. There continued to be no doubt in the minds of responsible officials of the federal government that the Indians were ultimately educable. These men admitted that the present state of many of the Indians was one of semi-barbarism, but they did not believe in a racial inferiority that was not amenable to betterment. "It is proved, I think, conclusively," Crawford remarked of the Indian race, "that it is in no respect inferior to our own race, except in being less fortunately circumstanced. As great an aptitude for learning the letters, the pursuits, and arts of civilized life, is evident; if their progress is slow, so has it been with us and with masses of men in all nations and ages." Circumstances and education alone made the difference between them and the whites; and Indian agents, missionaries, and traders contributed evidence that the Indians were susceptible of improvement. There would be no racial obstacle to their eventual assimilation into the political life of the nation.[29]

So schools for the Indians were advocated with even greater enthusiasm than Thomas L. McKenney and his pioneering missionary friends had displayed, as befitted an age in which education was considered the "universal utopia."[30] The promotion of schools as the agency to swing the Indians from a state considered to be barbarous, immoral, and pagan to one that was civilized, moral, and Christian took on new exuberance when the Indians were safely ensconced in the West, where the "experiment" could be carried out unhindered. Indian schools, Commissioner Crawford asserted in 1839, formed "one of the most important objects, if it be not the greatest, connected with our Indian relations. Upon it depends more or less even partial success in all endeavors to make the Indian better than he is."

28. CIA Report, 1840, serial 375, pp. 232–34. Crawford's vision was shared by the secretaries of war. See report of Joel R. Poinsett, December 5, 1840, *Senate Document* no. 1, 26–2, serial 375, p. 28; report of John C. Spencer, November 26, 1842, *Senate Document* no. 1, 27–3, serial 413, p. 190.

29. CIA Report, 1844, serial 449, p. 315; report of Thomas H. Harvey, October 8, 1844, ibid., p. 435; report of William Wilkins, November 30, 1844, *Senate Document* no. 1, 28–2, serial 449, p. 127.

30. The phrase is from a chapter heading in Arthur A. Ekirch, Jr., *The Idea of Progress in America, 1815–1860* (New York: Columbia University Press, 1944), p. 195.

The commissioner hammered tirelessly at this theme. "The greatest good we can bestow upon them," he said in 1842, "is education in its broadest sense—education in letters, education in labor and the mechanic arts, education in morals, and education in Christianity."[31]

The initial problem was how to intrigue the Indians, both the youths to be educated and their parents, into accepting the schooling. It was all too evident that simply duplicating white schools in the Indian country or sending Indians to the East for formal education was not the answer. Learning in letters alone was not appreciated by the Indians and did not give any practical advancement to young Indians, who became misfits within their own communities. The answer, rather, lay in manual labor schools, whose full importance was made explicit by Crawford:

> The education of the Indian is a great work. It includes more than the term imports in its application to civilized communities. Letters and personal accomplishments are what we generally intend to speak of by using the word; though sometimes, even with us, it has a more comprehensive meaning. Applied to wild men, its scope should take in much more extensive range, or you give them the shadow for the substance. They must at the least be taught to read and write, and have some acquaintance with figures; but if they do not learn to build and live in houses, to sleep on beds; to eat at regular intervals; to plough, and sow, and reap; to rear and use domestic animals; to understand and practise the mechanic arts; and to enjoy, to their gratification and improvement, all the means of profit and rational pleasure that are so profusely spread around civilized life, their mere knowledge of what is learned in the school room proper will be comparatively valueless. At a future day, more or less remote, when those who are now savage shall have happily become civilized, this important branch of Indian interest may be modified according to circumstances; but at present, when every thing is to be learned at the school, and nothing, as with us, by the child as it grows up, unconsciously and without knowing how or when, the manual labor school system is not only deserving of favor, but it seems to me indispensable to the civilization of the Indians; and their civilization, with a rare exception here and there, is as indispensable to real and true Christianity in them.[32]

This apotheosis of white cultural traits and insistence upon them, willy-nilly, for the Indians is an overpowering indication of the ethnocentric, paternalistic viewpoint of the white reformers. Once the Indians

31. CIA Report, 1839, serial 363, p. 343; CIA Report, 1842, serial 413, p. 386.
32. CIA Report, 1844, serial 449, p. 313.

accepted the new way of life, they would see the advantages of education in arts and letters, and the desire to attain it would motivate the Indians to attend and promote traditional schools. As civilization advanced, Christianity could be promoted, and moral improvement would follow. The desire for material well-being would stimulate industry, which would in turn accelerate the whole process. It was a wonderful white man's carousel.

The practical model for the Indian Office was the manual labor school established at the Methodist Shawnee mission in eastern Kansas in 1839, which seemed to embody all the characteristics needed to reach the goal. The school, built with church funds aided by substantial grants from the Indian civilization fund of the government, drew students from several tribes—Shawnee, Delaware, Kansas, Peoria, Potawatomi, Wyandot, Ottawa, and a scattering of others—and provided training for both boys and girls in useful agricultural and domestic skills, as well as in the English language.[33] Crawford considered the school "the strongest evidence I have yet seen of the probability of success, after all our failures, in the efforts made by benevolent and religious societies, and by the Government, to work a change in Indian habits and modes of life; while it is conclusive proof that these sons of the forest are our equals in capacity."[34] For its good work, and even more as a harbinger of greater things to come within the Indian country, the school won praise from the highest sources. Manual labor schools for the Indians became the goal of the War Department and the Indian Office.[35]

Two other principles in connection with manual labor education were adopted by the Indian Office. One was that Indian schools should teach girls as well as boys, if civilization were to be forwarded. When Crawford, early in his term of office, noted that more boys than girls were being educated, he asked, "Upon what principle of human action is this inequality founded?" And he set forth his argument in strong terms:

Unless the Indian female character is raised, and her relative position changed, such an education as you can give the males will be a rope

33. Valuable details on the founding and operation of the Shawnee mission school are given in Martha B. Caldwell, comp., *Annals of Shawnee Methodist Mission and Indian Manual Labor School* (Topeka: Kansas State Historical Society, 1939), and J. J. Lutz, "The Methodist Missions among the Indian Tribes in Kansas," *Transactions of the Kansas State Historical Society* 9 (1905–1906): 170–93. A good theoretical analysis of early missionary manual labor schools is Robert F. Berkhofer, Jr., "Model Zions for the American Indian," *American Quarterly* 15 (Summer 1963): 176–90.

34. CIA Report, 1840, serial 375, p. 243. Crawford got his information from a report of John B. Luce, November 11, 1840, ibid., pp. 387–88. See also the reports of the beginning of the school in CIA Report, 1839, serial 363, pp. 433–34.

35. Report of W. L. Marcy, December 5, 1846, *Senate Document* no. 1, 29–2, serial 493, p. 60; CIA Report, 1846, serial 493, p. 227.

of sand, which, separating at every turn, will bind them to no ame-
lioration. Necessity may force the culture of a little ground, or the
keeping of a few cattle, but the savage nature will break out at every
temptation. If the women are made good and industrious house-
wives, and taught what befits their condition, their husbands and
sons will find comfortable homes and social enjoyments, which, in
any state of society, are essential to morality and thrift. I would therefore advise that the larger proportion of pupils should be female.[36]

"The conviction is settled," he reiterated in 1841, "that the civilization of
these unfortunate wards of the Government will be effected through the
instrumentality of their educated women, much more than by their taught
men."[37] Although the commissioner's goals were never met, promotion of
female education continued.

A second principle, gradually developed during the decade, was that
Indian youths should be taught in the Indian country where they lived
and not sent off to eastern schools. This reversed the tradition of sending
select Indian boys to schools in the East, where it was supposed that they
could more quickly absorb the white man's civilization and take it back
to their tribes. Thus the Cherokees John Ridge and Elias Boudinot had
been educated at Cornwall, Connecticut, and many Indians had attended
Richard M. Johnson's Choctaw Academy in Kentucky.

Crawford advised from the first against sending Indians away from
home to distant schools, and in 1844 Secretary of War Wilkins argued that
education should be diffused as equally as possible through the whole tribe
by establishing common schools within the Indian country. The education
of a few individuals in a school away from their tribe did not promote the
designs of the government, Wilkins said, for he was afraid that men more
highly educated than the mass of the tribes might employ their talents for
selfish acquisition and oppression of their uneducated brothers. By 1846
the Indian Office had clearly decided to adhere to the new policy.[38] "The
practice so long pursued of selecting a few boys from the different tribes,
and placing them at our colleges and high schools," Commissioner William Medill repeated in 1847, "has failed to produce the beneficial results
anticipated; while the great mass of the tribe at home were suffered to remain in ignorance." He intended to discontinue the plan as soon as existing arrangements could be changed and apply the resources of the Indian

36. CIA Report, 1839, serial 363, p. 344.
37. CIA Report, 1841, serial 401, p. 241.
38. CIA Report, 1839, serial 363, p. 344; report of Wilkins, November 30, 1844, *Senate Document* no. 1, 28–2, serial 449, p. 127; report of Marcy, December 5, 1846, *Senate
Document* no. 1, 29–2, serial 493, p. 60.

Office solely to schools within the Indian country, where education could be extended to both sexes and generally spread throughout the tribe.[39]

To carry out the educational reform considerable money was expended in the Indian country. The civilization fund of $10,000 a year was apportioned among the various missionary societies in small amounts.[40] The effect of these allowances in stimulating contributions by missionary groups is hard to evaluate, for other federal funds also were poured into the mission schools. Chief among these were funds specified for education in treaties made with the Indians or designated from annuity money by the tribes themselves for educational purposes. Thus the Choctaw treaty of 1830 stipulated that the government would pay $2,000 annually for twenty years for the support of three school teachers, and the tribe voted in 1842 to apply $18,000 a year from its annuities to education.[41] A treaty with the Ottawas and Chippewas in 1836 specified that, in addition to an annuity in specie of $30,000 for twenty years, $5,000 each year would be granted for teachers, schoolhouses, and books in their own languages, and $3,000 more for missions. These payments were to run for twenty years and as long thereafter as Congress would continue the appropriation. In 1845, $68,195 was provided by treaties for Indian education, to which was added $12,367.50 from the civilization fund. Subsequent treaties added to the school funds available. A treaty with the Kansas Indians in 1846, for example, called for the investment of the sum paid for ceded lands, and $1,000 a year from the interest was directed to schools. The treaty of 1846 with the Winnebagos stated that $10,000 of the cession payment would be applied to the creation and maintenance of one or more manual labor schools.[42] To these government funds were added the money supplied by the missionary societies. The government also built schools and churches and supplied agricultural implements and domestic equipment that could be used in the sort of education advocated by white leaders of the 1840s.

Although the number of students in the Indian schools was small, the optimism of the Indian Office and the missionaries was not without foundation. The Choctaws, who were more interested in education than many of the tribes, offered an example of what was possible. They began to build

39. CIA Report, 1847, serial 503, p. 749. See also report of Marcy, December 2, 1847, *Senate Executive Document* no. 1, 30–1, serial 503, p. 70.

40. A year-by-year listing of expenditures from the fund for the period 1820–1842 appears in *House Document* no. 203, 27–3, serial 423. See also George D. Harmon, *Sixty Years of Indian Affairs: Political, Economic, and Diplomatic, 1789–1850* (Chapel Hill: University of North Carolina Press, 1941), appendix, table V, pp. 378–79.

41. Kappler, p. 315; P. P. Pitchlynn to William Armstrong, December 12, 1842, in CIA Report, 1843, serial 431, pp. 367–68.

42. Kappler, pp. 451–52, 553, 566; Harmon, *Sixty Years of Indian Affairs*, appendix, table VII, p. 381.

schools as soon as they arrived in the West. The missionaries of the American Board reported eleven schools with 228 Choctaw students in 1836, in addition to which there were five schools supported by the Choctaw Nation and the three district schools provided by the 1830 treaty. In 1842 a comprehensive system of schools was begun. Spencer Academy and Fort Coffee Academy were opened in 1844, Armstrong and New Hope academies two years later. The national council also supported four schools established earlier by the American Board. By 1848 the Choctaws had nine boarding schools supported by tribal funds, and neighborhood schools had been opened in many communities.[43] The commissioner of Indian affairs reported progress as well among the other tribes. The Cherokees especially made remarkable advances and had a better common school system than that of either Arkansas or Missouri.[44]

Comparative numbers give some indication of the progress, although reports were often incomplete. In 1842 forty-five schools (out of a total of fifty-two) reported 2,132 students enrolled. In 1848 there were sixteen manual labor schools with 809 students and eighty-seven boarding and other schools with 2,873 students; in 1849, although some reports were missing, a further increase in students was noted.[45]

These schools could not have existed without the devoted work of Christian missionaries, and Indian education was a beneficiary of the missionary impulse of the Protestant churches that was an important element in the reform ferment of the age. The Indian Office felt this influence strongly, for its goals and those of the missionary societies were identical: practical, moral, and religious education of the Indians that would bring both Christianity and civilization to the aborigines. Reliance on the missionaries, indeed, was uppermost in the minds of federal officials. Commissioner Crawford noted in his report of 1839: "No direction of these institutions [Indian schools] appears to me so judicious as that of religious and benevolent societies, and it is gratifying to observe the zeal with which all the leading sects lend themselves to this good work; discouragements do not seem to cool their ardor, nor small success to dissuade them from persevering efforts." So successful was the Methodist school in Kansas that the War Department was eager to support similar establishments directed by other religious groups, "equally zealous, no doubt, in spreading the light

43. Debo, *Choctaw Republic*, pp. 60–61; documents 69–72 in CIA Report, 1843, serial 431, pp. 367–72. Spencer Academy is a good example of the cooperation of several agencies in the Indian schools. It was started with $2,000 from the government's civilization fund and $6,000 from Choctaw annuities, and it was directed and run by Presbyterian missionaries. See W. David Baird, "Spencer Academy, Choctaw Nation, 1842–1900," *Chronicles of Oklahoma* 45 (Spring 1967): 25–43.

44. CIA Report, 1847, serial 503, p. 750; Foreman, *Five Civilized Tribes*, p. 410.

45. Document 83 in CIA Report, 1842, serial 413, pp. 520–22; CIA Report, 1849, serial 570, p. 956.

of the Gospel among the Indians, and equally disposed to advance their moral culture."[46]

Agents in the field who were close to the missionaries and their work strongly praised the efforts of the churches, and officials in Washington uncritically accepted the highly favorable reports sent in by the missionaries themselves. The eagerness to see success in these ventures, unwarranted as it might have been at times, reflects the utopian, reform-minded views of the age.[47]

The general reports of progress were highly optimistic. Government officials held firm to their views of the perfectibility of the Indians, of their ability to attain the civilization of the whites. They eagerly seized upon whatever evidence pointed in that direction, convinced as they were that the advances in education among some of the tribes proved conclusively that all Indians were amenable to such attainments, immediately or in the near future. They were sure their efforts had contributed to the good result, and they spoke in justification of the faith they had had. Only a few voices were raised in opposition, not to deny the possibilities or even some of the accomplishments, but to point to the slowness of the progress.

By the end of the decade success seemed assured and was in fact proclaimed from on high. Secretary of War W. L. Marcy in December 1848 reported: "No subject connected with our Indian affairs has so deeply interested the department and received so much of its anxious solicitude and attention, as that of education, and I am happy to be able to say that its efforts to advance this cause have been crowned with success. Among most of the tribes which have removed to and become settled in the Indian country, the blessings of education are beginning to be appreciated, and they generally manifest a willingness to co-operate with the government in diffusing these blessings." The schools, he concluded, afforded evidence that nearly all of the emigrated tribes were rapidly advancing in civilization and moral strength, and he gave full credit to the Indian Office for the improved condition of the numerous tribes. In the same year, William Medill, then commissioner of Indian affairs, acknowledged the earlier decline of the Indians and the disappearance of some aboriginal groups. "Cannot this sad and depressing tendency of things be checked, and the past be at least measurably repaired by better results in the future?" he asked. His

46. CIA Report, 1839, serial 363, p. 343; report of Joel R. Poinsett, December 5, 1840, *Senate Document* no. 1, 26–2, serial 375, p. 28.

47. See Epilogue, "The Harvest Unreaped," in Robert F. Berkhofer, Jr., *Salvation and the Savage: An Analysis of Protestant Missions and American Indian Response, 1787–1862* (Lexington: University of Kentucky Press, 1965), pp. 152–60, for a critical appraisal of the missionaries' success up to 1860. Reports of the missionaries appear in such sources as the *Annual Report* of the American Board of Commissioners for Foreign Missions and in the board's journal, *The Missionary Herald*, as well as in reports attached to the annual reports of the commissioner of Indian affairs.

answer was cautious but reassuring: "It is believed they can, and, indeed, it has to some extent been done already, by the wise and beneficent system of policy put in operation some years since, and which, if steadily carried out, will soon give to our whole Indian system a very different and much more favorable aspect."[48]

The optimism of the next commissioner of Indian affairs, Orlando Brown, knew no bounds, but his report of 1849 differed only in degree and not in kind from the enthusiastic appraisals of his predecessors. "The dark clouds of ignorance and superstition in which these people have so long been enveloped seem at length in the case of many of them to be breaking away, and the light of Christianity and general knowledge to be dawning upon their moral and intellectual darkness," he wrote. Brown gave credit for the change to the government's policy of moving the Indians toward an agricultural existence, to the introduction of the manual labor schools, and to instruction by the missionaries in "the best of all knowledge, religious truth—their duty towards God and their fellow beings." The result was "a great moral and social revolution" among some of the tribes that he predicted would be spread to others by adoption of the same measures. Within a few years he believed that "in intelligence and resources, they would compare favorably with many portions of our white population, and instead of drooping and declining, as heretofore, they would be fully able to maintain themselves in prosperity and happiness under any circumstance of contact or connexion with our people." In the end he expected a large measure of success to "crown the philanthropic efforts of the government and of individuals to civilize and to christianize the Indian tribes." He no longer doubted that the Indians were capable of self-government. "They have proved their capacity for social happiness," he concluded, "by adopting written constitutions upon the model of our own, by establishing and sustaining schools, by successfully devoting themselves to agricultural pursuits, by respectable attainments in the learned professions and mechanic arts, and by adopting the manners and customs of our people, so far as they are applicable to their own condition."[49]

This was a bit too much, for the Indians did not reach utopia. But it was quite in tune with the age, when zealous reformers saw no limit to the possibilities for ameliorating and perfecting the human condition, when the insane were to be cured, the slaves freed, the prisons cleansed, and women's rights recognized, and when Sunday schools would flourish. Government officials and their missionary allies hoped for no less for the American Indians.

48. Report of Marcy, December 1, 1848, *House Executive Document* no. 1, 30–2, serial 537, p. 84; CIA Report, 1848, serial 537, pp. 385–86.
49. CIA Report, 1849, serial 570, pp. 956–57.

CHAPTER II

New Structures
and Programs

Development of the Indian Department.

Proposals for an Indian State.

Annuities and Liquor Regulation.

The removal of the eastern Indians not only meant the relocation of tens of thousands of Indians in the Trans-Mississippi West, radically changing the distribution of the tribes with whom the United States government dealt, but it also necessitated a modification and codification of the laws and regulations governing Indian relations. The Indian bureaucracy (which had grown piecemeal during the previous decades) was regularized, an up-to-date trade and intercourse law was enacted, and plans were proposed for Indian government in the West. In addition, special problems growing out of annuity payments and the liquor traffic were once again directly countered with legislative remedies.

DEVELOPMENT OF THE INDIAN DEPARTMENT

The first step was congressional authorization in 1832 of a commissioner of Indian affairs to replace the head of the Indian Office appointed by the secretary of war on his own authority (Thomas L. McKenney and his two successors, Samuel S. Hamilton and Elbert Herring). Congress specified that the new official, who would be under the direction of the secretary of war, would manage all Indian affairs.[1] This formalization had been a dream

---

1. 4 *United States Statutes* 564.

of McKenney's, which he had promoted unsuccessfully for many years before he was removed from office in 1830.

The first to serve in the long line of commissioners extending up to the
1970s was Elbert Herring, who carried over from the older office and who
served until 1836. Herring was a politician with no experience in Indian
affairs, but he was an enthusiastic supporter of the removal policy and programs determined by Andrew Jackson and Lewis Cass. He fitted well into
the paternalistic, benevolent Christian reform pattern of the time and
urged the transformation of Indian society from a system of communal to
one of private property, concluding that the "absence of the *meum* and
tuum in the general community of possessions, which is the grand conser-
vative principle of the social state, is a perpetual operating cause of the *vis
inertiae* of savage life." He recommended a new political system for the
tribes, the education of Indian youth, and the introduction of Christianity,
"all centering on one grand object—the substitution of the social for the
savage state."[2] Herring's successor, Carey A. Harris, was likewise a firm
supporter of the removal policy. A Tennessee newspaperman and lawyer
who had become chief clerk in the War Department and a close associate
of Cass and Jackson, Harris served as commissioner for only two years,
when he was forced to resign because of a scandal arising out of speculation in Indian allotments.[3]

In 1834 Congress went far beyond the establishment of the commis-
sionership by undertaking a wholesale revamping of the Indian department and its activities. First, it put a firm legislative foundation under the
Indian service, made explicit provisions for Indian agents, whose status
had been somewhat irregular, and established systematic accounting procedures in order to eliminate the confusion and embarrassment that had
frequently arisen in financial matters. Second, it restated and codified Indian policy as it had been embodied in trade and intercourse laws during
the preceding four and a half decades of United States history, bringing to
culmination earlier legislation, ripened now. Third, it intended to fulfill
the pledges made to the Indians upon removal that adequate provision
would be made for their protection and for their government.[4]

The first and second of these measures were not revolutionary. Their

2. CIA Report, 1832, serial 233, p. 163; see also CIA Report, 1834, serial 266, pp.
238–39, 241. A brief biographical sketch of Herring is provided in Ronald N. Satz,
"Elbert Herring, 1831–36," in Robert M. Kvasnicka and Herman J. Viola, eds., *The Commissioners of Indian Affairs, 1824–1977* (Lincoln: University of Nebraska Press, 1979),
pp. 13–16.
3. Ronald N. Satz, "Carey Allen Harris, 1836–38," in Kvasnicka and Viola, *Commissioners of Indian Affairs*, pp. 17–22.
4. I use material here from Francis Paul Prucha, *American Indian Policy in the Formative Years: The Indian Trade and Intercourse Acts, 1790–1834* (Cambridge: Harvard
University Press, 1962), pp. 250–69.

ultimate source was earlier legislation based on past experience, as well as numerous recommendations made through the years to perfect United States policy toward the Indians. There were, moreover, important proximate sources through which the past was brought to focus on the present. Such were the detailed recommendations submitted to the secretary of war in February 1829 by Lewis Cass and William Clark, the report of the Stokes Commission sent out by the secretary of war in 1832 to investigate the new home allotted to the emigrating Indians, and finally, the report of the House Committee on Indian Affairs, which presented the draft of the new Indian bills to Congress in 1834.

The trade and intercourse laws from 1790 to 1802, with occasional later amendments, had grown little by little, and they needed to be augmented and pulled together in a single piece of legislation. This need, plus the frustrating difficulties arising from the lack of well-founded administrative procedures in the War Department for handling Indian affairs, struck Peter B. Porter with special force when he became secretary of war in the spring of 1828. "In the few weeks that have elapsed since I had the honor to be called to this Department," Porter wrote to Governor Cass in July 1828, "I have found no portion of its extensive and complicated duties so perplexing, and the performance of which has been less welcome, than those which appertain to the Bureau of Indian Affairs." This was not due to deficiencies in the character of the men charged with the duties, he asserted, but came rather from "the want of a well digested system of principles and rules for the administration of our Indian concerns." His purpose in writing Cass and in sending a similar letter to William Clark at St. Louis was to invite the two men to Washington to draw up a code of regulations for Indian affairs that could be presented to Congress for its action. "The long and intimate acquaintance which you have both had with the Indian character," he told them, "—your knowledge of their interests, their habits, wants, wishes and capabilities would render your aid and advice in the formation of such a system, peculiarly useful and desirable."[5]

Both Cass and Clark responded enthusiastically to Porter's proposal. Clark thought that the existing laws were "not sufficiently explicit & consistent" to punish offences against the laws and regulations, and Cass wanted "some established principles to regulate the discretion which now exists." Working together in Washington, they produced a long report, which Porter sent to the Senate on February 9, 1829.[6]

5. Porter to Cass, July 28, 1828, OIA LS, vol. 5, pp. 56–57 (M21, reel 5). See also report of the secretary of war, November 24, 1828, *Senate Document* no. 1, 20–2, serial 181, pp. 20–21.

6. Clark to Porter, August 27, 1828, OIA LR, St. Louis Superintendency (M234, reel 748); Cass to Porter, September 8, 1828, ibid., Michigan Superintendency (M234, reel 420). The report of Cass and Clark is in *Senate Document* no. 72, 20–2, serial 181.

In answer to Porter's demand for a bill that would "embrace the whole policy of the government, and comprise all its legislation on Indian intercourse, and every other subject connected therewith, in one statute," the two men submitted the draft of a bill with fifty-six sections. It was made up in large part of transcriptions—more or less literal—from previous laws, incorporating most of the intercourse act of 1802, a law of 1800 providing for visits of Indians to the seat of government, provisions of the law of 1816 excluding foreigners from the Indian trade, the law of 1817 providing for crimes committed in the Indian country, the law of 1818 concerning the manner of appointing Indian agents, the law of 1819 establishing an annual $10,000 civilization fund, the supplementary intercourse law of 1822, the provisions of 1824 designating sites for the trade, and sections of other laws that touched upon Indian trade, Indian agents, or the accounting for public funds. There was also much that was new: additions and modifications of earlier legislation embodying the views of Cass and Clark for ameliorating the existing state of affairs. These pertained to regularizing and specifying the appointment and duties of Indian department personnel and to improving methods for handling financial accounts. Discretionary power for agents in granting licenses was recommended, along with tighter restriction in general of access to the Indian country.

The proposed bill was accompanied by a set of "Regulations for the Government of the Indian Department." These in many places repeated the provisions in the bill but also added details of procedure for carrying the law into effect. There were sections governing the civil and fiscal administration of the Indian department, and others that prescribed the limits of agencies, listed the designated trading posts, and provided rules for treating with the Indians, paying annuities, issuing licenses, processing claims for indemnification for losses suffered by either race, using the civilization fund, prohibiting liquor, and accounting for funds.[7]

A third item was a bill to consolidate into one statute all the provisions for payment of annuities due from the United States to the Indians. This was a sensible proposal, intended to eliminate the unnecessary complications of accounting for funds under diverse headings.[8]

The work of Cass and Clark bore witness to their competence in Indian affairs. The proposed bills, it is true, included a few items that were no longer of current importance, but they provided adequately for a workable department and new legislation and regulations to correct evils not taken care of by the earlier laws. The men skillfully worked into one bill and one set of regulations diverse matters that had been scattered through the statutes and War Department directives. They attempted in their regulations

7. The regulations are printed ibid., pp. 75–82.
8. Ibid., pp. 52–57.

to codify existing practice where it was satisfactory and introduce new procedures where greater clarity or strength was needed. The proposed bill was accompanied by an extensive section-by-section commentary that made clear the thinking behind the proposals and gave insight into Indian affairs at the time.

The proposals were submitted to the Senate by Porter with the earnest recommendation that they receive early consideration. McKenney, too, praised them; the report was, he declared, "able and judicious," and the accompanying bill "ample and apposite," although he objected to the mode of accounting that Cass and Clark had proposed and offered alternative suggestions. McKenney picked out for special emphasis the provisions in the bill and regulations that would grant discretion to the agents in issuing licenses to traders. That this discretionary power was a crucial point in the regulation of Indian intercourse can be seen from the violent opposition it stirred up in the American Fur Company.[9] Congress took no action on the Cass-Clark report as it stood, but the recommendations were not ineffectual, for they served as a ready reference for those who advocated some updating of the laws governing relations with the Indians, and much of the report was incorporated into the bills that became law in 1834.

Removal invigorated the concern to update the legislative basis of Indian affairs. The Stokes Commission of 1832, besides investigating the land in the West, was charged to gather information that would be essential in developing a sound policy for governing future relations with the Indians. "In the great change we are now urging them [the Indians] to make," Secretary of War Cass warned the commissioners, "it is desirable that all their political relations, as well among themselves as with us, should be established upon a permanent basis, beyond the necessity for any future alteration. Your report upon this branch of the subject will be laid before Congress, and will probably become the foundation of a system of legislation for these Indians."[10]

The commissioners submitted a long and useful report, full of details on the condition of the western tribes and the character of the territory to be allotted to the emigrating Indians. They emphasized the necessity for governmental action to suppress hostilities among Indian groups and recommended in detail the military posts in the West that they considered essential. They noted the high prices charged the Indians for goods by white traders and urged that the government care for Indian wants by supplying annuities in goods at reasonable cost. The commissioners stressed the im-

9. CIA Report, 1829, serial 192, pp. 167–68; McKenney to John H. Eaton, January 21, 1830, OIA LS, vol. 6, pp. 237–38 (M21, reel 6).

10. Instructions of Cass, July 14, 1832, *House Executive Document* no. 2, 22–2, serial 233, pp. 32–37.

298 Indian Removal

portance of freeing the Indian country of white citizens and preventing whites from grazing their livestock or trapping on Indian lands. They strongly suggested the organization of the Indian territory and an annual grand council of Indians. So anxious were they to avoid contacts between the whites and the Indians that they recommended a neutral strip of land five miles wide between the lands of the two races on which all settlement was to be prohibited.[11]

President Jackson in his annual message of December 1833 called attention to the need for a reorganization of Indian affairs to meet new conditions. In response, the House Committee on Indian Affairs presented a full-scale report on May 20, 1834. The report relied heavily on the Cass-Clark proposals of five years earlier and on the report of the Stokes Commission, which had been submitted on February 10. Accompanying the report was a trio of bills—for organizing the Indian department, for a new trade and intercourse law, and for establishing a government for the Indians in the West.[12]

Because the authorization for a commissioner of Indian affairs in 1832 met the demand that had been made for a centralized office to handle Indian matters, the committee turned immediately to the problem of Indian superintendencies and agencies. They discovered legislative and administrative confusion. They found four superintendents, eighteen agents, twenty-seven subagents, and thirty-four interpreters on duty with the Indian department, drawing a total annual compensation of $57,222. They were dismayed at the lack of legal foundation for the offices that these men filled and insisted that the creation of the offices and the fixing of the salaries "should not be left to Executive discretion or to legislative implication." For help in drawing up a suitable bill, the committee turned to the secretary of war, asking him "to furnish them with a general bill, reorganising the Indian Department & in fact defining as far as possible the Indian service." Cass replied with alacrity and made arrangements to meet personally with the committee.[13]

The bill reported by the committee on May 20 withdrew the superintendence of Indian affairs from the governors of Florida and Arkansas territories, and from the governor of Michigan Territory as soon as a new

11. Report of commissioners, February 10, 1834, *House Report* no. 474, 23–1, serial 263, pp. 78–103.

12. Message of December 3, 1833, Fred L. Israel, ed., *The State of the Union Messages of the Presidents, 1790–1966*, 3 vols. (New York: Chelsea House, 1966), 1: 386–87; *House Report* no. 474, 23–1, serial 263.

13. House committee to Cass, February 25, 1834, OIA LR, Miscellaneous (M234, reel 435); Cass to committee, February 26, 1834, Office of the Secretary of War, Reports to Congress, vol. 3, National Archives, Record Group 107. No copy of a written report to the committee including a detailed bill could be found.

territory should be organized west of Lake Michigan. It continued the superintendency at St. Louis for all Indians west of the Mississippi who were not within the bounds of any state or territory. The superintendents were given general direction over agents and subagents, including the power to suspend them for misconduct. Authorized agencies were listed in the bill, a terminal date for others was set, and the rest were declared abolished. The establishment of subagencies, however, and the appointment of subagents was left in the hands of the president. The powers and responsibilities of the agents and subagents, especially in regard to issuing licenses, were extended. To care for miscellaneous needs, the president was empowered to require military officers to perform the duties of Indian agent. The limits of the agencies were to be determined by the secretary of war according to tribes or by geographical boundaries. The bill made provision, too, for hiring and paying interpreters, blacksmiths, and other mechanics.

A second concern of the committee in the Indian department bill was the payment of annuities; the bill provided that no payments be made on an individual basis, but that the whole annuity be paid to the chiefs or to other persons delegated by the tribes. If the Indians requested, the annuity could be paid in goods, and all goods for the Indians were to be purchased by an agent of the government and under sealed bids if time permitted—in an attempt to prevent the exorbitant markup on goods that the western commissioners had reported.

The bill contained additional items collected from previous legislation: the prohibition that no person employed in the Indian department could engage in trade with the Indians; authorization for the president to furnish domestic animals and implements of husbandry to the Indians in the West; and a grant of rations to Indians who visited military posts or agencies on the frontier. The bill also authorized the president to prescribe the necessary rules and regulations for carrying out the act. The committee pushed this bill as an economy measure, as well as a clarification of former uncertainties, and it submitted data to show that the bill would effect an annual saving of over $80,000. The bill became law on June 30 exactly as it had been submitted by the committee.[14]

The new legislation established a well-organized Indian department with a considerable reduction of personnel, effecting its economy in part by placing additional burdens upon the military officers on the frontier. The post commanders were often called upon to assume the duties of Indian agent, and the quartermaster officers were frequently responsible for the funds disbursed to the Indians in annuity payments. To govern the officers in these tasks the adjutant general sent them copies of the 1834

14. 4 *United States Statutes* 735–38.

TABLE 2: Field Organization of the Indian Department, 1837

ACTING SUPERINTENDENCY OF MICHIGAN	Upper Missouri Agency
Michilimackinac Agency	Upper Missouri Subagency
Saginaw Subagency	Council Bluffs Subagency
Sault Ste. Marie Subagency	Great Nemahaw Subagency
SUPERINTENDENCY OF WISCONSIN	Osage River Subagency
TERRITORY	ACTING SUPERINTENDENCY
Sac and Fox Agency	OF THE WESTERN TERRITORY
St. Peter's Agency	Choctaw Agency
Prairie du Chien Subagency	Creek Agency
Green Bay Subagency	Cherokee Agency
Lapointe Subagency	Osage Subagency
Crow Wing River Subagency	Neosho Subagency
SUPERINTENDENCY OF ST. LOUIS	MISCELLANEOUS
Fort Leavenworth Agency	Chickasaw Agency
Council Bluffs Agency	Ohio Subagency
	New York Subagency

Source: "Regulations Concerning Superintendencies, Agencies, and Subagencies, April 13, 1837," in *Office Copy of the Laws, Regulations, Etc., of the Indian Bureau, 1850* (Washington: Gideon and Company, 1850).

laws and special sets of regulations, and he directed them to follow instructions given them by the commissioner of Indian affairs, by order of the secretary of war.[15]

The second bill of the committee, which on June 30 became the intercourse law of 1834, was a good example of continuity in American Indian policy.[16] It offered no sharp break with the past but embodied, occasionally in modified form, the principles that had developed through the previous decades. One who has seen the provisions of the earlier laws feels much at home here. What changes did occur were generally the culmination of longterm agitation for correction of abuses. The committee in drawing up this bill relied heavily on the proposals made by Cass and Clark in 1829.

The act began with a definition of the Indian country. The principle of the earlier intercourse laws, in which "the boundary of the Indian country was a line of metes and bounds, variable from time to time by treaties," was rejected by the committee because the multiplication of treaties made it difficult to ascertain just what was Indian country at any given moment. Instead, the new law declared: "All that part of the United States west of the Mississippi, and not within the states of Missouri and Louisiana, or the

15. Circular to post commanders, July 12, 1834, Adjutant General's Office, Letters Sent, vol. 11, pp. 42–43, National Archives, Record Group 94.
16. 4 *United States Statutes* 729–35.

Territory of Arkansas, and also, that part of the United States east of the Mississippi river, and not within a state to which the Indian title has not been extinguished, for the purposes of this act, be taken and deemed to be the Indian country." The law accepted the removal of the Indians as an accomplished fact. The Indians in the southern states were no longer considered to be in Indian country, and in territories east of the Mississippi, as Indian titles were extinguished, the lands would cease automatically to be Indian country. West of the Mississippi the designation of Indian country could be changed only by legislative enactment.

The licensing system for trading with the Indians was continued, but it was strengthened by the grant of discretionary authority to the agents in issuing licenses and by the requirement that all trading be done at designated sites. The use of presidential authority to withhold goods from certain tribes and to revoke licenses to trade with them, which Cass and Clark had proposed as a means of bringing pressure to bear on the Indians when the public interest demanded it, became part of the new law. To protect the integrity of the Indian country, restrictions were made more explicit and fines were often increased. Other sections of previous laws were included—provisions for indemnification of thefts and damages, for bringing criminals to justice, for restricting the whiskey traffic, for use of military forces, and so on. The law in its final form differed little from the bill introduced by the committee.

In one respect the 1834 law marked a new direction in the relations of the United States with the tribes. The War Department in the past had been careful not to interfere in purely Indian squabbles. Although it deprecated the hostilities that frequently broke out between tribes, it had adopted a hands-off policy. In the law of 1834 the government committed itself to the opposite policy, as it had already done to some extent in particular treaties with the Indians. Hostilities had been stimulated by the closer contacts between tribes that resulted from the emigration of eastern Indians to the West, and these hostilities were an increasing cause of concern to frontiersmen and fur traders. Cass and Clark had argued in 1829 that "no well founded objection can be foreseen" to the president's use of military force to prevent or terminate hostilities between tribes. They based their proposal on the principle that "the relation of the government of the United States to the Indian tribes, is, in many respects, a paternal one, founded upon the strength and intelligence of the one party, and the weakness and ignorance of the other." They charged the Indians with wars "as ceaseless as they are causeless, originating they know not why, and terminating they care not when," arising often out of the desire of young men of a tribe to prove their valor. The government had a direct interest in suppressing such wars, both to protect American citizens who fell in the way of war parties and to preserve the Indians themselves. The law of 1834 gave the War Department statutory authorization, under the direction of the president, to use military force to end or prevent Indian wars.

A milestone in American Indian policy had been reached in 1834, and the United States looked to the future with an Indian policy that was considered reasonable and adequate. The two laws passed in 1834 summed up the experience of the past; they offered the well-grounded legal basis for the Indian service that had been so long in coming and embodied the principles for regulating contacts between whites and Indians that had proved necessary through the preceding decades. The continually changing boundaries of the Indian country that had kept Indian relations in a state of flux were now stabilized, it was hopefully assumed, by the removal of the Indians to the West. With a tempered enthusiasm the president and the secretary of war commended the nation for what had been accomplished and looked forward to less troubled times—although in 1834 the worst of the tribulations for the emigrating Indians were yet to come.[17]

PROPOSALS FOR AN INDIAN STATE

The third bill reported by the House Committee on Indian Affairs in 1834 was one for organizing a western territory to provide a political system for the emigrant Indians. It was one episode in continuing agitation on the part of well-meaning officials and reformers for a unified or confederated government for all the Indians in the West, an "Indian state" that might eventually become a regular part of the Union. The proposals reflected paternalistic white thinking, not Indian views, for many of the tribes rejected them.[18]

It is impossible to pinpoint an originator of the concept of the Indian state, for it had appeared in a variety of forms even before Indian removal became a national issue. An early proponent was the Reverend Jedidiah Morse, whose report in 1822 to Secretary of War Calhoun was full of innovative ideas. Morse thought in terms of a colony for the Indians in what is now Wisconsin and the Upper Peninsula of Michigan. "Let this territory be reserved exclusively for Indians," he wrote, "in which to make the pro-

17. The great influx of Indians into the West after the passage of the laws in 1834 soon indicated the need for changing some of the administrative arrangements, but change came slowly. See the recommendations made by T. Hartley Crawford to Joel R. Poinsett, December 30, 1839, *House Document* no. 103, 26–1, serial 365. The various changes are well described in Edward E. Hill, *The Office of Indian Affairs, 1824–1880: Historical Sketches* (New York: Clearwater Publishing Company, 1974).

18. A careful, heavily documented study of a century of such proposals is Annie Heloise Abel, "Proposals for an Indian State, 1778–1878," *Annual Report of the American Historical Association for the Year 1907,* 1: 87–104.

posed experiment of gathering into one body as many of the scattered and other Indians as choose to settle here, to be educated, become citizens, and in due time to be admitted to all the privileges common to other territories and States in the Union."[19] Official attention was turned in that direction by President Monroe. In his annual message of December 7, 1824, he spoke of the need to move the Indians to western lands, which would be divided into districts with "civil governments . . . established in each," and in his special removal message of January 27, 1825, he called for "a well-digested plan for their government and civilization" and for providing in the Indians' western territory "a system of internal government which shall protect their property from invasion, and, by the regular program of improvement and civilization, prevent that degeneracy which has generally marked the transition from the one to the other state." He then spoke at greater length about the government:

> The digest of such a government, with the consent of the Indians, which should be endowed with sufficient power to meet all the objects contemplated—to connect the several tribes together in a bond of amity and preserve order in each; to prevent intrusions on their property; to teach them by regular instruction the arts of civilized life and make them a civilized people—is an object of very high importance. It is the powerful consideration which we have to offer to these tribes as an inducement to relinquish the lands on which they now reside and to remove to those which are designated. It is not doubted that this arrangement will present considerations of sufficient force to surmount all their prejudices in favor of the soil of their nativity, however strong they may be.[20]

Monroe did not specify the nature of the government, but Calhoun's report, on which he based his special message, seemed to look in the direction of ultimate statehood, for it spoke of a system "by which the Government, without destroying their independence, would gradually unite the several tribes under a simple but enlightened system of government, and laws formed on the principles of our own." Congress showed interest in these proposals to constitute a regular territory for the Indians in the West, and Senator Thomas Hart Benton introduced a bill, drafted by Calhoun, that passed the Senate but failed in the House of Representatives.[21]

The matter came up again in the John Quincy Adams administration,

19. Jedidiah Morse, *A Report to the Secretary of War of the United States on Indian Affairs* (New Haven: S. Converse, 1822), appendix, p. 314.

20. James D. Richardson, comp., *A Compilation of the Messages and Papers of the Presidents, 1789–1897*, 10 vols. (Washington: GPO, 1896–1899), 2: 261, 281–82.

21. Calhoun report of January 24, 1825, ASP:IA, 2: 544. The congressional action is traced in Abel, "Proposals for an Indian State," p. 92.

and Secretary of War James Barbour prepared a bill which recommended among other things the establishment of a territorial government for the Indians, to be placed in the hands of the president, subject to the control of Congress. He suggested "a legislative body, composed of Indians, (to be selected in the early stages by the President, and eventually to be elected by themselves,) as well for the purpose of enacting such laws as would be agreeable to themselves, as for the purpose of exciting their ambition."[22] Although Adams and his cabinet concurred, no legislation was forthcoming. But the idea was by no means dead.

It was kept alive, to a large extent, through the efforts of the Baptist missionary Isaac McCoy. Many whites were concerned simply with the removal of the Indians from the East, but McCoy was interested in what would happen to them in the West. He early developed an obsession for Indian "colonization," urging the formation of an Indian colony where the tribes could be protected from the onslaughts of whites and led to a new civilized and Christianized existence. This vision of an Indian Canaan included plans for some sort of unified territorial government, supplied at first in the form of a few simple laws and regulations by the United States. McCoy had an idea of a single national Indian identity that would somehow absorb the separate tribes, and he envisaged his colony developing into a state of the Union.[23]

Thomas L. McKenney from his post in the War Department's Indian Office encouraged the missionary. He wrote to the secretary of war early in 1829: "It is my decided opinion, which I respectfully submit, that nothing can preserve our Indians, but a plan well matured and suitably sustained, in which they shall be placed under a Government, of which they shall form part, and in a colonial relation to the United States. . . . In a colony, of course, the existing divisions among the Tribes would be superseded by a general Government over the whole; and by a parcelling out of the lands among the families. . . . It does appear to me that as a first step in this business of Colonization, a general arrangement should be made in regard to the lands and the limits—a Government simple in its form, but effective, ought to be extended over those who have already emigrated."[24] The Stokes Commission of 1832, moreover, in its detailed report on conditions facing

22. ASP:IA, 2: 648.

23. George A. Schultz, *An Indian Canaan: Isaac McCoy and the Vision of an Indian State* (Norman: University of Oklahoma Press, 1972), pp. 78–100; William Miles, "'Enamoured with Colonization': Isaac McCoy's Plea of Indian Reform," *Kansas Historical Quarterly* 38 (Autumn 1972): 268–86. The crystallization of McCoy's plan came in his *Remarks on the Practicability of Indian Reform, Embracing Their Colonization* (Boston, 1827; 2d ed., New York, 1829).

24. McKenney to Peter B. Porter, January 31, 1829, OIA LS, vol. 5, pp. 289–90 (M21, reel 5).

the Indians in the West, suggested the organization of the Indian territory "for the sole purpose of enforcing the laws of the United States, as far as they are applicable to the Indian country," with a governor, secretary, marshal, prosecuting attorney, and judiciary to be set up at Fort Leavenworth. In addition, the commissioners called for an annual grand council of the Indians.

> Here distant tribes may meet to settle difficulties, make peace, renew their friendship, and propose salutary regulations for their respective tribes. Here, too, improvements in the arts could be exhibited, and the savage tribes permitted to see and taste the fruits of civilization; here, also, the Government could communicate instruction and advice to her red children. It is not improbable that the tribes may, ere long, adopt some general articles of confederation for their own republic not inconsistent with the wishes of Government.[25]

The extensive reorganization of Indian affairs that came in 1834 included a fundamental concern for an Indian state. The House committee intended its third bill to meet "the obligations of the United States to the emigrant tribes"; it was "to provide for the establishment of the Western Territory and for the security and protection of the emigrant and other Indian tribes therein." The three bills were considered "parts of a system," and the committee urged that they all be passed together.[26]

The third bill established boundaries for an Indian territory west of Arkansas and Missouri that would be reserved forever for the Indian tribes. It pledged the faith of the United States to guarantee the land to the Indians and their descendants. Each of the tribes was to organize a government for its own internal affairs, and a general council would be established as a governing body for the voluntary confederation of the tribes envisaged by the bill. The president would appoint a governor, who would have a veto over acts of the council, power to reprieve offenders sentenced to capital punishment (with pardoning power reserved to the president), and considerable authority in settling difficulties between tribes, executing the laws, and employing the military forces of the United States. The confederation would send a delegate to Congress, and the committee expressed a hope of eventual admission of the territory as a state into the Union.

The three bills of the committee, although introduced in the House on May 20, 1834, were not debated until June 24, close to the adjournment of

25. Report of commission, February 10, 1834, *House Report* no. 474, 23–1, serial 263, pp. 100–101.

26. The bill for the western territory is in *House Report* no. 474, 23–1, serial 263, pp. 34–37; discussion of the bill in the committee report is on pp. 14–22.

Congress on June 30. The lateness of the session may well have enabled
the first two bills to be pushed through without much change, but strong
opposition arose to the bill on the western territory, the most radical of the
three, which had no real precedents. After considerable and violent debate,
it foundered in the House and was postponed to the next session and to
ultimate failure.[27]

The bill was severely criticized. John Quincy Adams immediately as-
sailed it on the basis of unconstitutionality. "What consitutional right had
the United States to form a constitution and form of government for the
Indians?" he demanded. "To erect a Territory to be inhabited exclusively
by the Indians?" Samuel F. Vinton of Ohio spoke with much severity
against almost every part of the bill, charging that it would establish an
absolute military despotism in the West that would be in the hands of the
president ruling through the appointed governor. Critics like Adams and
Vinton were not to be hurried into accepting the bill and demanded that it
be postponed until it could be given full consideration. Adams admitted
that he had read neither the committee's report nor the bills before that
very day and had not suspected that any such bill as this was included
among them. The admission of an exclusively Indian state to the Union
was a seminal idea, he said, and might set a dangerous precedent. Was the
House prepared upon a half-hour's notice, he asked, "totally to change the
relations of the Indian tribes to this country?" He objected, too, to the power
given to the president by the bill—power that rightly belonged to Congress. William S. Archer of Virginia argued that the bill did not provide an
Indian government but would "establish and enforce the Government of
the United States within the sacred territory set apart as the exclusive
abode" of the Indians. Millard Fillmore of New York doubted the propriety
of the bill as a piece of legislation. To him it seemed more nearly an act of
treaty making. Horace Everett of Vermont calmly and ably defended the
report of the committee and the western territory bill, answering point by
point the arguments of the critics, denying in large part that the criticisms
had any validity when applied to the circumstances of the Indians and
their present state of civilization. Everett was seconded by other members
of the committee, but the demand to postpone consideration of the bill
was too strong to withstand.[28] The bill was taken up again at the beginning
of the second session of the Twenty-third Congress in December 1834, but
once again Congress adjourned before action was taken.[29]

There were repeated attempts to resurrect the idea of a western Indian
state. Isaac McCoy had not given up his dream, and he enlisted Senator

27. *House Journal*, 23–1, serial 253, pp. 645, 833, 834.
28. *Register of Debates in Congress*, 23d Congress, 1st session, pp. 4763–79 (June 25,
1834).
29. *House Journal*, 23–2, serial 270, pp. 65, 425, 430–33.

John Tipton of Ohio in his cause. The Senate considered a bill introduced by Tipton in 1836 that proposed "to unite the tribes as one people, and to allow them to meet annually by delegates to enact laws for the government of the whole, without infringing the rights of the tribes severally to manage their own internal affairs"—all subject to the approval of the president. The confederation would send a delegate to Congress. The argument of Tipton's Committee on Indian Affairs was couched in terms of the necessity of a system of government if the Indians were to improve their condition from a state of savagery to one of civilization.[30] In 1837 and again in 1839 the Senate passed bills to promote territorial organization of the Indians. But the House refused to approve the legislation, despite a strong push for the measure on the part of Everett and Caleb Cushing of Massachusetts.[31]

The executive branch of the government had endorsed the measure. President Jackson himself thought in terms of a confederacy of the southern Indians in the West, developing their own territorial government, which should be on a par with the territories of the whites and eventually take its place in the Union. He backed the suggestions of the commissioner of Indian affairs and the secretary of war for developing a confederated Indian government.[32]

In the end all the suggestions and recommendations and partial successes in Congress came to nothing. The arguments made against the bill in 1834 remained strong, and the House was unwilling to approve such an innovative measure as an Indian state in the Union. But even if the paternal plans for a regulated confederated government in the western territory

30. *Senate Report* no. 246, 24–1, serial 281. The whole report is an excellent statement of the McCoy proposal for removal and organization of the Indians west of Arkansas and Missouri.

31. Abel, "Proposals for an Indian State," pp. 97–98; Schultz, *Indian Canaan*, pp. 177–81, 188–95. To promote his vision of the territorial organization and development of Indians in the West, McCoy published four issues of *The Annual Register of Indian Affairs within the Indian (or Western) Territory*, 1835–1838. See the 1837 issue, pp. 52–56, for one set of arguments for territorial government. McCoy declared: "Most of the tribes within the Territory have expressed a desire to become united in one civil compact, and to be governed by laws similar to those of the United States." In 1844 the American Indian Mission Association, of which McCoy was secretary, submitted memorials to Congress again urging the establishment of a territory for Indians. *Senate Document* no. 272, 28–1, serial 434; *Senate Document* no. 76, 28–2, serial 451.

32. See Jackson to John Coffee, February 19, 1832, *Correspondence of Andrew Jackson*, ed. John Spencer Bassett, 6 vols. (Washington: Carnegie Institution of Washington, 1926–1935), 4: 406; message of Jackson, December 5, 1836, Israel, *State of the Union Messages*, 1: 465–66. Lengthy discussion of the matter of an Indian state is in CIA report, 1836, serial 297, pp. 385–95; see also CIA Report, 1837, serial 321, p. 566, and "Report of Mr. McCoy Relative to a Government for the Western Territory," ibid., pp. 618–24.

had passed congressional barriers, it is not likely that such an organization could have been set up effectively, for strong Indian groups were also vehemently opposed. If to many whites a unified Indian state seemed wise and feasible, to the Indians it violated tribal nationalism. The Five Civilized Tribes, the most politically sophisticated of the emigrated Indians, upon whom any successful confederated government would have had to depend, refused to consider such a move. Though they met in occasional intertribal councils, they held fast to their own tribal identities and independent governments, and their removal treaties gave a legal foundation to their position. The tribes were to have (as the Choctaw treaty, for example, provided) "the jurisdiction and government of all the persons and property that may be within their limits west, so that no Territory or State shall ever have a right to pass laws for the government of the Choctaw Nation of Red People and their descendants."[33] These nations established viable governments of their own, which they steadfastly protected against federal encroachment.

When a Cherokee delegation in 1838 expressed fears that a form of government might be imposed upon the Cherokees in the West that they were not prepared for and did not want, Secretary of War Poinsett assured them that "no form of government will be imposed upon the Cherokees without the consent of the whole nation, given in council, nor shall their country be erected into a territory without such previous concurrence." As the Choctaw delegate Peter Pitchlynn insisted in 1849, when the territorial idea surfaced again, the scheme was "fruitful of evil, and only evil, to all the Indian tribes." It was, he said, "beautiful in theory, but in practice, would be destructive to all the long cherished hopes of the friends of the red men, as it would introduce discord, dissensions, and strife among them," and he pointed to differences in land tenure, levels of civilization, language, and laws and customs.[34]

The very treaties on which the Indians depended for their independence, of course, provided opening wedges for the interposition of United States government action or influence. Laws passed by the Choctaw national council, for example, were to be "not inconsistent with the Constitution, Treaties, and Laws of the United States," and the prohibition on outside legislation excepted such laws "as may, and which have been en-

33. Kappler, p. 311; see also similar provision in Creek treaty of 1832, ibid., p. 343, and Cherokee treaty of 1835, ibid., p. 442.

34. Poinsett to John Ross and others, May 18, 1838, *House Document* no. 376, 25–2, serial 330, p. 3; "Remonstrance of Col. Peter Pitchlynn, Choctaw Delegate, against the passage of the bill to unite under one government the several Indian tribes west of the Mississippi river," January 20, 1849, *House Miscellaneous Document* no. 35, 30–2, serial 544. See also the memorial of Creek and Choctaw delegations, April 26, 1838, *Senate Document* no. 407, 25–2, serial 318.

acted by Congress, to the extent that Congress under the Constitution are required to exercise a legislation over Indian Affairs." The treaty, furthermore, obligated the United States "to protect the Choctaws from domestic strife and from foreign enemies."[35] But, in fact, no Indian territorial government or Indian state was set up.

ANNUITIES AND LIQUOR REGULATION

The settlement of the Indians in the Indian country west of the Mississippi and the new legislation organizing the Indian department did not eliminate all problems in Indian-white relations. The Indians, unfortunately, were not sequestered from contact with evil men. Traders under license were permitted in the Indian country, and they came to the emigrant Indians principally to provide goods in return for annuity money. Concern for the Indians in the 1840s included a critical attack upon the existing system of annuity payments and strenuous efforts to change the system.[36]

Commissioner of Indian Affairs T. Hartley Crawford, a state legislator and representative from Pennsylvania who took office in October 1838, complained in 1841: "The recipients of money are rarely more than conduit pipes to convey it into the pockets of their traders."[37] The annuities aggravated the very conditions that the Indian Office was trying to correct. So long as the Indians were assured of receiving their annual stipend, they did not exert themselves to earn a living, thus defeating the efforts of reformers to turn them into hard-working farmers. Much of the annuity money was spent for worthless goods or trivial objects, so that the bounty of the government was misappropriated. The annuity problem, furthermore, was closely tied to the problem of intemperance among the Indians, for the money was easily drained off into the pockets of whiskey vendors.[38]

The attack on the problem was made on several fronts, all aimed at directing the annuities toward the benefit of the Indians. A change was demanded, first, in the method of payment. The act of 1834 that reorganized the Indian department provided for payment to the chiefs, and the funds often did not reach the commonalty but were siphoned off by the chiefs and their friends for purposes that did not necessarily benefit the tribe as a whole. To correct this deficiency, Congress on March 3, 1847, granted dis-

35. Kappler, p. 311.
36. This section is based on Francis Paul Prucha, "American Indian Policy in the 1840s: Visions of Reform," in John G. Clark, ed., *The Frontier Challenge: Responses to the Trans-Mississippi West* (Lawrence: University Press of Kansas, 1971), pp. 93–101.
37. CIA Report, 1841, serial 401, pp. 238–39.
38. See, for example, the report of James Clarke, Iowa Superintendency, October 2, 1846, CIA Report, 1846, serial 493, p. 243.

cretion to the president or the secretary of war to direct that the annuities, instead of being paid to the chiefs, be divided and paid to the heads of families and other individuals entitled to participate, or, with the consent of the tribe, that they be applied to other means of promoting the happiness and prosperity of the Indians. The new law, in addition, struck boldly at the liquor problem. No annuities could be paid to Indians while they were under the influence of intoxicating liquor or while there was reason for the paying officers to believe that liquor was within convenient reach. The chiefs, too, were to pledge themselves to use all their influence to prevent the introduction and sale of liquor in their country. Finally, to protect the Indians from signing away their annuities ahead of time, the law provided that contracts made by Indians for the payment of money or goods would be null and void.[39]

The War Department immediately took advantage of the discretionary authority and sent instructions to superintendents and agents to pay the annuities in all cases to the heads of families and other individuals entitled to them.[40] Although there were complaints from parties adversely affected by the new policy, the Indian Office was well pleased. William Medill, Crawford's successor, declared in 1848, "in the whole course of our Indian policy, there has never been a measure productive of better moral effects."[41] Medill also aimed to cut down the Indian profligacy with annuity payments by dividing the annuities and paying them semi-annually and by encouraging the Indians to use them for worthwhile purposes that would lead to their civilization. The goal was always the same: "The less an Indian's expectations and resources from the chase, and from the government in the shape of money annuities," Medill said, "the more readily can he be induced to give up his idle, dissolute, and savage habits, and to resort to labor for a maintenance; and thus commence the transition from a state of barbarism and moral depression, to one of civilization and moral elevation."[42]

The influence of the traders upon the Indians and their catering to the

39. 9 *United States Statutes* 203–4.

40. William Medill to Thomas H. Harvey, August 30, 1847, CIA Report, 1847, serial 503, p. 756.

41. CIA Report, 1848, serial 537, p. 400. For the reaction of Thomas H. Harvey to the new legislation, see his report of October 29, 1847, CIA Report, 1847, serial 503, pp. 832–41. Commissioner Luke Lea in 1850, although he conceded "the general wisdom and justice of the policy," argued that it tended to reduce the position of the chiefs, through whom the government dealt with the tribes. CIA Report, 1850, serial 587, pp. 44–45.

42. CIA Report, 1847, serial 503, p. 746; CIA Report, 1848, serial 537, pp. 393–94, 400. See, however, the remarks of D. D. Mitchell, superintendent of Indian affairs at St. Louis, October 13, 1849, in which he criticized the semi-annual payment for small tribes. CIA Report, 1849, serial 570, p. 1068.

Indians' tastes for liquor and useless goods led to a proposal for a new "factory system." Commissioner Crawford broached the subject in his report of 1840. Emphatically asserting that he did not propose a return to the old factory system, which had been "rightly abolished," Crawford nevertheless called its principle valuable. Because of the increased annual disbursements to the Indian tribes, the improved facilities for transportation, the greater need of the Indians for protection as they became surrounded by white population, and the growing dependency of the Indians upon payments, he urged an alternative to the existing system that would be more beneficial to the Indians. He outlined his plan in some detail:

> I would make a small establishment of goods, suitable to Indian wants, according to their location, at each agency. I would not allow these goods to be sold to any one except Indians entitled to a participation in the cash annuities, and I would limit the purchases to their proportion of the annuity; so that the Government would, instead of paying money to be laid out in whiskey and beads, or applied to the payment of goods at two prices bought from others, meet the Indians to settle their accounts, and satisfy them that they received, in articles of comfort or necessity, the annuity due them for the year, at *cost*, including transportation. The Indians would be immensely benefited; and the expense would not be greater than that of the money-payments now almost uselessly made them.

Under such a system Crawford believed that the government Indian agents would gain the position of importance with the Indians that they ought to have. The Indians would look to the government as its best friend, for from it would come the goods they needed.[43]

In subsequent years Crawford repeated and strengthened his original recommendation. The House Committee on Indian Affairs took up the proposal in 1844 and reported a bill to authorize the furnishing of goods and provisions by the War Department, but the action died in the House. Crawford did not give up. His plan, he asserted, would increase the comfort of the Indians; the comfort in turn would be a "leading string . . . to conduct them into the walks of civilization," and general improvement of the Indians would soon be seen everywhere.[44] But when Crawford left office, his scheme died. It was too much to ask in an age of private enterprise that the government go back into the Indian trade. Control of the evils of the trade reverted to the old attempt to enforce the licensing system that had been part of the traditional setup.

43. CIA Report, 1840, serial 375, pp. 240–41.
44. CIA Report, 1842, serial 413, pp. 382–83; CIA Report, 1843, serial 431, p. 266; CIA Report, 1844, serial 449, pp. 312–13; *House Journal*, 28–1, serial 438, p. 1112.

A strong movement in that direction came in 1847, under the direction of Medill and Secretary of War W. L. Marcy. Although existing previous laws and regulations called for a careful surveillance of the traders and the elimination of those deemed unfit for dealing with the Indians, Medill found that lax enforcement had allowed licenses to be given to many persons who should never have been permitted to go into the Indian country. He insisted that licenses should be granted to "none but persons of proper character, who will deal fairly, and cooperate with the government in its measures for meliorating the condition of the Indians." He therefore drew up new and tighter regulations, which were promulgated by the War Department. The secretary of war reported in 1848 that the new regulations and the rigid supervision over the conduct of traders had put an end to many evils and abuses.[45]

All problems or obstacles in improving the Indians' condition seemed to stem from or to be aggravated by intemperance. The cupidity of white men, who were eager to sell vile concoctions to Indians at exorbitant prices, could not be struck at directly, and restrictions on the sale of liquor to Indians were impossible to enforce. A primary justification for removing the Indians to the West had been to place them in a home free from temptations. In an age of reform, when many considered excessive drinking an important factor in the problems of delinquency and dependency among the general public, temperance was to be one of the means that would open up "the fountains of hope" for Indians in the new lands.[46]

But removal alone did not prevent intemperance among the Indians. The whiskey vendors were if anything more virulent on the western frontier than in the settled regions of the East, and the means of stopping their nefarious commerce were less effective. In 1843 Crawford reported on the strenuous and unremitting exertions of the Indian department to prevent the use of ardent spirits by the Indians, describing attempts by the territories of Iowa and Wisconsin to prevent the trade. But his outlook was pessimistic that any final solution would come from legal enactments. His hope lay with the efforts of the tribes themselves, and he noted with pleasure that temperance societies had been organized in several of the tribes and that some tribes had passed laws of their own to put down the sale and use of whiskey.[47]

45. CIA Report, 1847, serial 503, pp. 750–51. The "Regulations Concerning the Granting of Licenses to Trade with the Indians," November 9, 1847, and the forms of licenses and bonds to be used are printed ibid., pp. 760–64. See also report of W. L. Marcy, December 1, 1848, *House Executive Document* no. 1, 30–2, serial 537, pp. 83–84.

46. CIA Report, 1840, serial 375, pp. 233–34. The temperance crusade is discussed in Alice Felt Tyler, *Freedom's Ferment: Phases of American Social History to 1860* (Minneapolis: University of Minnesota Press, 1944), pp. 308–50.

47. CIA Report, 1843, serial 431, pp. 270–71.

Crawford professed to see some signs of success. He and others worked diligently to promote temperance through education, but they did not neglect the frontal attack on the liquor trade that had long been a staple of American Indian policy. The law of 1832 creating the commissioner of Indian affairs had absolutely prohibited the introduction of liquor into the Indian country, and the trade and intercourse law of 1834 contained detailed provisions for prosecuting violators. But this legislation had not been completely successful, and the secretaries of war in 1843 and 1845 called for more.[48]

Finally, on March 3, 1847, Congress acted. In addition to the fines set by the act of 1834, the new law provided up to two years' imprisonment for anyone who sold or disposed of liquor to an Indian in the Indian country, and up to one year's imprisonment for anyone who introduced liquor, excepting such supplies as might be required for the officers and troops of the army. In all cases arising under the law, Indians were to be competent witnesses. The commissioner of Indian affairs and the secretary of war were not satisfied to let the law serve by itself, however. New regulations, dated April 13, 1847, were promulgated by the War Department, which called attention to the provisions of the new law and the pertinent sections of the law of 1834, then spelled out in detail just what duties were imposed by these laws upon the military officers and the Indian agents—who were enjoined to be vigilant in executing their duties and were threatened with removal from office if they did not succeed.[49]

Federal laws and regulations to control the liquor traffic had effect only within the Indian country and not in the adjoining states. In an attempt to prevent the Indians from crossing the line to obtain liquor, Secretary of War Marcy wrote a strong letter on July 14, 1847, to the governors of Missouri, Arkansas, and Iowa, invoking their aid. The stringent laws of Congress, he pointed out, failed to reach the most prolific source of the ills, which lay within the limits of the nearby states. He described the ills resulting from the trade and noted that the insecurity of frontier whites was often due to Indian retaliation for such injuries.[50]

The efforts to prevent whiskey from reaching the Indians met with limited success. But all the laws of Congress and the strenuous efforts of the

48. Report of J. M. Porter, November 30, 1843, *Senate Document* no. 1, 28–1, serial 431, p. 59; report of W. L. Marcy, November 29, 1845, *Senate Document* no. 1, 29–1, serial 470, p. 205. A thorough discussion of the evils of the liquor traffic among the Indians is Otto F. Frederikson, *The Liquor Question among the Indian Tribes in Kansas, 1804–1881* (Lawrence, Kansas, 1932).

49. 9 *United States Statutes* 203; regulations of April 13, 1847, CIA Report, 1847, serial 503, pp. 764–66.

50. Marcy to governors of Missouri, Arkansas, and Iowa, July 14, 1847, CIA Report, 1847, serial 503, pp. 767–69.

Indian agents and military officers on the frontier to enforce them did not end drunkenness. The frontier was too extensive and the profits to whiskey dealers too large to make complete prohibition possible. More reliance was urged upon a system of rewards and punishments operating directly on the Indians themselves, but even these were largely ineffective.[51] Abuse of liquor remained an abiding plague in Indian affairs.

51. CIA Report, 1848, serial 537, p. 402; CIA Report, 1849, serial 570, p. 939; report of W. L. Marcy, December 1, 1848, *House Executive Document* no. 1, 30–2, serial 537, pp. 83–84. See also Frederikson, *Liquor Question*, pp. 55–64, regarding the act of 1847 and its effect.

PART THREE

American Expansion and the Reservation System

The removal of the Indians from east of the Mississippi and their settlement beyond Arkansas and Missouri was accomplished by mid-century. The Five Civilized Tribes maintained their national identity in the Indian Territory and at varying rates overcame the trauma of their uprooting and emigration. The smaller tribes along the Missouri border were encouraged by government officials and Christian missionaries to strive for the good life, cultivating farms, learning mechanical arts, and educating their children in white schools. The Indians and the whites were generally at peace.

Just when the education and civilization of the border tribes seemed to be bearing such good fruit, however, dramatic events in the 1840s overturned the premises upon which American Indian policy had been based. The formal removal program had followed the earlier policy, more or less unplanned, of simply moving the Indians west out of the way of advancing white settlement. The definite line separating the Indian country from white lands, which had been defined in the intercourse law of 1796, had been gradually pushed westward, as the Indian tribes ceded land in exchange for annuities and for newly designated and newly guaranteed lands to the west. Some thought that the removals of the 1830s had culminated this process, and that in the "Western Territory" beyond Arkansas, Missouri, and Iowa the removed Indians would be finally secure behind a permanent line running from the Red River north and northeast to Lake Superior. Then, suddenly, before the end of the 1840s the concept of such a line was shattered, and it was not long before the barrier itself was physically destroyed. The expansion of the United States that in three short years added Texas (1845), the Oregon country (1846), and California and the rest of the Mexican Cession (1848), radically changed the relationship between the United States and the Indians.

The government now came face to face with new groups of Indians. There were the nomadic buffalo Indians of the northern and southern plains— Sioux, Cheyennes, Arapahos, Crows, Kiowas, Comanches, and Pawnees— warlike and untamed and uninterested in transforming themselves into English-speaking farmers. There were Indians like the Utes, Shoshonis, and Paiutes, subsisting at minimal levels in the mountains and in the wastelands of the Great Basin. There were the oasis Indians of the Southwest with their age-old patterns of life in the pueblos, warlike Apaches and Navajos raiding their peaceful Indian neighbors and the Mexican settlements, and numerous bands of California Indians, some affected by the Spanish mission experience but others living still undisturbed in the mountains. To the north were the Indians of the Pacific Northwest, fishing along the coast and hunting in the intermountain basins. These tribes were not totally unknown, of course, for early explorers had encountered and observed them; traders had met them on the Pacific coast, in the Rocky Mountains, and along the Santa Fe Trail; and some military reconnaissance expeditions had come upon Indian warriors.[1]

In Texas the white population that had created the Republic of Texas in 1836 had already challenged Indian occupation of the region. With the acquisition of the Oregon country and the Mexican Cession, American population in those areas swelled greatly, and the aboriginal inhabitants were increasingly pressed upon by aggressive pioneers who had scant concern for Indian rights of person or property. And to get to the riches of the Pacific coastal regions, emigrants cut across the hunting grounds of the plains Indians. The Indian country was invaded, crossed and crisscrossed, and it was no longer possible to solve the question of the Indians' destiny by the convenient scheme of repeated removal. The commissioner of Indian affairs in 1856 looked into the future with considerable perception. He saw railroads moving into the great plains as far as good lands extended and at the same time other railroads moving east from the Pacific coast settlements, followed in both cases by an active white population that would open farms and build cities.

When that time arrives, and it is at our very doors, ten years, if our country is favored with peace and prosperity, will witness the most of

---

1. These military encounters are described in Francis Paul Prucha, *The Sword of the Republic: The United States Army on the Frontier, 1783–1846* (New York: Macmillan Company, 1969); see especially chaps. 12 and 18.

it; where will be the habitation and what the condition of the rapidly wasting Indian tribes of the plains, the prairies, and of our new States and Territories?

As sure as these great physical changes are impending, so sure will these poor denizens of the forest be blotted out of existence, and their dust be trampled under the foot of rapidly advancing civilization, unless our great nation shall generously determine that the necessary provision shall at once be made, and appropriate steps be taken to designate suitable tracts or reservations of land, in proper localities, for permanent homes for, and provide the means to colonize, them thereon.[2]

So reservations—in most cases small parcels of land "reserved" out of the original holdings of the tribes or bands—developed as an alternative to the extinction of the Indians.[3] The reservations, however, were thought of as a temporary expedient, for whites dealing officially with the Indians in the 1850s all accepted the idea that the nation within its new continental limits would become the abode of enterprising and prosperous American citizens. They had no notion of a pluralistic society or a divided land occupied in part by European immigrants and their descendants and in part by American Indians adhering to their own customs. The goal was to ease the immediate conflicts between the two cultures and to prevent, as far as it was in their power to do so, the utter destruction of the weaker party. It was for this end that segregation on reservations and application of the intercourse laws were considered so essential for Texas, Utah, New Mexico, California, and the Pacific Northwest and that revision of the intercourse laws was incessantly called for to make them more applicable to the new conditions. But beyond protection and preservation there was the ultimate goal of transformation: to induce the Indians all to become cultivators of the soil, to adopt the white man's language, customs, and religion, and, finally, to be self-supporting citizens of the commonwealth, a goal that all but a few believed was entirely practicable if only the proper means were applied. Agriculture, domestic and mechanical arts, English education, Christianity, and individual property (land allotted in severalty) were the elements of the civilization program that was to be the future of the Indians.

The policy makers were firm in their views of what constituted humanitarian concern and benevolence for their Indian charges. Having judged the civilization programs among the Five Civilized Tribes and the border Indians as marked with signs of ultimate success, they saw no reason why the same

---

2. CIA Report, 1856, serial 875, p. 574.

3. Robert A. Trennert, Jr., *Alternative to Extinction: Federal Indian Policy and the Beginnings of the Reservation System, 1846–51* (Philadelphia: Temple University Press, 1975), covers only a half-dozen years and the region east of the Rockies, but the main title of the book can be applied much more broadly.

causes would not produce the same effects among the new tribes that had fallen under United States jurisdiction.

The United States government had only one pattern for dealing with Indians. It held that Indians retained title to the lands they occupied (although there was considerable question whether this principle applied to the Indians and land that came to the United States from Mexico) and that these titles could be extinguished only by treaties, which would specify the lands ceded and the payment to be made for them. Yet the treaties with most of the tribes with whom the government now came into contact, following a precedent already well established in the East, were not the result of negotiations between two sovereign and independent powers. They were instead a convenient and accepted vehicle for accomplishing what United States officials wanted to do under circumstances that were frequently difficult. By treaty the government could provide Indian segregation on small reservations, throwing open the rest of the territory to white settlement and exploitation. On the reservations the restrictions and protection of the intercourse laws could be applied to restrain if not prevent deleterious contacts between the two races and to protect the remaining rights of the Indians. By treaty, too, the United States sought to provide the means for transforming the life of the Indians, for the negotiations were used to gain the acquiescence, at least nominal, of the Indians to an agricultural existence and "moral improvement and education."

The system was applied with indifferent success. In many cases the treaty procedure came too late, after the destruction of the Indians was already far advanced, and the federal government was inexcusably slow in looking after Indian affairs in the remote regions of the Far West. The single pattern was applied with little appreciation of the varying Indian cultures it was supposed to replace, and on occasion the treaties signed in the field were not ratified by the Senate, leaving the status of the Indians and their lands in a sort of limbo. Often, application of the treaty provisions was possible only after resisting Indians had been overwhelmed and crushed by military force.

The men in the Indian service whose lot it was to seek solutions for the new Indian problems facing the nation after the territorial acquisitions of the 1840s took faltering steps, and Congress was no more sure-footed. But out of it all developed a reservation system that became a staple of United States Indian policy for the future.

CHAPTER 12

The Indian Office: Men and Policies

Department of the Interior. Commissioners

of the 1850s. An Expanded Indian Department.

Perennial Problems: Annuities and Liquor.

The Challenge of Scientific Racism.

The changed relations with the Indians that came with American expansion to the Pacific were accompanied by changes in the administration of Indian policy, for new conditions called for corresponding responses. Yet there were constants. Problems that had plagued the conduct of Indian affairs in the East, then in mid-America, reappeared in relations with the far western tribes. And the paternalistic concern for the transformation of the Indians continued, now applied to the newly contacted Indian groups.

DEPARTMENT OF THE INTERIOR

In 1849 Indian affairs were transferred from the War Department, which had been responsible for them since the beginning of the nation, to a newly created executive department called the Department of the Interior. Congress, in organizing the government after the Constitution had been adopted, had put Indian relations into the charge of the War Department with hardly a second thought, for the Revolutionary War had placed the Indians for the most part on the side of the British, and contact with them had been as adversaries. Henry Knox, who had been in charge of the War Department under the Articles of Confederation, continued in that position in Washington's cabinet, so there was a welcome continuity in dealing with the Indians. The seemingly interminable border conflicts between encroaching frontiersmen and resisting Indians, and the serious outbreaks of war in the Old Northwest in the 1790s and both north and south during the War of 1812 made it reasonable to keep Indian affairs under the secretary of war—even though the administration of them (through superintendents, agents, and factors) was a civilian operation. The officials of the Indian department were civilian employees of the War Department, not military men, except in rare temporary cases.

As circumstances changed and the Indians were no longer looked upon primarily as military foes, the logical reasons for having the secretary of war direct Indian affairs disappeared. What held the management of the Indians within the War Department was bureaucratic inertia and strong congressional disinclination to increase the size of the executive branch of the government by creating a new department and a new cabinet officer.

Agitation for an "interior" department began long before mid-century. Even when the national government was established there were proposals for a secretary of domestic affairs to balance a secretary of foreign affairs, but the decision at the time was for a Department of State, responsible for both domestic and foreign matters. The secretary of state, for example, was charged with management of the territories. Land business, because sale of the public domain was an essential element in the financial well-being of the nation, was appropriately placed under the secretary of the treasury. The rapid growth of the nation, however, soon put considerable stress on the national administrative organization, and by 1815 serious weaknesses appeared. Repeated moves were made to relieve the burdens of the existing departments by shifting offices that did not strictly pertain to them into some sort of "home department." All of the plans called for including Indian affairs within the new department.[1]

In light of the strong arguments for a new department, coming from successive presidents and from Congress itself, it is difficult to explain the delay and postponement over a period of more than a quarter-century. Some argued that the nation had gotten along without an interior department and opposed tampering with the structure. More important, perhaps, was the republican fear of gradual and imperceptible aggrandizement of federal power over domestic matters. It continued to be obvious, nevertheless, that it was incongruous to have the Patent Office in the State Department, the management of public lands under the Treasury, and—in an era when serious Indian wars were considered a thing of the past—Indian affairs in the War Department.

The eventual success in gaining a new department came largely as a result of America's expansion in the 1840s, the acquisition of the Oregon

1. For the history of agitation for an interior or home department, see Henry Barrett Learned, "The Establishment of the Secretaryship of the Interior," *American Historical Review* 16 (July 1911): 751–73.

Removal and Concentration

18. Andrew Jackson as the Great Father

The removal policy that forced the emigration of eastern Indians to regions west of the Mississippi is closely associated with President Andrew Jackson, for he vigorously pursued the policy. Jackson, who was severely criticized by opponents of removal, thought he was acting in a paternal fashion for the Indians' best interests. This contemporary cartoon shows the president and his "children."

19. John Ross

As principal chief of the Cherokee Nation, John Ross firmly opposed all removal measures of the federal government. Although only one-eighth Cherokee by blood, Ross won the support of a majority of the nation because of his staunch defense of Cherokee rights. This portrait of 1848 is by John Neagle.

20. Major Ridge

A group of Cherokees led by Major Ridge, his son John Ridge, and his nephew Elias Boudinot decided to accept removal as the only means to preserve the Cherokee Nation. In December 1835 the Ridge party signed the Treaty of New Echota, which provided for the removal of the whole nation.

The removal of the Indians caused a great public debate, and religious leaders were found on both sides. Jeremiah Evarts, secretary of the American Board of Commissioners for Foreign Missions, led the attack on the removal policy, charging that to carry it out against the rights and wishes of the Indians would be a great national sin. Isaac McCoy, a Baptist missionary, on the other hand, spent much of his life promoting the movement and colonization of the eastern Indians in the West.

21. Jeremiah Evarts

22. Isaac McCoy

23. Black Hawk, Sac Chief

The removal of Indians from the region north of the Ohio River proceeded without serious resistance. The one exception was the Black Hawk War of 1832. Black Hawk refused to give up his ancestral lands in Illinois east of the Mississippi, and when troops were sent to evict him, the war began. This painting by George Catlin catches the nobility and defiant spirit of the chief.

24. Osceola, Seminole

The Second Seminole War, 1835–1842, was a long-drawn conflict with few heroes. Osceola, presented in this portrait by George Catlin, was a leader in the Seminole resistance to removal. He was captured when he came in to parley in 1837 and died the next year while imprisoned at Fort Marion.

The "permanent Indian frontier" west of Missouri and Iowa was broken by emigrants moving across the plains to the Pacific coast. One of the strongest advocates of legally opening the plains to white settlement was Senator Stephen A. Douglas of Illinois, who wanted to tie the nation together by transcontinental railroads.

The invasion of California by Americans after the discovery of gold in 1848 was a disaster for the California Indians, who were no match for the aggressive whites. One man who tried to protect the Indians was Edward Fitzgerald Beale, who as special agent (1852–1854) sought to establish reservations for them in a form reminiscent of the old Spanish missions.

25. Stephen A. Douglas

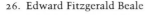

26. Edward Fitzgerald Beale

Treaties with Indians in the Pacific
Northwest in order to concentrate them
on reduced reservations were the work
largely of Isaac I. Stevens, governor of
Washington Territory. The treaty council of Stevens with the Flathead Indians
in July 1855 was sketched by Gusta-
vus Sohon.

27. Isaac I. Stevens

28. Flathead Treaty Council

Country and the Mexican Cession, which at a stroke greatly increased the "interior" concerns of the United States. The final move came from Robert J. Walker, Polk's secretary of the treasury, who for four years had experienced firsthand the overburdening of the existing departments. Walker proposed a new officer "to be called the Secretary of the Interior, inasmuch as his duties would be connected with those branches of the public service . . . associated with our domestic affairs." In the new establishment would repose the General Land Office taken from the Treasury Department, the Patent Office taken from the State Department, and the Pension Office and the Indian Office taken from the War Department. Walker argued most strongly in regard to the General Land Office, which with the increased public domain in California, Oregon, and New Mexico greatly increased the duties of the secretary of the treasury, and in regard to Indian matters. Of the latter he wrote:

> The duties now performed by the Commissioner of Indian Affairs are most numerous and important and must be vastly increased with the great number of tribes scattered over Texas, Oregon, New Mexico, and California, and with the interesting progress of so many of the tribes in Christianity, knowledge, and civilization. These duties do not necessarily appertain to war, but to peace, and to our domestic relations with those tribes. . . .
>
> This most important bureau, then, should be detached from the War Department, with which it has no necessary connexion.[2]

Walker prepared a bill, introduced on February 12, 1849, by Representative Samuel F. Vinton for the House Committee on Ways and Means. After small debate the measure passed the House by a considerable margin; the only substantial change was the substitution of Home Department for Department of the Interior in the title of the bill. The debate in the Senate was more pointed, for James M. Mason of Virginia and John C. Calhoun of South Carolina expressed the fear that the bill would tend to increase the powers of the federal government not specifically delegated to it by the Constitution. Other senators pointed out that the bill was adding no new duties but was merely giving better organization to those that already existed, and the bill passed the Senate by a vote of thirty-one to twenty-five. President Polk signed it on March 3, 1849, just as the Thirtieth Congress was ending and his Democratic administration was giving way to President Zachary Taylor and the Whigs.[3]

2. Report of R. J. Walker, December 9, 1848, *House Executive Document* no. 7, 30–2, serial 538, pp. 36–37.
3. *Congressional Globe*, 30th Congress, 2d session, pp. 514–18, 543–44, 669–80. Most of the debate concerned the duties of the secretary of the treasury and the need to divide them. The law is in 9 *United States Statutes* 395–97.

The law came to be because of the administrative burdens upon existing departments, especially the Treasury Department, and the new department was put together out of four parts that were sloughed off by others and did not fit together logically except that they all dealt with domestic matters. It was thus by chance, not by some sinister design, that the General Land Office, concerned with the disposal of the public domain in the interest of white settlers, and the Indian Office, responsible for protecting Indian rights to their land, came to be conflicting responsibilities of the same executive officer. The relation of the two responsibilities, however, was not lost on the sponsors of the bill, for Vinton saw a "peculiar fitness" in the arrangement, since "the business of the one was intimately interwoven with that of the other." Senator Jefferson Davis of Mississippi, who argued strongly for the bill, spoke of the incongruity of keeping the Indian bureau in the War Department. "When our intercourse with the Indian tribes was held under the protection of troops," he said, "and wars and rumors of wars came annually with the coming of grass, it was proper to place Indian relations under the War Department. Happily for them, honorably for us, the case has greatly changed, and is, I hope, before a distant day, to assume a character consonant with the relations of guardian and ward, which have been claimed by us as those existing between our Government and the Indian tribes. . . . War being the exception, peace the ordinary condition, the policy should be for the latter, not the former condition."[4]

There was no objection from the War Department about giving up its control of Indian affairs; no doubt the secretary was happy to be rid of the onerous duty. For the Indian Office, the new law of itself did not create any great problems. The work had been a civilian operation reporting to the secretary of war; it continued as it was, but reported now to the secretary of the interior. The lack of concern evidenced is remarkable in light of the excessive agitation that arose in the 1860s and 1870s about transfer of the Indian Office back to the War Department. The end of the 1840s was one of those times of rare tranquility on the frontier, when it was easy to believe that Indian wars were a thing of the past and that Indians were no longer a military matter. There seems to have been no sense of vested interests that sometimes hinder administrative changes.

When Indian disturbances broke out again in the 1850s, responsible people began to question whether military control of the whole Indian service might not be wise. In 1860, both Secretary of War John B. Floyd and Secretary of the Interior Jacob Thompson responded affirmatively to a Senate resolution asking about the expediency of moving Indian affairs back to

4. *Congressional Globe*, 30th Congress, 2d session, pp. 514, 678.

the War Department. As Thompson observed, the War Department had superior facilities for controlling and managing "the wild, roving, and turbulent tribes of the interior, who constitute the great majority of the Indians." The secretary, no doubt, would have welcomed handing on Indian problems to someone else, but a transfer bill introduced in May 1860 quickly died.[5]

COMMISSIONERS OF THE 1850S

If one counts Orlando Brown, the appointee of the Whig administration and the first commissioner of Indian affairs under the Department of the Interior, there were six commissioners in the dozen years during which the reservation system was developed in response to the problems created by American expansion. There was a rapid turnover of the high officers charged with managing Indian affairs as politicians of various stripes—generally without any special experience with Indians—stepped into the office amid the challenges from the expanded West. Yet a strong and consistent reservation policy developed to which the commissioners, whatever their background, adhered.

Brown's tenure was short. A leading Whig in Kentucky, a protégé of John Crittenden, and a man of literary and political talents, Brown had a disappointing career as commissioner. He had hoped for a cabinet post when Taylor became president and accepted the next highest opening, the Indian Office, only to find that Secretary of the Interior Thomas Ewing dominated the scene, both in handling Indian affairs and in handing out the patronage that the new department made available for hungry Whig office seekers. His humanitarian views about the progress of the emigrated Indians and his vision of a great social and moral revolution among them led him to believe that a like application of methods to the Indians in the newly acquired territories would produce like results. He accepted the framework for such a program from his predecessors—to concentrate the Indians in smaller areas in order to move them out of the way of the whites and to foster among them agriculture and the arts of civilized life. But Brown's unhappiness in his job led him to resign effective July 1, 1850.[6]

President Taylor appointed as Brown's successor a Mississippi lawyer and politician, Luke Lea, a man with no Indian experience who sought a federal job after failing in his bid for the governorship of Mississippi. Tay-

5. Floyd to Jefferson Davis, March 26, 1860, and Thompson to Davis, March 13, 1860, *Senate Report* no. 223, 36–1, serial 1040; *Senate Journal*, 36–1, serial 1022, p. 441.

6. CIA Report, 1849, serial 550, pp. 937–58; Robert A. Trennert, "Orlando Brown, 1849–50," in Robert M. Kvasnicka and Herman J. Viola, eds. *The Commissioners of Indian Affairs, 1824–1977* (Lincoln: University of Nebraska Press, 1979), pp. 41–47.

lor's sudden death on July 9, 1850, led to a shakeup in the cabinet. Ewing resigned as secretary of the interior, and his replacement, the Virginia Whig Alexander H. H. Stuart, left Indian matters largely in the hands of the Indian Office. Lea, like others before him, relied on the proposals of his predecessors in formulating his Indian policies. In the circumstances of the times, to be sure, he was sensitive to the demands of whites in the new territories, and he assumed without question the superiority of his own culture. "When civilization and barbarism are brought in such relation that they cannot coexist together," he wrote, "it is right that the superiority of the former should be asserted and the latter compelled to give way. It is, therefore, no matter of regret or reproach that so large a portion of our territory has been wrested from the aboriginal inhabitants and made the happy abodes of an enlightened and Christian people." Much of the conflict that had arisen, he declared, had been due to "the Indian's own perverse and vicious nature."[7]

Yet Lea adopted the unequivocal stand that the civilization of the Indians was a necessary and practicable goal of the federal government. Although he admitted the difficulties of the task and his own insufficiency in carrying it out, he declared that civilizing the Indians was "a cherished object of the government." He noted the critics who ridiculed any chance of success, but he was not to be turned aside. "It should be remembered . . . ," he said, "that to change a savage people from their barbarous habits to those of civilized life, is, in its nature, a work of time, and the results already attained, as evinced in the improved condition of several of our tribes, are sufficient to silence the most skeptical, and warrant the assurance that perseverance in the cause will achieve success." Any plan, he thought, would have to provide for the Indians' "ultimate incorporation into the great body of our citizen population."[8]

The immediate means to Lea's humanitarian end would be a national system of reservations, and in his first annual report he had worked out a clear statement of that policy in regard to "our wilder tribes."

> It is indispensably necessary that they be placed in positions where they can be controlled and finally compelled by sheer necessity to resort to agricultural labor or starve. Considering, as the untutored Indian does, that labor is a degradation, and that there is nothing worthy of his ambitions but prowess in war, success in the chase, and eloquence in council, it is only under such circumstances that his haughty pride can be subdued, and his wild energies trained to the more ennobling pursuits of civilized life. There should be assigned to

7. CIA Report, 1852, serial 658, p. 293; Robert A. Trennert, "Luke Lea, 1850–53," in Kvasnicka and Viola, *Commissioners of Indian Affairs*, pp. 49–55.
8. CIA Report, 1851, serial 613, pp. 273–74.

each tribe, for a permanent home, a country adapted to agriculture, of limited extent and well-defined boundaries; within which all, with occasional exception, should be compelled constantly to remain until such time as their general improvement and good conduct may supersede the necessity of such restrictions. In the mean time, the government should cause them to be supplied with stock, agricultural implements, and useful materials for clothing; encourage and assist them in the erection of comfortable dwellings, and secure to them the means and facilities of education, intellectual, moral, and religious.[9]

The beginning of Lea's term coincided with the appointment of Charles E. Mix as chief clerk in the Indian Office, a position second only to the commissioner and one of considerable influence, given its continuity in the midst of rapidly changing commissioners and the frequent absence of the incumbents from Washington. Mix was experienced, having entered the Indian Office as a clerk after the failure of his mercantile business in the Panic of 1837, and he had a reputation for integrity and efficiency. For eighteen years after his appointment in 1850 he was a force to be reckoned with, and he left the stamp of his views on Indian policy of the period. It is often difficult to determine how much of the work of the commissioners, including the writing of annual reports, was in fact the work of Mix.[10]

There can be no doubt, however, that much of the consistency of policy during the 1850s was due to this man. Mix in fact held the office of commissioner for a five-month period in 1858, and his report for that year marked him as strongly in favor of the reservation policy. His remarks formed a sort of paradigm of what was proposed during the decade. He noted "three serious, and, to the Indians, fatal errors" that had characterized past policy toward the Indians: "their removal from place to place as our population advanced; the assignment to them of too great an extent of country, to be held in common; and the allowance of large sums of money, as annuities, for the lands ceded by them." It was, he asserted, these mistakes in policy rather than any lack of capacity on the part of the Indians that had been responsible for the failure to "domesticate and civilize" them. By frequent changes in location and the holding of large bodies of land in common, the Indians were kept unsettled and failed to acquire experience in private property, and their large annuities fostered habits of indolence and profligacy and made them victims of unscrupulous traders

9. CIA Report, 1850, serial 587, pp. 35–36; see also CIA Report, 1852, serial 658, p. 300.

10. Harry Kelsey, "Charles E. Mix, 1858," in Kvasnicka and Viola, *Commissioners of Indian Affairs*, pp. 77–79. I have also profited from "Mr. Lincoln's Indian Bureau," an unpublished manuscript by Harry Kelsey, a copy of which was kindly supplied me by the author.

and speculators. The policy Mix advocated and helped to establish reversed, to some degree, all three of these "errors."[11]

Luke Lea served through President Millard Fillmore's term; he was replaced on March 24, 1853, by George W. Manypenny, an Ohio businessman and newspaper publisher who thus began a longterm interest in the welfare of the American Indians. Manypenny was a man of energy, intelligence, and honesty who won the enmity of western politicians for his courageous resistance to fraudulent claims against Indian annuities. He followed the tradition of his predecessors, and he no doubt felt the influence of Charles Mix.[12]

For the border tribes, who were blocking white expansion into Kansas and Nebraska, Manypenny wanted the Indians assigned to reduced reservations with provision for allotment of land in severalty. His commitment to a reservation system as a means of promoting the civilization of the Indians in the Far West was strong. Of the Indians in New Mexico and Utah, he wrote at the end of 1854: "Conventional arrangements are necessary . . . for the purpose of fixing them in proper locations, and giving to the department such influence and control over them as will enable it, as far as possible, to confine them thereon, and to induce them to resort to agriculture and kindred pursuits, instead of relying, as they now do, for support upon the uncertain and precarious supplies of the chase; and when that fails, upon the more hazardous and injurious practice of theft and plunder." Manypenny knew that no military force that might be sent to the territories could prevent depredations, unless by exterminating the Indians. The alternative was for the Indians to be "colonized in suitable locations, and, to some extent at least, be subsisted by the government, until they can be trained to such habits of industry and thrift as will enable them to sustain themselves."[13]

It was clear to Manypenny (as it was to Mix) that it was no longer possible to solve the question of the Indians' destiny by the convenient expedient of repeated removal. He hoped at first in dealing with the emigrated tribes along the border in Kansas and Nebraska to move them into the "colonies" established north and south, but he noted the Indians' resistance and ultimately promoted instead the assignment of permanent reservations, reduced in size to be sure, where the Indians already were.[14] The reservation policy that was developing in the 1850s, therefore, included as an essential component the establishment of fixed and permanent homes for the Indians.

11. CIA Report, 1858, serial 974, p. 354.
12. Robert M. Kvasnicka, "George W. Manypenny, 1853–57," in Kvasnicka and Viola, *Commissioners of Indian Affairs*, pp. 57–67.
13. CIA Report, 1854, serial 746, p. 222.
14. CIA Report, 1856, serial 875, p. 575.

Allotment of land in severalty was a necessary corollary of the reduced permanent reservations, and it was recommended strongly by Manypenny and his successors. The doctrine of private property was, of course, an essential part of the American way that the Indians had long been expected to accept. But it took on a special urgency as the reservation system got under way, for it lay "at the very foundation of all civilization."[15]

Manypenny faced the question of Indian civilization and Christianization more realistically than some of the workers in the field, who sent in accounts of rapid advancement in civilization among the tribes they served. The commissioner noted that after years of such flattering reports the Indians who had been under government supervision for all that time should have reached a high state of civilization. Yet that was far from the case. Nevertheless, he was mildly optimistic, following the long tradition of humanitarian concern for Indian betterment. He noted that "many have made an encouraging degree of progress, in acquiring the elements of a rude civilization," and that although much remained yet to be done "to secure and accomplish the full and complete regeneration of the Indians," the object was a noble one and fully deserving the attention and energies of the government and of "a great Christian people." His commitment to Christianity was firm, and his policy was suffused with his belief. He ended his annual report of 1854 with this statement: "As a Christian government and people, our obligations and duties are of the highest and holiest character, and we are accountable to the Maker of all men for the manner in which we discharge them. Having faithfully employed all the means placed within our reach to improve the Indian race, and preserve it from extinction, we can, with a good conscience and strong faith, leave the issue in the hands of our common Father."[16]

Manypenny served the full four-year term of Franklin Pierce's administration, something of a record for the 1850s. He was followed by James W. Denver, a representative from California, who served from April to December 1857 and again from November 1858 to March 1859, with Charles Mix serving in the interval. Denver's term was too short to influence Indian policy in any significant way, and Mix's management of affairs was no doubt pronounced.[17] Next came Alfred B. Greenwood, a Georgian by birth who had made his career in the frontier state of Arkansas. He, too, relied heavily on the chief clerk and worked diligently with him for an updating of Indian legislation. He accepted the policy of concentrating the Indians and recalled the belief of his predecessors that "the Indian possessed all the elements essential to his elevation to all the powers and sympathies which

15. The quoted phrase is from James W. Denver, CIA Report, 1857, serial 919, p. 292.
16. CIA Report, 1853, serial 690, p. 264; CIA Report, 1854, serial 746, pp. 230–31.
17. Donald Chaput, "James W. Denver, 1857, 1858–59," in Kvasnicka and Viola, *Commissioners of Indian Affairs*, pp. 69–75.

appertain to his white brother, and which only need proper development to enable him to tread with equal step and dignity the walks of civilized life." He asserted the wisdom of placing the Indians on reservations and introducing them to agriculture, then gradually restricting their possessions and finally dividing their reservations in severalty; and against critics who distrusted the system he expressed his confidence in its ultimate success.[18] But in the end Greenwood became entangled in the sectional crisis. Although he served out his term, he left Washington when Lincoln took office in April 1861 and actively served the South as a recruiter of Cherokee and Choctaw Indians for the Confederacy and as a member of the Confederate Congress.[19]

AN EXPANDED INDIAN DEPARTMENT

While the commissioners were developing and promoting a reservation policy for the Indians in the West, they were also concerned about the insufficiency of the administrative machinery they had to work with. Orlando Brown in 1849 noted "the present defective and inefficient organization" of his bureau. "However well adapted to the condition of things in 1834, when it was prescribed," he declared, "it is incompatible with the present state of affairs, and altogether inadequate to enable the Department to discharge, in a proper manner, the enlarged and more complicated trusts and duties now devolving upon it." He noted the movement of the eastern tribes to regions across the Mississippi, the increased transactions with the Indians under treaty stipulations, and the vast numbers of Indians added by the acquisition of Texas, Oregon, California, and New Mexico. One serious defect was the lack of a sufficient number of superintendents to handle Indian affairs in regions remote from the seat of government, regions where discretionary authority frequently needed to be exercised, and where superintendents could give "immediate and rigid supervision" to agents and subagents. Brown did not like to see the duties of agent and superintendent combined, nor did he like the ex officio arrangement by which territorial governors performed the duties of Indian superintendents. He boldly asked for "seven full and independent superintendencies"—four east of the Rockies, including Texas, and one each for Oregon, California, and New Mexico. Brown also pointed to the inadequate arrangement of agents and subagents. Only eleven agents were authorized by law, but subagents could be appointed at the discretion of the president,

18. CIA Report, 1860, serial 1078, pp. 249–50.
19. Gary L. Roberts, "Alfred Burton Greenwood, 1859–61," in Kvasnicka and Viola, *Commissioners of Indian Affairs*, pp. 81–87.

with the result that subagents often filled positions with duties and responsibilities that called for a full agent. He thought that if the salaries of the agents were increased, more competent men could be found for the agencies and many subagencies could be eliminated.[20]

Commissioner Brown, strongly supported by Secretary of the Interior Ewing, proposed to Congress the additional superintendents and agents that were needed. Separate bills were drawn up, one each for Oregon, California, New Mexico, and Texas. But the sectional controversy meant postponement of action on all but the Oregon bill, approved on June 5, 1850, which established an independent superintendency for Oregon and provided for three agents and the extension of the trade and intercourse laws over the territory.[21] Brown's successor, Lea, pushed for fulfillment of the Indian Office's proposals. Representative Robert W. Johnson, chairman of the Committee on Indian Affairs, offered amendments to the Indian appropriation bill that embodied the request. "The object of the series of amendments," he said, ". . . is to effect that reorganization of the Indian Department which the changed relations of our Government, her very considerable acquisition of territory, the increased number of tribes, and the amount of responsibility require." The amendments were included in the act, approved on February 27, 1851. At last, an expanded Indian department matched the expanded nation.[22]

The law repealed all previous authorization for Indian superintendents east of the Rockies and north of Texas and New Mexico and provided instead three superintendents for the Indians in those areas, to be appointed by the president with the advice and consent of the Senate. The president or the secretary of the interior was empowered to assign the superintendents to appropriate tribes. (The governor of Minnesota Territory, however, was to continue as ex officio superintendent until the president should direct otherwise.) In place of the twenty-three agents and subagents employed in the same region, the law authorized eleven Indian agents at a salary of fifteen hundred dollars a year and six other agents at a thousand dollars a year. The same law provided four agents for New Mexico and one for Utah and extended the intercourse laws over the tribes in those terri-

20. CIA Report, 1849, serial 550, pp. 952–56. Brown relied heavily on a report of W. Medill of December 30, 1846, written in response to a House request for information about possible changes in the public service for greater economy and efficiency, printed in *House Document* no. 70, 29–2, serial 500, pp. 10–14. See also the discussion of reorganization of the Indian department in Robert A. Trennert, Jr., *Alternative to Extinction: Federal Indian Policy and the Beginnings of the Reservation System, 1846–51* (Philadelphia: Temple University Press, 1975), pp. 45–60.

21. 9 *United States Statutes* 437.

22. *Congressional Globe*, 31st Congress, 2d session, pp. 616–19; 9 *United States Statutes* 586–87. See also Trennert, *Alternative to Extinction*, pp. 57–58.

tories. The Central Superintendency was established in place of the old St. Louis Superintendency, with responsibility for agents and Indians in present-day Kansas and Nebraska as well as the upper reaches of the Missouri, Platte, and Arkansas rivers. The Northern Superintendency assumed responsibility for the Indians in Wisconsin and Michigan and, after 1856, those in Minnesota. The Southern Superintendency replaced the old Western Superintendency and had charge of the Indians in the Indian Territory and the Osage Indians in southern Kansas.[23]

The separation of the territorial governors from ex officio duty as Indian superintendents, which was part of Orlando Brown's proposal, did not come at once. The problems that arose from this overburdening of frontier administrators, to say nothing of the frequent conflicts of interest, did not slacken; and with repeated recommendations from the Indian Office, Congress acted piece by piece. In 1850 a separate superintendency for Oregon was created. In 1856 the Minnesota Superintendency, in which the governor served as superintendent, was discontinued and its agencies added to the Northern Superintendency. And in 1857 the two offices were separated in the territories of Utah and New Mexico.[24]

If renovation was necessary in the field organization, the operation of the Indian service also loudly called for an overhaul. Some order, it is true, was achieved without legislative change when Charles Mix became chief clerk in 1850. Relying on an authorization of funds provided by Congress, Mix drew up a compilation of rules and regulations for the superintendents and agents in their multifarious business with the Indian Office. The 85-page pamphlet, entitled *Office Copy of the Laws, Regulations, Etc., of the Indian Bureau, 1850*, was a mélange of previous rules and directives. It included the intercourse law of June 30, 1834, in full, as well as the law of the same date organizing the Indian department. To these were added a series of so-called "revised regulations," issued from time to time by the secretary of war for carrying into effect the laws of 1834. These were intended to specify the boundaries and sites of existing superintendencies, agencies, and subagencies and to describe in detail the duties of the various officials and the procedures for carrying out trade regulations, for handling depredation claims, for managing the emigration of Indian groups, and for paying annuities. Similarly, detailed instructions about the revision of the inter-

23. A concise history of these superintendencies and the agencies attached to them is given in Edward E. Hill, *The Office of Indian Affairs, 1824–1880: Historical Sketches* (New York: Clearwater Publishing Company, 1974), pp. 28–31, 118–20, 174–75.

24. 9 *United States Statutes* 437; 11 *United States Statutes* 185. On territorial governors as ex officio Indian superintendents, see William M. Neil, "The Territorial Governor as Indian Superintendent in the Trans-Mississippi West," *Mississippi Valley Historical Review* 43 (September 1956): 213–37.

course laws in 1847 were included. The manual included copies of the numerous forms on which the various reports were to be submitted.[25]

The manual by itself might have been a dead letter had it not been for the zeal with which Mix managed the office. He called to task agents who did not follow the letter of the regulations, and in his long term in the Indian Office he was able to develop a uniformity of practice that had been badly needed amid the rapid turnover of personnel. The manual in its original form was rudimentary, without table of contents or index, but it remained as it was until 1869, when a few slight revisions were made.[26]

There was some gain in having the existing legislation and explanatory regulations set forth in a single place and a chief clerk on duty to see that the proper forms were used and that reports went through the proper channels. But clearly more was needed. It was the constant refrain of the commissioners of Indian affairs that new legislation was necessary. Thus Manypenny wrote in a typical statement in 1854: "Experience has proven the law approved June 30, 1834, 'to regulate trade and intercourse with the Indian tribes, and to preserve peace on the frontier,' to be inadequate to meet and dispose of all the varied questions and difficulties which frequently arise under, and grow out of, the existing state of our Indian relations."[27]

What bothered Manypenny, in addition to the general inapplicability of old laws to new circumstances, was the inadequacy of the law of 1834 to protect the persons and property of the Indians. He saw what was happening to the Indians as they succumbed to the pressures of the invading whites, and he remarked, "The rage for speculation and the wonderful desire to obtain choice lands, which seems to possess so many of those who go into our new territories, causes them to lose sight of and entirely overlook the rights of the aboriginal inhabitants." He concluded: "Humanity, Christianity, national honor, unite in demanding the enactment of such laws as will not only protect the Indians, but as shall effectually put it out of the power of any public officer to allow these poor creatures to be despoiled of their lands and annuities by a swarm of hungry and audacious speculators, attorneys, and others, their instruments and coadjutors."[28]

The same plea was made by Manypenny's successors.[29] Finally, in Feb-

25. *Office Copy of the Laws, Regulations, Etc., of the Indian Bureau, 1850* (Washington: Gideon and Company, 1850). The congressional authorization is in 9 *United States Statutes* 558.

26. The manual is discussed briefly in Kelsey, "Mr. Lincoln's Indian Bureau," pp. 25–27.

27. CIA Report, 1854, serial 746, p. 225. See also CIA Report, 1855, serial 810, p. 335.

28. CIA Report, 1856, serial 875, pp. 572–75.

29. CIA Report, 1857, serial 919, p. 300; CIA Report, 1858, serial 974, p. 364; CIA Report, 1859, serial 1023, pp. 389–90. See the long and detailed discussion about inequities and inadequacies in the existing laws in the report of Elias Rector, superintendent

ruary 1859, Congress directed the commissioner of Indian affairs "to prepare rules and regulations for the government of the Indian service, and for
trade and intercourse with the Indian tribes and the regulation of their affairs," which would have effect only when enacted by Congress. Commissioner Greenwood worked to comply with the request, but nothing came
of the effort.[30]

There was some growth in the office staff in Washington, but it was not
at all proportionate to the increased work that devolved upon the commissioners. Manypenny complained in 1856 that the work "had swelled to an
extent almost incredible." The tasks of the office had doubled since 1852,
yet the office staff remained the same size.[31]

PERENNIAL PROBLEMS: ANNUITIES AND LIQUOR

The question of the proper manner of paying annuities to the Indians was
reopened in the 1850s, as the pendulum of arguments swung back again to
an earlier position. The legislation of 1847, which provided for per capita
payment of the annuities rather than payment to the chiefs as the law of
1834 had directed, in its turn was now a cause of complaint. The praise
that had been showered on the 1847 law by Commissioner Medill, in the
minds of his successors in the 1850s, was sadly misplaced. Luke Lea, in his
first year in office, found "material objections" to the practice. Although
the law had allowed the tribes to set apart some of their annuity payments
for national and charitable purposes, in fact they had not done so. Nor did
he like the slighting of the chiefs that came with a per capita payment, for
it was through the chiefs that the government carried on business with the
tribes, and he thought they deserved a larger share than the "common Indians." Moreover, if the chiefs were passed by, their authority within the
tribes was weakened and disorder resulted. Congress took no action on
Lea's recommendations, however, and in 1857 James Denver raised the
same questions in a forceful way. He declared that the "great body of the
Indians can be managed only through the chiefs" and predicted that the per
capita payments would break down the domestic government of the Indians and thus foster lawlessness.[32]

The policy makers were caught between two contradictory positions

of the Southern Superintendency, September 24, 1857, CIA Report, 1857, serial 919, pp.
479–93.

30. 11 *United States Statutes* 401; CIA Report, 1859, serial 1023, pp. 389–90.
31. CIA Report, 1856, serial 875, pp. 571–72.
32. CIA Report, 1850, serial 587, pp. 44–45; CIA Report, 1857, serial 919, pp. 295–96.

and could not easily extricate themselves. They held, on one hand, that the tribes were independent governments (as far as domestic matters were concerned), for which the chiefs were essential figures who needed to be treated with special respect. On the other hand, they saw the abuses that crept in with the large payments to the chiefs, who could succumb to the pressures of outside manipulators interested in pocketing the annuity payments themselves. Thus Manypenny in 1853 condemned the conversion of the private debts of a few Indians into "national debts" to be paid out of the annuities.[33]

It was clear to the officials of the 1850s, however, as it would be to their successors through the decades, that annuities in *money*, whether paid directly to individuals or distributed through the chiefs, were an unmitigated evil. Instead of advancing the Indians toward civilization and self-support, the money was looked upon as a substitute for work, and the Indians became increasingly dependent on what amounted to a dole. Commissioner Manypenny declared that the money-annuity system had done "as much, if not more, to cripple and thwart the efforts of the government to domesticate and civilize our Indian tribes, than any other of the many serious obstacles with which we have had to contend." He wanted payments to the Indians to be in the form of goods, agricultural implements, and stock animals or in the form of "means of mental, moral, and industrial education and training."[34] As he set about to negotiate treaties with the Indians, he saw to it that payments were not permanent, but that they would gradually be reduced over a set period of years. Moreover, the payments were placed under the control of the president, who could use the funds as he saw fit to contribute to the civilization and improvement of the tribes. A set provision was inserted in most of the treaties in this or similar form:

All which several sums of money shall be paid to the said . . . tribes, or expended for their use and benefit under the direction of the President of the United States, who may, from time to time, determine, at his discretion, what proportion of the annual payments, in this article provided for, if any, shall be applied to and expended, for their moral improvement and education; for such beneficial objects as in his judgment will be calculated to advance them in civilization; for buildings, opening farms, fencing, breaking land, providing stock, agricultural implements, seeds, &c., for clothing, provisions, and merchandise; for iron, steel, arms and ammunition; for mechanics, and tools; and for medical purposes.[35]

33. CIA Report, 1853, serial 690, p. 261.
34. Ibid., pp. 260–61.
35. Treaty with the Oto and Missouri Indians, 1854, Kappler, p. 609.

Because, as Manypenny reported at the end of 1856, since March 4, 1853, fifty-two treaties had been entered into with various tribes (thirty-two already ratified and twenty still under consideration), his policy had significant effect. Moreover, the policy inaugurated in the previous decade of paying annuities semi-annually was revived. It appeared to have a good effect in countering the tendency of many Indians to spend their funds wastefully and then sink back into a long period of misery until the next annual payment arrived.[36]

An old problem, not unconnected with the receipt of annuity payments, was the liquor traffic to the Indians. Even the new and tighter strictures of the law of 1847 were not enough. "The appetite of the Indian for the use of ardent spirits," Manypenny lamented in 1855, "seems to be entirely uncontrollable, and at all periods of our intercourse with him the evil effects and injurious consequences arising from the indulgence of the habit are unmistakably seen. It has been the greatest barrier to his improvement in the past, and will continue to be in the future, if some means cannot be adopted to inhibit its use." The federal system was in large part to blame, for the federal government had done almost all it could to end the sale or use of liquor in the Indian country, but it could not legislate for the states and territories that were adjacent to or surrounded the tribal lands. All it could do was to urge proper legislation, but nothing truly effective was provided.[37]

THE CHALLENGE OF SCIENTIFIC RACISM

The men in the Indian Office held firm to the principles of Indian civilization that had carried over from earlier decades. They accepted without serious question the prevailing doctrine that Indians were fully human beings like their white neighbors, that they were emerging (in varying degrees) from a state of savagery or barbarism, and that it was the responsibility of a Christian nation and its government to take them in hand like a good father, punishing them when necessary but supplying them with the patterns and means of a civilized existence based on agriculture (ultimately with private property holdings) and providing teachers and missionaries for their moral, intellectual, and industrial advancement. They saw no philosophical conflict in their acceptance and promotion of an expanding white society that was moving into the vast regions acquired in the previous decade and their benevolent concern for the Indians who were threatened with being crushed by the American advance. They believed in the superiority of their way of life and hoped to convince—or compel—the

36. CIA Report, 1856, serial 875, p. 571; CIA Report, 1855, serial 810, pp. 336–37.
37. CIA Report, 1855, serial 810, p. 340; see also CIA Report, 1850, serial 587, p. 45.

Indians to accept it as the only alternative to extermination. The fact that partial extermination resulted from the contacts of the two races, notably in California, was not the result of plan but of the insufficiency of the reservations and other means offered and the slowness of the Indians to accept the salvation offered them so insistently. There is no indication that the policy makers departed from the norms and principles of the evangelical Christian society in which they lived, even though we know nothing about their personal involvement in the rising Christian revivalism that marked the decade of the 1850s in the North.[38]

They lived at a time, however, when the optimism of humanitarians in regard to the Indians' progress was challenged by the rise of the so-called American School of Ethnology, the first serious attempt to develop a scientific racism. This group of investigators and writers denied the unity of mankind and preached a multiplicity of races, some innately inferior to others. Caught between the biblical chronology of man's existence on earth (the Protestant divine James Ussher had set the creation of the world at 4004 B.C.) and clear evidence that distinct races had existed for thousands of years, these men rejected the monogenesis of traditional Judeo-Christian belief and opted for polygenesis, that is, separate creation of the white, black, red, brown, and yellow races. Much of their evidence was furnished by Samuel G. Morton, who collected and measured human skulls. In his *Crania Americana*, published in Philadelphia in 1839, he concluded that the Indians were a distinct race, whose characteristics were physical and not based merely on environment, and he wrote disparagingly about Indian capabilities.[39]

Whereas Morton was circumspect and careful not to appear to challenge biblical beliefs headon, his most famous follower, Dr. Josiah C. Nott of Mobile, was a polemicist and propagandist who delighted in stinging the clergy and other religious traditionalists. As early as 1844 he began to write

38. Only Manypenny came from the region where revivalism was strong, and he sounds most like the revivalists. Three commissioners—Brown, Lea, and Greenwood—were southerners, and southern tradition was a heavily biblical one, with unspeculative reliance upon religious fundamentals.

39. Samuel George Morton, *Crania Americana; or, A Comparative View of the Skulls of the Various Aboriginal Nations of North and South America, to Which Is Prefixed an Essay on the Varieties of the Human Species* (Philadelphia: J. Dobson, 1839), pp. 81–82. Morton repeated the same views in a talk before the Boston Society of Natural History in 1842, printed as *An Inquiry into the Distinctive Characteristics of the Aboriginal Race of America*, 2d ed. (Philadelphia: John Pennington, 1844). A good account of Morton and the American School is given in William R. Stanton, *The Leopard's Spots: Scientific Attitudes toward Race in America, 1815–1859* (Chicago: University of Chicago Press, 1960). I have also relied on Reginald Horsman, "Scientific Racism and the American Indian in the Mid-Nineteenth Century," *American Quarterly* 37 (May 1975): 152–68, although I disagree with his conclusions.

about the inferiority of non-Caucasian races, and in 1854, together with the Egyptologist George R. Gliddon, he published *Types of Mankind,* which gathered evidence that the races came from separate creations and were different in their capacities. "In America," the two wrote, "the aboriginal barbarous tribes cannot be forced to change their habits, or even persuaded to successful emigration: they are melting away from year to year. . . . It is as clear as the sun at noon-day, that in a few generations more the last of these Red men will be numbered with the dead." They saw the Indians of America as "one great family, that presents a prevailing type," and offered this description: "Small and peculiarly shaped crania, a cinnamon complexion, small feet and hands, black straight hair, wild, savage nature, characterize the Indian everywhere."⁴⁰

It should be noted that Nott and others of his stripe were more concerned with blacks than with Indians, and their arguments in favor of the existence of inferior races offered a scientific argument for slavery. That may help explain why Nott received favorable notice in some segments of the Democratic and southern press. The *Democratic Review* flirted with the new ideas, and the *Southern Quarterly Review* and *DeBow's Review* (published in New Orleans) openly accepted inherent differences in the races, heeding the animadversions of the ethnologists about Indians.⁴¹

The American School, however, made no perceptible headway against the views of the Indian policy makers, imbued as they were with the pervasive evangelical religious atmosphere of the day. Even in regard to the blacks, neither the North nor the South accepted the scientists' conclusions about the inferiority of blacks as a basis for action. The North could not accept a doctrine that lent comfort to slavery, and the South, with its deep commitment to religion, relied on the Bible for support of slavery, not on a science that would force rejection of the Bible.⁴² In regard to the In-

40. J. C. Nott and George R. Gliddon, *Types of Mankind; or, Ethnological Researches, Based upon the Ancient Monuments, Paintings, Sculptures, and Crania of Races, and upon Their Natural, Geographical, Philological, and Biblical History* (Philadelphia: Lippincott, Grambo and Company, 1854), pp. 69–70.

41. There is an extended discussion of the articles on the diversity of races and the inferiority of the Indian that appeared in these journals in Horsman, "Scientific Racism," pp. 160–64.

42. John S. Haller, Jr., *Outcasts from Evolution: Scientific Attitudes of Racial Inferiority, 1859–1900* (Urbana: University of Illinois Press, 1971), p. 78. See also Stanton, *Leopard's Spots,* pp. 193–95. Historians who assert that the makers of Indian policy were influenced by the American School are Reginald Horsman in "Scientific Racism," Thomas F. Gossett, in *Race: The History of an Idea in America* (Dallas: Southern Methodist University Press, 1963), and Russel B. Nye, in *Society and Culture in America, 1830–1860* (New York: Harper and Row, 1974). These authors do not offer convincing evidence that these views were the dominant ones and none at all to show that they formed the basis for government policy. See "Scientific Racism and Indian Policy," in

dians, the efforts to educate and Christianize them in the 1840s and after make it clear that the government policy makers and their missionary partners maintained a uniform—and in some cases a very strong—adherence to the traditional positions. There were few indications that they were aware of the new scientific theories, and if scientific racism was adverted to at all, it was rejected.

In 1851, the year Samuel Morton died, Commissioner Luke Lea made a typical assertion: "The history of the Indian furnishes abundant proof that he possesses all the elements essential to his elevation; all the powers, instincts, and sympathies which appertain to his white brother; and which only need the proper development and direction to enable him to tread with equal step and dignity the walks of civilized life. . . . That his inferiority is a necessity of his nature is neither taught by philosophy, nor attested by experience." George W. Manypenny noted the slowness of the Indians' progress, but he did not think ultimate success was impossible. "I believe," he said in 1855, "that the Indian may be domesticated, improved, and elevated; that he may be completely and thoroughly civilized, and made a useful element of our population." Both Lea and Manypenny, however, were aware of what the latter called "erroneous opinions and prejudices in relation to the disposition, characteristics, capacity, and intellectual powers of the race" and considered them obstacles and drawbacks in the rapid improvement of the Indians.[43] These men and their predecessors in the 1840s clearly did not accept the view of the Indian proposed by Morton, Gliddon, and Nott. They did not subscribe to the racist positions of *DeBow's Review*. Their viewpoints and their actions (especially in regard to education for the Indians) continued to follow the pattern of evangelical Christianity of the first decades of the century.

Thomas L. McKenney, appearing on the lecture circuit in the 1840s with lectures on the "origin, history, character, and the wrongs and rights of the Indians," held firm to monogenesis. He wrote:

> I am aware that opinions are entertained by some, embracing the theory of multiform creations; by such, the doctrine that the whole family of man sprang from one original and common stock, is denied. There is, however, but one source whence information can be derived on this subject—and that is the Bible; and, until those who base their

---

Francis Paul Prucha, *Indian Policy in the United States: Historical Essays* (Lincoln: University of Nebraska Press, 1981), pp. 180–97, which I draw on here.

43. CIA Report, 1851, serial 613, p. 274; CIA Report, 1855, serial 810, pp. 338, 340. For the views of Henry R. Schoolcraft, see Stanton, *Leopard's Spots*, p. 192; for those of Lewis Henry Morgan, see Carl Rezek, *Lewis Henry Morgan: American Scholar* (Chicago: University of Chicago Press, 1960).

convictions on Bible testimony, consent to throw aside that great land-mark of truth, they must continue in the belief that "the Lord God formed *man* of the dust of the ground, and breathed into his nostrils the breath of life, when he became a living soul." Being thus formed, and thus endowed, he was put by his Creator in *the* garden, which was eastward in Eden, whence flowed the river which parted, and became the four heads; and that from his fruitfulness his species were propagated.

The propagation of the entire human race from "an original pair," McKenney asserted, "is a truth so universally admitted, as to render any elaborate argument in its support superfluous." Because the Eden of Adam and Eve was not in America, the Indians could not have been indigenous to America. McKenney believed they were of Asiatic origin and had migrated to the New World by way of Bering Strait. He argued in his lectures against those who said that the Indian was irreclaimable.[44]

The American School of Ethnology is of interest primarily to historians of science. The polygenesis doctrine, on which the diversity of human species and the inferiority of the nonwhite races rested, was replaced by the evolutionary theories of Charles Darwin, whose *Origin of Species* was published in 1859.[45] Morton and Nott and their friends turned out to be scientific oddities, their cranial measurements relegated to the attic like the phrenology with which they flirted. The dominance of evangelical Protestant views in Indian policy after the Civil War was, if anything, stronger than it had been before.

44. Thomas L. McKenney, *Memoirs, Official and Personal: With Sketches of Travels among the Northern and Southern Indians* (New York: Paine and Burgess, 1846), 2: 14–15.

45. There was a strange recurrence in the 1970s of the notion of separate creation of the Indians among some Indians, who asserted that the Indians were always in the New World and did not migrate here. This appeared to be part of the movement to reassert the importance of Indianness.

CHAPTER 13

A Pathway to
the Pacific

Colonization of the Western Tribes.

Kansas-Nebraska and the Indians.

Military Action on the Plains.

The territorial acquisitions of the 1840s were both the result of and a stimulus to population movements to the Pacific slope. Although large numbers moved by sail around Cape Horn and others risked the shorter distance through the Isthmus of Panama, great hordes of emigrants chose the course across the continent. In 1843 the first mass movement to Oregon took place, jumping off from Independence, Missouri, and moving along the overland route to the Willamette Valley in Oregon. The spectacle was repeated in 1844 and 1845, and by 1848 more than fourteen thousand emigrants had impressed the Oregon Trail indelibly on the landscape and on the American consciousness. Some turned south from Fort Hall and sought California instead of Oregon; the trickle of immigrants became a torrent when news of the discovery of gold in California in 1848 reached the East.[1] Meanwhile, there was heavy traffic as well on the Santa Fe Trail, which had been laid out in 1822 and which became a major passageway to the Southwest and California.

---

1. There are plentiful statistics on the emigrants in John D. Unruh, Jr., *The Plains Across: The Overland Emigrants and the Trans-Mississippi West, 1840–60* (Urbana: University of Illinois Press, 1979). See chapter 5, "Emigrant-Indian Interaction," pp. 156–200.

COLONIZATION OF THE WESTERN TRIBES

These great movements of population had two effects on Indian affairs. In the first place, they cut directly through the lands of the Indians, making a wide swath that upset the ecological patterns by destroying large numbers of game (chiefly buffalo) and forcing the Indians to seek new hunting grounds; this in turn led to increased intertribal irritations. Although direct conflicts between the Indians and the Oregon and California emigrants were few, and in many cases the Indians offered vital assistance to the intruders, the ultimate result shook apart the existing economic and political structures on the plains into an irreparable shambles—which it became the responsibility of the federal government to deal with. In the second place, the increasing population of the West (the population of California in the census of 1850 was ninety-three thousand, that of Oregon Territory thirteen thousand, and that of Utah Territory eleven thousand) meant that the Indians were surrounded. No longer was it possible to keep moving the tribesmen vaguely "to the west." Whites and their lines of communication moved upon the Indians with seemingly inexorable force from both directions, east and west, and the process speeded up still more after the Civil War.

To meet the crisis, the officials of the federal government, whether Democrats of Whigs, had one solution. This was to free the great middle section of the plains of its Indian inhabitants by moving them to two great "colonies," one already well established in the south as the Indian Territory and a comparable one to be laid out north of the lines of travel.[2] The idea had been slowly developing. Commissioner of Indian Affairs T. Hartley Crawford in 1841 spoke of "an Indian territory in the northern part of Iowa" as a "counterpoise to the southwestern Indian territory," with a "dense white population . . . interposed between the two settlements." And his successor, William Medill, in 1848 noted that the government had "commenced the establishment of two colonies for the Indian tribes that we have been compelled to remove; one north, on the head waters of the Mississippi, and the other south, on the western borders of Missouri and Arkansas." These officials were thinking primarily of locations for the Indians transferred from east of the Mississippi, but no great mental gymnastics were required to expand the notion to the tribes of the plains. Medill in fact urged removing the Omahas and the Otos and Missouris, keeping the Pawnees north of the Platte, and restraining the Sioux to their northern

2. An old but still very useful treatment of this whole matter is James C. Malin, *Indian Policy and Westward Expansion* (Lawrence, Kansas, 1921). See also Robert A. Trennert, Jr., *Alternative to Extinction: Federal Indian Policy and the Beginnings of the Reservation System, 1846–51* (Philadelphia: Temple University Press, 1975).

regions. He looked forward to the day when "an ample outlet of about six geographical degrees will be opened for our population that may incline to pass or expand in that direction; and thus prevent our colonized tribes from being injuriously pressed upon, if not swept away."[3]

There were attempts as early as the mid-1840s to provide territorial organization for the central plains, looking toward the joining of the west coast with the east, the protection of the emigrants, and the populating of the region by whites. Secretary of War William Wilkins in 1844 recommended that the areas on both sides of the Platte be organized as a territory. Senator David Atchison of Missouri and Senator Stephen A. Douglas of Illinois introduced bills in 1844–1845 for organizing the region, and Douglas took pride in the fact that from that time forward he tirelessly advocated the measure. The Indian barrier set up with the removal of the Indians from east of the Mississippi was anathema to him. "It was obvious to the plainest understanding," he wrote later, "that if this policy should be carried out and the treaty stipulations observed in good faith it was worse than folly to wrangle with Great Britain about our right to the whole or any part of Oregon—much less cherish the vain hope of ever making this an Ocean-bound Republic. This Indian Barrier was to have been a colossal monument to the God terminus saying to christianity, civilization and Democracy 'thus far mayest thou go, and *no* farther.'"[4]

Orlando Brown enthusiastically adopted the earlier proposals, and Luke Lea said he concurred in the policy of his predecessors—"by a partial change in their [the Indians'] relative positions, to throw open a wide extent of country for the spread of our population westward, so as to save them from being swept away by the mighty and advancing current of civilization, which has already engulfed a large portion of this hapless race." There was an ample outlet south of the colonized tribes, he said, but another was needed farther north, "leading more directly towards our remote western possession."[5]

But the humanitarian concerns of the previous decade were not suddenly dropped in the face of the new circumstances and the imperious demands for some easing of the tensions caused by the migrating and expanding white population. All the proposals for colonization had a second

3. CIA Report, 1841, serial 401, p. 231; CIA Report, 1848, serial 537, pp. 388, 390.

4. Douglas to J. H. Crane, D. M. Johnson, and L. J. Eastin, December 17, 1853, *The Letters of Stephen A. Douglas*, ed. Robert W. Johannsen (Urbana: University of Illinois Press, 1961), pp. 269–70. The report of Wilkins is in *House Executive Document* no. 2, 28–2, serial 463, p. 124. There is a discussion of the attempts of Senators Atchison and Douglas to get Congress to organize Nebraska Territory in Malin, *Indian Policy and Westward Expansion*, pp. 38–40.

5. CIA Report, 1849, serial 570, p. 946; CIA Report, 1850, serial 587, p. 39. Lea repeated his statement of policy the next year in CIA Report, 1851, serial 613, p. 268.

component or argument: it was necessary to consolidate the Indians in order to preserve them and to civilize them. The interest in settling the Indians in circumstances where they could be "improved" by education and manual labor, which had been an essential part of the civilization plans from the beginning of the century, continued to be viewed as a kind of panacea for the Indian problem. Medill explicitly urged application of the old policy to the new situation. He wrote in 1848:

> The policy already begun and relied on to accomplish objects so momentous and so desirable to every Christian philanthropist, is, as rapidly as it can safely and judiciously be done, to colonize our Indian tribes beyond the reach, for some years, of our white population; confining each within a small district of country, so that, as the game decreases and becomes scarce, the adults will gradually be compelled to resort to agriculture and other kinds of labor to obtain a subsistence, in which aid may be afforded and facilities furnished them out of the means obtained by the sale of their former possessions. To establish, at the same time, a judicious and well devised system of manual labor schools for the education of the youth of both sexes in letters—the males in practical agriculture and the various necessary and useful mechanic arts, and the females in the different branches of housewifery, including spinning and weaving; and these schools, like those already in successful operation, to be in charge of the excellent and active missionary societies of the different Christian denominations of the country, and to be conducted and the children taught by efficient, exemplary, and devoted men and women, selected with the approbation of the Department by those societies; so that a physical, intellectual, moral, and religious education will all be imparted together.[6]

He recalled the case of other tribes, "not long since colonized," who a few years before had been nomads and hunters, opposed to labor, and distrustful of schools and missionaries, but who now desired to educate their children. He declared that they were "becoming prosperous and happy from having learned how to provide certain and comfortable support for themselves and their families by the cultivation of the soil and other modes of labor." But the biggest change he saw was in the condition of Indian women, who had been drudges and slaves but now were beginning to assume their true position as equals.[7]

Medill's successors sang the same song. Orlando Brown waxed eloquent about the effects of civilization and education among the tribes moved

6. CIA Report, 1848, serial 537, p. 386.
7. Ibid.

from the East and expected the same results if the same methods were applied to the more western Indians.[8] Luke Lea asserted: "If timely measures are taken for the proper location and management of these tribes, they may, at no distant period, become an intelligent and Christian people, understanding the principles of our government, and participating in all its advantages."[9]

The federal government took steps to carry out these designs—to open up the passage to the Far West and to promote the civilization of the Indians—by a series of Indian treaties in the early 1850s. The first of these was the Treaty of Fort Laramie, signed September 17, 1851, with the Sioux, Cheyennes, Arapahos, Crows, Assiniboins, Gros Ventres, Mandans, and Arikaras. The treaty was negotiated by David D. Mitchell, a onetime fur trader who was superintendent of Indian affairs at St. Louis and an active advocate of clearing a central passageway to the Pacific. He was aided by Thomas Fitzpatrick, Indian agent for the Upper Platte Agency. The Indians agreed to cease hostilities among themselves and "to make an effective and lasting peace." They recognized the right of the United States to establish roads and military posts in their territory, and they agreed to make restitution for wrongs committed on whites lawfully passing through their lands. The treaty spelled out in detail the boundaries for each of the tribes in an attempt, generally unsuccessful, to keep them apart. In return the United States promised to protect the Indians from white depredations and to pay annuities of fifty thousand dollars a year for fifty years (reduced to ten years, with a possible five-year extension, by an amendment proposed by the Senate and later ratified by the tribes). The annuities were to be paid in "provisions, merchandize, domestic animals, and agricultural implements, in such proportions as may be deemed best adapted to their condition by the President of the United States."[10]

Mitchell reported optimistically on the results of the treaty. He said that the presents distributed at the council satisfied the Indians for all past destruction of buffalo, grass, and timber caused by the emigrating whites. And he justified the large annuity because it was needed to save the Indians. He wrote: "Humanity calls loudly for some interposition on the part of the American government to save, if possible, some portion of these ill-fated tribes; and this, it is thought, can only be done by furnishing them the means, and gradually turning their attention to agriculture." The veteran Jesuit missionary Pierre-Jean DeSmet, who attended the council, spoke highly of the peaceful behavior of the Indians and approved the

8. CIA Report, 1849, serial 570, pp. 956–57.

9. CIA Report, 1851, serial 613, p. 268. See also CIA Report, 1850, serial 587, pp. 35–36.

10. Kappler, pp. 594–95.

treaty, which he said would be "the commencement of a new era for the Indians—an era of peace."[11]

The treaty was considered highly successful by the Americans, but the powerful Sioux with their Cheyenne and Arapaho allies, in a sense, dominated the conference. The treaty was a recognition of Sioux power and did little effectively to curb it, for the Sioux continued to expand their domination of the hunting grounds, and wars between them and the United States were not long in coming.[12]

In 1853 Thomas Fitzpatrick by himself negotiated a treaty with the southern plains tribes—Comanches, Kiowas, and Apaches—at Fort Atkinson on the Santa Fe Trail in southwestern Kansas. The provisions were similar to those of Fort Laramie: agreements of peace among the Indians and with the whites, right of passage through the territories for the whites, and permission for military and other posts on Indian lands. The annuities were set at eighteen thousand dollars a year for ten years, with a possible five-year extension; a special article provided that if the United States decided it would be wise to establish farms among the Indians for their benefit, the annuities could be changed into a fund for that purpose.[13]

Fitzpatrick had no trouble with the Indians about the rights of way through their country, which had long been conceded, although he heard strenuous objections to the military posts, which "destroy timber, drive off the game, interrupt their ranges, excite hostile feelings, and but too frequently afford a rendezvous for worthless and trifling characters." The Indians similarly objected to reservations of land for depots and roads, but Fitzpatrick saw no alternative and felt that the concessions finally made by the Indians were "extremely fortunate." He wrote in his report of 1853:

> In view of the fact that at no distant day the whole country over which those Indians now roam must be peopled by another and more enterprising race, and also of the consideration that the channels of

11. CIA Report, 1851, serial 613, pp. 288–90; Hiram Martin Chittenden and Alfred Talbot Richardson, *Life, Letters, and Travels of Father Pierre-Jean DeSmet, S.J., 1801–1873*, 4 vols. (New York: Francis P. Harper, 1905), 2: 675–84. For a detailed analysis of the ratification of the amendment reducing the annuities, see Harry Anderson, "The Controversial Sioux Amendment to the Fort Laramie Treaty of 1851," *Nebraska History* 37 (September 1956): 201–20.

12. Richard White, "The Winning of the West: The Expansion of the Western Sioux in the Eighteenth and Nineteenth Centuries," *Journal of American History* 65 (September 1978): 319–43, traces the powerful advance of the Sioux. The 1851 treaty council is used perceptively by Raymond J. DeMallie as a case study of treaty making in his "Touching the Pen: Plains Indian Treaty Councils in Ethnohistorical Perspective," in Frederick C. Luebke, ed., *Ethnicity on the Great Plains* (Lincoln: University of Nebraska Press, 1980), pp. 41–46.

13. Kappler, pp. 600–602.

commerce between the east and west will eventually, in part at least, pass through their country, it was regarded as incumbent to provide, as far as practicable, for any action the government might see proper to take upon the subject. Already the idea of a great central route to the Pacific by railway has become deeply impressed upon the public mind; and while many courses are contemplated two of them at least ·are designed to pass through this section of the country. Should the results of explorations now in progress determine it thus, the acknowledgment contained in this clause of the treaty may be found of inestimable value. It will afford all the concession necessary for locations, pre-emptions, reservations, and settlements, and avoid, besides, the enhanced costs of secondary treaties with these tribes. Moreover, it will open a rich vein of wealth in what is now a wilderness, and that, too, without additional public burden.[14]

KANSAS-NEBRASKA AND THE INDIANS

The agitation for a railroad to the Pacific, to which Fitzpatrick alluded in his report, was an important force in clearing the central region of its Indian inhabitants. Some sort of transcontinental road linking the Mississippi Valley with the Pacific, and thus with the riches of the Orient, had been urged by Asa Whitney in the mid-1840s; by 1853 the need was so universally agreed upon that Congress authorized surveys to determine the most appropriate route. The War Department sent out four scientific parties to investigate the possibilities in the north, in the south, and through the central regions. The search for a railroad route also had deep political implications, for each section had strong advocates of a railroad. A southern route would pass through Louisiana, Texas, and the Territory of New Mexico to California—politically organized areas that would offer protection and encouragement to settlement along the road. It was therefore incumbent upon the proponents of a central route to see that the lands through which it would pass were politically organized. And in addition to the need for a railroad, there was continued pressure for settlement of the lands west of the Indian frontier line from restless farmers who felt unjustly obstructed from the "normal" development of the West by the Indian barrier. Congress moved steadily toward creation of a Nebraska territory, which became the goal—one might almost say the obsession—of Senator Douglas.[15]

14. CIA Report, 1853, serial 690, pp. 362–63.
15. Douglas's role is well analyzed in Robert W. Johannsen, *Stephen A. Douglas* (New York: Oxford University Press, 1973), pp. 390–434. The complex issues involved in

In a letter dated December 17, 1853, to a convention for promoting Nebraska to be held in St. Joseph, Missouri, Douglas voiced his own aspirations and those of many in the nation.

> How are we to develope, cherish and protect our immense interests and possessions on the Pacific, with a vast wilderness fifteen hundred miles in breadth, filled with hostile savages, and cutting off all direct communication. The Indian barrier must be removed. The tide of emigration and civilization must be permitted to roll onward until it rushes through the passes of the mountains, and spreads over the plains, and mingles with the waters of the Pacific. Continuous lines of settlement with civil, political and religious institutions all under the protection of law, are imperiously demanded by the highest national considerations. These are essential, but they are not sufficient. No man can keep up with the spirit of this age who travels on anything slower than the locomotive, and fails to receive intelligence by lightning. We must therefore have Rail Roads and Telegraphs from the Atlantic to the Pacific, through our own territory. Not one line only, but many lines, for the valley of the Mississippi will require as many Rail Roads to the Pacific as to the Atlantic, and will not venture to limit the number. The removal of the Indian barrier and the extension of the laws of the United States in the form of Territorial governments are the first steps toward the accomplishment of each and all of those objects.[16]

Congress, hoping at last to satisfy both the North and the South in regard to the thorny question of slavery in the central area, passed the Kansas-Nebraska Act in May 1854, which, while repealing the Missouri Compromise prohibition on slavery, provided for two territories whose inhabitants themselves under "popular sovereignty" would decide for or

---

the Nebraska question are treated in Roy F. Nichols, "The Kansas-Nebraska Act: A Century of Historiography," *Mississippi Valley Historical Review* 43 (September 1956): 187–212, and James C. Malin, *The Nebraska Question, 1852–1854* (Lawrence, Kansas, 1953). The Indian aspects of the Nebraska territorial agitation get special attention in Roy Gittinger, "The Separation of Nebraska and Kansas from the Indian Territory," *Mississippi Valley Historical Review* 3 (March 1917): 442–61, and Malin, *Indian Policy and Westward Expansion*. See also Robert R. Russel, *Improvement of Communication with the Pacific Coast as an Issue in American Politics, 1783–1864* (Cedar Rapids, Iowa: Torch Press, 1948), pp. 150–67.

16. Douglas to J. H. Crane, D. M. Johnson, and L. J. Eastin, December 17, 1853, in Douglas, *Letters*, pp. 270–71. The letter was originally printed, with a long introduction, in James C. Malin, "The Motives of Stephen A. Douglas in the Organization of Nebraska Territory: A Letter Dated December 17, 1853," *Kansas Historical Quarterly* 19 (November 1951): 321–53.

against slavery. Whatever the ultimate motivations of the men who voted for the bill, the long agitation for territorial organization that culminated in the act provided a tremendous impetus to the new direction in Indian policy. While the territorial debate was engaging Congress in 1853–1854, in fact, the Indian Office was taking steps to free the region of Indian title and thus open it for settlement.

That difficult task was the responsibility largely of George W. Manypenny, a man whose humanitarian sentiments toward the Indians were frequently enunciated. Manypenny believed that for the Indians' sake the western territories should be organized and that the Indians should be placed as much as possible out of the paths of emigrants to the Pacific. "Objections have been urged to the organization of a civil government in the Indian country," he wrote in 1853; "but those that cannot be overcome are not to be compared to the advantages which will flow to the Indians from such a measure, with treaties to conform to the new order of things, and suitable laws for their protection."[17]

Under an authorization of Congress of March 3, 1853, Manypenny energetically moved ahead to fit the Indians into "the new order of things."[18] He visited most of the border tribes, held councils with them, and did his best to get agreement from them for the cession of their lands. The Indians were ill-disposed to such a measure, having been excited and irritated by exploring parties of whites already invading their territory. At first they were opposed to any sale at all, but eventually they agreed on condition that they could keep small reserves in the areas where they were then situated—a policy that the commissioner objected to, for he wished them to move out entirely.[19] In Washington between March 15 and June 5, 1854, he negotiated nine treaties with the Indians who lived along the eastern border of the new territories: Otos and Missouris, Omahas, Delawares, Shawnees, Iowas, Sacs and Foxes of the Missouri, Kickapoos, Kaskaskias, Peorias, Piankashaws, Weas, and Miamis.[20]

The treaties were pretty much of a piece; the Oto and Missouri treaty of March 5 can be taken as an example. It provided for the cession of the tribes' holdings west of the Missouri River and designated a reduced area

17. CIA Report, 1853, serial 690, p. 251. On Manypenny see Henry E. Fritz, "George W. Manypenny and *Our Indian Wards*," *Kansas Quarterly* 3 (Fall 1971): 100–104; and Robert M. Kvasnicka, "George W. Manypenny, 1853–57," in Robert M. Kvasnicka and Herman J. Viola, eds., *The Commissioners of Indian Affairs, 1824–1977* (Lincoln: University of Nebraska Press, 1979), pp. 57–67.

18. 10 *United States Statutes* 238–39.

19. CIA Report, 1853, serial 690, pp. 249–50.

20. Kappler, pp. 608–46. These tribes held about 15 million acres, all of which were ceded except for about 1,342,000 acres retained by the tribes in reduced reservations. CIA Report, 1854, serial 746, pp. 213–14.

within the old reservation to which the Indians agreed to remove within a year. A significant characteristic of this treaty, as of all these treaties, was the provision for allotting lands in the newly designated reserve in farm-sized plots to individual Indians. The president was given the discretionary authority to survey the land, set it off in lots, and assign the lots in specified amounts (a quarter-section to a family, 80 acres to single adults, and so on) to all Indians who were "willing to avail of the privilege" and would locate on the lots as a permanent home. There were to be regulations for bequeathing the land and restrictions on its lease or sale. If the Indians left the land to "rove from place to place," their patents would be revoked and their annuities withheld until they returned and "resumed the pursuits of industry." Any residue of land after all the Indians had received an allotment was to be sold for the benefit of the Indians.

In return, the United States agreed to pay the Otos and Missouris annuities on a sliding scale from twenty thousand to five thousand dollars over the next thirty-eight years. The president would decide what proportion, if any, was to be paid in money and what proportion expended for education and other means to civilization. Another twenty thousand dollars was granted to help the Indians to move, subsist for a year, and establish themselves on their farms. Moreover, the government would build a grist and saw mill and a blacksmith shop and for ten years would employ a miller, a blacksmith, and a farmer. Punishment in the form of withholding annuities was prescribed for anyone who would drink liquor or bring it into the Indians' lands. Thus were these Indians, who had been subjected to the civilizing policies of the government for a number of decades, to be finally incorporated into white society. The continued Indian residence in Kansas and Nebraska, however, was not intended to impede the westward movement of the whites, for the Indians agreed in the treaties to allow "all the necessary roads and highways, and railroads, which may be constructed as the country improves" to run through their lands, with just compensation to be paid in money.[21]

Good as the intentions of the federal officials were in attempting to provide permanent homes for the Indians in eastern Kansas and Nebraska (as much as possible on individual homesteads), they did not reckon fully with the special problems facing Kansas in the mid-1850s and with what Manypenny called "the wonderful desire to obtain choice lands" on the part of individuals, land companies, and railroads that "causes them to lose sight of and entirely overlook the rights of the aboriginal inhabitants." The conflict between the pro-slavery and anti-slavery forces that turned the

21. Clauses in the various treaties pertained to the special conditions of each tribe; the treaties with the Delawares and the Shawnees were the most complex. Most of the treaties made land grants to missionary societies who maintained schools for the Indians.

southern territory into Bleeding Kansas caught the hapless Indians in a devastating situation. As Manypenny neared the end of his tenure as commissioner, he described the pathetic conditions, which were beyond his power to control. The general disorder and the influx of lawless men and speculators slowed down the surveys and the selection of homes for the Indians. He lamented the hindrances to effective use of the means of civilization provided in the treaties.

> The schools have not been as fully attended, nor the school buildings, agency houses, and other improvements, as rapidly constructed as they might otherwise have been. Trespasses and depredations of every conceivable kind have been committed on the Indians. They have been personally maltreated, their property stolen, their timber destroyed, their possession encroached upon, and divers other wrongs and injuries done them. . . . In the din and strife between the anti-slavery and pro-slavery parties with reference to the condition of the African race there, and in which the rights and interests of the red man have been completely overlooked and disregarded, the good conduct and patient submission of the latter contrasts favorably with the disorderly and lawless conduct of many of their white brethren, who, while they have quarrelled about the African, have united upon the soil of Kansas in wrong doing toward the Indian![22]

Manypenny hoped that with the return of peace and order to the territory the good citizens would hasten to repair the wrong and injury done to the Indians by lawless men. But he was much too sanguine in his expectations. The Indian reserves were extraordinarily attractive to designing speculators; leaders of Indian factions made use of the uncertain times for their own benefit; and the federal government was powerless—or lacked the will to exert power—to fulfill its promises to protect the Indians, who had declared in the treaties of 1854 that they would abide by the laws of the United States in conflicts with citizens and expected to be protected and to have their own rights vindicated in turn by the United States.[23]

A special case was that of the Wyandot Indians, who had moved from Ohio in 1843 to a reserve at the mouth of the Kansas River. The Wyandots were highly acculturated to white ways, and some of their leaders played an important part in the agitation for a Nebraska territory. In January 1855

---

22. CIA Report, 1856, serial 875, p. 572.

23. A detailed and critical account of the conflicts over Indian lands in Kansas after 1854 is in Paul Wallace Gates, *Fifty Million Acres: Conflicts over Kansas Land Policy, 1854–1890* (Ithaca: Cornell University Press, 1954). What happened to the Indian reserves in Kansas is described in H. Craig Miner and William E. Unrau, *The End of Indian Kansas: A Study of Cultural Revolution, 1854–1871* (Lawrence: Regents Press of Kansas, 1977).

they negotiated a treaty with Manypenny in which they declared that, "having become sufficiently advanced in civilization, and being desirous of becoming citizens, it is hereby agreed and stipulated, that their organization, and their relations with the United States as an Indian tribe shall be dissolved and terminated." The Wyandots were declared to be citizens of the United States, and their land was divided among the members of the tribe. Despite the advances of the tribe, however, many Wyandots were not able to prosper under the new conditions, and in February 1867 this portion—including some who, "although taking lands in severalty, have sold said lands, and are still poor," and others who were "unfitted for the responsibilities of citizenship"—decided "to begin anew a tribal existence" and remove to the Indian Territory on land ceded by the Senecas.[24]

MILITARY ACTION ON THE PLAINS

The plans of federal officials for opening a wide passageway west through the plains were interrupted by Indian hostility, brought on by the inexorable pressure of white population sometimes compounded by the imprudent and foolish actions of a few men. Indian hostility became so general by the end of the 1850s that one could speak of a plains Indian barrier of Sioux, Cheyennes, Arapahos, Kiowas, and Comanches extending from the Mexican to the Canadian border. This barrier did not crumble until a decade or more after the Civil War. The United States army, maintaining small forts along the trails and in trouble spots in the West, at first followed a defensive strategy, acting the role of policeman. Then, as Indian raids multiplied, it modified its policy to consider the whole tribe or band responsible for the raids of its members, and it mounted offensive campaigns against them.[25]

The first encounter arose out of the chance Indian killing of a cow belonging to an emigrant Mormon on the trail near Fort Laramie. A rash young lieutenant, John L. Grattan, marched out of the fort on August 19, 1854, to arrest the Indian accused of the cow's death. When the Brulé chief Conquering Bear, at whose camp the culprit was sought, failed to deliver

24. Kappler, pp. 677–81, 960–63. The complicated story of the indefinite land grants to certain members of the tribe made when the Indians moved from Ohio and confirmed in the 1855 treaty—called Wyandot "floats"—is told in Homer E. Socolofsky, "Wyandot Floats," *Kansas Historical Quarterly* 36 (Autumn 1970): 241–304. See also Raymond E. Merwin, "The Wyandot Indians," *Transactions of the Kansas State Historical Society* 9 (1905–1906): 73–88.

25. The best discussion of this subject is Robert M. Utley, *Frontiersmen in Blue: The United States Army and the Indian, 1848–1865* (New York: Macmillan Company, 1967), pp. 108–41.

him, Grattan opened fire, killing the chief. The Sioux fought back and quickly destroyed Grattan and his whole detachment. Emboldened, other Indians attacked the trail along the Platte. The Indian Office criticized the army's action, for under the intercourse law there should have been recourse to the Indian agent for compensation for the butchered animal. But the army decided to teach the Sioux a lesson.[26]

Secretary of War Jefferson Davis placed Colonel William S. Harney in command, and in the summer of 1855 Harney and the troops he had assembled at Fort Kearny moved against the Brulés. Early in September they destroyed the Indians' village near Ash Hollow on the North Platte in western Nebraska. Harney reported heavy casualties for the Sioux: eighty-six killed, five wounded, and about seventy women and children captured. "Never for years," wrote one of the officers in his journal after the battle, "has there been such an utter rout and disorganization of a band of Indians." Then the troops marched through the heart of the Sioux lands from Fort Laramie to Fort Pierre on the Missouri. At Fort Pierre in March 1856 Harney held a council with the Sioux chiefs and cowed them into agreeing to refrain from hostilities.[27] But the harsh action did little to encourage genuinely peaceful sentiments among the Indians. Harney's expedition was simply the first major challenge to the powerful Sioux advance on the northern plains, a movement that paralleled the advance of white Americans into the same region.[28]

Cheyenne Indians, continuing their raids of the Pawnees despite the treaty at Fort Laramie in 1851, disturbed the central plains, and they soon became the target of army action. The Cheyennes struck at emigrants on the trail along the Platte, and the army planned an offensive for the spring of 1857. During May and June a column of troops under Colonel Edwin

26. Lloyd E. McCann, "The Grattan Massacre," *Nebraska History* 37 (March 1956): 1–25; CIA Report, 1854, serial 746, pp. 224, 304–6.

27. Report of Harney, September 5, 1855, *Senate Executive Document* no. 1, 34–1, serial 811, pp. 49–51; Ray H. Mattison, ed., "The Harney Expedition against the Sioux: The Journal of Capt. John B. S. Todd," *Nebraska History* 43 (June 1962): 89–130 (quotation from p. 114); "Council with the Sioux Indians at Fort Pierre," *House Executive Document* no. 130, 34–1, serial 859. The treaty signed by Harney with the Indians at Fort Pierre, an action not in accordance with Indian Office procedures, was rejected by the Senate.

28. White, "Winning of the West," pp. 341–42. White writes: "The warfare between the northern plains tribes and the United States that followed the Fort Laramie Treaty of 1851 was not the armed resistance of a people driven to the wall by American expansion. In reality these wars arose from the clash of two expanding powers—the United States, and the Sioux and their allies. If, from a distance, it appears that the vast preponderance of strength rested with the whites, it should be remembered that the ability of the United States to bring this power to bear was limited. The series of defeats the Sioux inflicted on American troops during these years reveals how real the power of the Tetons was."

Vose Sumner moved up the Platte while a parallel operation under Major John Sedgewick followed the Arkansas. The Indians disappeared before the troops advancing west, but then the columns joined and turned back east to invade the Cheyenne homelands. Along the Solomon River in western Kansas hostile Cheyennes were driven back, and in the followup operation a principal Cheyenne village was destroyed. At that point Sumner's command was called for duty in Utah, and he was forced to suspend his operations. But he had done enough to subdue the Indians. When the Indian agent for the Upper Arkansas met with the tribes to distribute presents in the summer of 1858, he noted that Sumner had worked "a wondrous change in their dispositions toward the whites." The Cheyennes especially were anxious for a new treaty. "They said they had learned a lesson last summer in their fight with Colonel Sumner," the agent reported; "that it was useless to contend against the white man, who would soon with his villages occupy the whole prairie. They had eyes and were not blind. They no longer listened to their young men who continually clamored for war."[29]

The Cheyennes' chastisement kept them quiet even during the Pike's Peak gold rush of 1858–1859, when hordes of gold seekers cut across the central plains from the Missouri to the Rockies. But the increased emigration and its effect upon the Indians gave the Indian Office one more argument for its reservation policy. Commissioner Alfred B. Greenwood noted at the end of 1859 the exasperation that the oncoming whites caused the Indians by dispersing or killing off the game. Only assurances that the government would not let them suffer, he thought, had kept the Indians peaceful. He continued:

> They have also been brought to realize that a stern necessity is impending over them; that they cannot pursue their former mode of life, but must entirely change their habits, and, in fixed localities, look to the cultivation of the soil and the raising of stock for their future support. There is no alternative to providing for them in this manner but to exterminate them, which the dictates of justice and humanity alike forbid. They cannot remain as they are; for, if nothing is done for them, they must be subjected to starvation, or compelled to commence robbing and plundering for a subsistence. This will lead to hostilities and a costly Indian war, involving the loss of many lives, and the expenditure of a much larger amount of money than

29. Report of Agent Robert C. Miller, August 17, 1858, CIA Report, 1858, serial 974, p. 450; S. L. Seabrook, "Expedition of Col. E. V. Sumner against the Cheyenne Indians, 1857," *Collections of the Kansas State Historical Society* 16 (1923–1925): 306–15. Pertinent documents are printed in LeRoy R. Hafen and Ann W. Hafen, eds., *Relations with the Indians of the Plains, 1857–1861* (Glendale, California: Arthur H. Clark Company, 1959), pp. 15–153.

would be required to colonize them on reservations, and to furnish them with the necessary facilities and assistance to enable them to change their mode of life.

Greenwood urged Congress to appropriate funds for the negotiation of new treaties with the tribes.[30]

While a precarious peace settled on the northern plains, the Kiowas and Comanches continued their raids on the Texas frontier. Although they suffered numerous casualties inflicted by United States cavalry and the Texas Rangers, the Indians kept up their hostility throughout the decade. Even an extensive summer campaign of regular troops in 1860 through southern Kansas and western Indian Territory failed to quench the fires.[31]

In the antebellum years neither the army with its offensive operations on the plains and its network of military posts nor the Indian Office with its treaties of peace and civilization and its commitment to a reservation system had completely opened the way for unharassed travel or settlement on the Great Plains.

30. CIA Report, 1859, serial 1023, p. 385.

31. These operations are described in detail in Utley, *Frontiersmen in Blue*, pp. 125–40. See also Brad Agnew, "The 1858 War against the Comanches," *Chronicles of Oklahoma* 49 (Summer 1971): 211–29, and the documents in Hafen and Hafen, *Relations with the Indians of the Plains*, pp. 191–299.

CHAPTER 14

Texas, New Mexico, and Utah

The Indian Situation in Texas.

Reservations for Texas Indians.

Indian Affairs in New Mexico.

Indians, Mormons, and Gentiles.

The developing reservation policy of the United States met severe tests in Texas and in the regions acquired from Mexico as a result of the Mexican War. There was no lack of resolve on the part of federal officials in Washington or the superintendents and agents they sent into the field. These men held fast to the notion that the Indians must be forced to end their nomadic habits and their raids against the settlements and accept a new existence by living within specified boundaries and depending for subsistence on cultivation of the soil and stock raising. Only thus would there be order in the land and the Indians be protected against extermination. But wherever the federal government turned there were special problems that were only slowly appreciated and that came close to shattering the humanitarian dreams of the policy makers. In Texas state autonomy and self-interest was the special obstacle, in New Mexico the long tradition of raiding the Mexican settlements, and in Utah the overriding presence of the Mormons.

THE INDIAN SITUATION IN TEXAS

The government's reservation policy in Texas failed utterly, for it could not be built securely on the foundation inherited from the Republic of Texas.[1]

1. For useful accounts of the history of federal Indian policy in Texas, see Lena Clara

After Texas gained its independence from Mexico in 1836, its Indian policy vacillated between two extremes. President Sam Houston, who served 1836–1838 and again 1841–1844, and the last president of the Republic, Anson Jones (1844–1846), followed a policy of friendship and conciliation, even in the face of continuing Indian raids upon the settlements. President Mirabeau Buonaparte Lamar, who served between Houston's two terms, on the other hand, was determined to remove or exterminate the Indians, and he organized volunteer troops and rangers to subjugate the hostile tribes. Cherokee Indians, who had peacefully moved into east Texas from Arkansas about 1820, were driven out of Texas by military force in 1839, and other immigrant Indians were threatened with a like fate.[2] Although agents and commissioners were appointed from time to time to deal with the Indians, the Republic of Texas acknowledged no Indian rights to the land, and the Indians roamed over the central and western regions of Texas, following their nomadic hunting life. They passed freely between Texas and lands still under Mexican jurisdiction, moreover, complicating the relations of Texas with Mexico.[3] When Texas was annexed in 1845, the United States inherited an unsolved Indian problem of serious dimensions.

The federal government worked under special handicaps. In the first place, the annexation provisions left control of the public lands in Texas in

---

Koch, "The Federal Indian Policy in Texas, 1845–1860," *Southwestern Historical Quarterly* 28 (January 1925): 223–34; 28 (April 1925): 259–86; 29 (July 1925): 19–35; 29 (October 1925): 98–127; George Dewey Harmon, "The United States Indian Policy in Texas, 1845–1860," *Mississippi Valley Historical Review* 17 (December 1930): 377–403; Alban W. Hoopes, *Indian Affairs and Their Administration: With Special Reference to the Far West, 1849–1860* (Philadelphia: University of Pennsylvania Press, 1932), pp. 178–99; and Robert A. Trennert, Jr., *Alternative to Extinction: Federal Indian Policy and the Beginnings of the Reservation System, 1846–51* (Philadelphia: Temple University Press, 1975), pp. 61–93. Valuable collections of documents are *Texas Indian Papers*, ed. Dorman H. Winfrey and James M. Day, 4 vols. (Austin: Texas State Library, 1959–1961); and *The Indian Papers of Texas and the Southwest, 1825–1916*, ed. Dorman H. Winfrey and James M. Day (Austin: Pemberton Press, 1966).

2. For the history of Indian affairs under the republic, see Anna Muckleroy, "The Indian Policy of the Republic of Texas," *Southwestern Historical Quarterly* 25 (April 1922): 229–60; 26 (July 1922): 1–29; 26 (October 1922): 128–48; 26 (January 1923): 184–206; and A. K. Christian, "Mirabeau Buonaparte Lamar," *Southwestern Historical Quarterly* 24 (July 1920): 39–80. On the Texas Cherokees, see Ernest William Winkler, "The Cherokee Indians in Texas," *Quarterly of the Texas State Historical Association* 7 (October 1903): 95–165; Albert Woldert, "The Last of the Cherokees in Texas, and the Life and Death of Chief Bowles," *Chronicles of Oklahoma* 1 (June 1923): 179–226; Dorman H. Winfrey, "Chief Bowles of the Texas Cherokee," *Chronicles of Oklahoma* 32 (Spring 1954): 29–41; Mary Whatley Clarke, *Chief Bowles and the Texas Cherokees* (Norman: University of Oklahoma Press, 1971).

3. Ralph A. Smith, "Indians in American-Mexican Relations before the War of 1846," *Hispanic American Historical Review* 43 (February 1963): 34–64.

the hands of the state, not the federal government as was the case with the other states and territories. That meant that the United States assumed responsibility for Indian affairs in the new state without ownership and jurisdiction over lands that could be granted and guaranteed to Indian tribes as reservations, and it was unable, without the consent of Texas, to extend the federal trade and intercourse laws (which applied to federally controlled Indian country) for the protection of the Texas Indians from white crimes, encroachment, and trade abuses.[4]

Second, by article 11 of the Treaty of Guadalupe Hidalgo at the end of the Mexican War in 1848, the United States accepted serious obligations. It agreed to restrain the Indians from incursions into Mexico and to exact satisfaction for incursions that could not be prevented. The treaty made it unlawful for inhabitants of the United States to purchase captives or property seized by the Indians in Mexico, and the United States government agreed to rescue Mexican captives brought into the country and return them to Mexico. In addition, the treaty declared: "The sacredness of this obligation shall never be lost sight of by the said Government, when providing for the removal of the Indians from any portion of the said territories, or for it's being settled by citizens of the United States; but on the contrary special care shall then be taken not to place it's Indian occupants under the necessity of seeking new homes, by committing those invasions which the United States have solemnly obliged themselves to restrain." A clause in the original treaty obliged the United States not to furnish firearms or ammunition to the Indians, but this was struck out by the Senate. The amendment, Secretary of State James Buchanan informed Mexico, was "adopted on a principle of humanity": if the Indians could not live by the chase, they were all the more likely to raid Mexican and American settlements for sustenance. Given the lack of federal control over the affairs of Texas and New Mexico, these stipulations were never effectively carried out, and the United States, with a sigh of relief, extricated itself from the responsibilities in the Gadsden Treaty of 1853. A large part of the payment under that treaty was considered an indemnity for Indian incursions.[5]

4. One of the conditions of annexation was that Texas "shall also retain all the vacant and unappropriated lands lying within its limits, to be applied to the payment of the debts and liabilities of said Republic of Texas, and the residue of said lands, after discharging said debts and liabilities, to be disposed of as said State may direct." 5 *United States Statutes* 798; 9 *United States Statutes* 108.

5. Treaty of Guadalupe Hidalgo, February 2, 1848, in Hunter Miller, ed., *Treaties and Other International Acts of the United States*, 8 vols. (Washington, GPO, 1931–1948), 5: 219–22, 251, 256; Gadsden Treaty, December 30, 1853, ibid., 6: 296–97. A full discussion is given in J. Fred Rippy, "The Indians of the Southwest in the Diplomacy of the United States and Mexico, 1848–1853," *Hispanic American Historical Review* 2 (August 1919): 363–96. See also Paul Neff Garber, *The Gadsden Treaty* (Philadelphia: University of Pennsylvania Press, 1923), pp. 25–40.

Finally, the military forces available to the federal government, by which it might have enforced by military might what persuasion and diplomacy failed to accomplish, were never numerous enough to patrol the long frontier lines and the even longer international boundary with anything more than minimal effect. In 1849 the army completed a string of posts along the Mexican boundary and at the same time established a cordon of forts along the line of Texas settlement from Fort Worth on the Trinity River to Fort Martin Scott west of Austin, with the purpose of keeping marauding Indians out of the settled areas. The frontier posts, manned largely by infantry, were unable to restrain the mounted Indians, nor were they effective in holding back the tide of white settlers. By 1851 the Texans had moved across the defense line and were demanding a new chain of posts. To satisfy them, Fort Belknap was established on the Brazos River west of Fort Worth, and a new series of posts appeared on a line running southwest to Fort Clark near the Rio Grande. Some of the earlier forts were closed and their men and supplies moved to the new establishments. With these forts and others built throughout the 1850s to protect communication lines, the troops tried valiantly but unsuccessfully to maintain peace.[6]

Despite the peculiarities of the situation, the federal government proceeded pretty much according to the main outlines of its developing policy for dealing with the new Indians it encountered as the result of western territorial acquisitions. In September 1845 it began by dispatching a peace commission to conciliate the Indians. The two commissioners, Pierce M. Butler and M. G. Lewis, called a council of the tribes in Texas for January 1846, but it was not until May that the Indians—Comanches, Anadarkos, Caddos, Lipans, and others—assembled on the Brazos River at a place called Council Springs. By that time the war with Mexico had commenced, and the need to keep the restive Indians peaceful was of great importance.[7] On May 15 the tribes signed a treaty with the traditional provisions: the Indians acknowledged themselves to be under the exclusive protection of

6. A brief summary of the military defense is given in Robert M. Utley, *Frontiersmen in Blue: The United States Army and the Indian, 1848–1865* (New York: Macmillan Company, 1967), pp. 71–75. A more detailed account appears in W. C. Holden, "Frontier Defense, 1846–1860," *West Texas Historical Association Year Book* 6 (1930): 35–64. See also Rupert Norval Richardson, *The Frontier of Northwest Texas, 1846 to 1876: Advance and Defense by the Pioneer Settlers of the Cross Timbers and Prairies* (Glendale, California: Arthur H. Clark Company, 1963); Averam B. Bender, *The March of Empire: Frontier Defense in the Southwest, 1848–1860* (Lawrence: University of Kansas Press, 1952).

7. Details of the negotiations are given in Butler and Lewis to William Medill, August 8, 1846, *Senate Report* no. 171, 30–1, serial 512, pp. 29–37. The report is printed also in *House Document* no. 76, 29–2, serial 500. For the record kept by a Cherokee Indian who accompanied Butler and Lewis, see Grant Foreman, ed., "The Journal of Elijah Hicks," *Chronicles of Oklahoma* 13 (March 1935): 68–99.

the United States and agreed to keep peace with the Americans and with other Indians; the United States assumed sole right to regulate trade and intercourse with them; the Indians agreed to give up all captives; punishment for crimes between Indians and whites was provided for (there was a separate article on horse stealing); the United States promised to erect trading houses and agencies on the borders of the tribes; special provision was made to prohibit the liquor traffic; and there was, finally, the usual provision, at the discretion of the president, for blacksmiths, schoolteachers, and "preachers of the gospel." Other articles, attempting to define the jurisdiction of the United States and the state of Texas in Indian affairs, were stricken out on the insistence of the Texas delegation in Congress, so that the treaty could at length be ratified and proclaimed on March 8, 1847.[8]

Even before ratification, initial steps were taken to provide for the Texas Indians. On March 3, 1847, Congress authorized $20,000 for presents, $3,650 for a special agent and two interpreters for a year, and $10,000 "to carry into effect the treaty with the Comanches and other tribes of Indians."[9]

The agent appointed, Robert S. Neighbors, was an especially happy choice. Neighbors, who had moved to Texas in 1836 when he was twenty, had served with distinction in the Texas Revolution and under the Republic of Texas (as army officer and Indian agent). He understood the Indians' situation, was sympathetic to their plight, and stood irrevocably committed to protecting their interests; he acted as an effective and persuasive diplomat under conditions that gave him little to work with.[10] Neighbors was a realist in appraising the situation. He wrote to the commissioner of Indian affairs soon after he took office:

> For the last few months our settlements have extended very rapidly, and, unless checked, will continue to do so; also, frequently large parties of surveyors penetrate many miles into the country now occupied by the Indians. These movements keep the Camanches and many other tribes in continual excitement; and unless some measures can be adopted by the department to check the surveyors, it will finally lead to serious difficulties. From these causes the Camanches are in a doubtful state of quietness, and there is no telling how soon there will be a general outbreak among them. The present

8. Kappler, pp. 554–56; Grant Foreman, "The Texas Comanche Treaty of 1846," *Southwestern Historical Quarterly* 51 (April 1948): 313–32.

9. 9 *United States Statutes* 204.

10. Kenneth F. Neighbours, "Robert S. Neighbors in Texas, 1836–1859: A Quarter Century of Frontier Problems" (Ph.D. dissertation, University of Texas, 1955); Neighbours, "Robert S. Neighbors and the Founding of Texas Indian Reservations," *West Texas Historical Association Year Book* 31 (1955): 65–74.

laws of Texas do not acknowledge that the Indians have any right of soil; and those persons holding land claims contend that they have the privilege of locating wherever they choose.[11]

Neighbors, nevertheless, believed that peace was possible. He called a great council of the tribes at the end of September 1847 in order to explain the treaty of 1846 and to allay their fears, and he persuaded Governor J. Pinckney Henderson of Texas to reinstate the laws of the Republic of Texas regarding intercourse with the Indians and to designate a temporary line above the settlements separating Indians from whites.[12] But with the withdrawal of heavy troop concentrations in Texas at the end of the Mexican War and the continued advance of the surveyors and settlers came new raids and hostility along the frontier.

RESERVATIONS FOR TEXAS INDIANS

There seemed to be only one practicable solution. Texas must grant lands for reservations on which the Indians could be settled and turned into farmers and where the federal government could protect them from lawless whites. All the responsible federal officials were of one mind on this. Neighbors in March 1849 outlined his own specifications for a workable plan: (1) a boundary line established by treaty, which would extinguish Indian claims to all the land needed by Texas; (2) acquisition from Texas by the United States of sufficient territory to establish a permanent location for the Indians; (3) extension of the federal trade and intercourse laws over the Indians of Texas; (4) a general agency, with at least three subagents; and (5) necessary military posts in the Indian country. John H. Rollins, the Whig who succeeded Neighbors when his term of office expired in 1849, came to the same conclusion: "Nothing short of a country for the Indians, over which the laws of the United States regulating our Indian intercourse and relations were extended, together with a temporary support for the Indians," he wrote, "could be safely adopted as a permanent policy." Like many others, he argued, too, on the basis of economy, asserting that "it would be incalculably less expensive to purchase a country for the Indians, remove them to it, and support them until they had made some advance in agriculture, than to deprive them by force of a country which they very

11. Neighbors to William Medill, June 2, 1847, CIA Report, 1847, serial 503, pp. 893–94. The full report, pp. 892–96, gives an excellent picture of the conditions and how Neighbors met them.

12. Neighbors to Medill, October 12, 1847, CIA Report, 1847, serial 503, pp. 903–6; Neighbors to Medill, November 18, 1847, *Senate Report* no. 171, 30–1, serial 512, pp. 9–10.

properly thought their own, to say nothing of the duty of humanity, or the sudden and violent interruption which a prolonged and uncertain war would cause to the prosperity and progress of this and other frontier States." George T. Howard, who became agent when Rollins died in September 1851, spoke of "the absolute necessity for some provision being made for the settlement of these Indians, and for supplying them with the necessary means to commence the cultivation of the soil." He believed so strongly in the need that he recommended buying or leasing land from private individuals if Texas did not grant some reservation lands. "Until a territory is procured for them," he wrote, "all attempts to control and civilize them will prove abortive." When Neighbors was reappointed special agent for Texas Indians in May 1853, he began to work with unabated energy for the realization of a reservation system.[13]

The agents on the spot, judging the conditions as they experienced them firsthand, were seconded by the commissioners of Indian affairs and the secretaries of the interior. These men in Washington no doubt were influenced by what the highly respected agents were proposing, but it cannot be overlooked that the plans for Texas reservations accorded precisely with the philosophy of the general government for handling Indian relations. The Indians were to be persuaded to stop their hunting over a vast area, claiming lands that were increasingly sought by white settlers; to settle as agriculturalists on limited reserves out of the way of the whites, where they would soon become self-sufficient again in the new economic pattern; and to adopt the cultural attributes of white civilization through education and Christianization. The statements of Medill, Brown, and Lea and their successors were not pious abstractions; these men advocated what they considered a practical solution, one that as Christian officials they had judged successful in dealing with tribes that had moved to the new frontier west of the Mississippi. They saw no reason to doubt its efficacy in dealing with the wild tribes of Texas.[14]

In 1850 Congress authorized two more agents to serve in Texas and thirty thousand dollars for procuring information, for collecting statistics, and for making treaties with and giving presents to the Indian tribes on the borders of Mexico. The instructions to the three-man commission appointed for these purposes—Charles S. Todd, Robert B. Campbell, and

13. Neighbors to William J. Worth, March 7, 1849, CIA Report, 1849, serial 550, p. 964; Rollins to C. S. Todd, March 25, 1851, CIA Report, 1851, serial 613, p. 518; Howard to Luke Lea, June 1, 1852, quoted in Hoopes, *Indian Affairs and Their Administration*, p. 187; Howard to Lea, August 15, 1852, CIA Report, 1852, serial 658, p. 430.

14. There is an especially pointed statement of this policy in CIA Report, 1848, serial 537, p. 386. For remarks on Texas Indian policy, see CIA Report, 1847, serial 513, pp. 751–52; CIA Report, 1848, serial 537, p. 408; CIA Report, 1849, serial 550, pp. 941–42; CIA Report, 1850, serial 587, p. 44.

Oliver Temple—said little about treaties but emphasized the necessity of gathering information about the attitude of the Indians toward the United States, about where to locate agencies, and about what kind of presents were necessary, information that would be useful guidance to the Indian Office in determining how to deal with the Indians of Texas. The commissioners were told to inquire into "everything relating to the character of the several tribes: their manners, habits, customs, mode of living—whether by agriculture, the chase, or otherwise; the extent of their civilization, their religion or religious ceremonies—whether Christian or Pagan; what their religious rites; whether marriages are held sacred among them, and whether a plurality of wives is tolerated." In addition, they were to report on the topography and resources of the country and the nature of Indian claims and tenure. Unfortunately, little came from the commission, for Congress refused to appropriate additional funds for it and abrogated its authority to negotiate treaties. Its report was brief and of limited value, but the commissioners did urge settling the Indians within definite boundaries, a "salutary and philanthropic policy [that] may tend to their civilization, by leading them to cultivate the soil, to acquire individual property, and domesticate themselves, so far at least as to become herdsmen, instead of living like wandering Arabs."[15]

Although Congress in 1850 extended the trade and intercourse laws over New Mexico and Utah territories, it did not do so for the state of Texas, and Lea felt obliged to instruct the agents in Texas: "You will . . . have no right to resort to force in the execution of your official duties; and an attempt to do so would not only be without the sanction of law, but might be regarded as derogatory to the rights and dignity of a sovereign State. Hence the means you will employ in carrying out the views and policy of the Government must be altogether of a mild and persuasive character." Lea pleaded for action in setting aside lands for the Indians. The amount of reserved territory, he asserted, would be small. Without it the Indians were forced either to starve or to steal, nor should Texas complain about depredations that the state itself was largely responsible for. The Indians, he said in 1851, "certainly have the right to live somewhere; and nowhere, more certainly, than on the lands which they and their fathers have occupied for countless generations." He insisted that reservations were "indispensable to a proper adjustment of Indian affairs" in Texas.[16]

15. 9 *United States Statutes* 555, 556; A. S. Loughery, acting commissioner of Indian affairs, to Todd, Campbell, and Temple, October 15, 1850, CIA Report, 1850, serial 587, pp. 153–55; Luke Lea to Todd, Campbell, and Temple, April 3, 1851, CIA Report, 1851, serial 613, pp. 301–2; Todd, Campbell, and Temple to Lea, August 23, .1851, ibid., pp. 302–6.

16. CIA Report, 1851, serial 613, p. 272; Lea to John H. Rollins, John A. Rogers, and Jesse Stem, November 25, 1850, ibid., p. 515; CIA Report, 1852, serial 658, p. 299.

As conditions worsened in Texas, the state finally saw the necessity of what federal officials had been requesting for almost a decade. After giving up hope that all Indians could be removed from the state, it moved slowly toward the reservation system. In 1851, a joint committee on Indian affairs of the Texas legislature proposed such a plan. The report, heavily influenced by the committee chairman (none other than Robert Neighbors, who had been elected to the house after his removal as Indian agent), offered the following proposal:

> The State could adopt no better or more humane plan to relieve our border citizens from the petty thefts and depredations committed by those Indians residing in our State in detached bands, and under the control of no direct agency by setting apart small tracts or parcels of land near the United States military posts selected on our frontier, to be occupied by these Indians, subject to the pleasure of the State. By adopting the plan proposed, they will at once settle down, cultivate the soil, turn attention to stockraising, etc., instead of depending on the chase, which, at least, affords an uncertain and scanty subsistence, and often drives them to acts of theft upon the stock of our citizens, to supply the deficiency required for the support of their old men and families.[17]

Little by little the idea matured, for the existing state of affairs could not continue much longer.

Finally, on February 6, 1854, the Texas legislature offered reservations for the Indians. The law provided that up to twelve leagues of land be set aside for use of the Indians within the state. The land, to be selected and surveyed by the United States, was to be laid out so far as possible in square tracts, numbering three or fewer, and these were to be located no more than twenty miles east or south of the northernmost line of United States military posts. Jurisdiction over the territory selected for the Indians was ceded to the United States government "so far as to enable it to extend any act of Congress now existing, or hereafter to be passed, regulating trade and intercourse with the Indian tribes," but the state retained its jurisdiction over non-Indians. The federal government was authorized to settle the Indians on the reserve, "exercise entire control and jurisdiction" over them, and establish necessary agencies and military posts. The lands would revert to the state should the Indians abandon them.[18]

---

17. *Senate Journals of the State of Texas,* 1851–1852, quoted in Harmon, "Indian Policy in Texas," p. 389. Harmon discusses the moves toward reservation grants on pp. 387–94.

18. Williamson S. Oldham and George W. White, *A Digest of the General Statute Laws of the State of Texas* (Austin: John Marshall and Company, 1859), pp. 238–39. By a

With these provisions, Neighbors and his superiors in Washington moved to establish their long-desired colonies. In the summer of 1854 the agent, in company with Captain R. B. Marcy of the United States army, selected two reserves. One, of 37,152 acres, was located at the main fork of the Brazos River about ten miles south of Fort Belknap. Another, of 18,576 acres, was located on the Clear Fork of the Brazos at Camp Cooper.[19] It took some time to gather the Indians, but in March 1855 the semi-agricultural tribes —Caddos, Wacos, Tawakonis, Anadarkos, Tonkawas, Keechies, and a few Delawares—began to colonize the Brazos reserve. In September Neighbors counted 794 Indians located there, and he spoke enthusiastically of their agricultural progress. "There can be no doubt of the success of the policy," he wrote, "and I would earnestly commend it to the fostering care of the general government as the most humane and economical that could possibly be followed, and one, that, in a very short time, will relieve our frontier forever from the scenes of murder and theft that have retarded the extension of civilization for so many years." The Brazos reservation appeared to fulfill all the agent's hopes, as year by year he reported more Indians settled, more fields under cultivation, and more crops harvested. The hopes were not only for tranquility on the frontier, but for the Indians' advancement as well, and Neighbors was not disappointed. "There has been great improvement for the last year in the moral and physical condition of the Indians now settled," he wrote in 1856. "They are gradually falling into the customs and dress of the white man; and by being well clothed, having houses to live in, and [being] relieved from the continued anxieties attending a roving life, their health has greatly improved, and they now, for the first time for several years, begin to raise healthy children." A school for the Indian children was successfully begun, too. The glowing reports, however, referred largely to the Brazos reserve; the Comanche reserve, with In-

---

law of February 4, 1856, Texas provided another five leagues of land west of the Pecos River as a reservation for the Indians in that area. Ibid., pp. 239–40. This third reservation was never established because the difficulties with the first two precluded extension of the reservation system in Texas, and Congress prohibited the use of appropriations for the new reservation. 11 *United States Statutes* 400; CIA Report, 1859, serial 1023, p. 383. By a law of July 28, 1856, Texas extended the intercourse laws of the United States insofar as they prohibited the introduction of liquor into the Indian country for a distance of ten miles from the boundary lines of the reservations. Oldham and White, *Laws of the State of Texas*, p. 240.

19. Kenneth F. Neighbours, "The Marcy-Neighbors Exploration of the Headwaters of the Brazos and Wichita Rivers in 1854," *Panhandle-Plains Historical Review* 27 (1954): 26–46; W. Eugene Hollon, *Beyond the Cross Timbers: The Travels of Randolph B. Marcy, 1812–1887* (Norman: University of Oklahoma Press, 1955), pp. 169–86; R. B. Marcy, *Thirty Years of Army Life on the Border* (New York: Harper and Brothers, 1866), pp. 170–214.

dians less ready to settle down, made much less progress, both in numbers and in agricultural production.[20]

The letters of Neighbors and the other agents convinced the officials in Washington for a time of the program's success. But the legal problems of protecting the Indians on the reservations were never solved. Although the Texas legislature had done what it could to provide federal jurisdiction over the reservations, Congress, for its part, never officially extended the trade and intercourse laws to Texas, so that federal officials had no weapon against the whites who were introducing liquor and in other ways abusing the Indians.[21]

The location of hundreds of Indians on the two reserves did not solve the Indian problem in Texas. Nonreservation Indians, many if not most of whom came into the state from Mexico, New Mexico, or Indian territory, continued their depredations. In the minds of the enraged Texans it was difficult to draw a sharp distinction between those Indians and Indians on the reservations. Indeed, many Texans believed that reservation Comanches were guilty of raids and other outrages. Tension increased as the border warfare heightened, for neither state nor federal officials were able to end the attacks. What hopes for peace there might have been were destroyed on December 27, 1858, when a group of whites attacked a party of peaceful Indians on a hunting expedition and murdered seven men and women in their sleep. Neighbors reported it as "the most cold-blooded murder of women and children that has ever transpired since the revolution made Texas a republic, and exceeds all the brutality attributed to the wild Comanches." He saw the act as part of an "organized conspiracy against the Indian policy of the general government, for the purpose of breaking up the reserves in Texas." The whites feared retaliation from the Indians, and some sought openly to attack the Indians on the reserves, who dared not leave their limits and clustered around the agency in fear.[22]

20. Neighbors to Charles E. Mix, September 10, 1855, CIA Report, 1855, serial 810, pp. 497–502; Neighbors to George W. Manypenny, September 18, 1856, CIA Report, 1856, serial 875, pp. 724–27; Neighbors to Mix, September 16, 1858, CIA Report, 1858, serial 974, pp. 524–27. Descriptions of the reservations are given in Kenneth F. Neighbours, "Chapters from the History of Texas Indian Reservations," *West Texas Historical Association Year Book* 33 (1957): 3–16. There is an account of the Comanche reservation in Rupert N. Richardson, "The Comanche Reservation in Texas," *West Texas Historical Association Year Book* 5 (1929): 43–65, and in his *The Comanche Barrier to South Plains Settlement: A Century and a Half of Savage Resistance to the Advancing White Frontier* (Glendale, California: Arthur H. Clark Company, 1933), pp. 211–66. For an account of the Indian-white contact focused on the Comanches, see T. R. Fehrenbach, *Comanches: The Destruction of a People* (New York: Alfred A. Knopf, 1974).

21. The agents and commissioners of Indian affairs continued to call for congressional action; see, for example, CIA Report, 1858, serial 974, pp. 359–60, 529–36.

22. Neighbors to J. W. Denver, January 30, 1859, CIA Report, 1859, serial 1023,

The futility of the government's reservation policy was soon apparent. In February 1859 Neighbors urged the immediate removal of the reservation Indians outside the borders of Texas to land recently obtained from the Choctaws and Chickasaws. Even if the United States poured in military forces to protect the reserves, the Indians under the circumstances could hardly progress in the arts of civilization. At the end of March the Indian Office directed the agents to make the move so that the Indians could be "protected from lawless violence, and effective measures adopted for their domestication and improvement," and accordingly instructions were sent in mid-June.[23] After a survey of the proposed lands with some of the chiefs and the superintendent of the Southern Superintendency, Elias Rector, who would assume responsibility for the Indians in their new home, the move was made. In August, protected by United States cavalry on the march, 1,050 Indians from the Brazos reserve and 380 Comanches migrated to Indian Territory—out of the "heathen land of Texas," "out of the land of the Philistines," as Neighbors described it to his wife.[24] Having seen his charges to the new reservation, Neighbors returned to Fort Belknap. He had long been under attack by certain Texans for his defense of Indian rights, and on September 14, 1859, as he went about his business in town, he was murdered by a stranger.[25]

The reservation as a panacea was thus strikingly ineffective in Texas. The federal government, unwilling to tangle with the Texans, who emphasized states' rights, was delayed in establishing reservations for the Indians because of state control of public lands. When, through a grant by the state, land was set aside for the Indians, the government proved unable to protect the settled Indians from lawless and aggressive Texas frontiersmen. Even if it had forced a showdown, the agitation and resulting tension would have weakened if not destroyed the conditions under which an agricultural civilization program, one of the primary goals of reservation life, would have

---

p. 595; numerous documents that tell the story of white aggression against the Indians are printed ibid., pp. 588–632.

23. Neighbors to Denver, February 14, 1859, CIA Report, 1859, serial 1023, p. 605; Mix to Neighbors, March 30, 1859, ibid., pp. 631–32; A. B. Greenwood to Neighbors, June 11, 1859, ibid., pp. 650–51.

24. Neighbors to Greenwood, July 24, 1859, ibid., p. 687; Neighbors to Lizzie A. Neighbors, August 8, 1859, quoted in Koch, "Indian Policy in Texas," p. 122; Kenneth F. Neighbours, "Indian Exodus out of Texas in 1859," *West Texas Historical Association Year Book* 36 (1960): 80–97. Texas in 1875 finally declared the reserves abandoned and provided for squatters and other homesteaders on the lands. John Sayles and Henry Sayles, *Early Laws of Texas,* 3 vols. (St. Louis: Gilbert Book Company, 1888), 3: 301–3.

25. Statement of M. Leeper, September 15, 1859, CIA Report, 1859, serial 1023, pp. 701–2; Kenneth F. Neighbours, "The Assassination of Robert S. Neighbors," *West Texas Historical Association Year Book* 34 (1958): 38–49.

been possible. The federal government chose to retreat instead, holding its policy intact.

The removal, of course, brought no peace to Texas. Marauding Indians devastated the settlements, and defense of the Texas frontier remained a serious problem until the ultimate subjugation of the southern plains tribes in the 1870s.

INDIAN AFFAIRS IN NEW MEXICO

The United States began its formal relations with the Indians of New Mexico during the Mexican War, and its relations in the first instance were primarily military.[26] The advance of General Stephen Watts Kearny into the region in 1846 as part of the American strategy in the Mexican War set the pattern for government action. Kearny's column came as a conquering army, promising to bring peace and order to a land torn by depredations and fear. The Pueblo Indians in their settled towns along the Rio Grande were beset by their hostile Navajo neighbors and threatened periodically by the warlike Apaches and Comanches raiding from the southern plains, and they hastened to greet the American soldiers with gestures of friendship. The Americans looked upon the Pueblos, who had been considered citizens by the Mexican government, as "civilized Indians," living in organized communities and dependent upon agriculture for subsistence.

Quite different were the "wild," more nomadic Apaches and Navajos, tending their sheep and horses but living in large part by raids on the Mexicans. It was these Indians who created such an uproar in the region and who were the basic problem for the United States government. Kearny came with a strong feeling of American superiority, which he expected the Indians to recognize, and he hoped to gain support for his occupation from the Mexicans by his offers of protection against the hostile Indians. He told the people of Las Vegas, the first major settlement he encountered, on August 15, 1846: "From the Mexican government you have never received protection. The Apaches and the Navajhoes come down from the mountains and carry off your sheep, and even your women, whenever they

26. The best studies of early Indian affairs in New Mexico are Trennert, *Alternative to Extinction,* pp. 94–130, and Hoopes, *Indian Affairs and Their Administration,* pp. 161–78. The place of Indian affairs in the whole political picture can be seen in Howard R. Lamar, *The Far Southwest, 1846: A Territorial History* (New Haven: Yale University Press, 1966), pp. 56–108. Military activities against the Indians are studied in Utley, *Frontiersmen in Blue,* pp. 142–74, and Bender, *March of Empire,* pp. 149–70. See also Averam B. Bender, "Frontier Defense in the Territory of New Mexico, 1846–1853," *New Mexico Historical Review* 9 (July 1934): 249–72, and "Frontier Defense in the Territory of New Mexico, 1853–1861," ibid. (October 1934): 345–73.

please. My government will correct all this. It will keep off the Indians, protect you in your persons and property." As he moved victorious to Santa Fe, he repeated his assurances, proclaiming that he would protect the peaceful inhabitants against the Indians.[27]

There was no trouble with the Pueblos, whose delegates met peacefully with Kearny and convinced him of their friendship. The other tribes were less easily handled. Colonel Alexander W. Doniphan moved into Navajo country and negotiated with the chiefs. An agreement was signed on March 22, for the Navajos were initially impressed by the American power and agreed to stop their raids against the Mexicans and to return captives and stolen property.[28] Peace seemed to be at hand as Kearny proceeded on to California and Doniphan into Mexico, leaving Charles Bent on the spot in charge of a provisional territorial government set up by Kearny. Bent made recommendations to the Indian Office for the appointment of agents and subagents and urged that a delegation of Indians be sent to Washington to impress them with the power of the United States. But the territory was not yet a part of the United States, and the Indian Office could not act. Continued military control was the only alternative.[29]

It did not take long for Indian unrest to reappear. Mexicans, unhappy with the American occupation, plotted to overthrow the government and enlisted Pueblo support. An uprising at Taos on January 19, 1847, killed Governor Bent and other officials and ended the idea of peaceful occupation, although the revolt was quickly put down by military force. Soon the wild Indians renewed their depredations, and Indian affairs in New Mexico deteriorated, as the success of Navajo and Apache raids emboldened other tribes to attack the Americans, especially along the Santa Fe Trail. American military force in New Mexico was not enough to guarantee the peace that Kearny had so sanguinely promised.[30]

The end of the Mexican War and the ratification of the Treaty of Guadalupe Hidalgo in 1848 did not greatly change the military picture in New Mexico, although the provision by which the United States agreed to stop Indian raids into Mexico added considerably to the responsibilities of the

27. W. H. Emory, "Notes of a Military Reconnaissance from Fort Leavenworth, in Missouri, to San Diego, in California," *Senate Executive Document* no. 7, 30–1, serial 505, p. 27; "Proclamation to the Inhabitants of New Mexico by Brigadier General S. W. Kearny," August 22, 1846, *House Executive Document* no. 19, 29–2, serial 499, pp. 20–21.

28. An account of Doniphan's expedition is in John Taylor Hughes, *Doniphan's Expedition: Containing an Account of the Expedition against New Mexico* (Cincinnati: U. P. James, 1847), reprinted in William Elsey Connelley, *Doniphan's Expedition and the Conquest of New Mexico and California* (Topeka, 1907), pp. 115–524. The text of the agreement appears on p. 307.

29. Trennert, *Alternative to Extinction*, p. 103.

30. Ibid., pp. 104–12.

army commanders. Lieutenant Colonel John M. Washington, the new military governor, intended to pacify the hostile tribes and then make them accept American control, in line with the conventional Indian policy of the day. "The period has arrived," he wrote to the War Department in February 1849, "when they [the Indians] must restrain themselves within prescribed limits and cultivate the earth for an honest livelyhood, or, be destroyed. . . . The particular location and extent of these limits and the inducements held out for a change from their present roving habits to the pursuit of agriculture, from the savage state to that of civilization, are well worthy of attention."[31]

The pacifying was no easy task. In all sections of the region Indian raids continued, and the citizens were enraged. "We are now," wrote one of them to the secretary of war in July 1849, "in actual war with four of the most powerful and numerous tribes on the continent, all living in close proximity to the territory and all making daily incursions into our settlements."[32] Prodded by such criticism, Governor Washington began a military operation against the Navajos in August, penetrating into their country. A first meeting with three chiefs broke up in a fight in which one Navajo was killed, but after a display of military force in Canyon de Chelly, Washington negotiated a treaty with other chiefs, who agreed to recognize American jurisdiction and to submit to the trade and intercourse laws, to return captives and stolen property and remain at peace, and to allow the federal government to determine their boundaries.[33] No sooner had the expedition returned to Santa Fe, however, than the Indians renewed their raids.

When the new Whig president Zachary Taylor entered office in 1849, the government provided for civilian administration of Indian affairs in New Mexico by transferring a midwestern agency to Santa Fe and appointing a South Carolina politician, James S. Calhoun, to be Indian agent.[34] Calhoun proved to be a man of marked ability who exhibited deep concern for the Indians and intelligently promoted an Indian policy that would end

31. Washington to Roger Jones, February 3, 1849, quoted ibid., p. 113.
32. Remarks of William S. Messervy, quoted ibid., p. 114.
33. Documents regarding Washington's Navajo expedition are in *House Executive Document* no. 5, 31–1, serial 569, pp. 104–15. The treaty is printed ibid., pp. 113–14. Continuing relations with the Navajos are studied in Frank D. Reeve, "The Government and the Navaho, 1846–1858," *New Mexico Historical Review* 14 (January 1939): 82–114. See also L. R. Bailey, *The Long Walk: A History of the Navajo Wars, 1846–68* (Los Angeles: Westernlore Press, 1964), pp. 14–20.
34. Calhoun's letter of appointment, April 7, 1849, is in *House Executive Document* no. 17, 31–1, serial 573, pp. 194–96. His early reports to the secretary of the interior and the commissioner of Indian affairs appear ibid., pp. 198–229. The standard work on Calhoun is Annie Heloise Abel, ed., *The Official Correspondence of James S. Calhoun While Indian Agent at Santa Fe and Superintendent of Indian Affairs in New Mexico* (Washington: GPO, 1915).

the troubles in the Southwest. He arrived in Santa Fe just as Governor Washington was preparing to launch his expedition into Navajo country, and he accompanied the troops in order to support the commander's attempt to impress the Indians with the authority of the United States. Before the year was out Calhoun had succeeded in negotiating with the Utes a treaty similar to that signed with the Navajos; it included promises by the Indians "to build up pueblos, or to settle in such other manner as will enable them most successfully to cultivate the soil, and pursue such other industrial pursuits as will best promote their happiness and prosperity," to cease their "roving and rambling habits," and to support themselves "by their own industry, aided and directed as it may be by the wisdom, justice, and humanity of the American people."[35]

Calhoun's proposal for adjusting Indian affairs in New Mexico was a display of military force that would end Indian depredations, then settlement of the Indians on reservations modeled after the Pueblo towns. The agent worked out a specific plan. Separated tracts of land, at least a hundred miles apart, would be assigned to the Navajos, Apaches, Utes, and Comanches. The Indians would be supplied with subsistence until they had learned to become self-sufficient. It would cost money, Calhoun admitted, but as he told the Indian Office, "to establish order in this territory, you must either submit to these heavy expenditures, or exterminate the mass of these Indians."[36]

Calhoun's plan depended on military force to keep the Indians on their reservations, and he called for the establishment of military posts in the Indian country. But he also demanded civilian agents for the tribes, to aid him in the civilizing aspects of his proposal. "The presence of Agents in various places in the Indian country," he told the commissioner of Indian affairs, "is indispensably necessary—their presence is demanded by every principle of humanity—by every generous obligation of kindness—of protection, and good government throughout this vast territory." He was especially insistent that agents be supplied to the Pueblos, not only to aid them in their agriculture, but to protect them from encroaching whites; and he urged the extension of the trade and intercourse laws to New Mexico so that the agents would have authority for their protective action.[37]

The hands of the commissioner of Indian affairs were tied, however, as long as New Mexico did not have a civil government and remained under military control, and the conflict between civilian and military officers over Indian affairs complicated an already difficult situation. The Indians

35. Kappler, pp. 585–87.

36. Calhoun to Orlando Brown, February 3, 1850, Abel, *Correspondence of Calhoun*, p. 141; Calhoun to Brown, March 30, 1850, ibid., p. 179.

37. Calhoun to Medill, October 15, 1849, ibid., pp. 56–57; Calhoun to Brown, November 16, 1849, ibid., pp. 78–81.

boldly kept up their attacks, and the army, forced to rely on infantry when cavalry were desperately needed against the mounted Indians, could do little but lament its own ineffectiveness. In addition, the strong movement of the New Mexicans for immediate statehood disturbed the Pueblos, who feared that the formation of a state before federal protection had been extended to them would result in loss of the civil and property rights they had enjoyed under Mexican rule and under American military government.[38]

Congress, caught up in the sectional controversy that emerged with the Mexican War, denied the New Mexican demands for statehood. Instead, on September 9, 1850, the Territory of New Mexico was established as part of the Compromise of 1850. The Senate, on January 7, 1851, confirmed the appointment of James S. Calhoun as first territorial governor and ex officio superintendent of Indian affairs, and at the end of February Congress authorized four Indian agents for New Mexico and extended the trade and intercourse laws over the territory.[39]

The military component of Indian affairs in New Mexico, nevertheless, continued to be of great moment. In November 1849 Secretary of War George W. Crawford detailed Colonel George A. McCall of the Third Infantry to investigate conditions in New Mexico. McCall's report of July 15, 1850, gave a detailed account of the geographical characteristics and agricultural capabilities of the land, of the Indians and their way of life, and of the possibilities of changing the ways of the various tribes. The Navajos he thought "might in a short time by judicious management be induced to give up their roving habits and settle themselves in permanent towns in the vicinity of their fields." At the other extreme, he wrote of the Jicarilla Apaches: "This band is considered as incorrigible, and it is believed they will continue to rob and murder our citizens until they are exterminated. I know of no means that could be employed to reclaim them." He noted how ignorant all the Indians were of the power of the United States and urged that groups of them be invited to Washington to see the "means and resources of the country to carry on a war."[40]

McCall's report called for military posts in the Indian country, and the War Department adopted his proposals. Colonel Edwin V. Sumner, who assumed military command in New Mexico, was directed to chastise the hostile Indians and move his troops out of the towns of the territory into the Indian country. Calhoun heartily agreed, for once the posts were estab-

38. The statehood movement is discussed in Trennert, *Alternative to Extinction*, pp. 122–23, and in more detail in Lamar, *Far Southwest*, pp. 73–82.

39. Abel, *Correspondence of Calhoun*, p. 296; 9 *United States Statutes* 447, 587.

40. On McCall, his work, and his reports, see George Archibald McCall, *New Mexico in 1850: A Military View*, ed. Robert W. Frazer (Norman: University of Oklahoma Press, 1968). The quotations are from pp. 100, 105, 108.

lished among the Indians, he could assign the agents to the tribes to begin the program of civilization. Sumner proceeded with the program. In 1851 he established Fort Union east of Santa Fe, as a depot for army supplies coming into the territory and as a base for troops sent out to protect the Santa Fe Trail, and Fort Defiance in the Navajo country. New posts near El Paso (Fort Fillmore) and at Valverde south of Albuquerque (Fort Conrad) placed more troops among the Indians.[41]

While the military policy was being implemented, Calhoun began placing his agents. Early in 1852 a Navajo agency was established at Fort Defiance and one was opened near Ojo Caliente for the southern Apaches. Here the agents began to distribute the seeds and farming implements that were to start the Indians on the way to becoming farmers.[42] At the time of Calhoun's untimely death in June 1852, the application of the new policy in New Mexico was well begun.

On July 1, 1852, a treaty was negotiated with the Mescalero Apaches including the typical provisions. The Indians declared "that they are lawfully and exclusively under the laws, jurisdiction, and government of the United States of America, and to its power and authority they do submit" and agreed to "perpetual peace and amity" with the government and people of the United States. The Indians bound themselves to treat Americans honestly and humanely, to allow free passage through their lands, and "to conform in all things to the laws, rules, and regulations" of the United States in regard to Indian tribes. Moreover, the treaty authorized the United States to "designate, settle, and adjust their territorial boundaries, and pass and execute in their territory such laws as may be deemed conducive to the prosperity and happiness" of the Indians. In return, the United States would grant to the Indians "donations, presents, and implements, and adopt such other liberal and humane measures as said government may deem meet and proper." Against the protestations of the Apache chiefs, the treaty included a provision that Indian raids into Mexico were to stop.[43]

However inappropriate such an idealistic treaty may have been in the circumstances, peace was maintained in New Mexico for two years; but Calhoun's successors were soon plagued with the old troubles. Although the Gadsden Purchase treaty eliminated the responsibility of the United

---

41. Sumner's operations and Calhoun's reaction are treated in Trennert, *Alternative to Extinction*, pp. 127–30. See also Robert M. Utley, "Fort Union and the Santa Fe Trail," *New Mexico Historical Review* 36 (January 1961): 36–48, and Bailey, *Long Walk*, pp. 25–39.

42. Data on the establishment of the agencies in the New Mexico Superintendency are given in Edward E. Hill, *The Office of Indian Affairs, 1824–1880: Historical Sketches* (New York: Clearwater Publishing Company, 1974), pp. 110–16.

43. Kappler, pp. 598–600.

States to prevent raids into Mexico, the new territory included more western Apaches within the boundaries of the United States—Indians who were not very amenable to the government's Indian policy.[44] In 1854 a war with the Jicarilla Apaches broke the peace, and other tribes were restless. The Utes attacked settlers on the upper Arkansas and Rio Grande, and military forces were sent out in early 1855 to subdue them. At the same time trouble with the Mescalero Apaches broke out, and army troops invaded their country. New military posts were built along the Rio Grande and in other trouble spots.[45]

The next move came from Congress, which in the summer of 1854 appropriated $30,000 for the negotiation of treaties with the Apaches, Navajos, and Utes in New Mexico. The money provided the opportunity to apply the policy that was maturing in the mind of the commissioner of Indian affairs, George W. Manypenny, who believed that the only solution was to extend to New Mexico (and to its sister territory, Utah) the system of reservations that was being developed elsewhere.[46]

David Meriwether, who had become governor in 1853, negotiated a series of treaties with the tribes in the summer of 1855, which embodied Manypenny's principles. All the treaties were quite similar, and the treaty with the Capote Utes on August 8 can be taken as an example. The Utes agreed to peaceful relations, a cession of all their land claims, and the acceptance of a specified reserve of about two thousand square miles at the headwaters of the San Juan River; but the more crucial articles imposed a regimen of civilization upon the Indians, who agreed to settle on the reservation within a year after ratification of the treaty and to "cultivate the soil, and raise flocks and herds for a subsistence." Furthermore, the president of the United States, at his discretion, could survey the reservation and allot parcels of land to individual Indian families. In return for the cession and the promises of the Indians, the United States would pay annuities: $5,000 annually for the first three years, $3,000 for the next three, and $2,000 for the following twenty years. The payments were to be made at the direction of the president, who could determine what proportion, if any, would be paid in money and what proportion might be expended for moral improvement and civilization. Additional articles prohibited the

44. See Ralph Hedrick Ogle, *Federal Control of the Western Apaches, 1848–1886,* with an introduction by Oakah L. Jones, Jr. (Albuquerque: University of New Mexico Press, 1970), pp. 31–45. This study was first published in *New Mexico Historical Review,* 1939–1940.

45. Utley, *Frontiersmen in Blue,* pp. 142–74, describes the military action in New Mexico, 1854–1861. The location of the posts is given in Francis Paul Prucha, *A Guide to the Military Posts of the United States, 1789–1895* (Madison: State Historical Society of Wisconsin, 1964).

46. CIA Report, 1854, serial 746, p. 222. The authorization for the treaties is in 10 *United States Statutes* 330.

making, selling, or using of spirituous liquors on the reservation and provided that the trade and intercourse laws would continue in force over the Indian lands.[47]

Here was a clear indication of the theoretical policy of the government to turn the Indians of the newly acquired territories into settled agriculturalists, no matter what the Indians' traditions and inclinations might be or what the capabilities of the land for farming. Meriwether reported that the Utes "very reluctantly consented to commence the cultivation of the soil for a subsistence"; but he had strong hopes that success with this relatively amicable band would have "a powerful effect upon all the other bands of this savage tribe."[48] Meriwether's chief concern in the treaties can be seen in his exultant report to Manypenny when he forwarded them: "Each treaty contains a stipulation requiring the Indians to *cultivate* the land assigned to them." The governor urged speedy action by the president and the Senate, but the Senate failed to approve the treaties. Yet the negotiations appear to have had some effect, for Manypenny reported at the end of 1856 that depredations in New Mexico had been less serious than in any of the previous years.[49]

On March 3, 1857, the position of superintendent of Indian affairs was separated from the territorial governor's office, and James L. Collins was appointed superintendent. In 1856 and again in 1857 Congress appropriated $47,500 for the Indian service in the Territory of New Mexico and "for making to the Indians in said Territory presents of goods, agricultural implements, and other useful articles, and in assisting them to locate in permanent abodes, and sustain themselves by the pursuits of civilized life." So even without ratification of the treaties Collins moved ahead with plans to concentrate the Utes on the San Juan and the Apaches along the Gila. The goal was to remove the Indians from the vicinity of the white settlements and to supervise them from nearby military posts. In 1859 Congress acted in regard to the Apaches, authorizing a reservation of one hundred square miles on or near the Gila River, and a small area was selected by the Indian Office and established by executive order.[50]

While plans for peaceful settlement of the Utes and the Apaches proceeded, the Navajos were engaged in war—predatory raids by the Indians and retaliation by federal troops. Only after a vigorous campaign in the winter of 1860–1861 were the Indians subdued and a peace negotiated. By

47. Kappler, vol. 5, p. 687.
48. Meriwether to Manypenny, August 14, 1855, ibid., p. 689. Kappler prints only two of the unratified treaties.
49. CIA Report, 1855, serial 810, p. 507; CIA Report, 1856, serial 875, p. 566. The action of the Senate on the treaties is in *Journal of the Executive Proceedings of the Senate*, 10: 31, 254–55.
50. 11 *United States Statutes* 79, 184, 185, 401.

then the Civil War had brought new circumstances, as both the military and civilian officials were forced to neglect Indian affairs for more pressing concerns.[51]

INDIANS, MORMONS, AND GENTILES

Indian affairs in Utah Territory, stretching from the Rocky Mountains to the Sierra Nevada north of the thirty-seventh parallel, were complicated by relations between the Mormons and the federal government. The Mormons were deeply interested in the Indians from a theological standpoint, for the Book of Mormon described them as Lamanites, descendants of Israelites who had migrated to the New World and who had fallen from grace. They were to be redeemed in the new age, and the Mormons actively sought Indian children for upbringing in their own families as a means of conversion.[52] The Mormons, moreover, had practical interests in Indian relations in the Great Basin, where the Utes, Shoshonis, and Paiutes occupied the lands into which Mormon immigrants poured in the 1840s and 1850s. The security and well-being of the Mormon settlements depended upon peaceful accommodation with the Indians, and Brigham Young repeatedly directed his followers to treat the Indians well. There was genuine concern for the civilization of the Indians that differed little from that exhibited by Christian humanitarians in the East, and Young appreciated the futility of war with the natives. "We have proved," he told the territorial legislature after two decades in Utah, "that the pacific, conciliatory policy is in every sense the better course for us to pursue. Experience has taught us that it is cheaper to feed the Indians than to fight them—a statement that has been so often repeated that it has become a recognized axiom among us." The peaceful policy, of course, did not always work, and Mormon frontiersmen experienced Indian wars and depredations as they encroached seriously upon the Indians.[53]

51. Utley, *Frontiersmen in Blue*, pp. 168–74. See also Frank McNitt, *Navajo Wars: Military Campaigns, Slave Raids, and Reprisals* (Albuquerque: University of New Mexico Press, 1972); and Bailey, *Long Walk*, pp. 83–142.

52. Mormon relations with the Indians are discussed in Juanita Brooks, "Indian Relations on the Mormon Frontier," *Utah Historical Quarterly* 12 (January–April 1944): 1–48; and Gustive O. Larson, "Brigham Young and the Indians," in Robert G. Ferris, ed., *The American West: An Appraisal* (Santa Fe: Museum of New Mexico Press, 1963), pp. 176–87. The setting of Indian affairs within the broader context of Mormon frontier development can be seen in Nels Anderson, *Desert Saints: The Mormon Frontier in Utah* (Chicago: University of Chicago Press, 1942). See also Leonard J. Arrington and Davis Bitton, *The Mormon Experience: A History of the Latter-Day Saints* (New York: Alfred A. Knopf, 1979), pp. 145–60.

53. Governor's message, January 22, 1866, in J. Cecil Alter, ed., "The Mormons and the Indians: News Items and Editorials from the Mormon Press," *Utah Historical Quar-*

Added to the problems of Indian-white relations common to all American frontiers was the question of Mormon domination of life in Utah, a serious irritant to the agents of the federal government who were responsible for Indian affairs there. The federal government, as the decade of the 1850s advanced, became greatly concerned that its authority in the territory was not respected by Brigham Young and the Mormons. Under these unfavorable circumstances, the United States attempted to provide an Indian policy in Utah.[54]

When the Mexican Cession was acquired by the Treaty of Guadalupe Hidalgo, the government transferred an older agency to Salt Lake just as it had moved an agency to Santa Fe. On April 7, 1849, John Wilson of Missouri was appointed to the Salt Lake post. His letter of appointment indicated how little the Indian Office knew about the Indians he was sent to serve, for he was issued no specific instructions and was asked instead to gather information about the tribes and their customs, their territory, their attitude toward whites, and whether the trade and intercourse laws could properly be applied.[55]

Little came of this early beginning; Wilson conferred with the Mormons in Utah in September, then he moved into California and soon resigned. A successor was appointed, but the Salt Lake Agency was abolished before he reached it. Some stability came with the establishment of the Territory of Utah in September 1850 and the appointment of Brigham Young as territorial governor and ex officio superintendent of Indian affairs.[56]

In February 1851 Congress extended the intercourse laws over Utah and provided an agent for the Utah Superintendency, who with two subagents reached Salt Lake City in the summer.[57] These men almost at once became embroiled in the controversies between Mormons and Gentiles (as the

---

terly 12 (January–April 1944): 65. For a brief account of the Walker War and the Gunnison massacre of 1853, for example, see Hoopes, *Indian Affairs and Their Administration*, pp. 141–46.

54. The best studies of Indian affairs in Utah before the Civil War are Dale L. Morgan, "The Administration of Indian Affairs in Utah, 1851–1858," *Pacific Historical Review* 17 (November 1948): 383–409, and Hoopes, *Indian Affairs and Their Administration*, chapter 5, "Indian Affairs in Utah, 1849–1860," pp. 131–59. Most of the pertinent documents are printed in "The Utah Expedition," *House Executive Document* no. 71, 35–1, serial 956, pp. 124–215.

55. William Medill to John Wilson, April 7, 1849, *House Executive Document* no. 17, 31–1, serial 573, pp. 182–84. Letters from Wilson dated Fort Bridger, August 22, 1849, and Great Salt Lake Valley, September 4, 1849, are printed ibid., pp. 104–12, 184–87.

56. Morgan, "Indian Affairs in Utah," pp. 383–84; Hoopes, *Indian Affairs and Their Administration*, pp. 131–34.

57. 9 *United States Statutes* 587; Jacob H. Holeman to Luke Lea, September 21, 1851, CIA Report, 1851, serial 613, pp. 444–46.

Mormons called all non-Mormons). The agent, Jacob H. Holeman, was especially critical of the Mormons. In November 1851 he wrote to the Indian Office from Salt Lake City to warn against the encroachments of the Mormons upon the Indians:

> I alluded in my report to the necessity of adopting such measures by the general government as would protect the Indians of this Territory; they are becoming very much excited by the encroachment of the Mormons, as they are making settlements throughout the Territory on all the most valuable lands, extending these settlements for near three hundred miles from this city. In the first settlements of this city and the adjoining country by the Mormons they at first conciliated the Indians by kind treatment; but when they once got a foothold, they began to *force their way;* the consequence was a war with the Indians, and in many instances, a most brutal butchery. This they fear will be the result wherever the Mormons may make a settlement. The Indians have been driven from their lands, and their hunting grounds destroyed, without any compensation therefor. They are in many instances reduced to a state of suffering bordering on starvation.

He felt that the Mormons were too self-interested to be allowed to have anything at all to do with the Indians officially.[58]

Holeman's correspondence continued to exhibit a strong prejudice against the Mormons, and the agent was in continual conflict with Young. His bias was not supported at first in Washington, however, and in 1853 he was replaced.[59] His successor died within a year, and the new agent, Dr. Garland Hurt, soon renewed Holeman's critical reports about the Mormons. Hurt was especially disturbed by the expansion of Mormon missions among the Indians and what he saw as a concerted drive to alienate the Indians from non-Mormons.[60]

Hurt took constructive steps to aid the Indians, and through his initiative the federal government began a program for Indians in Utah that paralleled its developing reservation system in other parts of the West. A great problem, however, was the lack of any treaty with the Indians by which some recognition of their lands and other rights against the whites might have been officially established. John Wilson had proposed that the Indian title to lands near the Great Salt Lake be extinguished "by treaty," and Agent Holeman had asserted that a treaty with the various tribes in Utah

58. Holeman to Lea, November 28, 1851, "Utah Expedition," pp. 128–29.
59. Conflict between the agent and the superintendent is treated in Morgan, "Indian Affairs in Utah," pp. 386–92.
60. Hurt to George W. Manypenny, May 2, 1855, "Utah Expedition," pp. 176–77.

would produce much good: "it would have the effect of preventing depredations on their lands, quieting their excitement against the whites, and ultimately save the Government from much trouble and expense."[61] Brigham Young was of the same mind. He wanted the government to promote schools and other measures to civilize the Indians, and he declared: "If previous to any such arrangements being made for their benefit it becomes necessary to enter into Treaty stipulations with them, then we should not delay that operation any longer, but go about it as speedily as possible."[62]

The Mormons were of course eager to have a valid title to their lands, which could come only with the extinguishment of Indian title by treaty, and they kept up pressure on Washington to arrange such a negotiation with the Indians. Commissioner Manypenny wanted to locate the Indians within specified boundaries and begin the process of civilization, and the Indian appropriation bill of July 31, 1854, spoke of distributing money appropriated for the Utah Indians "under treaty stipulations" or in some other way.[63]

But the movement for a treaty in Utah was abortive. Young provided estimates of goods needed for treating with the Indians, but in the end they were merely filed away because similar arrangements suggested for the Indians in New Mexico had been turned down by the Senate. Not until 1863 were any treaties signed with Indians in Utah Territory, and not until 1865 was a treaty negotiated (but never ratified) with the Utes.[64]

In the meantime, Hurt moved ahead with an alternative to formal reservations by establishing a farming system for the Indians' benefit. Building on some early moves by Brigham Young to provide farmers to instruct the Indians, Hurt undertook to teach them to farm in order to ease their destitution, an action cautiously approved by Commissioner Manypenny, who suggested hiring farmers on a temporary basis only. In late 1855 Hurt laid out a number of "reservations" where Indians were collected to farm. Although the agent forcefully justified his action, he was reined in, for he had spent money from contingent funds without official authorization. He thought such liberal action necessary to counteract Mormon missionary activity and to win over the Indians to a favorable view of the federal government.[65]

61. Wilson to Thomas Ewing, September 4, 1849, *House Executive Document* no. 17, 31–1, serial 573, p. 105; Holeman to Lea, September 21, 1851, CIA Report, 1851, serial 613, p. 446.

62. Young to Lea, November 30, 1851, OIA LR, Utah Superintendency (U/1–1852) (M234, reel 897, frame 217).

63. CIA Report, 1854, serial 746, p. 222; 10 *United States Statutes* 332.

64. Morgan, "Indian Affairs in Utah," p. 396; 10 *United States Statutes* 332; Kappler, pp. 848–53, 859–60.

65. Morgan, "Indian Affairs in Utah," pp. 397–401. Reports of Hurt's work are in CIA

In 1856 Congress appropriated $45,000 for the Utah Superintendency, and the financial strain on the farming program was eased, but the agent still had to maneuver around Brigham Young for the money. Hurt was convinced of the value of the farms. He attributed the tranquility on the frontier to his efforts to establish reservations for the Indians and to the introduction of a system of agriculture. "Though these reservations have been visited during this season by large bands of the wild Indians who live east of the Wasatch Mountains," he wrote to the commissioner of Indian affairs, "the influences which these farms exerted upon them through the home tribes, has enabled us to conduct our intercourse with them in a very tranquil manner."[66]

In addition to his repeated spats with the Gentile agents, Brigham Young did not get along well with the Indian Office in Washington. The governor complained of bureaucratic red tape that obstructed his handling of Indian affairs (believable even without any Mormon-Gentile antagonism), and Commissioner Manypenny suggested as early as 1854 that the ex officio superintendency be separated from the governor's office. He argued that Young's duties as head of the Mormon Church took much of his time and that the duties of Indian superintendent, which often had to be performed far from the seat of government, should properly be given to a different person.[67]

In 1857 relations between the United States and the Mormons in Utah approached a breaking point. Brigham Young's plan for a Mormon-dominated state, with economic and political as well as religious control, was in many ways a fact. Non-Mormons in Utah were antagonized, and their hostility spread across the nation. The announcement in 1852 that polygamy was a basic doctrine and practice of the Mormon Church added an emotional fervor to the cries of lawlessness and rebellion against the Mormons. President James Buchanan, over-hastily heeding complaints from a few federal officials in Utah and the public outcry, replaced Young as governor of Utah Territory with Alfred Cumming and sent a military expedition west to put down the alleged rebellion and to make sure that the new governor was accepted and respected. Congress on March 3, 1857, had already provided for independent superintendents of Indian affairs in

---

Report, 1855, serial 810, pp. 517–21; Hurt to Manypenny, August 30, 1856, "Utah Expedition," pp. 179–81.

66. 11 *United States Statutes* 79; Hurt to Denver, June 30, 1857, OIA LR, Utah Superintendency (H/685–1857) (M234, reel 898, frame 333).

67. Manypenny to Secretary of the Interior Robert McClelland, April 10, 1854, "Utah Expedition," pp. 165–66; CIA Report, 1854, serial 746, p. 225. Young's complaints about the attention—or lack of it—that he received from the Indian Office are strongly stated in Young to Manypenny, June 26, 1855, "Utah Expedition," pp. 170–75.

the western territories, and Jacob Forney was appointed to the new office for Utah Territory.[68]

As the Utah Expedition, commanded by Albert Sidney Johnston, moved toward Utah, the Mormons geared for war. Buchanan had neglected to inform Young of his replacement and of the military expedition, and the Mormon governor and his followers, when they received news of the advance of the troops, believed that the army was coming to destroy them. They prudently sought to engage the Indians on their side against the federal troops and the Gentile oppressors. Thus Young instructed one of the Mormon missionaries to the Indians in August 1857: "Continue the conciliatory policy towards the Indians, which I have ever recommended, and seek by works of righteousness to obtain their love and confidence, for they must learn that they have either to help us, or the United States will kill us both."[69]

In such an atmosphere of fear and hatred the Mountain Meadows massacre, one of the most brutal episodes in the long history of Indian-white conflicts in the West, occurred in September 1857. A company of emigrants from Arkansas and Missouri, passing through southern Utah to California, irritated both the Indians and the Mormons by their behavior. Encamped at a place called Mountain Meadows, they were besieged by hostile Indians. The Indians were aided by a number of Mormon men who, caught in the frenzy of the day, hoped to preserve the goodwill of the Indians and prevent the emigrants from carrying news to California that might stimulate an attack on the Mormons from that direction. Decoyed out of their encampment after giving up their arms in promise of safe conduct, the 120 emigrants were murdered by the Indians and the Mormons. Only 17 children were spared. Although Brigham Young by no means instigated or condoned the act, he tried to keep the Mormon participation in the affair quiet. The news of the massacre further fueled antagonism toward the Mormons.[70]

The "Mormon War" was in the end bloodless. The troops, arriving in the West too late in the year to move directly into Utah, wintered near Fort Bridger with some discomfort, for the Mormons had applied a scorched-earth policy to the vicinity. Conciliatory measures were begun, and Brigham Young, who had ordered the evacuation of Salt Lake City with direc-

68. There is a good account of the Utah Expedition and Mormon reaction to it in Leonard J. Arrington, *Great Basin Kingdom: An Economic History of the Latter-Day Saints, 1830–1900* (Cambridge: Harvard University Press, 1958), pp. 161–94.

69. Young to Jacob Hamblin, August 4, 1857, quoted in Brooks, "Indian Relations," p. 20.

70. A detailed critical study of the massacre is Juanita Brooks, *The Mountain Meadows Massacre* (Norman: University of Oklahoma Press, 1962; originally published in 1950). The author declares that Brigham Young was accessory after the fact.

tions to burn the city if the hostile troops moved in, agreed to accept peace. In the spring the troops passed peacefully through the nearly deserted city and established a military post (Camp Floyd) forty miles to the west, where they stayed until called back by the Civil War. Governor Cumming was amicably accepted by the Mormons, and Forney took over the duties of Indian superintendent.

Brigham Young continued to use his considerable influence with the Indians to further peaceful relations with them and to work for their civilization. When treaty negotiations with the Utes were undertaken in 1865, the agent did not hesitate to call upon Young for support.[71] Yet peaceful relations were not enough, for the white encroachment on Indian lands came faster than the government's plans for civilization and self-support could be carried out, and at the end of the decade many of the Indians were hungry, naked, and in desperate straits.

71. O. H. Irish to William P. Dole, June 29, 1865, CIA Report, 1865, serial 1248, pp. 317–20.

CHAPTER 15

California, Oregon, and Washington

A Reservation Policy for California.

Indian Affairs in the Oregon Country.

The Indians of Washington Territory.

The movement of American citizens to the Pacific coast and the incorporation of California and the Pacific Northwest into the American nation illustrate the deleterious effect upon the Indians of a policy applied from a great distance without a sound appreciation of local conditions and without adequate concern to protect Indian rights against the onslaught of American invaders on their aboriginal lands. Yet the government in the end applied to the Indians of the Pacific slope and the inland empire the same paternalistic patterns that marked the development of the reservation system in other parts of the nation.

A RESERVATION POLICY FOR CALIFORNIA

The relations of the United States with the Indians of California were particularly disastrous for the Indians, for the attempt of the federal government to protect them through treaty machinery was abortive, and the Indians were no match for the aggressive and often lawless gold seekers who flooded the region in 1849 and after.[1]

1. Indian policy in California has been well documented in William H. Ellison, "The Federal Indian Policy in California, 1846–1860," *Mississippi Valley Historical Review* 9 (June 1922): 37–67, and Alban W. Hoopes, *Indian Affairs and Their Administration:*

The United States, to begin with, was almost entirely ignorant of the Indians in the new acquisition. It knew neither the population, the number and organization of the bands and tribes, nor the status of the Indians under Mexico—a status that presumably was to be continued under the provisions of the Treaty of Guadalupe Hildalgo. The Americans, logically enough, grouped the Indians roughly into two categories. One was the mission Indians, who had come under the influence of Franciscan friars in the mission establishments that dotted the coast from San Diego to San Francisco Bay. These Indians had been drawn to live at the missions in order to be trained in agriculture, stock raising, and simple crafts, as well as to be instructed in Christianity. The missions enjoyed considerable prosperity and success. Stock was raised in large numbers there, and substantial yields of grain were harvested. The Indians, under the training and discipline of the priests, did the building, weaving, tanning, soap making, and other work needed to maintain the nearly self-sufficient communities. But by the time the Americans arrived the missions had been secularized by the Mexican government and the Indians by and large dispersed.[2] The rest of the native inhabitants were "wild Indians," who had little or no contact with whites and who subsisted by hunting, fishing, and gathering acorns. Estimates of the number of these two groups vary; a total of one hundred thousand at the time of American occupation may be a reasonable figure, representing a considerable decline from the estimated aboriginal population of more than three hundred thousand.[3]

With Special Reference to the Far West, 1849–1860 (Philadelphia: University of Pennsylvania Press, 1932), pp. 35–68. Some idea of Indian reaction to the policy in southern California can be gained from George Harwood Phillips, *Chiefs and Challengers: Indian Resistance and Cooperation in Southern California* (Berkeley: University of California Press, 1975). Accounts of the destruction of the Indians and their cultures are in Robert F. Heizer, ed., *The Destruction of the California Indians* (Santa Barbara: Peregrine Smith, 1974); Heizer, ed., *They Were Only Diggers: A Collection of Articles from California Newspapers, 1851–1866, on Indian and White Relations* (Ramona, California: Ballena Press, 1974); and Heizer and Alan J. Almquist, *The Other Californians: Prejudice and Discrimination under Spain, Mexico, and the United States* (Berkeley: University of California Press, 1971), pp. 23–91.

2. There has been a great deal of study of the missions and considerable controversy about whether their effect on the Indians was good or bad. An old but classic study is Herbert E. Bolton, "The Mission as a Frontier Institution in the Spanish-American Colonies," *American Historical Review* 23 (October 1917): 42–61. A survey of the historiography is John Francis Bannon, "The Mission as a Frontier Institution: Sixty Years of Interest and Research," *Western Historical Quarterly* 10 (July 1979): 303–22. For details on the California missions and missionaries, see the works of Maynard Geiger.

3. Ellison in "Federal Indian Policy in California," p. 40 and n., suggests "at least 100,000 or perhaps 125,000," basing his figure on contemporary reports and the estimates of ethnographers. A similar conclusion of "about 100,000," is given in Robert F. Heizer, "Treaties," in *Handbook of North American Indians*, vol. 8: *California*, ed.

After California was seized by United States troops under Stephen Watts Kearny in 1847, it was the military who first sought to establish some sort of official relations with the Indians and to prevent as much as possible the raids and counterraids between Indians and whites that threatened the peace of the country. Kearny, as military governor, hoped to conciliate the Indians by means of presents (which he urged the War Department to send), and in 1847 he appointed three subagents: John Sutter for Indians on the Sacramento River; Mariano G. Vallejo for those on the north side of San Francisco Bay; and J. D. Hunter for those at San Luis Rey.[4]

The federal government proceeded slowly in providing civil government for California, and it sought to determine as precisely as possible the actual state of affairs. In the spring of 1849 the president appointed Thomas Butler King to study conditions in California. The instructions to King from Secretary of State John M. Clayton included directions to secure information about "the number of the various Indian tribes which form a portion of the population of the Territories; their power, character and modes of life." King's report, dated March 22, 1850, offered scant help to the policy makers. He reported the impossibility of forming an accurate estimate of the number of Indians in the territory, but he noted that "the whole race seems to be rapidly disappearing." He greatly disparaged the Indians, who seemed to him "to be almost the lowest grade of human beings" without the slightest inclination to cultivate the land. "They have never pretended to hold any interest in the soil," he asserted, "nor have they been treated by the Spanish or American immigrants as possessing any." He did not think that the Mexican government had ever purchased any land from the Indians or otherwise extinguished their claims. But he suggested that it might be possible to collect the Indians and teach them the "arts and habits of civilization," although he did not hold out much hope for their preservation.[5]

Another official observer of Indian affairs was William Carey Jones, dis-

---

Robert F. Heizer (Washington: Smithsonian Institution, 1978), p. 701. The great work on the population of the California Indians has been done by Sherburne F. Cook; see his *The Conflict between the California Indians and White Civilization: Ibero-Americana*, nos. 21–24 (Berkeley: University of California Press, 1943); and *The Population of the California Indians, 1769–1970* (Berkeley: University of California Press, 1976).

4. Ellison, "Federal Indian Policy in California," p. 42; Hoopes, *Indian Affairs and Their Administration*, pp. 36–37. Documents on the appointment of, instructions to, and reports from the subagents can be found in two similar (though not identical) printings of government documents on the occupation of California: *Senate Executive Document* no. 18, 31–1, serial 557, and *House Executive Document* no. 17, 31–1, serial 573.

5. Clayton to King, April 3, 1849, *House Executive Document* no. 17, 31–1, serial 573, p. 11; Thomas Butler King, *California: Report of Hon. T. Butler King* (Washington: Gideon and Company, 1850), pp. 3–4. The report is also printed in *House Executive Document* no. 59, 31–1, serial 577.

patched to California to investigate the question of land titles. At the end of his instructions from the commissioner of the General Land Office, Jones was told explicitly what to look for: "You will make an inquiry into the nature of the *Indian rights* as existing under the Spanish and Mexican governments, and as subsisting when the United States obtained the sovereignty, indicating from authentic data the difference between the privileges enjoyed by the wandering tribes and those who have made actual settlements and established rancherias, and will report their general form, extent, and localities; their probable number, and the manner and form in which such rights have been regarded by the Spanish and Mexican governments."[6]

Jones's report was succinct. He declared that it was a constant principle of the Spanish colonial laws that the Indians "shall have a *right* to as much land as they need for their habitation, for tillage, and for pasturage." He noted that the mission Indians were to have rights to the land they used and that other grants were subject to these Indian rights. Nor did he believe a continuation of these principles would cause much inconvenience because of the small number of Indians involved. "A proper regard for long recognized rights, and a proper sympathy for an unfortunate and unhappy race," he said, "would seem to forbid that it should be abrogated, unless for a better." As for the "wild or wandering tribes," the Spanish recognized no title whatever to the soil.[7]

Influenced no doubt by these reports and intending to follow in California established principles of reservation policy, the government moved ahead, albeit somewhat clumsily, to provide enclaves of land for the Indians, as well as agents to look after their interests and conduct their relations with the United States.

In April 1849 a subagent, Adam Johnston, was appointed for the Sacramento and San Joaquin valleys. He appears to have managed his affairs competently and supplied officials in Washington with detailed reports about the state of affairs, but he soon faded into the background somewhat as Congress provided for commissioners and agents.[8] On September 28, 1850, Congress authorized the appointment of three agents for Indian tribes in California "to perform the duties now prescribed by law to Indian agents." Two days later it appropriated $25,000 to enable the president to

6. J. Butterfield to Jones, July 5, 1849, *House Executive Document* no. 17, 31–1, serial 573, p. 115.

7. William Carey Jones, *Report on the Subject of Land Titles in California: Made in Pursuance of Instructions from the Secretary of State and the Secretary of the Interior* (Washington: Gideon and Company, 1850), pp. 36–37.

8. Johnston's commission is given in *House Executive Document* no. 17, 31–1, serial 573, pp. 187–88. His reports are in *Senate Executive Document* no. 4, 33–special session, serial 688.

hold treaties with the California tribes; this sum was subsequently increased to $50,000.[9]

At this point there was considerable confusion. The act appointing the agents provided no appropriation for their salaries; the act authorizing treaties made no provision for treaty commissioners. The strange situation was resolved pragmatically: the men appointed as agents were charged with negotiating the treaties and paid from the treaty money. To this dual position of agent-commissioner, the president appointed Redick McKee of Virginia, George W. Barbour of Kentucky, and O. M. Wozencraft of Louisiana. These men arrived in California at the end of December and the beginning of January and set about energetically to negotiate treaties with the Indians. Their vague instructions stated that the goal of the government was to gain information about the Indians and their customs and "to make such treaties and compacts with them as may seem just and proper."[10] Operating as a group, the three men signed a treaty on March 19, 1851, with men whom they took to be the leaders of six tribes in the San Joaquin Valley, and on April 29 another treaty was made with sixteen tribes. Later, in order to speed the work, the commissioners split up, each moving to a designated region to continue the treaty making. By January 7, 1852, eighteen treaties had been negotiated and signed.[11]

The treaties were much alike. The Indians recognized the United States as sole sovereign over the land ceded to the United States by Mexico in 1848, and they placed themselves under the protection of the United States and agreed to keep peace. By each treaty a definite reservation was set aside for the tribes, and subsistence in the form of beef cattle was provided for them while they were moving and settling on the reservations. Annuities in the form of clothing, agricultural implements, and livestock were authorized, and farmers, blacksmiths, and schoolteachers were pro-

9. 9 *United States Statutes* 519, 558, 572.

10. CIA Report, 1850, serial 587, p. 42. The appointment letter is printed in *Senate Executive Document* no. 4, 33—special session, serial 688, p. 7; their instructions are in A. S. Loughery to McKee, Barbour, and Wozencraft, October 15, 1850, ibid., pp. 8—9. The reports of the three commissioners and journals of their activity appear in the same Senate document. See also Alban W. Hoopes, ed., "The Journal of George W. Barbour, May 1 to October 4, 1851," *Southwestern Historical Quarterly* 40 (October 1936): 145—53, and 40 (January 1937): 247—61; and Chad L. Hoopes, "Redick McKee and the Humboldt Bay Region, 1851—1852," *California Historical Society Quarterly* 49 (September 1970): 195—219.

11. The treaties are printed in Kappler, vol. 4, pp. 1081—1128. Official secrecy on the treaties was lifted by the Senate on January 18, 1905. A copy of the 1905 Senate printing of the treaties is in Records of the Office of Indian Affairs, Documents Relating to the Negotiation of Ratified and Unratified Treaties with Various Indian Tribes (T494, reel 8, frames 410—25), National Archives, Record Group 75. The idea that the secrecy was conspiratorial is considered and rejected in Harry Kelsey, "The California Indian Treaty Myth," *Southern California Quarterly* 55 (Fall 1973): 225—35.

vided for a period of years. The eighteen treaties set aside 11,700 square miles (7,488,000 acres) of land, about 7.5 percent of the state.[12]

The three commissioners did their work rapidly. Indeed, haste was necessary if conflicts between the onrushing whites and the Indians were to be prevented and the Indians protected in their rights. But they acted without the detailed knowledge of the Indians that modern anthropologists can provide. Although 139 tribes or bands were represented in the eighteen treaties, an enumeration in 1926 indicated that more than 175 tribes were not included in the treaties. Thirty years later, a study conducted under Indian Claims Commission litigation reported that of the 139 signatory groups, 67 were identifiable as tribelets, 45 were merely village names, 14 were duplicates spelled differently without the commissioners having been aware of the fact, and 13 were either unidentifiable or personal names.[13]

The irregularities, although indicative of the lack of precise information with which the whole process was carried out, in the end did not matter, for the Senate refused to ratify the treaties. There is some question whether, even at the beginning, a majority of the Senate intended to authorize treaties of cession rather than mere treaties of peace and friendship. A clearly worded measure introduced by John C. Frémont, one of California's first senators, "to treat with the Indian tribes of California having territorial claims in the State of California and to extinguish their land claims," with an appropriation of $100,000 for the negotiations, was substantially changed by the Committee on Indian Affairs. The new version made no mention of land claims, and the appropriation was excluded altogether from the authorization bill. There was considerable feeling in Congress that the California Indians had no land titles and therefore that no treaties were needed to extinguish them.[14]

---

12. These are calculations of Ellison, "Federal Indian Policy in California," p. 57, and they have been generally accepted by historians. The map of California in Charles C. Royce, *Indian Land Cessions in the United States*, Eighteenth Annual Report of the Bureau of American Ethnology, 1896–1897, part 2 (Washington: GPO, 1899), pl. 7, purports to show the lands ceded (all of California west of the Sierra Nevadas) and the reservations established, but the map is based on faulty information and assumptions. Heizer says: "There seems to be no basis whatsoever for this map beyond the vague impression of the U.S. Senate in 1852 that the California Indian tribes were agreeable to ceding to the United States the lands of California. Royce's map is, therefore, his own artifact deriving from the same assumption that the Senate made in 1852. But since it was already known in 1852 that many groups had not been treated with, either because they had not been encountered in the course of the wanderings of the three commissioners or because through lack of interpreters no communication was possible between the Americans and numbers of groups of native Californians, it must have been obvious that the 1851–1852 treaties did not, as was implied, cover the quieting of territorial claims ('title') of the Indians then living in the state." Heizer, "Treaties," pp. 703–4.

13. Heizer, "Treaties," p. 703.

14. Kelsey, "California Indian Treaty Myth," pp. 228–29.

But whatever the status of Indian titles, other aspects of the treaties drawn up by the three commissioners militated against their ratification. There was stong opposition from Californians, who saw large regions to be snatched from their grasp and reserved for the Indians, whom they despised. Furthermore, the costs of the treaties had grown to nearly a million dollars, far beyond the total of $50,000 that had been appropriated. The commissioners, working on the spot, had felt it necessary to contract for large numbers of cattle to feed the Indians, and they also provided for further subsistence and annuities in the treaties. Although Commissioner Luke Lea and the newly appointed superintendent of Indian affairs for California were solidly for ratification, the Senate voted with the opposition.[15]

The rejection of the treaties left Indian affairs in California in an uncertain state. For one thing, many of the claims made under the contracts let by the treaty commissioners were later declared fraudulent and never paid. More serious was the worsening condition of relations between the Indians and the miners and other settlers. This became the responsibility of Edward F. Beale, a highly competent and benevolent man with navy and army experience who was appointed the first Indian superintendent in California under congressional authorization of March 3, 1852.[16] Beale, arriving in San Francisco on September 16, immediately saw the urgency of the situation and quickly set about to give new shape to American policy. "The necessity of a speedy and permanent arrangement for this unhappy race is more apparent every day," he wrote at the end of October, "as our people are fast filling every habitable foot of ground in the entire state, to the exclusion of the original occupants." What he proposed was a considerable change from the traditional land cession and reservation policy embraced by the rejected treaties. He set forth his plan in brief tentative form as follows:

> In the first place, I propose a system of "military posts" to be established on reservations, for the convenience and protection of the

15. Ellison, "Federal Indian Policy in California," pp. 57–58. A strong statement about California opposition to the treaties is William H. Ellison, "Rejection of California Indian Treaties: A Study in Local Influence on National Policy," *Grizzly Bear* 37 (May 1925): 4–5, 86; 37 (June 1925): 4–5, supplement 7; 37 (July 1925): 6–7. Kelsey, "California Indian Treaty Myth," argues for the preeminence of the question of Indian land titles in the rejection of the treaties. A set of reprinted items is in George E. Anderson, W. H. Ellison, and Robert F. Heizer, *Treaty Making and Treaty Rejection by the Federal Government in California, 1850–1852* (Socorro, New Mexico: Ballena Press, 1978). The action of the Senate can be followed in the *Journal of the Executive Proceedings of the Senate*, vol. 8.

16. 10 *United States Statutes* 2–3. On Beale and his work, see Gerald Thompson, *Edward F. Beale and the American West* (Albuquerque: University of New Mexico Press, 1983), pp. 45–79; Richard E. Crouter and Andrew F. Rolle, "Edward Fitzgerald Beale and the Indian Peace Commissioners in California, 1851–1854," *Historical Society of South-*

Indians; these reservations to be regarded as military reservations or government reservations. The Indians to be invited to assemble within these reserves.

A system of discipline and instruction to be adopted by the agent who is to live at the post.

Each reservation to contain a military establishment, the number of troops being in proportion to the population of the tribes there assembled.

The expenses of the troops to be borne by the surplus produce of Indian labor.

The reservation to be made with a view to a change in location, when increase of white population may make it necessary.

A change of present Indian laws to be made, so as to suit the condition of this State and the proposed policy.[17]

Beale had in mind a reestablishment of the mission system on a secular basis, for he thought the missions had been an ideal means for channeling Indian labor into useful projects. "Every useful mechanic art, all necessary knowledge of agricultural pursuits, was here [at the mission] taught under a system of discipline at once mild, firm, and paternal," he wrote to Luke Lea. "It is this system, modified and adapted to the present time, which I propose for your consideration; nor can I conceive of any other which would preserve this unfortunate people from total extinction, and our government from everlasting disgrace."[18]

Beale began to implement his plan on a piece of land on the San Joaquin River, land passed over by the settlers as unworthy of their labor. Here he wanted to establish an Indian settlement. This should not be done by treaty, he insisted, and the land should be a *government* reservation to

---

ern California Quarterly 42 (June 1960): 107–32. An older biography of Beale is Stephen Bonsal, *Edward Fitzgerald Beale: A Pioneer in the Path of Empire, 1822–1903* (New York: G. P. Putnam's Sons, 1912).

17. Beale to Luke Lea, October 29, 1852, *Senate Executive Document* no. 4, 33–special session, serial 688, p. 374. Lea's own proposal was similar to what was being worked out in the central plains; he suggested forming the California Indians into "two grand colonies, to be suitably located: one in the northern and the other in the southern portion of the State." CIA Report, 1852, serial 658, p. 300.

18. Beale to Lea, November 22, 1852, *Senate Executive Document* no. 4, 33–special session, serial 688, p. 380. Phillips, in *Chiefs and Challengers*, pp. 128, 173, asserts that "the foundation of the reservation system that he [Beale] proposed to his superiors" was a report drawn up by a subagent appointed by Beale, Benjamin D. Wilson. The report is printed with an introduction and annotations in John Walton Caughey, ed., *The Indians of Southern California in 1852: The B. D. Wilson Report and a Selection of Contemporary Comment* (San Marino: Huntington Library, 1952).

which the Indians would have no title and from which they could be moved as occasion demanded.[19] He asked $500,000 to carry out his policy. His plea was that of a Christian humanitarian as he described the condition of the Indians:

> Driven from their fishing and hunting grounds, hunted themselves like wild beasts, *lassoed*, and torn from homes made miserable by want, and forced into slavery, the wretched remnant which escapes starvation on the one hand, and the relentless whites on the other, only do so to rot and die of a loathsome disease, the penalty of Indian association with frontier civilization. This is no idle declamation—I have seen it; and seeing all this, I cannot help them. I know that they starve; I know that they perish by hundreds; I know that they are fading away with a startling and shocking rapidity, but I cannot help them. Humanity must yield to necessity. They are not dangerous; therefore they must be neglected. I earnestly call the early attention of the government to this condition of affairs, and to a plan I have proposed in a previous letter for its relief. It is a crying sin that our government so wealthy and so powerful, should shut its eyes to the miserable fate of these rightful owners of the soil. What is the expense of half a million for the permanent relief of these poor people to a government so rich?[20]

Congress responded by authorizing the creation of five military reservations from the public domain that were not to exceed twenty-five thousand acres each. A quarter of a million dollars was appropriated to sustain the Indians and move them to the reservations.[21]

Beale enthusiastically pursued his plan, developing a promising reservation at Tejon Pass, but his work was checked by political opposition and by his own carelessness in his accounts.[22] Just as appropriations were being considered for California Indian affairs in May 1854, Beale was reported to be nearly $250,000 in arrears in his accounts. Although subsequent investigation exonerated him, the damage had been done. Congress cut the number of authorized reservations from five to three, which were to run between five and ten thousand acres each. Out of a total appropriation of $200,000 for continuing the removal and subsistence of the Indians, not more than $25,000 was to be used to extinguish competing white land

19. Beale to Lea, December 14, 1852, *Senate Executive Document* no. 4, 33–special session, serial 688, pp. 391–92.

20. Beale to Lea, November 22, 1852, ibid., p. 378.

21. 10 *United States Statutes* 238.

22. For the Tejon reservation, see Helen S. Giffin and Arthur Woodward, *The Story of El Tejon* (Los Angeles: Dawson's Book Shop, 1942), pp. 19–43.

titles to the reserved lands. While Congress was taking this action, Beale was removed from office.[23]

The plan that Beale had outlined, however, was continued by his successor, Thomas J. Henley, who was optimistic about the possibilities of the reservation system. He established Nome Lacke Reservation for Indians in the northern part of the state and then petitioned the government to restore the provision for five reserves. Congress agreed; it again authorized five reservations and appropriated $150,000 to move the Indians to the two additional reservations, which could be as large as 25,000 acres each. By September 1856 there were four permanent reservations: Tejon, Nome Lacke, Klamath (on the Klamath River), and Cape Mendocino (on the Pacific). In addition, three temporary farms had been established. Henley sent in glowing reports, the commissioner of Indian affairs looked optimistically at the developments, and Congress continued to provide large appropriations for the military reservation system.[24]

Doubts arose about the success of the California experiment, however. In 1858 a special agent, Godard Bailey, was dispatched to visit the reservations. His observations led him to conclude that Beale's plan of collecting the Indians on the reserves where they would be supported by their own labor was "a lamentable failure." He reported: "At present the reservations are simply government alms-houses, where an inconsiderable number of Indians are insufficiently fed and scantily clothed, at an expense wholly disporportioned to the benefit conferred. There is nothing in the system, as now practiced, looking to the permanent improvement of the Indian, or tending in any way to his moral, intellectual, or social elevation; the only attempts at anything of the sort that fell under my observation seeming to be rather the result of individual effort than to spring from the system itself."[25]

Congress in 1858 cut the appropriations for the removal and subsistence of the California Indians to $50,000—not enough to restore the reservations from their dilapidated condition. In these circumstances, Commissioner Charles E. Mix seriously challenged the favorable appraisal of his predecessors and asserted that "serious errors" had been committed. He

23. Ellison, "Federal Indian Policy in California," p. 63; 10 *United States Statutes* 332; *Congressional Globe*, 33d Congress, 1st session, pp. 1027–30, 1841–51, 1895, 1945, 1983.

24. Ellison, "Federal Indian Policy in California," pp. 64–65; 10 *United States Statutes* 698, 699; 11 *United States Statutes* 183, 330; Henley to George W. Manypenny, September 4, 1856, CIA Report, 1856, serial 875, pp. 787–97; Henley to J. W. Denver, September 4, 1857, CIA Report, 1857, serial 919, pp. 675–78. See also the annual reports of Manypenny in 1854, 1855, and 1856, and the report of J. W. Denver in 1857.

25. Bailey to Charles E. Mix, November 4, 1858, CIA Report, 1858, serial 974, pp. 649–57; quotation from p. 650.

thought that too much money had been expended and too much done for the Indians, with negligible results. He urged a system that would make the Indians self-sufficient without cost to the government. He wanted them put on good land and then forced to provide for themselves. All unauthorized whites were to be kept out, manual labor schools provided, and after a year the lands divided in severalty among the Indians. Mix's successor, A. B. Greenwood, closely followed this lead. Accepting Bailey's conclusions, as Mix had done, he asserted that "almost any change would be better than the present system as administered," and he recommended the abandonment of Beale's system and the repeal of the laws authorizing the superintendent and the agents in California, and their replacement by a system of two districts with precisely limited agents and other personnel. On June 19, 1860, a new law took effect that largely followed Greenwood's recommendations. It authorized the secretary of the interior to divide California into northern and southern districts. Two superintending agents were provided for, who could appoint a supervisor for each reservation "to instruct the Indians in husbandry," and no more than four laborers to aid each supervisor. The Indians were to be placed on small reservations, to which they would move by simple agreements, not by formal treaties.[26]

The new arrangement seemed little better than the old. President Lincoln's commissioner of Indian affairs, William P. Dole, a man with genuine concern for Indian rights whatever his other failings, found much to condemn when he took office in 1861. He saw the need for breaking up some of the reservations, for establishing others with more ample resources, and for correction of the "outrageous wrongs perpetrated, under color of law, against not only the property but also the persons and liberty of the Indians." None of the reserves in the southern district were free of white claims and none were adequate in extent to serve the Indians' needs, and in the northern district conditions were little better. The result was utter defeat of the purposes for which the reservations had been set up. Dole's analysis is an apt statement of the goals of the government's policy and a harsh, but justified, condemnation of conditions (seemingly beyond the will or power of the federal government to correct) that frustrated the goals.

Instead of being a retreat from the encroachments of the whites upon which they may concentrate and gradually become accustomed

26. CIA Report, 1858, serial 974, pp. 357–58; CIA Report, 1859, serial 1023, pp. 386–88; CIA Report, 1860, serial 1078, pp. 244–45; 12 *United States Statutes* 57. Instructions to the new superintending agents are printed in CIA Report, 1860, serial 1078, pp. 454–56.

to a settled mode of life, while *learning* the arts and advantages of civilization, and which at a proper time is to be subdivided and allotted to them in severalty, and thus a home furnished to each of them, around which shall cluster all those fond associations and endearments so highly prized by all civilized people, and they in a condition to appreciate the same, the reservation is a place where a scanty subsistence is doled out to them from year to year; they become accustomed to rely upon charity rather than their own exertions; are hemmed in by people by whom they are detested, and whose arts and customs they have neither the power nor inclination to acquire, and thus they become vagrants and vagabonds, accomplishing for themselves no desirable end, and are a nuisance to their white neighbors.[27]

The California Indians continued to live in a kind of limbo. Many of them settled on the reservations and developed a rancheria existence—little spots of poor land within the rich state to which they had no clear title and on which they were under constant threats of encroachment from white Americans. Their numbers declined by 1856, according to some estimates, to as few as twenty-five or thirty thousand.[28] These so-called "mission Indians" and their rights became a special subject of attention of the post-Civil War humanitarian Indian reformers.

The designation of the reservations in California under the rejected treaties, under Beale's and Henley's activities, and under the district superintending agents contributed to the development of the federal Indian reservation system, but the California experience was outside the main course of reservation history. The Indians were allowed no clear title to the land, and the small and scattered reserves of land presented quite a different situation from that on the Sioux reserve in Dakota, for example, or the Kiowa-Comanche reservation in Oklahoma set up by the treaties made by the peace commission in 1868, which fitted into the pattern of the northern and southern colonies advocated since the late 1840s.[29]

INDIAN AFFAIRS IN THE OREGON COUNTRY

The United States was slow to vindicate its claim to the Oregon Country, the vast area lying north of California and west of the Rocky Mountains,

27. CIA Report, 1861, serial 1117, pp. 639–40.
28. Cook, *Population of the California Indians*, p. xv.
29. Ellison, "Federal Indian Policy in California," argues that the California reservations were the origin of the United States reservation system and set the pattern for later reservation policy; Hoopes, *Indian Affairs and Their Administration*, follows his lead. These authors overlook the long history of setting aside lands with set boundaries for

and thus to assume responsibility for Indian relations in the area.[30] Although Yankee traders along the coast and occasional overland expeditions like those of Lewis and Clark and the Astorians gave the United States a claim to the region, the nation did not at first take much interest in such a remote spot. In 1818 the United States made an agreement of joint occupation for ten years with Great Britain, and in 1827 the agreement was extended. In the twenties and thirties, however, there was public agitation for the acquisition of Oregon. Representative John Floyd of Virginia tried to develop enthusiasm in Congress for Oregon and in December 1820 persuaded the House to appoint a committee to "inquire into the situation of the settlements upon the Pacific Ocean, and the expediency of occupying the Columbia River." The committee (with Floyd as chairman) submitted a report urging annexation that produced no tangible movement in regard to acquiring Oregon but did stir up public attention. In 1822 Floyd proposed another measure, and he continued to agitate for occupation of the Columbia River region. But the arguments in favor of the rich province were overcome by counterarguments that the Pacific region was too distant to be joined in one nation with the existing states.[31]

The agitation for Oregon did not cease. It was promoted by a Massachusetts school teacher, Hall Jackson Kelley, who carried on an extensive propaganda campaign that urged government support for a colony in Oregon to combat the growing influence of the British. His efforts to transplant a New England town to the Oregon wilderness came to nothing. A fellow New Englander, Nathaniel J. Wyeth, was little more successful, although he led a small party across the continent to the Willamette Valley in 1832 and left a journal of the expedition that is a valuable document on the westward crossing.[32]

---

specific tribes and the intention of leading the Indians to white civilization there. Note that Robert A. Trennert, Jr., *Alternative to Extinction: Federal Indian Policy and the Beginnings of the Reservation System, 1846–51* (Philadelphia: Temple University Press, 1975), does not mention California at all.

30. An authoritative general history of the region including an account of Indian affairs is Dorothy O. Johansen, *Empire of the Columbia: A History of the Pacific Northwest*, 2d ed. (New York: Harper and Row, 1967). Indian policy developments in Oregon and Washington are treated thoroughly in Hoopes, *Indian Affairs and Their Administration*, pp. 69–130.

31. *Annals of Congress*, 16th Congress, 2d session, p. 679. The report of Floyd's committee, in favor of occupying the Oregon Country, January 25, 1821, with a proposed bill is printed ibid., pp. 945–59. A detailed account of Floyd's activity is given in Charles H. Ambler, "The Oregon Country, 1810–1830: A Chapter in Territorial Expansion," *Mississippi Valley Historical Review* 30 (June 1943): 3–24.

32. On Kelley see Fred Wilbur Powell, *Hall Jackson Kelley: Prophet of Oregon* (Portland, Oregon: Ivy Press, 1917), and Powell, ed., *Hall J. Kelley on Oregon* (Princeton:

Of more significance for the settlement of Oregon and relations with the Indians was the work of Christian missionaries. In October 1831 four Indians of the Northwest appeared in St. Louis in the company of a group of traders. The story arose that they had come to seek missionaries to show them the road to heaven, and the publication of this story—in large part a fabrication—in the Methodist *Christian Advocate and Journal* in March 1833 pricked the Christian conscience.[33] Soon substantial missionary efforts aimed at Christianizing the Indians of Oregon and the establishment of permanent settlements there as a base of operation were under way. The first of these was a Methodist mission led by Jason Lee, who moved across the continent in 1834. Lee and his party established the first American agricultural community in the Willamette Valley. Supported by the Methodist Board of Missions and promoted by aggressive propagandizing in the East, the Methodist mission grew in size and by 1840 was a significant advertisement of the economic wonders of Oregon.[34]

The Methodists were followed by missionaries of the American Board of Commissioners for Foreign Missions. In 1835 Dr. Marcus Whitman and the Reverend Samuel Parker moved up the Missouri with a party of the American Fur Company and met with Indians in the Green River Valley. Encouraged by the reception the Indians gave them, Whitman returned east for helpers while Parker continued to the coast to seek out locations for missions. Whitman was authorized by the American Board to establish a mission among the Flatheads, and he and the Reverend Henry H. Spalding and their wives returned to the West in 1836. The Whitmans opened a mission among the Cayuse Indians at Waiilatpu, near Fort Walla Walla; the Spaldings set up one at Lapwai, in present-day Idaho, among the Nez Per-

---

Princeton University Press, 1932), which prints a number of Kelley's writings. For Wyeth's work, see "The Correspondence and Journals of Captain Nathaniel J. Wyeth, 1831–6," ed. F. G. Young, *Sources of the History of Oregon,* vol. 1, parts 3–6.

33. Two recent scholarly accounts of the story are in Clifford M. Drury, *Marcus and Narcissa Whitman and the Opening of Old Oregon,* 2 vols. (Glendale, California: Arthur H. Clark Company, 1973), 1: 28–50, and Alvin M. Josephy, Jr., *The Nez Perce Indians and the Opening of the Northwest* (New Haven: Yale University Press, 1965), pp. 93–103. Three older articles, presenting different views, are John Rothensteiner, "The Flat-Head and Nez Perce Delegation to St. Louis, 1831–1839," *St. Louis Catholic Historical Review* 2 (October 1920): 183–97; Francis Haines, "The Nez Perce Delegation to St. Louis in 1831," *Pacific Historical Review* 6 (March 1937): 71–78; and J. Orin Oliphant, "Francis Haines and William Walker: A Critique," ibid. 14 (June 1945): 211–16.

34. A careful study of Lee's mission is Robert J. Loewenberg, *Equality on the Oregon Frontier: Jason Lee and the Methodist Mission, 1834–43* (Seattle: University of Washington Press, 1976). See also Cornelius J. Brosnan, *Jason Lee: Prophet of the New Oregon* (New York: Macmillan Company, 1932). A brief, popular, and well-illustrated article is Michael Ames, "Missionaries' Toil for Soul and Survival: Introducing Christianity to the Pacific Northwest," *American West* 10 (January 1973): 28–33, 63.

ces. Another American Board mission was established at Fort Colville among the Spokanes.[35] Catholic missionaries, too, moved into the Oregon Country. Some came from Canada in response to appeals from French Canadians living in the Willamette Valley. Others, of whom the Jesuit Pierre-Jean DeSmet was the most famous, moved up the Missouri River. Father DeSmet opened a mission in the Bitterroot Valley in present-day Montana in 1841. These Catholic missions expanded in the interior regions of the Oregon Country, and the missionaries gained great influence with the Indians.[36]

The Protestant missions were less successful than the Catholic, in large part because of dissension among the missionaries. The discouraging reports led the American Board in 1842 to direct the closing of the Waiilatpu and Lapwai missions, keeping only the one among the Spokanes; but Whitman on a trip to the East in support of the missions won a reprieve.[37] Yet the missions did not prosper, and the Indians' lack of concern turned into hostility.

The missionary endeavors, especially the agricultural success of the Methodists in the Willamette Valley, building on the earlier agitation for the settlement of Oregon, helped to touch off a massive movement of Americans into Oregon. A migration of about a thousand emigrants left Independence, Missouri, in 1843 (guided by Marcus Whitman on his return from the East), and in the following years even larger companies swelled the American population in the Willamette Valley. By 1845 the population in Oregon was about six thousand, and the increase in American presence soon led to renewed pressure for sole American jurisdiction. The British, finding the fur trade declining and fearing the turbulent frontiersmen, moved from Fort Vancouver on the Columbia to Vancouver Island; and despite some braggadocio about "54° 40' or fight," the United States and Great Britain came to a peaceful agreement on June 15, 1846, by which the forty-ninth parallel boundary line was extended to the Pacific. The Oregon Country south of that line was now the undisputed posses-

35. The fullest and best account of the Whitmans is Drury, *Marcus and Narcissa Whitman.* See also Clifford M. Drury, *Henry Harmon Spalding, Pioneer of Old Oregon* (Caldwell, Idaho: Caxton Printers, 1936), and Clifford M. Drury, *Elkanah and Mary Walker: Pioneers among the Spokanes* (Caldwell, Idaho: Caxton Printers, 1940).

36. A thorough introduction to Catholic involvement with the Indians in the Pacific Northwest that is broader in scope than its title indicates is Robert Ignatius Burns, *The Jesuits and the Indian Wars of the Northwest* (New Haven: Yale University Press, 1966). On DeSmet, see H. M. Chittenden and A. T. Richardson, eds., *Life, Letters, and Travels of Father Pierre-Jean DeSmet, S.J., 1801–1873,* 4 vols. (New York: Francis P. Harper, 1905).

37. There is extended literature about the legend that Whitman "saved" Oregon by his trip to the East. An excellent analysis of the legend is in Drury, *Marcus and Narcissa Whitman,* 2: 375–86.

sion of the United States and its Indian affairs the concern of the federal government.

The United States government, however, was slow to accept its new responsibilities, and it made no immediate move to establish a territorial government or any administrative machinery to attend to Indian affairs. It is true that in 1842, while Oregon was still under joint occupation, Elijah White had been appointed Indian subagent for Oregon. He had successfully eased tensions between the whites and the Cayuse and Nez Perce Indians, but he made political enemies, and in 1845 he was removed from his position and not replaced.³⁸ The settlers, meanwhile, in good American fashion, in 1843 and 1845 had set up their own "provisional government," but they expected a formal territorial government to be set up. It was the Indian troubles in Oregon that finally produced some action in Congress.

When an epidimic of measles struck the Whitman mission, in which the whites under Dr. Whitman's care recovered while the Cayuse Indians ministered to by him died, the Indians were convinced that they had been poisoned as part of a missionary plot. On November 29, 1847, the Indians rose up against the mission and murdered Whitman, his wife, and a dozen others, taking captive the remaining women and children.³⁹ The outrage stirred up the people of Oregon, and in May the provisional legislature petitioned Congress for immediate territorial organization. The legislature noted, among other reasons for extending laws of the United States over the territory, that it had "no *power or right to treat with the Indian tribes,* nor means to pay them should we make a treaty," and that a general Indian war was likely. On August 14, 1848, President Polk signed the bill that created the Territory of Oregon, which made the governor ex officio superintendent of Indian affairs. The law specifically protected the rights of the Indians in the new territory "so long as such rights shall remain unextinguished by treaty between the United States and such Indians," and it vindicated the right of the United States to make laws and regulations regarding the Indians. As a stopgap measure, it provided funds for such presents to the Indians as might be required for the "peace and quietude of the country." Polk appointed as governor Joseph Lane, an able Kentucky politician, who was a hero of the Mexican War and later vice presidential candidate with Breckinridge in 1860. In the following March, Lane arrived in Oregon and declared the new government to be in operation. Lane's instruction of August 31, 1848, from the commissioner of Indian affairs di-

38. Hoopes, *Indian Affairs and Their Administration,* p. 70.

39. Drury, *Marcus and Narcissa Whitman,* 2: 205–65. For a history of the Cayuses, see Robert H. Ruby and John A. Brown, *The Cayuse Indians: Imperial Tribesmen of Old Oregon* (Norman: University of Oklahoma Press, 1972), and *The Spokane Indians: Children of the Sun* (Norman: University of Oklahoma Press, 1970).

rected him to collect information about the Indians in Oregon, the best arrangements for agencies, and the funds needed to manage Indian affairs in his territory.[40]

Lane observed the Indian situation by traveling through the territory, and he maintained a precarious peace. His views reflected the dominant white attitude toward Oregon's riches and the Indians who stood in the way of their exploitation. In his message to the Oregon legislature on July 17, 1849, he called attention to the wonders of the region and noted "how lavishly nature has bestowed her blessings on this favored land." Regarding the Indians, he told the legislators: "Surrounded as many of the tribes and bands now are, by the whites, whose arts of civilization, by destroying the resources of the Indians, doom them to poverty, want, and crime, the extinguishment of their title by purchase, and the locating them in a district removed from the settlements, is a measure of the most vital importance to them. Indeed, the cause of humanity calls loudly for their removal from causes and influences so fatal to their existence." Lane urged a memorial to Congress on the subject, and the Oregon legislature quickly responded with a long memorial dated July 20, 1849, that prayed for the purchase of the Indian lands and the removal of the Indians to some district "where their wretched and unhappy condition may be ameliorated."[41]

Lane's brief administration ended with the surrender by the Cayuses of the Whitman murderers, who were tried and executed in the summer of 1850. With the advent of Taylor's Whig administration, Democrat Lane was replaced as governor by John P. Gaines, who arrived in Oregon in August 1850. But by then Congress, following the urging of the territorial delegate from Oregon, Samuel R. Thurston, had made special provision for Indian affairs. Thurston's purposes were to extinguish all Indian title to lands west of the Cascade Mountains and to remove the Indians from that region to some location east of the mountains, and he urged that appropriate officials be appointed to handle Indian matters. Congress was sympathetic. On February 1, 1850, the House adopted Thurston's resolution, and on June 5 a law was approved that supported his desires. It called for the appointment of commissioners to negotiate treaties with the Oregon Indians to carry out his plans. Moreover, it removed the responsibility for

40. "Petition of Citizens of Oregon, praying that the laws of the United States may be extended over that Territory, &c.," *Senate Miscellaneous Document* no. 136, 30–1, serial 511, p. 4; 9 *United States Statutes* 323–31; William Medill to Lane, August 31, 1848, OIA LS, vol. 41, pp. 207–10 (M21, reel 41).

41. Lane to the secretary of war or commissioner of Indian affairs, October 22, 1849, *Senate Executive Document* no. 52, 31–1, serial 561, pp. 167–80; governor's message, July 17, 1849, ibid., p. 8; "Memorial of the Legislature of Oregon Praying for the Extinguishment of the Indian Title and the Removal of the Indians from Certain Portions of That Territory," July 20, 1849, *Senate Miscellaneous Document* no. 5, 31–2, serial 592.

Indian affairs from the territorial governor and authorized the appointment of a separate superintendent of Indian affairs, and it extended the intercourse law of 1834 over the Indians of Oregon Territory. One to three Indian agents were to be appointed by the president for Oregon.[42]

Anson Dart of Wisconsin was appointed superintendent, and three agents were named. Luke Lea instructed Dart to urge the Indians to live in peace and harmony among themselves, to induce them to engage in agricultural pursuits (encouraging them by prizes offered for the best crops), and to cooperate with the Christian missionaries working among the Indians without getting involved in sectarian disputes. The Indian, Lea said, has "but one alternative—early civilization or gradual extinction. The efforts of the government will be earnestly directed to his civilization and preservation, and we confidently rely upon their Christian teachers, that, in connection with their spiritual mission, they will aid in carrying out this policy." The adopted policy of the government toward the Indians of the West was repeatedly proclaimed. If the objectives of the civilization program for the Indians could be attained—"if they can be taught to subsist, not by the chase merely, a resource which must soon be exhausted, but by the rearing of flocks and herds, and by field cultivation, we may hope that the little remnant of this ill-fated race will not utterly perish from the earth, but have a permanent resting-place and home on some part of our broad domain, once the land of their fathers." Lea seemed to have no awareness that the Indians with whom Dart had to deal subsisted largely by fishing and that a change to an agricultural existence was neither wise nor easily accomplished.[43]

On October 25, 1850, three commissioners, including Governor Gaines, were appointed "to negotiate treaties with the several Indian tribes in the Territory of Oregon for the extinguishment of their claims to lands lying west of the Cascade Mountains." The goal of the government, they were told, was to free the land west of the Cascades entirely of Indian title and to move all the Indians to some spot to the east. Their instructions made it clear that the payments stipulated for the ceded lands were to be in objects beneficial to the Indians and that no part should be paid in money. The instructions specified agricultural assistance, hiring of blacksmiths and mechanics, employment of farmers to teach cultivation, physicians, and "ample provision for the purposes of education."[44]

The wishes of the Oregon settlers to clear the western part of Oregon of Indians, backed by the instructions of the federal government, ran up

42. *Congressional Globe*, 31st Congress, 1st session, p. 272; 9 *United States Statutes* 437.

43. Lea to Dart, July 20, 1850, CIA Report, 1850, serial 587, pp. 148–51.

44. A. S. Loughery, acting commissioner of Indian affairs, to J. P. Gaines, Alonzo H. Skinner, and Beverly S. Allen, October 25, 1850, CIA Report, 1850, serial 587, pp. 145–47.

against the Indians' adamant refusal to depart. The alternative was outlined by the commissioners:

> It will be impossible to remove the Indians of Willamette and lower
> Columbia valleys, without a resort to force, nor do we think it very
> desirable to do so. As before stated they are friendly and well disposed, they live almost entirely by fishing, and the wages they receive from the whites for their labor. They possess little or no skill as
> hunters or warriors. And to remove them from their fisheries and
> means of procuring labor from the whites would in our opinion insure their annihilation in a short time either from want or by the
> hands of their more warlike neighbors. General satisfaction we believe would be felt by the Indians and the citizens to allow them
> small reservations of a few sections and a portion of their fishing
> grounds.[45]

And this is what they provided in the six treaties they signed with the Indians in April and May 1851. Then the work of the commissioners was ended by an act of Congress of February 27, 1851, directing that all treaty making be carried on by regular officers of the Indian department, not by special commissioners. Superintendent Dart carried on the negotiations by himself. During the summer and fall of 1851 he signed thirteen treaties with Indian bands that freed more than six million acres of land of Indian title.[46]

For reasons that are difficult to pin down precisely, none of the treaties signed by the commissioners and by Dart were ever ratified. The failure to eliminate the Indians completely from west of the Cascades by providing residual reservations there for the tribes probably played an important part, for in this sense the treaties failed to accomplish what the congressional directive had stipulated. Some of the treaties, too, were negotiated with mere remnants of once more populous tribes. The Wheelappa band of Chinooks, with whom Dart signed a treaty on August 9, 1851, for example, had only two male survivors and a few women and children. And the cost of the annuities may have been another point of objection.[47]

45. Commissioners to Luke Lea, February 8, 1851, quoted in Hoopes, *Indian Affairs and Their Administration*, pp. 78–79. The commissioners made the same point when they submitted to the commissioner of Indian affairs the treaties containing provisions for reserved lands, contrary to the directions they had received. See commissioners to Lea, April 19 and May 14, 1851, CIA Report, 1851, serial 613, pp. 467–72.
46. The treaty making is discussed in detail in C. F. Coan, "The First Stage of the Federal Indian Policy in the Pacific Northwest, 1849–1852," *Oregon Historical Society Quarterly* 22 (March 1921): 46–65. In an appendix, pp. 65–89, Coan reprints the report of Dart to Lea, November 7, 1851, transmitting the treaties; also reprinted there are the few treaties that are extant. See also Hoopes, *Indian Affairs and Their Administration*, pp. 79–86.
47. Coan, "First Stage," pp. 59, 65.

The first round of treaties, then, did not bring a firm settlement of Indian problems facing the federal government in Oregon, and critical conditions remained. Whites moved into the territory in ever-increasing numbers, eager to lay their hands on the rich lands. Congress on September 27, 1850, by the so-called Donation Land Law, without concern for Indian titles, had provided grants of 320 acres to American citizens or prospective citizens who had resided in Oregon and cultivated the land for four years, and settlers felt entitled to take land wherever they chose.[48]

In the summer of 1853 Anson Dart resigned, and Joel Palmer, an Oregon pioneer, was appointed superintendent in his stead. Palmer, who served until August 1856, directed Indian affairs in Oregon in a critical period. As he took office troubles began with the Rogue River Indians, and a minor war raged through the summer and early fall of 1853. The Indians were subdued by army regulars and Oregon volunteers, and Palmer signed a treaty of cession with the Indians at Table Rock on September 10, 1853. By this treaty the Indians gave up their claims to land in Oregon and accepted a small section of their lands as a temporary reserve until a permanent reservation could be established. Annuities in the form of specified goods were provided, but article 7, added by the Senate, stipulated that the annuities at the discretion of the president could be used instead to establish farms for the benefit of the Indians. The treaty was ratified on April 12, 1854.[49]

With this success behind him, Palmer proceeded to negotiate a series of treaties with other tribes along the coast and with tribes in central Oregon that eliminated Indian title over much of the area between the Cascades and the coast, as well as a sizable section of the interior. Palmer had decided views about what the negotiations should include. In June 1853 he painted a bleak picture of the Indians' condition as they were pressed upon by the whites and as they succumbed to white vices and diseases, and then he set forth his proposal:

> If the benevolent designs of the government to preserve and elevate these remnants of the aborigines are to be carried forward to a suc-

---

48. 9 *United States Statutes* 496–500; James M. Bergquist, "The Oregon Donation Act and the National Land Policy," *Oregon Historical Quarterly* 58 (March 1957): 17–47. A contemporary reaction to the Donation Land Law was provided by the superintendent of Indian affairs in Washington Territory: "The inapplicability of the intercourse law, and its being in conflict with the act of Congress donating lands to settlers, &c., of September 27, 1850, renders it almost impossible to do anything without extinguishing their titles, and placing them in reservations where they can be cared for and attended to." Isaac I. Stevens to George W. Manypenny, December 26, 1853, *Senate Executive Document* no. 34, 33–1, serial 698, p. 6.

49. Kappler, pp. 603–5.

cessful issue, there appears but one path open. A home remote from the settlements must be selected for them. There they must be guarded from the pestiferous influence of degraded white men, and restrained by proper laws from violence and wrong among themselves. Let comfortable houses be erected for them, seeds and proper implements furnished, and instruction and encouragement given them in the cultivation of the soil. Let school-houses be erected, and teachers employed to instruct their children; and let the missionaries of the gospel of peace be encouraged to dwell among them. Let completeness of plan, energy, patience and perseverance characterize the effort; and, if still it fail, the government will have at least the satisfaction of knowing that an honest and determined endeavor was made to save and elevate a fallen race.[50]

The Palmer treaties were pretty much of a piece and fitted well into the pattern established throughout the West in the 1850s.[51] There was little indication in them that two sovereign equals were negotiating. For lack of other acceptable and established procedures, the treaties were the vehicle chosen to accomplish what the United States government wanted as it reacted to cries from western settlers and to the philosophical principles dominant in government circles. The Indians were to be moved out of the way of the whites—not, as in the case of the removal of the eastern tribes, to open spaces in the West, but to limited reserves within their old, more extensive territorial claims or to other specified locations within the territory. Most of the treaties were made with "confederated tribes and bands," an often more or less arbitrary grouping for convenience. In all of them the chiefs and headmen of these bands acknowledged "their dependence on the Government of the United States" and promised to stay on friendly terms with the citizens, sometimes consenting "to submit to, and observe all laws, rules, and regulations which may be prescribed by the United States for the government of said Indians." They agreed, moreover, to grant rights of way through their lands for roads and railroads. All claims of the Indians to lands were given up in return for small reservations within their old limits, but most of the Palmer treaties included a blanket agreement to move from these reserves to other locations selected by the government

50. Palmer to Manypenny, June 23, 1853, CIA Report, 1853, serial 690, p. 449. Palmer's annual report of October 8, 1853, is printed in *Oregon Historical Society Quarterly* 23 (March 1922): 28–38.

51. The treaties negotiated by Palmer and the Oregon Indians are printed in Kappler, pp. 606–7, 655–60, 665–69, 714–19, 740–42. C. F. Coan, "The Adoption of the Reservation Policy in the Pacific Northwest, 1853–1855," *Oregon Historical Society Quarterly* 23 (March 1922): 3–27, deals with the treaty making in Oregon and Washington territories.

"should the President at any time believe it demanded by the public good and promotive of the best interests of said Indians."

All the treaties spoke specifically of "civilization." Annuity payments for ceded lands, set for a limited term of years, were not to be in money, but in goods conducive to the agricultural development of the Indians and for their moral improvement and education. The United States, moreover, agreed to erect blacksmith shops, hospitals, and schoolhouses and to furnish for a period of years the necessary mechanics, physicians, and teachers. The treaties authorized the president to survey the reservations and assign lots in severalty to Indians "willing to avail themselves of the privilege, and who will locate thereon as a permanent home." An attack was made on the liquor menace by providing that annuities be withheld from Indians guilty of intemperance; and no annuities could be taken to pay the debts of individuals. Although government officials no doubt rejoiced in the framework of existence for the Indians envisaged in the treaties, the negotiations were in fact a nearly complete capitulation of the tribesmen to superior power.

The treaties signed by Palmer with the Indians in 1853 and 1854 were ratified and proclaimed in good time. When war broke out again in 1855, the Senate delayed ratification of the later treaties until the spring of 1859, causing incalculable problems in dealing with the Indians, who did not understand why the benefits promised them in the treaties were not forthcoming.

THE INDIANS OF WASHINGTON TERRITORY

On March 2, 1853, Washington Territory (initially bounded by the forty-ninth parallel to the north, the Rocky Mountains to the east, and the Columbia River and the forty-sixth parallel to the south) was broken off from Oregon Territory. Isaac Ingalls Stevens was appointed territorial governor and ex officio superintendent of Indian affairs. Stevens, from Massachusetts, was a West Point graduate with service in the Mexican War, who resigned his commission in March 1853 to accept the new position in the West; he was thirty-five years old. At his request the War Department placed him in charge of the party surveying the northern route for a Pacific railroad, and he met with Indian groups as he moved west from St. Paul to Olympia, the territorial capital.[52]

52. A scholarly biography of Stevens that pays close attention to his handling of Indian affairs is Kent D. Richards, *Isaac I. Stevens: Young Man in a Hurry* (Provo: Brigham Young University Press, 1979). Hazard Stevens, *The Life of Isaac Ingalls Stevens*, 2 vols. (Boston: Houghton, Mifflin and Company, 1900), is by his son and must be used with

Soon after Stevens's arrival he wrote to the commissioner of Indian affairs of the "urgent necessity" that treaties be made at once with the Indians west of the Cascades, for settlers were moving in rapidly and the Indians would be driven from their homes. He realized, however, that the
complete removal of the Indians from west of the Cascades was unrealis-
tic. He noted the attachment of the Indians to their hereditary residences
and that their customary means of subsistence by fishing would be seriously disrupted by removal into the interior. The solution was to provide
small reserves for them in their present locations. Stevens urged as well
treaties with the tribes in eastern Washington. "There is much valuable
land, and an inexhaustible supply of timber, east of the Cascades," he
wrote; "and I consider its speedy settlement so desirable that all impediments should be removed." Commissioner Manypenny strongly supported
the need for treaties; and Stevens, on a visit to Washington, D.C., in the
spring of 1854, added his own personal promotion of the idea. Congress
appropriated $45,000 for negotiating treaties with the Indians in Washing-
ton Territory and another $80,000 for holding a council with "the Black-
feet, Gros Ventres, and other wild tribes of Indians, immediately within or
adjacent to the eastern boundary of Washington Territory."[53]

Governor Stevens was an energetic and highly organized man, and his
career as superintendent of Indian affairs was marked by a series of dramatic councils with the Indians at which treaties of peace, cession, and
civilization were signed. In preparation for treating with the Indians, Stevens organized a commission, which met on December 7, 1854. The application of a pattern common to the whole nation is seen in the report of the
meeting, for the commission read and discussed the recent treaties made
by Commissioner Manypenny with the Otos and Missouris and with the
Omahas. After considerable discussion of reservations, fishing stations,
schools, and farms, George Gibbs, a talented Yale-trained lawyer and geolo-

---

caution because of its favorable bias, but it contains detailed accounts of the Indian councils. An account of the Indian tribes met on the way west is given in Stevens's report of
September 16, 1854, in CIA Report, 1854, serial 746, pp. 392–457; a final report appears
in *Reports of Explorations and Surveys, to Ascertain the Most Practicable and Economical Route for a Railroad from the Mississippi River to the Pacific Ocean*, vol. 12, book 1
(*House Executive Document* no. 56, 36–1, serial 1054). A useful description of the Washington Superintendency is James R. Masterson, "The Records of the Washington Superintendency of Indian Affairs, 1853–1874," *Pacific Northwest Quarterly* 37 (January
1946): 31–57.

   53. Stevens to Manypenny, December 26, 1853, *Senate Executive Document* no. 34,
33–1, serial 698, pp. 6–7; Stevens to Manypenny, December 29, 1853, ibid., pp. 13–14;
Manypenny to Robert McClelland, February 6, 1854, ibid., pp. 1–2; 10 *United States
Statutes* 330.

gist who was a member of the group, was delegated to prepare "a pro-
gramme of a Treaty" in accordance with the views of the commission.[54]

When the commission met again three days later, a draft of a treaty was
ready. Thus armed, the governor and his commissioners met on Christmas
Day with a number of tribes at Medicine Creek at the mouth of the Nisqually River. This was not to be a "negotiation" between two political
powers, of course, but an imposition upon the Indians of the treaty provisions Stevens brought with him, for he held a highly paternalistic view of
his relations with the tribes. As his wife remarked in a letter to her mother
that undoubtedly reflected her husband's opinions, the Indians "think so
much of the whites that a child can govern them." "Mr. Stevens," she said,
"has them right under his thumb—they are afraid as death of him and do
just as he tells them." On December 26 the governor spoke to the assembled Indians in a flowery and patronizing manner that expressed his
view of relations between the government and the tribesmen:

> This is a great day for you and for us. A day of Peace and Friendship
> between you and the Whites for all time to come. You are about to be
> paid for your lands, and the Great Father has sent me to-day to treat
> with you concerning the payment. The Great Father lives far off. He
> has many children: some of them came here when he knew but little
> of them or the Indians, and he has sent me to inquire into these
> things. We went through this Country last year, learned your num-
> bers and saw your wants. We felt much for you and went to the Great
> Father to tell him what we had seen. The Great Father felt for his
> children—he pitied them, and he has sent me here to-day to express
> those feelings, and to make a Treaty for your benefit.[55]

The prepared treaty was explained point by point to the Indians, who
signed it on December 26 without objection. The terms were very similar
to those in the treaties signed by Joel Palmer and the Oregon Indians, but
in addition to those terms, specific provision was made to protect the fishing rights of the Indians. The United States agreed to maintain for twenty
years an agricultural and industrial school for the children of the signatory
bands and for those of other tribes and bands, at a general agency to be set
up for the Puget Sound region. This treaty was promptly ratified.[56]

In quick succession, Stevens and his assistants signed similar treaties

54. "Records of the Proceedings of the Commission to hold Treaties with the Indian
Tribes in Washington Territory and the Blackfoot Country," Records of the Office of Indian Affairs, Documents Relating to the Negotiation of Ratified and Unratified Treaties
with Various Indian Tribes (T494, reel 5, frames 205–6).

55. Ibid. (frames 206–9). Margaret Stevens's letters of February 17 and 18, 1855, are
quoted in Richards, *Isaac I. Stevens*, p. 195.

56. Kappler, pp. 661–64.

with other groups of coastal Indians at Point Elliott (January 22, 1855), Point No Point (January 26), and Neah Bay (January 31). With that of Medicine Creek, these treaties cleared a wide area of land around Puget Sound, but they were not ratified until 1859.[57]

The summer and fall of 1855 were taken up by three great councils with the Indians in which Stevens, with his usual drive and energy, expected to impose on the Indians of the interior his vision of their future. The first was the Walla Walla Council in late May and early June, attended by Joel Palmer as well as Stevens and made up of delegations of Walla Walla, Cayuse, Umatilla, Yakima, and Nez Perce Indians. The Indians, aside from the generally friendly Nez Perces, were hostile, and concessions, including special cash annuities for the chiefs, had to be made to get signatures on the treaties. Two treaties were signed on June 9, one with the Walla Wallas, Cayuses, and Umatillas and a second with the Yakimas. Another on June 11 was signed with the Nez Perces. They contained the usual provisions for cessions, reservations, annuity payments, employment of mechanics, articles for agricultural development, and means for moral improvement and education. But the treaties were not the successes that Stevens assumed, for the chiefs were offended by the terms that the whites proposed and could see their crushing effect. The Jesuit missionary Joseph Joset commented: "The chiefs agreed to a mock treaty in order to gain time and prepare for war."[58]

In mid-July Stevens moved on to Hell Gate on the Clark Fork just beyond the northern end of the Bitterroot Valley for a council with Flathead, Kutenai, and Pend d'Oreille Indians. The treaty, similar to those at Walla Walla, was signed on July 16, 1855.[59] At Hell Gate, too, there was much agitation among the Indians as they argued about a proper location for the reduced reservation they were expected to accept. The deep Indian attachment for traditional homelands was not sufficiently appreciated by the whites, who looked chiefly at the economic potentialities of a reservation for sustaining the Indians in a peaceful agricultural existence, and the treaty was signed by the Indians with the understanding that the president would survey the region and designate an acceptable spot.[60]

57. Ibid., pp. 669–77, 682–85. Extracts from the proceedings at Point No Point are printed in Charles M. Gates, ed., "The Indian Treaty of Point No Point," *Pacific Northwest Quarterly* 46 (April 1955): 52–58.

58. Quoted in Burns, *Jesuits and the Indian Wars*, p. 79. There is an excellent account of the council and its background in Josephy, *Nez Perce Indians*, pp. 285–332; a shortened version is in Josephy, "A Most Satisfactory Council," *American Heritage* 16 (October 1965): 26–31, 70–76. The treaties are printed in Kappler, pp. 694–706.

59. Kappler, pp. 722–25.

60. The most thorough critical account of the council is in Burns, *Jesuits and the Indian Wars*, pp. 96–114. An incomplete version of the official minutes is in Albert J.

The final grand council was held in October with the Blackfeet, Flatheads, and Nez Perces at the mouth of the Judith River in present-day Montana. It fulfilled a need, observed by Stevens when he crossed the continent with the railroad survey expedition in 1853, for a treaty of peace between the often warring tribes of the northern Rockies; and the $80,000 appropriated by Congress in 1854 had been for this purpose. Joel Palmer and Alfred Cumming, superintendent of the Central Superintendency, were named with Stevens as commissioners for the treaty. Manypenny told them that the principal objects were the establishment of well-defined and permanent relations of amity between the Indians and the United States and between the tribes themselves. "A cordial, firm, and perpetual peace should be established," the commissioner of Indian affairs directed; "a well understood recognition by the Indians of their allegiance to the United States, and their obligation to obey its laws, should be obtained, and a high regard on their part for its justice, magnanimity and power, should be fostered or inculcated."[61]

After some false starts occasioned by a delay in the arrival of goods to be distributed as presents, the council was opened on October 16 by Stevens and Cumming with thirty-five hundred Indians in attendance; Joel Palmer did not come. The treaty, signed on October 17, began with formal statements of perpetual peace between the United States and the Indians and between the signatory tribes themselves and with other tribes. Boundaries were specified for common hunting grounds for the Indians for a period of ninety-nine years, and the lands belonging exclusively to the Blackfeet were described. The United States agreed to provide the Blackfeet with certain annuities and to instruct them in agricultural and mechanical pursuits, to educate their children, and in other aspects to promote their "civilization and Christianization." This treaty was ratified by the Senate on April 15, 1856.[62] But those signed at the Walla Walla and Flathead councils had to wait for ratification until March 1859, together with those signed with the western Washington tribes and Palmer's Oregon Indian treaties.

Stevens used the Indian councils to promote his interests in the north-

---

Partoll, ed., "The Flathead Indian Treaty Council of 1855," *Pacific Northwest Quarterly* 29 (July 1938): 283–314. See also Burns, "A Jesuit at the Hell Gate Treaty of 1855," *Mid-America* 34 (April 1952): 87–114.

61. Manypenny to Cumming, Stevens, and Palmer, May 3, 1855, CIA Report, 1855, serial 810, pp. 530–31.

62. Kappler, pp. 736–40. For accounts of the council, see Burns, *Jesuits and the Indian Wars*, pp. 117–23; John C. Ewers, *The Blackfeet: Raiders on the Northwestern Plains* (Norman: University of Oklahoma Press, 1958), pp. 214–22; and Alfred J. Partoll, ed., "The Blackfoot Indian Peace Council," *Frontier and Midland: A Magazine of the West* 17 (Spring 1937): 199–207.

ern railroad route. As he and his party traveled to the council sites, he continued to explore the land in terms of railroad possibilities. Even the military operations against the Indians were used for the same purpose, for, as he wrote in his final report on the survey, the military expeditions were always accompanied by one or two staff officers experienced in exploration, whose observations contributed materially to the knowledge of the country. Stevens was ever aware of the three tasks he was simultaneously engaged in: promoting a northern route for the transcontinental railroad, diligently working to build up a populous, enterprising white settlement in Washington Territory, and settling Indian affairs, by treaty and if need be by war. It is easy, in looking back to the 1850s, to see a serious conflict of interest in the governor-superintendent's position, but Stevens himself did not see it that way, for in his mind all were coordinated to produce a peaceful and prosperous region, of which he was an ardent advocate.

The delay in treaty ratification, which so seriously complicated Indian relations, was due primarily to the wars that broke out in 1855. Increasing penetration of their country by whites stirred up both the Rogue River Indians in Oregon and the Yakimas and their allies in central Washington. The simultaneous operations that resulted, the Rogue River War and the Yakima War, can be considered a single military endeavor. The troubles began while Stevens was still engaged in his council with the Blackfeet far to the east. Hostile acts by the Yakimas and the Oregon Indians, including the murder of Yakima Indian agent A. J. Bolen, called out volunteers to augment the military strength of the small regular army garrisons, and military operations continued in the two territories into the summer of 1856. The Rogue River and Umatilla hostiles in Oregon surrendered in June and were concentrated on the Coast Reservation. In Washington the interior Indians, joined by those around Puget Sound, carried on a longer struggle under the Yakima chief Kamiakin. Quarrels between Stevens and the military commander John Wool and recriminations over action of the volunteers did little to bring the war to a close, and military action brought only temporary pacification of the hostile Indians. Not until 1858, when defeat of a column under Lieutenant Colonel Edward J. Steptoe called forth strong punitive action by troops under Colonel George Wright, did peace return to the Northwest. After victories in the battles of Four Lakes and Spokane Plains, Wright traversed the Indian country, executing culprits accused of inciting attacks and, with the mediation of the Jesuit missionary Joset, gaining the submission of the defeated chiefs.[63]

63. The action in these wars can be followed in Robert M. Utley, *Frontiersmen in Blue: The United States Army and the Indian, 1848–1865* (New York: Macmillan Company, 1967), pp. 175–210; Burns, *Jesuits and the Indian Wars*, pp. 158–355. See also Robert Ignatius Burns, ed., "Pere Joset's Account of the Indian War of 1858," *Pacific North-*

The military action was decisive in Oregon and Washington. The Indians, unlike those in many parts of the nation, had moved beyond their guerilla warfare and, with well-defined war aims, met their enemy in open battlefield encounters, in which they were decisively defeated. The ending of the war opened the way for ratification of the treaties by the Senate on March 8, 1859. The movement to the reservations and the advance toward the white man's ways of life that those treaties specified became the lot of the Indians in the Pacific Northwest. "Reservation life proved fully as unhappy as they had expected," Robert Utley has written, "but the memory of Colonel Wright hung over them, and never again did they try to deflect their destiny by force of arms."[64]

The reservation policy that had determined Indian affairs in the Northwest was strongly supported by the successors of Palmer and Stevens. Absolom F. Hedges, who replaced Palmer in August 1856, envisaged self-supporting reservations and manual labor schools to civilize the Indians, although he was in office too short a time to accomplish much. On March 3, 1857, the separate superintendencies for Oregon and Washington were abolished and a joint superintendency provided, with James W. Nesmith as superintendent. Nesmith considered the ultimate civilization and Christianization of the Indians "utopian and impracticable." But he saw what happened when the whites and Indians were in contact and pleaded for ratification of the treaties so that the Indians could be placed on reservations where the intercourse laws could be enforced and peace and quiet maintained in the region.[65] The Presbyterian missionary Edward R. Geary, who replaced Nesmith in April 1859, had a more sanguine view of Indian advancement, holding firmly to the evangelical Christian view of Indian potentialities. "Amidst many failures," he wrote, "enough has been achieved to establish the improvability, intellectually, morally and socially, of the Indian race, and that the impediments to their elevation are not innate and peculiar, but such as would be found in any other portion of the human family, in the same conditions, and affected by the same influences." Geary noted the improvement that came with the final ratification of the treaties, but, because of Indian opposition, he could report little

---

west Quarterly 38 (October 1947): 285–307. Stevens's quarrels with the military are discussed in Kent Richards, "Isaac I. Stevens and Federal Military Power in Washington Territory," *Pacific Northwest Quarterly* 63 (July 1972): 81–86. Official documents on the wars are printed in *House Executive Document* no. 93, 34–1, serial 858, and in *House Executive Document* no. 76, 34–3, serial 906.

64. Utley, *Frontiersmen in Blue*, p. 209.

65. Hoopes, *Indian Affairs and Their Administration*, pp. 126–27; report of Nesmith, September 1, 1857, CIA Report, 1857, serial 919, pp. 605–6; report of Nesmith, August 20, 1858, CIA Report, 1858, serial 974, pp. 566–74.

progress in the education that he deemed so essential. Establishment of industrial schools, under the direction of religious men—"those who from a sentiment of humanity, guided and energized by the strong convictions of moral obligations, have devoted their lives to the efforts of Christian beneficence"—was his principal recommendation.[66]

66. Report of Geary, September 1, 1859, CIA Report, 1859, serial 1023, p. 753; report of Geary, October 1, 1860, CIA Report, 1860, serial 1078, pp. 408–9. The joint superintendency ended in early 1861.

PART FOUR

The
Civil War
Years

Indian affairs during the years of the Civil War were marked by two distinct situations. In the first place, the Civil War had a direct bearing on Indian relations in the Indian Territory and the neighboring state of Kansas. The defection of the slave-holding Indian nations from their treaty obligations to the Union and their signing of treaties of allegiance and alliance with the Confederate States of America brought them into the Civil War as formal participants, while loyal factions that fled to Kansas created additional problems for the federal government.

In the second place, this period in the West was one of continuing development and settlement, with throngs of whites moving into new areas in search of precious metals or agricultural riches. It was almost as though westerners were unaware of the great battle raging between the North and the South. The Pike's Peak gold rush of 1859 and the concurrent discoveries in Nevada were soon followed by the establishment of Colorado and Nevada territories in 1861; and Nevada achieved statehood in 1864. Then the mining frontiers moved rapidly both north and south, with political organization of new territories coming quickly in the wake of the first major strikes. Arizona Territory was created in 1863, and in the same year Idaho Territory was set up to satisfy the whites who had rushed into the Snake River region. New discoveries of precious metals in what is now western Montana led to thriving centers of population at Virginia City and Helena. In May 1864 Congress created Montana Territory. These advances cut deep into Indian lands, and the increased traffic they occasioned between the mining settlements and the more established sections of the country further exasperated the Indians. Meanwhile, growing white population on the central plains brought new pressure upon the Indian tribes there. Kansas grew in population from 107,206 in 1860 to 364,399 in 1870 and Nebraska (which became a state in 1867) from 28,841 to 122,993.

The Civil War years were filled with Indian-white conflicts growing out of white invasion of Indian lands. These serious encounters were aggravated by the weakening of federal authority in the West as regular troops were withdrawn and replaced by volunteers, who were often few in number, inexperienced in Indian control, and too frequently imbued with frontier hostility toward Indians. Yet the federal government, despite the fact that its energies were fully engaged in the great sectional struggle, could not totally ignore the Indians, and both the Indian service (working under the weight of a patronage system that placed political appointees in sensitive positions) and the army had to worry about the "second front."

The Lincoln government met the challenges by continuing the fundamental policies of the preceding decades: an absolute commitment to transformation of the Indians into the white man's civilization and the development of restricted reservations as the principal "first step" in that process. The principle was well expressed by the commissioner of Indian affairs in 1863 when he wrote to two special agents in Kansas in response to questions they had sent about allotment of Potawatomi lands: "The Government recognizes Indians who still continue their tribal organization as its wards, requiring and entitled to its protection and guardianship. It is the Policy of the Government to reclaim and civilize the Indians, and to induce them to abandon their tribal organizations and adopt the customs and arts of civilized society. That solution of all questions which relate to the disposition of the lands or other property which will most conduce to the desired result should be adopted."[1]

The special problems arising out of relations with the Five Civilized Tribes in the Indian Territory, the outbreak of Sioux Indians in Minnesota, and the subjugation of the Apaches and Navajos in New Mexico necessitated military action and in some cases military control, but in the end civilian management of the tribes by the Indian Office was vindicated.

Abraham Lincoln himself devoted little personal attention to Indian affairs. His own experience with Indians, like that of his predecessors, had been minimal. He had had little contact with Indians in Indiana and Illinois; and even his brief tour as a militia captain in the Black Hawk War

1. William P. Dole to Special Commissioners Wolcott and Ross, April 28, 1863, OIA LS, vol. 70, p. 494 (M21, reel 70).

had not furnished any real experience in dealing with Indians and their problems. In the Lincoln-Douglas debates of 1858, Douglas at Ottawa tried to make capital of Lincoln's desire to provide citizenship for "negroes, Indians and other inferior races." When Lincoln ignored the challenge about Indians, Douglas at Alton tried again, declaring that when the signers of the Declaration of Independence had said that all men were created equal, they "did not mean the negro, nor the savage Indians, nor the Fejee Islanders, nor any other barbarous race." Lincoln answered forthrightly, quoting from an earlier speech at Springfield: "I think the authors of that notable instrument intended to include *all* men. . . . They meant to set up a standard maxim for free society . . . [applicable] to all people, of all colors, every where."[2]

That Lincoln's humane principles applied to Indians there can be little doubt, but he held common white views about their destiny. In an address to a delegation of plains Indians at the White House in March 1863, he spoke of peace and the observation of treaties, but his advice to his "red brethren" was typical of his age: "The pale-faced people are numerous and prosperous because they cultivate the earth, produce bread, and depend upon the products of the earth rather than wild game for subsistence. . . . I can only say that I can see no way in which your race is to become as numerous and prosperous as the white race except by living as they do, by the cultivation of the earth."[3]

Lincoln could not give Indian problems high priority amid the other crises that filled his presidency; only when forced to look at them because of spectacular events such as the Sioux outbreak in Minnesota or the southern refugee Indian flight into Kansas or because of the prodding of reformers did he act personally in regard to the Indians. Mostly he left Indian matters in the hands of the secretary of the interior and, even more, the commissioner of Indian affairs.

2. *The Lincoln-Douglas Debates of 1858*, ed. Robert W. Johannsen (New York: Oxford University Press, 1965), pp. 45–46, 299, 304.

3. Report of the meeting in *Daily Morning Chronicle* (Washington), March 27, 1863, printed in *Collected Works of Abraham Lincoln*, ed. Roy P. Basler, 9 vols. (New Brunswick: Rutgers University Press, 1953–1955), 6: 151–52. A brief treatment of Lincoln and the Indians is Harry Kelsey, "Abraham Lincoln and American Indian Policy," *Lincoln Herald* 77 (Fall 1975): 139–48; a fuller treatment that is very critical of Lincoln is David A. Nichols, *Lincoln and the Indians: Civil War Policy and Politics* (Columbia: University of Missouri Press, 1978).

CHAPTER 16

The Southern Indians
and the Confederate States

Tribes in the Indian Territory. Indian

Treaties with the Confederacy. War in

the Indian Territory. Peace Council at

Fort Smith. Reconstruction Treaties.

When secession and the Civil War occurred, Indian affairs took on a new dimension, for the Indian country in the West was of strategic importance in the war. Of vital concern to both the North and the South was the attitude of the southern Indians—especially the Cherokees, Creeks, Choctaws, Chickasaws, and Seminoles—now living in the area to which they had been removed, north of Texas and west of Arkansas.[1]

TRIBES IN THE INDIAN TERRITORY

The Five Civilized Tribes, or at least significant portions of them, were southern in sympathy as well as location. They were dominated by mixed-bloods, many of whom were slave-owners, and cultural affinity to the

1. The most complete and thoroughly documented study of these Indians in the war is the series of three volumes by Annie Heloise Abel under the general title *The Slaveholding Indians* (Cleveland: Arthur H. Clark Company), vol. 1 (1915): *The American Indian as Slaveholder and Secessionist: An Omitted Chapter in the Diplomatic History of the Southern Confederacy*; vol. 2 (1919): *The American Indian as Participant in the Civil War*; and vol. 3 (1929): *The American Indian under Reconstruction*. I have relied upon these volumes as a guide to printed sources, and the volumes themselves contain copies of a great many documents. A shorter general article is Annie Heloise Abel, "The Indians in the Civil War," *American Historical Review* 15 (January 1910):

southern states as well as practical political interests tilted them toward the seceding states. Even so, it is difficult to understand how Indian groups so recently uprooted from their traditional lands by Georgia, Alabama, Mississippi, and Tennessee—action vigorously opposed and condemned by northern states—could now forswear their allegiance and treaty obligations to the Union and ally themselves with the South. Despite large Unionist factions, especially among the Creeks and the Cherokees, all of the Five Civilized Tribes signed formal treaties with the Confederate States of America, and some of the smaller Indian groups in the Indian Territory joined them in this switch of allegiance.

Geographical location had a significant influence. The Choctaws and Chickasaws were located along the Red River adjacent to Texas, and the Choctaws were bordered on the east by Arkansas. Thus caught in a vise between two ardent members of the Confederacy, there was little likelihood that they could maintain a neutral or Unionist position even if they had been inclined to do so. The Creeks and Seminoles and even more the Cherokees, located farther north, could for a while think of neutrality and at least hope for effective support and succor from the North. The Cherokees held out the longest, and only under extreme pressure did the Union faction, led by John Ross, succumb.

The Indian department officials in the Indian Territory at the outbreak of the Civil War were largely southern sympathizers, for the federal patronage system had long emphasized local men. The agents, the agency employees, and the traders were southerners, in many cases from Arkansas and Texas. Douglas H. Cooper, a Mississippian appointed Choctaw and Chickasaw agent by President Buchanan, became a key military officer of the Confederacy in the West, and even among the agents appointed by Lincoln when he took office there were southern men who worked for secession. Elias Rector, superintendent of the Southern Superintendency, which was responsible for the Indians south of Kansas, was a cousin and close associate of Henry Rector, secessionist governor of Arkansas, and worked closely with him in drawing the Indians into the Confederate fold.[2]

There were, moreover, financial considerations. The trust funds of the Indians, invested by the federal government for the benefit of the tribes,

---

281–96. See also Sammy D. Buice, "The Civil War and the Five Civilized Tribes: A Study in Federal-Indian Relations" (Ph.D. dissertation, University of Oklahoma, 1970); and Ohland Morton, "Confederate Government Relations with the Five Civilized Tribes," *Chronicles of Oklahoma* 31 (Summer 1953): 189–204; 31 (Autumn 1953): 299–322.

2. Abel, *Indian as Slaveholder*, pp. 59–60. William H. Garrett, Creek agent, was from Alabama; Robert J. Cowart, Cherokee agent, was from Georgia; Matthew Leeper, agent for the Indians in the Leased District, was from Texas; and Andrew J. Dorn, Neosho River agent, was from Arkansas. Ibid., p. 82 n.

were almost entirely in southern stocks and bonds. There was a fear, played upon heavily by the secessionists, that these funds would be forfeited if the tribes maintained their attachment to the North.[3]

The southern Indians questioned the genuineness of the support of their interests by Lincoln's Republican administration. They recalled the remark of William H. Seward in a Chicago speech during the presidential campaign of 1860—"The Indian territory, also, south of Kansas, must be vacated by the Indians"—and it was easy to build up this chance remark in a political speech into a policy of once again contracting their territories. They were aware, too, of the defenseless nature of their situation as far as northern military support was concerned. In the late 1850s the War Department, despite vigorous protests by the secretary of the interior, had persisted in a general withdrawal of troops from the Indian Territory. When the war broke out, the remaining Union forces were withdrawn, and the military posts were occupied by Confederate forces. The Indians were left at the mercy of the Confederacy, and southern officials were quick to capitalize on all the points in their favor.[4]

The election of Lincoln and the secession of the Deep South could not be ignored by the Indian nations. The first to react formally, and apparently on their own initiative, were the Chickasaws. At a special meeting of their national legislature, the tribe on January 5, 1861, issued a call to the Choctaw, Creek, Cherokee, and Seminole nations to send commissioners to an intertribal conference "for the purpose of entering into some compact, not inconsistent with the Laws and Treaties of the United States, for the future security and protection of the rights and Citizens of said nations, in the event of a change in the United States."[5] The conference met at the Creek Agency on February 17, with scanty attendance by the Creeks, Seminoles, and Cherokees and no Chickasaws or Choctaws. The tone of the meeting was one of caution, set by John Ross in his instructions to the Cherokee delegates, which warned against premature action and pointed to the obligations of their treaties with the United States.[6]

3. Ibid., p. 61; George Dewey Harmon, "The Indian Trust Funds, 1797–1865," *Mississippi Valley Historical Review* 21 (June 1934): 23–30. The use of the trust funds in Confederate arguments to the Indians can be seen in David Hubbard to John Ross and Ben McCulloch, June 12, 1861, *The War of the Rebellion: A Compilation of the Official Records of the Union and Confederate Armies*, 70 vols. (Washington: GPO, 1880–1901), series 1, 13: 497; henceforth cited as *Official Records*.

4. Abel, *Indian as Slaveholder*, pp. 52–59. Seward's speech is in *The Works of William H. Seward*, ed. George E. Baker, 5 vols. (Boston: Houghton, Mifflin and Company, 1853–1884), 4: 363.

5. Quoted in Abel, *Indian as Slaveholder*, pp. 68–69 n.

6. Instructions of John Ross to Cherokee delegation, February 12, 1861, quoted ibid., p. 71 n.

Meanwhile, the Choctaws were striking out on their own. In a meeting on February 7, 1861, they passed a series of resolutions expressing the sentiments of their General Council in regard to the political disagreement between the North and the South. The Choctaws deprecated the unhappy state of affairs and hoped that the differences between the sections could be honorably adjusted, but they took an unequivocal stand in the case that did not occur:

> *Resolved further*: That in the event a permanent dissolution of the American Union takes place, our many relations with the General Government must cease, and we shall be left to follow the natural affections, education, institutions, and interests of our people, which indissolubly bind us in every way to the destiny of our neighbors and brethren of the Southern States, upon whom we are confident we can rely for the preservation of our rights of life, liberty, and property, and the continuance of many acts of friendship, general counsel, and material support.

The Choctaws made a special bow of amity toward Arkansas and Texas and directed that a copy of the resolutions be sent to the governors of the southern states.[7] Although one small party, of which Peter Pitchlynn was a member, hoped to maintain neutrality, the bulk of the nation was strongly for the Confederacy, and it convinced or intimidated the opposition.[8]

The Chickasaws did not act until after the Civil War had broken out. On May 25, 1861, their legislature, with the approval of Governor Cyrus Harris, threw in their lot with the South. They saw the secession and war as the dissolution of the United States under the Constitution, thus freeing them from their treaty obligations, and noted the failure of the Lincoln government, "pretending to represent said Union," to protect them. They predicted a bloody war that they could not escape. "Our geographical position, our social and domestic institutions, our feelings and sympathies," their resolution read, "all attach us to our Southern friends." Their rights, they believed, would be recognized and protected by the Confederate States, and "as a Southern people we consider their cause our own." The Chickasaws made a strong point of the fact that "the current of the events of the last few months has left the Chickasaw Nation *independent*," free to form such alliances as seemed best to it. They appealed to the neighboring tribes

7. *Official Records*, series 1, 1: 682, quoted in full in Abel, *Indian as Slaveholder*, pp. 73–74.

8. Angie Debo, *The Rise and Fall of the Choctaw Republic* (Norman: University of Oklahoma Press, 1934), pp. 80–109. Pitchlynn's part is discussed in W. David Baird, *Peter Pitchlynn: Chief of the Choctaws* (Norman: University of Oklahoma Press, 1972), pp. 126–28.

to join them in defending their territory from "the Lincoln hordes and Kansas robbers, who have plundered and oppressed our red brethren among them, and who doubtless would extend towards us the protection which the wolf gives to the lamb should they succeed in overrunning our country."[9]

In the face of such a sympathetic movement of the Indians toward the Confederacy, the federal Indian Office offered little to reassure the Indians. Perhaps unaware of the secessionist action taken by the Choctaws and the Chickasaws (for communications with the Indian Territory were almost nonexistent after the departure of Unionist agents and federal troops), Indian Commissioner William P. Dole on May 11, 1861, addressed a circular letter to the chiefs of the Five Civilized Tribes, telling them that neither Lincoln nor any government agents had any intention of interfering with their domestic institutions and that an appeal had been made to the War Department to furnish them the protection called for in their treaties with the United States. It was an ineffectual statement, carried to the Indians by the new southern superintendent, William G. Coffin, who was delayed in getting to his post, and it showed the ineffectiveness of the Indian Office's attempt to get action from the War Department, which by that date more than had its hands full elsewhere.[10]

INDIAN TREATIES WITH THE CONFEDERACY

The Confederacy was much more energetic in its concern for Indian affairs. It saw at once the strategic necessity of drawing the Indian Territory into its camp and the need to act expeditiously before the withdrawn federal troops could be replaced by volunteers, who might shore up any sagging Union sentiment among the Indians.

The provisional government of the Confederate States on February 21, 1861, resolved to open negotiations with the Indian tribes in the West, and four days later it proposed appointing agents to those tribes. On March 15, a Bureau of Indian Affairs was created in the War Department, and the next day David Hubbard was nominated by President Jefferson Davis to head the bureau.[11] While this administrative machinery was being set up, the Department of State under Robert Toombs was promoting the appoint-

9. The resolution is in *Official Records*, series 1, 3: 585–87. The Chickasaw part in the Civil War and Reconstruction is told in Arrell M. Gibson, *The Chickasaws* (Norman: University of Oklahoma Press, 1971), pp. 227–46.

10. Dole to Indian chiefs, May 11, 1861, CIA Report, 1861, serial 1117, pp. 650–51; Dole to Caleb B. Smith, May 30, 1861, ibid., pp. 651–52. See also Abel, *Indian as Slaveholder*, pp. 80–82.

11. Abel, *Indian as Slaveholder*, pp. 127–28.

ment of a special diplomatic agent to deal with the Indian tribes west of
Arkansas. In May the provisional Congress passed an act for the protection
of the Indian tribes, under which Albert Pike was appointed special agent
for negotiating treaties with the Indians. A native of New England, Pike
had become a prominent lawyer in Arkansas; he had also gained military
experience in the Mexican War, and he was even a poet of some renown.
He was an excellent choice for dealing with the Indians, for he respected
their rights and was generous in the guarantees he wrote into the treaties
he signed with them.[12]

Pike failed in his first attempt to persuade John Ross to align the Cherokee Nation with the Confederacy, but he passed on to quick success with
the other tribes. The Creeks signed a treaty on July 10, 1861, the Choctaws
on July 12, and the Seminoles on August 1.[13] All these treaties began with a
preamble that indicated the Confederacy's offer "to assume and accept the
protectorate of the several nations and tribes of Indians occupying the
country west of Arkansas and Missouri, and to recognize them as their
wards, subject to all the rights, privileges and immunities, titles and guár-
anties, with each of said nations and tribes under treaties made with them
by the United States of America" and the Indians' agreement thereto. It
was a formal transfer of allegiance and loyalty from the Union to the Confederacy. The tribes, moreover, agreed to offensive and defensive alliances
with the South.

The treaties recognized the existing territorial limits of the tribes, and
they guaranteed fee simple ownership of the lands within the boundaries.
The lands were never to be included in any state or territory, nor would a
tribe, without its consent, be organized as a territory or state. In many respects the treaties were the same as the earlier treaties with the United
States; but the new treaties were more generous to the tribes, and the tone
was one of conciliation rather than dictation, for Pike promised the Indians many things that they had been contending for with the United
States. The Indians were allowed more control of their trade, property
rights in slaves were guaranteed, and financial benefits were promised. It
was necessary for the rights of the Indians to be clearly recognized when
Indian alliances were so desperately sought by the Confederacy.

The treaties, as Pike negotiated them, contained a provision for Indian
delegates in the Confederate Congress, and the Choctaw-Chickasaw treaty
provided for ultimate statehood (to which the Creeks, Seminoles, and

12. Ibid., pp. 129–41. For a biography of Pike, see Walter L. Brown, "Albert Pike,
1809–1891" (Ph.D. dissertation, University of Texas, 1955).

13. The treaties are printed in *Official Records*, series 4, 1: 426–43, 445–66, 513–27.
They are exhaustively analyzed in Abel, *Indian as Slaveholder*, pp. 157–80. See also
Kenny A. Franks, "An Analysis of the Confederate Treaties with the Five Civilized
Tribes," *Chronicles of Oklahoma* 50 (Winter 1972–1973): 458–73.

Cherokees could be joined). President Davis objected to both these provisions as impolitic and unconstitutional, and the treaties were amended to leave the decision on delegates and admission of states to the House of Representatives and to Congress.[14]

Pike moved on from his success with these major tribes, which he treated with great solicitude, to negotiate with the lesser tribes in the Indian Territory. He went first to the Wichita and Comanche tribes in the Leased District, a region west of the ninty-eighth meridian that the United States in 1855 had rented from the Choctaws and Chickasaws for the settlement of Wichita Indians and other tribes and that passed under jurisdiction of the Confederate States by the Choctaw-Chickasaw treaty of July 12. These tribes were less important to the cause of the South than the Five Civilized Tribes and received few concessions. The two treaties, signed on August 12, were primarily treaties of peace and of promoting civilization, in large part to satisfy the citizens of Texas, who were ravaged by Indian raids. They contained little if anything to distinguish them from treaties made by the United States with the western tribes except, of course, that the Indians placed themselves "under the laws and protection of the Confederate States of America." They were full of the rhetoric of paternalism—promising the Indians their reserves "as long as grass shall grow and water run," providing for livestock and agricultural assistance, and asking of the tribes only "that they will settle upon their reserves, become industrious, and prepare to support themselves, and live in peace and quietness."[15]

The Cherokees were still outside the southern fold, but as Pike was negotiating in the west, John Ross abandoned his neutral stance and threw in his lot with the Confederacy. This was a surprising move, for Ross had formally declared his neutrality and his intention of holding firm to his treaty relationship with the United States. He had answered the pressures from Governor Rector of Arkansas firmly but politely, and to a Texas commission that visited him he reiterated his neutral stand. On May 17, 1861, in fact, Ross issued a formal proclamation of neutrality, reminding the Cherokees of their obligations to the United States and urging them to abstain from partisan discussions and actions.[16] When the Confederate Indian

14. Davis message of December 12, 1861, James D. Richardson, comp., *Compilation of the Messages and Papers of the Confederacy: Including the Diplomatic Correspondence, 1861–1865*, 2 vols. (Nashville: United States Publishing Company, 1905), 1: 149–51. The ratification action of the Confederate Congress is printed with each treaty in *Official Records*.

15. *Official Records*, series 4, 1: 542–54. See also Arrell M. Gibson, "Confederates on the Plains: The Pike Mission to Wichita Agency," *Great Plains Journal* 4 (Fall 1964): 7–16.

16. "Proclamation to the Cherokee People," May 17, 1861, *Official Records*, series 1, 13: 489–90.

commissioner, David Hubbard, tried to win Ross over in June by suggesting that the southern states had treated Indians far better than the northern and that the only hope for preserving the money, property, and slaves of the Cherokees lay in joining the Confederacy, the chief replied: "A comparison of Northern and Southern philanthropy, as illustrated in their dealings toward the Indians within their respective limits, would not affect the merits of the question now under consideration, which is simply one of duty under existing circumstances. I therefore pass over it, merely remarking that the 'settled policy' of former years was a favorite policy with both sections when extended to the acquisition of Indian lands, and that but few Indians now press their feet upon the banks of either the Ohio or the Tennessee."[17]

But there were strong forces undermining Ross's position of neutrality. The factionalism of the Cherokees was revived. The old treaty party, now led by Stand Watie and his nephew Elias C. Boudinot and supported by many half-bloods, among whom most of the slave-owners were found, were sympathetic to the southern cause. Ross's great dream of unity in the Cherokee Nation might be shattered if a North-South split grew, and he could lose his position of leadership if the Confederacy chose to deal with Watie, as indeed Pike hinted in June that it might do. Ross's position, moreover, was seriously weakened when federal troops withdrew from the Indian Territory in April 1861 and Confederate forces controlled the surrounding areas. Unionist Indian agents and northern missionaries had departed, and the treaties Pike had made with the other tribes still further undercut Ross. The attractive offers made by Pike no doubt also played a part, for the Confederate agent was promising things that Ross had sought for years to obtain from the federal government without success. And then, the decisive Confederate victory at Wilson's Creek near Springfield, Missouri, on August 10, 1861, made Confederate success in its bid for separation from the North seem possible.[18]

On August 21, at a national conference of the Cherokee Nation attended by nearly four thousand men, Ross announced his decision "to

17. David Hubbard to John Ross and Ben McCulloch, June 12, 1861, *Official Records*, series 1, 13: 497–98; John Ross to David Hubbard, June 17, 1861, ibid., pp. 498–99.

18. Analyses of Ross's change of mind are in Gary E. Moulton, *John Ross: Cherokee Chief* (Athens: University of Georgia Press, 1978), pp. 171–73, and Morris L. Wardell, *A Political History of the Cherokee Nation, 1838–1907* (Norman: University of Oklahoma Press, 1938), pp. 133–38. There has been much speculation about the genuineness of Ross's adherence to the Confederacy; he himself protested after the war that he had always at heart been loyal to the United States and was forced by circumstances to ally with the South. A refutation of that position was made by Albert Pike in a letter to the commissioner of Indian affairs, February 17, 1866, quoted in Abel, *Indian as Slaveholder*, pp. 134–40 n. The letter is a good statement of Pike's activities in 1861.

adopt preliminary steps for an alliance with the Confederate States." The council quickly passed resolutions supporting the chief. Pike was notified of the change of heart and asked to return to work out a formal treaty.[19]

At the same time, in accord with Pike's request, Ross invited the leaders of the Osages, Shawnees, Senecas, and Quapaws to Park Hill, his estate in the Cherokee Nation, and these tribes on October 2 and 4 signed treaties with the South. They placed themselves under the protection of the Confederate States forever and were guaranteed their property and other rights; in return they agreed to "make themselves parties to the existing war between the Confederate States and the United States of America, as the allies and wards of the former" and to furnish warriors for the war.[20] These small tribes, located in the northeastern section of the Indian Territory, were to block a Union invasion from the north.

The treaty with the Cherokees came finally on October 7. It was similar to those with the other Five Civilized Tribes and included the promises made by Pike: Cherokee Nation control over its lands, the right to incorporate other tribes into the nation, rights of self-government, control over the appointment of agents, a Cherokee court, a delegate in the House of Representatives, and provision for sale of the Neutral Lands, which the Cherokees owned in Kansas. As a kind of anti-climax, the Cherokee Council on October 31 adopted a declaration of independence, written by Pike, that stated the reasons for joining the Confederacy and declared the Cherokees a "free people, independent of the Northern States of America and at war with them by their own act."[21]

WAR IN THE INDIAN TERRITORY

The deep concern of the Confederacy to sign treaties with the tribes in the Indian Territory, of course, was not abstract concern for Indian rights and welfare but rested in part on the need for military alliance and aid in order to prosecute the war. This was uppermost in Pike's mind, for even before the provisional congress had adopted its bill for protection of the Indian country Pike had pointed out the absolute necessity of securing the territory militarily. He probably expected in fact to be appointed military com-

19. Ross's address and the council's resolutions are included in Joseph Vann to William P. Ross, August 21, 1861, *Official Records*, series 1, 3: 673–76. See also Abel, *Indian as Slaveholder*, pp. 217–27.

20. *Official Records*, series 4, 1: 636–66.

21. Ibid., pp. 669–87. A summary of the treaty is in Wardell, *Cherokee Nation*, pp. 139–41. The "Declaration of the people of the Cherokee Nation of the causes which have impelled them to unite their fortunes with those of the Confederate States of America," October 28, 1861, is in *Official Records*, series 1, 13: 503–5.

mander rather than diplomatic agent, and it was not long before he got such an appointment.[22]

Meanwhile, on May 13, 1861, the Confederacy assigned Brigadier General Ben McCulloch as military commander in the Indian Territory, with orders to prevent a federal invasion from Kansas or elsewhere and to engage the services of Indian troops to augment his white regiments. Although McCulloch could not persuade Ross to desert his neutrality at that time, he was successful with the other major tribes, and Pike's treaties with them provided for Indian troops to fight with the Confederacy. Even before the treaties were signed, many Choctaws and Chickasaws were recruited by Douglas Cooper, and after the treaties the recruiting of Indian troops went forward rapidly. Stand Watie had organized troops before the Cherokee treaty, and by the end of July 1861 a large Confederate Indian force was in the field. After the Cherokee treaty, a regiment of Cherokee "home guards" under Colonel John Drew was accepted by McCulloch. Then on November 22, 1861, the Indian Territory was established as a separate military department, with Albert Pike commanding as a brigadier general.[23]

The successful recruiting and organization of military commands among the Indians could not hide the division within some of the tribes between northern and southern factions. The Choctaws and Chickasaws were strong supporters of the South, but the Cherokees and the Creeks were seriously rent by the tenacity of Union factions. The full-blood Cherokees of the Ross party had joined the South without enthusiasm under the press of circumstances, and latent Union sentiment came to the surface whenever conditions seemed promising. Among the Creeks large numbers led by Opothleyohola resisted attempts to force them into the southern camp and fled as refugees into Kansas, where similar discontented refugees from other tribes joined them.[24]

It appeared to the loyal Indians that they had been abandoned by Lincoln and the North, and the president gave grounds for such a judgment by his vacillation and delay.[25] When Lincoln at length in January 1862 decided to retake the Indian Territory, he faced grave problems. Chief among these

22. Abel, *Indian as Slaveholder*, pp. 131–32.
23. Ibid., pp. 143–44, 207–15, 252 n.
24. The divisions of the tribes and the secret organizations—Pins or Keetoowah Society among the Cherokees, for example, supporting the Union and circles of the Knights of the Golden Circle among the tribes supporting the Confederacy—are discussed in Wardell, *Cherokee Nation*, pp. 121–23, and Abel, *Indian as Slaveholder*, pp. 86 n, 135 n, 216.
25. A detailed study that is very critical of Lincoln's actions in regard to the Indians is David A. Nichols, *Lincoln and the Indians: Civil War Policy and Politics* (Columbia: University of Missouri Press, 1978).

were the thousands of Indian refugees in Kansas. They crowded across the border in a state of destitution, for which there seemed to be no remedy. An army surgeon in February 1862 described them in this fashion:

> It is impossible for me to depict the wretchedness of their condition. Their only protection from the snow upon which they lie is prairie grass, and from the wind scraps and rags stretched upon switches; some of them had some personal clothing; most had but shreds and rags, which did not conceal their nakedness; and I saw seven, ranging in age from three to fifteen years, without one thread upon their bodies. . . . Why the officers of the Indian department are not doing something for them I cannot understand; common humanity demands that more should be done, and done at once, to save them from total destruction.[26]

The southern superintendent, William G. Coffin, who was with the refugees at their camp on the Verdigris River, reported, "The destitution, misery, and suffering amongst them is beyond the power of any pen to portray; it must be seen to be realized."[27]

At length the Indian Office moved to provide aid. Commissioner William P. Dole went to Kansas in late January. He found that Major General David M. Hunter was doing the best he could to assist the refugees with army provisions, but in mid-February Hunter ran out of supplies and turned over the problem to the Indian department. Dole wired the secretary of the interior: "Six thousand Indians driven out of Indian territory, naked and starving. General Hunter will only feed them until 15th. Shall I take care of them on the faith of an appropriation?" When Secretary of the Interior Caleb B. Smith told him to go ahead, Dole began to purchase supplies on credit for the Indians.[28] Congress sustained that action and on July 5 provided that the annuities of the hostile Indians in the Indian Territory should be applied for the relief of the refugees.[29] The solution of the refugee problem, however, was not relief, but return of the Indians to their homes in the Indian Territory and protection of them there.

26. A. B. Campbell to James K. Barnes, February 5, 1862, CIA Report, 1862, serial 1157, pp. 295–96.

27. W. G. Coffin to Dole, February 13, 1862, ibid., p. 289. A comprehensive study of the refugee problem is Edmund J. Danziger, Jr., "The Office of Indian Affairs and the Problem of Civil War Indian Refugees in Kansas," *Kansas Historical Quarterly* 35 (Autumn 1969): 257–75. See also Dean Banks, "Civil War Refugees from Indian Territory in the North, 1861–1864," *Chronicles of Oklahoma* 41 (Autumn 1963): 286–98.

28. The action is described in a report of Dole to Smith, June 5, 1862, CIA Report, 1862, serial 1157, pp. 291–93, to which other pertinent documents are attached.

29. *Congressional Globe*, 37th Congress, 2d session, p. 815; 12 *United States Statutes* 528.

Lincoln's ultimate decision to invade the Indian Territory was entangled in the serious political and military squabbles that engulfed Kansas. At the center of these was James H. Lane, an adventurous politician from Indiana who moved to Kansas in 1855. He had built up a strong political following but managed to quarrel with everyone who might hinder his ascent to power. As senator from the new state of Kansas, he persistently nagged Lincoln in order to get what he wanted. He was appointed brigadier general of volunteers (without resigning his Senate seat) and promoted an expedition into the Indian Territory manned by Indian troops and led by him. The Indian expedition was obstructed and delayed by disagreements between Lane and Hunter, who commanded the Kansas Department and who hoped to lead the expedition himself, and not until June 1862 was it ready to move. By then Hunter had been replaced by Brigadier General James G. Blunt, a friend of Lane's. The expedition was less grandiose than Lane had originally proposed, and its object was limited "to open the way for friendly Indians who are now refugees in Southern Kansas to return to their homes and to protect them there."[30]

As the expedition moved south under Colonel William Weer, the Confederate Indian forces were in sad disarray. The serious Confederate defeat at the Battle of Pea Ridge in Arkansas in April, in which General McCulloch was killed, had a dispiriting effect, and quarrels between Pike and General T. C. Hindman (who had taken over McCulloch's troops) further hindered effective operations. The advancing expedition moved easily into Tahlequah, the Cherokee capital. John Ross, arrested by the invading army, went north to Kansas with his family and other Cherokee refugees and then on to Washington and Philadelphia, where he waited out the war. During the late summer and fall the Union forces generally routed the Confederates they met, and large numbers of Indians deserted to the Union side. Only Stand Watie's soldiers seemed to hold together.[31]

The refugee problem was not solved by the invasion from Kansas; in fact, the returning army brought with it additional Indians fleeing the destruction in their homeland. John Ross made use of his exile to importune the president to do something for the refugees, although his efforts were impeded by lingering doubts about his loyalty to the Union. No immediate action was forthcoming. General Blunt wanted immediate removal, for the problem of caring for the refugees was staggering, but the officials of the Indian Office did not want the refugees to be sent back until they could be protected adequately from raids and from further suffering, and white sol-

30. L. Thomas to H. W. Halleck, March 19, 1862, *Official Records*, series 1, 8: 624. A full discussion of Lane and the Kansas problems is provided in Albert Castel, *A Frontier State at War: Kansas, 1861–1865* (Ithaca: Cornell University Press, 1958). The organization of the expedition is discussed in Abel, *Indian as Participant*, pp. 91–123.

31. Ibid., pp. 125–201.

diers hesitated to act vigorously in the Indian cause. The situation was further complicated by traders and contractors in Kansas who prospered by supplying provisions to the refugees. Finally in May 1864—under pressure from Senator Lane, who strongly advocated the Indians' return, and aware of the expense of maintaining the Indians in Kansas—Congress appropriated funds to move the Indians back into the Indian Territory and to aid destitute Indians. Under Superintendent Coffin's care, five thousand Indians were removed in June 1864, and Lincoln authorized funds to help them until they were able to fend for themselves.[32]

The last years of the war were disastrous for the Indian Territory. Guerilla warfare caused widespread destruction, and political disorganization resulted in corruption and exploitation.[33] The ground gained by the Five Civilized Tribes, as they had developed economically and socially in the Indian country between removal and the Civil War, was lost. The physical destruction was enormous, and the factionalism and political upheaval were equally demoralizing. The Indians were considered by many northerners to have lost all rights by their adherence to the Confederacy. But the Confederacy, which had made such grand promises of protection and financial benefits, had been unable to live up to those promises. When the war ended, mammoth problems of reconstruction faced the Indian Territory.

PEACE COUNCIL AT FORT SMITH

The United States government intended to deal strongly with the tribes that had joined the Confederacy. The Indians had thrown over their treaty obligations and concluded formal alliances with the South, and many of them had fought tenaciously for the Confederate cause. Stand Watie was the last Confederate general to surrender.

The government's sentiment toward these wayward tribes was expressed in a bill for the consolidation of the Indian tribes and the establishment of a civil government in the Indian Territory, passed by the Senate on March 2, 1865. The bill, sponsored by Senator James Harlan of Iowa, was on its

32. Nichols, *Lincoln and the Indians*, pp. 54–64: 13 *United States Statutes* 62. Ross's dealings with the Lincoln administration are treated in Gary E. Moulton, "John Ross and W. P. Dole: A Case Study of Lincoln's Indian Policy," *Journal of the West* 12 (July 1973): 414–23.

33. For the military history of the war see Abel, *Indian as Participant*, pp. 243–335, and Lary C. Rampp and Donald L. Rampp, *The Civil War in the Indian Territory* (Austin: Presidial Press, 1975). The failure of the Confederacy to live up to its treaties with the Indians and furnish adequate protection is analyzed in Kenny A. Franks, "The Implementation of the Confederate Treaties with the Five Civilized Tribes," *Chronicles of Oklahoma* 51 (Spring 1973): 21–33, and "The Confederate States and the Five Civilized Tribes: A Breakdown of Relations," *Journal of the West* 12 (July 1973): 439–54.

surface a proposal for territorial organization of the Indian Territory to bring it within the regular political framework of the United States. But behind such purpose lay the desire to open the rich lands to white exploitation. By territorial organization the unique proprietorship of all the lands that the removal treaties of the 1830s had placed forever in the hands of the Five Civilized Tribes would be shattered and the riches of the territory opened to all. The avarice for Indian lands that appeared in the 1850s fulfilled the prophecy of Jeremiah Evarts, who in opposing removal of the Indians in 1829, had written: "Twenty five years hence, there will be 4,000,000 of our population west of the Mississippi, and fifty years hence not less than 15,000,000. By that time, the pressures upon the Indians will be much greater from the boundless prairies, which must ultimately be subdued and inhabited, than it would ever have been from the borders of the present Cherokee country."[34]

Typical of the expansionist views were those of Robert J. Walker, territorial governor of Kansas, who had noted in his inaugural address of May 27, 1857, that the Indian Territory was "one of the most salubrious and fertile portions of this continent," admirably suited for growing cotton, and that it "ought speedily to become a State of the American Union." The treaties with the Indians were no obstacle, he thought, for like those of Kansas they could be replaced, and by selling their lands to whites the Indians could become "a most wealthy and prosperous people." Perhaps the western parts could be set aside for the Indians, and the eastern sections could be a white state. Of great importance to Walker was the need to cross the Indian Territory with railroads, to join Kansas with the Gulf of Mexico, and to join the Mississippi Valley to the Pacific coast.[35] President Buchanan in his first annual message to Congress had remarked on the rapid advance of the Five Civilized Tribes "in all the arts of civilization and self-government" and looked forward to the day, not far distant, when they would be "incorporated into the Union as one of the sovereign States."[36] This was not merely a Democratic dream, of course, for Seward's call for vacating the Indian Territory of Indians came from a prominent Republican who became secretary of state in Lincoln's cabinet.

34. Jeremiah Evarts, *Essays on the Present Crisis in the Condition of the American Indians: First Published in the National Intelligencer, under the Signature of William Penn* (Boston: Perkins and Marvin, 1829), p. 100. Evarts's predictions on population were close; the census of 1860 showed 4,536,475 persons west of the Mississippi; that of 1880 showed 11,259,360.

35. Quotations from John Ross, "Message of the Principal Chief of the Cherokee Nation to the National Committee and Council in General Council Convened," October 5, 1857, CIA Report, 1857, serial 919, pp. 509–10.

36. Message of December 8, 1857, in Fred L. Israel, ed., *The State of the Union Messages of the Presidents, 1790–1966*, 3 vols. (New York: Chelsea House, 1966), 1: 966.

Although the Confederate States made much of such expansionist statements in their campaign to woo the southern Indian tribes by pointing out the dangers that lay in store for them under the Union, the South was driven by the same greed (disguised as it might have been while the Confederate States needed the Indian alliances). Even Albert Pike, whose concern for the Indians has been noted, could voice less benevolent intentions; in his report to President Jefferson Davis on the negotiation of the treaties with the Indian tribes, he concluded:

> If it should seem to any one that too much is conceded to any of these Indians, let him but learn the great extent and the varied resources of the Indian country, with its fine streams, its splendid scenery, its soil unexcelled in the world for fertility, its vast undulating prairies, on which all the herds of the world could feed, its capabilities to produce grain of every kind, hemp, tobacco, cotton, fruit, wine and wool; its immense basins of coal, its limestones, marbles, granite, iron, lead and salt, which will make it some day the very finest State of the Confederacy, and he will begin to comprehend that the concessions made the Indians are really far more for *our* benefit than for *theirs*; and that it is *we*, a thousand times more than they, who are interested to have this country, the finest, in my opinion, on the continent, opened to settlement and formed into a State.[37]

And the treaty with the Choctaws and Chickasaws, as Pike negotiated it, provided for their admission as one of the Confederate States, to which the other tribes could be joined.

Indian Commissioner Dole, to his credit, fought strenuously to prevent a territorial organization that would destroy the treaty guarantees made by the federal government. He saw no advantage in the innovation for governing the Indians, and he noted that the action would be "at variance with our long established Indian policy." Although he admitted that there was some question about the force of treaty obligations toward Indians who had joined the Confederacy, Dole insisted that the obligations were intact toward Indians who had remained loyal and that to violate them would "constitute a gross breach of national faith." Dole, however, was unable to stop the growing movement in Congress to organize the Indian Territory and the parallel proposal to remove the Indians from Kansas and concentrate them in part of the territory. Through Senator Lane's efforts, in fact, Congress in March 1863 attached to the Indian appropriation bill a provision for removal.[38]

37. Pike, "Report of the Commissioner of the Confederate States to the Indian Nations West of Arkansas," quoted in Gibson, "Confederates on the Plains," pp. 15–16.
38. Abel treats these movements in *Indian under Reconstruction*, pp. 235–41 and

On February 4, 1865, Lane offered a resolution directing an inquiry into the expediency of organizing a territorial government for the country lying between Kansas and Texas. On February 20, Senator James Harlan, who with Lane was a member of the Indian Committee, reported a bill. It was never debated in the House, but its sponsors were able to push it through the Senate before adjournment, and the "Harlan Bill" became an important expression of opinion from the Senate, which might later have to ratify treaties of peace with the Indian tribes of the Confederacy. The bill directed the establishment of a regular territory with set boundaries and a government similar to that in other territories. Executive officers were to be appointed by the president of the United States. A council elected by the tribes would share legislative power with the governor. A delegate would represent the territory in the United States Congress. According to an amendment offered by Senator James Doolittle, the arrangement would go into effect by means of treaties with the tribes.[39]

The United States called the tribal leaders to a conference at Fort Smith, Arkansas, in September 1865. There the Indians met with a special commission headed by Dennis N. Cooley, whom Andrew Johnson had appointed commissioner of Indian affairs in place of Dole in July. Cooley, who was from Dubuque, Iowa, was a friend and associate of Harlan, now secretary of the interior. Associated with Cooley on the commission were Elijah Sells, head of the Southern Superintendency, who had replaced Coffin in May; Thomas Wister, a well-known Quaker from Pennsylvania; General W. S. Harney; and Colonel Ely S. Parter, a Seneca Indian and aide-de-camp to General Ulysses S. Grant, who later became commissioner of Indian affairs. The secretary of the commission was Charles E. Mix of the Indian Office.[40]

---

nn. Dole's statements are from Dole to Caleb Smith, March 17, 1862, quoted ibid., pp. 235–36 n. The authorization of removal is in 12 *United States Statutes* 793.

39. *Congressional Globe*, 38th Congress, 2d session, pp. 589, 915, 1021–24, 1058, 1303–6, 1308–10. The provisions of the bill are printed ibid., pp. 1021–22. Abel, *Indian under Reconstruction*, pp. 244–66, quotes extensively from the Senate debates of February 23, 24, and March 2, 1865, and discusses the matter fully on pp. 218–67. Senator Lafayette S. Foster of Connecticut spoke strongly against the bill, arguing in terms reminiscent of the debate against removal in 1830 that the measure would be a violation of trust and a breach of faith.

40. The "Report of D. N. Cooley, as President of the Southern Treaty Commission," October 30, 1865, and the "Official Report of the Proceedings of the Council with the Indians of the West and Southwest, Held at Fort Smith, Arkansas, in September, 1865," are printed in CIA Report, 1865, serial 1248, pp. 480–96 and 496–537. A brief sketch of Cooley is Gary L. Roberts, "Dennis Nelson Cooley, 1865–66," in Robert M. Kvasnicka and Herman J. Viola, eds., *The Commissioners of Indian Affairs, 1824–1977* (Lincoln: University of Nebraska Press, 1979), pp. 99–108.

The goal of the commission was well summarized in a telegraph from Harlan to Cooley en route to Fort Smith: "The President is willing to grant them peace; but wants land for other Indians, and a civil government for the whole Territory." Cooley also carried to Fort Smith a copy of the Harlan Bill and a long letter of instructions from Secretary Harlan.[41]

When the conference opened on September 8, only the loyal factions of the tribes were on hand, for the secessionists were meeting at Armstrong Academy in the Choctaw Nation. But Cooley proceeded anyway to address the gathering as though he were talking to Confederate Indians, telling them they had forfeited their annuities and rights to land in the Indian Territory but that the president was willing to make new treaties with them. The delegates were startled by what they heard, for none of them had come with authority from their tribes to make treaties, but the next day Cooley continued in his course. He outlined for the Indians in seven points the stipulations that were to be included in the treaties.

1. Each tribe must enter into a treaty for the permanent peace and amity with themselves, each nation and tribe, and with the United States.

2. Those settled in the Indian territory must bind themselves, when called upon by the government, to aid in compelling the Indians of the plains to maintain peaceful relations with each other, with the Indians in the territory, and with the United States.

3. The institution of slavery, which has existed among several of the tribes, must be forthwith abolished, and measures taken for the unconditional emancipation of all persons held in bondage, and for their incorporation into the tribes on an equal footing with the original members, or suitably provided for.

4. A stipulation in the treaties that slavery, or involuntary servitude, shall never exist in the tribe or nation, except in punishment of crime.

5. A portion of the lands hitherto owned and occupied by you must be set apart for the friendly tribes in Kansas and elsewhere, on such terms as may be agreed upon by the parties and approved by government, or such as may be fixed by the government.

6. It is the policy of the government, unless other arrangement be made, that all the nations and tribes in the Indian territory be formed into one consolidated government after the plan proposed by the Senate of the United States, in a bill for organizing the Indian territory.

41. Harlan to Cooley, August 24, 1865, quoted in Roberts, "Cooley," p. 103; Harlan to commissioners, August 16, 1865, quoted in full in Abel, *Indian under Reconstruction*, pp. 219–26.

7. No white person, except officers, agents, and employés of the government, or of any internal improvement authorized by the government, will be permitted to reside in the territory, unless formally incorporated with some tribes, according to the usages of the band.[42]

The loyal Indians present argued that they had not willingly overturned their allegiance to the United States but had done so only under pressure. The Cherokees could point to their National Council's action in February 1863 revoking the treaty with the Confederate States and abolishing slavery. But Cooley was not easily turned aside from his position. He was especially harsh toward John Ross, whom he refused to acknowledge as principal chief of the Cherokee Nation. The conference underscored again the divisions within the tribes.

The Indian delegates, aside from their insistence that they were not authorized to negotiate new treaties with the United States, were strongly opposed to some of the points Cooley proposed. They were hesitant about incorporating the blacks into their nations, and they were especially hostile to the scheme of a territorial government that had been the heart of the Harlan Bill. Only Elias C. Boudinot, representing the southern Cherokees, was willing to accept territorial organization, a goal he continued to work for. The best that Cooley's commission could accomplish at Fort Smith was an agreement of amity between the tribes and the United States. In it the Indians acknowledged once more that they were under the exclusive jurisdiction of the United States, and they canceled and repudiated the treaties they had made with the Confederacy. In its turn the United States promised peace and friendship and renewed protection of the tribes.[43] The formal treaties would have to come later.

Secretary Harlan's concern about reconstruction of the tribes in the Indian Territory that had participated in the Civil War should not obscure the general continuity of his Indian policy with that of earlier officials. His long instructions to Cooley's commission included sections dealing with the western tribes that were part and parcel of the reservation system developed in the previous decade. Harlan was convinced that the nomadic Indians would have to be narrowly concentrated on reservations to be out of the way of a growing white population, and he instructed the commissioners in case they had occasion to deal with tribes to the west:

> You will impress upon them, in the most forcible terms, that the advancing tide of immigration is rapidly spreading over the country, and that the government has not the power or inclination to check it.

42. CIA Report, 1865, serial 1248, pp. 482–83.
43. The agreement is printed in the minutes of the council, CIA Report, 1865, serial 1248, pp. 514–15. Kappler prints it among unratified treaties, pp. 1050–52.

Our hills and valleys are filling up with an adventurous and rapidly increasing people, that will encroach upon and occupy the ancient abodes of the red man. Such seems to be an inevitable law of population and settlement on this continent. It leads to collisions, always followed by lamentable results, and sometimes by bloody and devastating wars. It is for the interest of both races, and chiefly for the welfare of the Indian, that he should abandon his wandering life and settle upon lands reserved to his exclusive use, where he will be protected in his rights and surrounded with every kindly and elevating influence by a paternal government.[44]

The western Indians were to be assigned tracts of land as remote as possible from the routes of whites to the West. Although Harlan admitted that "a sudden transition from a savage and nomadic life to the more quiet and confining pursuits of civilization is not to be expected," the lands were to be suitable for the ultimate adoption of pastoral and agricultural life. He insisted that the government would have to furnish the assistance necessary for a transition to a new way of life and improvement of the Indians' moral and intellectual condition. "The nation cannot adopt the policy of exterminating them," he said. "Our self-respect, our Christian faith, and a common dependence on an all-wise Creator and benefactor forbid it. Other nations will judge our character by our treatment of the feeble tribes to whom we sustain the relation of guardian. Morally and legally there is no distinction between destroying them and rendering it impossible for them to escape annihilation by withholding from them adequate means of support." Harlan was an active Methodist, as was Cooley, and this concern for Indian salvation and transformation cannot be dismissed as mere cant and hypocrisy. It was understood by Harlan and by the commissioners to whom he addressed it as in conformity with the worldview they had inherited— an acceptance of the inevitable (that is, Providential) advance of the white population and its culture, with efforts to protect and sustain the Indians until they should be able to cope with the onrush and be subsumed by it.[45]

Cooley's commission did not negotiate treaties with the western tribes. That work was accomplished in October, the month following the Fort Smith council, by a special United States commission. The treaties signed

44. Harlan to commissioners, August 16, 1865, in Abel, *Indian under Reconstruction*, p. 224.

45. Ibid., p. 225. Abel says the object of the Harlan bill was "nothing more and nothing less than capitalistic exploitation of southern Indian preserves," and she speaks freely of "cant and hypocrisy" in Cooley's invocation of a beneficent Great Spirit in his address to the assembled delegates at Fort Smith (pp. 183, 227). But this is to misunderstand the evangelical Protestant heritage in which Harlan, Cooley, and their associates, as well as the leaders of the Five Civilized Tribes, worked.

on the Little Arkansas with the Cheyennes, Arapahos, Comanches, Kiowas, and Kiowa-Apaches included the provisions Harlan had outlined in his instructions.[46]

The Fort Smith council adjourned on September 21, to meet again at the call of the secretary of the interior. In Washington in the spring and early summer of 1866 the representatives of the Five Civilized Tribes met with Cooley, Sells, and Parker and signed new treaties with the United States. The treaties had common provisions and built upon the points laid out by Cooley at Fort Smith, but considerable modifications were made to meet the protestations of the Indians. The tribes gave up sections of their land to make homes for Indians to be removed from Kansas and elsewhere; slaves were emancipated and slavery forever prohibited, and provisions were made for the freedmen; stipulations were included for a general council of all the tribes in the Indian Territory (looking toward territorial government, but for the present stopping short of it); and rights of way for railroads were provided for. The Seminoles gave up their entire territory and accepted a new region to the east. The Choctaws and Chickasaws sold their interests in the Leased District to the United States. The Creek land was cut in two. But the Cherokees, although they sold the Neutral Lands and the Cherokee Strip and gave the United States an option on the Cherokee Outlet, lost none of their lands; they agreed to admit other Indians to their territories west of the ninety-eighth meridian, however. The Choctaw-Chickasaw treaty and that of the Cherokees included provisions for survey of their lands and allotment of them in severalty whenever approved by the tribal councils.[47]

The treaties were signed with reunited tribes, although the divisions were by no means all healed. Among the Choctaws and Chickasaws there was little trouble, for there had been no fundamental split into loyal and secessionist parties. The Creeks and Seminoles patched up their divisions and sent national delegations to Washington to negotiate with the govern-

---

46. Kappler, pp. 887–95.

47. The treaties are printed in Kappler as follows: Seminole, March 21, 1866, pp. 910–15; Choctaw and Chickasaw, April 28, 1866, pp. 918–31; Creek, June 14, 1866, pp. 931–36; Cherokee, July 19, 1866, pp. 942–50. There is detailed coverage in Abel, *Indian under Reconstruction*, pp. 301–63. See also the following articles on the separate treaties: Harry Henslick, "The Seminole Treaty of 1866," *Chronicles of Oklahoma* 48 (Autumn 1970): 280–94; Gail Balman, "The Creek Treaty of 1866," ibid., pp. 184–96; Marion Ray McCullar, "The Choctaw-Chickasaw Reconstruction Treaty of 1866," *Journal of the West* 12 (July 1973): 462–70; Paul F. Lambert, "The Cherokee Reconstruction Treaty of 1866," ibid., pp. 471–89.

MAP 6: The Indian Territory, 1866–1888

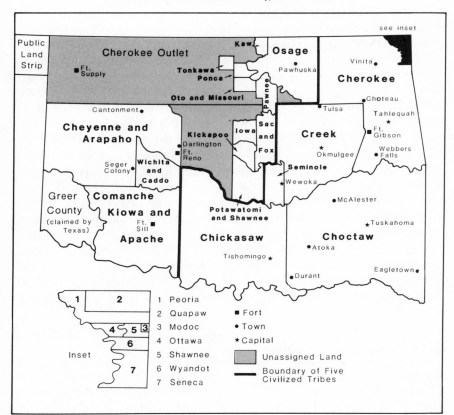

ment. But among the Cherokees hostile factions persisted, and both groups were on hand in Washington. On March 3, 1865, the northern Cherokees, acting through the National Council, sent a delegation led by Ross, who was in ill health and close to the end of his life. A southern delegation, led by Elias C. Boudinot and William P. Adair, sought its own ends. Cooley dealt with both delegations, but he was favorably inclined toward the southern group, for it was sympathetic with his proposals for a territorial government and his encouragement of railroad development in the Indian Territory. He was not averse to considering a division of the Cherokee Nation into northern and southern parts, however. Cooley sent a treaty made with the southern delegates to the president in May, justifying his action at great length in an anti-Ross pamphlet he published at the same time entitled *The Cherokee Question*. But President Johnson refused to forward the treaty to the Senate. The commissioner of Indian affairs was then forced to come to terms with the northern delegation, with whom he finally signed the treaty that was ratified by the Senate. The treaty represented compromises on both sides. The southern faction was offered a degree of autonomy in the Canadian District, lying between the Arkansas and Canadian rivers, but the unity of the nation was preserved. John Ross died on August 1, 1866, and new leadership was found for the distracted nation.[48]

The Civil War was a crucial experience in the history of the southern Indians. Even though they could argue that their attachment to the Confederacy was the result of abandonment by the Union and duress from the Confederate government, it placed them in the position of conquered foes at the end of the war. Politicians in the North like Lane and Harlan were ready to use the occasion to bring about a fundamental change in the relations of the Cherokees and other nations with the United States. In this they were largely frustrated for the time being by the Indians, who managed to keep intact most of their national autonomy for another three decades. But northern sentiment in the post-Civil War years, even among notable friends of the Indians, never quite shook off the conviction that the treaty rights of the Indians had been destroyed by the tribes' defection, and the movement for territorial organization gathered momentum as the century progressed.[49]

48. There is an extended account of the treaty negotiations and the relations of the factions in Wardell, *Cherokee Nation*, pp. 194–207, and in Abel, *Indian under Reconstruction*, pp. 345–63. Cooley's pamphlet is *The Cherokee Question: Report of the Commissioner of Indian Affairs to the President of the United States, June 15, 1866, Being Supplementary to the Report of the Commissioners Appointed by the President to Treat with the Indians South of Kansas, and Which Assembled at Fort Smith, Ark., in September, 1865* (Washington: GPO, 1866). The pamphlet is reprinted, with introduction and notes to refute its anti-Ross position, in Joseph B. Thoburn, ed., "The Cherokee Question," *Chronicles of Oklahoma* 2 (June 1924): 141–242. The heated nature of the conflict between the two Cherokee parties can be seen in the small "pamphlet war" they conducted in the summer of 1866; the pamphlets are conveniently listed in Lester Hargrett, *The Gilcrease-Hargrett Catalogue of Imprints* (Norman: University of Oklahoma Press, 1972), pp. 55–56. Ross's last days are treated in Moulton, *John Ross*, pp. 184–96.

49. Some useful information on post-treaty reconstruction in the separate Indian nations is in M. Thomas Bailey, *Reconstruction in Indian Territory: A Story of Avarice, Discrimination, and Opportunism* (Port Washington, New York: Kennikat Press, 1972); Ohland Morton, "Reconstruction in the Creek Nation," *Chronicles of Oklahoma* 9 (June 1931): 171–79; and Hanna R. Warren, "Reconstruction in the Cherokee Nation," ibid. 45 (Summer 1967): 180–89.

CHAPTER 17

Indian Conflicts:
A Series of Other Wars

Sioux Uprising in Minnesota.

War in the Southwest.

Bosque Redondo—The Great Experiment.

Sand Creek.

The Civil War was accompanied by a series of other wars that the United States government was forced to fight concurrently—wars with the Sioux in Minnesota and Dakota, with the Apaches and Navajos in Arizona and New Mexico, and with the Cheyennes, Arapahos, Kiowas, and Comanches in Kansas and eastern Colorado. Unlike the action of the southern tribes in the Indian Territory, which was an inextricable part of the Civil War, the Indian wars in the north and west were only indirectly related to the main event. They nevertheless put an additional strain on the resources of the Lincoln administration and were significant events in the history of the government's relations with the Indian tribes.

SIOUX UPRISING IN MINNESOTA

On August 18, 1862, without warning, the Sioux Indians of Minnesota rose up in fury against the white settlers. This was an outbreak of peculiar violence, and it tested severely the Indian policy of the federal government.[1]

1. The standard and best account of the Sioux uprising is William Watts Folwell, *A History of Minnesota*, 4 vols. (St. Paul: Minnesota Historical Society, 1921–1930), 2: 109–301. An excellent narrative that skillfully weighs the evidence and includes many illustrations is Kenneth Carley, *The Sioux Uprising of 1862* (St. Paul: Minnesota Historical Society, 1961). Briefer accounts of value are Roy W. Meyer, *History of the Santee*

Minnesota was the homeland of important Indians: in the north bands of Chippewas (Ojibwas) and in the south the Santee Sioux (Mdewakanton, Sisseton, Wahpeton, and Wahpekute bands). As white population moved into the Midwest in the 1830s and 1840s, these Indians were still relatively isolated and not immediately within the plans of the advancing whites, for they were beyond the Mississippi River, that chimerical boundary that was supposed to mark the western limits of American settlement. In 1837, it is true, the Chippewas ceded their Minnesota lands east of the Mississippi below the mouth of the Crow Wing River and the Sioux a thin triangle south of the Chippewa cession.[2] But for a dozen years or more, the rich agricultural lands of the Sioux in what is now the southern half of Minnesota were left undisturbed. With the admission of Wisconsin into the Union (1848), however, and the subsequent establishment of Minnesota Territory (1849), pressures began to mount for freeing more lands in Minnesota for settlement. The cry for the "Sulands" could not long be ignored.

On July 23, 1851, at Traverse des Sioux, the chiefs of the Wahpeton and Sisseton bands of the Upper Sioux ceded their lands in southern and western Minnesota for $1,665,000 in cash and annuity goods. Two weeks later, at Mendota across from Fort Snelling, the Lower Sioux (Mdewakanton and Wahpekute) signed away the southeastern quarter of Minnesota for $1,441,000. In return for some twenty-four million acres of rich land, the Sioux, in addition to the promised annuities, were provided with two reservations twenty miles wide stretching along both sides of the upper Minnesota River. The treaties, negotiated by Luke Lea, commissioner of Indian affairs, and Alexander Ramsey, governor and ex officio superintendent of Indian affairs in Minnesota Territory, were in large part designed by fur traders, of whom Henry Hastings Sibley, longtime trader with the Sioux at Mendota and later first governor of the state of Minnesota, was the most prominent. The traders, to whom the Indians were heavily in debt, wanted treaties that would provide funds for canceling those debts, and most of the cash payments stipulated by the government went into the traders' pockets, not into the hands of the Indians.[3]

Sioux: United States Indian Policy on Trial (Lincoln: University of Nebraska Press, 1967), pp. 109–54; Edmund Jefferson Danziger, Jr., *Indians and Bureaucrats: Administering the Reservation Policy during the Civil War* (Urbana: University of Illinois Press, 1974), pp. 95–130; and Theodore C. Blegen, *Minnesota: A History of the State* (Minneapolis: University of Minnesota Press, 1963), pp. 259–84. A popular account that emphasizes stories of settlers caught in the war is C. M. Oehler, *The Great Sioux Uprising* (New York: Oxford University Press, 1959). Military aspects of the war are treated in Louis H. Roddis, *The Indian Wars of Minnesota* (Cedar Rapids, Iowa: Torch Press, 1956).

2. Chippewa Treaty of St. Peters, July 29, 1837, and Sioux Treaty of Washington, September 29, 1837, Kappler, pp. 491–94.

3. Kappler, pp. 588–93. For the role of traders and politicians in the treaties, see

The treaties were also "civilizing" treaties, for the small reservations were intended to be the site of increased agricultural development for the Indians. The treaties had the usual agricultural, educational, and general civilization provisions. As the Indians moved to the reservations in 1853 and 1854, agency buildings were erected at both the Upper Sioux Agency and the Lower Sioux Agency, and the agent divided his time between them. Here the successive agents, aided by Christian missionaries, worked to change the Indians into white farmers. Joseph R. Brown, who became agent in September 1857, was especially active. He had had long experience as a fur trader and was married to a woman of Sioux blood, and he proceeded energetically to lead the Indians down the road of civilization envisaged in the 1851 treaties. "Sufficient progress has been made," he reported in 1858, "to dispel all doubt of the capacity of the Sioux for a thorough transformation from a state of heathen barbarism to that of civilized and useful members of community"—although he realized that the transformation would be a slow and painful process. Convinced that only individual ownership of land would make true civilization possible, Brown proposed to allot eighty-acre plots to individual families as a step toward private property and ultimate citizenship. Then in 1858 new treaties further restricted the reservations, as the lands lying north of the Minnesota River were ceded to the United States. These treaties endorsed Brown's program and provided for the allotment of eighty acres to heads of families and single individuals over twenty-one. The secretary of the interior, moreover, was given discretionary power over expenditure of the annuities, to use them in a way "best calculated to promote their interests, welfare, and advance in civilization."[4] The theory behind the system was well stated by Brown's successor: "The theory, in substance, was to break up the community system among the Sioux; weaken and destroy their tribal relations; individualize them by giving each a separate home and having them subsist by industry—the sweat of their brows; till the soil; make labor honorable and idleness dishonorable; or, as it was expressed in short, '*make white men of them*,' and have them adopt the habits and customs of white men."[5]

Although there were encouraging reports of success in the civilization program, there was in fact a deep division among the Sioux and growing hostility between the "farmer" Indians and the "blanket" Indians, who intended to keep their old ways. Persecution of the agriculturalists by the

---

Lucile M. Kane, "The Sioux Treaties and the Traders," *Minnesota History* 32 (June 1951): 65–80, and Meyer, *Santee Sioux*, pp. 72–87.

4. Report of Joseph R. Brown, September 30, 1858, CIA Report, 1858, serial 974, pp. 401–9; Kappler, pp. 781–89.

5. Thomas J. Galbraith to Clark W. Thompson, January 27, 1863, CIA Report, 1863, serial 1182, p. 398.

traditional party made it difficult for them to adhere to the programs of the agents and the missionaries. The superintendent of the Northern Superintendency wrote in the summer of 1860: "There is no doubt that at the present time a great struggle for ascendancy is taking place among the Sioux between the civilized or improvement Indians who have adopted our habits and customs and those who still retain the savage mode of life."[6] Conditions were becoming ripe for an explosion.

The Indians had specific grievances. The Great Father's promises in the treaty negotiations had never fully materialized, for the sums listed were drained away to pay traders' debts, and the Indians were further irritated by the attempts to substitute goods for money payments. In 1861, under the spoils system, the superintendent of the Northern Superintendency, the Sioux agent, and many of the agency employees were swept out of office to make room for Republicans who had aided the party effort in the 1860 election. Joseph Brown was replaced as agent by Thomas J. Galbraith, a man of no Indian experience who was characterized by an arrogance and inflexibility that boded ill for the handling of a delicate and dangerous situation. The Sioux, moreover, had been emboldened by the Spirit Lake Massacre in 1857, in which a renegade band of Wahpekutes under Inkpaduta raided and murdered settlers in northern Iowa and southern Minnesota. The perpetrators had not been punished, and the Indian Office had backed down from its initial purpose of strict punishment for the crimes.[7]

The Civil War, of course, had a decided effect. Withdrawal of regular troops was not unnoticed by the Indians. Although the men were replaced in part by Minnesota volunteers, the number of companies was cut in half and the new soldiers were inexperienced. The Sioux were restless, and there were rumors that the war would put an end altogether to the money coming from the federal government. Many men at the time also suspected machinations of Confederate agents among the Indians. Galbraith hinted darkly that rebel sympathizers had created disaffection among the Indians at his agency; Secretary of the Interior Caleb Smith feared a general Indian uprising in the West, and he suspected that British traders from Canada, in sympathy with the South, were at work. "I am satisfied," he wrote in November 1862 in a discussion of the causes of the Minnesota outbreak, "that the chief cause is to be found in the insurrection of the southern States." Ultimately these fears were admitted to have been groundless, but it is easy to see how they could have arisen in the excitement of the times.[8]

6. William J. Cullen to Alfred B. Greenwood, July 16, 1860, quoted in Meyer, *Santee Sioux*, pp. 107–8.

7. Folwell, *Minnesota*, 2: 223–25, 400–415; Meyer, *Santee Sioux*, pp. 97–101.

8. Galbraith to Thompson, January 27, 1863, CIA Report, 1863, serial 1182, p. 401; report of Smith, November 29, 1862, *House Executive Document* no. 1, 37–3, serial 1157, pp. 7–10.

All these proximate causes were built upon the fundamental opposition of large numbers of the Sioux to the civilization program. Agent Galbraith declared: "The radical moving cause of the outbreak is, I am satisfied, the ingrained and fixed hostility of the savage barbarian to reform, change, and civilization." He condemned the Sioux culture out of hand and saw behind it the working of the Devil. Nevertheless, his analysis of the cause of the war was not far different from that of Chief Big Eagle, an active participant in the conflict, who commented later on the causes of the uprising:

The whites were always trying to make the Indians give up their life and live like white men—go to farming, work hard and do as they did—and the Indians did not know how to do that, and did not want to anyway. It seemed too sudden to make such a change. If the Indians had tried to make the whites live like them, the whites would have resisted, and it was the same with many Indians. The Indians wanted to live as they did before the treaty of Traverse des Sioux—go where they pleased and when they pleased; hunt game wherever they could find it, sell their furs to the traders, and live as they could.[9]

In 1862 there was unreasonable delay in the annuity payments. This would have remained only an irritation, no doubt, had not the Indians come to depend so heavily on the annuities. Because of bad crops they were in a state of near starvation. The agent and the missionaries made some moves to provide subsistence for the tribes, but at the time of the outbreak many of the Indians were desperate. In early August at the Upper Agency serious violence was prevented only by a show of military force from Fort Ridgely and a reluctant agreement by Galbraith to issue supplies (although he wanted to wait until the money annuities had arrived so that supplies and cash could be distributed together). On August 15 at the Lower Agency hungry and angry Indians were turned away because neither the agent nor the traders were willing to supply them. Trader Andrew Myrick said, "So far as I am concerned, if they are hungry let them eat grass."

The outbreak began with a simple enough event. On August 17, for inconsequential reasons and without premeditation, four Indians killed five white settlers in Acton Township. The Indians knew that the rash action would bring retaliation by the whites, and the chiefs debated about what course to pursue. In the end they decided for war. Led by Little Crow on

9. Galbraith to Thompson, January 27, 1863, CIA Report, 1863, serial 1182, p. 397; "Chief Big Eagle's Story," in Kenneth Carley, ed., "As Red Men Viewed It: Three Indian Accounts of the Uprising," *Minnesota History* 38 (September 1962): 129. Big Eagle also noted the abuses of the traders, the replacement of the agent and the superintendent, the rumors that the Union was losing the Civil War and that it would be a good time for the Indians to regain their lands, and intratribal politics.

August 18 the Indians stormed the Lower Agency in a surprise attack. Among those killed was Andrew Myrick, whose body was found with grass stuffed in his mouth. The outbreak spread rapidly, as the Indians decimated the outlying settlements and attacked Fort Ridgely and the town of New Ulm.

Panic seized the frontier in Minnesota and the neighboring states and territories, and official Washington picked up the exaggerated reports.[10] Commissioner Dole called the action "the most atrocious and horrible outbreak to be found in the annals of Indian history." He noted the Acton murders and reported:

And now followed a series of cruel murders, characterized by every species of savage atrocity and barbarity known to Indian warfare. Neither age, sex, nor condition was spared. It is estimated that from eight hundred to one thousand quiet, inoffensive, and unarmed settlers fell victims to savage fury ere the bloody work of death was stayed. The thriving town of New Ulm, containing from 1,500 to 2,000 inhabitants, was almost destroyed. Fort Ridgely was attacked and closely besieged for several days, and was only saved by the most heroic and unfaltering bravery on the part of its little band of defenders until it was relieved by troops raised, armed, and sent forward to their relief. Meantime the utmost consternation and alarm prevailed throughout the entire community. Thousands of happy homes were abandoned, the whole frontier was given up to be plundered and burned by the remorseless savages, and every avenue leading to the more densely populated portions of the State was crowded with the now homeless and impoverished fugitives.[11]

The state of Minnesota and the United States reacted quickly to the outbreak. On August 19 Governor Ramsey placed Henry Sibley in command of a relief expedition; Sibley, with hastily gathered militia and volunteers, moved against the Indians. Ramsey pleaded with Washington for federal aid, but President Lincoln could not easily release men from the conduct of the Civil War. The serious problems of defense against the Indians—both real and imagined—did not disappear in the Northwest, how-

10. The absurdity of the panic can be seen in Milo M. Quaife, "The Panic of 1862 in Wisconsin," *Wisconsin Magazine of History* 4 (December 1920): 166–95.

11. CIA Report, 1862, serial 1159, pp. 170–71. Dole's estimates of casualties were high. No exact figures are available, but about 500 seems reasonable for massacred civilians and soldier deaths. Folwell analyzes the various estimates in an appendix in *Minnesota*, 2: 391–93; he notes that in the New York draft riots of July 1863 "more than twice as many murders were committed and much more property was destroyed by white savages than by Indians during the outbreak of 1862." Ibid., p. 213.

ever, and after the Second Battle of Bull Run, Lincoln, who for political as well as military reasons wanted to get rid of General John Pope, created a Department of the Northwest and sent Pope to command it.[12] The general arrived in St. Paul on September 16 and immediately took a hard line toward the Indians. "It is my purpose utterly to exterminate the Sioux if I have the power to do so," he wrote to Sibley, "and even if it requires a campaign lasting the whole of next year. Destroy everything belonging to them and force them out to the plains, unless, as I suggest, you can capture them. They are to be treated as maniacs or wild beasts, and by no means as people with whom treaties or compromises can be made."[13]

The Indians, although they had the initial advantage of surprise, were in the end no match for the forces of Sibley and Pope. A decisive victory by Sibley at Wood Lake on September 23 was the end of organized fighting by the Sioux in Minnesota. Indians who remained hostile fled west, and friendly chiefs arranged for the release of white captives. Large numbers of Sioux were captured or surrendered, and day by day more Indians, many of them on the point of starvation, gave themselves up.

Cries of vengeance filled the air, and a five-man military commission was quickly appointed to try the captive Indians. The commission worked with great haste; in ten days it tried 392 prisoners, condemning 303 to death. Pope and Sibley wanted the condemned men executed at once, and they telegraphed the names to Lincoln for confirmation of the sentences. Lincoln would not move so precipitously; he directed that the full records of the trials be sent to him for review.

The president was pressured greatly from both sides. Pope was adamant for a speedy execution. "The example of hanging many of the perpetrators of the late outrages," he declared, "is necessary and will have a crushing effect." Governor Ramsey hinted that private vengeance would take over if official action was denied, and private citizens and the newspapers of Minnesota warned the president of dire consequences if he failed to carry out the executions. Senator Morton Wilkinson and Minnesota Representatives Cyrus Aldrich and William Windom worked desperately to prevent a presidential pardon. In the Senate, Wilkinson regaled the members with lurid

12. The story of the Department of the Northwest is told in detail in Robert Huhn Jones, *The Civil War in the Northwest: Nebraska, Wisconsin, Iowa, Minnesota, and the Dakotas* (Norman: University of Oklahoma Press, 1960). See also Richard N. Ellis, *General Pope and U.S. Indian Policy* (Albuquerque: University of New Mexico Press, 1970), pp. 1–51.

13. Pope to Sibley, September 28, 1862, *The War of the Rebellion: A Compilation of the Official Records of the Union and Confederate Armies*, 70 vols. (Washington: GPO, 1880–1901), series 1, 13: 686 (hereafter cited as *Official Records*). See also Pope to Sibley, September 17, 1862, ibid., pp. 648–49.

stories of murdered men and violated women and got approval of a resolution requesting information from the president regarding evidence on the condemned prisoners.[14]

In a formal protest to Lincoln against a pardon of the convicted Sioux, the Minnesota legislators expressed the sentiments of their constituents:

> We *protest against the pardon* of these Indians, because, if it is done, the Indians will become more insolent and cruel than they ever were before, believing, as they certainly will believe, that their great father at Washington either justified their acts or is afraid to punish them for their crimes.
>
> We *protest against it* because, if the President does not permit these executions to take place under the forms of law, the outraged people of Minnesota will dispose of these wretches without law. These two peoples cannot live together. We do not wish to see mob law inaugurated in Minnesota, as it certainly will be, if you force the people to do it. . . .
>
> You can give us peace, or you can give us lawless violence. We pray you, sir, in view of all that we have suffered, and of the danger which still awaits us, *let the law be executed; let justice be done* our people.[15]

But calmer, more reasonable voices also were heard. The lawyers whom Lincoln assigned to study the trial transcripts were shocked by what they found—short trials, reliance on hearsay evidence, denial of due process and of counsel—and rejected many of the findings of the military commission. Henry B. Whipple, Espicopal Bishop of Minnesota, despite the unpopularity of his views in Minnesota, stood up strongly for careful justice, and he appealed to Lincoln through Senator Henry Rice: "We cannot hang men by the hundreds. Upon our own premises we have no right to do so. We claim that they are an independent nation & as such they are prisoners of war. The leaders must be punished but we cannot afford by an wanton cruelty to purchase a long Indian war—nor by injustice in other matters purchase the anger of God.[16]

14. John Pope to H. W. Halleck, October 10, 1862, ibid., series 1, 13: 724; *Congressional Globe*, 37th Congress, 3d session, p. 13. Lincoln's part is treated in David A. Nichols, *Lincoln and the Indians: Civil War Policy and Politics* (Columbia: University of Missouri Press, 1978), pp. 76–128. Nichols is harsh in his judgment of Lincoln, although he admits the humaneness of Lincoln's action in regard to the execution of the Sioux.

15. *Senate Executive Document* no. 7, 37–3, serial 1149, p. 4. The statement is full of lurid details about Indian atrocities.

16. Whipple to Rice, November 12, 1862, Whipple Papers, Minnesota Historical Society, quoted in Nichols, *Lincoln and the Indians*, p. 104. Whipple describes his opinions and actions in his autobiography, *Lights and Shadows of a Long Episcopate* (New York: Macmillan Company, 1899), pp. 105–32.

The strongest voice was that of Commissioner Dole, who understood the hysteria on the frontier and did not criticize Sibley and Pope but called for reasonable action. "I cannot reconcile it to my sense of duty to remain silent," he wrote to the secretary of the interior. Dole admitted that the Indians had committed "horrible and atrocious crimes" at which the country was justly incensed; but "an indiscriminate punishment of men who have laid down their arms and surrendered themselves as prisoners," he said, "partakes more of the character of revenge than the infliction of deserved punishment; that it is contrary to the spirit of the age and our character as a great, magnanimous, and Christian people." Dole had no exalted views of the Indians, but he believed that only the leaders should be punished, not the rank and file who followed them in blind obedience, and he urged a middle course upon the administration. He pleaded with Smith to "prevent the consummation of an act which I cannot believe would be otherwise than a stain upon our national character, and a source of future regret." Secretary Smith sent the plan to Lincoln with his endorsement of the "humane views" of the commissioner.[17]

It was not an easy question for Lincoln. He decided finally to uphold the sentence of death for only thirty-nine of the convicted men, and on December 6 he sent Sibley their names. He laid out the basis for his decision to the Senate. "Anxious to not act with so much clemency as to encourage another outbreak, on the one hand, nor with so much severity as to be real cruelty, on the other," Lincoln said, "I caused a careful examination of the records of the trials to be made, in view of first ordering the execution of such as had been proved guilty of violating females. Contrary to my expectations, only two of this class were found. I then directed a further examination, and a classification of all who were proven to have participated in *massacres*, as distinguished from participation in *battles*."[18] One of the thirty-nine men was reprieved at the last minute; the thirty-eight were hanged at Mankato in a spectacle attended by a large crowd on December 26, 1862.

Mass execution was not the only thing Minnesotans wanted. They demanded the total removal of the Sioux from the state. Citizens of St. Paul, in a memorial to the president, offered typical arguments: "The Indian's nature can no more be trusted than the wolf's. Tame him, cultivate him, strive to Christianize him as you will, and the sight of blood will in an

17. Dole to Caleb B. Smith, November 10, 1862, CIA Report, 1862, serial 1157, pp. 213–14; Smith to Lincoln, November 11, 1862, Lincoln Papers, Library of Congress (microfilm reel 43, no. 19500).
18. Lincoln to the Senate, December 11, 1862, *Senate Executive Document* no. 7, 37–3, serial 1149, pp. 1–2; Lincoln to Sibley, December 6, 1862, *Collected Works of Abraham Lincoln*, ed. Roy P. Basler, 9 vols. (New Brunswick: Rutgers University Press, 1953–1955), 5: 542–43.

instant call out the savage, wolfish, devilish instincts of the race." Only if the Indians were removed from the state could Minnesotans feel secure. It was a question "simply whether the Indian or the white man shall possess Minnesota."[19]

The Lincoln administration acquiesced. On March 3, 1863, Congress authorized the removal of the Sioux from the state, requiring that they be located outside the limits of any existing state. Dole and Secretary of the Interior John P. Usher (who had replaced Smith in January 1863) picked a spot near Fort Randall on the upper Missouri. In May and June 1863 the Sioux who had been encamped at Fort Snelling in the wake of the uprising were loaded on steamboats for the long journey down the Mississippi and up the Missouri to their new reservation at Crow Creek. It was a miserable, barren spot, and after three years the Sioux were moved to a new and better reservation at the mouth of the Niobrara River in Nebraska. Meanwhile, the convicted Indians not executed at Mankato were moved to a prison in Davenport, Iowa; only later were they allowed to join their families in Nebraska.[20]

The hapless Winnebago Indians were caught in the removal uproar. Having already been moved from their Wisconsin homes—to Iowa in 1840, to the Crow Wing River in Minnesota in 1849, and then to Blue Earth County, Minnesota, in 1855—they were now forced to relocate again in order to satisfy the cries of Minnesotans against Indians in their midst on lands coveted for their own use. By a law of February 21, 1863, Congress authorized their removal, and they quickly followed on the heels of the departing Santees, locating next to the Sioux reservation at Crow Creek. The Winnebagos were unhappy in the new spot, and they moved en masse to the Omaha reservation in Nebraska in 1864. The Indian Office recognized the fait accompli and purchased part of the Omaha reserve as a permanent home for the wandering Indians.[21]

The Sioux who fled Minnesota during the outbreak of 1862 were not quickly pacified. They roamed the Dakota prairies and found some support among the Yankton and Yanktonai Indians. General Pope feared a new attack by these Indians on the Minnesota frontier, and he mounted a punitive expedition into Dakota Territory against them. In 1863 General Sibley moved west from Minnesota, while General Alfred Sully proceeded up the Missouri. They scattered the Indians they met, but the expeditions settled

19. Memorial, *Senate Executive Document* no. 7, 37–3, serial 1149, p. 5.

20. 12 *United States Statutes* 819–20; *House Report* no. 13, 37–3, serial 1173. Details on the removal are given in William E. Lass, "The Removal from Minnesota of the Sioux and Winnebago Indians," *Minnesota History* 38 (December 1963): 353–64, and Danziger, *Indians and Bureaucrats*, pp. 11–30.

21. 12 *United States Statutes* 658–60; Kappler, pp. 872–73.

nothing. In 1864 Sully led another expedition into Dakota, where he was joined by Minnesota forces. In the Battle of Killdeer Mountain on July 28, 1864, the Sioux were defeated. Military posts were established along the Missouri, and the Indian raids gradually ceased.[22]

On February 19, 1867, the Sisseton and Wahpeton Sioux in Dakota signed a treaty in Washington according to which two reservations were established for them. One was a triangle of land in what is now the north-eastern corner of South Dakota (Sisseton Reservation), and the other extended south from Devils Lake in North Dakota. The treaty, designed to promote civilization among the Indians, called for the allotment of the reservations in quarter-section tracts. It further specified that Congress would take steps from time to time to enable the Indians to return to an agricultural life, "including, if thought advisable, the establishment and support of local and manual-labor schools; the employment of agricultural, mechanical, and other teachers; the opening and improvement of individual farms; and generally such objects as Congress in its wisdom shall deem necessary to promote the agricultural improvement and civilization of said bands."[23]

WAR IN THE SOUTHWEST

The drive in the 1850s against the warlike Indians in New Mexico and Arizona that promised success in pacifying them was ended by the outbreak of the Civil War. Many regular army troops were withdrawn from the scattered garrisons, leaving the Indians free to renew their raids against the inhabitants of the region. And the Confederate attempts to control the area by military expeditions and the organization of territory government created new confusion, for all Union forces had to be mobilized to meet the challenge of the southern attack.[24]

The Confederate invasion began with a move up the Rio Grande from El Paso by troops under John R. Baylor of the Texas Mounted Rifles, and the Union forces gave way. Forts Buchanan and Breckinridge near Tucson were abandoned, and then Fort Fillmore on the Rio Grande was evacuated and its troops attempted to march to Fort Stanton. On the way they surren-

22. A brief, well-documented account of these expeditions is in Robert M. Utley, *Frontiersmen in Blue: The United States Army and the Indians, 1848–1865* (New York: Macmillan Company, 1967), pp. 270–80. See also Folwell, *Minnesota*, 2: 265–301.

23. Kappler, pp. 957–59. The history of the Sioux on these reservations is told in detail in Meyer, *Santee Sioux*.

24. Confederate operations in the Southwest are discussed in Ray C. Colton, *The Civil War in the Western Territories: Arizona, Colorado, New Mexico, and Utah* (Norman: University of Oklahoma Press, 1959), pp. 3–99, which thoroughly exploits the documents printed in *Official Records*.

dered to Baylor, and Fort Stanton, unreinforced, was also abandoned. Baylor, in the flush of victory, set up a Confederate Territory of Arizona (composed of all of New Mexico south of the thirty-fourth parallel) and proclaimed himself governor. At the end of the year, a major Confederate military advance into the region was begun under the command of General Henry Hopkins Sibley, a former United States officer who had fought in New Mexico against the Indians in the 1850s.[25]

To meet this attack Brigadier General Edward R. S. Canby had to rely on New Mexico volunteers and a handful of remaining regulars. They were no match for Sibley, who advanced up the Rio Grande. On February 21, 1862, the Union forces were defeated at the Battle of Valverde, north of Fort Craig, and the Confederates, largely unimpeded, moved on to Albuquerque, which they took on March 2, and then to Santa Fe on March 10. The only remaining obstacle to control of all New Mexico was the great depot of supplies at Fort Union. But the invading army did not make it. Union forces, augmented by feisty Colorado volunteers under Major John M. Chivington, routed the Confederate army at Glorieta Pass on March 28, and the southerners retreated down the Rio Grande, never to return.[26]

A new phase in the history of New Mexico began in August 1862 with the arrival on the Rio Grande of a column of California volunteers under Brigadier General James H. Carleton, who on September 18 replaced Canby in command of the Department of New Mexico. For the rest of the war Carleton was the dominant figure in New Mexico. A man of ability and zeal, he was also arrogant and arbitrary, and he stubbornly pushed for the fulfillment of his vision of what New Mexico needed. With the Confederate threat removed, the new commander turned his attention to subduing the Indians. Joining with an old associate, Colonel Christopher (Kit) Carson of the New Mexico cavalry, Carleton set out to accomplish his objective: to end once and for all the depredations of the Apaches and the Navajos. To do this Carleton intended to adopt the guerilla tactics of the Indians themselves. "The troops must be kept after the Indians," he wrote in 1863, "not in big bodies, with military noises and smokes, and the gleam of arms by day, and fires, and talk, and comfortable sleeps by night; but in small parties moving stealthily to their haunts and lying patiently in wait for

25. Baylor's work, especially his harsh policy of extermination against the Indians, is treated in Martin Hardwick Hall, "Planter vs. Frontiersman: Conflict in Confederate Indian Policy," in Essays on the American Civil War, ed. William F. Holmes and Harold M. Hollingsworth (Austin: University of Texas Press, 1968), pp. 45–72. For a detailed narrative of Sibley's campaign, see Hall, Sibley's New Mexico Campaign (Austin: University of Texas Press, 1960).

26. In addition to Colton's and Hall's books, see Max L. Heyman, Jr., Prudent Soldier: A Biography of Major General E. R. S. Canby, 1817–1873 (Glendale, California: Arthur H. Clark Company, 1959), pp. 137–87.

them; or by following their tracks day after day with a fixedness of purpose that never gives up." He intended to make no treaties short of total surrender, and when subjugation was achieved to move the Indians to an isolated reservation away from all contact with the white inhabitants of the territory, where they could be supported by the government until they could be transformed into agriculturalists and enlightened by teachers and Christian missionaries.[27]

Carleton turned first to the Mescalero Apaches of south central New Mexico. These Indians had been subdued in the mid-1850s, and Fort Stanton had been erected on the Rio Bonita in May 1855. But when the post was abandoned in the face of Confederate attack in 1861, the Apaches began to prey upon the white settlers. "This condition of the tribes is truly disheartening to the citizens," Indian Agent Lorenzo Labadi wrote in September 1862. "There is no security for life or property, and unless the government takes immediate steps to stop these depredations the country will be stripped of every species of property it now contains. The only permanent remedy for these evils is in the colonization of these Indians. Reservations should be at once located and the Indians forced to reside upon them."[28]

The general moved vigorously. He ordered Carson to reactivate Fort Stanton and directed the officers to kill the Indian men and capture the women and children, and to hold no council of peace with them. If the chiefs wanted peace, they would have to go to Santa Fe to submit. "The whole duty can be summed up in a few words," he told Carson: "The Indians are to be soundly whipped, without parleys or councils."[29] The troops kept up incessant pressure on the Apaches, and in November the chiefs appeared with the agent at Santa Fe to make peace. There Carleton revealed what he had in store for them. He had established a new military post (Fort Sum-

27. An extensive collection of documents concerning Carleton's operations in New Mexico, 1862–1865, that he furnished to the Doolittle Committee, is printed in the committee's report, *Condition of the Indian Tribes: Report of the Joint Special Committee, Appointed under Joint Resolution of March 3, 1865* (Washington: GPO, 1867; also printed as *Senate Report* no. 156, 39–2, serial 1279), pp. 98–322. The quotation is from Carleton to Edwin A. Rigg, August 6, 1863, ibid., p. 124. A biography of Carleton that treats him favorably is Aurora Hunt, *Major General James Henry Carleton, 1814–1873: Western Frontier Dragoon* (Glendale, California: Arthur H. Clark Company, 1958). An excellent brief account of Carleton's New Mexico career is Utley, *Frontiersmen in Blue*, pp. 231–60. Kit Carson's role can be followed in Edwin L. Sabin, *Kit Carson Days, 1809–1869*, rev. ed., 2 vols. (New York: Press of the Pioneers, 1935), 2: 694–724 and reprinted documents in appendix, pp. 846–91; and Clifford E. Trafzer, *The Kit Carson Campaign: The Last Great Navajo War* (Norman: University of Oklahoma Press, 1982).

28. Labadi to J. L. Collins, September 25, 1862, CIA Report, 1862, serial 1157, pp. 391–92. Labadi was speaking of the Navajos as well as of the Apaches.

29. Carleton to Joseph R. West, October 11, 1862, and Carleton to Carson, October 12, 1862, *Condition of the Indian Tribes*, pp. 99–101.

ner) on the Pecos River in eastern New Mexico at a spot called Bosque Redondo, after the round grove of cottonwoods there. The Indians who
wanted peace were to move to the Bosque Redondo and take up a life of
agriculture; the government would provide their subsistence and protect
them until they could raise crops for themselves. By the end of March 1863
more than four hundred Apaches—the great bulk of the tribe—were at
Fort Sumner. "My purpose," Carleton wrote to the adjutant general, "is to
have them fed and kept there under *surveillance:* to have them plant a
crop this year; to have them, in short, become what is called in this country a *pueblo.*" There missionaries could teach them the Gospel and open a
school for the children, and the agent could instruct them in farming.[30]

Carleton next gave his attention to the Navajos, a far more numerous
tribe with an estimated ten thousand people, compared with the four or
five hundred Mescaleros. His plan for them, however, was the same as for
the Apaches: to subdue the hostile elements of the tribes and move all to
some distant reservation. The goal was similar to that preached by his
predecessor, Canby, who had declared at the end of 1861 that there was "no
choice between their absolute extermination or their removal and colonization at points so remote from the settlements as to isolate them entirely from the inhabitants of the Territory."[31] But whereas Canby probably
had in mind some section of the traditional Navajo lands, Carleton soon
decided that the Navajos as well as the Apaches were to settle at the
Bosque Redondo.

While Colonel Carson was rounding up the Mescaleros, the offensive
against the Navajos began with the establishment of Fort Wingate in western New Mexico in October 1862. Navajo chiefs responded by appearing in
Santa Fe in December to seek peace, but Carleton let them know that he
had no faith in their promises and sent them home. In April 1863 he informed two leading peace chiefs, Delgadito and Barboncito, that the peaceful Indians would have to be clearly separated from the warring tribesmen—in short, that they would have to move to the Bosque Redondo.
When the chiefs rejected the proposal to move so far from home, Carleton
issued an ultimatum, directing the commander at Fort Wingate to tell

30. Carleton to Carson, November 25, 1862, and Carleton to Lorenzo Thomas,
March 19, 1863, ibid., pp. 101–2, 106. Carleton wrote to Bishop John B. Lamay of Santa
Fe asking for a priest "of energy, and of all those qualities of patience, good temper, as-
siduity and interest in the subject so necessary in one who is wanted to teach the Indian
children now at Fort Sumner, not only the rudiments of an education, but the principles
and truths of Christianity." Carleton to Lamay, June 12, 1863, ibid., p. 112. An account of
the Apaches is given in C. L. Sonnichsen, *The Mescalero Apaches* (Norman: University
of Oklahoma Press, 1958), pp. 89–119.

31. Canby to assistant adjutant general, Western Department, December 1, 1861,
Official Records, series 1, 4: 77–78. Canby's Indian campaigns are described in Heyman,
Prudent Soldier, pp. 113–36, 157–60.

them that they would have until July 20 to come in. "We have no desire to make war on them and other good Navajoes," Carleton said, "but the troops cannot tell the good from the bad; and we neither can nor will tolerate their staying as a peace party among those against whom we intend to make war." After the deadline, *"every Navajo that is seen will be* considered hostile and treated accordingly."[32]

Carleton meant just what he said, and he began to lay plans for an invasion of the Navajo country. On June 15, 1863, he ordered Kit Carson to move into the area and "to prosecute a vigorous war upon the men of this tribe until it is considered at these Head Quarters that they have been effectually punished for their long continued atrocities." The army was to have only one message for the Indians: "Go to Bosque Redondo, or we will pursue and destroy you. We will not make peace with you on any other terms."[33]

As winter set in, Carleton planned an attack into the Canyon de Chelly, the final citadel of the Navajos. The Indians could not withstand the insistent attacks and the destruction of their crops, orchards, and livestock. After the invasion, they surrendered in large numbers, for they faced starvation and had lost all hope of turning back the determined white soldiers. By mid-March six thousand had come in. They were transported across New Mexico to the reservation on the Pecos in a Long Walk that recalled the Cherokees' Trail of Tears more than a quarter-century before. By the end of 1864, three-fourths of the total tribe—some eight thousand people—were at the Bosque Redondo. The remainder, refusing to surrender, fled westward to the deserts, out of contact with the settlements.[34]

Carleton was now ready to begin the massive experiment in Indian transformation that he had outlined for his superiors in September 1863:

> The purpose now is never to relax the application of force with a people that can no more be trusted than you can trust the wolves that run through their mountains; to gather them together, little by little,

32. Carleton to J. Francisco Chavez, June 23, 1863, *Condition of the Indian Tribes*, p. 116. An extensive collection of documents on the campaign against the Navajos with accompanying scholarly commentary is Lawrence C. Kelly, *Navajo Roundup: Selected Correspondence of Kit Carson's Expedition against the Navajo, 1863–1865* (Boulder, Colorado: Pruett Publishing Company, 1970).

33. General Orders no. 15, Headquarters, Department of New Mexico, June 15, 1863, and Carleton to Carson, September 19, 1863, in Kelly, *Navajo Roundup*, pp. 21–22, 52.

34. The campaign in the Canyon de Chelly and the surrender of the Navajos is described ibid., pp. 80–158. See also L. R. Bailey, *The Long Walk: A History of the Navajo Wars, 1846–68* (Los Angeles: Westernlore Press, 1964), pp. 145–71. A collection of stories of the Long Walk handed down among the Navajos is presented in Ruth Roessel, ed., *Navajo Stories of the Long Walk Period* (Tsaile, Arizona: Navajo Community College Press, 1973). A census of Indians at the Bosque Redondo, December 31, 1864, is given in *Condition of the Indian Tribes*, pp. 264–65.

on to a reservation, away from the haunts, and hills, and hiding-places of their country, and then to be kind to them; there teach their children how to read and write; teach them the arts of peace; teach them the truths of Christianity. Soon they will acquire new habits, new ideas, new modes of life; the old Indians will die off, and carry with them all latent longings for murdering and robbing; the young ones will take their places without these longings; and thus, little by little, they will become a happy and contented people, and Navajo wars will be remembered only as something that belongs entirely to the past. Even until they can raise enough to be self-sustaining, you can feed them cheaper than you can fight them.[35]

BOSQUE REDONDO—THE GREAT EXPERIMENT

There was much in favor of Carleton's dream to turn the Bosque Redondo into a model reservation. The site was distant enough from the concentrations of white settlement to prevent contact between the two races, and the open plains in which it was located made it difficult for Indians to flee unnoticed. The land along the Pecos was suitable for irrigated farming, and Carleton estimated that enough food could be grown to feed the large number of Indians. In fact, a good beginning was made. The Apaches were put to work to build irrigation ditches, prepare fields, and plant crops, and when the Navajos arrived, they too worked hard to make the reservation livable. Carleton was sanguine about the possibilities, and he looked ahead ten years to see the Navajos as the "happiest and most delightfully located pueblo of Indians in New Mexico—perhaps in the United States."[36]

Carleton's actions, of course, were not motivated solely by concern for Indian welfare, genuine as that may have been. Like others of his time, he was not unmindful of the rich possibilities of the land vacated by the Indians when they gathered on restricted reservations. As he turned over his immense file of correspondence in October 1865 to the congressional committee headed by Senator James Doolittle that was sent west to investigate Indian troubles, he called attention to documents that spoke of the mineral wealth of the Indian lands and remarked that unless the Indians, who

35. Carleton to Lorenzo Thomas, September 6, 1863, *Condition of the Indian Tribes,* p. 134.

36. Carleton to Lorenzo Thomas, March 6, 1864, ibid., p. 163. The development of the Bosque Redondo reservation and the difficulties encountered there are told in detail in Gerald Thompson, *The Army and the Navajo: The Bosque Redondo Reservation Experiment, 1863–1868* (Tucson: University of Arizona Press, 1976), and Lynn R. Bailey, *Bosque Redondo: An American Concentration Camp* (Pasadena: Socio-Technical Books, 1970).

did not mine the metals, were removed to reservations, the riches could not be safely exploited by the whites. The question, he said, was "shall the miners be protected and the country be developed, or shall the Indians be suffered to kill them and the nation be deprived of its immense wealth?" And as the Navajos came in for transfer to Fort Sumner in March 1864, he wrote to the adjutant general: "By the subjugation and colonization of the Navajo tribe, we gain for civilization their whole country, which is much larger in extent than the State of Ohio, and, besides being by far the best pastoral region between the two oceans, is said to abound in the precious as well as in the useful metals." But he pressed this argument in part at least in order to persuade the federal government to appropriate sufficient funds to make possible the transformation in living that he envisaged for the Navajos at the Bosque Redondo. "When it is considered what a magnificent pastoral and mineral country they have surrendered to us—a country whose value can hardly be estimated," he wrote, "the mere pittance, in comparison, which must at once be given to support them, sinks into insignificance as a price for their natural heritage."[37]

Carleton had a number of strong supporters. James L. Collins, former superintendent of Indian affairs for New Mexico, continued to promote the project, and Henry Connelly, the governor of New Mexico Territory, no doubt relieved that the Navajo problem was being solved, accepted Carleton's evaluation of the scheme. Kit Carson, of course, had only praise for the reservation. "A new era dawned upon New Mexico," he wrote about Carleton's policy at the end of his campaign, "and the dying hopes of the people were again revived." He urged a gentle but firm hand in leading the Indians "into the habits or customs of civilized life" and predicted that the Navajos at the Bosque Redondo in a few years would "equal if not excel our industrious Pueblos, and become a source of wealth to the Territory instead of being as heretofore its dread and impoverishers."[38]

It was not to be. Almost from the start weaknesses in the scheme began to appear, and outspoken critics condemned the operation. The chief of the critics was Michael Steck, former Mescalero Apache agent who had replaced Collins as superintendent in March 1863. Although Steck favored the settlement of the Apaches at Fort Sumner and thought they could prosper there, he came to oppose strongly the movement of thousands of Navajos to the same reservation. Carleton had noted that the Apaches and Navajos were related and spoke the same language, but Steck asserted that the two tribes had been "inveterate enemies, and it is folly to suppose

37. Carleton to James R. Doolittle, October 22, 1865, and Carleton to Lorenzo Thomas, March 6 and 12, 1864, *Condition of the Indian Tribes*, pp. 98, 163, 166–68.

38. Carson to assistant adjutant general, Department of New Mexico, May 20, 1864, in Kelly, *Navajo Roundup*, pp. 157–58; Utley, *Frontiersmen in Blue*, pp. 245–46.

MAP 7: The Long Walk of the Navajo Indians

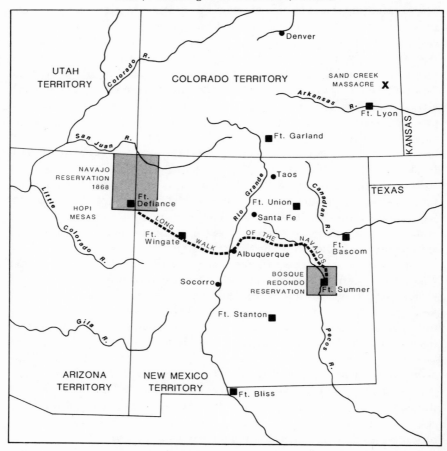

that they can agree upon the same reservation after having been so long at war." More important, the Bosque Redondo reservation, to his mind, was unequal to the demands of its large population, and millions of dollars would be required from the Treasury of the United States to give them subsistence. Steck wanted a reservation for the Navajos to be established on the Little Colorado River near their own country, where they would be contented and could to a large extent provide for themselves. The continuing controversy between the general and the superintendent obstructed any smooth operation of the reservation.[39]

39. Steck to William P. Dole, December 10, 1863, and October 10, 1864, CIA Report, 1864, serial 1220, pp. 324–31, 351–52. See also Edmund J. Danziger, Jr., "The Steck-

Even without the squabbling, there were problems on the reservation. The Navajos, used to a largely pastoral existence, objected to being cooped up on farms, with no provisions for extensive flocks and herds. They objected to Carleton's plans to have them live in concentrated villages, when they were used to smaller and more mobile units of habitation. But it was the forces of a harsh nature that ultimately destroyed the Bosque Redondo experiment. It is possible that with good crops and thus adequate food supplies the discontent of the Indians could have been overcome. But year after year the crops failed, destroyed by insects or drought. Goods supplied by the government were never adequate, and reduced rations were frequently the lot of the Indians. The Navajos were destitute, demoralized, and weakened by disease—far from the happy farmers that Carleton had predicted. Nor was the general able to develop his plans for education.[40] The reservation life, moreover, did not bring an end to Indian raiding in New Mexico, for dissident Apaches and Navajos still struck the settlements, and as conditions worsened at the Bosque Redondo, members of both tribes slipped away to join in the depredations.

To add to Carleton's troubles there were political murmurings against him in New Mexico Territory. The huge demand for supplies at Fort Sumner raised prices in the territory, and Carleton had to bear the brunt of the criticism. The Santa Fe *New Mexican*, a Republican newspaper fighting the Democrats who supported Carleton, ran numerous articles criticizing the general, and the legislature petitioned the federal government for his removal.[41] Early in January 1865, Carleton struck back in the propaganda war with a pamphlet entitled *To the People of New Mexico*, in which he presented his reasons for establishing the reservation. He noted the failure of all past attempts to subjugate and pacify the Navajos and declared that his plan was logically the best—as plain "as that two and two make four." Then he answered point by point the criticisms that had been directed at

Carleton Controversy in Civil War New Mexico," *Southwestern Historical Quarterly* 74 (October 1970): 189–203.

40. In pleading for funds for schools, Carleton wrote to the secretary of the interior: "The education of these children is the fundamental idea on which must rest all our hopes of making the Navajoes a civilized and Christian people. . . . You can figure to your own mind, 3,000 intelligent boys and girls with no one to teach them to read or write. Here is a field for those who are philanthropic which is ample enough to engage their attention and be the object of their charities for many years." Carleton to the secretary of the interior, March 30, 1865, *Condition of the Indian Tribes*, p. 224.

41. Long extracts from the *New Mexican* are printed with commentary in William A Keleher, *Turmoil in New Mexico, 1846–1868* (Santa Fe: Rydal Press, 1952) pp. 440–58. Extracts from the memorial of the legislature, January 21, 1866, are printed ibid., pp. 455–56. Keleher's book also contains a great many documents dealing with the whole New Mexico Indian problem; see pp. 275–512.

him. In the end he urged the New Mexicans to "wait patiently and hopefully until this great experiment has been thoroughly tested."[42]

The "great experiment" failed. New crop disasters precluded cutting the tremendous costs of maintaining the reservation Indians, and the dissatisfaction of the Navajos increased. On December 21, 1866, General Ulysses S. Grant instructed the commander of the Department of the Missouri to turn over the Navajos, "now held as prisoners" at the Bosque Redondo, to the Indian Office, but it was ten months before the actual transfer was accomplished on October 21, 1867. By that time General Carleton had given up his command in New Mexico for service in the Department of Texas. The Indian Office, unfortunately, was even less prepared financially than the War Department to continue the operation, and it announced at the end of 1867 that it was prepared to take care of the Indians at the Bosque Redondo for only three months and then additional appropriations would be necessary.[43] The New Mexico superintendent, A. B. Norton, who had been appointed in February 1866, described the dismal failure of the reservation:

> The soil is cold, and the alkali in the water destroys it. The corn crop this year is a total failure. Last year 3,000 bushels only was raised in 3,000 acres, and year before last six thousand bushels; continually growing worse instead of better. The self-sustaining properties of the soil are all gone. The Indians now dig up the muskite [mesquite] root for wood, and carry it upon their galled and lacerated backs for 12 miles. . . . What a beautiful selection is this for a reservation. It has cost the government millions of dollars, and the sooner it is abandoned and the Indians removed the better.

Norton insisted that the Indians stayed there only by force. "Free them from military control and fear," he said, "and they would leap therefrom as the bird from its open cage." His strong recommendation was to send them back to their homeland.[44]

Congress authorized a Peace Commission in 1867, which, though mainly concerned with the hostile tribes on the southern and northern plains, also

---

42. Gerald E. Thompson, ed., "'To the People of New Mexico': Gen. Carleton Defends the Bosque Redondo," *Arizona and the West* 14 (Winter 1972): 347–66.

43. Thompson, *Army and the Navajo*, pp. 123–50. See CIA Report, 1867, serial 1326, part 2, p. 12.

44. Norton to N. G. Taylor, August 24, 1867, CIA Report, 1867, serial 1326, part 2, p. 190. The problems of supplying subsistence at the Bosque Redondo were the concern of the commissary general of subsistence, who wrote on January 16, 1868, that reports from his subordinates "clearly indicate that the selection of that location as a place for the attempt to civilize these Indians was unfortunate, and that it ought not to be further continued, but that some more suitable location should be selected and the Indians transferred to it." *House Executive Document* no. 248, 40–2, serial 1341, p. 8.

turned its attention to the Navajos. General William T. Sherman and Samuel Tappan, members of the commission who were sent to the Bosque Redondo, met with the Indians in late May 1868 and heard from them about the terrible conditions on the reservation and their earnest desires to return home. They could see for themselves the tragedy of the enforced stay at Fort Sumner, and on June 1 they signed a treaty with the Navajo chiefs providing for the Indians' return west. Boundaries were set for a reservation there; $150,000 was provided for removal and for the purchase of livestock; and all the customary stipulations for advancing the Indians in civilization were included.[45]

There was little problem in the return trip of the Navajos to their old lands, for they were eager to go, and they rejoiced as they saw the familiar landmarks. But it was not a simple return to the past, for the years at the Bosque Redondo left an indelible mark on the tribe. The Indians' clothing and housing had been influenced by the close contact with whites on the reservation, and a new sense of tribal unity had been fostered. More fundamentally, the Navajos put behind them their longtime raiding and depredations and settled on the reservation to work out their future. There was never again a Navajo war.[46]

SAND CREEK

When the Indians in Minnesota rose up against the white settlers in 1862, there was great consternation, for whites feared a widespread conspiracy among the Indians to attack all along the frontier while the nation was

45. John L. Kessell, "General Sherman and the Navajo Treaty of 1868: A Basic and Expedient Misunderstanding," *Western Historical Quarterly* 12 (July 1981): 251–72; Thompson, *Army and the Navajo*, pp. 151–57; Kappler, pp. 1015–20. The pervasiveness of the civilization policy of the government is seen here. Although the situation of the Navajos in New Mexico was quite different from that of the northern plains tribes who signed the Treaty of Fort Laramie in 1868, the provisions for selecting homesteads, for school attendance, and the like were almost identical.

46. Thompson, *Army and the Navajo*, pp. 158–65, analyzes the effects of the Bosque Redondo experience. An authoritative study of the Navajos, in a much-quoted statement, asserted in 1946: "Fort Sumner was a major calamity to The People; its full effects upon their imagination can hardly be conveyed to white readers. Even today it seems impossible for any Navaho of the older generation to talk for more than a few minutes on any subject without speaking of Fort Sumner. Those who were not there themselves heard so many poignant tales from their parents that they speak as if they themselves had experienced all the horror of the 'Long Walk,' the illness, the hunger, the homesickness, the final return to their desolated land. One can no more understand Navaho attitudes—particularly toward white people—without knowing of Fort Sumner than he can comprehend Southern attitudes without knowing of the Civil War." Clyde Kluckhohn and Dorothea Leighton, *The Navaho* (Cambridge: Harvard University Press, 1946), pp. 9–10.

engaged in the great struggle of the Civil War. There were, in fact, scattered
raids along the emigrant and mail routes crossing the plains, and the general restlessness among the Sioux, Cheyennes, and Arapahos worried the
Indian Office and the War Department and unnerved the territorial officials in the West, even though there was no general uprising.[47]

In 1861, at Fort Wise on the upper Arkansas, peaceful chiefs, including
Black Kettle and White Antelope of the Cheyennes and Little Raven of the
Arapahos, had agreed to give up the lands assigned them in the Treaty of
Fort Laramie of 1851 and accept a reservation along the Arkansas. The
land of the reservation was to be allotted in severalty to individual members of the tribes in order to promote "settled habits of industry and enterprise." The treaty provided annuities for fifteen years, totalling $450,000,
to be spent at the discretion of the secretary of the interior for agricultural
development among the tribes, and land for the support of schools. The
Indians who signed the treaty agreed to induce the portions of the tribes
not represented to join them in this great step toward civilization.[48]

The chiefs who agreed to the Fort Wise Treaty had no success in drawing others to such a radical change in their way of life, and most of the
Indians continued to rely on hunting the buffalo that still roamed between
the Platte and the Arkansas. Governor John Evans of Colorado Territory
hoped to draw all the Indians to a great council in September 1863, where
they would agree to settle on the upper Arkansas reservation, but no one
appeared, for the traditional chiefs rejected the concept of the treaty. With
the failure of the council, Evans expected and planned for war.[49] In this aggressive policy he was eagerly joined by the military commander of the
District of Colorado, Colonel John M. Chivington, the hero of Glorieta

---

Henry F. Dobyns and Robert C. Euler, in *The Navajo People* (Phoenix: Indian Tribal Series, 1972), pp. 35–36, assert: "'The Long Walk' became a central fact of Navajo psychol-
ogy for the next century, the foundation stone of Navajo-White relationships, and a fundamental conceptual watershed between the remote and increasingly meaningless past,
and the actuality of United States domination. The United States forcefully pacified the
Navajos and their 'Long Walk' drove that fact home to them."

47. The military action on the plains is described in Utley, *Frontiersmen in Blue*,
pp. 281–99, and in Donald J. Berthrong, *The Southern Cheyennes* (Norman: University
of Oklahoma Press, 1963), pp. 174–244. The Indian Office's concern is treated in Danziger, *Indians and Bureaucrats*, pp. 21–47. An excellent firsthand account of the guarding of the telegraph lines and the emigrant trail west of Fort Laramie is provided in William E. Unrau, ed., *Tending the Talking Wire: A Buck Soldier's View of Indian Country,
1863–1866* (Salt Lake City: University of Utah Press, 1979).

48. Kappler, pp. 807–11. This treaty is a splendid example of the government's sincere but unreasonable expectations of inducing the nomadic plains Indians to settle
down on individual lots as agriculturalists.

49. A scholarly biography of Evans that is favorable to the governor is Harry E. Kelsey, Jr., *Frontier Capitalist: The Life of John Evans* (Denver: State Historical Society of
Colorado and Pruett Publishing, 1969); see pp. 115–53.

Pass. Chivington, a Methodist minister turned soldier and politician, enjoyed unusual autonomy while his superiors were occupied with the Civil War.

The Civil War did not seriously interrupt the great migration of people to the West. The explosion of the mining frontier that followed the strikes in Colorado in 1858 continued unabated and largely unconcerned with the dramatic events taking place in the East. Stage and freight lines moved west across Kansas, and the burgeoning traffic of men and materials continued to cut sharply into the hunting grounds of the Indians, who reacted with sporadic raids on stations and settlements. Although the raids were often isolated and of limited destruction, the depredations over a wide area made it difficult to separate hostile Indians from peaceful ones. It was enough to alarm the Colorado settlements to the point of panic, and Evans and Chivington urged military action to crush the offending Indians and restore security to the territory.

One group of Cheyennes under Black Kettle and White Antelope, joined by a small number of Arapahos, wanted peace with the whites. These Indians met with Governor Evans and Colonel Chivington at Camp Weld near Denver on September 28, 1864. The whites sought only to determine the attitude of the Indians and made no formal peace arrangements, but their remarks were interpreted by the chiefs to mean peace, and the Indians turned in their arms at Fort Lyon (the former Fort Wise) and moved north to a camp along Sand Creek. There on the morning of November 29 they were attacked without warning by Colonel Chivington with troops of the First Colorado Cavalry and one-hundred-day enlistees of the Third Colorado Cavalry. Black Kettle raised an American flag and a white flag before his tent to indicate the peaceful nature of the camp, and White Antelope stood with his arms folded in a peaceful gesture as the whites advanced, but to no avail. The soldiers slaughtered the defenseless Indians in a most brutal manner, killing men, women, and children indiscriminately and mutilating in revolting fashion the bodies of those who fell. Black Kettle and others escaped, but about one hundred and fifty Indians, including White Antelope, were killed in this Sand Creek Massacre.[50]

50. The literature on Sand Creek is extensive, for the complexity of the event and of its origins has puzzled and intrigued historians and popular writers. Useful accounts are Stan Hoig, *The Sand Creek Massacre* (Norman: University of Oklahoma Press, 1961); Raymond G. Carey, "The Puzzle of Sand Creek," *Colorado Magazine* 41 (Fall 1964): 279–98; Janet Lecompte, "Sand Creek," ibid., pp. 315–35; and Lonnie J. White, "From Bloodless to Bloody: The Third Colorado Cavalry and the Sand Creek Massacre," *Journal of the West* 6 (October 1976): 535–81. For a discussion of the historical controversies about Sand Creek, see Michael A. Sievers, "Sands of Sand Creek Historiography," *Colorado Magazine* 49 (Spring 1972): 116–42; background information is supplied in William E. Unrau, "A Prelude to War," ibid., 41 (Fall 1964): 299–313, and Harry Kelsey, "Background to Sand Creek," ibid. 45 (Fall 1968): 279–300.

The atrocities at Sand Creek were celebrated with jubilation in Denver, where the returning volunteers were cheered in the streets and in the theaters as they displayed the grisly trophies of the campaign. But the savage treatment of the peaceful Indians brought nothing but revulsion and outcry in the East. There was no dearth of information, for three formal investigations of the event collected extensive testimony and spread it before the public in official reports. Here was a barbaric affair that sickened those who had hoped for Christian treatment of the Indians.

First on the scene was the Joint Committee on the Conduct of the War, which was directed by the House of Representatives on January 10, 1865, to investigate Sand Creek. In March the committee heard testimony in Washington, gathered affidavits, correspondence, and official reports, and added testimony from Chivington in Denver. The report, signed by Senator Benjamin F. Wade, was a devastating condemnation. Its description of the massacre was lurid and its criticism harsh. The soldiers, it said, "indulged in acts of barbarity of the most revolting character; such, it is to be hoped, as never before disgraced the acts of men claiming to be civilized." It spoke of the "fiendish malignity and cruelty of the officers who had so sedulously and carefully plotted the massacre" and accused Chivington of deliberately planning and executing "a foul and dastardly massacre which would have disgraced the veriest savage among those who were the victims of his cruelty."[51] Then a military fact-finding commission led by Samuel F. Tappan met in Denver to investigate the conduct of Colonel Chivington.[52]

At the same time the Joint Special Committee of Congress, headed by Senator Doolittle, undertook its study of the condition of the western Indians. One part of the committee, assigned to study Kansas, the Indian Territory, and the territories of Colorado, New Mexico, and Utah, made a special investigation of Sand Creek. It, too, took testimony in Washington in March and then traveled west to Fort Riley, Fort Lyon, and Denver, where interviews were held with participants and other interested parties.[53]

The voluminous hearings furnished tremendous ammunition for those who were aghast at the government's handling of Indian affairs and wanted immediate reform. No matter that the testimony on Sand Creek was often contradictory, that evidence was admitted without any critical norms, and that the investigators made no claim to objectivity.[54] No matter that the

51. "Massacre of Cheyenne Indians," in Report of the Joint Committee on the Conduct of the War, *Senate Report* no. 142, 38–2, serial 1214, pp. iii–v. Appended to the report are more than one hundred pages of testimony.

52. "Proceedings of a Military Commission Convened by Special Orders No. 23, Headquarters District of Colorado, Denver, Colorado Territory, Dated February 1, 1865, in the Case of Colonel J. M. Chivington, First Colorado Cavalry," *Senate Executive Document* no. 26, 39–2, serial 1277, pp. 2–228.

53. "The Chivington Massacre," *Condition of the Indian Tribes*, pp. 26–98.

54. Carey, "Puzzle of Sand Creek," pp. 297–98, points out the weaknesses in the

attack was undertaken by local troops and was not the result of official United States policy or plans. The Sand Creek Massacre became a cause célèbre, a never-to-be-forgotten symbol of what was wrong with United States treatment of the Indians, which reformers would never let fade away and which critics today still hold up to view.[55]

Sand Creek intensified Indian hostilities on the plains if it did not, indeed, set off new Indian warfare. Black Kettle and others who escaped were aided by the Northern Cheyennes and Arapahos and by the Comanches and Kiowas, and the Indians fought off the troops sent out to quiet them. The army planned an extensive campaign, but humanitarian outcries over Sand Creek and the desire of the Indians themselves for peace led to negotiations. A United States commission met with chiefs of the Cheyennes and Arapahos, Comanches, Kiowas, and Kiowa-Apaches on the Little Arkansas River. On October 14, 1865, the Cheyennes and Arapahos present signed a treaty in which they agreed to give up their lands in Colorado and accept a reservation which lay partly in Kansas and partly in the Indian Territory. Although they were permitted to range over their old lands, they agreed not to disturb the roads, military posts, and towns of the white. The government agreed to pay annuities for forty years. Three days later a similar agreement was concluded with the Kiowa-Apaches, and on the following day one with the Comanches and Kiowas, who were to get a reservation in the Indian Territory and in the panhandle of Texas. The treaties, although they brought a temporary peace, did not solve the problem because the reservations to be established never materialized. The control of Texas over its lands nullified the agreement with the Comanches and Kiowas, and Kansas refused to allow a reservation within its boundaries.[56]

At the end of the Civil War, when full attention could once more be directed to Indian problems, the nation was ready for a major overhaul of Indian policy.

---

techniques of the groups that investigated Sand Creek. He concludes: "Not one of the examining bodies can be credited with having done a reputable job of distinguishing between the valid testimony of eye-witnesses and the second-hand accounts of special pleaders, or of cutting through the jungle of half-truths, exaggerations, and untruths to determine, beyond reasonable doubt, what actually happened before, at, and after Sand Creek."

55. The Sand Creek Massacre gets emphatic treatment, for example, in Helen Hunt Jackson, *A Century of Dishonor* (New York: Harper and Brothers, 1881), pp. 343–58, and Dee Brown, *Bury My Heart at Wounded Knee* (New York: Holt, Rinehart and Winston, 1970), pp. 67–102. For a novelized treatment, see Michael Straight, *A Very Small Remnant* (New York: Alfred A. Knopf, 1963).

56. Kappler, pp. 887–95; Berthrong, *Southern Cheyennes*, pp. 224–44; William H. Leckie, *The Military Conquest of the Southern Plains* (Norman: University of Oklahoma Press, 1963), pp. 23–26.

CHAPTER 18

The Indian System
and Its Critics

Commissioner Dole and the Reservation System.

Protests against the Indian System.

Proposals for Military Control.

Lincoln's Republican administration, replacing the long rule of the Democrats (broken only by the Whig interlude of Zachary Taylor and Millard Fillmore) was much concerned about political patronage, and the Department of the Interior was full of rich plums. Caleb B. Smith, picked by Lincoln to be secretary of the interior, was an Indiana lawyer and politician who led his state's delegation to the Republican National Convention in Chicago in 1860, gave a seconding speech for Lincoln's nomination, and worked hard to deliver Indiana to Lincoln in the election. He had no real interest in the job or in the Washington bureaucracy, knew nothing about Indian affairs, and resigned as soon as an opportunity presented itself. Smith left much of the work of the Interior Department in the hands of John Palmer Usher, also from Indiana, who had been appointed assistant secretary of the interior in November 1861 and who succeeded him as secretary in January 1863. Usher was more interested in railroad affairs than in Indian matters, and though he appeared to hope sincerely for the welfare of the Indians, he did little or nothing to counteract the political and economic pressures that impinged upon Indian interests.[1]

1. On Smith, see Louis J. Bailey, "Caleb Blood Smith," *Indiana Magazine of History* 29 (September 1933): 213–39, and Richard J. Thomas, "Caleb Blood Smith: Whig Orator and Politician—Lincoln's Secretary of Interior" (Ph.D. dissertation, Indiana University, 1969). A generally favorable biography of Usher is Elmo R. Richardson and Alan W.

COMMISSIONER DOLE AND THE RESERVATION SYSTEM

The focus of federal Indian affairs during the Civil War era was William P. Dole, who served as commissioner of Indian affairs during the whole of Lincoln's administration—a longer term than any commissioner until William A. Jones (1897–1904). Dole, like Smith and Usher, had been a longtime resident of Indiana, although he had moved to Illinois in 1854, and he, like them, got his appointment as a reward for active campaigning for Lincoln. He was a personal friend of the president, and no doubt Lincoln agreed with his major Indian policies and actions. Although he knew nothing about Indians when he entered office, he took his responsibilities seriously and was considerably more than a political hack, despite his eager appointment of relatives and political friends to offices within his patronage. It was he who faced the crucial issues of the Confederate Indians, the refugees from the Indian Territory, the Minnesota Sioux outbreak, and long-continuing problems inherited from earlier administrations.[2]

The basic concern of Dole's administration was the extension and reform of the reservation system. In this he was no doubt influenced considerably by Charles Mix, who continued to hold his job as chief clerk in the Indian Office amid the political vicissitudes of the times. But Dole also had his own ideas. He wanted to isolate the Indian from contact with white settlements, and he wrote in his first annual report: "There seems to be no means by which he can be secured from falling an easy victim to those vices and temptations which are perhaps the worst feature of our civilization, and to which he seems to have an almost irresistible inclination." He noted that the multiplication of small reservations, notably in California and in Kansas, meant that the Indians would soon be entirely surrounded by whites. His recommendation was to concentrate the In-

---

Farley, *John Palmer Usher, Lincoln's Secretary of the Interior* (Lawrence: University of Kansas Press, 1960). The authors conclude, p. 63: "In dealing with the Indian tribes, he could not free himself from the traditional bonds of politics and patronage or resist the pressure of local attitudes." A harsh picture of Usher is presented in David A. Nichols, *Lincoln and the Indians: Civil War Policy and Politics* (Columbia: University of Missouri Press, 1978).

2. Because Dole managed Indian affairs, studies of government relations with the Indians during the Civil War concentrate on him. The most useful ones are those of Harry Kelsey: "William P. Dole and Mr. Lincoln's Indian Policy," *Journal of the West* 10 (July 1971): 484–92; "William P. Dole, 1861–65," in Robert M. Kvasnicka and Herman J. Viola, eds., *The Commissioners of Indian Affairs, 1824–1977* (Lincoln: University of Nebraska Press, 1979), pp. 89–98; and the manuscript, "Mr. Lincoln's Indian Bureau," a copy of which was kindly furnished me by the author. See also Donovan L. Hofsommer, "William Palmer Dole: Commissioner of Indian Affairs," *Lincoln Herald* 75 (Fall 1973): 97–114.

dians, moving those on the scattered reservations into larger reservations and then excluding all whites except "such soldiers and officers as may be actually required in order to preserve peace among the Indians, enforce the necessary police regulations, instruct the young, and render the necessary aid to adults while acquiring a knowledge of the arts of civilized life."[3] Dole hoped to apply his principle to the Indians in Kansas and went personally to Kansas to treat with them.

The concentrated reservation plan also entered into Dole's consideration of the problems arising from conflicts between the plains Indians and the advancing whites. "The white and the red man cannot occupy territory in common," he asserted in 1864, and he proposed to set aside three to five large blocks of the public domain for Indian use, "selected with especial reference to their adaptation to the peculiar wants and requirements of the Indians, and protected by the most stringent legislation against encroachments by the whites." The Indian Territory looked like the best place to Dole, and he assumed that the Indians who joined the Confederacy would have to make room after the war for other Indians who might be moved there. The congressional action in 1862 that authorized the president to abrogate treaties with the Indians "in a state of actual hostility to the government" opened the possibility of using lands in the Indian Territory for such a concentration.[4] Although Dole himself actually accomplished little, either with the settled Indians in eastern Kansas or with the plains Indians still active in the western part of the state, the policy of concentrating these Indians in the Indian Territory was in the end carried out.

Despite his inexperience, Dole immediately saw that an improvement could be made in the reservation system by recognizing "cattle husbandry as a means of subsistence for the Indians, equal in importance with the tillage of the soil." He realized that the arid conditions west of the hundredth meridian made agriculture a risky business, and he hoped to furnish the Indian, "who is naturally more of a herdsman than a cultivator," with a source of subsistence when crops failed. Treaties with the western tribes like the Shoshonis and Utes made during Dole's administration called specifically for provision of stock for herding or in general for goods judged by the president to be "suitable for their wants and condition either as hunters or herdsmen."[5]

Dole continued his predecessors' drive for allotment of Indian lands. "It seems perfectly manifest to me," he wrote in 1863, "that a policy designed

3. CIA Report, 1861, serial 1117, pp. 646–47; CIA Report, 1862, serial 1157, pp. 169–70; CIA Report, 1863, serial 1182, pp. 129–30; CIA Report, 1864, serial 1220, p. 149.

4. CIA Report, 1864, serial 1220, p. 149; 12 *United States Statutes* 528. Dole's views are also expressed in CIA Report, 1862, serial 1157, pp. 179–80.

5. CIA Report, 1861, serial 1117, p. 638; Kappler, pp. 849, 852, 858, 860.

to civilize and reclaim the Indians within our borders, and induce them to adopt the customs of civilization, must of necessity embrace, as one of its most prominent features, the ideas of self-reliance and individual effort, and, as an encouragement to those ideas, the acquisition and ownership of property in severalty." He saw a chance to improve the system, however, by insisting that allotments not be granted indiscriminately but only to an Indian who had demonstrated interest and ability—as "a special mark of the favor and approbation of his 'Great Father,' on account of his good conduct, his industry, and his disposition to abandon the ancient customs of his tribe, and engage in the more rational pursuits of civilization." The treaties negotiated during his administration all had some provision for individual ownership of Indian land.[6]

Dole acted out the role of the Great Father, and part of the role was that of teacher. The education and thereby the civilization of the Indians was not forgotten amid the pressure of other duties, and the place of religion in the process was still a prime consideration. Dole paid attention to the schools in his reports, accepting and promoting the manual labor boarding school as the ideal. He wrote to a friend in 1862:

> The best schools are the labor schools and *the more labor the better*. Book learning is useless to an Indian if he has not habits of industry with it. If he does not work for his living after he leaves school but returns to the chase or depends upon annuities and his wife's labor he is the *worse* for all we have expended on him, generally and very generally, at that. What I want then is a farm with a farmer whose heart is in it to teach the boys to work only mixing enough of books with it for a change and to make it of interest caring very little except that they should be taught to be self-sustaining. I have thought deeply about this . . . and have come to the conclusion that an honest, upright, true-hearted missionary, I care not of what church, who will with his family settle down with or near some of these people and by example and kindness teach them the arts of husbandry &c. &c. will do more good than all the traveling agents in the Union.[7]

Dole made his most significant mark on Indian policy by his insistence on the use of treaties to protect Indian rights. Whatever might be thought about the inappropriateness of dealing with nomadic Indian bands as sovereign nations, Dole was concerned about the question of Indian rights to

6. CIA Report, 1863, serial 1182, p. 130; see also CIA Report, 1861, serial 1117, p. 647.

7. Dole to Elijah White, June 9, 1862, Letterbook, Dole Papers, Huntington Library. Dole's reliance on missionaries in educational work is noted in CIA Report, 1861, serial 1117, p. 645.

land, especially in the huge area of the Southwest acquired from Mexico. The commissioner could see little sense in arguing about the Indian title to land in the Mexican Cession, for he believed that the Indians had moral if not legal rights to the land. He met squarely the argument that the Spanish and Mexicans had not recognized title for the nomadic tribes and therefore that the United States should not. "If this position is correct," he said in his report of 1861, "it would seem to follow that the policy so long pursued by our government in negotiating treaties with the Indians, and thus extinguishing their titles to land within our borders, has been radically wrong; for as the Indians occupied the territory of both nations prior to the advent of the European races upon this continent, it seems clear that they held lands in the territory of Mexico and the United States by precisely the same tenure." He believed that the transfer of the lands in the Southwest to the United States placed the Indians "within the protection of the general policy established by the United States for the government of other tribes" and that it would be an anomaly to treat the Indians in the Mexican Cession any differently from other Indians.[8]

The Indians of California, especially, needed attention, and Dole pressed for a just land settlement for them against the opposition of local citizens who did not want to see Indian rights to land secured. He painted a dismal picture of the Indians' condition in California, beset by encroaching whites and with no place of refuge or security. "The great error in our relations with the California Indians," he wrote in 1862, "consists . . . in our refusal to recognize their usufructuary right in the soil, and treat with them for its extinguishment; thereby providing for them means of subsistence until such time as they shall be educated to conform to the widely altered circumstances by which they are surrounded." Dole conceded that it was perhaps too late to make treaties, but he wanted the government to "do voluntarily that justice which we have refused to acknowledge in the form of treaty obligations." But Congress refused to cooperate, and nothing was done for California except a reorganization in 1864 by which the dual superintendencies established in 1860 were replaced by a single superintendent, who was to have charge of no more than four reservations, each with its own agent.[9]

Dole recognized an obligation on the part of the government to provide for destitute Indians—whether there were treaty arrangements calling for

8. CIA Report, 1861, serial 1117, p. 637.
9. CIA Report, 1862, serial 1157, p. 191; 12 *United States Statutes* 530; 13 *United States Statutes* 39. For an account of Indian-white conflicts in California during the Civil War, see Leo P. Kibby, "California, the Civil War, and the Indian Problem: An Account of California's Participation in the Great Conflict," part 2, *Journal of the West* 4 (July 1965): 384–403.

support or not. Senator John Sherman of Ohio did not agree, pointing out that no relief was proposed for whites driven out of the South, and asked, "Why, then, should we extend relief to Indians, when no one would call for that relief to loyal white people?" But Dole's concerns were more humane. Where he saw need, as among the refugee Indians in Kansas, Dole spent the money from other Indian accounts and then insisted that Congress pay it back.[10]

Dole busied himself also with questions of Indian trust funds, moneys appropriated in payment of land cessions that were invested, largely in state bonds, by the United States government for the benefit of the Indians. In the previous administration $871,000 of these securities had been stolen (Dole said "abstracted"), and the commissioner wanted them to be replaced. He argued, sensibly enough, that the loss should not be borne by the Indians, who were "dependent pupils and wards of this government," but by the government that had undertaken to invest the funds as guardian and custodian, and he urged that Congress appropriate at least the interest due the Indians on such bonds as a measure of manifest justice and wise policy. He advocated, moreover, the investment of all Indian trust funds in United States bonds rather than in those of the individual states. Congress on July 12, 1862, authorized the secretary of the treasury to credit each of the Indian tribes to which the stolen bonds pertained the sum of those funds, and it appropriated money to pay 5-percent interest on them. But this provision did not apply to the Cherokees and Potawatomis, and at the end of the year Dole recommended similar provisions for them and measures to prevent further "abstraction" of Indian funds. He continued to urge prudent investment and reinvestment of the Indians' money.[11]

PROTESTS AGAINST THE INDIAN SYSTEM

The politicization of the Indian service, which reached some sort of a zenith in Lincoln's administration precisely when the Civil War turned public and official attention away from Indian affairs, and the rampant corruption that accompanied it intensified the abuses that the Indians had long suffered. Although there was no concentrated movement for Indian

10. Kelsey, "Mr. Lincoln's Indian Bureau," pp. 78–82; *Congressional Globe*, 37th Congress, 2d session, p. 2149.
11. CIA Report, 1861, serial 1117, pp. 644, 817; CIA Report, 1862, serial 1157, pp. 194–95; CIA Report, 1863, serial 1182, pp. 156–57; CIA Report, 1864, serial 1220, p. 190; 12 *United States Statutes* 539–40. There is a long report on the stolen bonds in *House Report* no. 78, 36–2, serial 1105. See also George Dewey Harmon, "The Indian Trust Funds, 1797–1865," *Mississippi Valley Historical Review* 21 (June 1934): 29–30.

reform during the war years, private individuals kept the issue alive. Two men were especially insistent: John Beeson, an Oregonian who already had to his credit a long history of agitation on behalf of the Indians, and Protestant Episcopal Bishop of Minnesota Henry Benjamin Whipple.

Beeson was an Englishman who came to America in 1830 and settled in Illinois in 1834. Two decades later he was struck by the "Oregon fever" and moved in 1853. When the Rogue River War broke out between the Indians and the white settlers, Beeson's deep religious convictions led him to defend the Indians and to charge that the war was the result of white aggression. Such nonconformity with frontier attitudes made Beeson's life in Oregon impossible, and he returned to the East, where he devoted much of his time to promotion of Indian causes. He published in New York in 1857 *A Plea for the Indians*, in which he gave a history of the Oregon war and condemned the white savages for destroying the Indians, and in 1859 he spoke at Fanueil Hall in Boston, where he shared the platform with Edward Everett, Wendell Phillips, and other reformers in an appeal for Indian rights. In the following year he began publication of *The Calumet*, meant to be a vehicle for promoting reform in Indian affairs. Only one issue of the journal came from the presses, however, for the secession crisis turned attention away from Indian matters.[12]

The Civil War did not curb all of Beeson's activities. Firmly convinced that the war was not caused by slavery but was "an extension of the unneighborly, unChristian, and destructive practice which for generations had been operating against the Aborigines," he insisted that redress of Indian wrongs was "the first step in the order of national reform and self preservation." The reformer was received sympathetically by Lincoln, and in a meeting in 1864 the president told him: "My aged Friend. I have heard your arguments time and again. I have said little but thought much, and you may rest assured that as soon as the pressing matter of this war is settled the Indians shall have my first care and I will not rest untill Justice is done to their and your Sattisfaction."[13] Beeson interviewed other national

---

12. John Beeson, *A Plea for the Indians, with Facts and Features of the Late War in Oregon* (New York, 1857; rev. ed., 1859); Beeson, *Are We Not Men and Brethren? An Address to the People of the United States* (New York: National Indian Aid Office, 1859). For my discussion of Beeson and Whipple, I draw on Francis Paul Prucha, *American Indian Policy in Crisis: Christian Refomers and the Indian, 1865–1900* (Norman: University of Oklahoma Press, 1976), pp. 4–10. An autobiographical sketch by Beeson is in *Calumet* 1 (February 1860): 4–9. A useful sketch of Beeson appears in Robert Winston Mardock, *The Reformers and the American Indian* (Columbia: University of Missouri Press, 1971), pp. 10–14.

13. Beeson to Lincoln, November 18, 1862, Department of the Interior, Indian Division, Letters Received, Miscellaneous, National Archives, Record Group 48. Lincoln's statement is quoted in Beeson to E. P. Smith, June 25, 1873, OIA LR, Miscellaneous P–520 (M234, reel 466, frame 302).

leaders, memorialized Congress, and organized public meetings in the eastern cities. When his funds ran out, he returned to Oregon in 1865, but his interest in Indian reform flared up periodically as he joined his voice to others who took up the cause of the Indians.[14]

Paralleling Beeson's activities was the more influential agitation of Bishop Whipple, whose stature as an Indian friend eventually made him a correspondent and confidant of important national leaders and whose powerful voice condemning wrongs could not be ignored as could the more fanatical utterances of Beeson. Whipple, after serving in a parish in Rome, New York, and for two years among the poor on the south side of Chicago, was elected the first Protestant Episcopal Bishop of Minnesota in 1859. In 1860 he took up residence at Faribault, which was his home for the rest of his life. Having thus been thrust into contact with both the Chippewas and the Sioux on that still primitive frontier, the new bishop investigated the condition of the Indians and became painfully aware of the injustices in the government's Indian system. He began an active crusade to right the wrongs suffered by the Indians, bombarding government officials all the way up to the president himself with letters and memorials.[15]

Whipple began his campaign while Buchanan was still in office. In a letter to the president he insisted that civilization and Christianization were the only hope for the Indians. He castigated the present condition of the Indian service, with the illegal sale of liquor and corruption prevalent among the traders. He predicted a Sioux uprising unless reforms were forthcoming. "Again and again I had declared publicly," he wrote, "that as certain as any fact in human history, a nation which sowed robbery would reap a harvest of blood."[16]

Whipple renewed his crusade with the Lincoln administration, attempting first to influence Caleb Smith, the new secretary of the interior, and

14. Beeson wrote many letters to government officials, in some of which he sought government employment as a special commissioner to the Indians. Examples are cited in Prucha, *American Indian Policy in Crisis*, p. 6 n. Beeson suggested using phrenology to pick out suitable agents, "such as have the requisite amount of benevolence, conscientiousness and intellect." *Plea for the Indians*, p. 126. In 1875 Beeson again proposed that Indian agents be "tested by the science of phrenology" so that appointments could be based on "native qualities and approved character." Address to the People of the United States, September 23, 1875, copy inclosed in Beeson to President Hayes, October 15, 1877, OIA LR, Miscellaneous (M234, reel 475). In 1862 Beeson suggested that the Indian Office organize a band of Indian singers to travel around the country giving concerts; this would do more to civilize the Indians, he said, "than all the Armies and Missionaries put together." Kelsey, "Mr. Lincoln's Indian Bureau," p. 101.

15. Whipple's career as an Indian reformer can be followed in his autobiography, *Lights and Shadows of a Long Espicopate* (New York: Macmillan Company, 1899), and in the Henry B. Whipple Papers, Minnesota Historical Society.

16. Whipple, *Lights and Shadows*, p. 105; Whipple to Buchanan, April 9, 1860, ibid., pp. 50–53.

Superintendent Clark Thompson and Agent Thomas Galbraith, the new
political appointees in charge of Minnesota Indians.[17] Then he appealed to
President Lincoln himself in a letter of March 6, 1862, writing "freely with
all the frankness with which a Christian bishop has the right to write to
the Chief Ruler of a great Christian Nation." He pointed to the rapid deterioration that had taken place among the tribes since they had signed away
much of their lands in treaties with the United States, and he especially
excoriated the Indian agents, who were selected to uphold the honor and
faith of the government without any attention to their fitness. "The Congressional delegation desires to reward John Doe for party work," the
bishop charged, "and John Doe desires the place because there is a tradition
on the border that an Indian Agent with fifteen hundred dollars a year can
retire upon an ample fortune in four years." He asked for simple honesty,
for agency employees who were men "of purity, temperance, industry, and
unquestioned integrity" rather than "so many drudges fed at the public
crib." He wanted the Indian to be treated as a ward of the government, with
aid in building a house and opening a farm and with adequate schools for
his children. And he insisted that law be provided for the Indians as it was
for the whites. Whipple was not ready to submit a detailed plan for a new
Indian system, but he urged instead that a commission of three men be
appointed to investigate Indian affairs and propose a new plan to remedy
the evils, a commission of men who would be "so high in character that
they are above the reach of political demagogues."[18]

Lincoln graciously acknowledged the communication and passed the
matter to the secretary of the interior, who indicated his agreement with
Whipple. "No one who has any knowledge of the manner in which their
[the Indians'] business is managed," Smith wrote, "can ignore the fact that
they are made victims of the avarice of those who are brought in communication with them, and that the Agents, selected by the United States, to
protect their interests, in many instances become the willing instruments
of designing men, who enrich themselves by obtaining the money which
the government intended should be expended for the benefit of the Indians." But he noted that the agents were usually local men who were not
well known to the president, and he excused himself from further consideration of the matter by sending Whipple's letter to the committees of Indian affairs in the House and Senate, with a recommendation that action
be taken to remedy the situation.[19]

Whipple's main concern was to end the evils caused by political ap-

17. Nichols, *Lincoln and the Indians,* pp. 132–33.
18. Whipple to Lincoln, March 6, 1862, *Lights and Shadows,* pp. 510–14.
19. Lincoln to Whipple, March 27, 1862, and Smith to Whipple, March 31, 1862,
Whipple Papers.

pointment of incompetent and corrupt men in the Indian service, which he believed could be done by the appointment of a commission "of some pure, large hearted & clear headed men to carry into effect the provisions of Congress." But he saw also, as he told Lincoln, "the absolute necessity of providing a government for your Indian wards," so that the good would feel its protection and the bad fear its punishment.[20]

Whipple worked hard with the two senators from Minnesota, Morton S. Wilkinson and Henry M. Rice, and with Representative Cyrus Aldrich, who chaired the House Committee on Indian Affairs. Rice alone seemed sympathetic, and he admitted that the problems would exist "so long as Agents and Superintendents, even Commissioners are appointed as rewards for *political service*." He was not sanguine, however, about correcting the system, and he confessed to Whipple that he feared "the demagogue, the politician, & those *pecuniarally interested*." From Wilkinson and Aldrich the bishop did not get even sympathy, for they openly expressed doubts that the Indians would profit much from any attention. Wilkinson saw no sense in trying to educate or convert the Indians until they had learned habits of industry: "Labor is the great civilizer." Aldrich bluntly told the bishop, "I do no[t] entirely agree with your views with regard to the capacities of the Indian race. . . . It is very questionable to my mind whether under the most favorable circumstances the native Aborigine 'to the manor born' is capable of attaining a high or even mediocre state of civilization." Whipple nevertheless held adamantly to his position. "If the world were against me," he had written to Rice, "I know I am right & I will never yield." He intended to appeal to the people if he could make no headway with Congress or the executive.[21]

The Sioux uprising tragically fulfilled Whipple's premonitions of serious trouble if the Indian system were not reformed. His zeal for the rights and welfare of the Indians was not cooled by the war. He went immediately to the scene of the disaster, taking care of the wounded and comforting the bereaved. He then took a courageous stand in support of the Indians by publishing in the St. Paul newspapers a plea to his fellow citizens not to wreak vengeance on the Indians, whose uprising had been the result of intolerable evils worked upon them by the Indian system. He went personally to Washington to plead with Lincoln for clemency for the Indians condemned to death by the military commission.

Working through Senator Rice, Whipple continued to urge the president

20. Whipple to Smith, April 10, 1862, and Whipple to Lincoln, April 16, 1862, ibid.
21. Separate letters of Whipple to Wilkinson, Rice, and Aldrich, April 30, 1861; Rice to Whipple, April 22 and 26, 1862; Wilkinson to Whipple, May 8, 1862; Aldrich to Whipple, June 12, 1862; Whipple to Rice, April 30, 1862, ibid. Aldrich presented a somewhat more sympathetic attitude toward reform in a letter to Whipple, June 26, 1862, ibid.

to bring about a wholesale reform in Indian affairs. Lincoln heard the appeal and in his state of the union address of December 1, 1862, told Congress: "I submit for your especial consideration whether our Indian system shall not be remodeled. Many wise and good men have impressed me with the belief that this can be profitably done."[22] This favorable reaction encouraged Whipple, who wrote to Lincoln, "With all my heart I thank you for your recommendation to have our whole Indian system reformed. It is a stupendous piece of wickedness and as we fear God ought to be changed." He kept hammering on the idea that a commission should be appointed to set up the reforms. To his cousin, General Henry W. Halleck, he wrote shortly after Lincoln's message: "This Indian system is a sink of iniquity. The President has recommended reform. You have his ear. Do, for the sake of these poor victims of a nation's wrong, ask him to put on it [the commission] something better than politicians."[23]

Lincoln continued to recommend reform in his annual messages, and Commissioner Dole was not unsympathetic. But Congress, too busy with the war and much concerned about vested interests in the current Indian system, took no action.[24] Senator Rice reported ruefully in February 1863: "I have no hope of anything being done to improve the condition of the Indians by this Administration." And Senator Wilkinson justified postponement of action on the basis that he was "greatly perplexed as to the details of the system to be adopted" and that any new system would take long and careful thought. The new representative from Minnesota, Ignatius Donnelly, took up Whipple's cause, but he expected nothing but hostility from those whose frauds he uncovered, and he urged the bishop to keep up his fight to arouse public opinion.[25]

Whipple returned to the charge in October 1864 with a blistering attack on the Indian system in the *North American Review*. It was a long recitation of fraud and corruption on the part of politically appointed men who entered upon their duties "with only one thought, and that is plunder." "The school is a miserable sham," the bishop declared, "the agricultural funds are wasted by improvidence, the annuity goods are lessened by fraud in the purchase or by theft after they are received, and the implements of

22. Fred L. Israel, ed., *The State of the Union Messages of the Presidents, 1790–1966*, 3 vols. (New York: Chelsea House, 1966), 2: 1074. Rice wrote to Whipple after his meeting with Lincoln: "I will do my best—Alas! the poor Indian is kept in a savage state by a great government—and his condition renders him, not an object of pity, but of plunder." Rice to Whipple, November 27, 1862, Whipple Papers.

23. Whipple to Lincoln, December 4, 1862, and Whipple to Halleck, December 4, 1862, Whipple Papers.

24. Messages of December 8, 1863, and December 6, 1864, Israel, *State of the Union Messages*, 2: 1092–93, 1104.

25. Rice to Whipple, February 3, 1863; Wilkinson to Whipple, March 1, 1863; Donnelly to Whipple, June 12, 1864, Whipple Papers.

husbandry are worthless." Whipple continued to insist, moreover, that a system of law should be provided for the Indians. "The Indians have been placed under conditions where their rude patriarchal government is destroyed or cannot be exercised," he charged. "We have recognized them as an independent nation, and then left them without a vestige of government or law. . . . The only human being in the United States who has none of the restraints or protection of law is the treaty Indian."[26]

It would be hard to show that the corruption and fraud in the Indian service was notably worse in the Civil War era than it had been in the 1850s. The insistent demands of Manypenny and others for revision of the intercourse laws for the protection of the Indians from sharpers who cheated them was indication enough of unsavory conditions. But cries for reform were largely unheeded until public opinion on some broad scale picked up the outcries. Bishop Whipple reported that on one of his trips to Washington to plead the Indians' cause before the president and the cabinet, Secretary of War Stanton had said to General Halleck, "What does Bishop Whipple want? If he has come here to tell us of the corruption of our Indian system and the dishonesty of Indian agents, tell him that we know it. But the Government never reforms an evil until the people demand it. Tell him that when he reaches the heart of the American people, the Indians will be saved."[27]

What reached the heart of the American people were spectacular events like the Sioux uprising of 1862 with its massacre of unsuspecting whites— and even more, Sand Creek with its massacre of unsuspecting Indians. The reports of official investigative bodies into the causes of continuous warfare on the plains, coming after the Civil War had ended, energized a reform movement of much broader scope than was possible for the single voice of a John Beeson or a Henry Whipple, though both men, especially Whipple, continued to be heard.

PROPOSALS FOR MILITARY CONTROL

The renewal and continuation of Indian hostilities through the Civil War period made it almost inevitable that the question of military control of Indian affairs should be a vital issue, and transfer of the Indians from the civilian Indian Office to the army was advanced as a practical "reform." Dole fought against any such move. In some cases, of course, he had to

26. Henry B. Whipple, "The Indian System," *North American Review* 99 (October 1864): 452–54.

27. Whipple, *Lights and Shadows*, p. 144. Whipple used this story in his preface to Helen Hunt Jackson's *A Century of Dishonor: A Sketch of the United States Government's Dealings with Some of the Indian Tribes* (New York: Harper and Brothers, 1881).

acquiesce in military management of the Indians. General Carleton's grand scheme for solving the Indian problems in New Mexico by concentrating the Apaches and the Navajos at the Bosque Redondo rested upon army responsibility during most of the experiment. Dole's hands were tied, for the Indian Office had no means at its disposal to give the large numbers of Indians subsistence.

Another challenge, more in theory this time than in practice, came from General Pope, whose encounter with the Indians in Minnesota had made him an instant Indian specialist. While engaged with hostile Indians, Pope's military commanders dealt with the Indians (including prisoners and captives) without much concern for the Indian Office, but Pope also wanted a general overhaul of federal Indian policy. In a letter to General Halleck on September 23, 1863, Pope strongly criticized existing policy and called for agreements with the hostile Indians that would be treaties of peace only, with no purchase of lands and no annuities of any kind. "Such conditions," he said, "only exhibit (in the eyes of the Indians) weakness on the part of the Government, and lead necessarily to the very hostilities they are intended to prevent. They stimulate the cupidity of unscrupulous men, both traders and others, and finally lead to that system of swindling and wrong to the Indians in which have originated nearly all of our Indian difficulties."[28]

Pope's most ambitious statement was the plan he drew up and forwarded to Secretary of War Stanton in February 1864.[29] The general was on strong ground as he painted in black colors the existing conditions of Indian affairs: the evils attendant on avaricious whites surrounding Indian reservations or having contact with more remote Indians who came in each year for annuity payments, the excesses of the liquor trade, and the accumulation of payments made to Indians in the pockets of traders and whiskey dealers. To these abuses he attributed the Indian outbreaks. He asserted that "our Indian policy has totally failed of any humanizing influence over the Indian, has worked him a cruel wrong, and has entailed a very great and useless expense upon the government," and he urged "a radical change in our whole Indian policy." He objected to "the principle of remunerating the Indian for land taken from him."

Pope's plan was twofold. For the "reserve and annuity Indians" along the frontier, he proposed to move them "with or without their consent" to some reservation within the settled portions of the country, take away

28. Pope to Halleck, September 23, 1863, *The War of the Rebellion: A Compilation of the Official Records of the Union and Confederate Armies*, 70 vols. (Washington: GPO, 1880–1901), series 1, 22: part 2, pp. 569–70 (hereafter cited as *Official Records*).

29. Pope to Stanton, February 6, 1864, *Official Records*, series 1, 34: part 2, pp. 259–63; the document is also printed in CIA Report, 1864, serial 1220, pp. 568–73.

their arms, stop the payment of their annuities, and spend any money due or appropriated for them in building villages and supplying them with food and clothing. The Indian here "would be placed under the most favorable circumstances to apply to him the influences of civilization, education, and Christianity with hopes of successful results, and without the surroundings which have hitherto made such instruction impossible." Pope hoped that by the second generation the Indians would be humanized and, if not made into good citizens, at least turned into harmless members of the community. "So long as Indians retain their tribal organization, and are treated in their corporate and not their individual capacity, the change of habit and of ideas necessary to effect this result or to humanize the Indians cannot be accomplished, nor can these results ever be obtained under any circumstances until the Indian is no longer an object of cupidity to the whites."

For the "wild Indians" of the West with whom treaties had not yet been made, Pope proposed military control. All these Indians should be gathered at some point beyond the "western limits of the great fertile region between the Mississippi river and the Rocky mountains," where the army would be left to deal with them without treaties and "without the interposition of Indian agents." Pope saw no reason to treat the Indians as sovereign nations with territorial rights. Treat them completely as wards of the government, he insisted, with the western tribes under complete military control and the partially civilized ones cared for far away from the disruptive forces they were encountering on the frontiers.

In addition to these general proposals there were specific proposals for the reform of trade regulations. Pope recognized the obvious fact, repeatedly enunciated by the commissioners of Indian affairs, that the existing trade and intercourse laws were ineffective and unenforcible in much of the Indian country. His solution, again, was tight military control of the traders.[30]

Although many of Pope's ideas—such as the need to educate and assimilate the Indians and the need for revision of the trade laws—had long been espoused by the Indian Office and although Dole was ready to admit that evils existed in the present system, the Indian Office refused to consider the general's plan. Dole at first simply ignored it, but when General Halleck arranged for its publication in the *Army and Navy Journal* and sent his cousin Bishop Whipple to promote the plan with the commissioner and with the president, Dole felt obliged to reply.[31] This he did in his annual report of 1864, in which he printed Pope's plan and his own refutation

30. Pope to Assistant Secretary of War C. A. Dana, September 9, 1864, enclosing Pope to Halleck, May 11, 1864, *Official Records*, series 1, 41: part 3, pp. 124–26.
31. See Halleck to Pope, April 14, 1864, *Official Records*, series 1, 34: part 3, p. 159.

of it. He admitted that serious mistakes had occurred in the management of Indian affairs, that the Indians had suffered great wrongs, and that Indian wars had resulted, but he charged that it would be difficult to demonstrate that any other policy would have had better results. He challenged Pope's assumption that there were lands in the West forever out of the way of white expansion and pointed not only to the immense expense that would be incurred by placing the Indians in areas where there were no means of subsistence but also to the dangers of bringing together mutually hostile tribes. He ridiculed the idea of easily removing Indians from their homelands without their consent, calling attention to the military operations in Florida, Oregon, California, and New Mexico occasioned by such attempts. Nor was Dole convinced that abuses and unwholesome contacts would be obviated by military control. "I have yet to learn," he said, "that the greed of military contractors is any less than is that of contractors drawn from the ranks of civilians; or that camp-followers and the 'hangers-on' around the military posts are more virtuous than are the classes of whites who assemble around our Indian reserves under the present policy."[32]

Dole insisted that it was best to stick with the policy then in effect, which, he declared, had been "gradually improving by experience." The plan of concentrating the Indians on reservations was relatively new and may not have brought all the results intended, but it was "a step in the right direction." He noted that under its operation many of the smaller tribes had been united, and that this was a beginning toward eventual consolidation of the various tribes into a single political organization; but he admitted that it would be a slow process and require patient and persevering effort. He concluded: "I freely confess that the subject is to my mind beset with difficulties, but at the same time am convinced that the object which all profess to seek, viz: ultimate reclamation and civilization of the Indian, is best to be attained by steadily persevering in our present policy, amending it from time to time as experience may suggest, and, as rapidly as may be found practicable, concentrating the Indians upon portions of the public domain suited to their wants and capacities."[33]

Dole's eloquent plea for continuing the treaty system was an outright rejection of Pope's contention that the military should be given arbitrary control of the Indians, to do what was considered necessary with or without their consent. Dole's position was that there should be a mutual understanding between the Indians and whites about the boundaries of the Indian territory, the laws that were to be applied to Indians, and "the reciprocal duties and obligations resting upon each race, whether regarded as

32. Dole to J. P. Usher, April 6, 1864, CIA Report, 1864, serial 1220, pp. 573–75.
33. Ibid., p. 575.

individuals or distinct communities." And he compared two methods by which that mutual understanding could be arrived at:

> First, by availing ourselves of our overwhelming numerical, physical, and intellectual superiority, we may set apart a country for the use of the Indians, prescribe the laws by which they shall be governed, and the rules to be observed in the intercourse of the two races, and compel a conformity on the part of the Indians; or, secondly, we may, as has been the almost universal practice of the government, after resorting to military force only so far as may be necessary in order to induce the Indians to consent to negotiate, bring about this understanding through the instrumentality of treaties to which they are parties, and as such have yielded their assent.[34]

Dole recognized that the overwhelming power of the United States enabled the government to adopt either of these methods, and the use of that power in imposing treaty agreements upon tribes who were not really free to give or withhold assent may have blurred any substantial difference between Dole's two methods. Yet the distinction that Dole saw was based on significant theoretical principles. The military plan advanced by Pope, he argued, entirely ignored the independence of the Indians and reduced them to absolute subjection, whereas the treaty system did not altogether deprive them of "their sense of nationality and independence as a people." Moreover, arbitrary military control would lead the Indians to regard the whites as "merciless despots and tyrants, who have deprived them of their homes and liberties," whereas treaties, although they rested on a recognition that the Indians as belligerents could not cope with the United States, might lead the Indians toward friendship and a gradual appreciation of the advantages and blessings of civilization. Dole asserted that the military plan was put forward for economic rather than humanitarian reasons, and he disputed even the economic benefits of it. He concluded that the advantages of the second method "seem so apparent that I can hardly realize that the former is seriously advocated." He remained firmly convinced that no better system could be found "for the management of the Indians" than the system then followed: "the fixing of the rights, duties, and obligations of each race towards the other through the instrumentality of treaties."[35]

In thus taking an adamant stand against turning the Indians over to the War Department, Dole maintained an essential principle of federal Indian policy at a time when it might have been easy to gain substantial public as well as official support for a transfer. It was an initial victory against a

---

34. CIA Report, 1864, serial 1220, p. 150.
35. Ibid.

campaign for turning Indian affairs over to military men that was to continue into the post–Civil War decades. More significantly, Dole refused to consider Pope's recommendation to end the treaty system, cancel annuity payments, and manage the Indians without in any way seeking their consent or legally establishing Indian rights and government responsibilities.[36]

There were not, then, any radical reforms in Indian affairs in the Civil War era. The federal government continued and advanced the reservation system that had been accepted during previous decades as the best solution to the intense problems facing the nation in its relations with the Indian tribes, and Dole and Lincoln met the special crises that arose with what they believed to be fair-mindedness and humanity. But the public furor that erupted over Sand Creek as the Civil War ended did not allow for careful distinctions in placing blame. Commissioner Dole bore much of the criticism aimed against the evils in Indian affairs, to which the Colorado massacre called attention, and a few weeks after Lincoln's assassination, he was forced out of office. Secretary of the Interior Usher also resigned. Andrew Johnson's appointees, James Harlan and Dennis N. Cooley, whose work we have already seen, filled the offices of secretary of the interior and commissioner of Indian affairs.

36. Pope's plan and Dole's rejection of it are discussed in Richard N. Ellis, *General Pope and U.S. Indian Policy* (Albuquerque: University of New Mexico Press, 1970), pp. 31–51. I do not agree with Ellis's strong charge that Dole "completely distorted Pope's proposals."

The
Peace Policy

The Civil War was an economic conflict between competing agrarian and industrial societies and a great nationalistic drive on the part of the North to crush rising southern nationalism and thus preserve the Union. But it was also a great Christian crusade, a moral mandate fulfilled, a wiping away of the hideous blot of sinful slavery from the conscience of the nation. The emotional intensity of the northern endeavor was heightened still more by the religious dimensions of the struggle. It was God's work: "Mine eyes have seen the glory of the coming of the Lord. He is trampling out the vintage where the grapes of wrath are stored." The evil of chattel slavery, holding in bondage black brothers made in God's image, fired the abolitionists. Rejected at first by more prudent and traditional men, abolitionism spread in subtle and diverse ways. No matter how much politicians might protest that they urged no moves against slavery where it was protected by the Constitution, and that it was only the extension of slavery they abhorred, the question of the ultimate morality of slavery could not be quieted. Even before the Emancipation Proclamation it was clear that the Civil War was indeed a war to end slavery and to recover for the Christian nation the uprightness—in its own eyes and in the eyes of the world—it had lost by clinging to the monstrous practice of human bondage. In a Senate speech in January 1864, Senator James R. Doolittle of Wisconsin asserted his belief that "we shall come out of this struggle with slavery utterly done away with; that we shall be redeemed and regenerated as a people; that we shall stand hereafter, as we have stood heretofore, in the vanguard of the civilized nations—the power of all other powers on earth."[1] The Civil War, despite the carnage and destruction, was, in the minds of many, America's finest hour. The war reinforced the evangelical aspiration and sentiments of the nation, touching many with a new revivalist ardor that could not be suddenly cooled by Appomattox.

The end of the Civil War freed new energies, and America embarked upon expansion and development of a scope that few in antebellum days would have thought possible. Northern industry, stimulated by the war and encouraged by sympathetic and benevolent legislators, absorbed the energies and talents of many men, and the exuberance that came when the crushing burden of war was removed covered over the traumas of that past event. Exploitation of land and mineral resources moved at new speeds, and transcontinental railroads, rapidly becoming a reality, tied the nation together in new unity.

Evangelical reformism thrived in this new and ebullient atmosphere. The evils of slavery had been crushed, and radical reconstruction, with new amendments to the Constitution and military occupation of the defeated South, sought to guarantee a secure place in the nation for the freedmen—who also engaged the interests of the benevolent (Generals O. O. Howard, Samuel C. Armstrong, and Clinton B. Fisk come to mind) who were working to ease the transition from the life of a slave to that of a free citizen of the republic.

Yet evils still abounded that reforming spirits could not ignore. One of the most obvious and pressing at war's end was the condition of the Indians, now made manifest as never before. Even before the war had run its course, the trail of post–Civil War Indian reform had begun, for the massacre at Sand Creek in November 1864 became a popular symbol of what was wrong in the Indian service, and a great humanitarian outcry was the result.

The concern was fed by official reports of injustice toward the Indians, and the nation witnessed an upsurge of Christian sentiment demanding Christian justice for the Indians that would be proper to a Christian nation. This was a restatement of the paternal concern for Indian welfare that had existed for decades, and the program demanded little that was new. What was new was the totality of the agitation against perceived wrongs and the intensity with which evangelical Christians moved into Indian affairs. The Indian Office, officially charged with managing Indian affairs, seemed incapable of the task in the period of chaos and crisis. Congressional committees undertook to investigate Indian wrongs, and a carefully picked

1. William Frederick Doolittle, comp., *The Doolittle Family in America* (Cleveland: Sayers and Waite Printing Company, 1901–1908), p. 673.

special commission of civilians and military officers was established to propose and implement remedies.

The formal answer to the demands for reform came in the administration of Ulysses S. Grant. It has been called "Grant's peace policy," but the principles it embodied antedated 1869 and continued to the end of the century and beyond. The peace policy was almost as many-faceted as the Indian problem it hoped to solve. Basically it was a state of mind, a determination that since the old ways of dealing with the Indians had not succeeded, a new emphasis on kindness and justice was in order. Because states of mind do not begin and end abruptly with the passage of a law, the establishment of a commission, or a military disaster, but change more subtly and grow until they dominate an era, the peace policy cannot be precisely dated, nor can it be rigidly defined.[2]

An official description of the policy in its early days appeared in a statement in 1873 by Grant's secretary of the interior, Columbus Delano, that listed the aims and purposes of the administration's policy. In the first place, Delano noted, the policy aimed to place the Indians on reservations. There they could be kept from contact with frontier settlements and could be taught the arts of agriculture and other pursuits of civilization through the aid of Christian organizations cooperating with the federal government, and there "humanity and kindness may take the place of barbarity and cruelty." Second, the policy sought to combine with such humane treatment "all needed severity, to punish them for their outrages according to their merits, thereby teaching them that it is better to follow the advice of the Government, live upon reservations and become civilized, than to continue their native habits and practices." Third, it meant a determination to see that the supplies furnished to the Indians were of high quality and reasonably priced so that funds appropriated for the Indians would not

2. I use here material from Francis Paul Prucha, *American Indian Policy in Crisis: Christian Reformers and the Indian, 1865–1900* (Norman: University of Oklahoma Press, 1976), pp. 30–33. A number of other historians have studied the peace policy or particular aspects of it, and each has his own definition of what the policy included. The following are important works: Robert H. Keller, Jr., *American Protestantism and United States Indian Policy, 1869–82* (Lincoln: University of Nebraska Press, 1983); Peter J. Rahill, *The Catholic Indian Missions and Grant's Peace Policy, 1870–1884* (Washington: Catholic University of America Press, 1953); Robert Lee Whitner, "The Methodist Episcopal Church and Grant's Peace Policy: A Study of the Methodist Agencies, 1870–1882" (Ph.D. dissertation, University of Minnesota, 1959). The peace policy is discussed thoroughly as well in these books: Henry E. Fritz, *The Movement for Indian Assimilation, 1860–1890* (Philadelphia: University of Pennsylvania Press, 1963); Robert Winston Mardock, *The Reformers and the American Indian* (Columbia: University of Missouri Press, 1971); and Loring Benson Priest, *Uncle Sam's Stepchildren: The Reformation of United States Indian Policy, 1865–1887* (New Brunswick: Rutgers University Press, 1942).

be squandered. Fourth, through the aid of religious organizations, it aimed to procure "competent, upright, faithful, moral, and religious" agents to distribute the goods and to aid in uplifting the Indians' culture. Finally, "through the instrumentality of the Christian organizations, acting in harmony with the Government," it intended to provide churches and schools that would lead the Indians to understand and appreciate "the comforts and benefits of a Christian civilization and thus be prepared ultimately to assume the duties and privileges of citizenship." Forty years later, a formal description of the peace policy spoke broadly of "such legislation and administration in Indian affairs as by peaceful methods should put an end to Indian discontent, make impossible Indian wars, and fit the great body of Indians to be received into the ranks of American citizens."[3]

Underlying this new departure in Indian policy was the conscious intent of the government to turn to religious groups and religion-minded men for the formulation and administration of Indian policy. The peace policy might just as properly have been labeled the religious policy. Building on the long history of close relations between the federal government and missionary groups in Indian matters, the nation now went far beyond simple cooperation of church and state in educational and religious activities. It welcomed official church societies and church-related individuals into fuller partnership; and to a large extent these groups came to dominate official government policy and administration of Indian affairs, at first by direct participation, then by stirring up and channeling public opinion. In turning to religious organizations, the federal government abdicated much of its responsibility. Specific governmental functions were handed over to the churches, a development that indicated not only the failure of the governmental processes in regard to the "Indian question" but also the pervasive moral and religious influences on the national outlook.

Paradoxically, the period in which the peace policy was inaugurated was a time of Indian wars, and military force was employed to crush the resisting tribes. The need for troops in active service against Indians led to a vociferous demand that all Indian affairs be turned over to the army, which might be able to better control and manage the Indians than the civilian champions of the peace policy could and which might end the fraud that continued to mark the provision of goods to the Indians. The drive to transfer the Indian Office from the Interior Department to the War Department nearly succeeded. That the movement was halted is an indication of the depth of the nation's Christian humanitarianism.

3. Report of the Secretary of the Interior, 1873, *House Executive Document* no. 1, part 5, 43–1, serial 1601, pp. iii–iv; Merrill E. Gates, "Peace Policy," in Frederick Webb Hodge, ed., *Handbook of American Indians North of Mexico*, 2 vols. (Washington: GPO, 1907–1910), 2: 218–19.

The administrative structures of the peace policy introduced under Grant, it is true, largely failed, but the spirit of the policy did not die with them. The secretary of the interior in 1882 denied that the peace policy was connected with or dependent upon formal church participation in managing Indian affairs. "I do not know what you mean by the peace policy," he told the secretary of the Methodist board of missions. ". . . If how-ever, you mean that peace is better than war and that civilization and labor are better for the Indian than his past and present condition, I agree with you."[4] In the decade and a half from 1865 to 1880 the principles of peace and civilization were refined and reformulated into a consistent and gener-ally agreed upon program that in the following two decades would be en-acted into law.

4. Henry M. Teller to J. M. Reid, August 5, 1882, *Report of the Board of Indian Com-missioners*, 1882, p. 53.

CHAPTER 19

Stirrings
of Reform

Doolittle Committee.

Indian Peace Commission.

Civilization for the Indians.

Reform Impulses.

As demands for Indian reform burst out with new energy, a full-scale reform movement developed that substantially influenced relations between the federal government and the Indian tribes. Congress prepared the way with formal investigations of evil conditions in the West.[1]

DOOLITTLE COMMITTEE

On March 3, 1865, Congress created the Joint Special Committee "to inquire into the present condition of the Indian tribes, and especially into the manner in which they are treated by the civil and military authorities of the United States."[2] The committee, composed of three senators and four representatives, was chaired by Senator James R. Doolittle and is commonly called the Doolittle Committee. The chairman, a longtime active Baptist described by his family biographer as "the ideal type of cultured, Christian gentleman," was a good choice to head such a reform committee. He was a deeply religious man who saw in the American republic the

1. This chapter uses material from Francis Paul Prucha, *American Indian Policy in Crisis: Christian Reformers and the Indian, 1865–1900* (Norman: University of Oklahoma Press, 1976), pp. 14–29.
2. 13 *United States Statutes* 572–73.

special guidance of Divine Providence and who boldly proclaimed that the Declaration of Independence was "the new gospel of man's redemption" and the Fourth of July "the birthday of God's Republic, second only in history to the birth of Christ."[3]

Doolittle's committee split into three groups and toured the West to investigate conditions among the Indians. In addition, the committee sent a detailed questionnaire to military commanders, Indian agents, and others acquainted with the West asking about causes of the deterioration of the Indians, the best forms of land tenure, the effects of schools and missions, the use of annuities, and whether the Indian Office should be transferred to the War Department. The voluminous answers were attached to the committee's report, which, after long delay, was submitted on January 26, 1867. The committee noted that, except for the tribes in the Indian Territory, the Indian population was rapidly declining as the result of disease, intemperance, war, and the pressure of white settlement. The wars, it asserted, came in large part because of "the aggression of lawless whites." Viewing the loss of Indian hunting grounds as an important cause of decay, it spoke of the powerful effect of the railroads on the destruction of the buffalo. Although the committee decided that the Indian service should stay in the Interior Department, it recommended a system of five inspection districts, each to be served by a three-man inspection committee composed of an assistant commissioner of Indian affairs, an army officer, and a person chosen by the president on the recommendations of church groups or missionary boards.[4]

The importance of the Doolittle Committee lay, not in immediate legislation, but in the effect its report had upon the Christian conscience of reform-minded humanitarians in the East. Its bulky appendix was full of charges of fraud and corruption indicating the need for a new policy. The statements were inconsistent, the charges often unsubstantiated, and the facts many times in error. The large volume hardly presented an accurate

---

3. William Frederick Doolittle, comp., *The Doolittle Family in America* (Cleveland: Sayers and Waite Printing Company, 1901–1908), p. 692. The other members were Lafayette S. Foster of Connecticut and James W. Nesmith of Oregon from the Senate and Asahel W. Hubbard of Iowa, William Higby of California, Lewis W. Ross of Illinois, and William Windom of Minnesota from the House.

4. *Condition of the Indian Tribes: Report of the Joint Special Committee, Appointed under Joint Resolution of March 3, 1865* (Washington: GPO, 1867; also printed as *Senate Report* no. 156, 39–2, serial 1279), pp. 3–10. There is a summary and analysis of the responses to the questionnaire in Donald Chaput, "Generals, Indian Agents, Politicians: The Doolittle Survey of 1865," *Western Historical Quarterly* 3 (July 1972): 269–82. In March 1866 Doolittle had introduced a bill to establish just such a system of inspection as the committee recommended. The bill passed the Senate, but the House did not act on it. See Doolittle's support of the measure and debate on it in *Congressional Globe*, 39th Congress, 1st session, pp. 1449–50, 1485–92.

picture of the "condition of the Indian tribes," but no matter, for it furnished ammunition for those seeking a change.[5]

Even while the Doolittle Committee was formulating its report, renewed warfare in the West drove home the need for some better Indian policy. War broke out along the Bozeman Trail, which had been built through the Powder River hunting grounds of the Sioux to link the new mining regions of Montana with the Oregon Trail near Fort Laramie. The state of siege in which the Indians held the military posts established in 1865 and 1866 to protect the miners' wagon trains caused apprehension, but few saw it as a prelude to white defeat. Then on December 21, 1866, a rash lieutenant, William Fetterman, ignoring the admonitions of his superiors not to go beyond the protective range of Fort Phil Kearny, was ambushed by the Indians. He and his command of eighty men were wiped out, and the Fetterman Massacre made clear in the East the seriousness of the Indian situation in the West.[6] A special committee appointed to investigate the disaster reinforced the conclusions of the Doolittle Committee.[7]

The central plains, too, were on fire, and the news of the Fetterman ambush and of raiding parties into Texas brought near panic. To prevent what he believed would be a major outbreak in the spring of 1867, General Winfield Scott Hancock moved to overawe the Indians by striking at a Cheyenne village. The action only stirred up the Indians more, and the peace of the spring turned into war as the hostile Indians terrorized the regions on both sides of the Platte.[8]

Responsible officials agreed that a crisis had arrived in Indian policy, that the past ways of dealing with the Indians had not worked and were especially unsuited for post-Civil War conditions. They saw the inexorable movement of waves of white population, against which the Indians were defenseless. "Unless they fall in with the current of destiny as it rolls and surges around them," wrote General Grant's aide-de-camp, Ely S. Parker, who later became commissioner of Indian affairs, "they must succumb and be annihilated by its overwhelming force." Commissioner of Indian Affairs

5. A very critical analysis of the Doolittle report that points to the political motivation of many of the statements contained in it and charges that it was "incomplete and largely misleading" is Harry Kelsey, "The Doolittle Report of 1867: Its Preparation and Shortcomings," *Arizona and the West* 17 (Summer 1975): 107–20.

6. There is a useful analysis of the military situation in Robert A. Murray, *Military Posts in the Powder River Country of Wyoming, 1865–1894* (Lincoln: University of Nebraska Press, 1968), pp. 3–12, 73–101. Red Cloud's part in the Indians' fight against the road is discussed in James C. Olson, *Red Cloud and the Sioux Problem* (Lincoln: University of Nebraska Press, 1965), pp. 27–57.

7. CIA Report, 1867, serial 1326, pp. 2–3. Reports of the members of the commission are in *Senate Executive Document* no. 13, 40–1, serial 1308.

8. See reports in *Senate Executive Document* no. 13, 40–1, serial 1308; *House Executive Document* no. 240, 41–2, serial 1425.

Nathaniel G. Taylor declared in similar vein that the millions of whites advancing upon the Indians would "soon crush them out from the face of the earth, unless the humanity and Christian philanthropy of our enlightened statesmen shall interfere and rescue them." Both Parker and Taylor agreed, despite cries to the contrary in the press and in the utterances of some public figures, that "the sentiment of our people will not for a moment tolerate the idea of extermination."[9]

A recommendation with two closely related elements crystallized in the reports and statement of 1867. First was a reservation scheme by which the Indians of the plains would be moved out of the way of the whites who seemed about to crush them. Although this was by no means a novel idea, officials now asserted the urgency and absolute necessity of such an arrangement in order to save the Indians. The Indians should be made to move to the reservations, where they would be given livestock, agricultural implements, and spinning and weaving equipment to enable them to move toward self-support; schooling in letters and industry; and missionary instruction in Christianity; and where they could be isolated from all whites except government employees and others permitted on the reservations. The second element in the recommendation was for a special commission made up of respected citizens of integrity (Parker wanted to add also some of the "most reputable educated Indians, selected from the different tribes") to select and designate suitable ample reservations and then work to persuade the Indians to move to them.[10]

INDIAN PEACE COMMISSION

Out of these threads came the United States Indian Peace Commission, a congressional creation intended to take the business of negotiating with the Indians out of the hands of the executive and give it instead to a special group of civilian and military leaders with interest and competence in Indian affairs. The act of Congress of June 20, 1867, that established the commission, designating the civilian members of the commission and leaving to the president the responsibility of naming the military component, set its tasks in unmistakable language. The body had authority to call together the chiefs of the warring tribes, find the causes of hostility, and negotiate treaties that would "remove all just causes of complaint on their part, and at the same time establish security for person and property along the lines of railroad now being constructed to the Pacific and other thoroughfares of

9. Taylor to W. T. Otto, July 12, 1867, and Parker to Grant, January 24, 1867, *Senate Executive Document* no. 13, 40–1, serial 1308, pp. 5–6, 42–49.
10. Ibid.; see also Lewis V. Bogy to O. H. Browning, February 4, 1867, ibid., pp. 7–11.

travel to the western Territories, and such as will most likely insure civilization for the Indians and peace and safety for the whites." For Indians who did not then occupy reservations under treaty agreements, the commissioners were to select reservations that would become their permanent homes. But there was an iron hand in this velvet glove: if the commissioners failed to get the Indians to settle on reservations and thus secure peace, the secretary of war was authorized to call for volunteers for "the suppression of Indian hostilities."[11]

The men chosen by Congress were a humanitarian lot. The chairman of the commission was Nathaniel G. Taylor, who had been appointed commissioner of Indian affairs by President Johnson on March 26, 1867. Born in Happy Valley, Tennessee, Taylor had graduated from Princeton in 1840, practiced law, and served in the House of Representatives both before and after the Civil War. He made a name for himself as a Union man and won praise for his efforts to succor East Tennessee refugees during the Civil War. When Taylor, a man of deep religious sentiment who served for a time as a Methodist minister, retired from the Indian Office, he devoted himself to farming and preaching the gospel. Taylor had strong views about Indian policy, which dominated his annual reports and the initial report of the Peace Commission; there was not the slightest doubt in his mind about either the obligation or the possibility of civilizing the Indians in a Christian pattern.[12] Seconding him was a Bostonian who had moved to Colorado, Samuel F. Tappan, a noted supporter of Indian rights with a tinge of fanaticism in his makeup, who had chaired the military commission investigating Colonel Chivington and Sand Creek. Aligned with them was Senator John B. Henderson of Missouri, chairman of the Senate Committee on Indian Affairs and sponsor of the legislation that had created the commission. A fourth was John B. Sanborn, a native of Minnesota, who had risen to the rank of major general in the army and who in 1867 was out of the service and practicing law in Washington. He had served on the commission that investigated the Fetterman Massacre. These four men had been named explicitly in the law that established the commission.[13]

11. 15 *United States Statutes* 17. See the discussion in *Congressional Globe*, 40th Congress, 1st session, pp. 756–57.

12. "Nathaniel G. Taylor," in Oliver P. Temple, *Notable Men of Tennessee from 1833 to 1875: Their Times and Their Contemporaries* (New York: Cosmopolitan Press, 1912), p. 199; *Biographical Directory of the American Congress*, s.v. Taylor, Nathaniel G. See also William E. Unrau, "Nathaniel Green Taylor, 1867–69," in Robert M. Kvasnicka and Herman J. Viola, eds., *The Commissioners of Indian Affairs, 1824–1977* (Lincoln: University of Nebraska Press, 1979), pp. 115–22.

13. Representative William Windom of Minnesota had been named as a member of the commission, but he begged off because of other duties and suggested Tappan in his place. *Congressional Globe*, 40th Congress, 1st session, p. 756.

In addition to these the president appointed three army officers, well-qualified men with considerable experience in the West and, though firm believers in military control of the Indians, not averse to attempts at peace maneuvers. General William T. Sherman was in command of the Division of the Missouri and had overall responsibility for peace on the frontier. With him was Major General Alfred H. Terry, commander of the Department of Dakota, a scholarly young man of forty who had an excellent military record. The third general was William S. Harney, then retired in St. Louis, who had served on the Indian frontier and had many personal friends among the Indians. An extra member was Major General Christopher C. Augur, commander of the Department of the Platte, who at first substituted for Sherman but then became a regular member of the commission. A reasonable mixture of military firmness and humanitarian leniency, the commission boded well for a successful move toward peace.[14]

The Peace Commission went right to work. After an organizational meeting in St. Louis in August it moved up the Missouri, determined to council with the Indians and arrive at some peaceful understanding with them. A meeting with delegations of Sioux and Northern Cheyennes at North Platte, however, settled nothing, for Red Cloud and the Indians from the Powder River region did not attend. After announcing a new meeting at Fort Laramie for November, the commission returned to St. Louis and turned its attention to the southern plains. At Medicine Lodge Creek in southern Kansas in October 1867 it signed treaties with the Cheyennes, Arapahos, Kiowas, Comanches, and Kiowa-Apaches that assigned the Indians to two reservations in the western part of the Indian Territory, where the United States would furnish rations and other goods needed to turn them into happy farmers.[15] There was less success in the north, for Red Cloud refused to come in to Fort Laramie, declaring that he would not consider peace until the military forts along the Bozeman Trail were removed. The commission decided on a new council in the spring and adjourned.

On January 7, 1868, the commission submitted its first report, which was clearly from Taylor's hand although it was signed by all the members.[16] The report was a jeremiad, a denunciatory tirade against the evils in

14. For a view of the Peace Commission and its work through military eyes, see Robert G. Athearn, *William Tecumseh Sherman and the Settlement of the West* (Norman: University of Oklahoma Press, 1956), pp. 171–85, 196–211, 227–28; and John W. Bailey, *Pacifying the Plains: General Alfred Terry and the Decline of the Sioux* (Westport, Connecticut: Greenwood Press, 1979).

15. Kappler, pp. 977–89. A detailed story of the negotiations of the treaties from the reports of newspapermen who covered the event is Douglas C. Jones, *The Treaty of Medicine Lodge: The Story of the Great Treaty Council as Told by Eyewitnesses* (Norman: University of Oklahoma Press, 1966).

16. "Report to the President by the Indian Peace Commission," January 7, 1868, CIA

the Indian system. It found that an Indian sought to gain all his ends by war, the only means he knew. "If he fails to see the olive-branch or flag of truce in the hands of the peace commissioner, and in savage ferocity adds one more to his victims, we should remember that for two and a half centuries he has been driven back from civilization, where his passions might have been subjected to the influences of education and softened by the lessons of Christian charity." In councils with the Indians the commission inaugurated "the hitherto untried policy in connection with Indians, of endeavoring to conquer by kindness."[17]

The commissioners sought to understand Indian behavior in terms of white behavior under similar circumstances. They saw no inherent warlikeness in the Indians—only a reaction to evils that would be expected of whites themselves. "If the lands of the white man are taken," the report said, "civilization justifies him in resisting the invader. Civilization does more than this: it brands him as a coward and a slave if he submits to the wrong. Here civilization made its contract and guaranteed the rights of the weaker party. It did not stand by the guarantee. The treaty was broken, but not by the savage. If the savage resists, civilization, with the ten commandments in one hand and the sword in the other, demands his immediate extermination."[18]

The commission accepted the charge to remove the causes of complaint on the part of the Indians, but they found it "no easy task." "We have done the best we could under the circumstances," it reported, "but it is now rather late in the day to think of obliterating from the minds of the present generation the remembrance of wrong." The indictment of past policy was almost complete. "Among civilized men war usually springs from a sense of injustice. The best possible way then to avoid war is to do no act of injustice. When we learn that the same rule holds good with Indians, the chief difficulty is removed. But it is said our wars with them have been almost constant. Have we been uniformly unjust? We answer unhesitatingly, yes."[19]

The evangelical sentiment that suffused the report is seen best in the goal for the Indians that it proposed. There was no hint that the Indians should be protected to live forever as Indians; that would seem to fly in the face of God's plan for the progress of the republic. "We do not contest the

Report, 1868, serial 1366, pp. 486–510. The report is also printed in *House Executive Document* no. 97, 40–2, serial 1337. There is a good discussion of the Peace Commission and its work in Henry George Waltmann, "The Interior Department, War Department, and Indian Policy, 1865–1887" (Ph.D. dissertation, University of Nebraska, 1962), pp. 134–55.

17. CIA Report, 1868, serial 1366, pp. 487, 489.
18. Ibid., p. 492.
19. Ibid., p. 502.

every-ready argument that civilization must not be arrested in its progress by a handful of savages," the commission noted. "We earnestly desire the speedy settlement of all our territories. None are more anxious than we to see their agricultural and mineral wealth developed by an industrious, thrifty, and enlightened population. And we fully recognize the fact that the Indian must not stand in the way of this result. We would only be understood as doubting the purity and genuineness of that civilization which reaches its ends by falsehood and violence, and dispenses blessings that spring from violated rights."[20]

The solution was simple enough. The Indians must accept the civilization of the whites. "The white and Indian must mingle together and jointly occupy the country, or one of them must abandon it. If they could have lived together, the Indian by this contact would soon have become civilized and war would have been impossible. All admit this would have been beneficial to the Indian." To transform the Indians, to break down the antipathy of race, the commission set forth its recommendations: districts in the West set aside for the Indians, organized as territories, where agriculture and domestic manufactures should be introduced as rapidly as possible; schools to teach the children English; courts and other institutions of government; farmers and mechanics sent to instruct the Indians; and missionary and benevolent societies invited to "this field of philanthropy nearer home." The report declared: "The object of greatest solicitude should be to break down the prejudices of tribe among the Indians; to blot out the boundary lines which divide them into distinct nations, and fuse them into one homogeneous mass. Uniformity of language will do this—nothing else will. As this work advances each head of a family should be encouraged to select and improve a homestead. Let the women be taught to weave, to sew, and to knit. Let polygamy be punished. Encourage the building of dwellings and the gathering there of those comforts which endear the home."[21]

As practical suggestions, the commissioners recommended that money annuities be abolished forever and that domestic animals and agricultural and mechanical implements be substituted, that the intercourse laws be thoroughly revised, and that all agents and superintendents be relieved of office and only the competent and faithful reappointed. They declared that since peace, not war, with the Indians was the object, Indian affairs should be under civilian and not military control, and they recommended the formation of an independent Indian department.[22] It was the old program rejuvenated by a crusading zeal.

20. Ibid., p. 492.
21. Ibid., pp. 503–4.
22. Ibid., pp. 507–9. The generals as well as the civilians signed the full report, including the statement that Indian affairs belong under civilian control. But General Sher-

CIVILIZATION FOR THE INDIANS

Settlement with the northern tribes came at Fort Laramie in 1868. The way had been prepared by the government's willingness to withdraw its posts from the Powder River country, for as the Union Pacific moved westward, it would soon be possible to supply a new route to Montana west of the Big Horn Mountains. Little by little the tribes came in. A treaty was signed with the Brulé Sioux on April 29, with the Crows on May 7, and with the Northern Cheyennes and Northern Arapahos on May 10. But the other bands of Sioux appeared only slowly to affix their signatures to the treaty. The offending forts were dismantled and burned during the summer, and Red Cloud finally signed the treaty in November. The treaty set aside the Great Sioux Reserve west of the Missouri River in Dakota, and the chiefs agreed to settle at the agencies and accept reservation life. Meanwhile, the commissioners had gone about their business of negotiating with other western tribes at Fort Sumner, New Mexico, and Fort Bridger, Utah. All the treaties followed a common pattern supplied by the commission, with certain local or tribal variations. They were political documents of significance, for they declared that war between the tribes and the United States would "forever cease" and that peace between the parties would "forever continue," made arrangements for the punishment of wrongdoers, and established reservations with well-defined boundaries on which the Indians agreed to reside.[23]

The modern concern of Indians to protect a community land base has led to an emphasis on the land arrangements of these treaties (especially the 1868 treaty with the Sioux at Fort Laramie) that distorts their meaning in the context of the circumstances under which they were signed. These treaties were reformist documents aimed at attaining the humanitarian civilizing goals of the Peace Commission, even though the reforming tendencies were probably not well understood by the Indians and have been overlooked by historians because they were not effective. The treaties were intended to turn the nomadic warriors into peaceful farmers, and if the established reservations did not contain 160 acres of tillable land for each person (provided "a very considerable number of such persons shall be disposed to commence cultivating the soil as farmers"), the government agreed to set apart additional arable land adjacent to the reservations.

---

man later asserted that the report did not accurately reflect the officers' views. "We did not favor the conclusion arrived at," Sherman explained, "but being out-voted, we had to sign the report." Sherman to E. G. Ross, January 7, 1869, quoted in Waltmann, "The Interior Department, War Department, and Indian Policy," p. 149.

23. Kappler, pp. 998–1024.

Heads of families who wished to farm were authorized to select 320 acres, to be recorded in a "land book." Such land would no longer be held in common but "in the exclusive possession of the person selecting it, and of his family so long as he or they may continue to cultivate it." Single adults could similarly claim 80 acres. Indians who convinced the agent that they intended in good faith to cultivate the soil for a living were to receive seeds and agricultural implements for three or four years and instructions from the farmer, provided by the treaty. If more than one hundred Indians began to farm, an additional blacksmith was to be provided. To stimulate enterprise, the sum of five hundred dollars annually for three years was authorized as awards for the ten persons each year who were judged by the agent to have grown the most valuable crops.

"In order to insure the civilization of the tribes," these treaties declared, ". . . the necessity of education is admitted." The Indians pledged themselves to compel their children between the ages of six and sixteen, both boys and girls, to attend school, and the agent was charged to see that this stipulation was strictly complied with. For each thirty students who could "be induced or compelled to attend school," the government would provide a teacher "competent to teach the elementary branches of an English education." The provision was to continue for not less than twenty years, by which time, presumably, a large part of the tribes would be civilized and self-sufficient. To further encourage self-reliance, preference was to be given to Indians in the hiring of farmers, blacksmiths, millers, and other employees authorized by the treaties.

These treaties were a triumph of theory and faith over hard reality. Aside from the fact that cultivation of the soil in quarter- or half-section plots was infeasible in most of the area covered by the treaties and that successful enterprise tended to be in grazing rather than in agriculture, the Indians concerned were not prepared to conform suddenly to the philanthropists' views of the good life of English education and neat farms.

Taylor's faith and philosophy again showed clearly in his annual report of 1868, in which he devoted a long section to the questions "Shall our Indians be civilized? And how?" He began with the assumption that the Indians had rights; to deny that would "deny the fundamental principles of Christianity." The crucial question was how best to protect those rights and at the same time harmonize them with white interests. It was a question, he admitted, that had "long trembled in the hearts of philanthropists and perplexed the brains of statesmen," but he did not hesitate to propose an answer. He wrote: "History and experience have laid the key to its solution in our hands, at the proper moment, and all we need to do is to use it, and we at once reach the desired answer. It so happens that under the silent and seemingly slow operations of efficient causes, certain tribes of our

Indians have already emerged from a state of pagan barbarism, and are to-day clothed in the garments of civilization, and sitting under the vine and fig tree of an intelligent, scriptural Christianity."[24]

The historical examples were the Cherokees, Choctaws, Chickasaws, Creeks, and Seminoles, who had once, as savages, terrorized the colonial frontiers but who now lived as Christian and enlightened nations. "Thus the fact stands out clear, well-defined, and indisputable," Taylor concluded, "that Indians, not only as individuals, but as tribes, are capable of civilization and of christianization. Now if like causes under similar circumstances always produce like effects—which no sensible person will deny—it is clear that the application of the same causes, that have resulted in civilizing these tribes, to other tribes under similar circumstances, must produce their civilization." And what were these means? Reduction of territory, causing the Indians to resort to agricultural and pastoral pursuits; settlement in fixed locations; introduction of private property; and the work of Christian missionaries among the Indians.[25] Uniting Christian philanthropy with philosophy, Taylor had found a solution to the Indian problem. In this he was fully supported by Secretary of the Interior Orville H. Browning, whose views corresponded with those of the commissioner.[26]

The peace party could at first claim success, and for a time there were no serious disturbances. Then in August 1868 a group of Cheyennes with a few Arapahos and Sioux shattered the agreements made at Medicine Lodge Creek by an outbreak on the Salina and Solomon rivers in Kansas. Roving war parties killed and burned and raped on the frontiers of Kansas and Colorado. General Sherman increased military control in the West. He had been named by Congress to disburse the funds appropriated for carrying out the treaties, and although the secretary of the interior had stated that relations between his department and the Indians were to remain unchanged, Sherman had acted otherwise. In August he created two military districts, one for the Sioux under General Harney and one for the Cheyennes, Arapahos, Kiowas, and Comanches under General W. B. Hazen. The army officers were to act as "agents" for the Indians not on reservations.[27]

When the Peace Commission met again in Chicago in October, there was no longer agreement. Senator Henderson was detained in Washington

24. CIA Report, 1868, serial 1366, p. 476.

25. Ibid., pp. 477–78.

26. Maurice G. Baxter, *Orville H. Browning: Lincoln's Friend and Critic* (Bloomington: Indiana University Press, 1957), pp. 202–5.

27. William H. Leckie, *The Military Conquest of the Southern Plains* (Norman: University of Oklahoma Press, 1963), pp. 63–87; Olson, *Red Cloud and the Sioux Problem*, p. 78.

over the business of President Johnson's impeachment, and only Taylor and Tappan were left to defend a conciliatory position. The others had been convinced by the summer's warfare that military force was needed to coerce the hostile Indians, and the resolutions they passed reversed much of the previous report. The commissioners now urged provisions at once to feed, clothe, and protect the tribes "who now have located or may hereafter locate permanently on their respective agricultural reservations," and they urged that treaties with these tribes be considered to be in force whether ratified or not. The depredations committed by the Indians, the resolutions declared, justified the government in abrogating clauses of the Medicine Lodge treaties that gave the Indians the right to hunt outside their reservations. Military force should be used to compel Indians to move to the reservations. The tribes, insofar as existing treaties permitted, should no longer be considered "domestic dependent nations," and the Indians should be individually subject to the laws of the United States. Finally, in a sharp reversal of its previous stand, the commission recommended transferring the Bureau of Indian Affairs to the War Department. Commissioner Taylor, as chairman, signed the resolutions, but it was obvious from his annual report that he vigorously disagreed with them.[28]

Generals Sherman and Sheridan decided on a winter campaign to drive the tribes to their reservations, and they determined to harry and kill those who refused to settle down, with none too great care in separating those who were actually hostile from those who hoped to remain at peace. Lieutenant Colonel George A. Custer attacked the sleeping village of Black Kettle's Cheyennes on the Washita River on November 27, killing more than a hundred, including Black Kettle, and taking women and children prisoners. And Sheridan ordered a sweep against other Cheyenne villages downriver toward Fort Cobb, where Kiowas and Comanches had turned themselves in and promised peace. Hostile Cheyennes and Arapahos were pursued south until most of them were defeated and returned to the reservation. But the reservations for many of these southern plains Indians were merely places to recoup their strength between raids.[29]

REFORM IMPULSES

The report of the Peace Commission and the continuing warfare on the plains both gave new impetus to reformers interested in the Indians—the

28. Resolutions dated October 9, 1868, CIA Report, 1868, serial 1366, pp. 831–32.

29. Leckie, *Military Conquest of the Southern Plains*, pp. 88–132. A sympathetic history of Sheridan and his aggressive action against the Indians is Carl Coke Rister, *Border Command: General Phil Sheridan in the West* (Norman: University of Oklahoma Press, 1944).

warfare because it reemphasized the urgency to do something radical to end conditions that caused war, the report because it gave hope that the government would listen to men and women who promoted peace and justice. A deep impression was made on a number of reformers who had not been notably interested in Indian affairs before. Some were abolitionists, whose reforming zeal for the cause of the slaves made them fit subjects for appeals in behalf of another oppressed minority. One of these was Lydia Maria Child, who wrote when she read the Peace Commission's report: "I welcomed this Report almost with tears of joy. 'Thank God!' I exclaimed, 'we have, at last, an Official Document, which manifests something like a right spirit toward the poor Indians! Really, this encourages a hope that the Anglo-Saxon race are capable of civilization." Child countered at considerable length the argument that the Indians could not be civilized, for she was convinced of the unity of mankind.[30] "Nothing can ever change my belief that human nature is essentially the same in all races and classes of men," she wrote two years later, "and that its modifications for good or evil are to be attributed to the education of circumstances. My faith never wavers that men can be made just by being treated justly, honest by being dealt with honestly, and kindly by becoming objects of kindly sympathy."[31]

Other abolitionists—notably Wendell Phillips—took up the cause of Indian reform, adding the abused Indians to a long list of reform causes promoted in the *National Standard*, Phillips's personal sounding board.[32] Yet the direct effect of abolitionist leaders on post–Civil War Indian reform was slight, even though Child, Phillips, and other antislavery crusaders spoke out occasionally on Indian affairs. Partly because they had already expended a large part of their reservoir of reforming energies, partly because they did not center their whole attention on Indian reform but kept active in a variety of movements, and partly because they did not create effective or enduring organizations through which to channel their work, they did

30. Lydia Maria Child, *An Appeal for the Indians* (New York: William P. Thomlinson, n.d.), p. 3; the essay first appeared in the *National Anti-Slavery Standard*, April 11, 1868.

31. Child to Aaron Powell, *National Standard*, August 27, 1870, p. 4, quoted in Robert Winston Mardock, *The Reformers and the American Indian* (Columbia: University of Missouri Press, 1971), p. 16. Child criticized some aspects of the Peace Commission's report, however: she objected to forcing English upon the Indians and to the punishment of polygamy. "We have so long indulged in feelings of pride and contempt toward those we are pleased to call 'subject races' that we have actually become incapable of judging them with any tolerable degree of candor and common sense." *Appeal for the Indians*, p. 8.

32. The Reform League, which Phillips helped to found in 1870, and its journal, the *National Standard* (which replaced the *National Anti-Slavery Standard*), supported blacks, Chinese immigration, women's rights, temperance, and prison reform, as well as Indian rights. Irving H. Bartlett, *Wendell Phillips, Brahmin Radical* (Boston: Beacon Press, 1961), pp. 370–71.

not shape the course of Indian policy. But this is not to deny their importance in helping to stir up public interest, in attracting other reformers to
the cause, and in contributing substantial weight to the whole movement.[33]

The Indians and the Indian wars also drew the attention of Alfred Love
and his Universal Peace Union, which added humanitarian treatment of
the Indians to its other peace-orientated reforms. The organization at its
convention in Washington in January 1868 sent a petition to Congress on
Indian matters, adding its voice to the growing concern, although Indian
activities were only a small part of the Union's work.[34]

The stirring reports of the serious state of Indian affairs brought still
other responses. The condemnation of evil and proposals for good struck
sympathetic chords among many persons of humanitarian and philanthropic bent, who turned to Indian reform once they had been awakened to
the needs. One such response was the formation in 1868 of the United
States Indian Commission in New York City under the instigation of Peter
Cooper. The purpose of this collection of Protestant ministers and other
benevolent gentlemen was "to array on the side of justice and humanity
the influence and support of an enlightened public opinion, in order to secure for the Indians that treatment which, in their position, we should demand for ourselves." These men condemned the failure of the government
to fulfill its treaty obligations, the outrages upon Indians by white citizens
and soldiers (especially Sand Creek), the degradation and deterioration of
the Indians by venereal disease brought in with military troops in Indian
country, and the lack of honest and faithful Indian agents. Once the nation
was informed about Indian wrongs, they thought, "their united voice will
demand that the honor and the interests of the nation shall no longer be
sacrificed to the insatiable lust and avarice of unscrupulous men."[35] Cooper,
an industrialist turned philanthropist, had a long history of humanitarian
concern, including antislavery agitation, and his Cooper's Union in New
York City not only offered industrial classes but provided a forum for

33. Mardock, in *Reformers and the American Indian* and in "The Anti-Slavery Humanitarians and Indian Policy Reform," *Western Humanities Review* 12 (Spring 1958):
131–45, argues that most of the men and women who took up the Indian cause after the
Civil War had previously been involved with the antislavery movement, but the evidence
in his own writings tends to disprove this. It is certainly not true that the *leaders* in the
post-Civil War Indian reform movement had been *leaders* in the antislavery movement.
The abolitionists cited by Mardock (Lydia Maria Child, Wendell Phillips, and Henry
Ward Beecher) had no sustained effect on Indian reform after the war.

34. See Robert Winston Mardock, "Alfred Love, Indian Peace Policy, and the Universal Peace Union," *Kansas Quarterly* 3 (Fall 1971): 64–71.

35. Memorial to Congress, July 14, 1869, *House Miscellaneous Document* no. 165,
40–2, serial 1350. The formation of the commission is described in Mardock, *Reformers
and the American Indian*, p. 33.

reform speakers of many persuasions. Vincent Colyer, an officer of the New York YMCA, served as secretary of the Indian Commission, and the Reverend Henry Ward Beecher was a prominent member. John Beeson supported the commission and urged that it be allowed to nominate commissioners and other persons employed in Indian affairs, and Bishop Whipple at a meeting on October 19 read a report on the condition of the tribes.[36] When General Hazen requested a visitor to study the conditions of the Kiowa and Comanche Indians at Fort Cobb, the commission sent Colyer to investigate.[37]

Of all the groups concerned about a Christian approach to Indian policy, none was more symbolic (if not actually influential) than the Society of Friends. The Quakers from colonial days on showed an interest in just and humane treatment of the Indians, and the story of William Penn's peaceful dealings with the Indians was repeated so widely that it became embedded in the general American consciousness in mythic form. There were few Americans, moreover, who were not acquainted with Benjamin West's painting of Penn's legendary treaty with the Indians in one of its manifold reproductions.[38] Although the Quakers' active Indian work in antebellum days was largely with the tribes in New York State, and although their concern for the blacks and the antislavery movement far overshadowed their interest in the Indians, the Quakers easily shifted to a new concern for Indians when the conditions after the Civil War demanded it. They offered a statement of principles in 1866 that, although it was probably not widely circulated, could have served as a platform for the new Christian peace policy: "From the earliest period at which the Religious Society of Friends had intercourse with the Indians, it has been their endeavor to treat them with kindness and justice, to guard them against the imposition and fraud to which their ignorance exposed them; to meliorate and improve their condition; and to commend the benign and heavenly principles of the Christian religion to their approval and acceptance by an upright example consistent therewith." The statement contrasted "the history of much of the public and more private dealings with the Indians," which it found "stained by fraud and bloodshed," with such pacific and religious behavior. Coercion and violence had failed to civilize and Christianize the Indians and thus to secure peace and harmony, and the Quakers asked whether it would not be well "for government and its officers to try the effect of just

36. Mardock, *Reformers and the American Indian*, pp. 33–34.
37. Leaflet of the commission, February 3, 1869.
38. Ellen Starr Brinton, "Benjamin West's Painting of Penn's Treaty with the Indians," *Bulletin of Friends' Historical Association* 30 (Autumn 1941): 99–189; Clyde A. Milner II, *With Good Intentions: Quaker Work among the Pawnees, Otos, and Omahas in the 1870s* (Lincoln: University of Nebraska Press, 1982), pp. 6–7.

and pacific measures; to substitute for the sword the benign and winning persuasion which flows from the spirit of the Gospel, and teaches us to do to others as we would that they should do to us."[39]

When disturbances on the frontier in the late 1860s attracted the attention of the nation, the Quakers did not fail to react. The conference of the Yearly Meetings of the Liberal Quakers (Hicksite) at Baltimore in 1868 sent a memorial to Congress praying "that the effusion of blood may cease, and that such just and humane measures may be pursued as will secure a lasting peace, and tend to the preservation and enlightenment of those afflicted people, whom we regard as the wards of the nation." The assembly urged "benevolent efforts to improve and enlighten the Indians" and that only persons "of high character and strict morality" be sent among them as agents. The next year, shortly after the release of the Peace Commission's report, these Quakers renewed their appeal to Congress for the Indians. "Let the effort be made in good faith," they said, "to promote their education—their industry—their morality. Invite the assistance of the philanthropic and Christian effort, which has been so valuable an aid in the elevation of the Freedmen, and render it possible for justice and good example to restore that confidence which has been lost by injustice and cruelty." The memorial strongly opposed turning over the Indian Office to the military and expressed a common worry among religious men about the venereal dangers that lurked at military posts. "May you be enabled, as representatives of a Christian nation," the Quakers ended their address to Congress, "to legislate respecting the Indians in the fear of the Almighty, and be guided by His wisdom."[40] A similar memorial was sent by the Orthodox Friends.

By 1869 the Indians were in the forefront of reformers' minds. The drive to protect them from avarice and corruption and to draw them ultimately into the Christian civilization of the humanitarians gathered momentum as one group after another turned with new interest toward them. The administration of Ulysses S. Grant, remembered for the opprobrious corruption called Grantism, paradoxically brought to fruition a policy dominated by evangelical Protestant men and principles.

39. *A Brief Sketch of the Efforts of Philadelphia Yearly Meeting of the Religious Society of Friends, to Promote the Civilization and Improvement of the Indians* (Philadelphia: Friends' Book Store, 1866), pp. 1, 55–56.

40. *Memorial of the Religious Society of Friends . . . Now Assembled in Conference in the City of Baltimore, of the Six Yearly Meetings or General Assemblies of Our People* [1868]; Memorial of Religious Society of Friends, January 21, 1869, *House Miscellaneous Document* no. 29, 40–3, serial 1385.

CHAPTER 20

Structures of
the Peace Policy

The Board of Indian Commissioners.

Churches and the Agencies.

Failure of the Structures.

The End of Treaty Making.

The demand of religiously motivated men and women for reform in Indian affairs could not be disregarded. The evangelical outcry led not only to national consciousness of the flagrant evils in the Indian service and the wars in the West but to most unusual administrative developments. The governmental structures that marked the peace policy were a remarkable manifestation of reliance of the "Christian nation" on professedly Christian men and principles in an attempt to establish the just and humane administration that was so ardently called for in the 1860s.[1]

THE BOARD OF INDIAN COMMISSIONERS

The first sign of the change came from President Grant himself, who in his inaugural address on March 4, 1869, declared: "The proper treatment of the original occupants of this land—the Indians—is one deserving of careful study. I will favor any course toward them which tends to their civilization and ultimate citizenship."[2] Encouraged by this clear sign of willing-

---

1. In this chapter I draw on Francis Paul Prucha, *American Indian Policy in Crisis: Christian Reformers and the Indian, 1865–1900* (Norman: University of Oklahoma Press, 1976), pp. 33–71.

2. *Inaugural Addresses of the Presidents of the United States from George Washington 1789 to Richard Milhous Nixon 1969* (Washington: GPO, 1969), p. 121.

ness to listen to Christian advocates, a group of Philadelphia philanthropists determined to press for an independent commission to watch over Indian affairs, an idea that had frequently been recommended as a means of rectifying the corruption and attendant evils in the Indian service.[3] The leader in this effort was William Welsh, who exemplified the Christian humanitarians upon whom the new policy depended. An Episcopalian layman, who with his brothers had amassed a sizable mercantile fortune, Welsh devoted much of his apparently boundless energy to public service. "Into how many of the secular interests of the community Mr. Welsh threw the weight of his influence, and the vigor of his active powers, I do not know," the Reverend M. A. DeWolfe Howe said in a memorial sermon for Welsh in 1878. "He spent no effort in winning popular favor. I think he would have refused any office in the exercise of which he could not hope to accomplish some positive religious good. He did not feel that he had time for any occupation in which he could not advance the cause and kingdom of Christ."[4]

Welsh, in 1868, called a meeting of like-minded men, and a committee representing different religious bodies was appointed to call upon the president and the secretary of the interior. The committee told Grant that although the government could do something by itself to aid the Indians, "without the co-operation of Christian philanthropists the waste of money would be great, and the result unsatisfactory." If philanthropists could be associated with the secretary of the interior, "the lost confidence of Congress could be regained, the Indians made more hopeful, and the whole Christian community aroused to co-operate with the Government in 'civilizing, Christianizing, and ultimately making citizens of the Indians.'"[5] Prominent among the group speaking thus candidly to the president was a friend of Grant's, George Hay Stuart, a wealthy Philadelphia merchant

3. See, for example, Henry B. Whipple, "What Shall We Do with the Indians" (1862), in *Lights and Shadows of a Long Episcopate* (New York: Macmillan Company, 1899), p. 518. A treaty with the Chippewas in 1863 had authorized the president to appoint a board of visitors from Christian denominations to attend annuity payments and to report regularly on the qualifications and behavior of persons living on the reservation. Kappler, p. 854. Instructions from the commissioner of Indian affairs to the committee are in CIA Report, 1863, serial 1182, pp. 458–59. The Joint Special Committee under Senator Doolittle had recommended inspection boards, and in 1868 the New York reform group called the United States Indian Commission had memorialized Congress to appoint unpaid, politically independent men to work in Indian affairs. *House Miscellaneous Document* no. 165, 40–2, serial 1350.

4. M. A. DeWolfe Howe, *Memorial of William Welsh* (Reading, Pennsylvania, 1878), p. 21.

5. The report of the committee is printed in *Taopi and His Friends; or, the Indians' Wrongs and Rights* (Philadelphia: Claxton, Remsen and Haffelfinger, 1868), pp. 73–84. The quotations are from pages 76 and 78.

who had been active in Presbyterian church work, temperance and anti-slavery movements, Sunday school work, and the Young Men's Christian Association. Stuart was, as the editor of his autobiography asserted, "a Christian merchant who is at once zealously Christian and diligently a man of business," whose joy it was "to testify everywhere and to all men of his love of the Saviour."[6]

On March 24, 1869, Grant and Secretary of the Interior Jacob D. Cox cordially received the delegation and accepted their ideas. Stimulated by Welsh's continuing efforts, Congress on April 10, 1869, authorized the president to "organize a board of Commissioners, to consist of not more than ten persons, to be selected by him from men eminent for their intelligence and philanthropy, to serve without pecuniary compensation," who under the president's direction should "exercise joint control with the Secretary of the Interior" over the disbursement of Indian appropriations.[7]

The establishment of this Board of Indian Commissioners, through a series of fortuitous concatenations, set post–Civil War Indian policy ever more firmly in the pattern of American evangelical revivalism. The chain of religious reformers from Charles G. Finney, the great revivalist preacher, to the board was remarkable but very clear. That it was so is indisputable testimony to the grip that religious thought had upon the public councils of the day.

Revivalism, so often associated with its rural manifestations in the Second Great Awakening of the decades after 1800, came to the fore again in the 1850s as an urban phenomenon. The years 1857–1858 were its high point, as widely publicized interdenominational revival meetings took place in the major cities of the United States that were attended by throngs of businessmen and others. These revivalist stirrings exhibited what later became major themes of American Protestantism—lay leadership, a drive toward interdenominational cooperation, and emphasis, not on theological argument, but on ethical behavior, which supported an intense concern for social reform.[8]

The outstanding manifestation and agent of the new awakening was the Young Men's Christian Association. Founded in England in 1844, the YMCA movement spread quickly in America after associations were organized in Montreal and Boston in 1851. The YMCA was the product of the successive waves of revivals that swept the nation in the nineteenth century. It reflected Finney's pragmatic concern for ethical action *now*, and it

6. Introduction by Robert Ellis Thompson to *The Life of George H. Stuart: Written by Himself* (Philadelphia: J. M. Stoddart and Company, 1890), pp. 20–21.

7. 16 *United States Statutes* 40.

8. The fullest account of this revival is Timothy L. Smith, *Revivalism and Social Reform in Mid-Nineteenth-Century America* (Nashville: Abingdon Press, 1957).

was a laymen's organization of unabashed interdenominational scope. "In all this," says the modern historian of the movement, "the Y.M.C.A. mirrored American Protestantism. Its faith rested upon a naive belief in the Bible as the unique, supernatural repository of all truth, knowledge, and morality. Its God was that of the Book, especially concerned for sinners whose day-to-day conduct failed to measure up to current Protestant usage. The Association was, for the most part, a move by the 'better' people in behalf of those for whom they felt a real compassion and responsibility."[9]

The revivals of 1857–1858 had a far-reaching effect upon the YMCA, for it had been the most important promotional agency for those nationwide revivals. Out of such circumstances came the YMCA's great work during the Civil War, the United States Christian Commission.[10]

When the war began, the YMCA directed its attention to the Union soldiers. Immediately after the Battle of Bull Run on July 21, 1861, the New York association sent two of its leaders, one of them Vincent Colyer, "to minister to the temporal and spiritual necessities of the wounded and dying men who crowded the hospitals in and near the capital."[11] The association organized a continuing mission to the soldiers, but Colyer soon became convinced that a national organization was needed to care for the religious needs of the troops. He and his New York supporters issued a call to associations across the country to appoint "army committees" and for these committees to meet in New York. In mid-November 1861 a convention of delegates from fifteen associations met in New York. On November 16 the convention established the twelve-member Christian Commission, which was to take charge of the army work of the YMCA and to act as a clearing house for religious work with the troops. Most of those appointed to the commission were YMCA leaders. The chairman was George H.

---

9. C. Howard Hopkins, *History of the Y.M.C.A. in North America* (New York: Association Press, 1951), pp. 45–46. Hopkins's volume is a thorough scholarly treatment of the YMCA; see also L. L. Doggett, *History of the Young Men's Christian Association* (New York: International Committee of Young Men's Christian Associations, 1896), and Sherwood Eddy, *A Century with Youth: A History of the Y.M.C.A. from 1844 to 1944* (New York: Association Press, 1944). The YMCA, with some internal controversy, limited its membership to members of "evangelical churches." Although in 1869 it defined what it meant by evangelical—maintaining the Holy Scriptures as "the only infallible rule of faith and practice," belief in the divinity of Christ, and belief in Christ as "the only name under heaven given among men whereby we must be saved from everlasting punishment"—it refused to name the churches that were evangelical. But clearly it excluded Unitarians and Universalists on one hand and Roman Catholics on the other, to say nothing of Jews and nonbelievers. There is a good discussion of the matter in Hopkins, *Y.M.C.A.*, pp. 362–69.

10. Hopkins, *Y.M.C.A.*, pp. 81–84.

11. Cephas Brainerd, *The Work of the Army Committee of the New York Young Men's Christian Association, Which Led to the Organization of the United States Christian Commission* (New York, 1866), quoted in Hopkins, *Y.M.C.A.*, p. 88.

Stuart, then president of the Philadelphia YMCA and chairman of the YMCA Central Committee.

The commission directed an army of volunteer workers who collected funds and materials, and it sent delegates into the hospitals and army camps to distribute stores, circulate good reading material among the men, aid chaplains in encouraging prayer meetings and discouraging vice, and assist surgeons on the battlefield. It was motivated by a sincere and open love of Christ and represented "the forces of Christianity developed and exemplified amid the carnage of battle and the more perilous tests of hospital and camp."[12]

The Christian Commission worked closely with the government. It sought and received the approbation and commendation of the president, the secretaries of war and navy, and the army generals. It set a useful pattern of a committee of distinguished men, without government positions and without pay, who took over duties and activities that might well have been considered the responsibility of government officials and who worked closely (though not always without friction) with both civilian and military officers.

The idea of the Christian Commission and the work it had done was much in the air when the Board of Indian Commissioners was conceived and organized. And when it came time to appoint the board, Grant called upon his old friend Stuart, who went to Washington to advise the president. "Stuart," Grant told him, "you and Welsh have got me into some difficulty by the passage of this bill which requires me to appoint a Board of Commissioners, and I have sent for you to help me." When Stuart asked how he could be of use, Grant replied, "I want you to name some likely men from the different sections of the country, and representing various religious bodies, who will be willing to serve the cause of the Indians without compensation." The industrialist obliged, suggesting men from Boston, New York, Philadelphia, Pittsburgh, Chicago, and St. Louis. Grant added a name of his own and insisted that Stuart himself be on the board.[13]

Secretary Cox, in inviting men to serve on the board, noted that the pur-

12. Edward P. Smith, *Incidents of the United States Christian Commission* (Philadelphia: J. B. Lippincott and Company, 1869), p. 5. The work of the commission can be traced also in Lemuel Moss, *Annals of the United States Christian Commission* (Philadelphia: J. B. Lippincott and Company, 1868), and in the commission's *Annual Report*, issued 1863–1866. A useful secondary account is M. Hamlin Cannon, "The United States Christian Commission," *Mississippi Valley Historical Review* 38 (June 1951): 61–80.

13. Stuart, *Life of George H. Stuart*, pp. 239–41. On the back of a telegram from Secretary of the Interior Cox to Stuart, April 13, 1869, seeking his consultation on the formation of the board, Stuart wrote: "Asked & went to Washington on receipt & helped to form the Indian Board of Commissioners *nearly all* of whom were named by me." George Hay Stuart Papers, Library of Congress.

pose was "that something like a Christian Commission should be established having the civilization of the Indians in view & laboring to stimulate public interest in this work."[14] In fact, the continuity between the old Christian Commission of the Civil War, which had ended its labors on January 1, 1866, and the new Board of Indian Commissioners was striking. Stuart's work as national chairman of the Christian Commission made him think largely of his coworkers in the commission when he supplied Grant with a list of names for the board. William E. Dodge, appointed from New York, was a businessmen whose life had paralleled Stuart's. An active Presbyterian, with antislavery, temperance, Sunday school, foreign mission, Bible Society, and YMCA interests and engagements, Dodge had organized the New York Branch of the Christian Commission in 1862 and presided at its fund-raising meetings. He was a deeply religious man, firmly impressed with the fundamental articles of the Calvinist creed.[15] Another New Yorker on the original Board of Indian Commissioners was Nathan Bishop, who had served as chairman of the executive committee of the New York Branch of the Christian Commission. He was a Baptist educator and philanthropist, active in a variety of church societies and organizations. From Chicago came John V. Farwell, a leading dry goods merchant and a supporter of the revivalist Dwight L. Moody, who had been chairman of that city's branch of the Christian Commission; and from Boston, Edward S. Tobey, a Congregational shipping magnate, who had been chairman of the Christian Commission there.[16]

The Board of Indian Commissioners thus comprised a good number of wealthy Christian gentlemen with recent firsthand experience, and generally applauded success, in a public philanthropic enterprise of notable extent, an enterprise that had sought and received aid for a good cause from people of goodwill across the nation and in which the cooperation between lay figures and the government had been very close. These old associates of Stuart were joined by William Welsh, who fittingly was chosen first chairman of the board, and by the Pittsburgh industrialist Felix R. Brunot. Brunot, who replaced Welsh as chairman on November 17, 1869, had a background in YMCA service, support of temperance and Sunday obser-

14. Cox to William Welsh, April 15, 1869, printed in *Taopi and His Friends*, pp. 82–83. A similar letter to William E. Dodge is in D. Stuart Dodge, *Memorials of William E. Dodge* (New York: Anson D. F. Randolph and Company, 1887), p. 168.

15. See Dodge, *Memorials of William E. Dodge*; Richard Lowitt, *A Merchant Prince of the Nineteenth Century: William E. Dodge* (New York: Columbia University Press, 1954); and Carlos Martyn, *William E. Dodge: The Christian Merchant* (New York: Funk and Wagnalls, 1890).

16. *Dictionary of American Biography*, s.v. Bishop, Nathan, by Thomas Woody, and Tobey, Edward Silas, by Sidney Gunn; John V. Farwell, Jr., *Some Recollections of John V. Farwell* (Chicago: R. R. Donnelley and Sons, 1911).

vance, and other good works that was similar to Stuart's. Other members of the first board were Robert Campbell, a St. Louis merchant and banker suggested by Stuart, and Henry S. Lane of Indiana, chosen by Grant to fulfill political obligations. The Quaker John D. Lang was appointed in 1870.[17]

The relation of the board to the churches was not defined in the law, but it was obviously very close. Although the original members were not official representatives of their particular denominations, they all reflected the dominant Protestant character of American Christianity. And when new members were appointed after 1875, they asserted that they had been nominated by and therefore represented their particular churches.[18] There were no Roman Catholics on the board, even though Catholics were heavily involved in Indian missionary work, and it seems reasonable to suppose that none would have been welcome.[19]

The work to which the Board of Indian Commissioners was to devote its attention was spelled out in considerable detail in a letter sent to the members on May 26, 1869, by Ely S. Parker, commissioner of Indian affairs. Acknowledging their desire for the "humanization, civilization, and Christianization of the Indians," Parker posed a series of questions for

17. Clinton B. Fisk, who became chairman of the Board of Indian Commissioners in 1874, had been a member of the Christian Commission. The Reverend Edward P. Smith, commissioner of Indian affairs 1873–1875, had served as field secretary of the commission. Hiram Price, named commissioner of Indian affairs in 1881, had served on the commission's Iowa committee.

18. Clinton B. Fisk said at his first meeting of the board in January 1875: "Most of us who are here today, I believe, are here by the nomination of the religious bodies which we represent." *Report of the Board of Indian Commissioners*, 1874, p. 123. In 1878, A. C. Barstow, then board chairman, testified: "He [President Grant] asked each of the religious bodies to recommend to him an able man to act upon the Board of Indian Commissioners. I represented upon the board the American Board of Commissioners for Foreign Missions." And E. M. Kingsley declared: "I have been a member of the Board of Indian Commissioners by the nomination of the Presbyterian Board of Foreign Missions, since, I think, February, 1875." *Senate Miscellaneous Document* no. 53, 45–3, serial 1835.

19. Some weak attempts to involve Catholics centered on the Reverend George Deshon, a Paulist priest who had been a classmate of Grant's at West Point. When asked about the matter in 1896, Deshon replied: "Prest Grant never offered to put a Catholic in the Board of Indian Comrs. . . . F. D. Dent, Grant's brother in law, and who was a long time in the White House, asked me if I would be willing to be one of the Commissioners, and I declined. He said Grant would appoint me if I would consent. I did not see that I could do the least good in that crowd of bigots who would ignore me and bolster themselves by serving with a Catholic man on the board and therefore I declined." Joseph A. Stephan to George Deshon, January 15, 1896, and Deshon to Stephan, January 18, 1896, Papers of the Bureau of Catholic Indian Missions, 1896, District of Columbia, Marquette University Library. See also references to Father Deshon and the peace policy in Peter J. Rahill, *The Catholic Indian Missions and Grant's Peace Policy, 1870–1884* (Washington: Catholic University of America Press, 1953). Not until 1902 were Catholics allotted positions on the board.

their consideration. It was an awesome list, which must have frightened the members; and it indicated the kinds of problems the Grant administration was interested in. What should be the legal status of the Indians and what were their rights and obligations under existing laws and treaties? Should treaties continue to be made with the tribes, and if not, what sort of legislation would be required? Should Indians be placed on reservations, and how could this be accomplished? Should a distinction be made in dealing with the localized, civilized Indians and the roving tribes of the plains and mountains? What line should be drawn between civil and military rule of the Indians? Were changes required in the trade and intercourse laws because of changed conditions in the country? And what changes should be made in the procedures for purchasing goods for the Indians and in methods of paying annuities? In order to carry out effectively its duties, the board was given authority to inspect the agencies and the records of the Indian Office, to be present at annuity payments and at councils with the Indians, to supervise the purchase of goods and to inspect the purchases, and to offer advice in general on plans for civilizing the Indians and on the conduct of Indian affairs.[20]

The powers were not clear and strong enough to satisfy William Welsh, who wanted the full joint control with the secretary of the interior that he thought had been directed by Congress. He feared that the board had been relegated to "a mere council of advice," and being unwilling "to assume responsibilities without any power of control," he resigned from the board only a month after its organization.[21]

The rest of the board entered upon its duties with energy and goodwill. The board appointed a purchasing committee (Stuart, Dodge, Farwell, and Campbell, all businessmen of competence and integrity) to cooperate with the government in purchasing supplies for the Indian department, and three of the members (Brunot, Bishop, and Dodge) made an extensive trip to the Indian country during the summer. At the end of the year, despite

20. Parker to board members, May 26, 1869, *Report of the Board of Indian Commissioners*, 1869, pp. 3–4. Grant in an order of June 3, 1869, promulgated regulations for the board. Ibid., pp. 4–5. The members of the board were all called to Washington for a meeting at which the questions were posed and arrangements made. The minutes of the early meetings of the board, from May 26, 1869, to February 3, 1870, are printed in *Minutes of the Board of Indian Commissioners* (Washington: H. Polkinhorn and Company, 1870). They give an excellent picture of how the board got under way, of meetings with government officials, of the appointment of Colyer as paid secretary, and so on. The complete minutes of the board, correspondence, and other records are in Records of the Office of Indian Affairs, Records of the Board of Indian Commissioners, National Archives, Record Group 75.

21. William Welsh, *Indian Office: Wrongs Doing and Reforms Needed* (Philadelphia, 1874), pp. 1–2.

problems of organization arising from Welsh's resignation, the ill health of some of the members, and the pressure of other duties, the board submitted a long and outspoken report, largely the work of Brunot. The report was a powerful denunciation of past Indian relations and, although it admitted that recommendations should not be the "result of theorizing," a remarkably complete prospectus of policies and programs to come.

The righteous indignation of these Christian philanthropists pervaded the report:

> While it cannot be denied that the government of the United States, in the general terms and temper of its legislation has evinced a desire to deal generously with the Indians, it must be admitted that the actual treatment they have received has been unjust and iniquitous beyond the power of words to express.
>
> Taught by the government that they had rights entitled to respect; when those rights have been assailed by the rapacity of the white man, the arm which should have been raised to protect them has been ever ready to sustain the aggressor.
>
> The history of the government connections with the Indians is a shameful record of broken treaties and unfulfilled promises.
>
> The history of the border white man's connection with the Indians is a sickening record of murder, outrage, robbery, and wrongs committed by the former as a rule, and occasional savage outbreaks and unspeakably barbarous deeds of retaliation by the latter as the exception.

The cause was clear: "Paradoxical as it may seem, the white man has been the chief obstacle in the way of Indian civilization. The benevolent measures attempted by the government for their advancement have been almost uniformly thwarted by the agencies employed to carry them out." The board saw no inherent problem in the Indians themselves, who had been made suspicious, revengeful, and cruel by the treatment they had received from the whites. They denied that the Indians would not work and pointed to the example of the Five Civilized Tribes and the Yankton Sioux. "The reports of the Indian Bureau," they asserted with the optimism of true reformers, "will be found to abound in facts going to prove that the Indian, as a race, can be induced to work, is susceptible of civilization, and presents a most inviting field for the introduction of Christianity."[22]

For men with little experience in Indian affairs, the members of the board confidently set forth preliminary recommendations for future dealings with the tribesmen. They urged that Indians be collected on small

22. *Report of the Board of Indian Commissioners,* 1869, pp. 7–9.

contiguous reservations making up a large unit that would eventually become a state of the Union. On the reservations the Indians should be given land in severalty, and tribal relations should be discouraged. They recommended the abandonment of the treaty system and the abrogation of existing treaties "as soon as any just method can be devised to accomplish it." Money annuities should cease, for they promoted idleness and vice. The board urged the establishment of schools to teach the children English and wanted teachers nominated by religious bodies. Christian missions should be encouraged and their schools fostered. "The religion of our blessed Saviour," they said, "is believed to be the most effective agent for the civilization of any people." They insisted upon an honest observation of treaty obligations, appointment of agents "with a view to their moral as well as business qualifications, and aside from any political consideration," and fair judicial proceedings for Indian criminals. "The legal status of the uncivilized Indians," they decided, "should be that of wards of the government; the duty of the latter being to protect them, to educate them in industry, the arts of civilization, and the principles of Christianity; elevate them to the rights of citizenship, and to sustain and clothe them until they can support themselves."[23]

It was just the sort of platform one would expect from the Christian merchant princes who made up the Board of Indian Commissioners. Whether they were conscious of it or not, they intended to apply to the "uncivilized" Indians of the plains and mountains the same prescriptions made for more eastern Indians in antebellum days.

The tours of board members of the West enabled them to gather firsthand information on which to base their continuing recommendations. If they carried with them their own prejudices and saw Indian matters from their own perspective, they nevertheless furnished an element of articulate concern for the Indians that could be ridiculed and often pushed aside but never completely ignored. Especially hard working was Felix Brunot. "Mr. Brunot saw that the task before him was tremendous," his sympathetic biographer recorded. "There was a race to civilise, there were agents to humanise, and there was a great nation to educate in the principles of Christian love toward an oppressed and heathen race." For five years Brunot spent his life on the work of the board—traveling to New York and Washington for meetings and consultations, writing articles and letters to stir up concern for the Indians, drawing up the reports of the board, and visiting the Indian tribes in the West during the summer months.[24] The secretary of the board, Vincent Colyer, in the first year alone submitted reports on the condition of the Indians he visited in Kansas, the Indian Ter-

23. Ibid., p. 10.
24. Charles Lewis Slattery, *Felix Reville Brunot* (New York: Longmans, Green and Company, 1901), pp. 147–48.

ritory, Texas, New Mexico, Arizona, and Colorado, as well as a long report on the Indians of Alaska. In 1871 he submitted another long report on the Apaches of New Mexico and Arizona.[25]

Of more practical significance than the investigative reports of members was the board's work in supervising the purchase of supplies for the Indians in an attempt to end the fraud and corruption in the Indian service. Poor goods were contracted for at high prices, and merchants and their friends grew rich by cheating the government and the Indians. In July 1870 Congress directed the board to inspect all goods purchased for the Indians, and the experienced businessmen who made up the special purchasing committee worked year after year to correct abuses. The committee was optimistic—it was convinced, it reported in 1871, "that all 'Indian rings' can be broken up, and that the wards of the nation, who have been so long the victims of greedy and designing men, ought and must be treated in a manner worthy of the highest moral obligations of a Christian government." Even with the loopholes that provided opportunity for continuing fraud, substantial savings and a rise in the quality of goods resulted from the committee's supervision.[26]

Meanwhile, the executive committee of the board examined the accounts and vouchers presented to the Indian Office for payment, a duty given to the board by Congress in 1871. The task was onerous and had not been solicited by the board, but it was an essential part of sharing responsibility with the secretary of the interior in the disbursement of funds. Millions of dollars' worth of bills and vouchers were examined each year, and the committee rejected those that were improper or unreasonable. Although the secretary of the interior frequently overruled the committee's decisions, the vigilance of these philanthropists saved the government large sums of money.[27]

25. *Report of the Board of Indian Commissioners,* 1869, pp. 30–55, 81–164; ibid., 1871, pp. 32–86. The 1871 report was printed separately as *Peace with the Apaches of New Mexico and Arizona: Report of Vincent Colyer, Member of the Board of Indian Commissioners, 1871* (Washington: GPO, 1872).

26. 16 *United States Statutes* 360; *Report of the Board of Indian Commissioners,* 1870, pp. 21–23; ibid., 1871, p. 161. See the reports of the purchasing committee in the annual reports of the board. The report for 1875, pp. 19–24, is a long recital of specific cases that revealed "the tricks, subterfuges, evasions, and combinations" that the purchasing committee experienced, and its attempts to defeat them. George H. Stuart, who served as chairman of the committee, tells of its work in *Life of George H. Stuart,* pp. 242–45.

27. 16 *United States Statutes* 568. In 1871, for example, the executive committee examined 1,136 vouchers, representing a cash disbursement of $5,240,729.60, of which it rejected or suspended $153,166.20. In 1873 it examined 1,656 vouchers, representing disbursement of $6,032,877.65, of which 39 vouchers representing $426,909.96 were turned down as fraudulent or questionable. *Report of the Board of Indian Commissioners,* 1871, p. 11–12; ibid., 1873, p. 9.

Still another function of the board was its liaison with the missionary societies engaged in Indian work. At a meeting in Washington each winter the board met with representatives of the missionary groups to discuss Indian matters. These conferences, which were usually attended by the commissioner of Indian affairs, were a valuable forum for promoting Indian reform, and they served to confirm and strengthen the religious reform sentiment of the day. They brought the evangelical churches into semiofficial association with the men who formulated Indian policy and furnished a useful platform from which to preach the reforms devised.[28]

CHURCHES AND THE AGENCIES

The second structural component of Grant's peace policy was the apportionment of the Indian agencies among church groups, with the understanding that the missionary boards would nominate the agents and other employees at the agencies. By such an arrangement, it was hoped, the evils resulting from dishonest and incompetent agents would be obviated. This extreme measure, an admission by the government that it was unable to carry out its obligations by ordinary procedures, was a striking example of the conviction in public as well as private circles that only by emphasis on moral and religious means would the Indians be led along the path to civilization.

The roots of the program were diverse. It was perhaps an obvious conclusion that if evils were caused because bad men were appointed agents, then the evils could be corrected by appointing good men. If religious men had provided such a positive influence for good among the Indians as missionaries and teachers, certainly the good effects could be increased by broadening the scope of their activities. Bishop Whipple had recommended such a move, and army officers noted that missionaries had often succeeded with the Indians where military and civilian officers had failed.[29]

The postwar allotment of agencies to religious bodies began with the Quakers. The memorial from the Baltimore assembly of the seven Yearly Meetings of Friends in January 1869 indicated a renewed concern for In-

28. Reports of the winter missionary conferences are included in the *Report of the Board of Indian Commissioners*, except that of 1872, which was published separately as *Journal of the Second Annual Conference of the Board of Indian Commissioners with the Representatives of the Religious Societies Cooperating with the Government, and Reports of Their Work among the Indians* (Washington: GPO, 1873). Catholic missionaries, except in a few isolated instances at the beginning, did not attend the conferences.

29. Robert H. Keller, Jr., *American Protestantism and United States Indian Policy, 1869–82* (Lincoln: University of Nebraska Press, 1983), pp. 20–21. Keller's work is the best general study of this aspect of the peace policy.

Peace Policy and Indian Wars

29. Henry B. Whipple

The Protestant Episcopal Bishop of Minnesota, Henry B. Whipple, was a longtime reformer in Indian affairs. Whipple pleaded with President Lincoln to change the conditions of fraud and corruption in the Indian service, and he took the side of the Indians after the outbreak in Minnesota of 1862. His interest in Indian affairs continued through the rest of the century.

The Peace Commission authorized by
Congress in 1867 negotiated treaties with
the Indians on both the southern and
northern plains in an attempt to bring
peace to the West by locating the tribes
on reservations. The members of the
commission were, left to right, Alfred H.
Terry, William S. Harney, William T.
Sherman, Nathaniel G. Taylor, Samuel F.
Tappan, and Christopher C. Augur. In the
center is a Sioux woman.

The Peace Commission met with Cheyenne, Arapaho, Kiowa, Comanche, and
Kiowa-Apache Indians at Medicine Lodge
Creek in southern Kansas in October
1867. The treaties signed there provided
for reservations for the Indians in the
western part of the Indian Territory. This
drawing is by Hermann Stieffel.

The peace policy after the Civil War is associated with the presidency of Ulysses S.
Grant. This peace medal was produced at
that time for presentation to the Indians;
it is full of messages and symbols of peace
and an agricultural life.

30. Medicine Lodge Creek Treaty Council

31. United States Indian Peace Commission

32. Grant Indian Peace Medal

33. Felix R. Brunot

35. Ely S. Parker

34. William T. Sherman

Brunot, Sherman, and Parker played key roles in the peace policy. The first, as head of the Board of Indian Commissioners, directed the work of that reforming group. The second represented the military point of view that the Indians needed to be handled with force and not by ineffective good wishes. The third, a Seneca Indian, was Grant's first commissioner of Indian Affairs, who helped to inaugurate the peace policy.

The Modoc War of 1873 was a severe test of the peace policy. When a peace commission led by General Canby met with the Modocs on Good Friday 1873, the Modoc leader Captain Jack killed Canby by shooting him at short range, and other members of the commission were killed or wounded. Captain Jack was later executed for the murder, and the Modoc tribe was exiled to the Indian Territory.

36. Edward R. S. Canby

37. Captain Jack, Modoc

38. Carl Schurz

Schurz, a political refugee from Germany, was a notable political reformer. As secretary of the interior in President Hayes's administration (1877–1881), he took an active part in Indian affairs. He hoped by education and the individualization of Indian land holdings to enable the Indians to make their way in American society.

39. Cartoon of Carl Schurz

By reform of the Indian Bureau, Secretary Schurz hoped to diffuse military attacks upon civilian control of Indian affairs. Thomas Nast, in *Harper's Weekly* for January 25, 1879, pokes fun of Schurz's endeavors, which in the end were more successful than the cartoon suggests.

41. Chief Joseph, Nez Perce

40. George Armstrong Custer

Custer, the "boy general" of the Civil War, was flamboyant and impetuous. The annihilation of his troops of the Seventh Infantry at the Battle of the Little Bighorn in June 1876 stunned the nation. The subsequent military campaigns to chastise the Indians destroyed the power of the Indians on the northern plains and forced them to reservations.

Chief Joseph received national attention when he led the flight of the Nez Perce Indians from the military forces of the United States in 1877. After his surrender to General Nelson A. Miles, he was taken to the Indian Territory, where he insistently demanded return to his homeland in the Pacific Northwest, a plea sympathetically supported by many reformers.

dians, and on January 25 a delegation of Quakers met with president-elect Grant to urge an Indian policy based on peace and Christianity and the selection of religious employees for the agencies as far as practicable. To this group Grant is said to have replied: "Gentlemen, your advice is good. I accept it. Now give me the names of some Friends for Indian agents and I will appoint them. Let us have peace." A similar committee of Philadelphia Friends also visited Grant. The committees were impressed with his cordial attitude and his apparently earnest desire to begin a more peaceful and humane policy toward the Indians.[30]

Grant moved quickly to implement the Quakers' proposal. On February 15, 1869, Ely S. Parker, then Grant's aide-de-camp, wrote to Benjamin Hallowell, secretary of the Quaker conference, asking for a list of Quakers whom the Society of Friends would endorse as suitable persons to be Indian agents. He added that Grant also wished to assure him "that any attempt which may or can be made by your Society, for the improvement, education, and Christianization of the Indians, under such Agencies, will receive . . . all the encouragement and protection which the laws of the United States will warrant him in giving."[31] The Quakers, after some hesitation about accepting posts on the distant and exposed frontier, responded favorably, and by mid-June both the Orthodox and Hicksite Friends had appointed superintendents and agents and organized special comittees to deal with Indian matters. The Hicksite Friends were given the Northern Superintendency, comprising six agencies in Nebraska; the Orthodox Friends received the Central Superintendency, comprising the Indians in Kansas and the Kiowas, Comanches, and a number of other tribes in the Indian Territory. Secretary of the Interior Cox noted: "The Friends were appointed not because they were believed to have any monopoly of honesty or of good will toward the Indians, but because their selection would of itself be understood by the country to indicate the policy adopted, namely, the sincere cultivation of peaceful relations with the tribes and the choice of agents who did not, for personal profit, seek the service, but were sought for it because they were at least deemed fit for its duties."[32]

30. T. C. Battey in introduction to Lawrie Tatum, *Our Red Brothers and the Peace Policy of President Ulysses S. Grant* (Philadelphia: John C. Winston and Company, 1899), pp. 17–18; *Report of the Joint Delegation Appointed by the Committees on the Indian Concern of the Yearly Meetings of Baltimore, Philadelphia and New York* (Baltimore: J. Jones, 1869). The Quakers' concern in Indian matters is well treated in Rayner W. Kelsey, *Friends and the Indians, 1655–1917* (Philadelphia: Associated Executive Committee of Friends on Indian Affairs, 1917); see especially pp. 162–99.

31. The letter is printed in Kelsey, *Friends and the Indians*, p. 168, and appears in many of the Quaker reports; it was considered the basic authorization for their participation.

32. Report of the Secretary of the Interior, 1869, *House Executive Document* no. 1,

For the other agencies Grant appointed army officers, a move that was not surprising in light of the reduction of the army that had come in 1868. He did this for reasons of economy, since the officers otherwise would be on pay but not on duty; and they were thought to be a "corps of public servants whose integrity and faithfulness could be relied upon, and in whom the public were prepared to have confidence." But this solution to the problems of political patronage was soon upset, for Congress on July 15, 1870, forbade army officers to accept civil appointments. Although such action can be explained by the desire of spoilsmen to regain a foothold in the Indian service by means of political appointments, there had been strong opposition to the army officers on the part of reform elements as well. The massacre of Piegan Indians by troops under Colonel E. M. Baker on January 23, 1870, an action approved by General Sheridan, caused a great humanitarian outcry. Such was the effect of army attempts to civilize the Indians, the critics declared. In the House of Representatives, during debate on the Indian appropriation bill, Daniel Voorhees of Indiana pointed to the "curious spectacle" of the president of the United States "upon the one hand welcoming his Indian agents in their peaceful garments and broadbrims coming to tell him what they had done as missionaries of a gospel of peace and of a beneficent Government, and upon the other hand welcoming this man, General Sheridan, stained with the blood of innocent women and children!"[33]

Vincent Colyer, secretary of the Board of Indian Commissioners, was convinced that missionaries and soldiers as agents formed an inconsistent combination. Fearing, however, that if the army officers were removed the evils of political appointments would return, he began a campaign to enlist other denominations besides the Quakers in the Indian service. With the approval of Cox and Grant, Colyer sought help from the various missionary boards, and he slowly gained their support. His goal was clearly a humanitarian one. He contended against army control because that would mean only policing the Indians, not reclaiming or civilizing them, and by extended church control the efforts of the politicians to regain their sway would be thwarted.[34]

41–2, serial 1414, p. x. Quaker participation is treated in Clyde A. Milner II, *With Good Intentions: Quaker Work among the Pawnees, Otos, and Omahas in the 1870s* (Lincoln: University of Nebraska Press, 1982).

33. Report of the Secretary of the Interior, 1869, p. x; 16 *United States Statutes* 319; *Congressional Globe*, 41st Congress, 2d session, p. 1581. See the discussion of the Piegan incident in Robert W. Mardock, *The Reformers and the American Indian* (Columbia: University of Missouri Press, 1971), pp. 67–73.

34. Colyer's view and his successful efforts to enlist other denominations to nominate agents are seen in his correspondence with officials of the various churches, printed

President Grant's motives are more difficult to isolate. Some observers credited his experience as a young army officer in the Pacific Northwest for his concern to right the wrongs suffered by the Indians. His own religious views and religious experience were hardly strong enough to have been a dominant element in his policy making, yet it seems reasonable that his desire to end the warfare that had so long marked Indian-white relations led him to accept the Quakers and other sincerely religious men as instruments to that end. At any rate, Grant justified his initial action in his first annual message to Congress. "The Society of Friends is well known as having succeeded in living in peace with the Indians in the early settlement of Pennsylvania, while their white neighbors of other sects in other sections were constantly embroiled," he said. "They are also known for their opposition to all strife, violence, and war, and are generally noted for their strict integrity and fair dealings. These considerations induced me to give the management of a few reservations of Indians to them and to throw the burden of the selection of agents upon the society itself. The result has proven most satisfactory." When the army agents were removed, it was a logical step to expand the system, to offer the agencies to other religious groups, who could be expected "to Christianize and civilize the Indian, and to train him in the arts of peace."[35]

Commissioner of Indian Affairs Parker strongly endorsed the scheme. "The plan is obviously a wise and humane one," he remarked. "Under a political management for a long series of years, and the expenditure of large sums of money annually, the Indians made but little progress toward that healthy Christian civilization in which are embraced the elements of material wealth and intellectual and moral development. . . . Not, therefore, as a denier resort to save a dying race, but from the highest moral conviction of Christian humanity, the President wisely determined to invoke the coöperation of the entire religious element of the country, to help, by their labors and counsels, to bring about and produce the greatest amount

---

in *Report of the Board of Indian Commissioners*, 1870, pp. 93–100. The sense of urgency and the pressure put on the missionary boards can be seen in the correspondence of Colyer, Cox, and Delano with the Reverend John C. Lowrie, secretary of the Presbyterian mission board, August–December 1870, in American Indian Correspondence, MS In 25 B–1–C, Presbyterian Historical Society, Philadelphia.

35. Fred L. Israel, ed., *The State of the Union Messages of the Presidents, 1790–1966*, 3 vols. (New York: Chelsea House, 1966), 2: 1199, 1216–17. Henry G. Waltman, in "Circumstantial Reformer: President Grant and the Indian Problem," *Arizona and the West* 13 (Winter 1971); 323–42, attempts to evaluate Grant's personal contribution to the reform of Indian policy. He concludes that "Grant was a well-intentioned, but shortsighted and inconsistent would-be Indian reformer whose identification with the Peace Policy was, in some respects, more symbolic than substantial."

of good from the expenditure of the munificent annual appropriations of money by Congress, for the civilization and Christianization of the Indian race."[36] These high-sounding sentiments were not mere rhetoric. Grant and Parker were convinced that a peace policy must work. The assignment of the agencies to the churches appeared to be a wonderful solution, in tune with the idealistic, humanitarian sentiments of the day.

Vincent Colyer, so much involved in the formulation and promotion of the scheme, was soon at work allotting the agencies to the various denominations. The only enunciated principle appeared at the end of 1870 in Grant's annual message to Congress, in which he declared his determination "to give all the agencies to such religious denominations as had heretofore established missionaries among the Indians, and perhaps to some other denominations who would undertake the work on the same terms, i.e., as a missionary work." But this was much too vague to be satisfactory, and Colyer was forced to make an initial division on the basis of his own scanty information about the agencies and the missionary work being performed at them. Colyer's original plans, which he admitted were "simply suggestions," were modified when the agencies were actually assigned, and changes in apportioning the agencies occurred throughout the existence of the policy.[37]

The distribution caused immediate dissatisfaction, and one religious group after another complained about being slighted or overlooked. The vagueness of criteria for appointment was partly to blame. Different principles were proposed, as they fitted the purposes of the churches concerned. One argument was that an agency belonged to whichever group had started the first mission there, whether or not it had been a success. Catholics insisted that agencies, according to Grant's statement, should be assigned to churches that had missionaries at them in 1870 and, if more than one group was represented, to the one that had been there first. At other times Catholics argued that the Indians themselves should choose which denomination they wanted. A Baptist member of the Board of Indian Commissioners proposed distribution according to denominational size, for the Baptists felt cheated in getting fewer agencies than the Episcopalians and Presbyterians, who had fewer adherents. The board argued that no church

36. CIA Report, 1870, serial 1449, p. 474.
37. Israel, *State of the Union Messages*, 2:1216; Colyer to Cox, August 11, 1870, *Report of the Board of Indian Commissioners*, 1870, p. 98. There is a listing of the assigned agencies and the number of Indians at each in CIA Report, 1872, serial 1560, pp. 461–62, and a slightly different listing in *Report of the Board of Indian Commissioners*, 1872, pp. 29–46. For a tabular listing of apportionments for 1870, 1872, and 1875, with a complete list of agencies assigned to each group and a statement of previous missionary efforts at each agency, see Keller, *American Protestantism and Indian Policy*, appendix 1, pp. 219–22.

TABLE 3: Distribution of Indian Agencies to Church Groups, 1872

Church	Agency	State or Territory	Number of Indians
AMERICAN BOARD OF COMMISSIONERS FOR FOREIGN MISSIONS	Sisseton	Dakota Territory	1,496
BAPTIST	Cherokee	Indian Territory	18,000
	Creek	Indian Territory	12,300
	Walker River	Nevada	6,000
	Paiute	Nevada	2,500
	Special	Utah Territory	3,000
			41,800
CATHOLIC	Tulalip	Washington Territory	3,600
	Colville	Washington Territory	3,349
	Grande Ronde	Oregon	870
	Umatilla	Oregon	837
	Flathead	Montana Territory	1,780
	Grande River	Dakota Territory	6,700
	Devils Lake	Dakota Territory	720
			17,856
CHRISTIAN	Pueblo	New Mexico Territory	7,683
	Neah Bay	Washington Territory	604
			8,287
CONGREGATIONAL	Green Bay	Wisconsin	2,871
	Chippewas of Lake Superior	Wisconsin	5,150
	Chippewas of the Mississippi	Minnesota	6,455
			14,476
FRIENDS (HICKSITE) Northern Superintendency	Great Nemaha	Nebraska	313
	Omaha	Nebraska	969
	Winnebago	Nebraska	1,440
	Pawnee	Nebraska	2,447
	Oto	Nebraska	464
	Santee Sioux	Nebraska	965
			6,598
FRIENDS (ORTHODOX) Central Superintendency	Potawatomi	Kansas	400
	Kaw	Kansas	290
	Kickapoo	Kansas	598
	Quapaw	Indian Territory	1,070
	Osage	Indian Territory	4,000
	Sac and Fox	Indian Territory	463
	Shawnee	Indian Territory	663
	Wichita	Indian Territory	1,250
	Kiowa	Indian Territory	5,490
	Upper Arkansas	Indian Territory	3,500
			17,724

TABLE 3, *continued*

Church	Agency	State or Territory	Number of Indians
LUTHERAN	Sac and Fox	Iowa	273
METHODIST	Hoopa Valley	California	725
	Round Valley	California	1,700
	Tule River	California	374
	Yakima	Washington Territory	3,000
	Skokomish	Washington Territory	919
	Quinaielt	Washington Territory	520
	Warm Springs	Oregon	626
	Siletz	Oregon	2,500
	Klamath	Oregon	4,000
	Blackfeet	Montana Territory	7,500
	Crow	Montana Territory	2,700
	Milk River	Montana Territory	19,755
	Fort Hall	Idaho Territory	1,037
	Michigan	Michigan	9,117
			54,473
PRESBYTERIAN	Choctaw	Indian Territory	16,000
	Seminole	Indian Territory	2,398
	Abiquiu	New Mexico Territory	1,920
	Navajo	New Mexico Territory	9,114
	Mescalero Apache	New Mexico Territory	830
	Tularosa or Southern Apache	New Mexico Territory	1,200
	Moquis Pueblo (Hopi)	Arizona Territory	3,000
	Nez Perce	Idaho Territory	2,807
	Uintah Valley	Utah Territory	800
			38,069
PROTESTANT EPISCOPAL	Whetstone	Dakota Territory	5,000
	Ponca	Dakota Territory	735
	Upper Missouri	Dakota Territory	2,547
	Fort Berthold	Dakota Territory	2,700
	Cheyenne River	Dakota Territory	6,000
	Yankton	Dakota Territory	1,947
	Red Cloud	Dakota Territory	7,000
	Shoshone	Wyoming Territory	1,000
			26,929
REFORMED DUTCH	Colorado River	Arizona Territory	828
	Pima and Maricopa	Arizona Territory	4,342
	Camp Grant	Arizona Territory	900
	Camp Verde	Arizona Territory	748
	White Mountain or Camp Apache	Arizona Territory	1,300
			8,300

TABLE 3, *continued*

Church	Agency	State or Territory	Number of Indians
UNITARIAN	Los Pinos	Colorado Territory	3,000
	White River	Colorado Territory	800
			3,800
		Total	239,899

Source: CIA Report, 1872, serial 1560, pp. 461–62.

had a *right* to any agency, and that the quality of work done by the churches or the simple resolution of competing claims might call for a change. The welfare of the Indians, it insisted, was paramount to the benefit to be received by any church. Sometimes the rival groups were left to work out exchanges and other agreements among themselves.[38]

What the government wanted from the churches was a total transformation of the agencies from political sinecures to missionary outposts. The religious societies were expected not only to nominate strong men as agents but to supply to a large extent the subordinate agency personnel. Teachers especially were desired, men and women with a religious dedication to the work that would make up for the low pay and often frightening conditions. The churches, too, it was assumed, would pursue more energetically and more effectively the strictly missionary activities already begun now that conflicts between government agents and missionaries would no longer be an obstacle. The commissioner of Indian affairs, in fact, asserted in 1872 that "the importance of securing harmony of feeling and concert of action between the agents of the Government and the missionaries at the several agencies, in the matter of the moral and religious advancement of the Indians, was the single reason formally given for placing the nominations to Indian agencies in the hands of the denominational societies."[39] Agency physicians, interpreters, and mechanics, if they were of solid moral worth, could all contribute to the goal of civilizing and Christianizing the Indians.

Utopia seemed to be within grasp. The reports of the secretaries of the interior, the commissioners of Indian affairs, the Board of Indian Commissioners, and Grant himself rang loud with praise for the new policy.

38. Keller, *American Protestantism and Indian Policy*, pp. 34–35.
39. CIA Report, 1872, serial 1560, p. 461.

FAILURE OF THE STRUCTURES

Both the Board of Indian Commissioners and the church-run agencies, despite the early praise, were soon in trouble. The romantic ideal of depoliticizing the Indian Office and the administration of the agencies by the appointment of high-minded, religiously motivated individuals ran up against the hard rock of practical operations within an old political system. The Board of Indian Commissioners felt the pressures first. As the board members began their work, all seemed to go smoothly, and the secretaries of the interior lauded their efforts and "the healthful effect of their influence and advice."[40] But the board soon found that its attempts to do good were blocked by powerful forces and its advice and recommendations ignored or contradicted. Goodwill and integrity on the part of the board's members met greed in the "Indian ring" and corruption among public officials. The board underwent a crisis in 1874 from which it only slowly recovered.

The problem was one of authority. Could there in fact be "joint authority" between the Department of the Interior and the quasi-private group of unpaid, philanthropic businessmen? Brunot, conscientiously trying to find out precisely what power the board had in supervising expenditures, submitted the documents relating to the board to the attorney general for a ruling. Although the ruling upheld the board's authority, in practice its recommendations were often set aside. Many disbursements, moreover, were not cleared through the board at all, and contracts were awarded without competitive bids.[41]

One element in the conflict was an attack on Commissioner of Indian Affairs Parker for alleged questionable dealings in procuring Indian supplies. The attack, led by William Welsh, who had lost none of his interest in Indian affairs by his resignation from the board, resulted in a congressional investigation of the Office of Indian Affairs. The investigating committee found "irregularities, neglect, and incompetency," but it exonerated Parker of fraud or corruption. Nevertheless, Parker resigned in July 1871, charging the whole affair to the enmity of those "who waxed rich and fat from the plundering of the poor Indians"; he declared it was "no longer a pleasure to discharge patriotic duties."[42] Although the *Nation* exulted that

40. Report of the Secretary of the Interior, 1870, *House Executive Document* no. 1, 41–3, serial 1449, p. ix; ibid., 1871, *House Executive Document* no. 1, part 5, 42–2, serial 1505, p. 3.

41. *Report of the Board of Indian Commissioners*, 1873, pp. 6–9. Congress in 1872 provided that the board's approval was not a prerequisite for payment of vouchers. 17 *United States Statutes* 186.

42. Welsh, *Indian Office*; William Welsh, *Summing Up Evidence before a Commit-*

a revolution had taken place by "the complete overthrow of a most gigantic system of wrong, robbery, hypocrisy, greed, and cruelty, and in the triumph of right, of official integrity, of administrative economy, and of the principles of a Christian civilization," the oppressive pressures on the board did not end.[43] Parker's forced resignation was countered by the forcing from office of Vincent Colyer, the board's secretary, whose investigation and reports on Indian affairs in the Southwest had won him the enmity of Secretary of the Interior Columbus Delano.[44]

By 1874 matters had come to an impasse, and all the original members of the Board of Indian Commissioners resigned. "It was obvious, towards the close of 1873," Brunot's biographer wrote, "that the original members of the Board of Indian Commissioners could not serve much longer. They freely gave of their busy lives for the sake of the Indians, but when they found repeatedly during the last year that their recommendations were ignored, that bills, laboriously examined by them and rejected by them, were paid, that gross breaking of the law in giving contracts was winked at, and that many important matters were not submitted to them at all, then they decided that their task was as useless as it was irritating."[45]

The passing of the original members marked the end of one phase of the board's existence; the new members appointed in 1874, although they dif-

---

tee of the House of Representatives, Charged with the Investigation of Misconduct in the Indian Office (Washington: H. Polkinhorn and Company, 1871); House Report no. 39, 41–3, serial 1464, pp. ii; Norton P. Chipman, Investigation into Indian Affairs, before the Committee on Appropriations of the House of Representatives: Argument of N. P. Chipman, on Behalf of Hon. E. S. Parker, Commissioner of Indian Affairs (Washington: Powell, Ginck and Company, 1871); "Writings of General Parker," Publications of the Buffalo Historical Society 8 (1905): 526–27. Arthur C. Parker, The Life of General Ely S. Parker (Buffalo: Buffalo Historical Society, 1919), pp. 150–61, has nothing but praise for Parker's career as commissioner of Indian affairs. A detailed and balanced account of the investigation of Parker and of his conflict with Welsh and the Board of Indian Commissioners appears in William H. Armstrong, Warrior in Two Camps: Ely S. Parker, Union General and Seneca Chief (Syracuse: Syracuse University Press, 1978), pp. 152–61.

43. Nation 13 (August 17, 1871): 100–101.

44. In October 1871 Brunot had refused an offer of the position of commissioner of Indian affairs, perhaps suspecting even then that conditions were hostile to the reforms he envisaged. Delano to Brunot, October 17, 1871, Records of the Board of Indian Commissioners, Minutes of Board Meetings, vol. 1, p. 61; Brunot to Delano, October 19, 1871, ibid., p. 62. Grant wrote to Stuart about the matter: "I will be careful that no one is apt'd Ind. Com. who is not fully in sympathy with a humane policy towards the indians. I will see too that he has the full confidence of the Peace [Board of Indian] Commissioners." Grant to Stuart, July 22, 1871, George Hay Stuart Papers, Library of Congress.

45. Slattery, Brunot, p. 217. See also Dodge, Memorials of William E. Dodge, pp. 177–78.

fered little from the old in background and religious outlook, were less inclined to set themselves up in opposition to the official government departments.[46] The old board members had attempted what was perhaps impossible: to assume direct responsibility for Indian finances and for Indian policy in general. But the seeds they planted would germinate and blossom later. The new board, weak though it was, continued the idea that the moral and religious sentiments of the nation should be represented in the formulation and administration of Indian policy. Brunot and his colleagues were the first example of highly motivated men in a corporate, united attempt to change the course of government action from outside the administrative structure. The idea would not die; it lived on in the reform sentiment that came to dominate the 1880s and 1890s.

The assignment of agencies to churches that had looked so promising in principle did not work well in practice. Fundamentally, the missionary societies were not prepared to handle the tremendous responsibility suddenly cast upon them. It was not as simple as many sanguine persons had thought to supply competent Christian men to run the agencies. Such men were not available in large numbers, and the missionary boards were none too astute in selecting agents. Amid the words of praise for the new system in the official reports were clear indications that men of inadequate character and competence had been appointed. In 1873 the Board of Indian Commissioners noted that "a vastly better class of men" had been given to the Indian service and that "at the present time a large majority of the agents are, it is believed, honest men." But the basic criticism remained: some of the agents were men with no real sympathy for the missionary effort. Of the eight hundred agency employees under control of the churches, many did not display Christian character, and some of them were from the worst social classes in the country. Until such difficulties were overcome, the work of Christianization would yield little fruit.[47]

Nor were the auxiliary services of education and missionary work effectively pursued, for most of the missionary boards found that providing for the Indian service was a distasteful responsibility. Among many of the churches, the Indians had to compete with foreign infidels, who captured the imagination of the communicants and most of the missionary funds.

---

46. Congressional debates on the board and its continued existence and on internal dissension within the board are discussed in Loring Benson Priest, *Uncle Sam's Stepchildren: The Reformation of United States Indian Policy, 1865–1887* (New Brunswick: Rutgers University Press, 1942), pp. 47–52. Priest takes too limited a view of the board's work and its successes, however.

47. Report of the Secretary of the Interior, 1872, *House Executive Document* no. 1, part 5, 42–3, serial 1560, p. 9: *Report of the Board of Indian Commissioners, 1871*, p. 11; ibid., 1873, pp. 24–25. For a heavily documented account of troubles in the peace policy agencies, see Keller, *American Protestantism and Indian Policy*, pp. 107–25.

In truth, the internal effectiveness of the whole policy was open to serious doubt, although the demands of the agencies were met differently by the different churches. The Quakers and the Episcopalians, who helped to originate the peace policy, met the challenge most effectively. The Roman Catholics, although they felt they were persecuted, also performed well. The Methodists, who had been most favored in the distribution of the agencies, did the least.[48]

Equally serious as the lack of sustained interest on the part of the churches was the interdenominational rivalry. Maintaining a position against a conflicting group was, unfortunately, often a more powerful motivation than concern for the welfare of the Indians. Examples of these fights abounded; they were all disedifying if not scandalous. If many could be explained by pettiness and denominational bias, the conflict between the Protestant mission groups and the Roman Catholics was nothing less than flagrant bigotry. The peace policy of Grant came at a time when Protestant missionary interest in the Indians was waning and Catholic activity in Indian missions and the Indian schools had begun a remarkable upsurge. This changing relation in the strength of the rival mission groups in itself explains much of the friction, for the Protestants, whose long dominance had not been seriously challenged before, now faced a threat from growing "Romanism."[49]

In its origins, the peace policy, both in the Board of Indian Commissioners and in the plan for allotting the agencies to the churches, was a Protestant affair. When the allotments were made, the Catholics were shocked to receive only seven agencies; on the basis of their previous missionary work they had expected thirty-eight. Their leaders protested, but to respond to Catholic complaints once the assignments had been made would have meant taking agencies away from groups to which they had been given. In order to protect their own interests against what appeared to them as a unified bloc of Protestants, therefore, the Catholics in 1874 organized a central agency, the Bureau of Catholic Indian Missions, to direct the work of the missions in the field and to lobby in Washington for

48. Keller, *American Protestantism and Indian Policy*, pp. 47–66, gives a denomination-by-denomination evaluation of the Protestant performance. For an evaluation of the Quaker agents of the Northern Superintendency, see Milner, *With Good Intentions*. For the work of the Methodists, see Robert Lee Whitner, "The Methodist Episcopal Church and Grant's Peace Policy: A Study of the Methodist Agencies, 1870–1882" (Ph.D. dissertation, University of Minnesota, 1959). Whitner concludes, p. 281: "The record of the Missionary Society of the Methodist Episcopal church as a participant in the peace policy was largely a failure. It did little to improve the service or the condition of the Indians. It did much to perpetuate sectarianism and intolerance and bigotry in America."

49. There are extended discussions of denominational conflict in Keller's book and Whitner's dissertation. See also the account in Priest, *Uncle Sam's Stepchildren*, pp. 31–36.

mission needs. The conflicts were numerous on the reservations, where Catholic and Protestant agents and missionaries carried on quite un-Christian feuds.[50]

Much was made of the question of religious liberty. Did assignment of an agency to a particular religious group exclude other denominations from the reservation? The Catholics, particularly, cut off by apportionment from a number of reservations where they had traditionally done missionary work, insisted on the right to preach and to teach the Indians on reservations officially assigned to Protestants. The controversy grew to considerable proportions, and no solution seemed in sight until a Protestant group in turn was excluded from carrying on its ministrations to Indians at a Catholic agency. Then the whole matter took on a new light, and ultimately a regulation from Secretary of the Interior Carl Schurz in 1881 declared that Indian reservations would be open to all religious denominations, except where "the presence of rival organizations would manifestly be perilous to peace and order" or where treaty stipulations would be violated.[51]

But religious liberty was not very broadly conceived in nineteenth-century America. The Mormons, who had done a good deal of missionary work among the Indians, did not participate in the peace policy. Nor were the southern branches of the great Protestant denominations allotted agencies, even though the Southern Methodists, for example, had been active Indian missionaries. What was more serious was the complete disregard for the religious views and the religious rights of the Indians themselves. Quakers, Methodists, Episcopalians, and all the other Protestants, fighting for the religious liberty of their own groups on the reservations, made no move to grant so much as a hearing to the Indian religions. The record of the Catholics was no better. They criticized Protestant bigotry and called for freedom of conscience, but that freedom did not extend to native religions, which were universally condemned. The missionaries were not in-

50. Strong Catholic attacks on Grant's policy appeared in *Address of the Catholic Clergy of the Province of Oregon, to the Catholics of the United States, on President Grant's Indian Policy, in Its Bearings upon Catholic Interests at Large* (Portland, Oregon: Catholic Sentinel Publication Company, 1874); and *Catholic Grievances in Relation to the Administration of Indian Affairs: Being a Report Presented to the Catholic Young Men's National Union, at Its Annual Convention, Held in Boston, Massachusetts, May 10th and 11th, 1882* (Richmond, Virginia, 1882). A thorough study of the Bureau of Catholic Indian Missions and of the work of the Catholics under the peace policy in the Sioux agencies in Rahill, *Catholic Indian Missions and Grant's Peace Policy.*

51. Rahill, *Catholic Indian Missions and Grant's Peace Policy,* pp. 273–307; R. Pierce Beaver, *Church, State, and the American Indians: Two and a Half Centuries of Partnership in Missions Between Protestant Churches and Government* (St. Louis: Concordia Publishing House, 1966), pp. 157–61; Keller, *American Protestantism and Indian Policy,* pp. 177–84. Schurz's statement is quoted in Rahill, p. 306.

terested in the Indians' right to maintain and defend their own religion. By religious freedom they meant liberty of action on the reservations for their own missionary activities.

It quickly became clear that the assignment of agencies to the churches did not solve the "Indian problem." Good intentions of Christian men were not enough to correct evils of a complex nature or overcome a long history of mismanagement. Failure to study or appreciate the Indian side of the question, to adopt or build upon the societal forms that persisted in the Indian communities, weakened all the missionary efforts. And although most of the church groups professed a sincere regard for the well-being and advancement of the Indians, all this was thought of completely in terms of transforming them into acceptable Christian citizens. Catholics and Protestants alike saw little worth preserving in the Indian groups they sought to convert and civilize.

Internal weaknesses and dissensions in the various missionary groups together with the interdenominational bickering and open conflict alone would have doomed the policy. But external forces, too, were at work. The policy of church agencies would have brought difficulties in times of the highest moral rectitude in government circles; in fact, it was attempted in a decade noted in American history as a low point in public morals. "Grantism" became a term for fraud and corruption in high federal office, and the Indian service was one of the more lucrative areas in which politicians and spoilsmen could grow rich. It is understandable that rapacious individuals would not stand idly by when the source of rich spoils was cut off by the missionary policy. Almost from the very start of the program, pressures of political patronage were at work, undermining the system. Secretary of the Interior Cox, a man of integrity and one of the architects of the peace policy, resigned in October 1870. Under his successor, Columbus Delano, the Interior Department provided one scandal after another, and Delano was forced to resign in 1875. During his term he made it clear to the churches that he had the final say in the appointment of agents, and he frequently presented agents to the missionary boards for their rubber-stamp approval. Being a "good Christian brother," he told the Board of Indian Commissioners, was "not enough to make a man a satisfactory agent."[52]

The White House, too, manipulated agency appointments for political friends, and even the Board of Indian Commissioners on occasion interfered for special appointments. More subtle but even more significant were the pressures exerted by Congress, many of whose members and their constituents did not understand or could not abide a church-dominated Indian service. If the agents themselves were church-appointed, at least room among the subordinate officials on the reservations could be made for a

52. *Report of the Board of Indian Commissioners*, 1870, p. 112.

friend in need of a job. Missionary boards did not know just how to counteract senatorial pressure for or against confirmation of particular individuals and often gave in rather than fight the issue. Senators frequently insisted that agents be appointed from men who lived in the state concerned,
thus severely limiting the churches' freedom of choice. But politicians
were not the only group with unclean hands. Church leaders, too, were not
above some conniving to satisfy friends of the church.[53]

Public denunciation of the peace policy was rare in the East, where the
press was favorable to the humane attempt to deal with the Indians. If
Grant was attacked, little or nothing was said about Indian policy. Western
opinion, though not unanimous, was hostile. In areas where Indians were
close at hand and often warlike, "peace" policies did not win much support. Extermination of the Indians was openly advocated; but a Montana
paper declared sarcastically that the government would never allow any
more punitive expeditions against the Indians because "some poor red-
skinned pet of the Government, with its Quaker policy would get hurt,
and tender-hearted philanthropists in the east would be thrown into con-
vulsions of grief."[54] How much the rabid utterances of the western press
affected the course of the policy is difficult to determine. Extreme ranting
most likely only confirmed the eastern humanitarians in their resolve.
Voter influence on representatives in Congress was not uniform, for western delegations did not vote as a bloc in opposition to the Grant policies.[55]

When Rutherford B. Hayes succeeded Grant in 1877, the policy of
church-appointed agents was clearly on a downhill course. Carl Schurz,
the reform-minded Liberal Republican whom Hayes appointed secretary of
the interior, developed quite a different tone from that of the previous administration, and the religious character of the men in office did not seem
any longer to be of prime importance. The board of inquiry that Schurz
appointed soon after taking office to investigate irregularities in the Indian
service criticized the appointment of agents "because of a sentiment"
rather than on the basis of business qualifications, and it said that to en-
trust the church-appointed agents with such great power and responsibility was to "undertake through pigmies the solution of a problem that has
engaged the best efforts of statesmen and philanthropists ever since the
days of the republic." Although admitting that it was possible for business

---

53. Keller, *American Protestantism and Indian Policy*, pp. 93–97.

54. *Montanian* (Virginia City), August 24, 1871, quoted ibid., p. 99. For other western
views see the discussion in Keller, pp. 98–101, and Henry E. Fritz, *The Movement for
Indian Assimilation, 1860–1890* (Philadelphia: University of Pennsylvania Press, 1963),
pp. 109–19.

55. Keller, *American Protestantism and Indian Policy*, pp. 103–5, discusses early
congressional debate on the peace policy.

acumen and religious convictions to coexist, the board asserted that religious convictions alone were not enough to stem the corruption in the Indian service or to prevent the avarice of contractors and frontiersmen.[56]

The churches became less and less involved in appointing the agents, and the denominations that had been in the forefront in instigating the policy became disillusioned and withdrew. The Friends, finding cooperation with the Indian Office impossible and suffering from a general weariness, resigned from the duty of supplying agents.[57] The Episcopalians, too, lost interest, and their nominations were ignored. In 1882, when the secretary of the Methodist board, J. M. Reid, wrote to Secretary of the Interior Henry M. Teller to inquire why the nominations for the Michigan and Yakima agencies had not been honored, the secretary replied that he would no longer consult religious bodies in the appointment of Indian agents. "I do not believe," he said, "that the government has discharged its duty when it shall have made its appropriations and then turned the matter over to the churches of the land to deal with as their different interests may dictate."[58] So the Methodists, like all the rest, were, as the chairman of the Board of Indian Commissioners remarked, "mustered out of the service."

THE END OF TREATY MAKING

A concomitant movement for fundamental change in American Indian policy that culminated early in Grant's administration was an attack on the treaty system. From President Grant down, reformers called for abandonment of the system that had been an essential element in the relation between the United States government and the Indian tribes from the inception of the nation. Those who had some historical sense realized that the treaties at first had been a good deal more than "a mere form to amuse the quiet savages, a half-compassionate, half-contemptuous humoring of

56. *Report of Board of Inquiry Convened by Authority of Letter of the Secretary of the Interior of June 7, 1877, to Investigate Certain Charges against S. A. Galpin, Chief Clerk of the Indian Bureau, and Concerning Irregularities in Said Bureau* (Washington, GPO, 1878), p. 63.

57. Tatum, *Our Red Brothers*, pp. 285–86; Kelsey, *Friends and the Indians*, pp. 184–85, 196. An account of the Friends' difficulties under Hayes is in *Extracts from the Minutes of a Convention of Delegates from the Seven Yearly Meetings of Friends Having Charge of the Indians in the Northern Superintendency* (Philadelphia, 1878).

58. J. M. Reid to H. M. Teller, July 31, 1882, and Teller to Reid, August 5, 1882, printed in *Report of the Board of Indian Commissioners, 1882*, pp. 52–54. The discussion at the meeting of the Board of Indian Commissioners and the church groups at which these letters were read indicated that the policy had come to an end with all the groups.

unruly children," as Commissioner Francis A. Walker observed in 1873.
The Indians at one time had had enough power to make a favorable cession
of lands a diplomatic triumph for the United States. "The United States
were clearly the stronger party in every such case," Walker noted; "but the
Indians were, in the great body of instances, still so formidable, that to
wrest their lands from them by pure, brutal violence would have required
an exertion of strength which the government was ill prepared to make."[59]

Early in the nineteenth century perceptive men had seen the incongruity of treating the Indian tribes as equals, but the decisions of Chief
Justice John Marshall in the Cherokee cases strengthened the position of
the Indian tribes. Then, as demands for reform in Indian affairs grew during and immediately after the Civil War, the treaty system came under increasing scrutiny. The attack was part of the movement to end Indian
tribal organization and make Indians wards of the government and then
ultimately individualized citizens. The disparities between the United
States and the tribes were noted along many lines. A statement drawn up
by Bishop Whipple and sent to the president in 1862 by the General Conference of the Episcopal Church declared that it was "impolitic for our
Government to treat a heathen community living within our borders as an
independent nation, instead of regarding them as wards." Whipple's statement two years later in the *North American Review* was even stronger.
"Our first dealing with these savages is one of those blunders which is
worse than a crime," he wrote. "We recognize a wandering tribe as an independent and sovereign nation. We send ambassadors to make a treaty as
with our equals, knowing that every provision of that treaty will be our
own, that those with whom we make it cannot compel us to observe it,
that they are to live within our territory, yet not subject to our laws, that
they have no government of their own, and are to receive none from us; in
a word, we treat as an independent nation a people whom we will not permit to exercise one single element of that sovereign power which is necessary to a nation's existence." Ostensibly the United States government and
the Indians were the parties to the treaties, Whipple said, but in actuality
the *"real* parties" were the Indian agents, the traders, and the politicians,
and the real design was to pay worthless debts due to traders and to create
places where political favorites could be rewarded.[60]

Reformers, moreover, blamed the treaty system for the conflicts and
wars that arose between the Indians and whites over land. In stinging
words, Felix Brunot indicted the whole system:

59. Francis A. Walker, *The Indian Question* (Boston: James R. Osgood and Company,
1874), pp. 8–9.
60. Whipple, *Lights and Shadows*, p. 139; Henry B. Whipple, "The Indian System,"
North American Review 99 (October 1864): 450–51.

The United States first creates the fiction that a few thousand savages stand in the position of equality in capacity, power, and right of negotiation with a civilised nation. They next proceed to impress upon the savages, with all the form of treaty and the solemnity of parchment, signatures and seals, the preposterous idea that they are the owners in fee of the fabulous tracts of country over which their nomadic habits have led them or their ancestors to roam. The title being thus settled, they purchase and promise payment for a portion of the territory, and further bind themselves in the most solemn manner to protect and defend the Indians in the possession of some immense remainder defined by boundary in the treaty, thus becoming, as it were, *particeps criminis* with the savages in resisting the "encroachments" of civilisation and the progressive movement of the age. Having entered into his last-named impracticable obligation, the fact of its non-performance becomes the occasion of disgraceful and expensive war to subdue their victims to the point of submission to another treaty. And so the tragedy of war and the farce of treaty have been enacted again and again, each time with increasing shame to the nation.[61]

Brunot's colleagues on the Board of Indian Commissioners echoed his sentiments. The board in its first report recommended unequivocally: "The treaty system should be abolished." And it went a step further in proposing that when a "just method" could be devised, existing treaties should be abrogated. Individual members of the board, in their inspection reports, repeated the same principle.[62] The highest government officials agreed with the reformers. Commissioner Parker, who had a long career of upholding the rights of the Seneca tribe to which he belonged, declared flatly in 1869 that the treaty system should no longer be continued. He considered the Indians to be wards of the government, whose title to the land was a "mere possessory one," and he condemned the treaty procedures for falsely impressing upon the tribes a notion of national independence. "It is time," he said, "that this idea should be dispelled, and the government cease the cruel farce of thus dealing with its helpless and ignorant wards." President Grant told the Board of Indian Commissioners that he believed the treaty system had been a mistake and ought to be abandoned.[63]

Before the reformers could organize effectively enough to bring an end to treaty making, however, the system was destroyed by Congress for rea-

61. Slattery, *Brunot*, p. 156.

62. *Report of the Board of Indian Commissioners*, 1869, p. 10; see also John V. Farwell to Brunot, November 4, 1869, ibid., pp. 28–29.

63. CIA Report, 1869, serial 1414, p. 448; minutes of May 27, 1869, Minutes of the Board of Indian Commissioners, vol. 1, pp. 6–7.

sons that had little to do with humanitarian reform. The end came as the result of a conflict of authority between the House of Representatives and the Senate. The fundamental problem was that making treaties was a function of the president and the Senate, and if dealings with the Indians were confined to treaties the House of Representatives was left out completely except to appropriate funds for arrangements it had no hand in making.

One crucial point at issue was the disposition of Indian lands. The Indian Office, by negotiating treaties with the Indians, could manipulate Indian land cessions in the interests of railroads or land companies. The territory freed of Indian title would not revert to the public domain and thus not become subject to the land laws that frontier settlers had fought to gain in their own interests. By means of the treaty process, one-fourth of the lands of Kansas passed from Indian ownership to individuals, land speculating companies, and railroads without ever becoming part of the public domain or coming under congressional control. Such disposal denied settlers the benefits of the Homestead Act of 1862 and gave no voice to the popularly elected House of Representatives, where land reform sentiment was strongest.[64] The most celebrated case was a treaty signed with the Osages in 1868 by which eight million acres of land was to be sold to railroad interests at about twenty cents an acre. News of the treaty precipitated strong opposition in the House, and the treaty was defeated. This was a striking example of what could happen to the public land system, and congressional opponents of the treaty-making power made full use of it in their attacks upon the defenders of the system.[65]

Another problem arose in 1869 in connection with the treaties negotiated in 1867 by the Peace Commission. The Senate inserted into the Indian appropriation bill for fiscal year 1870 certain funds necessary for implementing the treaties, but the House refused to concur. The Fortieth Congress ended on March 4, 1869, without providing any funds for the Indian Office for the year beginning July 1. When the new Congress met, the impasse continued until a compromise was reached whereby Congress voted a lump sum of two million dollars over and above the usual funds

64. Paul Wallace Gates, *Fifty Million Acres: Conflicts over Kansas Land Policy, 1854–1890* (Ithaca: Cornell University Press, 1954), pp. 6–8.

65. The debate in the House over the Osage treaty appears in *Congressional Globe*, 40th Congress, 2d session, pp. 3256–66. Gates discusses the matter fully in *Fifty Million Acres*, pp. 194–211. But he does not notice the other groups in opposition to the treaty-making power, and he attributes the end of treaty making too exclusively to the Osage land question. Furthermore, he writes from the standpoint of the settlers, as though their interests were always to be considered paramount. The Indian Office (aside from the temptations to fraud) could very well have negotiated for the sale of Indian lands, with the sale money to be used for the benefit of the Indians, rather than turning all the lands over to the public domain to be homesteaded without cost by white settlers.

"to enable the President to maintain the peace among and with the various tribes, bands, and parties of Indians, and to promote civilization among said Indians, bring them, where practicable, upon reservations, relieve their necessities, and encourage their efforts at self-support." The House, refusing to give up its principle of demanding equal voice with the Senate on Indian matters, added a provision that the legislation should not be construed to ratify or approve any treaty made since July 20, 1867. This was a meaningless action legally because the treaties had already been ratified by constitutional procedures, but it assuaged the pique of the House over its inferior position. A similar statement was included in the Indian appropriation bill for 1871, with the added provision that nothing should "affirm or disaffirm any of the powers of the Executive and Senate over the subject." Inadvertently, this disclaimer was omitted from the final engrossed bill, but it was formally passed with the appropriation act for the next fiscal year.[66]

The House realized that it was making little headway, for it was ultimately forced to approve the appropriations needed to carry out treaties ratified by the Senate, and the provisos tacked on to the bills had little if any legal effect. For the House to get an equal voice in Indian affairs the treaty system would have to be abolished altogether. Although some members of the House argued that such a move would be unconstitutional, their position was weakened by a decision of the Supreme Court that acts of Congress could supersede or abrogate treaties. The Senate was willing to end treaty making if treaties already ratified were held inviolate, so the way was cleared for the necessary legislation, which came finally in an obscure clause in the Indian appropriation act of March 3, 1871. Added to a sentence providing funds for the Yankton Indians was the statement: "*Provided*, That hereafter no Indian nation or tribe within the territory of the United States shall be acknowledged or recognized as an independent nation, tribe, or power with whom the United States may contract by treaty; *Provided*, further, That nothing herein contained shall be construed to invalidate or impair the obligation of any treaty heretofore lawfully made and ratified with any such Indian nation or tribe."[67]

The end of treaty making created a paradox. The question of what constitutional basis the federal government had for dealing with the Indians (aside from trade) had been answered largely by pointing to the treaty-

66. 16 *United States Statutes*, 40, 570. Debate on the matters is in *Congressional Globe*, 40th Congress, 3d session, pp. 1698–1708, 1813, 1891; 41st Congress, 1st session, pp. 170–73, 417–18, 557–73; 41st Congress, 2d session, pp. 1575–81, 4971–73, 5606–8.
67. 16 *United States Statutes* 566. See Laurence F. Schmeckebier, *The Office of Indian Affairs: Its History, Activities, and Organization* (Baltimore: Johns Hopkins Press, 1927), pp. 58–66; Priest, *Uncle Sam's Stepchildren*, pp. 95–99.

making power. Now Congress struck down this chief constitutional basis. As a matter of fact, however, the old processes could not be completely abandoned. Whether or not a group of Indians was recognized as "an independent nation, tribe, or power," dealings between it and the United States called for formal agreements by which Indian consent was obtained. This was especially true in land cessions. Such agreements differed from the treaties chiefly in that they were ratified not by the Senate alone but by both houses of Congress. Even legislative terminology showed that the old ways and attitudes had not been erased by the law of 1871. An act of May 1, 1876, for example, provided payment for a commission "to treat with the Sioux Indians for the relinquishment of the Black Hills country in Dakota Territory."[68] Congress did not simply legislate for the Indians as for other inhabitants of the United States, in the way Andrew Jackson and others following him had wanted.

The abolition of treaty making, only to be replaced by agreement making, did not satisfy reformers who objected to the perpetuation of tribal existence that such agreements acknowledged. Objectionable, too, was the continuation of treaty arrangements that had been concluded prior to 1871, for these still rested upon a basis of tribal sovereignty. The humanitarians concerned with the Indians' rights insisted that treaty rights of the past be respected at all costs—but to consider the Indians simultaneously both sovereign peoples and wards of the government, as Commissioner Edward P. Smith pointed out in 1873, involved "increasing difficulties and absurdities." "So far, and as rapidly as possible," Smith declared, "all recognition of Indians in any other relation than strictly as subjects of the Government should cease." He admitted, however, that this would require "radical legislation."[69] By 1876 problems arising in the Indian Territory, where the Five Civilized Tribes had maintained a strong national existence, led the secretary of the interior to assert that the sooner the idea of treating with the various tribes in the Indian Territory as though they possessed a sort of independent power and nationality were done away with, the earlier would some practical solution for their government be reached. And Commissioner J. Q. Smith was even more pointed in his remarks: "There is a very general and growing opinion that observance of the strict letter of treaties with Indians is in many cases at variance both with their best interests and with sound public policy."[70]

68. 19 *United States Statutes* 45.
69. *CIA Report, 1873, serial 1601,* p. 371.
70. *Report of the Secretary of the Interior, 1876, House Executive Document* no. 1, part 5, 44–2, serial 1749, p. viii; CIA Report, 1876, serial 1749, p. 389. A strong, detailed criticism of the treaty system appeared in Elwell S. Otis, *The Indian Question* (New York: Sheldon and Company, 1878), pp. 117–97.

Old ways did not change as easily as the legal forms. Even outside the Indian Territory, tribal leaders in some cases continued to exercise more authority on the reservations than the Indian agents, who were supposed to be directing the destinies of the nation's wards. Criticism of tribal authority and objections to consulting with the chiefs about government policy grew rather than diminished after the abolition of the treaty system.[71]

71. George E. Hyde, *A Sioux Chronicle* (Norman: University of Oklahoma Press, 1956), gives numerous examples of the conflict and tension between the agents and the Sioux tribal leaders. See also Priest, *Uncle Sam's Stepchildren*, pp. 102–4.

CHAPTER 21

Military
Challenge

Indian Wars.

The Army and the Indian.

The Transfer Issue.

The End of the Military Phase.

The period of the post-Civil War peace policy was marked, paradoxically, by continual Indian wars. Neither the philanthropists on the Board of Indian Commissioners nor the agents appointed by the churches were able to reverse conditions that led to Indian resistance, and the civilian men who dominated the Indian Office did not succeed in eliminating the need for military action. The promoters of the peace policy, in fact, developed a modus vivendi with the army, a fragile balance between the Indian Office and the War Department. Indian Commissioner Ely S. Parker in the early days of the peace policy spoke of "a perfect understanding" between the officers of the two departments. He summarized the policy of the government in the following terms: "that they [the Indians] should be secured their legal rights; located, where practicable, upon reservations; assisted in agricultural pursuits and the arts of civilized life; and that Indians who should fail or refuse to come in and locate in permanent abodes provided for them, would be subject wholly to the control and supervision of military authorities, to be treated as friendly or hostile as circumstances might justify."[1]

1. CIA Report, 1869, serial 1414, p. 447. There is a tremendous literature on the post-Civil War Indian wars. The best scholarly survey is Robert M. Utley, *Frontier Regulars: The United States Army and the Indian, 1866–1891* (New York: Macmillan Company, 1973), on which I have confidently relied. The wars with the plains Indians are popularly

Francis A. Walker, Parker's successor, likewise saw no inconsistency in making use of soldiers when Indians needed chastisement, while at the same time pursuing the peace policy on the reservations. Walker had little patience with recalcitrant Indians and little sympathy for their situation, and he had no qualms about using military men to restrain refractory tribesmen. He insisted that such action was neither an abandonment of the peace policy nor disparagement of it. The reservation policy from the beginning, he said, demanded "that the Indians should be made as comfortable on, and as uncomfortable off, their reservations as it was in the power of the Government to make them," and he saw the use of military force not as war but as discipline.[2]

The limited use of military police power that Walker envisaged in 1872, however, gave way to all-out war. The military encounters of the 1860s with the Apaches and Navajos in the Southwest, with the Cheyennes and Arapahos in the central plains, and with the Sioux in the Powder River Valley along the Bozeman Trail turned out to be, not the final examples of Indian wars cut short by the peace policy, but the beginning of a decade or more of desperate fighting in the West. This resurgence of violence brought into question the very foundation on which the policy of peaceful relations was based and created a strong movement for military management of the Indians in place of civilian control—a movement that came close to swamping the peace policy altogether.

INDIAN WARS

On the southern plains the Kiowas and Comanches, for whom raiding had become a way of life, would not say confined to the reservation assigned to them by the Treaty of Medicine Lodge Creek. Led by aggressive leaders like Satanta and Satank, these Indian left the reservation time and again to raid across the Red River into Texas. Lawrie Tatum, the Iowa Quaker farmer who had been sent to the Kiowas as agent in 1869 under the peace

---

treated in Ralph K. Andrist, *The Long Death: The Last Days of the Plains Indian* (New York: Macmillan Company, 1964). Some of the material in this chapter is taken from Francis Paul Prucha, *American Indian Policy in Crisis: Christian Reformers and the Indian, 1865–1900* (Norman: University of Oklahoma Press, 1976), pp. 72–102, 123–25, 234–36.

2. Walker discussed his views on Indian policy at great length in CIA Report, 1872, serial 1560, pp. 391–493; the quotation is from p. 394. See also Francis A. Walker, *The Indian Question* (Boston: James R. Osgood and Company, 1874), which reprints part of his 1872 report and two articles dealing with the Indian question in general and with Indian citizenship.

policy, tried desperately to make a nonviolent policy work. He seemed for a while to make some headway; but he resorted to withholding rations to force the chiefs to return white captives taken on the raids, and ultimately, when such coercion proved insufficient to restrain the Indians, he called for military assistance. Having thus violated the basic tenets of the peaceful Quakers, he got into trouble with his superiors, and at the end of March 1873 he resigned. Periodic promises of peace on the part of the Indians, interspersed with murderous raids off the reservation, kept the Red River frontier in a state of turmoil. The Cheyennes, too, joined in the depredations, and in June 1874 an attack by Kiowas, Comanches, and Cheyennes on a trading establishment at Adobe Walls in the Texas panhandle signaled the beginning of a full-scale war. Strong columns of troops were sent into the western part of the Indian Territory and into the Staked Plains of northwestern Texas to corral and subdue the Indians and force them to the reservations. But not until June 1875 were the last of the hostiles rounded up, the Red River War brought to a close, and the Indian prisoners of war sent to Fort Marion, Florida. With the defeat of the three tribes peace finally came to the southern plains.[3]

The peace policy was severely tried also by the Modoc War, a flaring up of hostilities along the Oregon-California border in 1872–1873 that grew out of Indian resistance to white pressures on their homelands.[4] The Modocs lived around Tule Lake, which stretched across the border, and they included in their lands along the southern edge of the lake a forbid-

3. Utley, *Frontier Regulars*, pp. 207–33; William H. Leckie, *The Military Conquest of the Southern Plains* (Norman: University of Oklahoma Press, 1963), pp. 133–235. There are many details on the conflict in W. S. Nye, *Carbine and Lance: The Story of Old Fort Sill* (Norman: University of Oklahoma Press, 1937). The Quaker agent's own story is in Lawrie Tatum, *Our Red Brothers and the Peace Policy of President Ulysses S. Grant* (Philadelphia: John C. Winston and Company, 1899). See also Lee Cutler, "Lowrie Tatum and the Kiowa Agency, 1869–1873," *Arizona and the West* 13 (Autumn 1971): 221–44.

4. The best histories of this war are Keith A. Murray, *The Modocs and Their War* (Norman: University of Oklahoma Press, 1959), and Erwin N. Thompson, *Modoc War: Its Military History and Topography* (Sacramento: Argus Books, 1971); Thompson's book is a detailed analysis of the military action prepared originally for the National Park Service. A more popular account is Richard H. Dillon, *Burnt-Out Fires: California's Modoc Indian War* (Englewood Cliffs, New Jersey: Prentice-Hall, 1973). Jeff C. Riddle, *The Indian History of the Modoc War and the Causes That Led to It* (San Francisco, 1914), is an account written, with the help of D. L. Moses, by the son of Frank and Tobey Riddle, interpreters in the negotiations between the whites and the Modocs. Official documents dealing with the war and the trial of the murderers from both War Department and Interior Department files are printed in "Modoc War," *House Executive Document* no. 122, 43–1, serial 1607. See also "Report of A. B. Meacham, Special Commissioner to the Modocs, upon the Late Modoc War," CIA Report, 1873, serial 1601, pp. 442–50.

ding region of lava beds, a remarkable stronghold against attacking forces. The Modocs were little affected by the mining frontier, for no gold was found in their vicinity, but their grasslands attracted ranchers, who soon clamored to have the Indians out of the way. In 1864, in response to these white cries, the United States government negotiated a treaty with the Indians by which they were moved to a reservation twenty-five miles to the north.[5] They had to share the reservation with the Klamath tribe; and the Modocs, on alien ground and outnumbered by the Klamaths, were restless and unhappy. One of the Modoc leaders, called Captain Jack by the whites, soon led his followers back to their old homes along Lost River, which ran into Tule Lake from the north. But white ranchers had moved there in the Indians' absence, and the return of Captain Jack and his band caused consternation and panic. Early negotiations with Captain Jack, endeavoring to get him to return to the reservation, came to nothing.

When Grant became president in 1869, he appointed as superintendent of Indian affairs for Oregon a faithful Republican named Alfred B. Meacham, an ardent temperance man moved by deep reforming instincts. Born in Indiana in 1826, Meacham had migrated to California during the gold rush and had then moved on to Oregon. As Indian superintendent he was a staunch supporter of Grant's peace policy and undertook to carry out its reform principles. He talked Captain Jack into returning to the reservation, but pressures from the Klamath Indians and the Indian agent drove Captain Jack again to Lost River in April 1870. The use of army troops in an attempt to force the Modocs back to the reserve led in 1872 to armed conflict, and the Modoc War was under way. The Indians holed up in the lava beds, from which the army without enthusiasm and without success sought to dislodge them, even though General Edward R. S. Canby, commanding the Department of the Columbia, himself assumed direction of the campaign.

To overcome this expensive and embarrassing impasse, a peace commission, headed by Meacham, was appointed on January 29, 1873. But negotiations made little progress. The Modocs themselves were divided, and the army tightened the pressure on the area held by the Indians. Captain Jack, his hand forced by more desperate members of his band, at length agreed to the treacherous murder of General Canby and the peace commissioners when they came unarmed to the next council. On Good Friday, April 11, 1873, the deed was done. At a signal from Captain Jack the Indians rose up armed, and Jack himself, drawing a pistol he had concealed under his coat, shot General Canby at pointblank range. The Reverend Eleasar Thomas, a member of the peace commission, was quickly killed,

5. Kappler, pp. 865–68.

too, by an Indian named Boston Charley. Meacham, who started to flee when the trouble broke out, was grazed by bullets and fell unconscious. He was partially scalped when a cry that soldiers were coming drove off his assailant, and he was found still alive when the rescuers arrived and eventually recovered. The other member of the commission escaped unharmed.

The disaster shocked the nation. Much of the sympathy that had supported the Modocs, who had been far outnumbered by the soldiers in the conflict, was destroyed, and cries for vengeance against the murderers resounded. The army intensified its drive until at last, giving up before hopeless odds, the Indians surrendered. Some of the criminals were granted amnesty for aiding in the capture of Captain Jack, but six of the Modocs were sentenced to death by a military commission at Fort Klamath.[6] On October 3, Captain Jack and three of his companions were executed at Fort Klamath; two lesser participants had their sentences commuted by President Grant to life imprisonment at Alcatraz.

The Modoc murders touched off a nationwide attack on Grant's peace policy. Western opposition was intense, and even supporters of the policy were stunned by the murder of the commissioners and agreed that stiff punishment was in order. It did not take long, however, for the peace advocates to renew their insistent urging that the peace policy be continued, and they spoke strongly against recurring white attacks upon the Indians —which, they charged, deserved as strict an accounting as that meted out to the Modocs. Meacham himself held no grudge against the Indians and devoted the rest of his life to Indian reform. He toured the lecture circuit with talks of his Modoc adventure, founded a journal devoted to Indian matters, *The Council Fire*, and served the government on special commissions.[7]

After the sentences of the military tribunal had been executed, the remaining 153 Modocs were exiled from their homeland. They were taken by the army to Fort McPherson, Nebraska, and there turned over to agents of the Interior Department, who moved them to the Indian Territory and placed them in charge of the Quapaw Agency. "The Indian is greatly attached to his tribal organization," Secretary Delano asserted, "and it is be-

6. "Proceedings of a Military Commission Convened at Fort Klamath, Oregon, for the Trial of Modoc Prisoners," *House Executive Document* no. 122, 43–1, serial 1607, pp. 131–83.

7. Biographical details are found in Meacham's own writings: *Wigwam and Warpath: or the Royal Chief in Chains* (Boston: John P. Dale and Company, 1875); *Wi-ne-ma (The Woman-Chief) and Her People* (Hartford: American Publishing Company, 1876); and "The Tragedy of the Lava-Beds," in T. A. Bland, *Life of Alfred B. Meacham* (Washington: T. A. and M. C. Bland, 1883). The fullest account of Meacham's life and works is Edward Sterl Phinney, "Alfred B. Meacham, Promoter of Indian Reform" (Ph.D. dissertation, University of Oregon, 1963).

lieved that this example of extinguishing their so-called national existence and merging their members into other tribes, while in reality a humane punishment, will be esteemed by them as the severest penalty that could have been inflicted, and tend by its example to deter hostile Indians in future from serious and flagrant insurrection."[8] The Modocs lived quietly and productively as farmers in the Indian Territory until in 1909 those who were left were allowed to return to the Klamath reservation in Oregon.

In Arizona and New Mexico the Apaches carried on a continual guerilla war with the troops sent to subdue them. Attempts to isolate friendly groups from those who continued depredations led to strong criticisms from local whites, who feared that the "feeding stations" were merely refugees for marauding Indians. On April 30, 1871, a force of Tucson citizens attacked the unsuspecting Apaches at Camp Grant, murdered and mutilated them, and carried off children into slavery. The Camp Grant Massacre speeded up attempts to apply the peace policy in Arizona, and in July 1871 Vincent Colyer was dispatched there to make peace with the Apaches and establish them on reservations. The outraged Arizonans ridiculed Colyer's attempts, but a good many Apaches gathered at temporary reservations set up at military posts, and General O. O. Howard, following in Colyer's path, made peace with the Chiricahua chief Cochise and induced more Indians to come into the agencies. A system of reservations was established, and a sizable number of Apaches gathered at them. Still the raiding continued, and in 1872–1873 General George Crook mounted a successful offensive against the bands. More Apaches settled on the reservations, and for several years peace was maintained in Arizona. Despite conflict between John Clum, the young civilian agent who assumed control of the San Carlos Agency in 1874, and the army officers, the Apaches were concentrated at San Carlos. The peace, however, did not end the raids into Mexico, carried on from both Arizona and New Mexico. Under Victorio, a Warm Springs Apache, the frontier was again terrorized until the chief was killed in 1880. And then new leaders, of whom Geronimo became the best known, continued the guerilla warfare until they too were tracked down. Geronimo finally surrendered in 1886.[9]

8. Report of the Secretary of the Interior, 1873, *House Executive Document* no. 1, part 5, 43–1, serial 1601, pp. ix–x.

9. Utley, *Frontier Regulars*, pp. 170–74, 192–98, 369–93. Colyer's report on the Apaches was printed in pamphlet form as *Peace with the Apaches of New Mexico and Arizona: Report of Vincent Colyer, Member of the Board of Indian Commissioners, 1871* (Washington: GPO, 1872). Specialized writings on the Apache wars are numerous. A comprehensive work is Dan L. Thrapp, *The Conquest of Apacheria* (Norman: University of Oklahoma Press, 1967). A recent scholarly biography of Geronimo is Angie Debo, *Geronimo: The Man, His Time, His Place* (Norman: University of Oklahoma Press, 1976).

Another challenge to civilian control of the Indians came in the conflicts with the Sioux. The Treaty of Fort Laramie in 1868 had left unceded lands in the Powder River country as hunting lands of the Sioux, but it had also set aside the Great Sioux Reserve west of the Missouri River in Dakota, and the chiefs had agreed to settle at the agencies and accept reservation life. Many of the Indians, lured by the government's rations, went to the agencies, but some, like Sitting Bull, remained on the unceded lands and refused to settle down. The nonreservation Indians were considered "hostile," for they occasionally raided Montana settlements and fought the advancing railroad surveyors who entered their lands. The Sioux were irritated, too, by the invasion of the Black Hills by a military expedition under George A. Custer in 1874 that confirmed the rumors that gold was there and stimulated the miners to invade the forbidden hills.

As long as the Indians were able to subsist by hunting in the Powder River Valley, it was impossible to control them fully. Only on the reservations would they be completely dependent upon the United States, and in December 1875 runners were sent to the Sioux to announce that all who were not at the agencies by January 31, 1876, would be hunted down by the army and brought in by military force. The midwinter deadline made compliance impossible, but in any event the Indians did not intend to obey. On February 1, 1876, the secretary of the interior declared that all Indians not on the reservations were to be considered hostile and asked the secretary of war to take appropriate action. General Sheridan, now in command of the Division of the Missouri, wanted a winter campaign, but delays prevented a full-scale attack until April and May, when three columns moved in toward the Sioux and their Cheyenne allies. One column headed eastward from Fort Ellis in Montana, a second moved north along the old Bozeman Trail from Fort Fetterman, and a third, including part of the Seventh Cavalry under Custer, traveled west from Fort Abraham Lincoln on the Missouri. Seriously underestimating the size of the opposing Indian force, Custer launched a premature attack on the Indian camp on the Little Bighorn on June 25, and he and his entire force were annihilated.[10]

News of the disaster on the Little Bighorn arrived in the East just as the centennial of the signing of the Declaration of Independence was being celebrated. The report stunned the nation, and heavy army reinforcements

10. Perhaps more has been written about Custer's battle than about any other Indian-related event in United States history. A well-documented survey of the whole conflict with the Sioux is Utley, *Frontier Regulars*, pp. 236–95. Utley also provides an excellent brief survey of the Little Bighorn battle that illuminates the strategy and tactics used in *Custer Battlefield National Monument, Montana* (Washington: National Park Service, 1969). A reasonable, detailed account is Edgar I. Stewart, *Custer's Luck* (Norman: University of Oklahoma Press, 1955). A recent reinterpretation is John S. Gray, *Centennial Campaign: The Sioux War of 1876* (Fort Collins, Colorado: Old Army Press, 1976).

were sent into Montana to hunt down the bands of Sioux and Cheyenne who had scattered after the fight. Such pressure was more than the Indians could withstand, and little by little during the fall and winter the bands surrendered at the agencies. Even the most recalcitrant at length came in. Crazy Horse with a band of more than a thousand surrendered at Camp Robinson, Nebraska, on May 6, 1877. Sitting Bull with his adherents fled into Canada determined never to submit to reservation life, but finally he, too, came back and gave up in July 1881. The Sioux war had accomplished what the peace policy had been unable to; it had forced the Indians to abandon their hunting grounds and accept government control on the reservations.

The defeat of the Sioux did not end all military action in the north, however. The traditionally peaceful Nez Perces in 1877 startled the nation with a new military conflict. When the Nez Perce Reservation had been reduced in 1863, some of the Indians, mostly those who had resisted the attempts to convert them to Christianity, refused to accept the treaty. Chief Joseph was among these "nontreaty" Indians, and he and his band continued to live in their beloved Wallowa Valley in eastern Oregon. Increasing white encroachments there laid the groundwork for trouble, and the United States was eager to persuade these tribesmen to join their relatives on the Lapwai Reservation in Idaho. It seemd a hopeless endeavor. Two special commissions sent to investigate the matter in 1873 reached contrary conclusions about the appropriateness of forcing the band to move, and in 1876 a new group made another attempt to reach a solution. This commission recommended that, as long as it remained peaceful, Joseph's band be allowed to remain in the Wallowa Valley, with troops sent in to ensure order. If the band did not quietly settle down there, it should be forced to move to the reservation. General Howard was given responsibility for the peace, and in a series of meetings with Chief Joseph he finally won the Indian's consent to go to Lapwai.[11]

Before the movement could be accomplished, hostilities broke out. In June 1877 young men of the band, avenging the murder of an Indian by whites, killed a party of settlers. General Howard's troops were ordered in and war began. The Indians' choice was flight. By skillful maneuvers, Joseph and the military leaders of the band moved east through the Lolo Pass into the Bitterroot Valley of Montana, down into Yellowstone Park, and then north, seeking to reach asylum in Canada. Pursued by Howard's soldiers and with occasional military encounters, the fleeing Indians executed one of the great military movements in history. They had almost

11. CIA Report, 1877, serial 1800, pp. 405–8; "Report of Civil and Military Commission to Nez Perce Indians, Washington Territory and the Northwest," December 1, 1876, ibid., pp. 607–13.

reached their objective when they were cut off by troops from Fort Keogh under General Nelson A. Miles. With many warriors dead and the rest exhausted and the women and children cold and starving, Chief Joseph surrendered at the Bear Paw Mountains on October 5.[12]

In 1878 and 1879, Bannocks, Shoshonis, and Paiutes in Idaho, Nevada, and eastern Oregon, upset by increasing white pressures on their lands, rose up in minor wars against the whites. Military expeditions directed by General Howard tracked down the hostiles through the rugged country of the Rockies and Great Basin and forced them back to their reservations.[13]

In neighboring Colorado, the Utes faced similar encroachment. By a treaty of 1868 they had been guaranteed a reservation in the western quarter of Colorado. Two agencies were to be maintained, one on the White River for bands in the north and the other on the Los Pinos River for three bands in the south, and provisions were made for education, for individual homesteads, and for stock, seeds, and implements to start the Utes on the road toward civilization.[14] The expanding mining frontier in Colorado soon encroached upon the reserved lands, however, and a United States commission, headed by Felix Brunot of the Board of Indian Commissioners, succeeded in gaining from the Indians in 1873 a large cession of land in the southern part of the reservation. The Utes remained at peace and under Chief Ouray exhibited loyalty and friendship to the United States. But white pressures upon their lands did not let up; and after Colorado had become a state in 1876 they became incessant as the state's inhabitants, its government, and the press shouted in ever louder chorus, "The Utes must go!" The tension between the two races was aggravated by government failures to provide promptly the goods and services promised in the treaties.

A violent outbreak might have been avoided but for a change in agents at the White River Agency in 1878. In that year, Agent H. E. Danforth, a nominee of the Unitarians under the peace policy, was replaced by Nathan C. Meeker. Meeker, born near Cleveland, Ohio, in 1817, had had

12. Utley, *Frontier Regulars*, pp. 296–321. The Nez Perces and the war have received much attention from historians. Histories of the tribe that include accounts of the conflict and its aftermath are Francis Haines, *The Nez Perces: Tribesmen of the Columbia Plateau* (Norman: University of Oklahoma Press, 1955), and Alvin M. Josephy, Jr., *The Nez Perce Indians and the Opening of the Northwest* (New Haven: Yale University Press, 1965). Histories specifically of the war are Merrill D. Beal, *"I Will Fight No More Forever": Chief Joseph and the Nez Perce War* (Seattle: University of Washington Press, 1963), and Mark H. Brown, *The Flight of the Nez Perce* (New York: G. P. Putnam's Sons, 1967). See also Mark H. Brown, "The Joseph Myth," *Montana: The Magazine of Western History* 22 (Winter 1972): 2–17.

13. Utley, *Frontier Regulars*, pp. 322–32.

14. Kappler, pp. 990–93. A comparison of this Ute treaty of 1868 with the one made in 1863 (ibid., pp. 856–59) indicates the new emphasis on means to promote civilization.

an intriguing career. Something of a visionary, he became converted to the agrarian socialism of Fourier and lived for several years in a phalanx in Ohio. For a while he served as agricultural editor of the *New York Tribune*, but he had not lost his utopian dreams. On a trip to the West in 1869 Meeker determined to set up an ideal agricultural community, and with Horace Greeley's enthusiastic support he founded Union Colony in eastern Colorado. The community, soon named Greeley, prospered, but Meeker himself seemed always to be in debt. When he was offered the Indian agency at White River, therefore, he saw it as a way to a sure income. But he also looked upon it as an opportunity to try his agricultural principles as a solution to the Indian problem—to build a Union Colony among the Utes. Meeker moved the agency downriver to a spot more suitable for his agricultural plans and began to plow, fence, and irrigate the meadows favored by the Indians as grazing grounds for their ponies. He met adamant opposition from some members of the tribe, who had no interest in farming and who objected to Meeker's plowing up their lands. When the agent realized their growing antagonism, he called for military support, and troops under Major Thomas T. Thornburgh were dispatched to strengthen his position. Thornburgh's troops were attacked as they entered the reservation, and the major and eleven of his soldiers were killed. At the same time, the agency was assaulted; Meeker and eight others were killed, and Meeker's wife and daughters were taken captive. It was a tragic ending for a good man whose obstinacy and lack of understanding of the Indians brought his death. Even Clinton B. Fisk, chairman of the Board of Indian Commissioners, who might have been expected to sympathize with the aggressive civilizing program Meeker had attempted, declared the agent "destitute of that particular tact and knowledge of the Indian character which is required of an agent; a man of too many years to begin with, unhappily constituted in his mental organization for any such place." Fisk viewed Meeker's whole administration as a failure.[15]

Although the uprising, the work of a small group of Indians, was quickly quieted through the good offices of Ouray and the concentration of additional troops in the area, the effect upon the Coloradans was electrifying. It was just the occasion they sought to demand a war of extermination

15. The Ute problems and the conflict they led to at White River are discussed in CIA Report, 1879, serial 1910, pp. 82–98. Two studies that treat the episode in detail are Robert Emmitt, *The Last War Trail: The Utes and the Settlement of Colorado* (Norman: University of Oklahoma Press, 1954), and Marshall Sprague, *Massacre: The Tragedy of White River* (Boston: Little, Brown and Company, 1957). See also the documents in *Senate Executive Document* no. 31, 46–2, serial 1882; *House Executive Document* no. 83, 46–2, serial 1925; *House Miscellaneous Document* no. 38, 46–2, serial 1931. Fisk's statement appears ibid., p. 45.

against the Utes. Secretary of the Interior Schurz moved at once to prevent
an expensive and destructive war, which he was sure would come if the
situation of the Utes in Colorado could not be radically changed. He sent a
special agent to get back the captives and then to obtain the surrender of
the guilty Indians. Schurz was chiefly interested in a plan for long-range
settlement of the difficulties, a plan he expressed in succinct terms: "settlement of the Utes in severalty, so as to promote the civilization of the
Indians, and to open the main part of the Ute reservation to development
by white citizens, thus removing a source of constant irritation between
the latter and the Utes." An agreement was signed in Washington on
March 6, 1880, by representatives of the Ute tribe that provided for removal of the White River Utes to the Uintah Reservation in Utah and for
the band of Uncompahgre and Southern Utes to settle on lands on the
Grand and the La Plata rivers.[16]

THE ARMY AND THE INDIAN

The Indian wars made the army an agent of the United States government
in the control and management of Indians that was on a par, or at least
almost so, with the Indian Office. And the ultimate goal of the two services was the same; to locate the Indians on reservations with set boundaries, where they could be educated and trained for American citizenship.
It was in methods and the nature of their tasks that the Interior Department and the War Department differed.[17]

The post-Civil War army, composed of officers and men who stayed
with the army as a career at the end of the sectional struggle, entered a
period of rapid professionalization. The commanding officers had their
eyes set on European models of what an up-to-date army preparing for conventional warfare should be. The schools and the manuals and theorists
like Emory Upton sought to change the American military forces into a
thoroughly modern and professional organization.

But the actual work of the postwar army was Indian fighting, a highly
unorthodox warfare, which the army somehow considered not its primary
mission but only a passing phase. So the military men were not well geared
to meet the enemy they actually confronted, an enemy with quite uncon-

16. Report of the Secretary of the Interior, 1879, *House Executive Document* no. 1,
part 5, 46–2, serial 1910, pp. 16–19. The quotation is from "Agreement with Ute Indians
of Colorado," *House Report* no. 1401, 46–2, serial 1937, p. 2. The agreement is in *Senate
Executive Document* no. 114, 46–2, serial 1885; it is also printed as part of the law in 21
United States Statutes 200–202.

17. For discussion of the army's role I have relied chiefly on Utley, *Frontier Regulars*,
pp. 44–58.

ventional characteristics. To begin with, the Indians could not readily be classified as hostile or friendly, so the enemy was seldom clearly identified. Who was friend and who was foe was never absolutely resolved, for the lines of division shifted rapidly, and the Indians wore no sharply distinguishing uniforms and did not draw up in organized array.

Moreover, the army did not develop a sharp ideological stand of hostility toward its Indian foes. Although the soldiers and their officers saw the horrors of savage warfare, they could also view the Indians through eyes that recognized the fraud, corruption, and injustice heaped upon the tribes. "Ambivalence, therefore," Robert Utley has noted, "marked military attitudes toward the Indians—fear, distrust, loathing, contempt, and condescension, on the one hand; curiosity, admiration, sympathy, and even friendship, on the other."[18] Humanitarians in the East, harping on Sand Creek (which was not a work of the regular army) or the Piegan Massacre and picking up exasperated statements of General Sherman and General Sheridan about refractory bands of Indians, charged that the army's policy was one of extermination. Such accusations were wide of the mark, for the impulse to civilize the Indians was as strong in the army as it was among humanitarian reformers and government officials.[19]

Some military men, in fact, were noted for their sincere concern for the Indians and their welfare and have been labeled "humanitarian soldiers."[20] Outstanding, perhaps, was General George Crook, a man who served in the West for a third of a century and who had a well-deserved reputation as an aggressive Indian fighter. But he also developed a philosophy of Indian relations based on honesty, justice, and concern for Indian civilization. He supported the Ponca Indians in their flight from the Indian Territory, spoke out in support of the Cheyenne chief Dull Knife and of the Bannock Indians in their conflicts with the United States, and during his second tour of Arizona, 1882–1886, worked out a positive program for the economic welfare of the Apaches that sought to convert them into capitalistic farm-

18. Ibid., p. 45.

19. See, for example, General Sherman's views in a letter "to a friend in Washington," April 17, 1873, in *Army and Navy Journal* 10 (April 26, 1873): 586–87. Sherman's policies and actions are well described in Robert G. Athearn, *William Tecumseh Sherman and the Settlement of the West* (Norman: University of Oklahoma Press, 1956). On Sheridan, see Carl Coke Rister, *Border Command: General Phil Sheridan in the West* (Norman: University of Oklahoma Press, 1944). A highly complimentary view of the army generals by a reformer is the statement of William Welsh in *Journal of the Second Annual Conference of the Board of Indian Commissioners with the Representatives of the Religious Societies Cooperating with the Government, and Reports of Their Work among the Indians* (Washington: GPO, 1973), pp. 47–48.

20. This theme has been developed in two articles by Richard N. Ellis, "The Humanitarian Soldiers," *Journal of Arizona History* 10 (Summer 1969): 53–66, and "The Humanitarian Generals," *Western Historical Quarterly* 3 (April 1972): 169–78.

ers.[21] In his later years, Crook's views toward Indian policy were almost indistinguishable from those of the civilian reformers with whom he came to have close contact. Crook believed firmly in the Indians' competence to survive and advance if given a chance. "I wish to say most emphatically," he wrote, "that the American Indian is the intellectual peer of most, if not all, the various nationalities we have assimilated to our laws, customs, and language. He is fully able to protect himself, if the ballot be given and the courts of law not closed against him." When the general died in 1890, he was eulogized as "a tower of strength to all who labored for Indian civilization."[22]

Another western commander of moderate views was General John Pope, who changed the exterminationist views he had expressed at the time of the Sioux outbreak in Minnesota in 1862. His long subsequent career in the West—he commanded the Department of the Missouri from 1870 to 1883—taught him much about the Indians and about the shortcomings of existing Indian policy. Although he directed campaigns against the warring Indians, he voiced concern for their future, relieved their suffering at the end of the wars, and sought to protect them from rapacious whites. His goal, like that of the reformers, was the eventual assimilation of the Indians into white society. General Oliver Otis Howard, too, was more than an Indian fighter. Known as the "Christian general" and renowned for his work as head of the Freedmen's Bureau, Howard approached the Indians with deep religious sentiments. His piety irritated some of his associates, but he sincerely hoped for peaceful means of dealing with the Indians. Like so many others, he concluded that there would be no lasting end to Indian troubles until the Indians got land in severalty and protection of the law and were assimilated into American culture. He pushed for Indian education and for an end to the reservation system.[23] Other officers—like Benjamin Grierson, who cooperated closely with the

---

21. James T. King, "George Crook: Indian Fighter and Humanitarian," *Arizona and the West* 9 (Winter 1967): 333–48. King asserts that Crook "conceived and put into practice one of the most enlightened Indian policies in the history of the American frontier" and that his career provides "insight into the element of humanitarianism which lies neglected among the more martial characteristics of the military frontier." See also King, "'A Better Way': General George Crook and the Ponca Indians," *Nebraska History* 50 (Fall 1969): 239–56. Crook's own story has been edited by Martin F. Schmitt, *General George Crook: His Autobiography* (Norman: University of Oklahoma Press, 1946).

22. Crook to Herbert Welsh, January 3, 1885, printed in *Letter from General Crook on Giving the Ballot to Indians* (Philadelphia, 1885), a leaflet distributed by the Indian Rights Association; *Report of the Indian Rights Association*, 1890, pp. 52–53.

23. Ellis, "Humanitarian Generals," pp. 169–70, 174–76; Richard N. Ellis, *General Pope and U.S. Indian Policy* (Albuquerque: University of New Mexico Press, 1970), pp. 230–42: John A. Carpenter, *Sword and Olive Branch: Oliver Otis Howard* (Pittsburgh: University of Pittsburgh Press, 1964), pp. 267–68.

MAP 8: The United States Army and the Indians—
The Plains and Mountains, 1865–1880

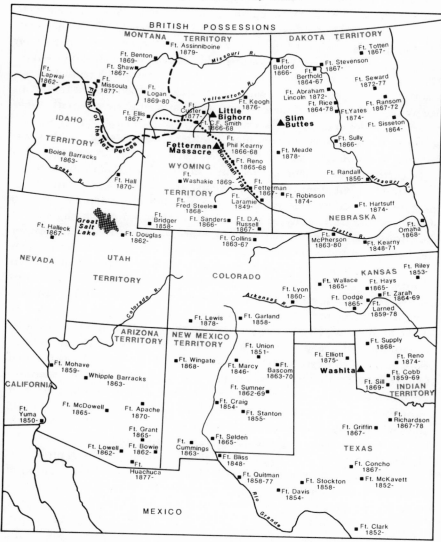

Quaker agent among the Kiowas and Comanches, Ranald Mackenzie, who fed the defeated and starving Indians, and Richard Henry Pratt, whose assignment to care for the prisoners of the Red River War started him on a lifelong career in Indian education and assimilation—add further testimony.

The work of troops in the West was more that of a police force than of a conventional army, as Commissioner Francis A. Walker had discerned: not war, but discipline. The basic unconventionality was that Indian warfare was guerilla warfare—stealth, cunning, and ambush in small parties were the rule. The Indians refused to engage in long-drawn battles and often faded away before a white force rather than engage it, and this quality won the admiration of the army. A sympathetic General Nelson A. Miles wrote: "The art of war among the white race is called strategy, or tactics; when practised by the Indians it is called treachery. They employed the art of deceiving, misleading, decoying, and surprising the enemy with great cleverness. The celerity and secrecy of their movements were never excelled by the warriors of any country. They had courage, skill, sagacity, endurance, fortitude, and self-sacrifice of a high order."[24]

To carry out its mission against such an enemy, with inadequate numbers stretched out thinly over an extensive frontier, the army built small military posts all over the West, tiny outposts housing a company or two of soldiers, as a warning to the Indians and as stations from which forays of detachments could march out when occasion demanded. As Felix Brunot told Red Cloud and other chiefs at a council at Fort Laramie in 1871, when trouble arose "the Great Father put war-houses all through the Indian country."[25] In the 1860s and 1870s the Trans-Mississippi West was dotted with scores of these forts, each established in response to some military problem or the clamor of settlers for protection.

The problem with this strategy was that the army was not large enough to man a fort at every critical spot. Yet the alternative, concentration of troops at a few strategic locations from which soldiers could be dispatched in strength to trouble spots, was impossible, both politically (because settlers wanted soldiers close at hand for protection and as a market for their produce) and practically (because the army did not have the means of rapid deployment). Even from the dispersed posts, the army usually moved only after the Indians had struck, dispersed, and disappeared. The army in the first decades after the Civil War was unable to solve its logistical problems. It was, as one officer remarked, like a chained dog, "within the length of the chain irresistible, beyond it powerless." The army's chain was its wagon train supply line.[26]

In an attempt to overcome its deficiencies, the army used surprise attacks on Indian villages, and sometimes it resorted to campaigns during

24. Nelson A. Miles, *Serving the Republic: Memoirs of the Civil and Military Life of Nelson A. Miles* (New York: Harper and Brothers, 1911), pp. 117–18.

25. CIA Report, 1871, serial 1505, p. 440. The locations of the regular army posts are indicated in Francis Paul Prucha, *A Guide to the Military Posts of the United States, 1789–1895* (Madison: State Historical Society of Wisconsin, 1964).

26. G. W. Baird, "General Miles's Indian Campaigns," *Century Magazine* 42 (July 1891): 351, quoted in Utley, *Frontier Regulars*, p. 48.

the winter, when the Indians were accustomed to curtail their operations and were often ill-prepared to beat back an attacker. Such tactics were "total war," for the women and children were nearly always intermingled with the fighting men and often took part in the fighting. The inability to distinguish between combatants and noncombatants raised questions that greatly disturbed the humanitarians and many military leaders as well. Another tactic was to employ Indians against other Indians, a common occurrence in all the Indian wars. Tribal rivalries and enmity made it possible to use Crows and Pawnees, for example, against the Sioux. General Crook in Arizona used scouts from the same tribe he was fighting.

Military leaders, unable to set aside planning and organization of the army for future possible wars with conventional enemies, stumbled along in their campaigns against their unconventional Indian foes, whom they were trying more to control than to destroy. The punishment they meted out often fell on the innocent as well as on the guilty, for the two were difficult to distinguish, and this destruction blackened the record of the army. Yet neither in theory nor in fact was the result extermination or genocide. It is impossible to establish an accurate record of Indian deaths in the post-Civil War Indian wars, but the casualties on both sides from armed conflict were in total small.[27] The tragedy was in the destruction of the Indians' traditional way of life, which was the conscious goal of both military and civilian officials.

THE TRANSFER ISSUE

Military actions against hostile Indians led to renewed agitation for transferring the Indian Office to the War Department.[28] This was a serious challenge to civilian control of Indian affairs, for the proposals did not envisage

27. Don Russell, "How Many Indians Were Killed?" *American West* 10 (July 1973): 42–47, 61–63. Russell concludes: "Weighing all factors, it seems improbable that more than 3,000 Indians were killed in all the U.S. Army's fights. Even if all the wildest claims be taken at face value, the total would not exceed 6,000. That is by no means the 'policy of exterminating Indians, tribe by tribe' alleged by those entirely ignorant of Indian warfare. Remember, too, that these small figures are to be compared, not with the number of Indians existing at any one time, whether 700,000 in 1492 or 250,000 in 1890, but rather with the total number of Indians who lived during the entire century" (p. 47).

28. Loring B. Priest, *Uncle Sam's Stepchildren: The Reformation of United States Indian Policy, 1865–1887* (New Brunswick: Rutgers University Press, 1942), pp. 15–27, treats the transfer issue with special emphasis on congressional action and public opinion. A brief survey article is Donald J. D'Elia, "The Argument over Civilian or Military Indian Control, 1865–1880," *Historian* 24 (February 1962): 207–25. A discussion of the issue in the early postwar years, with special emphasis on Kansas, is in Marvin H. Garfield, "The Indian Question in Congress and in Kansas," *Kansas Historical Quarterly* 2 (February 1933): 29–44.

a simple return to conditions that existed before the creation of the Department of the Interior in 1849. The earlier period had hardly been a period of *military* control; the Indian Office had been a civilian enterprise under the direction of a civilian commissioner of Indian affairs, with civilian superintendents (often ex officio the governors of the territories) and civilian agents and other agency personnel. Only on relatively rare occasions had army officers filled the posts of Indian agents, and conflicts between the two services, although both were under the single jurisdiction of the secretary of war, had frequently occurred.[29] Persons in the 1860s and 1870s who knew the history of the Indian service did not advocate a simple transfer of the bureau from one department to another with little change in outlook, activities, or character of personnel. They proposed putting the Indians into the hands of army men on active military duty. A complete transfer was urged, and General Sherman provided a description of the plan:

> Each military post has its quartermaster and commissary, who can, without additional cost, make the issues directly to the Indians, and account for them; and the commanding officer can exercise all the supervision now required of the civil agent, in a better manner, because he has soldiers to support his authority, and can easily anticipate and prevent the minor causes which have so often resulted in Indian wars. In like manner, our country is divided into military departments and divisions, commanded by experienced general officers named by the President, who can fulfill all the functions now committed to Indian superintendents; and these, too, have near them inspectors who can promptly investigate and prevent the incipient steps that are so apt to result in conflict and war.[30]

General Grant himself had casually recommended such a change in 1866, and when he became president, he had followed his convictions by appointing army officers to most of the Indian agencies. This seemed so reasonable to him that he did little theorizing about the matter. As humanitarian activity increased, however, the arguments for military control had to be expounded more explicitly. The military men and their supporters asserted that the proposals of the Indian reformers could not be carried

29. Francis Paul Prucha, *Broadax and Bayonet: The Role of the United States Army in the Development of the Northwest, 1815–1860* (Madison: State Historical Society of Wisconsin, 1953), pp. 93–95.

30. Sherman to W. A. J. Sparks, January 19, 1876, *House Report* no. 354, 44–1, serial 1709, p. 9. It should be noted that in the face of criticism against military control, Sherman later suggested that the War Department could employ civilian agents for the peaceful tribes and use military ones only for warlike tribes. Sherman to Alvin Saunders, November 27, 1878, *Senate Miscellaneous Document* no. 53, 45–3, serial 1835, p. 220.

out by mere moral suasion. Sherman, reviewing the work of the Peace Commission in assigning the Indians to reservations, wrote: "To labor with their own hands, or even to remain in one place, militates with all the hereditary pride of the Indian, and *force* must be used to accomplish the result." The War Department, he argued, was the only branch of the government that could act with the promptness and vigor necessary to carry out the plans and purpose of the commission. Nor could he abide a divided command. He wrote his brother John in the summer of 1868 that he would have to spend the rest of his days on the Indian frontier "unless the Indians are wholly taken charge of by the War or Interior Dept."[31]

Secretary of War J. M. Schofield similarly argued that it was inefficient and uneconomical to split the responsibility for Indian affairs between two departments. If the Interior Department could manage the Indians by itself, all right; but if the army was needed to protect the railroads and settlements, why not let the army officers act as Indian agents and save the expense of employing civilians. The army officers, moreover, with their military reputation and commissions at stake, could be depended upon for an honest administration of Indian affairs.[32]

As the peace policy progressed and the Indian agencies were handed over to representatives of the religious denominations, the opponents of civilian control found a rich field for criticism. Each failure of the peace policy, each act of Indian hostility, could be used to show that the humanitarians from the East, who had little contact with the wild Indians of the West, were unfit to formulate and carry out a practical Indian policy. Instances of failure by peaceful methods were taken to be automatic proof that Indian affairs belonged in the hands of the military.

Strong support of the army came from the West, where frontier governors, legislators, and newspaper editors called for aggressive military action against the Indians.[33] Nor did transfer lack support in the East. After the Fetterman disaster the *Nation* recommended transfer as the "primal remedy for our evils." Lamenting the *divisum imperium* that marked Indian management, it supported Sherman's stand of sole military control.

31. Report of Sherman, November 1, 1868, *House Executive Document* no. 1, 40–3, serial 1367, pp. 5–6; Sherman to John Sherman, July 30, 1868, William T. Sherman Papers, Library of Congress.

32. Report of Schofield, November 20, 1868, *House Executive Document* no. 1, 40–3, serial 1367, pp. xvii–xviii.

33. Garfield, "The Indian Question," pp. 29–37, 44. Memorials to Congress from the Kansas legislature in 1869 and 1874 urging transfer are in *Senate Miscellaneous Document* no. 29, 40–3, serial 1361, and *Senate Miscellaneous Document* no. 75, 43–1, serial 1584. Similar memorials from the California legislature in 1876 and 1878 are in *House Miscellaneous Document* no. 92, 44–1, serial 1701, and *House Miscellaneous Document* no. 19, 45–2, serial 1815.

What could the troops do if they had sole responsibility, the editor asked. "The answer is," he declared, "the troops could *corral* the Indians; they could keep them away from the emigrant routes; could establish a healthful state of non-intercourse; could remove the temptations to plunder by forcing the Indians away from certain prescribed regions. In this way they would effectually police the 'short route' to Montana and the Pacific."[34]

The Protestant churches were strongly committed to the Interior Department and its civilian peace program and universally opposed transfer, but the Catholic position was mixed. Catholic missionaries, squeezed out of some reservations by the allotment of agencies under Grant's peace policy, hoped that army control might give them a free hand to operate where they chose. Felix Brunot asserted that all denominations opposed transfer "except the Roman Catholics," and Indian Commissioner E. A. Hayt, in a personal letter to the secretary of the Baptist Home Missionary Society in 1878, remarked, "If the transfer to the Army takes place, which seems extremely probable, the Catholics boast that they will then be allowed to go to every agency in the United States, and I think their boast is not an empty one." The Bureau of Catholic Indian Missions, it is true, aligned itself with the Indian Office in opposing transfer, but strong Catholic voices called for a return of the Indian service to the War Department.[35]

There was continuing support for transfer in the House of Representatives, and Congress considered the issue for more than a decade. Debate first arose at the end of January 1867, when a bill for transfer passed the House by a narrow margin. Although western senators urged the need of force to manage Indian affairs, the Senate defeated the bill. The report of the Peace Commission against transfer, signed as it was by Generals Sherman, Augur, and Terry, dampened the agitation for the measure, but when the commission reversed its decision the way was cleared for a new attempt, and on December 8, 1868, a new transfer bill, introduced by Representative James Garfield, passed the House by a substantial margin. The Senate again refused to conform, despite attempts made in February 1869 to add an amendment to the Indian appropriation bill that would provide for transfer. Then, the inauguration of Grant's peace policy made any strong movement toward military control out of the question for the time being. Military actions like that of Major Baker against the Piegans in

34. *Nation* 4 (January 17, 1867): 52. But note that the journal had modified its position by 1879; see ibid. 28 (January 2, 1869): 7–8.

35. Charles Lewis Slattery, *Felix Reville Brunot, 1820–1898* (New York: Longmans Green, 1901), pp. 229–30; Hayt to S. S. Cutting, June 3, 1878, Records of the Office of the Commissioner of Indian Affairs, vol. 1878, p. 113, National Archives, Record Group 75; Peter James Rahill, *The Catholic Indian Missions and Grant's Peace Policy, 1870–1884* (Washington: Catholic University of America Press, 1953), pp. 120–21, 160, 204–5. See also *Council Fire* 1 (July 1878): 98.

January 1870 were made the most of by critics of the army's handling of Indian affairs and no doubt had an important effect upon the outcome of the issue. The increased incidence of Indian hostilities in the 1870s, however, kept the issue alive, and political considerations in the election year of 1876 again made the transfer measure an important one, even before the Custer massacre added new fuel. On April 21, 1876, the House passed a new measure, but the bill failed once again in the Senate, which continued to side with the civilian reformers.[36]

The failure of Congress to pass a transfer measure, despite incessant agitation on the part of military supporters, was due to the desperate struggle to maintain civilian control—and with it the peace policy—that came from the humanitarian Christian reformers. The peace policy had been launched in fear of military control of Indian affairs and developed in an atmosphere of constant threat that army dominance would be reasserted. Such insecurity kept the reformers alert to the least wind blowing in the direction of army control; their outbursts against the army made the arguments of the advocates of transfer seem moderate and mild-mannered by comparison.

At first everything seemed promising. The Joint Special Committee on the Condition of the Indian Tribes in its report of 1867, after weighing carefully the arguments for and against the transfer of the Indian Office, concluded unanimously that Indian affairs should remain in the Department of the Interior. The Peace Commission, likewise, after a careful analysis of conditions in the West, decided against transfer in its initial report of January 7, 1868. "If we intend to have war with them [the Indians] the bureau should go to the Secretary of war," it declared. "If we intend to have peace it should be in the civil department." The commission felt that the chief tasks of the Indian Office were to educate and instruct the Indians in peaceful acts. "The military arm of the government," it flatly asserted, "is not the most admirably adapted to the discharge of duties of this character." Not one army man in a thousand, the commissioners thought, would like to teach Indian children to read and write or Indian men to farm.[37] But renewal of war in the West that summer led to reversal of the commission's stand in its meeting at Chicago in October.

36. *Congressional Globe*, 39th Congress, 2d session, pp. 891–98, 1712–20; ibid., 40th Congress, 3d session, pp. 17–21, 39–43, 880–83, 1376–78; *Congressional Record*, 4: 2657–74, 2682–86, 3962–65; *House Report* no. 240, 44–1, serial 1708; *House Report* no. 354, 44–1, serial 1709. There is extensive and valuable testimony from both sides about the army and the Indians and specifically the transfer issue in *House Report* no. 384, 43–1, serial 1624.

37. *Condition of the Indian Tribes: Report of the Special Joint Committee* (Washington: GPO, 1867), pp. 6–7; "Report of the Indian Peace Commissioners," January 7, 1868, *House Executive Document* no. 97, 40–2, serial 1337, pp. 20–21.

To counteract this change of mind on the part of such a distinguished group, which would threaten the hopeful goals of the reformers, Commissioner of Indian Affairs Taylor, who as president of the Peace Commission had refused to vote for transfer when the commission as a whole reversed its position, issued a powerful report. His eleven-point indictment of military control of Indian matters, issued as part of his annual report on November 23, 1868, exhausted the arguments of the civilian reformers. This comprehensive and forceful statement was a manifesto to which later militants could add little. Like many other reformers, however, Taylor was abler in pointing out the evils he considered inherent in military control than in offering convincing proof that civilian control could furnish the answer to the Indian problem. In a strange mixture of reformers' rhetoric, evangelical preaching against evil, and innuendoes about the motives of the military men, he set forth his arguments. That the intemperance of his language and the absurdity of some of his charges might weaken his position seems not to have crossed his mind.

Taylor argued that transfer would mean the maintenance of a large standing army in peacetime, an expensive undertaking and one contrary to the republican principles of the nation. Previous military management of the Indians, he charged, had been a failure and must "in the very nature of things, always prove a failure," for soldiers were trained for war and were not competent to teach the arts of civilization. "Will you send professional soldiers, sword in one hand, musket in the other, and tactics on the brain," he asked, "to teach the wards of the nation agriculture, the mechanic arts, theology and peace? You would civilize the Indian! Will you send him the sword? You would inspire him with the peaceful principles of Christianity! Is the bayonet their symbol? You would invite him to the sanctuary! Will you herald his approach with the clangor of arms and the thunder of artillery?" Taylor, like most of the reformers, had an obsessive fear of the demoralizing influences and diseases that came to Indians who associated with the soldiers at military posts. "If you wish to exterminate the race," he wrote in one flight of rhetoric, "pursue them with ball and blade; if you please, massacre them wholesale, as we sometimes have done; or, to make it cheap, call them to a peaceful feast, and feed them on beef salted with wolf bane; but for humanity's sake, save them from the lingering syphilitic poisons, so sure to be contracted about military posts." As for the reversal of opinion in the Peace Commission, Taylor charged that to the military men's desire for more power.[38]

Grant's acceptance of the peace policy presented to him by the religion-minded reformers for a time quieted the fears of military dominance, and the early agreements about dividing authority over the reservation and the

38. CIA Report, 1868, serial 1366, pp. 467–75.

hostile nonreservation Indians brought a temporary truce. But the rise in hostilities in the West and the consequent attacks on the peace policy brought renewed defense from the anti-military party. In order to gain information from the reservations in support of its own position, the Board of Indian Commissioners on August 1, 1875, sent a circular letter to each agent, asking whether military forces were stationed at or near the agency, what the troops were used for, and how the Indians reacted to the military presence. The agent was to report his own judgment on the influence of the troops "in respect to morality, good order, and progress in civilization" and to furnish other information "bearing upon the wisdom of increasing or diminishing the use of the Army in the management of Indian affairs." In a related question, the agents were asked about the use of Indian police and whether they might replace military forces. The replies substantiated the anti-military leanings of the board. Nearly all the agents who had had experience with troops near the reservations reported that the Indians viewed the troops with dislike and apprehension and that the effect of the common soldiers upon the moral condition of the Indian was universally bad.[39]

The board could thus report its views with confidence. The work now, it insisted, was to educate and civilize the Indians, not to subdue them, and this was eminently civilian, not military work. Charging that the men who enlisted in the army during times of peace were "among the most vicious of our population," the board asserted that when a military post and an agency were close together bad results were certain to follow. Moreover, the army acted arbitrarily and with the use of force, which in itself led to more Indian hostilities. So, the members righteously concluded: "We cannot see any benefit whatever that is likely, or even possible, to result from relegating the care of the Indians to the Army. The Army is admirable in its place, but its function is not that of civil government in a republic like ours."[40]

Commissioner of Indian Affairs Edward P. Smith backed the board. In a long discussion of the whole transfer issue, he argued that the Peace Commission had voted against transfer in 1868 and that conditions in 1875 called for it even less. He noted that at five-sixths of the agencies no soldiers were needed, and at half of the remainder troops were required only to assist the agent in arresting turbulent men. "So far, then, as eleven-twelfths of the Indian agencies are concerned," he concluded, "the question of putting them under the control of the War Department has no more pertinency than that of putting the almshouse and city schools under the metropolitan police." Rather, the very process of civilization was hindered

39. *Report of the Board of Indian Commissioners*, 1875, pp. 64–103.
40. Ibid., pp. 14–15.

by the presence of the soldiers. "The first lesson to be given the Indian is that of self-support by labor with his own hands—the last lesson which a man in uniform teaches," he said. And he added the usual little piece on "the inevitable demoralization of intemperance and lewdness" which the soldiers brought to Indian reservations. But Smith was more than willing that the onerous task of supplying the Indian agencies be taken over by the army.[41]

A few reformers faltered. William Welsh, who had taken such an active part in initiating the peace policy, finally despaired of ridding the Indian service of graft and came out for army control, but he was almost alone, and his defection brought other men back into the fray. Felix Brunot, then no longer on the Board of Indian Commissioners, published an open letter, dated May 22, 1876, to his former colleague on the board, William E. Dodge, that was a new testimonial to the anti-military policy. He pointed once more to the good effects of the peace policy and counted up the acres plowed, the cattle raised, and the Indian children in school. And he ridiculed the idea that military control would mean economy, one of the chief arguments of the army men. Most of the agencies were not even near a military post; and he asked whether it was intended to move the Indians to the forts or the forts to the reservations. "If it is merely proposed to detach army officers from the posts to perform the duties of agents," he added, "I reply that any one acquainted with the nature of those duties must be aware that the agent can have time for nothing else, and if there are enough superfluous officers of a proper rank who can be spared from the posts to perform them, the army needs to be reduced." Bishop Whipple wrote to thank Brunot for his stand: "I think your manly letter at the time Mr. Welsh was disposed to turn our Indians over to the army prevented it."[42]

The crisis that came with Custer's defeat brought the reformers back into the fight. The Board of Indian Commissioners made a great stir about the question of economy in its report of 1877, providing comparative figures to show that costs had been greater under the War Department than under the Interior Department. But it did not want such practical issues to crowd out the main issue. "In all our dealings with the Indians, in all our legislation for them," it declared, "their civilization and ultimate citizenship should be the one purpose steadily pursued. That is the only aim worthy of us as a great Christian nation. And the attainment of this end will hardly be possible by military means." In the following year, the board repeated once again all the old arguments, emphasizing now, however, that the Indians themselves were opposed to transfer to military control. The Five Civilized Tribes publicly denounced the proposed transfer. The dele-

41. CIA Report, 1875, serial 1680, pp. 520–23.
42. Slattery, *Brunot*, pp. 233, 236–37.

gates of these nations in the capital met on February 12, 1878, to oppose a new transfer bill and addressed a long memorial to Congress in which they praised the peace policy inaugurated under Grant and echoed the reformers' pleas for keeping the Indians out of the hands of the military. "Do you desire to save from further destruction your Indian population?" they asked Congress. "Is it your purpose to civilize and christianize them, so as to prepare them eventually for citizenship? Then in the name of civilization, christianity, and humanity, we earnestly ask you to make no change in the present general management unless it be to create an independent Indian department."[43]

In this campaign the opponents of transfer had the support of the *Council Fire*. Alfred B. Meacham was particularly aggressive, and he wrote in May 1878:

> What means the clamor for a transfer of the Indian to the War Department?
>
> It means to make business for the War Department. No well-informed man will assert that it is for *the good of the Indian*. Everybody knows better. Those who clamor for change give as a reason that by so doing we will get rid of the Indian rings. This is all bosh. The Indian rings are no worse than the army rings.... If West Point is the only institution which graduates honest men then our Christian civilization is a lie. It is an insult to our peace-loving people to intimate that military men are superior to civilians in business integrity.

For the defeat of transfer—"that unwise and barbarous measure"—the journal took much of the credit. Former Commissioner of Indian Affairs George W. Manypenny also entered the lists, although a bit late to affect the outcome of the contest, with a detailed recital of military inhumanity to the Indians in a book called *Our Indian Wards*.[44]

The opposing sides were careful to seek supporting evidence from their friends. The Board of Indian Commissioners sent its questionnaire of 1875 to the civilian agents who were part of the Interior Department structure

43. *Report of the Board of Indian Commissioners*, 1877, pp. 5–6; ibid., 1878, pp. 9–16; *The Indians Opposed to the Transfer Bill: United Action of the Delegations of the Cherokee, Creek, Seminole, Chickasaw, and Choctaw Nations in Opposition to the Measure: They Protest against It, and Give Their Reasons for So Doing* (Washington: Gibson Brothers, 1878), p. 10.

44. *Council Fire* 1 (May 1878): 66; 6 (March 1883): 38–39; 6 (October 1883): 139–40. Manypenny wrote: "It is submitted that the facts given ought to silence, now and hereafter, the clamor in which military officers have indulged against the civil administration of Indian affairs, and forever dispose of the question of the restoration of the Indian bureau to the war department—a theme on which these officers (with but few exceptions) have indulged, with an assurance amounting to audacity." *Our Indian Wards* (Cincinnati: Robert Clarke and Company, 1880), p. xxv; see also pp. 373–94.

and who would have been eliminated under the army's proposals. No wonder the respondents were almost unanimous in asserting that what was needed was civilian effort to educate and civilize the Indians. The House Committee on Military Affairs in 1876, on the other hand, seeking advice on the expediency of transferring the Indian service to military control, sent its questionnaire to sixty high-ranking army officers, all but two of whom recommended the transfer as a measure of "expediency, wisdom, and economy." Not until 1878 was there an attempt by an investigating group to get both sides of the story, and then the report was a four-to-four split.[45]

When the campaign for transfer was renewed in Congress in 1878, the Senate succeeded once more in stopping a transfer amendment added to the Indian appropriation bill. A joint committee appointed to investigate the subject, after exhaustive testimony that repeated endlessly all the old arguments on both sides, could not overcome its partisan differences and submitted two reports—the Democrats urging transfer and the Republicans opposing it. By that time the issue had lost much of its urgency, and later congressional action was half-hearted and indecisive.[46]

Much of the credit for the victory against transfer belongs to Carl Schurz, whose reform of the Indian Office weakened one of the main lines of attack by military men against Interior Department control. Schurz publicly stood up to the generals who criticized civilian administrators. On the other side, in 1876, just at a crucial point when military advocates seemed to be winning, the impeachment of Secretary of War William Belknap for malfeasance in office and his subsequent resignation gave the opponents of War Department control a new argument. Did the nation, they asked, want Indian affairs turned over to such a corrupt office? One representative spoke of the spectacle of the "House marching to the Senate for the impeachment of the head of that Department, a Department all bad and worse with every revelation, and at the same time giving it new privileges and powers and fresh responsibilities."[47]

In all events, the humanitarians had won. The Board of Indian Commissioners rejoiced in 1879 that the "general sentiment of the country sustained our views and Congress refused to endorse a measure so fraught with evil and so subversive of the good results of the last ten years of hu-

45. *Report of the Board of Indian Commissioners*, 1875, p. 64; *House Report* no. 354, 44–1, serial 1709, pp. 4–5; *Senate Report* no. 693, 45–3, serial 1837.

46. *Congressional Record*, 7: 3876–77, 4192–4200, 4234–39, 4685–86; *House Report* no. 241, 45–2, serial 1822; *Senate Miscellaneous Document* no. 53, 45–3, serial 1835.

47. *Congressional Record*, 4: 2658. See the discussion of Schurz's role in Claude Moore Fuess, *Carl Schurz: Reformer* (New York: Dodd, Mead and Company, 1932), pp. 255–57, and Hans L. Trefousse, *Carl Schurz: A Biography* (Knoxville: University of Tennessee Press, 1982), pp. 242–47.

mane policy adopted by the government." Schurz, in his final report as secretary of the interior in 1880, renewed once more the arguments for civilian handling of the Indian service, but he noted how little military significance there was then in Indian affairs, and his tone indicated that he knew the fight was over.[48]

While the transfer issue was being debated, an alternative to the either-or proposition of Interior Department or War Department management of Indian affairs was also considered. A recommended solution to the disturbing conflict was that the Indian Office be elevated into an independent department on a par with Interior and War, although this was less satisfactory to military proponents than to civilian reformers. Commissioner Taylor, after his long condemnation of the threatened transfer in 1868, admitted that Indian affairs had not been much more satisfactory under the Interior Department than they had under the War Department prior to 1849. "There is too much cargo for the capacity of the vessel," he wrote, "and too much vessel and freight for the power of the machinery. We have crammed into a bureau, which under the supervisory and appellate power is a mere clerkship, all the large, complex, difficult and delicate affairs that ought to employ every function of a first-class department." The remedy was simple: launch a new Department of Indian Affairs. It was an intelligent and reasonable suggestion—one indicated by the Peace Commission in January 1868 as its own ultimate preference.[49]

The idea frequently recurred, but it made little headway. An independent department as the solution to fraud and graft in the Indian service was pushed by Felix Brunot and the original Board of Indian Commissioners in 1874, and the administration's failure to give the proposal a hearing was used as an excuse by the board for resigning en masse. The report of the joint committee in 1879 noted the proposal and recommended it because the committee viewed the Indian Office as important enough that its chief should communicate directly with the president. The committee, however, did not urge immediate legislation on the subject. Carl Schurz alluded to the idea in his final report; he was favorably inclined but not sure that it would be wise to enlarge the size of the cabinet.[50] The proposal never got the aggressive support needed to make it a reality.

The transfer issue was the greatest challenge that the peace program of

48. *Report of the Board of Indian Commissioners*, 1879, p. 8; Report of the Secretary of the Interior, 1880, *House Executive Document* no. 1, part 5, 46–3, serial 1959, pp. 16–19.

49. CIA Report, 1868, serial 1366, p. 474; "Report of the Indian Peace Commissioners," January 7, 1868, *House Executive Document* no. 97, 40–2, serial 1337, p. 21. See also S. F. Tappan to William T. Sherman, February 8, 1868, William T. Sherman Papers, Library of Congress.

50. *Senate Report* no. 693, 45–3, serial 1837, p. xix; Report of the Secretary of the Interior, 1880, *House Executive Document* no. 1, part 5, 46–3, serial 1959, p. 19.

the Christian Indian reformers had to meet. The persistent advocacy of military management of Indian affairs was an explicit denial that civilian methods, on which the peace policy depended, could succeed. The contest kept the air filled with charges and countercharges, forced the reformers to defend their policy both in theory and by practical accomplishments, and kept the public agitated over the Indian question. Scraping by with the narrowest of victories in Congress, the reformers stuck to their position until the succession of crises passed and they were able to begin anew with an aggressive humanitarian program for turning the Indians into standardized Americans.

THE END OF THE MILITARY PHASE

The military phase of Indian relations had practically ended by the early 1880s, at the same time that the church-appointed agency program of the peace policy collapsed. General Sherman, in his final report as general of the army, October 27, 1883, noted the changed situation:

> I now regard the Indians as substantially eliminated from the problem of the Army. There may be spasmodic and temporary alarms, but such Indian wars as have hitherto disturbed the public peace and tranquillity are not probable. The Army has been a large factor in producing this result, but it is not the only one. Immigration and the occupation by industrious farmers and miners of land vacated by the aborigines have been largely instrumental to that end, but the *railroad* which used to follow in the rear now goes forward with the picket-line in the great battle of civilization with barbarism, and has become the *greater* cause.[51]

Four great transcontinental lines cut across the West, and branch lines and lesser railroads crisscrossed the country that had once been the sole domain of the Indians. The logistical problems that had hampered the United States army's supply in the Trans-Mississippi West and made the mobile Indians more than an even match were solved by the railroads. The rapid extension of the lines made it possible to transport troops and supplies quickly to areas where they were needed. The increase in western settlement, moreover, made it advisable to abandon many of the small outposts. Secretary of War Robert T. Lincoln noted at the end of 1884 that "the Army has enjoyed almost complete rest from active field operations," and he remarked about the "unprecedented quiet among the Indians."[52]

51. *House Executive Document* no. 1, 48–1, serial 2182, pp. 45–46.
52. Report of the Secretary of War, 1884, *House Executive Document* no. 1, part 2, 48–2, serial 2277, p. 5.

The railroads, so emphasized by Sherman, had another effect. They speeded the destruction of the buffalo on the plains and thereby destroyed the Indians' independence and ability to wage war. At the end of the Civil War, great herds of buffalo blackened the landscape. By the mid-1870s the buffalo were largely gone in Kansas, and after 1883, the year of the last large kill, nearly all the herds vanished. New tanning methods and cheap transportation increased the market for buffalo hides, and hunters with their high-powered rifles covered the plains, slaughtering the huge beasts by the thousands and often leaving the flesh to rot and the bones to whiten on the plains.[53] The slaughter was applauded by both the civilian and the military officers of the government concerned with the Indians, for the disappearance of the Indians' means of subsistence would force them into the dependent condition that was to be the first step toward their transformation into hard-working, self-supporting farmers. Secretary of the Interior Delano wrote as early as 1874: "The buffalo are disappearing rapidly, but not faster than I desire. I regard the destruction of such game . . . as facilitating the policy of the Government, of destroying their hunting habits, coercing them on reservations, and compelling them to begin to adopt the habits of civilization." In the same year General Sheridan suggested that the Texas legislature award medals to the buffalo hunters in gratitude. "These men have done more in the last two years, and will do more in the next year, to settle the vexed Indian question," he said, "than the entire regular army has done in the last thirty years. They are destroying the Indian's commissary."[54] The end of the buffalo meant the end of the life that the plains Indians had known and was a fundamental condition for establishing the reservation system for the once-nomadic Indians.

53. The buffalo have been thoroughly treated in general studies that all include material on their destruction and the effect it had on the Indians. See, for example, Francis Haines, *The Buffalo* (New York: Thomas Y. Crowell Company, 1970); Thom McHugh, *The Time of the Buffalo* (New York: Alfred A. Knopf, 1972); David A. Dary, *The Buffalo Book: The Full Saga of the American Animal* (Chicago: Swallow Press, 1974). The slaughter of the buffalo is treated specifically in E. Douglas Branch, *The Hunting of the Buffalo* (New York: D. Appleton-Century Company, 1929; reprint with introduction by J. Frank Dobie, Lincoln, University of Nebraska Press, 1962), and Wayne Gard, *The Great Buffalo Hunt* (New York: Alfred A. Knopf, 1959).

54. *House Report* no. 384, 43–1, serial 1624, p. 99; Mari Sandoz, *The Buffalo Hunters: The Story of the Hide Men* (New York: Hastings House, 1954), p. 173, quoted in Utley, *Frontier Regulars*, p. 413.

CHAPTER 22

Reservation Policy

Consolidation of Reservations.

Indian Resistance to Removal.

Revision of Reservation Policy.

The post-Civil War Indian Office and the Indian reformers inherited a reservation policy that had developed gradually during the previous decades, and the concentration of Indians on reservations was the underpinning of Grant's peace policy.[1] Commissioner Ely S. Parker's question to the new Board of Indian Commissioners asking whether the Indians should be placed on reservations received a unanimous affirmative answer. The board declared in its first report:

> The policy of collecting the Indian tribes upon small reservations contiguous to each other, and within the limits of a large reservation, eventually to become a State of the Union, and of which the small reservations will probably be the counties, seems to be the best that can be devised. Many tribes may thus be collected in the present Indian territory. The larger the number that can be thus concentrated the better for the success of the plan; care being taken to separate hereditary enemies from each other. When upon the reservation they should be taught as soon as possible the advantage of individual ownership of property; and should be given land in severalty as soon

1. This chapter is taken largely from Francis Paul Prucha, *American Indian Policy in Crisis: Christian Reformers and the Indian, 1865–1900* (Norman: University of Oklahoma Press, 1976), pp. 107–31.

as it is desired by any of them, and the tribal relation should be discouraged.[2]

CONSOLIDATION OF RESERVATIONS

The views of the Board of Indian Commissioners accorded well with those of responsible men in Grant's administration. Secretary of the Interior Jacob D. Cox looked not to a new reservation policy but to "an enlarged and more enlightened application of the general principles of the old one." He saw two objects in the policy: "First, the location of the Indians upon fixed reservations, so that the pioneers and settlers may be freed from the terrors of wandering hostile tribes; and second, an earnest effort at their civilization, so that they may themselves be elevated in the scale of humanity, and our obligation to them as fellowmen be discharged." Cox, in agreement with the Board of Indian Commissioners, saw that larger concentration would obviate many of the evils that arose when small reservations were surrounded by the unscrupulous frontier whites, and he hoped that moving less advanced tribes into contact with more civilized ones would have a beneficial result. He was sanguine about the prospects of concentrating the tribes in the Indian Territory and the organization of a territorial government over them. In the north and west of the Rockies he wanted the same sort of development, although he realized that there it would take more time.[3]

With Columbus Delano, Cox's successor, consolidation of tribes in the Indian Territory became almost an obsession, and he began to play a numbers game, trying to fit all the Indians into one large reservation. He counted 172,000 Indians outside the Indian Territory, occupying 96,155,785 acres—558 acres per capita. Inside the Indian Territory he found only one person to every 630 acres. "Could the entire Indian population of the country, excluding Alaska and those scattered among the States . . . be located in the Indian Territory," he decided, "there would be 180 acres of land, *per capita*, for the entire number, showing that there is ample area of land to afford them all comfortable homes." At the same time he candidly admitted that the acres given up by the assembling tribes could be thrown open to white settlement and cultivation. He wanted the Indians to realize that if they did not cooperate in this scheme to preserve them in the consoli-

2. *Report of the Board of Indian Commissioners*, 1869, pp. 3, 9; minutes of May 26, 1869, Minutes of the Board of Indian Commissioners, vol. 1, p. 4, National Archives, Record Group 75.

3. Report of the Secretary of the Interior, 1869, *House Executive Document* no. 1, 41–2, serial 1414, pp. viii–ix.

dated reservation, they would inevitably be inundated or crushed by the rapidly growing tide of white emigration.[4]

In this work of reducing the Indians' reservations, Felix Brunot of the Board of Indian Commissioners played a large part. Negotiations with the Crows, carried on in 1873 by Brunot, which were intended to move the Indians from their reservation on the Yellowstone River in southern Montana to one in the Judith Basin and reduce their lands by four million acres, delighted the people of Montana. The territorial governor thanked Brunot for his work and attributed the success of the negotiations to "the ability and patience by which the negotiations were conducted, aided by the friendly feeling that has been brought about by the humane policy of the President towards the Indian tribes." To the disappointment of the whites, Congress failed to ratify the agreement, and the Crows stayed for the time being on their lands along the Yellowstone. But the case shows both the sincere desire of humanitarians like Brunot to reduce the Indians' land holdings and how the "friendly feeling" that was a conscious part of the peace policy worked toward the ultimate dispossession of the Indians.[5]

An even more personal involvement of Brunot in reducing the reservations came in his dealings with the Utes. Ouray, chief of the Utes, was steadfast at first in his refusal to sell any lands. When Brunot met Ouray at a council in 1872, the chief told him of the capture of his young son fifteen years before by a party of Cheyennes and Arapahos. Brunot and the secretary of the Board of Indian Commissioners, Thomas Cree, undertook to recover the long-lost son, who was found in Texas and united with his father in the office of the board in Washington. The young Indian, unfortunately, died on his way home. "But the gratitude which he [Ouray] felt toward Mr. Brunot and Mr. Cree," Brunot's biographer wrote, "did what a special commission could not do, and when Mr. Brunot told him he thought it right for him to sell a portion of his reservation, Ouray threw all his strong influence in favour of the sale, though a year before he intended opposition to the bitter end." Brunot did "what neither commissioners nor armies could accomplish"; after six days of patient negotiation on his part the Utes ceded five million acres, the southern half of their reservation in southwestern Colorado.[6]

Secretary Delano remarked in 1873 that the efforts of the Indian Office

4. Ibid., 1871, *House Executive Document* no. 1, part 5, 42–2, serial 1505, pp. 6–7; ibid., 1872, *House Executive Document* no. 1, part 5, 42–3, serial 1560, pp. 5–7.

5. Charles Lewis Slattery, *Felix Reville Brunot, 1820–1898* (New York: Longmans, Green and Company, 1901), pp. 207–13. The agreement is in Kappler, vol. 4, pp. 1142–47.

6. Slattery, *Brunot*, pp. 191–92, 214–15. The agreement of September 13, 1873, is in Kappler, vol. 1, pp. 151–52. The story of Ouray's lost son is told in Ann W. Hafen, "Efforts to Recover the Stolen Son of Chief Ouray," *Colorado Magazine* 16 (January 1939): 53–62.

had been "unremitting," and he continued to urge the Indians to exchange reservations lying within the range of advancing settlements and railroad construction for other locations. Even the Sioux in Dakota and Montana did not escape his solicitous attention. He noted the unproductive soil and the severity of the winters in those northern regions, conditions that hindered all attempts to improve the Indians' condition through agriculture and grazing. Rejecting the older idea of a northern as well as a southern reserve, he wanted to move these northern Indians en masse to the Indian Territory, where "both climate and soil are so favorable for the production of everything necessary to sustain and make them comfortable." Delano lamented the obstinacy of the Sioux, who refused to move, but he thought that time would ultimately overcome their objections.[7]

Delano's plans did not die when he was forced out of office in 1875. His successor, Zachariah Chandler, continued to urge them, although he was willing to use a reservation in Minnesota and another in the southern part of Washington Territory in addition to the Indian Territory as the new permanent homes for the scattered Indians. He also seemed less enthusiastic about what all this would do for the Indians and more concerned about saving money and trouble for the government. His report of 1876 neatly summed up the arguments:

> Briefly, the arguments are all in favor of the consolidation; expensive agencies would be abolished, the Indians themselves can be more easily watched over and controlled, evil-designing men be the better kept away from them, and illicit trade and barter in arms, ammunition, and whiskey prevented; goods could be supplied at a great saving; the military service relieved; the Indians better taught, and friendly rivalry established among them, those most civilized hastening the progress of those below them, and most of the land now occupied as reserves, reverting to the General Government, would be open to entry and sale.[8]

It might be suspected that men like Delano, whose record was none too clean, were more interested in freeing Indian lands for white exploitation than in Indian welfare, but they no doubt honestly believed that the Indians had to be moved from their present situations if they were to survive

7. Report of the Secretary of the Interior, 1873, *House Executive Document* no. 1, part 5, 43–1, serial 1601, pp. vii–viii; ibid., 1874, *House Executive Document* no. 1, part 5, 44–2, serial 1639, p. xii.

8. Ibid., 1876, *House Executive Document* no. 1, part 5, 44–2, serial 1749, p. vi. Chandler was merely repeating the arguments and proposals put forth by Commissioner of Indian Affairs John Q. Smith in his annual report, CIA Report, 1876, serial 1749, pp. 385–87. Two years later Commissioner E. A. Hayt drew up a bill to consolidate the tribes further. CIA Report, 1878, serial 1850, p. 440.

and advance. It was the almost universal opinion of the age and a doctrine that went back clearly as far as Thomas Jefferson. Views like Delano's on Indian consolidation were accepted as part of the humanitarians' package of Indian reform. "Since the inauguration of the present Indian policy," the Board of Indian Commissioners declared in 1876, "this board has not ceased to recommend the consolidation of agencies where it can be effected without infringing existing treaties. The time has now arrived when the Government must, if it would see an impulse given to the work of Indian civilization, take decided ground and prompt action upon this important subject." The board was convinced that "the public sentiment in and out of Congress will see the great advantage of this important advance movement in Indian civilization." Tribes that occupied small reservations and had made little progress, if moved to large reservations, would profit from the encouragement of their more advanced brethren and would learn by daily observation "that thrift, enterprise, and energy do always produce their legitimate fruits of civilization and self-dependence." Moreover, a system of law could be more easily introduced, early allotment of land could be provided, and tribal relations could be broken up. Such action, the board concluded, would "go far toward the successful solution of the Indian problem, which has so long perplexed our nation, puzzled our statesmen, and disturbed our philanthropists."[9]

INDIAN RESISTANCE TO REMOVAL

The theorists who elaborated schemes for consolidating all the Indians in one big reservation reckoned too little with the Indians, whom they were so willing to move around like pieces on a chessboard. The Indians were deeply attached to their homelands, and the topographical and climatic conditions were psychologically if not physically of tremendous importance to their well-being. Sioux, long acclimated to the northern plains, foresaw only misery and disaster if they had to move to the actually better lands in the Indian Territory. In the 1870s, while government officials and humanitarians were concocting fine schemes to remove the Indians to a few large reservations in order to save money and at the same time speed

9. *Report of the Board of Indian Commissioners*, 1876, pp. 4–6. The board repeated its recommendations in subsequent years. In 1878, a resolution submitted to the Senate asserted that there were 300,000 Indians on 300,000,000 acres of public land in the United States, or about 1,000 acres for each Indian, whereas whites were restricted to a 160-acre homestead for a family. The creation of four Indian reservations or territories was proposed, two west of the Rockies and two east, with the provision that Indians who cut loose from the tribe could take out homesteads where they were. *Senate Miscellaneous Document* no. 16, 45–2, serial 1785.

the civilization process, three disastrous removals propelled the issue into the public consciousness.

The most famous removal was that of the Ponca Indians from their reservation along the Missouri River to the Indian Territory. It was, in fact, the spark that ignited a new flame of concern for the rights of the Indians. The cause was just, the propaganda arising from it was spectacular, and the interest of eastern philanthropists in the Indians burned with new intensity.[10]

The Poncas, a small peaceful Siouan tribe, in 1865 had been guaranteed a reservation of 96,000 acres along the Missouri north of the Niobrara River. Three years later, however, the United States in the Fort Laramie treaty with the Sioux—without consulting the Poncas—ceded the entire Ponca reservation to the Sioux, the Poncas' traditional enemies.[11] Although the United States admitted that the transfer to the Sioux had been a mistake, the government's resolution of the problem was not to restore the lands, which might have irritated the Sioux, but to remove the Poncas to the Indian Territory. Over their objections, the Indians in 1877 were escorted south by federal troops and settled on the Quapaw reserve.

The hardships of the journey and the change in climate brought great misery and many deaths to the Poncas, and even after they had found a new and more favorable location within the Indian Territory, they remained restless and unhappy and longed to return to their old home in the north. "I am sorry to be compelled to say," Commissioner of Indian Affairs Ezra Hayt lamented, "the Poncas were wronged, and restitution should be made as far as it is in the power of the government to do so." Secretary of the Interior Schurz echoed these sentiments, but Congress paid no heed to the reports, and the Indians' condition remained precarious.[12]

One of the chiefs, Standing Bear, could endure the situation no longer. Taking along the body of his dead son, who had succumbed to malaria, and followed by a small portion of the tribe, he started out in January 1879 to return north. Reaching Nebraska early in the spring, the group settled

10. The story of Ponca removal is traced in Earl W. Hayter, "The Ponca Removal," *North Dakota Historical Quarterly* 6 (July 1932): 262–75; and Stanley Clark, "Ponca Publicity," *Mississippi Valley Historical Review* 29 (March 1943): 495–516. An account by one of the men who fought for the Poncas' rights, with reprints of important documents, is Zylyff [Thomas Henry Tibbles], *The Ponca Chiefs: An Attempt to Appeal from the Tomahawk to the Courts* (Boston, 1880; reprinted with an introduction by Kay Graber, Lincoln: University of Nebraska Press, 1972). An excellent account of the Ponca affair and the reaction of the reformers is in Robert Winston Mardock, *The Reformers and the American Indian* (Columbia: University of Missouri Press, 1971), pp. 168–91.

11. Kappler, pp. 875–76, 998.

12. Report of the Secretary of the Interior, 1877, *House Executive Document* no. 1, part 5, 45–2, serial 1800, pp. vii–viii; CIA Report, 1877, serial 1800, pp. 417–19. The quotation from Hayt is in CIA Report, 1878, serial 1850, p. 467.

down for the time being with the Omaha Indians, their longtime friends. The plight of Standing Bear and his followers had by this time become a public issue, and a group of citizens of Omaha, encouraged by General Crook, took up their case. When federal troops arrived to arrest the runaways and return them to the Indian Territory, prominent lawyers of the city drew up a writ of habeas corpus to prevent the chief's return, and on April 30 the matter was brought before Judge Elmer S. Dundy of the United States District Court. In the celebrated case of *Standing Bear* v. *Crook*, Judge Dundy ruled that "an Indian is a 'person' within the meaning of the laws of the United States, and has, therefore, the right to sue out a writ of habeas corpus in a federal court." Since he could find no authority for forcing the Poncas back to the Indian Territory, Dundy ordered their release.[13]

The Ponca affair had important repercussions on Indian reform, for a man much involved in the origins of the Standing Bear case in Omaha soon mounted a campaign in the East to stir up public support for the Poncas. He was Thomas Henry Tibbles, one of the strangest characters in the history of Indian reform. Tibbles had been a member of John Brown's band in Kansas, a guide and scout on the plains, an itinerant preacher, a Pullman car conductor, and a newspaper reporter. When the Poncas returned north, he was an assistant editor of the Omaha *Herald*. According to his own testimony, he was the prime mover in the Standing Bear case, and after the chief's release he resorted to the lecture platform to keep the Ponca issue alive. Accompanied by Standing Bear and Suzette LaFlesche, an Omaha Indian girl known as Bright Eyes, he appeared in Chicago and in several eastern cities to relate the wrongs of the Poncas, condemn the government for its actions, and appeal for support of the Indians' cause.[14]

The greatest success of Tibbles was in Boston, where a group of prominent men (including John D. Long, governor of Massachusetts, and Frederick O. Prince, mayor of Boston) organized the Boston Indian Citizenship Committee to fight for the rights of the Poncas and other Indians. The principal thrust of the group's program was to demand respect for the Indians' rights, including the return to their original reservation, and to denounce the federal government for its part in the Ponca removal. Tibbles fitted well into the program and spoke to enthusiastic audiences in Boston. Bright Eyes and Standing Bear, appearing on stage in Indian dress, added a strong personal touch to the proceedings.

The bête noire of Tibbles and the Boston reformers was Secretary of the Interior Carl Schurz, who had assumed his duties just as the actual move-

13. 25 *Federal Cases* 695–701. The quotation is at 700–701.
14. *Dictionary of American Biography,* s.v. Tibbles, Thomas Henry, by W. J. Ghent; publisher's preface in Thomas Henry Tibbles, *Buckskin and Blanket Days; Memoirs of a Friend of the Indians* (Garden City, New York: Doubleday, 1957). Autobiographical material appears in *Buckskin and Blanket Days* and in Zylyff, *Ponca Chiefs.*

ment of the Poncas to the Indian Territory got under way. In public speeches and published letters, the Boston committee and its supporters on one side and Secretary Schurz on the other engaged in acrimonious debate in which neither side adhered strictly to the facts. The atrocity stories of Tibbles and Bright Eyes were countered by Schurz's descriptions of the favorable condition of the Poncas in the Indian Territory. At a public meeting in Boston on December 3, 1880, presided over by Governor Long, Tibbles delivered an enthusiastically received diatribe against Schurz and his handling of the Ponca case, and other speeches were made by Long, Prince, Bright Eyes, and Wendell Phillips. Schurz replied to the talks in an open letter to Governor Long dated December 9, 1880, in which he urged that justice be accorded the government officials as well as the Indians; he argued that to move the Poncas back to Dakota, as the Boston group demanded, would cause new misery to the Indians and open the door to white invasions of the Indian Territory. This brought a long and denunciatory reply from Boston renewing the charges against the secretary.[15]

Schurz was also engaged in a public exchange with Helen Hunt Jackson, who had heard Tibbles and Bright Eyes in Boston in November 1879 and became a zealous convert to the cause of Indian reform. Schurz quashed an attempt to carry the Standing Bear case to the Supreme Court, and he urged Jackson and her friends, who were collecting funds for further legal action on Indian rights, to use the money for Indian education rather than pour it into the pockets of attorneys in futile cases.[16]

Still another of Schurz's opponents was Senator Henry L. Dawes of Massachusetts, with whom he tangled over the accidental killing of Standing Bear's brother, Big Snake, at the Ponca agency on October 31, 1879.[17] In a Senate inquiry into the killing, Dawes insinuated that the government had plotted the shooting of the Ponca chief; he then alluded to Schurz's German background: "It has been a relief to me, however, in examining

15. T. H. Tibbles, *Western Men Defended: Speech of Mr. T. H. Tibbles in Tremont Temple, Boston, Mass., December, 1880* (Boston: Lockwood, Brooks and Company, 1880); Schurz to Long, December 9, 1880, *Speeches, Correspondence and Political Papers of Carl Schurz*, ed. Frederic Bancroft, 6 vols. (New York: G. P. Putnam's Sons, 1913), 4: 50–78; Schurz to Edward Atkinson, November 28, 1879, ibid., 3: 481–89; *Secretary Schurz: Reply of the Boston Committee, Governor John D. Long, Chairman: Misrepresentations Corrected and Important Facts Presented* (Boston: Frank Wood, 1881).

16. The exchange of letters is printed in Helen Hunt Jackson, *A Century of Dishonor: A Sketch of the United States Government's Dealings with Some of the Indian Tribes* (New York: Harper and Brothers, 1881), pp. 359–66. Another expression of Schurz's views appears in his brief statement "The Removal of the Poncas," *Independent* 32 (January 1, 1880): 1.

17. Reports on the killing of Big Snake are printed in *Senate Executive Document* no. 14, 46–3, serial 1941. See also the testimony in *Senate Report* no. 670, 46–2, serial 1898, pp. 245–51. A useful article is J. Stanley Clark, "The Killing of Big Snake," *Chronicles of Oklahoma* 49 (Autumn 1971): 302–14.

our treatment of these weak and defenseless people, to find that these methods are not American in their origin, but bear too striking a resemblance to the modes of an imperial government carried on by espionage and arbitrary power. They are methods which I believe to be unique, and which I trust will never be naturalized."[18] In reply Schurz addressed an open letter to Dawes and gave every senator a copy on his desk as his only means of replying to Dawes's privileged congressional remarks. The letter was a devastating refutation of the senator's charges. The agitation in the Big Snake affair was, said Schurz, a new illustration of the fact that it was "difficult to exaggerate the malignant unscrupulousness of the speculator in philanthropy hunting for a sensation."[19]

The verbal combat between the reformers and the secretary of the interior did not prevent the working out of a solution to the Ponca problem, although nearly every move of the administration was subject to critical attack. A special Senate committee investigating the Ponca removal strongly condemned the government's action but split over a remedy. The majority report advocated returning the Poncas to their old home, whereas a minority report sided with Schurz in recommending that the Indians be indemnified but kept in the Indian Territory.[20] At the end of 1880 President Hayes appointed a special commission to confer with the Poncas, both those in the Indian Territory and those in Nebraska, and to recommend action. The commission, headed by General George Crook and made up of General Nelson A. Miles, William Stickney of the Board of Indian Commissioners, and William Allen of Boston, recommended that the Poncas in the Indian Territory remain there and that provision be made for those who wanted to stay in the north with Standing Bear. The decision of the commission was in accord with a declaration of wishes presented to the president by a delegation of Poncas from the Indian Territory on December 27, 1880, that indicated their desire to remain on the lands they then occupied and to relinquish all interest in their former reservation on the Missouri.[21]

18. *Congressional Record*, 11: 1958.

19. Carl Schurz, *An Open Letter in Answer to a Speech of Hon. H. L. Dawes, United States Senate, on the Case of Big Snake* (Washington, 1881). The letter, dated February 7, 1881, is printed also in *Speeches of Schurz*, 4: 91–113. The quotation is from p. 102. An account of the controversy, based in large part on the Dawes Papers in the Library of Congress, is in Loring Benson Priest, *Uncle Sam's Stepchildren: The Reformation of United States Indian Policy, 1865–1887* (New Brunswick: Rutgers University Press, 1942), pp. 78–79. Schurz's biographer, Claude Moore Fuess, in *Carl Schurz: Reformer* (New York: Dodd, Mead and Company, 1932), pp. 252–77, believes that Schurz was completely vindicated in his conflicts with the humanitarian reformers.

20. *Senate Report* no. 670, 46–2, serial 1898.

21. The commission's report and a copy of its proceedings are in *Senate Executive Document* no. 30, 46–3, serial 1941. Included is a minority report submitted by Allen,

Hayes recommended that immediate action be taken in line with the Crook commission report and the Ponca request. At last Congress acted; on March 3 it appropriated $165,000 to enable the secretary of the interior "to indemnify the Ponca tribe of Indians for losses sustained by them in consequence of their removal to the Indian Territory, to secure to them land in severalty on either the old or new reservation, in accordance with their wishes, and to settle all matters of difference with these Indians." All that remained was to gain Sioux approval for the Poncas of Standing Bear's party to remain in the north, and this was accomplished by a special agreement drawn up with a Sioux delegation in Washington in August 1881.[22]

The controversy over the Poncas between Schurz and the reformers, although it kept the country much alive to Indian problems, was unfortunate, for it obscured the fundamental agreement of both sides in their desire to promote justice for the Indians. In large part, no doubt, the attacks on Schurz by the evangelical reformers reflected the fundamental differences of the two parties. Schurz was a severely practical and unsentimental man. His program was one of "policy," not of religious motivation. A man more different in background and outlook from the general run of Indian reformers can hardly be imagined, yet Schurz's Indian policy—attack upon corruption and inefficiency in the Indian Office, support of civilian as opposed to military control of Indian affairs, allotment of land in severalty and sale of "surplus" lands, and an aggressive educational program for Indians—were all in line with what the friends of the Indian came to espouse so ardently later in the 1880s.

Senator Dawes, for his part, learned the danger of opposing the administration. After Schurz left office, Dawes wrote concerning the new secretary of the interior, Samuel J. Kirkwood, who had defended Schurz's position on the Poncas: "Of course we widely differ from him but an open conflict with this new administration, as with the last, on the Indian policy, must be avoided if possible, or we shall be very much disabled. . . . Let us, Boston and all, try to pull with Washington, but to be sure and pull the hardest!"[23] The reform groups learned, too, to base their arguments on sound information and not to be carried away, as they had been in the first flush of their reform enthusiasm, by such exaggerated tales as those told by Tibbles and Bright Eyes.[24]

---

who was unwilling to believe that the Indians had genuinely decided to stay in the Indian Territory.

22. Hayes letter of February 1, 1881, *Senate Executive Document* no. 30, 46–3, serial 1941, pp. 1–4; 21 *United States Statutes* 422; agreement with Sioux, *House Executive Document* no. 1, 47–1, serial 2018, pp. 39–40.

23. Dawes to Allen, August 11, 1881, Dawes Papers, quoted in Priest, *Uncle Sam's Stepchildren*, p. 79.

24. Tibbles, whose first wife died in 1879, married Bright Eyes in 1881.

Another celebrated case that illustrated the weakness of the consolidation policy was the flight of a band of Northern Cheyennes from the Indian Territory in 1878.[25] Following military action on the northern plains after Custer's defeat, a party of these Indians had been placed on the reservation of the Southern Cheyennes and Arapahos near Fort Reno. The Indians suffered greatly in their new home, and the subsistence supplied by the government was inadequate. On September 9, 1878, about three hundred of them led by chiefs Dull Knife and Little Wolf fled the reservation and headed north to join their friends the Sioux. When troops of the United States army were sent to stop the Indians and return them to the Indian Territory, the flight became a running fight, and the Cheyennes killed a number of settlers in their passage through Kansas.

When the Indians reached the Platte, they separated into two groups. One of them under Dull Knife moved westward toward Fort Robinson; the party surrendered on October 23 and was imprisoned at the fort. The post commandant received orders to transport the Indians back to the Indian Territory, but they steadfastly refused to go, and the officer attempted to freeze and starve them into submission. Able to endure the torture no longer and frightened by the seizure of one of their leaders, the Indians broke out of their quarters on the night of January 9. Weakened by the ordeal of their imprisonment, they were easy prey for the soldiers who pursued them, and fifty or sixty men, women, and children were killed in flight. Some were captured and returned to the south, while Dull Knife and others escaped to the Sioux. The other group, led by Little Wolf, had continued north, hoping to reach Montana. They were induced to surrender on March 25, 1879, and were taken to Fort Keogh, where they were allowed to remain.

Commissioner Hayt blamed the affair upon unwarranted dissatisfaction on the part of the Indians and asserted that Dull Knife's band contained "the vilest and most dangerous element of their tribe." With elaborate statistics he attempted to prove that the Indians had not been maltreated or underfed in the Indian Territory.[26] But other evidence soon became available. A select committee of the Senate appointed to investigate the case

25. A full account of the event is given in George Bird Grinnell, *The Fighting Cheyennes* (New York: Charles Scribner's Sons, 1915), chapters 19–20. Mari Sandoz, *Cheyenne Autumn* (New York: McGraw-Hill Book Company, 1953), tells the story of the Indians in dramatic style. See also Verne Dusenberry, "The Northern Cheyenne," *Montana Magazine of History* 5 (Winter 1955): 23–40.

26. CIA Report, 1878, serial 1850, pp. 455–57. Hayt's views were supported by Secretary Schurz in Report of the Secretary of the Interior, *House Executive Document* no. 1, part 5, 45–3, serial 1850, pp. vii–ix. See also CIA Report, 1879, serial 1910, pp. 80–82, and a letter of T. J. Morgan, April 23, 1890, *Senate Executive Document* no. 121, 51–1, serial 2686, pp. 2–9.

returned a critical report in June 1880 based on abundant testimony taken at Fort Reno and on interviews with Indians imprisoned in Kansas. Its findings sharply contradicted Hayt's report and described the government's lack of compliance with treaty agreements and the disastrous conditions that resulted from the shortage of supplies. "It is impossible to say," the committee reported, "that these were or were not the causes that led three hundred Indians in a body to escape from the Territory and to return to Dakota. They were doubtless provoking causes to that hegira, but the Indians were also strongly impelled by a longing desire to return to their native country, and by a feeling of disgust towards their new location." The committee noted, too, that the band had left the reservation not as a marauding party but simply with the intention of escaping to their former homes, and that they had begun to fight only when attacked by the army. The handling of Dull Knife's band at Fort Robinson was severely condemned.[27]

The committee's conclusion was decisive: there was no hope of civilizing Indians and making them self-supporting in a location where they were discontented. Unless they were living in a place they could look upon as home, it was unlikely that they would ever gain the independence of feeling that would lead them to work for their own living. "If they are compelled to accept a prison as a home," the report said, "they will naturally prefer to compel the keepers to feed and clothe them. They will remain pensioners upon our humanity, having lost all pride of character and all care of anything except to live." Moreover, the concentration of Indians in large numbers in one place was out of line with the changing relations between the government and the Indians. "They are already surrounded and separated into limited districts by the intervening white settlements," the senators noted, "and the time is near at hand when they must become members of the same communities with the white people."[28]

Ironically, at the very time Dull Knife and Little Wolf were fleeing north, another band of Northern Cheyennes led by Little Chief was moving south into the Indian Territory from western Nebraska. This group, too, was severely dissatisfied with its new surroundings and in the summer of 1879 sent a delegation to Washington to beg permission to join their tribesmen at Fort Keogh. Although Commissioner Hayt reported that the delegation was induced to return cheerfully to the Indian Territory, the case was by no means closed. In 1881, after continued petitioning, Little Chief's band was transferred to the Sioux reservation at Pine Ridge, and in

27. *Senate Report* no. 708, 46–2, serial 1899, pp. xvi–xviii. The failure of the attempt to force the Cheyennes into white agricultural patterns is studied in Ramon Powers, "Why the Northern Cheyenne Left Indian Territory in 1878: A Cultural Analysis," *Kansas Quarterly* 3 (Fall 1971): 72–81.
28. *Senate Report* no. 708, 46–2, serial 1899, p. xxi.

1883, under congressional authorization, the Northern Cheyennes still in the Indian Territory were allowed to follow.[29]

The Sioux reservation in Dakota did not completely satisfy the Cheyennes, however, and little by little they drifted west into Montana to join their brethren, for whom a reservation, eventually extended to the Tongue River, had been established by executive order on November 26, 1884. No attempts were made to restrain this voluntary migration of the Indians. Captain J. M. Bell, acting agent at Pine Ridge, urged in 1886 that the departing Cheyennes be brought back by force or imprisoned when they arrived at Fort Keogh. "Until measures of this kind are adopted," he reasoned, "they will continue roaming from place to place, and will accomplish nothing in the way of civilization." But Commissioner of Indian Affairs Hiram Price demurred, and Secretary of the Interior L. Q. C. Lamar declared: "These straying Indians, a restless element at their old agencies, appear to be satisfied in their new location, and it is not deemed advisable to force them to return to the Sioux Reservation."[30] This was a clear admission of the failure of the concentration policy.

Still another example of the impossibility of forcing northern Indians into the Indian Territory was the case of Chief Joseph's band of Nez Perces. When these Indians surrendered to General Miles in northern Montana in October 1877, Miles had promised that they could return to Idaho in the spring to settle down peacefully on the reservation. General Sherman overruled this humane decision. Declaring that the Indians were prisoners of war and that they "should never again be allowed to return to Oregon or to Lapwai," Sherman directed that the Nez Perces be imprisoned at Fort Leavenworth until they could be turned over to the Indian Office for disposition.[31] Transported down the Yellowstone and the Missouri to Fort Leavenworth, the miserable Indians were encamped in unhealthy lowlands along the river, where, ill provided for and pining for the clear mountain streams of their homeland, they succumbed to sickness, and many died.

29. The story of Little Chief and of the transfer of the Cheyennes to Dakota can be traced in CIA Report, 1880, serial 1959, p. 109; CIA Report, 1881, serial 2018, pp. 41–42; CIA Report, 1882, serial 2100, p. 50; CIA Report, 1883, serial 2191, p. 39.

30. Executive order in *House Document* no. 153, 55–3, serial 3807, p. 145; letters of J. M. Bell, J. D. C. Atkins, and L. Q. C. Lamar, in *Senate Executive Document* no. 212, 49–1, serial 2341. The movement of the Cheyennes on their own accord from Pine Ridge to Tongue River upset the supply of subsistence, and the Indian Office repeatedly asked Congress for aid in relieving the Indians' misery. See *Senate Executive Document* no. 208, 48–1, serial 2168; *House Executive Document* no. 17, 49–1, serial 2387; *Senate Executive Document* no. 212, 49–1, serial 2341; and *Senate Executive Document* no. 121, 51–1, serial 2686.

31. Report of Sherman, November 7, 1877, *House Executive Document* no. 1, 45–2, serial 1794, p. 15.

Commissioner Hayt had noted in his report for 1877 that "humanity prompts us to send them back and place them on the Nez Perce reservation." Yet he saw an "insuperable difficulty in the way." The murder of whites by members of Chief Joseph's band at the beginning of the outbreak meant that the Indians would find neither peace nor safety in their old haunts. Indictments had in fact been issued in Idaho for certain Nez Perces, and the memory of the murders would continue to be an obstacle to the return of the band. "But for these foul crimes," Hayt asserted, "these Indians would be sent back to the reservation in Idaho. Now, however, they will have to be sent to the Indian Territory; and this will be no hardship to them, as the difference in the temperature between that latitude and their old homes is inconsiderable." The Nez Perces at Fort Leavenworth were turned over by the army to agents of the Indian Office, and on July 21, 1878, they headed south to be settled on a section of the Quapaw Reservation. It was hoped that there, under the guidance of the Quaker agent, the desolate Indians would soon become self-supporting, as the Modocs had done in the same location.[32]

The Indians did not recover, and more of the band sickened and died. Two members of the Board of Indian Commissioners who visited them in August 1878 found Joseph absolutely averse to remaining in the Indian Territory. "Seldom have we been in councils where the Indians more eloquently or earnestly advocated their side of the question," they reported. "Joseph's arraignment of the Army for alleged bad faith to him after the surrender of himself and people to General Miles was almost unanswerable."[33] The commissioners ordered medical supplies for the Indians and made arrangements for a better tract of land on the Quapaw reserve for the Nez Perces, but these actions hardly struck at the heart of the matter.

When Hayt visited Joseph the following October, he was informed in unmistakable terms of the chief's dissatisfaction. The Indian insisted that he had been promised by Miles and Howard that he would be allowed to return to Idaho and that he had surrendered under that condition, and he complained about the quality of the region selected for his people in the Indian Territory. Hayt, like all who came in contact with the Nez Perce leader, was impressed with his intelligence, character, and integrity, and he tried to convince the chief that his people were prevented from returning to Idaho for their own protection and welfare. He attempted a limited accommodation, moreover, by taking Joseph west on a trip of exploration to

32. CIA Report, 1877, serial 1800, p. 409. Two thoroughly documented studies of the Nez Perces in the Indian Territory are J. Stanley Clark, "The Nez Perces in Exile," *Pacific Northwest Quarterly* 36 (July 1945): 213–32, and Berlin B. Chapman, "Nez Perces in Indian Territory: An Archival Study," *Oregon Historical Quarterly* 50 (June 1949): 98–121.
33. *Report of the Board of Indian Commissioners*, 1878, pp. 47–48.

seek a better spot for his band. A place on Salt Creek in the Cherokee Outlet near the Poncas seemed to please the chief, and Hayt believed that he would agree to settle there. Hayt had been accompanied by E. M. Kingsley, a member of the Board of Indian Commissioners, who was favorably impressed with Joseph's argument about Miles's promise and about bad conditions in the Indian Territory. "This statement is believed to be true in the main," Kingsley noted, "and, if so, Joseph stands before the American people a victim of duplicity; his confidence wantonly betrayed; his substance pillaged; an involuntary exile from home and kindred; his 'cause' lost; his people rapidly wasting by pestilence; an object not of haughty contempt or vulgar ridicule, but of generous, humane treatment and consideration."[34]

The wheels of justice moved very slowly and none too surely. Still reluctant to send the Indians back among hostile frontiersmen, the government in June settled the Nez Perces on the new tract in the Cherokee Outlet. Joseph was not reconciled. He told the reformer Alfred B. Meacham in July: "You come to see me as you would a man upon his deathbed. The Great Spirit Chief above has left me and my people to our fate. The white men forget us, and death comes almost every day for some of my people. He will come for all of us. A few months more and we will be in the ground. We are a doomed people."[35] Such dire predictions were not fulfilled, and the tribe's condition improved as the Indians engaged in agriculture and stock raising; but the basic dissatisfaction remained.

Finally in 1883 arrangements were made for the return of thirty-three women and children to Idaho. Philanthropists, encouraged no doubt by this break in the government's position, carried on a campaign to return the rest of the Nez Perces to the Pacific Northwest, and numerous memorials were sent to Congress for that purpose.[36] Congress now acted. A law of July 4, 1884, authorized the secretary of the interior to remove the Nez Perces from the Indian Territory if he judged proper. In May 1885, 118 of the band settled on the Lapwai Reservation in Idaho, where they were warmly received by friends and relatives. The remaining 150, because of continuing threats from Idaho citizens against some of them, were sent on to the Colville Reservation in Washington, where adjustment was slow.[37] Chief Joseph's eternal hope that he might eventually return to the Wallowa Valley was never fulfilled.

34. CIA Report, 1878, serial 1850, pp. 464–65; *Report of the Board of Indian Commissioners*, 1878, p. 51.

35. *Council Fire* 2 (October 1879): 145.

36. The memorials can be traced through the indexes to the House and Senate *Journals*, 48th Congress, 1st session. Some of the memorials came from citizens of Kansas, who may have been moved as much by a desire to free the Cherokee Outlet as by philanthropic motives.

37. 23 *United States Statutes* 90, 378; CIA Report, 1885, serial 2379, p. 57.

REVISION OF RESERVATION POLICY

The cases of the Poncas, southern Cheyennes, and Nez Perces uncovered evils in forced removals that no one could hide and that policy makers could not ignore, whatever theoretical advantages there might have been in moving small tribes to large reservations and consolidating the agencies. Men who had held firmly to a removal policy were forced by the course of events to change their ground. Carl Schurz noted in 1880 that when he had taken charge of the Department of the Interior three and a half years earlier, the prevailing opinion seemed to be that it was best for the Indians to be gathered together where they could be kept out of contact with the whites and where their peaceful conduct could be ensured by a few strong military posts. He had accepted that view himself, but as he learned more from experience he realized that it was a "mistaken policy." In his new wisdom, he argued that it was more in accordance with justice as well as experience to respect the home attachments of the Indians and to introduce them to agricultural and pastoral pursuits in the lands they occupied, provided the lands were capable of sustaining the tribe. Moreover, he began to see that large reservations would become impracticable as the pressure of white settlement increased. "The policy of changing, shifting, and consolidating reservations," he declared, ". . . was therefore abandoned."[38]

In 1881, however, Schurz's successor Kirkwood tried to return to a policy of consolidation. He counted 102 reservations west of the Mississippi, occupied by about 224,000 Indians. Attached to these reservations were sixty-eight agencies, and nearby, for the protection of the whites and the Indians, were thirty-seven military posts. The expenses of this multiplication of agencies and forts disturbed Kirkwood. He believed that, if all the Indians could be gathered together into four or five reservations, the savings would be great and the benefit to the Indians proportionate. He urged Congress to appoint a commission to make recommendations about consolidation.[39]

Kirkwood could not reverse the new trend of thought. The humanitarian reformers resolved in 1884 that "careful observation has conclusively proved that the removal of Indians from reservations which they have long occupied, to other reservations far distant from the former and possessing different soil and climate, is attended by great suffering and loss of life." The reformers were moving rapidly away from support of any kind

38. Report of the Secretary of the Interior, 1880, *House Executive Document* no. 1, part 5, 46–3, serial 1959, pp. 3–4.
39. Report of the Secretary of the Interior, 1881, *House Executive Document* no. 1, part 5, vol. 1, serial 2017, pp. v–vi.

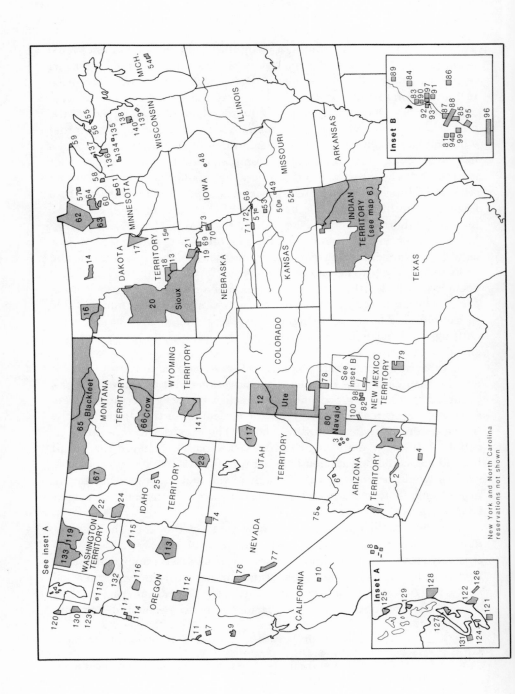

Inset B

Inset A

See inset A

WASHINGTON TERRITORY

MONTANA TERRITORY

Blackfeet

65

66 Crow

WYOMING TERRITORY

IDAHO TERRITORY

OREGON

NEVADA

CALIFORNIA

UTAH TERRITORY

Ute

COLORADO

Navajo

ARIZONA TERRITORY

NEW MEXICO TERRITORY

See inset B

DAKOTA TERRITORY

Sioux

NEBRASKA

KANSAS

INDIAN TERRITORY (see map 6)

TEXAS

MINNESOTA

IOWA

MISSOURI

ARKANSAS

WISCONSIN

ILLINOIS

MICH.

New York and North Carolina reservations not shown

MAP 9: Indian Reservations, 1880

ARIZONA TERRITORY
1. Colorado River
2. Gila River
3. Moqui Pueblo
4. Papago
5. White Mountain
6. Suppai

CALIFORNIA
7. Hoopa Valley
8. Mission
9. Round Valley
10. Tule River
11. Klamath River

COLORADO
12. Ute

DAKOTA TERRITORY
13. Crow Creek
14. Devils Lake
15. Flandreau
16. Ft. Berthold
17. Lake Traverse
18. Old Winnebago
19. Ponca
20. Sioux
21. Yankton

IDAHO TERRITORY
22. Coeur d'Alene
23. Ft. Hall
24. Lapwai
25. Lemhi

INDIAN TERRITORY
26. Arapaho and Cheyenne
27. Cherokee
28. Chickasaw
29. Choctaw
30. Creek
31. Kansas
32. Kiowa and Comanche
33. Modoc
34. Nez Perce
35. Osage
36. Ottawa
37. Pawnee
38. Peoria
39. Ponca
40. Potawatomi
41. Quapaw
42. Sac and Fox
43. Seminole
44. Seneca
45. Shawnee
46. Wichita
47. Wyandot

IOWA
48. Sac and Fox

KANSAS
49. Black Bob
50. Chippewa and Munsee
51. Kickapoo
52. Miami
53. Potawatomi

MICHIGAN
54. Isabella
55. L'Anse
56. Ontonagon

MINNESOTA
57. Bois Forte
58. Fond du Lac
59. Grand Portage
60. Leech Lake
61. Mille Lac
62. Red Lake
63. White Earth
64. Winnebagoshish

MONTANA TERRITORY
65. Blackfeet
66. Crow
67. Jocko

NEBRASKA
68. Iowa
69. Niobrara
70. Omaha
71. Oto
72. Sac and Fox
73. Winnebago

NEVADA
74. Duck Valley
75. Moapa Valley
76. Pyramid Lake
77. Walker River

NEW MEXICO TERRITORY
78. Jicarilla Apache
79. Mescalero Apache
80. Navajo

Pueblos
81. Jemez
82. Acoma
83. San Juan
84. Picuris
85. San Felipe
86. Pecos
87. Cochiti
88. Santo Domingo
89. Taos
90. Santa Clara
91. Tesuque
92. San Ildefonso
93. Pojoaque
94. Zia
95. Sandia
96. Isleta
97. Nambe
98. Laguna
99. Santa Ana
100. Zuni

NEW YORK
101. Allegany
102. Cattaraugus
103. Oil Spring
104. Oneida
105. Onandaga
106. St. Regis
107. Tonawanda
108. Tuscarora

NORTH CAROLINA
109. Cheoah Boundary
110. Qualla Boundary

OREGON
111. Grande Ronde
112. Klamath
113. Malheur
114. Siletz
115. Umatilla
116. Warm Springs

UTAH TERRITORY
117. Uinta Valley

WASHINGTON TERRITORY
118. Chehalis
119. Colville
120. Makah
121. Nisqually
122. Puyallup
123. Shoalwater
124. Squaxin Island
125. Lummi
126. Muckleshoot
127. Port Madison
128. Snohomish or Tulalip
129. Swinomish
130. Quinaielt
131. Skokomish
132. Yakima
133. Columbia

WISCONSIN
134. Lac Court Oreilles
135. Lac du Flambeau
136. La Point (Bad River)
137. Red Cliff
138. Menominee
139. Oneida
140. Stockbridge

WYOMING TERRITORY
141. Wind River

Source: Annual Report of the Commissioner of Indian Affairs, 1880.

of reservation system, whether scattered or consolidated, and urged now that the Indians be given the right to take homesteads on the lands they had traditionally occupied. Consolidation of the Indians in the Indian Territory met strong objections also from the white population in Missouri, Kansas, Texas, and Arkansas, who fought the concentration of more Indians in their vicinity. Although in fact they had nothing to fear from the Indians, the fuss they raised convinced Secretary of the Interior Lamar in 1885 that the scheme was impracticable. "The policy of change and unsettlement," he said, "should give way to that of fixed homes with security of title and possession, and hereafter the civilizing influences and forces already at work among the Indians should be pushed forward upon the lands which they now occupy."[40]

Yet the idea of Indian removals and concentration within the Indian Territory could not be completely scotched. Commissioner of Indian Affairs J. D. C. Atkins in the late 1880s, in the hope of easing white pressure upon vacant lands within the territory, advocated anew filling up the area by moving in various Indian groups. He met violent opposition from the reformers. "We ought by this time to have learned something from the experience in regard to such removals," one wrote. "Nearly all of our wars have originated in irritations growing out of them; our pauperizing policy of feeding and clothing Indians grew out of them, as this was an inducement offered, and it would be difficult to find a tribe whose removal has not proved to be a long step backward in their progress. The Commissioner should make a study of the past before he urges to its adoption this policy which has been fruitful of evil, and evil alone, hitherto."[41]

But if consolidation of reservations was given up as a realizable ideal, reduction of the existing reservations continued to be strongly pushed. Secretary Kirkwood, although he preferred consolidation, at least wanted to cut the size of those reservations that were "entirely out of proportion to the number of Indians thereon." Henry M. Teller, a former senator from Colorado, who followed Kirkwood as secretary of the interior, strongly advocated such reduction. He admitted the necessity of the reservations but did not think their size should be disproportionate to the needs of the Indians. "Very many of these reservations," he noted, "contain large areas of valuable land that cannot be cultivated by the Indians, even though they were as energetic and laborious as the best class of white agriculturists. All such reservations ought to be reduced in size and the surplus not needed

40. *Lake Mohonk Conference Proceedings,* 1884, pp. 15–16; Report of the Secretary of the Interior, 1885, *House Executive Document* no. 1, part 5, vol. 1, 49–1, serial 2378, pp. 27–28. Lamar largely repeats CIA Report, 1885, serial 2379, pp. 8–12.

41. CIA Report, 1886, serial 2467, pp. 88–90; Charles C. Painter, *The Proposed Removal of Indians to Oklahoma* (Philadelphia: Indian Rights Association, 1888), p. 6.

ought to be bought by the government and opened to the operation of the homestead law, and it would then soon be settled by industrious whites, who, as neighbors, would become valuable auxiliaries in the work of civilizing the Indians residing on the remainder of the reservation." The reduced lands should be vested in the tribe in fee simple. Teller urged that his plan be adopted for the Crow reservation in Montana Territory. Of the 4,713,000 acres in that reserve, Teller estimated that at least three million could be disposed of, leaving the Indians about 600 acres apiece, enough for them to become self-sufficient in agriculture or stock raising. Proceeds from the sale of the surplus lands, if properly used to buy herds for the Crows, could make the Indians self-supporting in a few years.[42]

The reformers continued to see great advantages in such a program. The pressure of the whites on Indian lands would be lessened if not entirely removed, the land left in Indian hands could be given a sure title, proceeds from the sale of the excess lands could replace direct appropriations for Indian subsistence and welfare, and the Indians would be driven closer to an agricultural pattern.

42. Report of the Secretary of the Interior, 1881, *House Executive Document* no. 1, part 5, vol. 1, 47–1, serial 2017, pp. v–vi; ibid., 1882, *House Executive Document* no. 1, part 5, vol. 1, 47–2, serial 2099, p. viii; ibid., 1884, *House Executive Document* no. 1, part 5, vol. 1, 48–2, serial 2286, pp. xiii–xiv. The Crow reservation, however, was not reduced until 1891.

CHAPTER 23

The Indian Service:
Policies and Administration

An Array of Commissioners. Fraud and

the "Indian Rings." Inspectors and

Special Agents. Policies and

Programs. Law and Order.

The Indian service, upon which rested much of the responsibility for solving the "Indian problem" of the post-Civil War decades, was itself a large part of the problem. The fraud and abuses that Bishop Whipple had railed against in the early 1860s became a much-publicized national concern in the years that followed, and the Indian service was a primary example of the corruption that tainted Grant's administration. To protect and aid the Indians without at the same time curtailing the expansion of white population in the West created a problem of major dimensions for the Indian Office. Commissioner Dennis Cooley saw it clearly as he neared the end of his term. He wrote in 1866:

It does not seem a great task to attend to the business of directing the management of about three hundred thousand Indians; but when it is considered that those Indians are scattered over a continent, and divided into more than two hundred tribes, in [the] charge of fourteen superintendents and some seventy agents, whose frequent reports and quarterly accounts are to be examined and adjusted; that no general rules can be adopted for the guidance of those officers, for the reason that the people under their charge are so different in habits, customs, manners, and organization, varying from the civilized and educated Cherokee and Choctaw to the miserable lizard-eaters of Arizona; and that this office is called upon to protect the Indians, whether under treaty stipulations or roaming at will over his wild hunting-grounds, from abuse by unscrupulous whites, while at the same time it must concede every reasonable privilege to the spirit of enterprise and adventure which is pouring its hardy population into the western country; when these things are considered, the task assigned to this bureau will not seem so light as it is sometimes thought.[1]

The tensions would have taxed the abilities of wise and competent men. Yet, somehow, in spite of all the experiments with philanthropic advisers and church-related agents, the men who ran the Indian service, although they promoted the civilization programs that had become a standard element of Indian policy, left much to be desired.

AN ARRAY OF COMMISSIONERS

In the first decade and a half after the Civil War, the period in which the Indian peace policy took form, ten men held the office of commissioner of Indian affairs, if one counts the short period in which William P. Dole carried over into Andrew Johnson's administration. This was an average tenure of about a year and a half, a very short time given the reform ferment and the frontier turmoil of the time. Commissioner Cooley, who directed the crucial work of dealing with the Indian nations in the Indian Territory after the war, was appalled by the waste and corruption of the Indian service, but Congress was too busy with other matters to pay attention to the call for reform. Cooley's successor, Lewis Vital Bogy, a flexible Missouri politician, failed to win confirmation from the Senate, which accused him of fraudulent contracts for Indian goods. More significant in directing Indian affairs was Nathaniel G. Taylor, the Methodist minister and Tennessee politician whose humanitarian sentiments put a strong stamp of Christian philanthropy on Indian Office documents and activities, but whose convictions on Indian perfectability often got in the way of his grasp of the present situation. Ely S. Parker, the Seneca, who formally began the peace policy of Grant, resigned under a cloud in 1871, just as the program was getting under way.[2]

The peace policy was then directed by a group of commissioners with

1. CIA Report, 1866, serial 1284, pp. 1–2.
2. For Bogy, see William E. Unrau, "Lewis Vital Bogy, 1866–67," in Robert M. Kvasnicka and Herman J. Viola, eds., *The Commissioners of Indian Affairs, 1824–1977* (Lincoln: University of Nebraska Press, 1979), pp. 109–14, and William E. Unrau, "Politics, Bureaucracy, and the Bogus Administration of Indian Commissioner Lewis Vital Bogy, 1866–1867," *American Indian Law Review* 5 (Summer 1977): 185–94.

strong views about Indian policy and the civilization of their charges. The first of these, Francis A. Walker, was an anomaly. A brilliant economist and statistician who had directed the Ninth Census, Walker was appointed to the Indian Office to keep him on the government payroll when census salary appropriations were cut. Although he had no previous Indian experience, he quickly grasped the situation and the needs of the office. In spite of the fact that he held office only temporarily—from late 1871 to early 1873—he wrote a long and forceful annual report in 1872 (later incorporated with two other essays into a book called *The Indian Question*) in which he advanced his philosophy of firmness in settling Indians on definite reservations and a strong commitment to protecting their rights once they arrived there. A practical man with little trace of the sentimentality that marked Christian reformers like Nathaniel Taylor, Walker nevertheless had strong humanitarian instincts and deep concern for fair treatment of the Indians. At the end of his term he wrote:

> In good faith and good feeling we must take up this work of Indian civilization, and, at whatever cost, do our whole duty by this unhappy people. Better that we should entail a debt upon our posterity on Indian account, were that necessary, than that we should leave them an inheritance of shame. We may have no fear that the dying curse of the red man, outcast and homeless by our fault, will bring barrenness upon the soil that once was his, or dry the streams of the beautiful land that, through so much of evil and of good, has become our patrimony; but surely we shall be clearer in our lives and freer to meet the glances of our sons and grandsons, if in our generation we do justice and show mercy to a race which has been impoverished that we might be made rich.[3]

Edward P. Smith, who succeeded Walker, was the epitome of a peace policy commissioner. He was the son of a clergyman who, after obtaining a degree from Yale, entered the seminary and in 1856 was ordained a Congregational minister. His baptism in public good works came when he was with the United States Christian Commission during the Civil War as the commission's general field agent with the Army of the Cumberland; later he was field secretary for the central office of the commission. After 1866 he worked with the American Missionary Association in New York City and was nominated by that body to be an Indian agent under the peace policy, and in February 1871 he became agent of the Chippewas in Minnesota.

3. Francis A. Walker, "The Indian Question," *North American Review* 116 (April 1873): 388. See also Francis A. Walker, *The Indian Question* (Boston: James R. Osgood and Company, 1874); CIA Report, 1872, serial 1560, pp. 391–493; H. Craig Miner, "Francis A. Walker, 1871–73," in Kvasnicka and Viola, *Commissioners of Indian Affairs*, pp. 135–40.

He was strongly recommended for the position of commissioner of Indian affairs by Secretary Delano and by the Board of Indian Commissioners and was appointed to that office on March 20, 1873, bringing with him a commitment to the reforms urged by the Christian humanitarians. He held no brief with Indians as sovereign tribes and promoted incessantly the movement toward individual allotment of land, American law for the Indians, and progress toward self-support; and in true missionary fashion he continually reported in optimistic terms the advancement he saw among the Indians. Ironically, Smith fell victim himself to the demand for reform, for his actions as Chippewa agent in regard to timber sales led to a formal investigation. Although he was cleared of any wrongdoing in the Chippewa affair, he was attacked again during an investigation of charges of fraud against the Red Cloud agent in 1875, and in December of that year he resigned.[4]

John Q. Smith, who followed, continued the reform principles of his predecessors, but he left no strong mark on the office or on Indian affairs. His term, from December 1875 to September 1877, was a high point for charges of fraud against the Indian service, and although he himself escaped any charges of personal corruption, he was removed from office soon after Carl Schurz became secretary of the interior.[5]

Smith's successor was Ezra A. Hayt, a businessman from New Jersey with close ties to the Board of Foreign Missions of the Reformed Church, which had secured his appointment on the Board of Indian Commissioners in 1874. He was an effective member of the board and during most of his time on it was chairman of the purchasing committee. In that capacity he came into conflict with the Indian Office. Following an investigation of flour purchased for Indians in the Indian Territory, over which Hayt and Commissioner J. Q. Smith strongly disagreed, President Grant demanded that Hayt resign from the board, which he did on January 20, 1877. Schurz, seeking a man of high integrity to replace Smith as commissioner of Indian affairs, appointed Hayt to the position. Hayt carried out his duties with energy and aggressive promotion of a civilization program for the Indians. When he suffered the usual attacks from persons critical of all Indian Office actions and was blamed for disturbances (the Northern Cheyenne and the Ute troubles, for example) that had their roots in earlier administrations, he was strongly backed by Schurz. But when evidence of irregularities at the San Carlos Agency were uncovered that incriminated him, Hayt became a liability in Schurz's campaign of reform, and the secretary removed him from office at the end of January 1880.[6]

4. Richard C. Crawford, "Edward Parmelee Smith, 1873–75," in Kvasnicka and Viola, *Commissioners of Indian Affairs*, pp. 141–47.
5. Edward E. Hill, "John Q. Smith, 1875–77," ibid., pp. 149–53.
6. Roy E. Meyer, "Ezra A. Hayt, 1877–80," ibid., pp. 155–66.

Under such circumstances, the Hayes administration sought a man of unassailable integrity. It found him in a Michigan representative, Roland E. Trowbridge, whose background showed no interest in Indians but whose college classmate and close friend was Rutherford B. Hayes. Honesty was Trowbridge's hallmark, and he suffered no charges of corruption. But he made no innovations in the service, and illness forced long absences from his duties. After less than a year in office and without even signing the annual report (which was submitted by the acting commissioner, H. R. Clum), Trowbridge resigned in March 1881.[7]

FRAUD AND THE "INDIAN RINGS"

These commissioners, including two ordained Protestant ministers and other upright Christian gentlemen of close church affiliation, were unable to stem the abuses that plagued the Indian service, for they faced conditions that stimulated fraud and corruption in official Indian-white relations. As land cessions multiplied and the money and other goods due the Indians increased, the chances for unscrupulous whites to cash in on the payments grew almost without bounds. Disposition of such resources as timber from Indian reservations offered still other opportunities for robbing the Indians through fraudulent contracts. Not only was this a matter of plain injustice to the nation's wards, but cheating the Indians of their rightful due frequently led to reprisals. Supplying goods to the Indians—a multimillion dollar business by the 1870s—was the chief arena for illegal and unjust economic gain at the expense of the government and the Indians. There seemed to be endless ways of cheating by the supply of inferior or insufficient goods for full or inflated prices, and the huge transportation costs of moving masses of goods from eastern markets to the far distant and often isolated agencies offered still other prizes. Although it was never possible to put one's finger on them precisely, "Indian rings"— some sort of conspiratorial aggregation of suppliers and Indian service personnel and sometimes corrupt Indian leaders—seemed to be everywhere.[8]

The creation of the Board of Indian Commissioners was one attempt to correct the evils by having an independent, disinterested group of high-minded businessmen supervise the purchase of Indian goods. The purchasing committee of the board performed valuable and to some extent effec-

7. Michael A. Goldman, "Roland E. Trowbridge, 1880–81," ibid., pp. 167–72.

8. Although charges against *the* "Indian ring" or against "Indian rings" were widespread, there was no agreement about who precisely was involved. For one study of their operations, see George H. Phillips, "The Indian Ring in Dakota Territory, 1870–1890," *South Dakota History* 2 (Fall 1972): 345–76.

tive service by checking the bids and inspecting the goods supplied, and the board was optimistic. It reported in 1871 "that all 'Indian rings' can be broken up, and that the wards of this nation, who have been so long the victims of greedy and designing men, ought and must be treated in a manner worthy of the highest moral obligations of a Christian government." But it soon enough discovered the "tricks, subterfuges, evasions, and combinations" of the men who became rich from the Indian business.[9]

One of these subtle schemes was described by George Stuart, who chaired the first purchasing committee of the board:

> I . . . soon discovered how it was that the "Indian Ring" was enabled to make such immense profits out of the annual supplies furnished to the government for its Indian wards. The advertisements for such goods specified certain classes, number one, number two, etc., each class containing several articles, so that the bidders had to bid for the whole of a class of goods, and the lowest *total* bid obtained the award. At the foot of the advertisement specifying the several classes, it was stated that "the government reserves the right to diminish or increase the quantity taken of any of the articles of any class." On further examination, I found [that] a bidder who was said to have made a large fortune out of the government had bid about half-price for a large quantity of goods called for by one article in one of the classes, and nearly double its market value for an article in the same class of which a very small quantity was called for. On this class his bid was, very naturally, the lowest. Finally, I found that he ultimately supplied a very small quantity of the article for which he had bid half-price, and a very large quantity of the article for which he had bid nearly double its market value.[10]

No matter how much the board's supervising functions may have helped, the failure of the board to break through entrenched corruption meant that it was not the solution to the problem. Nor did the church nomination of agency personnel provide a satisfactory answer by furnishing presumably honest men to deal with the Indians, for evils continued to crop up, and even Christian gentlemen in the office of commissioner of Indian affairs were forced from office because tainted by corrupt practices for which they may or may not have been personally responsible.

A special case that received much publicity showed the continuing problem: charges leveled against Red Cloud Agent J. J. Saville by Chief Red

9. *Report of the Board of Indian Commissioners,* 1871, p. 161; ibid., 1878, pp. 19–24. The latter gives specific cases.

10. George Hay Stuart, *The Life of George Hay Stuart: Written by Himself,* ed. Robert Ellis Thompson (Philadelphia: J. M. Stoddart, 1890), pp. 242–43.

Cloud and highly publicized by the noted Yale paleontologist, Othniel C. Marsh.[11] When Marsh was in Dakota hunting fossils, Red Cloud complained to him about the ill treatment he received and showed him samples of bad supplies furnished by the government. Marsh in turn took the complaints to the Board of Indian Commissioners and to the public at large. The board called for an investigation, and Secretary Delano, not wanting to be left out, cooperated with the president of the board in appointing a special committee to investigate the charges.[12] The whole affair was pretty much a fiasco. Red Cloud admitted that the samples he had shown Marsh were not typical of goods the Indians received. Marsh himself was less than completely helpful to the investigating committee, filing his complaints in the form of a pamphlet addressed to the president of the United States that he released to the press before the committee received it. He had laid the matter directly before the president, he said, because he had "no confidence whatever in the sincerity of the Secretary of the Interior or the Commissioner of Indian Affairs." Delano's response, also printed as a pamphlet, questioned Marsh's competence and judgment in the case and blamed the affair on attempts of the press to injure him.[13]

The committee determined that Red Cloud's samples were not representative of goods issued the Sioux, but it did find inferior supplies and agreed that the government and the Indians were being defrauded. The committee members recommended replacing the contractors for pork and flour and generally tightening the supply procedures. They thought, too, that Saville should be removed as agent, not because they found him guilty of fraud but because of lax administration that made fraud possible. Commissioner Edward P. Smith considered the committee's report a vindication of the Indian Office, however, and little came of the inquiry except the public airing of conditions in the Indian service that plainly called for remedy.[14]

The first significant moves came with the appointment of Carl Schurz as secretary of the interior. A reformer of long standing, Schurz was deter-

11. An excellent discussion of the case is in James C. Olson, *Red Cloud and the Sioux Problem* (Lincoln: University of Nebraska Press, 1965), pp. 179, 183–84, 189–98. The most important documents are in *Report of the Special Commission Appointed to Investigate the Affairs of the Red Cloud Indian Agency, July, 1875* (Washington: GPO, 1875). Marsh's side of the affair is recounted in Charles Schuchert and Clara Mae LaVene, *O. C. Marsh: Pioneer in Paleontology* (New Haven: Yale University Press, 1940), pp. 145–68.

12. Minutes of April 28 and 29, 1875, Minutes of the Board of Indian Commissioners, National Archives, Record Group 75.

13. O. C. Marsh, *A Statement of Affairs at Red Cloud Agency: Made to the President of the United States* (n.p., 1875); *Documents Relating to the Charges of Professor O. C. Marsh of Fraud and Mismanagement at the Red Cloud Agency* (n.p., 1875).

14. CIA Report, 1875, serial 1680, pp. 538–39.

mined to end the fraud and the conditions that made it possible. He noted in his first report, among other problems, "the temptations to fraud and peculation in furnishing and distributing supplies; [and] the careless and blundering management of agents, removed from immediate supervision." Schurz was a realist and knew that correction of the evils he saw would require time, patient labor, and "above all things, an honest and efficient Indian service."[15] The key, as always, was the character of the men who managed Indian affairs, and Schurz moved quickly, beginning at the top. After Commissioner J. Q. Smith, who had been carried over from the previous administration, resigned under pressure, Schurz turned to investigate the work of the chief clerk of the Indian Office, S. A. Galpin. A special committee of three, appointed by Schurz, not only judged specific charges against Galpin but reviewed broadly the whole operation of the Indian Office. Its report, dated December 31, 1877, found much carelessness and mismanagement to condemn all along the line, and Galpin was removed from office.[16]

But Schurz did not succeed completely. Even his carefully picked commissioner of Indian affairs, Ezra Hayt, proved a disappointment in the end, and the problem of finding proper men to conduct an absolutely honest and efficient service remained.

INSPECTORS AND SPECIAL AGENTS

One special remedy that was used to ease the problem was a corps of inspectors to keep tab on operations in the field and to give the central headquarters closer supervision over the activities of the agents and other personnel on the reservations. First put into effect in 1873, the provision for Indian inspectors rested on earlier recommendations. The Doolittle Committee's major practical suggestion for eliminating abuses had been a system of five inspection districts, each to be served by a three-man commission. Senator Doolittle's bill incorporating the inspection provisions passed the Senate in March 1866, but it never came to vote in the House.[17]

15. Report of the Secretary of the Interior, 1877, House Executive Document no. 1, part 5, 45–2, serial 1800, pp. x–xii.

16. Report of the Board of Inquiry Convened by Authority of the Secretary of the Interior of June 7, 1877, to Investigate Certain Charges against S. A. Galpin, Chief Clerk of the Indian Bureau, and Concerning Irregularities in Said Bureau (Washington: GPO, 1878). There is an account of the episode in Loring Benson Priest, Uncle Sam's Stepchildren: The Reformation of United States Indian Policy, 1865–1887 (New Brunswick: Rutgers University Press, 1942), pp. 68–69.

17. Senate Journal, 39–1, serial 1236, pp. 235, 243, 246. See Doolittle's support of the measure and debate on it in Congressional Globe, 39th Congress, 1st session, pp. 1449–50, 1485–92.

The supervisory duties envisaged by Doolittle were then carried out in part by the Board of Indian Commissioners. Because the board's unofficial status led to conflict with the official bureaucracy, however, that group did not function well as the watchdog it was intended to be, except to some extent in its supervision of the purchase of Indian goods. An inspection mechanism within the Indian Office itself was needed, and the Board of Indian Commissioners, in fact, in its report of 1872 called for a "board of inspectors" of at least five persons to be appointed by the president from names recommended by the annual meetings of the various religious denominations.[18]

In January 1873, when the Indian appropriation bill reached the Senate, Senator William M. Stewart of Nevada offered an amendment as an added section of the bill. He proposed that the president detail an army officer to visit each agency every six months to examine the agency and its reservation and to report back to the president how its business was conducted, how the money was spent, how the Indians were being treated, and what progress they were making in civilization. The officer would be given authority to investigate all records and to examine agents and others under oath. When objections arose against such use of army officers and the conflict that was likely to occur between the two branches of government, Stewart proposed a substitute amendment by which the president would appoint "a person" to inspect the agencies every six months. To a suggestion that the Board of Indian Commissioners could fulfill the function, he replied: "The present Indian commission is composed of very nice men, very well-disposed men, men whom I have every reason to have the highest confidence in, so far as I know, but they are old men, they are not very active men; they have not seen all the reservations; they cannot give you this information, they cannot make this examination." After agreeing that the superintendencies as well as the agencies should be inspected and haggling over the number of inspectors and the salary to be paid them, the Senate on January 10 passed an amendment providing for no more than five inspectors, with annual salary of $3,000 plus traveling expenses. The inspectors would have power not only to inspect all records but to suspend superintendents, agents, and agency employees and appoint others in their places, subject to the president's approval.[19]

When the amendment reached the House of Representatives, the inspection scheme was combined with the question of whether the superintendencies should be continued. Added to the Senate amendment when it was reported to the House by the Committee on Appropriations was a clause abolishing all superintendencies as of June 30, 1873, and using the

18. *Report of the Board of Indian Commissioners*, 1872, p. 19.
19. *Congressional Globe*, 42d Congress, 3d session, pp. 436, 439–40, 480–81.

funds provided for their salaries to pay the inspectors. Some members pointed to the continuing need for superintendents in some parts of the country, but Representative Aaron A. Sargent of California, the chief advocate of the amendment, noted that the Board of Indian Commissioners in its 1872 report had recommended the discontinuation of the superintendencies; he thought it would be "unjust to this board, and rather a dangerous experiment, to adopt one part of their suggestions [inspectors] and reject the other." At any rate, he wanted to see if the country could not get along without "this expensive machinery of superintendents and superintendents clerks." The House concurred in the abolition of all superintendencies, of which there were eight at the time.[20]

This attack on the superintendencies as unnecessary was not a new thing. Congress in 1870 had authorized the president "to discontinue any one or more of the Indian superintendencies, and to require the Indian agents of such superintendencies to report directly to the commissioner of Indian affairs." In the following year it had charged the president to dispense with agents and superintendencies when feasible. The moves came from a desire for economy, ever present in Indian appropriations, but they were also due no doubt to changing conditions on the frontier. When diplomatic relations with the tribes were uppermost and treaty negotiations an important element in the handling of Indian affairs by the United States, the superintendents played a large role, for they often took part in the treaty making. With the developing reservation system and the emphasis on changing patterns of Indian life, the agent on the reservation assumed a new and more important role in directing the Indians toward civilization.[21]

In 1873 the measure that came out of the conference committee was a compromise. The appointment, pay, number, and duties of the inspectors were left untouched, for the House had concurred in this part of the Senate amendment. But the bill now directed that only four of the eight superintendencies be abolished. The president was to have authority to assign the four remaining superintendents over such agencies as he thought proper and to dispense with all of them at his discretion. In this form the measure became law on February 14, 1873.[22] The Indian service now had its board of inspectors.

20. Ibid., pp. 916–17. The recommendation of the Board of Indian Commissioners is in *Report of the Board of Indian Commissioners, 1872*, p. 19. Congress in 1873 authorized the following superintendencies: two east of the Rockies, one each for Oregon and California, and one each for the territories of Washington, New Mexico, Arizona, and Montana. 17 *United States Statutes* 438.

21. 16 *United States Statutes* 360–61, 545; Paul Stuart, *The Indian Office: Growth and Development of an American Institution, 1865–1900* (Ann Arbor: UMI Research Press, 1979), pp. 73–78.

22. *Congressional Globe*, 42d Congress, 3d session, p. 1079; 17 *United States Statutes* 463.

The Indian inspectors were hardly a panacea, but they provided an instrument that, with the right personnel and the right use, could facilitate reform and a tighter and more formal organization of the service. Inspections had of course been carried on before by special agents or commissioners appointed for particular one-time duties, but the inspectors authorized in 1873 were a new element between the agencies and the Washington office—men who, unlike the superintendents, viewed headquarters rather than the agents as the object of their first loyalty. Even though the number of inspectors was reduced to three in 1875 and the semi-annual inspection of each agency was no longer required, the new office hastened the demise of the remaining superintendencies, the last of which was closed in January 1878. Then in 1880 the number of inspectors was raised again to five. In addition, Congress in 1878 authorized two special agents and in 1882 doubled the number. These men were used to strengthen the inspection service.[23]

In 1873, when the inspectors were authorized, the system of church management of the agencies and superintendencies was in full force, and the first inspectors were chosen from men connected with the church-run agencies, with consequent interdenominational rivalry. Later inspectors were chosen from former agents and superintendents. The inspectors performed a great variety of tasks, although their primary function was to monitor the activities of the agents and make sure that laws and regulations were obeyed. They were used frequently to investigate specific complaints lodged against agents, often by whites in the neighborhood who charged discrimination against their economic interests. They aided in the removal of tribes (for example, the Ponca removal of 1877). They helped in problems resulting from the dissolution of the superintendencies, negotiated with tribes for railroad rights of way through the reservations, and made recommendations about transfers of personnel.[24]

At first the inspectors and the special agents both reported to the commissioner of Indian affairs, but in 1880 Schurz directed the inspectors to report directly to him. Because the legislation authorizing the Indian inspectors called for reports to be sent to the president, Schurz reasoned that in legal effect he acted for the president in the matter and should get the reports. Under his direction the work of the inspectors became more routinized, for he required them to report regularly on their activities. As in-

---

23. 18 *United States Statutes* 422–23; 20 *United States Statutes* 60; 21 *United States Statutes* 116; 22 *United States Statutes* 70. Stuart, *Indian Office*, chapters 6–9, discusses the work of the inspectors and the part they played in the formalization and institutionalization of the Indian Office.

24. Stuart, *Indian Office*, pp. 80–81, 87–96. Details on the inspection at three agencies, 1873–1906, are given on pp. 101–18.

structions to the inspectors became more detailed, their reports in turn became more patterned. In 1883 a formal set of instructions was issued.[25]

POLICIES AND PROGRAMS

As they struggled to control and improve the administration of Indian affairs, the commissioners, despite their diversity of background and short tenures, nevertheless had a uniform policy. All of them, in varying degrees, continued the promotion of Indian civilization that was the corollary of the reservation system. And in this they had the support of their superiors, the secretaries of the interior. Although in the period from the Civil War to 1880 no major legislative enactments effected the reforms advocated by humanitarians and their supporters in the government, the proposals that were to mark the last two decades of the nineteenth century began to assume a form that was generally agreed upon. By the end of Carl Schurz's administration in the Interior Department, the formulations were ready for the intensive campaign that followed to get Congress to enact them into law.

The policies were based on an increasingly clear realization that the expansion of the white population across the nation had forever doomed the Indians' traditional way of life. Ignatius Donnelly, then a young representative from Minnesota, predicted the outcome before the Civil War had ended. He saw white population closing in on the Indians from both the east and the west. "With the termination of our great war, now near its close," he said in the House on February 7, 1865, "a migration will spring up of which the world has as yet known no parallel; and in a few short years every tract capable of settlement and cultivation will pass into the occupancy of the white man. What is to become of the Indians as the races of the world thus draw together from the opposite shores of the continent?" Dennis Cooley in 1866 saw the white population "rapidly crowding westward upon the Indians, either in the search for farming lands or for the precious minerals; and the people who have held these lands are compelled to give way before the advancing tide." He saw a continued increase in the difficulties, for there was no way to avoid the collision. "It is the law of nature and of the progress of mankind," he said, "and its operation cannot be stayed."[26]

The movement of railroads westward and the climactic event of the completion of the Union Pacific transcontinental line in 1869 greatly

25. Ibid., pp. 82–83.
26. *Congressional Globe*, 38th Congress, 2d session, appendix, p. 61; CIA Report, 1866, serial 1284, p. 2.

speeded the process. "The completion of one of the great lines of railway to the Pacific coast has totally changed the conditions under which the civilized population of the country come in contact with the wild tribes," Secretary Cox noted in that year. "Instead of a slowly advancing tide of migration, making its gradual inroads upon the circumference of the great interior wilderness, the very center of the desert has been pierced. Every station upon the railway has become a nucleus for a civilized settlement, and a base from which lines of exploration for both mineral and agricultural wealth are pushed in every direction." The inevitability of the advance was taken for granted; the westward course of white population could not—and should not—be stopped or delayed by the Indians. Francis Walker lectured the humanitarian reformers in 1872 that they should exert themselves "not feebly and futilely to attempt to stay this tide, whose depth and strength can hardly be measured, but to snatch the remnants of the Indian race from destruction before it."[27]

The first step in saving the Indians from destruction had been the reservation system, which sought to remove the Indians from the path of the onrushing whites; by 1880 the pattern of reservations was set, although some of them would later be reduced again in size. But once that measure was accomplished, proposals for how to treat the Indians now confined to the reservations became the important elements of United States Indian policy. The Indians, having lost the independence and freedom that marked their aboriginal existence, now became in fact the wards and dependents of a paternal government, and the officials of the Department of the Interior and the Indian Office accepted that fact. They saw it as their responsibility to provide the means for the Indians to move from their traditional life to the white man's civilization—and to force this change upon the Indians for their own good. Commissioner Walker expressed the conclusion with his usual forcefulness:

> The Government should extend over them a rigid reformatory discipline, to save them from falling hopelessly into the condition of pauperism and petty crime. Merely to disarm the savages, and to surround them by forces which it is hopeless in them to resist, without exercising over them for a series of years a system of paternal control, requiring them to learn and practice the arts of industry at least until one generation has been fairly started on a course of self-improvement, is to make it pretty much a matter of certainty that by far the larger part of the now roving Indians will become simply vagabonds in the midst of civilization, forming little camps here and there over the

27. Report of the Secretary of the Interior, 1869, *House Executive Document* no. 1, 41–2, serial 1414, p. vii; CIA Report, 1872, serial 1560, p. 397.

face of the Western States, which will be festering sores on the communities near which they are located; the men resorting for a living to basket-making and hog-stealing; the women to fortune-telling and harlotry.[28]

When Carl Schurz left office, almost a decade later, he expressed the same concern and recommended strong government control. "Nothing is more indispensable," he said, "than the protecting and guiding care of the Government during the dangerous period of transition from savage to civilized life. . . . [The Indian] is overcome by a feeling of helplessness, and he naturally looks to the 'Great Father' to take him by the hand and guide him on. That guiding hand must necessarily be one of authority and power to command confidence and respect. It can be only that of the government which the Indian is accustomed to regard as a sort of omnipotence on earth. Everything depends upon the wisdom and justice of that guidance."[29]

A list of priorities in Indian policy emerged during the 1870s that the secretaries of the interior and the commissioners of Indian affairs, aided and abetted by reform sentiment (such as that expressed in the reports of the Board of Indian Commissioners), all espoused. They were set forth in excellent summary form by Schurz in 1879:

1. To set the Indians to work as agriculturists or herders, thus to break up their habits of savage life and to make them self-supporting.

2. To educate their youth of both sexes, so as to introduce to the growing generation civilized ideas, wants, and aspirations.

3. To allot parcels of land to Indians in severalty and to give them individual title to their farms in fee, inalienable for a certain period, thus to foster the pride of individual ownership of property instead of their former dependence upon the tribe, with its territory held in common.

4. When settlement in severalty with individual title is accomplished, to dispose, with their consent, of those lands on their reservations which are not settled and used by them, the proceeds to form a fund for their benefit, which will gradually relieve the government of the expenses at present provided for by annual appropriations.

5. When this is accomplished, to treat the Indians like other inhabitants of the United States, under the laws of the land.

To Schurz these elements of an Indian policy would solve the problems without injustice to the Indians or hindrance to the development of white

28. CIA Report, 1872, serial 1560, p. 399.
29. Carl Schurz, "Present Aspects of the Indian Problem," *North American Review* 133 (July 1881): 8–9.

settlement. The Indians would be raised to a high level of civilization because of the stimulus of individual ownership of property. The policy would not deprive them by force of what belonged to them but would induce them to part with, for a just compensation, lands they did not need and did not cultivate, which could then be opened to progress and improvement.[30]

The policies and programs carried out or recommended by the Indian Office and its supporters continued to rest upon a belief that the Indians were fully capable of adopting civilized ways. Although there were always voices raised against the competence of the Indians and ridicule made of attempts to raise the "savages" to the level of the whites, the dominant official views remained strong in the Christian humanitarian tradition, echoing in many ways such classic statements as those of Commissioner Taylor in 1868. This, of course, was to be expected from the commissioners who by experience and religious outlook were cast in the same mold. Among the most optimistic was Commissioner E. P. Smith, who in 1874 and 1875 was ready to declare large numbers of the Indians ready to be absorbed as citizens into American society. His successor, J. Q. Smith, though more aware of the long road ahead for many Indians, declared in 1876: "From the fact that for so long a period Indian civilization has been retarded, it must not be concluded that some inherent characteristic in the race disqualified it for civilized life. It may well be doubted whether this be true of any race of men. Surely it cannot be true of a race, any portion of which has made the actual progress realized by some of our Indians. They can and do learn to labor; they can and do learn to read. Many thousands to-day are engaged in civilized occupations." Carl Schurz, more hardheaded than the sentimental philanthropists with whom he sparred, held the same opinion. "That all the Indians on this northern continent have been savages and that many of them are savages now is true," he wrote in 1879; "but it is also true that many tribes have risen to a promising degree of civilization, and there is no reason to doubt that the rest, if wisely guided, will be found capable of following their example."[31]

Mundane policies of law and land allotment and self-support were not the only forces at work. Suffusing all was the powerful spirit of Christianity, and missionaries continued to be the primary agents of the government's program for Indian improvement. The assignment of agencies to Christian denominations gave the greatest momentum to the drive, but that was a result, not the cause, of the Christian philanthropic spirit. The

30. Report of the Secretary of the Interior, 1879, *House Executive Document* no. 1, part 5, 46–2, serial 1910, pp. 5–6.
31. CIA Report, 1874, serial 1639, pp. 313, 316; CIA Report, 1875, serial 1680, pp. 527–31; CIA Report, 1876, serial 1749, pp. 384–85; Report of the Secretary of the Interior, 1879, *House Executive Document* no. 1, part 5, 46–2, serial 1910, p. 4.

peace policy enlisted the kind of aid "for which the Government has no substitute," E. P. Smith said, "and without which all effort for civilization will drag heavily until it is abandoned." Then he put his finger on the peculiarly American manifestation of religious aid:

> No movement for changing the character and habits and prevailing condition of a people or a class can attain anything worthy the name of success without calling for the help which a volunteer benevolent or religious organization outside of the Government alone can give. The Sanitary and Christian Commissions of the war, Prison Associations, Children's Aid and other Relief Societies, and the multitude of benevolent organizations which the Government and the States call to their aid whenever any work of humanity or recovery of man is to be undertaken, bear abundant testimony to the prevailing opinion on this subject which has grown out of experience.[32]

The missionaries, whose aid was so generally praised, continued to play an especially important role in educating the Indians; one of the motives behind the allotment of agencies to religious denominations had been to encourage the educational and other work of the missionaries on the reservations by eliminating conflict between them and agents. It is difficult, however, to determine exactly the proportion of Indian school work done by church groups. The United States supplied funds to tribes for their own schools in accord with treaty specifications and used some funds designated for "civilization" for school support. In 1870 Congress for the first time appropriated money "for the support of industrial and other schools among the Indian tribes not otherwise provided for." The sum of $100,000 was provided, but the Indian Office that year expended only $37,597, and the money was reappropriated for later use. Money spent for schools rose only slowly until after 1880, when the sums advanced dramatically, reaching $2,277,557 in fiscal year 1893. Even though the government thus became firmly committed to maintaining a system of public schools for the Indians, it continued to rely for much Indian education on mission schools on a contract basis in which the church groups built the schoolhouses and supplied the teachers in return for an annual per capita payment for the students they enrolled. A considerable number of schools, in addition, were supported entirely by the churches.[33]

---

32. CIA Report, 1875, serial 1680, p. 524.
33. 16 *United States Statutes* 359; Stuart, *Indian Office*, pp. 119–34. A useful history and analysis of school development and expenditures is provided in the Report of the Indian School Superintendent (John H. Oberly) for 1885, CIA Report, 1885, serial 2379, pp. 75–127.

LAW AND ORDER

Much of the program of civilization, Christianization, and education, of course, was no more than a continuation and intensification of ideas long promoted by officials and others interested in Indian affairs. Newer was the emphasis on law for the Indians. It had been an assumption of United States Indian policy that the tribes were political entities within which law and order were maintained by Indian custom or law. But the traumatic changes brought by reservation life and the stepped-up attacks on Indian tribalism and Indian ways that were part of the reform movement brought with them a general disorganization and disintegration of Indian societies. "A serious detriment to the progress of the partially civilized Indians," the Board of Indian Commissioners declared in 1871, "is found in the fact that they are not brought under the domination of law, so far as regards crimes committed against each other." The board admitted that Indian tribes differed greatly among themselves and that all were not yet suited to white legal norms. "But when they have adopted civilized costume and civilized modes of subsistence," it said, "we owe it to them, and to ourselves, to teach them the majesty of civilized law, and to extend to them its protection against the lawless among themselves."[34]

A sharp blow at the traditional status of the Indian tribes was the legislation of 1871 declaring that thereafter no Indian tribe would be recognized as an independent nation with whom the United States could contract by treaty. Although agreements still were concluded that were no different from previous treaties except in mode of ratification, the formal end of treaty making and the conscious intention thereby to denigrate the power of the chiefs resulted in a loss of old systems of internal order without the substitution of anything in their place. Francis A. Walker clearly defined the problem:

> While the Act of 1871 strikes down at a blow the hereditary authority of the chiefs, no legislation has invested Indian agents with magisterial power, or provided for the assembling of the Indian *demos.* There is at this time no semblance of authority for the punishment of any crime which one Indian may commit against another, nor any mode of procedure, recognized by treaty or statute, for the regulation of matters between the government and the several tribes. So far as the law is concerned, complete anarchy exists in Indian affairs; and

34. *Report of the Board of Indian Commissioners*, 1871, pp. 7–8; see also ibid., 1873, p. 6. In this section I use material from Francis Paul Prucha, *American Indian Policy in Crisis: Christian Reformers and the Indian, 1865–1900* (Norman: University of Oklahoma Press, 1976), pp. 201–8, 329–31.

nothing but the singular homogeneity of Indian communities, and the almost unaccountable spontaneity and unanimity of public sentiment within them, has thus far prevented the attention of Congress and the country being called most painfully to the unpardonable negligence of the national legislature in failing to provide a substitute for the time-honored policy which was destroyed by the Act of 1871.[35]

Walker's successor, who inherited the problem, was no less concerned, and he recommended the application of United States courts to the Indian territories as a substitute for the former tribal authority. This became the common cry of reformers both in and out of the government. Even among white men, they asserted, civilization would not long exist without the guarantees of law. How, then, could there be any hope of civilizing the Indians without law? "That the benevolent efforts and purposes of the Government have proved so largely fruitless," the commissioner of Indian affairs declared in 1876, "is, in my judgment, due more to its failure to make these people amenable to our laws than to any other cause, or to all other causes combined." From all sides the refrain sounded. Bishop William Hare, the Episcopal missionary among the Sioux, wrote in 1877: "Wish well to the Indians as we may, and do for them what we will, the efforts of civil agents, teachers, and missionaries are like the struggles of drowning men weighted with lead, as long as by the absence of law Indian society is left without a base." Indians, too, were appealed to, and the commissioner of Indian affairs in 1878 said that Chief Joseph, the famous Nez Perce leader, believed that the greatest need of the Indians was a system of law by which controversies among Indians and between Indians and whites could be settled without appealing to physical force.[36]

A bill was introduced in Congress early in 1879 that authorized the president to prescribe police regulations for the Indian reservations and that provided for the laws of the respective states and territories relating to major crimes to be in force on the reservations. Both Schurz and Hayt strongly supported the measure. The latter declared: "A civilized community could not exist as such without law, and a semi-civilized and barbarous people are in a hopeless state of anarchy without its protection and sanctions. It is true the various tribes have regulations and customs of their own, which, however, are founded on superstition and ignorance of the usages of civilized communities, and generally tend to perpetuate feuds and keep alive animosities. To supply their place it is the bounden

35. Walker, *The Indian Question*, pp. 12–13.
36. CIA Report, 1873, serial 1601, pp. 372–73; CIA Report, 1875, serial 1680, pp. 517–18; CIA Report, 1876, serial 1749, pp. 387–88; CIA Report, 1878, serial 1850, p. 465. Bishop Hare is quoted in CIA Report, 1883, serial 2191, p. 7.

duty of the government to provide laws suited to the dependent condition of the Indians."[37] Congress could not be persuaded to enact the bill, but agitation kept the idea strong, and increasing pressure arose for law as a necessary means to bring about the reform and civilization among the Indians that humanitarians wanted. Under the paternal care of the United States, the Indians were to be introduced to white concepts of law.

A new agency of law that developed in the 1870s, which became a regular element on the reservations, was an Indian police force, quasi-military units under the command of the agents that emerged as substitutes for the authority of the chiefs or for military control of the reservations.[38] Some sort of police force was necessary in the best-ordered societies, it was argued, and to think that the Indian reservations, whose traditional tribal governments were weakened by the white reformers' attacks, could get along without law enforcers was absurd. It was all very well to condemn military management of Indian affairs, but if army troops were not on hand, the agent had to find some other way to back up his decisions.

The idea of a constabulary force of Indian policemen arose spontaneously on several reservations. Indians enrolled by the army as scouts had performed well, and it was not a difficult step to conceive of Indians as a temporary or even a permanent civilian corps. When Benjamin F. Lushbaugh became agent of the Pawnees in 1862, he was immediately annoyed by the frequent thefts, chiefly of horses, by young men of the tribe, and he organized a makeshift Indian police force to facilitate the recovery of property. In 1872–1873 a group of Navajo policemen, placed under a war chief, served well in preventing depredations and in expediting the return of stolen stock. Similar expedients for preserving order were used with success among the Klamaths, the Chippewas in Wisconsin, the Sioux, and the Blackfeet.[39]

The Apache police force established by John P. Clum, the extraordinary young agent at the San Carlos Reservation, was the best example. Clum had been nominated by the Dutch Reformed Church, which had been allotted the agency under Grant's peace policy and which, having no missionaries of its own willing to accept the hazards of the post, had turned to Rutgers College to find recruits. Clum had attended there briefly before

37. Report of the Secretary of the Interior, 1879, *House Executive Document* no. 1, part 5, 46–2, serial 1910, pp. 12–13; CIA Report, 1879, serial 1910, pp. 105–6.

38. An excellent, thorough treatment of Indian police and Indian judges is William T. Hagan, *Indian Police and Judges: Experiments in Acculturation and Control* (New Haven: Yale University Press, 1966).

39. Lushbaugh to Charles E. Mix, September 15, 1862, CIA Report, 1862, serial 1157, p. 266; Oakah L. Jones, Jr., "The Origins of the Navajo Indian Police, 1872–1873," *Arizona and the West* 8 (Autumn 1966): 225–38; Hagan, *Indian Police and Judges*, pp. 25–27, 39–40.

going west with the United States Weather Service, and former classmates recommended him for the position. He arrived at San Carlos on August 8, 1874, a cocky twenty-two year old "with instructions to assume *entire* control of the San Carlos agency." This meant forcing out the military and setting up his own enforcement agency. Two days after his arrival, Clum held a big talk with the Apaches and explained his plans. "I then told them that I intended to appoint some Indians as police-men," he later wrote; "that we would establish a supreme court for the trial of offenders; that I would preside as chief justice, and four or five Apache chiefs would serve as assistant justices; that Indians would be called as witnesses at the trials. Under this system, all Apache offenders would be arrested by Apache police, brought before an Apache court, with Apaches as witnesses, and, if convicted, sentenced by Apache judges, and finally delivered into the custody of Apache guards." The self-government plan worked, and Clum controlled the volatile Apaches without the aid of the army. The Indian Office and the Dutch Reformed Church supported him, and his Apache police were accepted as an integral part of the agency.[40]

The Board of Indian Commissioners raised the question of Indian police formally in its report for 1874. In a section entitled "Enforcement of Order," it noted that the power of the chiefs was limited and that outside intervention was resented. The result was that although the wild tribes had treaty obligations to maintain order, to educate their children, to apprehend and deliver offenders for punishment, and to labor for their own support, no machinery existed to enforce these stipulations and they had remained nugatory. The solution would be a "police or constabulary force" made up of the Indians themselves. Noting the successful attempts along this line at various reservations, the board concluded that there was abundant evidence to prove that a small, disciplined, and well-instructed police force of Indians would be a safe and effective means of preserving order and of assisting the tribe in enforcing its treaty obligations. And such a force in many cases, the board asserted, would obviate the necessity of a military post near the agency.[41]

In the following year the board moved ahead vigorously with its scheme. On August 1, 1875, it sent a circular letter to all the Indian agents as part of

40. Woodworth Clum, *Apache Agent: The Story of John P. Clum* (Boston: Houghton Mifflin Company, 1936), pp. 119–21, 132, 134–35. Clum's annual reports appear in the annual reports of the commissioner of Indian affairs, 1874–1877. Clum in later life wrote about his Apache police in "The San Carlos Apache Police," *New Mexico Historical Review* 4 (July 1929): 203–19; 5 (January 1930): 67–92. For a detailed, heavily documented account of Clum's career as agent, with emphasis on his struggle with the military, see Ralph Henrick Ogle, *Federal Control of the Western Apaches, 1848–1886* (Albuquerque: University of New Mexico Press, 1970).

41. *Report of the Board of Indian Commissioners*, 1874, p. 9.

its campaign against military control of the reservations. After requesting information about the existence of military forces in their vicinity and the effect of the troops on the Indians, the letter posed a specific question about Indian police: "Would the organization of an armed Indian police, under proper restrictions and discipline, for the enforcement of order, arrest of criminals, and the prevention of incursions of evil-disposed persons upon your reservation, prove safe or advisable; and to what extent would such an organization supersede the necessity of a military force?" A number of the agents saw no need for a police force because their charges were peaceful and well-ordered, and some believed that the Indian distaste for taking punitive action against other Indians would make such a police force useless, but the great majority replied favorably, some even enthusiastically. Agents who had already employed Indians as police of one sort or another pointed to the success of their efforts.[42]

It took some time for the work of the board to bear fruit. Commissioner Hayt picked up the recommendation in 1877 and urged the creation of a general system of Indian police. He noted the successes where such police had already been tried and the practice of using police in Canada. The police system, he said, would relieve the army from police duty on Indian reservations, would save lives and property, and would "materially aid in placing the entire Indian population of the country on the road to civilization." But Congress, where supporters of military control of the reservations were numerous and influential, held back. Finally, on May 27, 1878, a system of Indian police got congressional authorization. A section of the Indian appropriation act provided $30,000 to pay for 430 privates at $5 a month and fifty officers at $8 a month, "to be employed in maintaining order and prohibiting illegal traffic in liquor on the several Indian reservations." By the end of the year, the commissioner reported success at the thirty agencies where police forces had been organized, and in 1879 Congress doubled the number of policemen authorized. By 1880 there were police at forty agencies and a decade later at fifty-nine.[43]

The police were immediately useful to the agents as an extension of their authority. The tasks they performed were in many cases hardly police duties at all. An Indian policeman was the "reservation handyman." The police served as couriers and messengers, slaughtered cattle for the beef ration, kept accounts of births and deaths in the tribe, and took censuses for the agent; and they augmented the labor force of the agency by building roads, clearing out irrigation ditches, and doing other chores. In all this

42. Ibid., 1875, pp. 64–103.

43. CIA Report, 1877, serial 1800, pp. 398–99; CIA Report, 1878, serial 1850, pp. 471–72; CIA Report, 1880, serial 1959, pp. 88–89; CIA Report, 1890, serial 2841, pp. xc–xciv; 20 *United States Statutes* 86, 315.

they contributed substantially to the smooth operation of the agency. Routine labor, however, did not obscure the enforcement of order, which had been foremost on the minds of advocates of the police system. The Indian police were armed and often mounted, at the beck and call of the agent when disorder threatened or force was needed to see that rules and regulations on the reservation were properly observed. The police arrested or turned back intruders on the Indian lands and tore out the squatters' stakes, arrested horse thieves, escorted surveying parties, and served as scouts. They acted as guards at annuity payments, preserved order at ration issues, protected agency buildings and other property, and returned truant children to school. They searched for and returned lost or stolen goods, prevented depredations in timber, and brought whiskey sellers to trial. They arrested Indians for disorderly conduct, drunkenness, wife beating, and theft, and reported the comings and goings of strangers on the reservation.[44]

The reformers soon became aware, if they had not been from the start, that these duties and responsibilities of the Indian police were means to an end of greater worth than day-to-day good order on the reservations. The police were to become important chiefly for their moral influence. The police force on a reservation impressed the Indians with the supremacy of law; it discouraged the traditional practice of personal revenge; it imbued a sense of duty and personal responsibility, subjected the policemen themselves to strict discipline and self-control, and inspired them with a pride of good conduct; it taught respect for the personal and property rights of others; by strengthening the authority of the government agent against that of the chiefs, it prepared the Indians for the dissolution of their tribal relations and pushed them forward toward incorporation into American society. The Indian police taught by good example as well as by the enforcement of precepts. They were expected to have only one wife and to dress in the accepted white man's costume, with short hair and unpainted faces. The police force, Commissioner Hiram Price commented in 1881, was "a perpetual educator."

All in all, the Indian police worked remarkably well in fulfilling the reformers' designs. Four years after the program began, the commissioner of Indian affairs reported: "Tried as an experiment, it has proved a decided success. It has accomplished all that was claimed for it, and at many agencies has become an absolute necessity." Compared with white police forces throughout the country, he declared two years later, the Indian police could not be surpassed for faithfulness and the impartial performance of duty. And this was all the more remarkable considering that the police

44. Hagan, *Indian Police and Judges*, pp. 69–81. See also the annual reports of the commissioner of Indian affairs.

were asked to enforce against members of their own race laws made by white officials, many of which went strongly against established practices and customs, often of a religious nature.[45] The success rested to a large extent on the fact that the police forces often paralleled or replaced similar institutions within the tribes themselves. The soldier societies that had regulated much of tribal life had performed functions not unlike those assigned to the Indian police, and wittingly or unwittingly, agents drew their policemen from the membership of such societies.[46]

There were, of course, some nay sayers. The strongest argument made against the Indian police was that they gave too much power to the agent. The chairman of the House Committee on Indian Affairs in 1880 argued strongly against the continuation of the police on that basis. "This provision turns him [the Indian] over, bound hand and foot, to the agents," he said. "These men had authority before almost without restriction, except as they are restricted by the want of physical force. Now we give them eight hundred men armed and equipped, and thus the fullest authority is allowed with fearful power to execute not known laws, but the will of the agent."[47] There was no doubt that an obedient police force in the hands of an authoritarian or unscrupulous agent would be a dangerous thing. But isolated examples of dangerous behavior did not outweigh the overwhelmingly favorable impression made by the Indian police on white observers.[48]

Part of the agitation for law for the Indians came, not from fear of disorders within the Indian societies, which the Indian police might ease, but from the difficulties of protecting Indians from crimes perpetrated upon them by white aggressors. The instrument that was supposed to offer protection from such attacks was the Indian Trade and Intercourse Act of 1834, with its array of restrictions upon white contacts with Indians and penalties for violating them. Like the officials in the 1850s, who lamented the inapplicability of the old law to changed conditions, the secretaries and commissioners of the 1860s and 1870s saw urgent need for revision. Commissioner Cooley in 1866 began the refrain: "The intercourse laws,

45. CIA Report, 1882, serial 2100, pp. 35–36; CIA Report, 1884, serial 2287, p. 12. See also CIA Report, 1890, serial 2841, pp. xci–xciv, for extracts of agents' reports praising the Indian police.

46. Clark Wissler, *Indian Cavalcade; or, Life on the Old-Time Indian Reservations* (New York: Sheridan House, 1938), pp. 128–29; Hagan, *Indian Police and Judges*, p. 161.

47. *Congressional Record*, 10: 2487. Several other members of the House spoke strongly in favor of the police, and the objection was not sustained. See the debate, ibid., pp. 2487–89.

48. George E. Hyde, *A Sioux Chronicle* (Norman: University of Oklahoma Press, 1956), generally supports the critics' position, but Hagan's *Indian Police and Judges* gives a more sober and favorable evaluation of the police.

passed over thirty years since, and apparently sufficient at that time, before the tide of emigration had begun to set strongly towards the frontier, and while none but occasional hunters or trappers interfered with the occupancy of the country by the Indians, are insufficient now, when the white population west of the Mississippi begins to number its millions." A typical echo was that of Columbus Delano in 1874, who declared that the provisions of the act of 1834 were "entirely inadequate to meet the present requirements of the service" and that experience had shown that the law was no longer sufficient to protect the Indians.[49]

The problem was twofold. First, the Indians needed more effective protection against crimes committed against their persons and property by whites. What was called for was "a plain, comprehensive code, by which the superintendents and agents may dispense justice within their jurisdictions, and the infliction of appropriate penalties may be rendered certain, whether the offender be red or white." The longtime discrimination in favor of whites could not escape notice. "In too many cases, indeed almost universally," the commissioner wrote in 1866, "where a white offender against the rights or life of an Indian is brought into our courts through the efforts of the agent, he is sure of acquittal; but reverse the case, and the Indian almost surely suffers. It does seem practicable," he concluded, "to improve upon this condition of things." Secretary Delano, almost a decade later, pointed to the same problems.[50]

The second major concern was the inadequacy of the regulations for trade with the Indians. Indiscriminate granting of licenses to American citizens was a norm, and Congress in fact in 1866 had reinforced the principle by authorizing any loyal citizen to trade with the Indians. Such looseness aggravated the problems, for the Indian Office had authority neither to restrict the number of traders nor eliminate those judged unfit or unable to supply the Indians fairly and adequately.[51]

The result in both cases was severe irritation of the Indians, who sought revenge against the abuses and kept the frontier in turmoil. But more important, in the minds of the reformers, the situation left the Indians in an anomalous state in regard to law. The failure of Congress to act in providing a code of law for the Indians led Commissioner E. P. Smith in 1875 to

49. CIA Report, 1866, serial 1284, pp. 16–17; Report of the Secretary of the Interior, 1874, *House Executive Document* no. 1, part 5, 43–2, serial 1639, p. viii. See also CIA Report, 1867, serial 1326, part 2, p. 5; CIA Report, 1871, serial 1505, p. 422.

50. CIA Report, 1866, serial 1284, p. 17; Report of the Secretary of the Interior, 1874, *House Executive Document* no. 1, part 5, 43–2, serial 1639, p. viii. See the plea for better law for the Indians, both among themselves and in relation to whites, in CIA Report, 1874, serial 1639, pp. 324–25.

51. 14 *United States Statutes* 280; CIA Report, 1866, serial 1284, p. 17; CIA Report, 1877, serial 1800, pp. 404–5.

recommend the "divorcement of the United States and Indians as 'citizens of a domestic sovereignty within our borders,' and the transfer of the Indians and their property to the States where they reside." This could be done at once, he thought, in New York and for some of the Indians in Michigan, Wisconsin, and Minnesota; it could be done for others as soon as they were advanced enough in civilization to be treated as ordinary citizens.[52]

All the plans and the progress that came from them in implementing the peace policy fell short of the firm legislative enactments that were the ultimate goal of the reformers. Again and again the commissioners and the secretaries of the interior, supported and urged forward by church and other reform groups, had recommended legal support of land allotment, a system of courts, and increased educational facilities for Indians. To a large extent their exhortations were ineffective at the time, but they were not in vain. The ideas espoused in the 1860s and 1870s became the platform for a concentrated and successful drive in the next two decades that transformed the relations between the United States government and the Indians.

52. CIA Report, 1875, serial 1680, pp. 519–20. This was close to the policy of "termination" of the 1950s, although that term was not used.

Illustration
and Map Credits
Volume I

1. American Numismatic Society, New York City. 2. Charles Allen Munn Collection, Fordham University Library, Bronx, New York; Frick Art Reference Library print no. 21170. 3. New-York Historical Society, New York City, negative no. 1111. 4. National Archives, Washington, D.C. 5. New-York Historical Society, negative no. 6282 (painting by Edward Savage). 6. U.S. Signal Corps photograph no. 111–SC–90825 (from an engraving in Benson L. Lossing, *The Pictorial Field-Book of the War of 1812*) in the National Archives. 7–9. Independence National Historical Park Collection, Philadelphia. 10. Nebraska State Historical Society, Lincoln. 11. Library of Congress, Washington, D.C. 12. Architect of the Capitol, Washington, D.C. 13. In the collection of the Corcoran Gallery of Art, Washington, D.C., bequest of James C. McGuire. 14. National Archives. 15. State Historical Society of Wisconsin, Madison, negative no. WHI (x3) 35374 (from Marcius Willson, *American History*). 16. American Numismatic Society. 17. Chicago Historical Society, Chicago. 18. William L. Clements Library, University of Michigan, Ann Arbor. 19. Philbrook Art Center, Tulsa, Oklahoma. 20. National Anthropological Archives, Smithsonian Institution, Washington, D.C. (from a McKenney and Hall lithograph). 21. E. C. Tracy, *Memoir of the Life of Jeremiah Evarts, Esq.* (Boston: Crocker and Brewster, 1845), frontispiece (after a painting by Samuel F. B. Morse). 22. Kansas State Historical Society, Topeka. 23–24. National Portrait Gallery, Smithsonian Institution, Washington, D.C., on loan from the National Museum of American Art. 25. Illinois State Historical Library, Springfield. 26. California Historical Society, San Francisco; photograph by Edouart, San Francisco. 27. Hazard Stevens, *The Life of Isaac Ingalls Stevens* (Boston: Houghton Mifflin Company, 1900), frontispiece. 28. National Anthropological Archives,

Smithsonian Institution. 29. Library of Congress (photograph by George Prince, 1898). 30. Smithsonian Institution. 31. U.S. Signal Corps photograph no. 111–SC–87714 in the National Archives. 32. American Numismatic Society. 33. Charles Lewis Slattery, *Felix Reville Brunot*, frontispiece. 34–36. Library of Congress. 37. U.S. Signal Corps photograph no. 111–SC–82311 (photograph by Louis Heller, 1873) in the National Archives. 38. Library of Congress, Brady collection. 39. *Harper's Weekly*, January 25, 1879. 40. National Archives, photograph no. 111–B–4990. 41. U.S. Signal Corps photograph no. 111–SC–96773 (D. F. Barry photograph, 1877) in the National Archives.

MAP CREDITS

The maps in this volume were drawn by the Cartographic Laboratory, University of Nebraska–Lincoln. The following sources were drawn upon for the maps. 1. Edgar Bruce Wesley, *Guarding the Frontier: A Study in Frontier Defense from 1814 to 1825* (Minneapolis: University of Minnesota Press, 1935), p. 39; Herman J. Viola, *Thomas L. McKenney: Architect of America's Early Indian Policy, 1816–*

1830 (Chicago: Swallow Press, 1974). 2. *The American Heritage Pictorial Atlas of United States History* (New York: American Heritage Publishing Company, 1966), p. 148; Charles C. Royce, comp., *Indian Land Cessions in the United States*, Eighteenth Annual Report of the Bureau of American Ethnology, 1896–1897, part 2 (Washington: Government Printing Office, 1899), appropriate state plates. 3. R. David Edmunds, *The Potawatomis: Keepers of the Fire* (Norman: University of Oklahoma Press, 1978), p. 245; Royce, *Indian Land Cessions*. 4. *American Heritage Pictorial Atlas of United States History*, p. 148; Royce, *Indian Land Cessions*. 5. Arrell Morgan Gibson, *The American Indian: Prehistory to the Present* (Lexington, Massachusetts: D. C. Heath and Company, 1980), p. 313; Royce, *Indian Land Cessions*. 6. John W. Morris, Charles R. Goins, and Edwin C. McReynolds, *Historical Atlas of Oklahoma*, 2d ed. (Norman: University of Oklahoma Press, 1976). 7. Gerald Thompson, *The Army and the Navajo* (Tucson: University of Arizona Press, 1976), p. xii. 8. Francis Paul Prucha, *A Guide to the Military Posts of the United States, 1789–1895* (Madison: State Historical Society of Wisconsin, 1964). 9. *Annual Report of the Commissioner of Indian Affairs*, 1880.